WRITE ME A FEW OF YOUR LINES

WRITE ME A FEW OF YOUR LINES

A Blues Reader

Edited by Steven C. Tracy

University of Massachusetts Press *Amherst*

Printed in the United States of America
LC 99-18332
ISBN 1-55849-205-4 (cloth); 206-2 (pbk.)
Designed by Dennis Anderson
Set in Electra and Gill Sans by Keystone Typesetting, Inc.
Printed and bound by Sheridan Books, Inc.

Library of Congress Cataloging-in-Publication Data

Write me a few of your lines : a blues reader / edited by Steven C. Tracy.
p. cm.
Includes bibliographical references and index.
Discography: p.
ISBN 1-55849-205-4 (cl. : alk. paper). — ISBN 1-55849-206-2 (pbk. : alk. paper)
1. Blues (Music)—History and criticism. I. Tracy, Steven C. (Steven Carl), 1954– .
ML3521.W75 1999
781.643—dc21 99-18332
CIP

British Library Cataloguing in Publication data are available.

Contents

Part 2. Before and Alongside the Blues

Part 3. Folklore and the Blues

Part 4. The Blues and Religion

Prologue

IN HER blues-based novel *Their Eyes Were Watching God,* Zora Neale Hurston carves out a mythic space in words that establishes the "lowly" front porch of the rural, small-town general store at day's end as the place where the politically and socially powerless become the lords of sound. There and then, away from enforced animal existence and the invasive senses of the whites, the subjected (objects) become the subjects through their linguistic panache, wit, and creativity. The created become the creators, and the master of the spoken word reigns. Theirs is an existence and power beyond the imagination of their temporal lords, the heirs of the concept of an aristocracy inherently superior in intelligence and feeling to the lower classes, the mob, who are to be distrusted, tolerated, and above all ruled by the refined few. It is a story as old as the American genesis, this condescension and enslavement, and it is, to a great degree, a myth of inferiority that is forcefully dispelled musically, poetically, and spiritually by this century's humbly towering art form, the blues.

One could argue, in fact, that the blues are a triumphant artistic culmination of American democratic ideals, transcending the shameful actualities of American existence that threatened (and threaten) to overwhelm and eradicate the glorious identity projected in the most optimistic speeches and documents of its little more than two-century history. Indeed, what meaning does the word "freedom" have in a country that enslaves, and who better to interpret that meaning, to identify the soul and energy of that idea and ideal, than those from the quarters, bottoms, and ghettoes of the American landscape, whose language, skill, and creativity burst forth in brilliant song more potent, but less indiscriminately violent, than bomb or rocket's red glare? When Reformation leader Martin Luther wrote, "Whatever your heart clings to and confides in that is really your God," he was not thinking of the blues as we know it, writing as he did so long before its creation. And yet what songs have presented the human soul clinging to the salvation of art by confiding both openly and covertly the sin, shame, and sorrows as well as the successes and joys of humankind more fully than the blues, with their resounding creativity and energy and hopefulness and fecundity? Centuries later, Luther's namesake, Martin Luther King, Jr. wrote that "[a] riot is at bottom the language of the unheard," knowing that behind that physical riot percolated the riot-in-music, the riotous music, of the African American vernacular tradition that had always endured, so beautifully expressing the turmoil concretized in the whips and lashes of outrageous misfortune in the rural South and the sirens, flames, and shards of glass of urban rioting. And the impulse to utter that turmoil, to recast it in the figurative and the mundane as well as the literal and the fantastic, was a method of resistance, a strategy for survival, and a means of transcendence that has helped re-form our world as we know it.

As we cast about at the close of the millennium for a meaning in this final century which pivots toward the next, seeking a pulse beat by which to measure the rhythm, health, and strength of the age, we would do well to paraphrase some nomenclature from our well-meaning ancestors of the 1920s and consider the compelling arguments for labeling our century "the blues age." When at the turn of the twentieth century W.E.B. Du Bois identified the problem of the color line as the defining predicament of our time, this visionary reconnoitered the field on which would be acted out some of the most dramatic dilemmas, successes, and failures in politics, art, and science in these past one hundred years. All of our progress in these areas must be considered in the context of the potential emergence of America into its ideal identity as it has evolved in our understanding from 1776 until the present, and thus all of the events and non-events of the twentieth century are touched by that defining idealism.

Not only that, but as one surveys the achievements of the twentieth century and identifies not only superficial influences but a spiritual philosophy behind them, it is easy to see that philosophy embodied in what many would see as an unlikely place, though their skepticism is (or should be) in fact a violation of what America is or believes in in its ideal state. The blues is the music of a people emerging from the second American revolution into the turmoil of what should have been a Reconstruction of not only our country's social, political, and economic infrastructure, but of our country's moral and ethical framework as well. Set adrift in a morass of societal immorality and menace—as Charles Brown would wistfully sob in "Drifting Blues," his post–World War II lamentation, "drifting like a ship out on the sea"—African Americans generated a new type of music for themselves that would express both continuity with and dissociation from the past. Rooted in what they had experienced and fought for, it was also a declaration of independence and identity, an assertion of artistic individuality expressing the hardships, successes, and dreams of many African Americans as they moved forward into what was for them unfamiliar regions that effectively gerrymandered them into subordinacy. This, of course, was not the first time that African Americans had found themselves "poor . . . and a long ways from home," so the coping strategies were already in place in the vernacular music, especially in the covert allegories of the anti-spirituals. We are reminded of the typological bent of the Puritans who saw themselves as types of the Israelites, God's chosen people, the failure of European Protestantism laying behind them, journeying across a vast desert (ocean) to reach the Promised Land of the New World, exiles in a howling wilderness struggling against all adversity to bring into being the City of God on Earth. The emphasis in the spirituals on reaching the Promised Land, and the centrality of the figure of Moses, attests to the relevance and appeal of this typology to enslaved African Americans eager to express, but cautious to mask, their yearning for freedom in this world. Then, in Reconstruction and post-Reconstruction times, with an expanded field of secular musical expression available, another genre came forth, one that is traditional and contemporary, expressive of sorrow, happiness, and optimism; one that frequently deals with mundane difficulties and concerns in a way that evokes identification and, through that, relief and happiness; one that subtly embodies the ardent desire to achieve the rights to life, liberty, and the pursuit of happiness.

When twentieth-century modernists began seeking to find expression for the shambles of a world they believed they had inherited—that "heap of broken images" that T. S. Eliot described, or Ezra Pound's "accelerated grimace"—they were labeled a Lost Generation by Gertrude Stein, who saw in them an ennui, a restlessness, a disillusionment that threatened to bring their world to a stagnant halt. Still, these artists sought through their art to begin to piece back together the world so blasted by violence, treachery, illusion, and hypocrisy by transforming the usable past into a transformed and transforming present. The directive from Pound was to make it new and make it whole. Pound was essentially an archaeologist bent on reconstructing our perception of past history so as to radically alter our present. And that shred of hope in the face of the tremendous weight of accumulated moral, ethical, social, and political outrages and indignities is characteristic of the source and spirit of the blues, as is the transformation of the legacy of the slaves from one of perceived shame and degradation to one of resilience, hope, dignity, creativity, and humanity. What the generation of the 1920s called "the jazz age" was in many ways a bastard use of the term, one that was energized by the perception of the primitivism and raw passion of the music, the heat, but gave little credit to the light generated by the music and musicians themselves. The more crucial relevances of the blues tradition to times past, present, and future, not wholly evident to many then, have more fully spread themselves before us today.

At millennium's end, at millennium's beginning, it is difficult to conceive an art form that more brilliantly and directly expresses the angst and the optimism of the twentieth century, in lyrics and music that have become more pervasively influential, and in spirit more expressive of the emergence of vernacular culture to its significant level of importance, culturally and sociopolitically, than the blues. The lords of sound have indeed not only sung themselves into existence, but into ascendancy, and made a firmament of the front porch.

Acknowledgments

NOBODY can really adequately repay Bessie Tucker for her harrowing depiction of a brush with death in "Got Cut All to Pieces," or Elmore James for the transcendent anguish of "Something Inside Me," or Pete Johnson and Joe Turner for the irresistible drive of "Roll 'Em Pete." For what it took to live their experiences, conceive the performances, develop the skill and artistry, and generate the performances there is no sufficient remuneration. As with any art, we can only enjoy, marvel, and try to help keep it alive by passing it on in the manner best available to us. This book is another of my attempts to enjoy, marvel at, and pass on the art of people whose music has rarely been out of my waking mind since Canned Heat's "Going up the Country" led on to Henry Thomas's "Bull Doze Blues," and Memphis Minnie, Lucille Bogan, Big Bill Broonzy, Blind Blake, Howlin Wolf, Muddy Waters, and on and on and on, as I sensed instinctively that this was my art for life. To all the thousands of blues performers whose strains have produced so much pleasure in my life, people who I never met or got to thank personally, this book is dedicated.

Then there are those blues performers with whom I have been able to strike up personal relationships and whose music I have gotten to know intimately as part of their lives and mine: Pigmeat Jarrett, James Mays, Big Joe Duskin, and Albert Washington. These are the men who most forcefully taught me not to forget that the blues are by and about human beings with real lives, and that I must never allow what graced my ears to permit me to close my eyes to the experiences that formed a long prelude to the three minutes of artistic ecstasy spinning at 78 revolutions per minute under the heavy arm of my parents' nearly abandoned Victrola. They also let me perform with them, and helped teach me how to play the blues with conviction and integrity. Along with my band, the Crawling Kingsnakes—Phil Buscema, Hudson Rivers III, Dudley Radcliff, and Richard Berry—they have made my performing life very rich and satisfying.

All of these blues musicians have inspired the writers whose works are included here to write intelligently, beautifully, and passionately about this intelligent, beautiful, passionate art form. To those writers I also dedicate this book, since they have also helped lead me to this place from which, perhaps, I can help direct others whose budding interest in the blues has sparked a search for a better understanding of its origin, nature, and meanings.

They have championed the blues with an intelligence and vigor that has been of great service to blues lovers everywhere, and I feel honored to have my name appear in a book with such distinguished contributors.

A special word of appreciation for Jack Coughlin, with whom I have collaborated since I have been in Amherst and whose love and appreciation for the music is obvious in his sensitive portraits of blues performers. He read and commented on some of the original material included in this manuscript, as did Dudley Radcliff and Cathy Tracy, and they all assisted in helping me push it out the door and into the public arena. Once the University of Massachusetts Press indicated an interest, the prospectus was examined by Jeff Todd Titon and James Smethurst, both of whom made extremely useful suggestions with regard to the scope and structure of the volume. My sincerest gratitude for their thoroughness and expertise.

Special thanks also go out to Bruce Wilcox and others at the University of Massachusetts Press, especially Wendy Bergoffen and Chris Hammel. They enthusiastically accepted my proposal for the book and helped ease it into existence. The folks at *Living Blues Magazine* graciously helped me track down some addresses for some potential contributors that I might not otherwise have found, and I gratefully acknowledge their aid. I also acknowledge the generous support of Dean Lee Edwards of the College of Humanities and Fine Arts at the University of Massachusetts Amherst, and my colleagues in the Department of Afro-American Studies, whose scholarly activity is a constant source of knowledge and inspiration.

Finally, I must thank my wife, Cathy, my children, Michelle and Michael, and my parents, Edward and Jean, who have put up with and supported my efforts to write and teach about, promote, and perform the blues. I love them, and I hope that I deserve them.

Steven C. Tracy
University of Massachusetts at Amherst

WRITE ME A FEW OF YOUR LINES

Introduction

AFRICAN-AMERICAN

What we are talking about here begins here. Not just African—blues music did not originate or develop on African soil. Not just American—before the colonial North American slave trade began in 1526, there was no music like the blues on these shores either. African-American

And it begins not in a *static* place, but in a nexus, a locus of energy, a place of violence, and turmoil, and confrontation, and sacrifice, and restlessness, and frustration, and accommodation, and perseverance, and creativity, and enrichment, and transcendence; a place where the plantation ledgers and bills of sale of the architects of this country's political and social system were examined and (un)balanced and found wanting; a place perhaps where the highest ideals of this democracy—personal freedom; exaltation of the masses; the embracing of the spirit of the revolutionary moment and improvisatory celebration in the context of a comfortably loose but securely established structure that welcomes all comers and allows all identities to exist and flourish—are most sweetly and rhythmically exemplified. And yet we must go back to Africa in order to examine who and what it was that existed *there* that was brought *here* to create that which was much greater than the sum of its mechanical parts.

From the primary source of the North American slave trade, the West African savannah region, come the characteristics of African musical performance that have influenced the techniques of African American music over the centuries. We hear the predominance of percussion and percussively played instruments; the antiphonal (call and response) musical and lyric patterns; the vocal and inflectional manipulation, including growling, buzzing, and straining to achieve emotional tension and complexity; the manner of stretching—flattening and inflating—the boundaries of pitches in improvisational and organically decorative fashion, including the flatted thirds and sevenths referred to by some commentators as "blue" notes; the improvisational lyric moments which serve to embrace the immediacy of event, ritual, and artistic moment; the syncopation set up in relation to a metronomic sense that produces a sense of swing and trickster-like willful improvisation weaving in and out of the nodes of regularity; the instruments, particularly of the savannah stringed-instrument tradition, including the kora, halam, and konting (perhaps sources for the banjo), privileged in the New World in some ways by the suppression of drumming, and above all the RHYTHM so dominant in the music, particularly the complex polyrhythmic elements so common in the blues.

Furthermore, the figure of the griot (also called jali, the Mandingo term for singer), whose important role as music-maker in African societies where Islamic influence and strong chief-based authority are most powerful, is mirrored in some ways in the figure of the blues performer in this country. Witness the musicians' function as purveyor of traditional material, frequently learned from fathers and uncles but also other male and female community members, and conversely as improvisational innovators extending and renewing that tradition; their status as professional, semi-professional, or amateur musician, sometimes a wandering bard, sometimes community-based member; their role as singer of songs of praise, history, and genealogy, of ritual, and gossip and insult—these are ways in which they can resemble the figure of the blues singer, though there are clearly differences as well. The blues singer, for example, is not much of a genealogist, nor a historian describing the ancestral history of a tribal chief's or important person's family, though taken together the blues chart a group psychic history in their own way.

Altogether, these points drive home an insistent case for survivals of a variety of techniques and situations that produce a music that is similar not superficially, but modally—the manner of producing and achieving the music is remarkably similar—to African music. And in some ways its communal function is similar as well. We encounter it invoking and producing a spirit which invites involvement and communication both bodily and spiritually, producing unity of performance and sound while acknowledging and affirming counter-rhythmic countercurrents which are nonetheless integrated into the unified whole. For example, we find the music being used in conjunction with daily activities, and considered a part of daily ritual and meaning, rather than always being separated into an isolated artistic space. But beyond that, there are perhaps subtle ways in which the soul and spirit of African societies inform the ethos of the blues, in ways that are long-forgotten, unconscious, and intangible yet just as surely a part of its technical and visceral landscape.

Of course, there is a long musical passage from the first arrival of the slaves in this country and the emergence of the blues, probably sometime in the last two decades of the nineteenth century. It is a passage marked by interludes of reels and square dances, work songs and field hollers, spirituals and jubilees, coon songs and ragtime, ballads and game songs that preceded and/or existed alongside the blues, living on in the repertoires of songsters and "music physicianers" out to make a buck and wing on front porch or in back alley, on street corner or in country juke joint. We have immediately recognizable ancestors of the blues vocal style, especially in the work songs—apparently African-derived, secularized group labor songs with their antiphonal structure, highly rhythmic, heavily accented cadences, and improvised or traditional lyrics dealing most frequently with love or hard work and strung together in loosely, frequently emotionally connected units—and the field hollers—themselves similar to work songs but individualized, somewhat freer and more decorative in their vocal lines. However, they are still not quite the blues, even if we have examples of blues singers like Texas Alexander, Bessie Tucker, and Son House singing hollers or holler- or work song-like blues.

It wasn't until, apparently, some time in the 1880s that the form we recognize as the blues first emerged, and until 1890 that Gates Thomas collected a lyric in South Texas that was somewhat like the blues, the same year W. C. Handy identifies as the year when he himself first heard the blues. By the turn of the century numerous collectors, folklorists, and performers—Howard Odum and Ma Rainey among them—had noted the presence of the blues among southern African Americans. Just why the blues emerged at this particular time is hard to say without resorting to mere conjecture and, perhaps, oversimplification. Certainly African American music had been changing generationally even as it maintained its strong links with the past, but the newest generational shift, which brought to majority the first generation of African Americans born outside of slavery (and hence placed them in a strange yet familiar Reconstruction and post-Reconstruction world for which there was no ancestral experience), may well have been the major sociopolitical force that made this new blues form and expression necessary, functional, and attractive. When combined with African-derived modalities adapted and transformed on American soil, European-derived strophic/stanzaic lyric organization, and common blues-ballad harmonic accompaniment pattern, there was created the chronological, geographical, musical, and spiritual space in which the blues could be midwifed into existence.

Of course, the earliest "blues singers" appear not to have been singers of only blues but performers and entertainers who drew upon folk sources—ballads, hollers, spirituals, dance tunes, etc.,—and popular sources—minstrel songs/coon songs (often themselves folk-derived), ragtime, and popular sheet music. Their performances at country dances, medicine shows, white functions, and on the streets or in back-country juke joints provided a range of functions, from dance accompaniment to social commentary to parody, as is so clearly evident in the works of such performers as Henry Thomas, Frank Stokes, and Jim Jackson. Clearly the blues was taking its place beside other African American music in the late nineteenth and early twentieth centuries, and it was poised to gain its ascendancy in terms of popular mass consumption with the sheet music publication of Hart Wand's "The Dallas Blues" and W. C. Handy's "The Memphis Blues" (both published in 1912) and the criminally delayed entry of the African American blues singer into the arena of recorded music.

It was the initiative and drive of Perry Bradford, the reluctant "bravery" of Fred Hager, and especially the emergent power of the women's blues tradition in the voice of Mamie Smith that finally ushered African American blues to the turntable. Pianist-composer-entrepreneur Bradford, who had experienced some success with his *Made in Harlem* revue, initially took two of his compositions ("That Thing Called Love" and "You Can't Keep A Good Man Down") and revue star Mamie Smith to the Victor label, which rejected Smith for fear of alienating its white customers by recording an African American artist. Bradford then moved on to Fred Hager at the OKeh label, who reluctantly agreed to record the sides by Smith when Hager's first choice, Sophie Tucker, was unavailable. Based on that record's success, Smith was brought back into the studio on August 10, 1920, to record the first blues record by an African American, "Crazy Blues" and "It's Right Here For You (If You Don't Get It . . . Tain't No Fault O' Mine)." These titles must have surely also reflected the company's initial hesitance to record and release music by African American artists, as well as the African American press's calls for African American record releases and for the support of the African American public to purchase them. When the record sold 75,000 copies in its first month of release, convincing record companies of the commercial viability of such a product, the craze for female vaudeville blues singers was on.

These vaudeville blues, though, were different from the "folk" blues that African Americans had been singing and folklorists had been collecting in the rural South. Those folk blues were frequently performed by nonprofessional, sometimes itinerant, musicians in informal situations that allowed for great flexibility or informality in the musical and lyric structure of the song while still observing certain general traditional structural guidelines. The most common musical structure sauntered somewhere in the direction of twelve bars or measures, employing a I-IV-V chord pattern and utilizing a variety of lyric patterns, several sometimes used side by side in the same song. The most common lyric patterns in the blues are: one "line" or thought repeated in roughly the same language three times (AAA); one line repeated twice and then answered or completed or somehow resolved by a third, rhyming, line (AAB); one line sung and then completed by a rhyming line repeated twice (ABB); one line sung, followed by a different line that rhymes, and then followed by another different line that rhymes (ABC); and one line sung, followed by a different rhyming line, leading to a refrain that carries over from stanza to stanza (AB refrain). One such pattern is not necessarily employed exclusively in any given song. For example, Ma Rainey's recording of "See See Rider" employs ABB, AAB, and ABC stanzas. Many of the thoughts termed "lines" might actually be heard or transcribed as two "lines" since a strong medial caesura is frequently characteristic in the vocal performance of the blues line, which of course has ramifications for the textual transcription of blues lyrics. In addition to the common twelve-bar patterns, eight-bar patterns were common in the tradition as well, featuring a variety of lyric patterns (AB; AB refrain).

Unfettered by the length limitations of the 78-rpm record, performances could and would frequently exceed their roughly three minute length, and could be more loosely and associationally—and occasionally—constructed than the blues recorded in the studio for popular consumption, which themselves tended to develop over the years toward more tightly and/or logically plotted story lines or themes. Folk blues were performed with a specific audience present and in mind, and with an expectation of immediate feedback, and the character of the songs frequently depended in part upon the audience for their content, directions, and dynamics of performance. Finally, these folk blues included formula-like phrases and lines that were employed by many singers, in a way not exactly identical to but similar to the oral-formulaic usages described by Milman Parry and Albert Lord in their descriptions of oral epic poets. Common lines or phrases such as "woke up this mornin" or "I'm goin away" were used to set certain ideas or themes in motion in relation to traditional models, in the context of which the singer could generate any number of completions of the traditional language to accomplish his or her individual purpose. Such techniques can give individual songs a simultaneously traditional and individual feel, emphasizing both the communal and personal aspects of blues lyrics.

By contrast, the vaudeville blues that were first brought to record by Mamie Smith, Lucille Hegamin, Lillyn Brown, Lavinia Turner, and Daisy Martin frequently had a number of characteristics that set them apart from the folk blues. The songs were often composed by professional tunesmiths and were thus somewhat stylized, though some vaudeville blues singers did compose their own blues and many of their songs did draw in some way on traditional lines and phrases. In addition to the twelve-bar structure, they often also featured introductory lyric or narrative passages or eschewed the twelve-bar structure for 16-, 24-, or 32-bar structures. The singers themselves were in numerous instances professional stage performers who appeared in revues and stage shows, singing pop songs, dancing, and/or performing comedy skits as well, though sometimes these roles might have been foisted upon them as a result of their status as African American women in an entertainment medium. Their accompanists were frequently trained professional jazz musicians performing somewhat sophisticated arrangements, though improvisation was of course present to varying degrees. And finally, the songs' lengths were crafted to fit on one side of a 78 (though certainly two-sided songs were possible, obviously the song would have to start over again for part two, and the intervening time and effort it took to turn over the record surely broke up the performance into two distinct parts rather than providing a continuous whole). These were the first blues produced for popular consumption on record, and for a number of years—and 1923–1926 was their heyday—singers such as Mamie Smith, Lucille Hegamin, Clara Smith, Victoria Spivey, Rosa Henderson, and the two most outstanding exponents of the genre—Ma Rainey and Bessie Smith—enthralled listeners with their tales of women's woes and triumphs, declaring from the stages of cabarets, theaters, and tent shows their (pop-) blues messages of weariness, frustration, defiance, and liberation. At times, especially in the cases of Ma and Bessie, they declaimed with such power and style that, no matter how pop- influenced the arrangement or lyrics, they struck to the heart of the deepest blues. The fact that they presented in sometimes frank and graphic terms the voices of a marginalized segment of American (and African American) society anxious to explore both inter- and intracommunity grievances and issues speaks to one of the functions of commercially-recorded vaudeville blues.

In the meantime, male country blues and folk performers continued to entertain across the South, making no inroads in the recording industry until the 1923 guitar solos by Sylvester Weaver and 1924 sides by Reece Du Pree, Daddy Stovepipe, Stovepipe No. 1, Papa Charlie Jackson, and Ed Andrews. However, it was the phenomenal success of Blind Lemon Jefferson in 1926 that proved that male country blues artists (and female country blues artists as well) could produce profit for record companies, sending company agents and representatives into the fields in search of country blues talent in a variety of geographical areas. Such forays began to provide a picture of a number of different regional blues style tendencies that were tied in a number of ways to conditions in the geographical location: the source in Africa of slaves brought to that area; the relations and interactions between blacks and whites in the area; the proximity and access to other kinds of music; the popularity and/or dominance of a particular area performer; and the access to commercial blues recordings are among the most important determinants producing regional tendencies—though they are not absolute determinants.

For example, we tend to associate Mississippi Delta blues with insistent, jagged polyrhythms, harsh and raspy vocal timbre, limited melodic range, and unrestrained intensity, all characteristics of Mississippi blues legend Charlie Patton and his "pupils" Son House and Willie Brown. And yet other excellent Mississippi blues performers such as Tommy Johnson, Skip James, Mattie Delaney, and John Hurt lack one or more of these "typical" characteristics. In Texas, reels, play party songs, work songs, and field hollers were prominent in the work of older generation Texas-area performers such as Henry Thomas, Texas Alexander, Bessie Tucker, Rambling Thomas, and King Solomon Hill. Among the younger Texas-area artists of the 1920s and 1930s, a lighter, mid-tempo, ragtime-influenced (but not dynamically flashy) music—with a steady, thumping bass, ornamental and rhythmically free treble part, and voice timbre that was less harsh than the "typical" Mississippi blues singer—prevailed. And yet above it all, similar in some ways and yet gloriously different, was the daunting figure of the virtually uncopyable Blind Lemon Jefferson. In the southeast states, dazzling guitar technique—polyrhythmic syncopated bounce and flashy chords and runs borrowed from ragtime music—smooth vocals, and sometimes boastful, lighthearted, double-entendre lyrics were common, crafted most beautifully by the influential Blind Blake, along with Gary Davis, Willie Walker, and Blind Boy Fuller, with a strong twelve-string guitar contingent including Barbecue Bob and Blind Willie McTell located in and around Atlanta. One could similarly enumerate these types of regional tendencies for areas such as Tennessee, with their great jug bands, St. Louis, and Alabama, as well as for blues and boogie woogie piano styles represented by the Thomas family, Roosevelt Sykes, Walter Davis, and Albert Ammons, Pete Johnson, and Meade Lux Lewis, and then move on to the great harmonica players, such as Bullet Williams, Jaybird Coleman, Eddie Mapp, Blues Birdhead and others.

Suffice it to say that there was a broad variety of blues styles, styles that began to coalesce into a smaller number of urban blues styles by drawing on the work of a number of urban blues pioneers of the 1930s and 1940s. There were the smooth, wistful vocals and beautifully integrated instruments of Leroy Carr and Scrapper Blackwell; the suave sophistication and pioneer virtuoso guitar work of the melismatic Lonnie Johnson; the Bluebird beat band blues of Big Bill Broonzy, slide guitar wizard Tampa Red, powerhouse pianist Big Maceo, and harmonica ace Sonny Boy Williamson (all distinctive vocalists in their own rights), and the Chicago through Memphis hard-bitten fireworks of Memphis Minnie. The World War II era found T-Bone Walker crystallizing the contributions of Blind Lemon, Lonnie Johnson, Scrapper Blackwell, and jazz pioneers Django Reinhardt and Charlie Christian into his own distinctive and influential single-string style, and the shouting of Kansas City's Big Joe Turner, the bluesy crooning of Nat King Cole-inspired Charles Brown, and the gospel and gospel-influenced stylings of Sister Rosetta Tharpe and Dinah Washington all pointing toward the predominant trends in blues, rhythm and blues, and the rock and roll to come. All of these styles were produced and/or influenced by increasing urbanization, greater use of amplification, and wider employment of larger ensembles, leading the metamorphosis of the blues from its rural roots to the varied expression of urban artists such as Muddy Waters, Little Walter, and Elmore James in Chicago; Howlin' Wolf, Junior Parker, and Little Milton in Memphis; the T-Bone Walker-influenced guitarists B. B. King or Albert King, Freddy King, Gatemouth Brown, and Albert Collins; and the blues, rhythm and blues, and soul stylings of Big Maybelle, Esther Phillips, Jimmy Reed, Slim Harpo, Professor Longhair, Fats Domino, Ruth Brown, and Wilson Pickett; and contemporary performers such as Otis Clay, Sugar Blue, Robert Cray, and Millie Jackson.

Through it all, the blues singer has provided both a personal and communal voice that encompassed the varied experiences of the African American in a racist society. "The blues started from slavery," Memphis Slim stated authoritatively in a conversation with Big Bill Broonzy and Sonny Boy Williamson, and indeed the blues is imbued with the lash of slavery, the empty promises of Reconstruction, the indignities of Jim Crow, and the continuing inequities inherent in American society. Blues performers themselves have defined the blues in their own songs—"the blues ain't nothin but a woman lovin a married man," "a low-down shakin chill," "a botheration on your mind"—but just as surely as the blues are rooted in these kinds of specific immediate experiences, they also draw upon a historical and emotional backdrop about which B. B. King has commented, "After you have lived in the [Jim Crow] system for so long, then it don't bother you openly, but way back in your mind it bugs you." Blues performers may not, in fact, always be describing solely their own experiences in their songs. Sometimes they spin out narratives of the experiences of relatives, friends, neighbors, or other community members, or experiences that any community member *could* have had, or experiences that reflect a symbolic rather than a literal reality, but almost all the songs are in the first person, in the first person, as if the experience had been the singers' own. Some songs like "Just a Dream" by Big Bill Broonzy portray the desire for some condition or circumstance that doesn't exist, like a welcome for a Black man from the president in the White House. But whoever had the actual experiences, by drawing on traditional vocal and performing techniques adapted to and altered based upon the singer's creativity and abilities; by using traditional lyric "formulas" and stanzas transformed to relate to contemporary experiences; and by tapping into characteristics of expression and performance that can be seen as part of a kind of "blues persona," blues performers can be seen as purveyors of both personal and communal, contemporary and historical, realities and visions. First person singular on the surface, first person plural down deep, multi-tensed in their echoes of the past, soundings of the present, and reverberations in the future. Unifiers.

Direct, immediate, insinuating, sensual, potent—something foxy and fine, moving on bulldog-hug-a-hound legs that have strutted and sashayed around the block (and across the ocean) enough times to know the blues by rote. Pigmeat built on an old hog frame—twelve sweet measures of humanity large enough to fit us all, but tight like that just the same. Full of mojos and turnrows and power and pain, distilled exquisitely into sweet showers of rain. A creative ritualistic celebration delivering high-born syncopators to the still-promised land. The Blues.

A Note on the Readings

THIS book is not, nor is it intended to be, the initiation or climax of the reader's blues experience. The performance itself, live or recorded, is the thing, must always be the alpha and the omega, and this work but a brief passage along the way. All the authors whose works are included herein would affirm this principle, for all have dedicated parts of their lives to enjoying, exploring, and/or championing the cause of the blues. The first exposure, therefore, must be to the moan, the trill, the wail, the words—the expression—and these pieces are always intended to lead back to the performances of the people who inspired them, as they have continued to inspire so many throughout their first century of existence.

Those who are familiar with the literature on the blues will doubtless find inclusions and exclusions with which to quibble. I have, in fact, quibbled with—even harshly berated—myself quite a bit, and expect to continue to do so. I have striven to include authors male and female, African American and otherwise, academic and nonacademic, in order to ensure a variety of sources and perspectives on the material. Is there enough here about the origins, development, and varied subject matter of the blues, about style, issues of gender and racism, the nature of performances and the crucial element of audience participation, and the extent of the influence that the blues has exerted over other musics and art forms, enough variety to do total justice to the subject matter? The answer is, of course not. However, in the end I had to agree to fix the text in its current concrete form and let my own hindsight second-guessing begin, trusting that I had weighed the important issues carefully enough to generate a useful volume that will, with its deliberately extensive bibliography, discography, and videography, point the direction for future research and exploration beyond the covers of this sizable but all-too-brief collection.

Choosing what to include in this volume has been an exceedingly difficult task. A good bit has been written on the blues, especially in the last thirty years, by a number of distinguished commentators, many of whom are included in this work. In fact, the authors whose work has been included here might have been equally well represented by a number of other book excerpts or articles on other aspects of the blues tradition, and readers are most definitely encouraged to use this volume as a starting point for reading the entire works from which these selections have been taken. In the process of choosing, matters of manuscript length and permissions cost have been a factor, but not the absolute determinant, of what and how much appears here, but the more significant criteria of social, political, artistic, and aesthetic significance and the extent of the contribution of the work to the dialogue on the blues has been foremost in this sometimes frustrating process. I also found that I was unable to track down some authors whose work I wished to include, and whose work therefore does not appear here. Just as difficult has been the task of excluding very worthy authors whose work has made valuable contributions to discussions about the blues and could justifiably have been placed among these pages, foremost among them Richard Wright, Bill Ferris, Frances Davis, Albert Murray, Rosetta Reitz, and Robert Palmer. Because of the various criteria for inclusion that left this volume without contributions by those authors, I can only direct the readers to the bibliography and the entries under their names with the promise that attention to their work will repay itself many times over.

And about subject matter: If I were going to add other sections, for example, they might deal with new directions for the blues as they are manifested in the soul-blues as represented by such labels as Malaco that are too frequently promoted and accepted primarily among African American audiences; rock-blues of the type that emerged with John Mayall, Cream, Paul Butterfield, and Canned Heat and have been represented more recently by Stevie Ray Vaughan, the Fabulous Thunderbirds, and even Blues Traveler; or the "new traditionalism" of African American acoustic artists such as Keb Mo. And what about the emergence and reemergence of many fine women blues artists on the scene, such as Etta James, Irma Thomas, Bonnie Raitt, Shemekia Copeland, Angela Strehli, Debbie Davies, and others? I would refer readers to the blues magazines currently in publication that, with various approaches and aesthetics, do among them a fine job of covering these various segments of the recent and current blues scene. Or there might be a substantial section on the themes and subject matter of the blues, a topic that has been well explored by Paul Oliver, Paul Garon, Sam Charters, and others in some depth. Had we but space enough and coin, this might be a much larger volume, but it would be priced right out of readers' hands.

I have not included excerpts from blues lyrics themselves, though some are included in the works presented here. This was a difficult decision on my part because, as I have already stated, I believe we must always go back to the performances themselves. My decision was guided and influenced by the very real possibility of a companion volume to this work of transcriptions of blues lyrics. Obviously, the best way to encounter blues lyrics is in performance, but there is value to transcribing the lyrics for more leisurely and meticulous consideration as well—though that whole approach to and process of transcription is fraught with dangers and difficulties. In the meantime, readers should most definitely consult the volumes of transcriptions listed in the bibliography. The same can be said for interviews with blues performers, which also may constitute a companion volume in the future. For now, the valuable interviews listed in the bibliography can serve as important supplements to this volume.

Defining the Blues—Useful/Interesting/Provocative Definitions

THE following brief excerpts are intended to hint at the variety of definitions of and approaches to the blues. These definitions will prepare the reader for a number of issues that will be raised in the text, serving as a provocative prelude to the selections contained herein.

The blues started from slavery.

—Memphis Slim

I'm from the lowland, the swamp. I'm from where the blues came from, and that's where I'm going before it ends up and something happens to me. I'm going back to the lowlands—that's where the blues came right off, that old country farm.

—Wild Child Butler

Oh I was in my room, I bowed down to pray
Say the blues come along and they drove my spirit away.

—Eddie "Son" House

[The blues are] a phylogenetic recapitulation . . . of species experience.

—Houston Baker

For me to sing the blues that I learned in Mississippi I have to go back to my sound and not the right chords as the musicians have told me to make. . . . The real blues is played and sung the way you feel and no man or woman feels the same way every day.

—Big Bill Broonzy

The Blues always impressed me as being very sad, sadder even than the Spirituals, because their sadness is not softened with tears, but hardened with laughter, the absurd, incongruous laughter of a sadness without even a god to appeal to.

—Langston Hughes

Creole began to tell us what the blues are all about. They were not about anything very new. He and his boys up there keeping it new, at the risk of ruin, destruction, madness, and death, in order to find new ways to make us listen. For, while the tale of how we suffer, and how we are delighted, and how we may triumph is never new, it always must be heard. There isn't any other tale to tell, it's the only light we've got in all this darkness.

—James Baldwin

You know the blues ain't nothin but a low-down shakin achin chill
Well if you ain't had em honey, I hope you never will.

—Eddie "Son" House

I got the railroad blues, got boxcars on my mind
And the girl I'm lovin, she sure done left this town.

—Yank Rachell

Whiskey straight will drive the blues away.

—Mississippi John Hurt

I woke up this mornin with the blues three different ways
Had two minds to leave you, only one to stay.

—Charlie Lincoln

The blues are sung not because one finds oneself in a particular mood but because one wants to put oneself into a certain mood. The song is the Nommo which does not reflect but creates the mood.

—Janheinz Jahn

People if you hear me hummin on this song both night and day
I'm just a poor boy in trouble tryin to drive these blues away.

—Walter Davis

. . . an impulse to keep the painful details and episodes of a brutal experience alive in one's aching consciousness, to finger its jagged grain, and to transcend it, not by the consolation of philosophy but by squeezing from it a near-tragic, near-comic lyricism.

—Ralph Ellison

Blues you roll and tumble, you made me weep and sigh
Made me use cocaine and whiskey but you wouldn't let me die.

—Sara Martin

Like the waves of the sea coming one after another, always one after another, like the earth moving around the sun, night, day-night, day-night, day-forever, so is the undertow of black music with its rhythm that never betrays you, its strength like the beat of the human heart, its humor and its rooted power.

—Langston Hughes

Did you ever feel lonesome just to hear your good man's name?
If the jinx is upon you the blues fall like showers of rain.

—Ora Brown

. . . a desperate search for language: Not for the language stolen from their ancestors, or for the language to which they are still not allowed full access, but for a new, exalted and *secret* language which takes shape dreamily in primordial gestures and cries.

—Franklin Rosemont

I've got a disposition and a way of my own
When my man starts kicking I let him find another home
I get full of good liquor, walk the streets all night
Go home and put my man out if he don't act right
Wild women don't worry
Wild women don't have them blues.

—Ida Cox

Yet the most astonishing aspect of the blues is that, though replete with a sense of defeat and down-heartedness, they are not intrinsically pessimistic; their burden of woe and melancholy is dialectically redeemed through sheer force of sensuality, into an almost exultant affirmation of life, of love, of sex, of movement, of hope. No matter how repressive was the American environment, the negro never lost faith in or doubted his deeply endemic capacity to live.

—Richard Wright

Old bald-headed four-eyed ofays popping their fingers . . . and they don't know yet what they're doing. They say "I love Bessie Smith." And don't even understand that Bessie Smith is saying "Kiss my ass, kiss my black unruly ass. . . ." If Bessie Smith had killed some white people she wouldn't have needed that music."

—Leroi Jones

[Everybody thinks of] the bluesman as bein' stupid, illiterate, not able to think for himself, that's why he's singin' these dirty, lowdown songs. They don't realize that THEY'RE the one that's stupid because they have been taught that these songs was dirty, they was filthy, they was no good. . . . Because you read a lot about the conditions in which the blues came about. And your parents probably didn't read about it and didn't care about it. They didn't want to hear about the nigger because he's just a dirty, lowdown, nasty, filthy, diseased NIGGER. And if you don't do somethin' for him, he's gonna starve. They didn't realize this nigger was takin' care of HIM. It's twisted all the way around. . . . I AM the privileged character. I'm the one wearin' the crown, even though it don't show. I'M the king, see.

—Johnny Shines

1

Africa and the Blues

WHEN African American Countee Cullen queried "What is Africa to me" in his famous poem "Heritage" and then produced a litany of varied, frequently conflicting images and ideas that flitted and flared across his haunted and confused consciousness, he was exposing a central perplexity in the construction of African American self-perception, comprehension, and enlightenment. The intermixture of cultures African and European that accompanied the frequently covert miscegenation that often horrified American society-at-large produced a hybrid blend quite unlike what had preceded it, yet similar: a reunion with an intimate and seductive stranger. How indeed did Africa influence daily behavior and infinite perspective, and could one separate the myths about Africa—its primitivism, exoticism, barbarism, backwardness—from the reality in order to arrive at a reasonable and appreciative conception of its contributions to the culture of African Americans, and through them Americans and the world?

The literature dealing with the influence of Africa on the blues is marked by controversy inherent to a topic that is necessarily impressionistic and subjective. In 1959, Alan P. Merriam wrote that "our understanding of African music in relation to African culture is almost non-existent," and thus judgments about how Africa infused African American music with its distinctive vitality necessarily partial and deficient. However, from early on, from vague assumptions about the nature of an African aesthetic that infused African American music, we have moved toward an increasingly more concrete and balanced examination of elements of African thought and experience that seem to have endured and survived the Middle Passage and the crucibles of slavery, Reconstruction, post-Reconstruction, the Jim Crow system, and the civil rights struggle.

The attempts of prominent anthropologists such as Richard Alan Waterman, Melville J. Herskovits, William R. Bascom, and Merriam to force a closer, more minute and informed examination of the relationship of African culture to African American culture, preceded by ardent calls from the African American community by people like scholar-Pan Africanist W.E.B. Du Bois, certainly helped focus and intensify discussions. Waterman wisely asserted that "the answer to the question of derivation may well depend largely on the initial direction of approach to the problem," highlighting the need for the opinions of African scholars whose perspective and angle of approach may yield different insights and results. Janheinz Jahn's provocative work does precisely that, asserting that the concepts of an African culture and philosophy independent of European and Middle Eastern influences can best explain the nature, function, and aesthetic of the blues tradition. And while some would argue that Jahn overgeneralizes about certain philosophic concepts, the definitions of which, as Alan Dundes pointed out, some scholars would wish to dispute, overemphasizes particular religious concepts and systems (in this case, those of the Bantu of Ruanda) at the expense of others, and overstates his case in his ardor to trumpet African autonomy, his ideas can valuably serve to reorient Western readers as they seek to understand the blues.

The desire for a more detailed "scientific" understanding and discussion of the relation of African to African American music suggested a need for greater coordination and classification in the debate. Alan Lomax's Cantometric analysis schema, while clearly still subjective, is an attempt at systematic comparison that generally aims at responding to Merriam's lament that too frequently studies had been "affective rather than analytical." Armed with thirty-seven rating scales and an intimate knowledge especially of African American music, Lomax's conclusion that African American musics of the United States "adhere closely to the core Black African model," while subjective, is still persuasive. Paul Oliver's pioneering *Savannah Syncopators* presented readers with an intelligent scholar with an intimate knowledge of the blues tradition and a probing, vigilant curiosity interacting with the concrete details of African life and ideas. The exchange included here from *Living Blues* magazine offers Oliver's concise summary of his points in that book and his disagreements with Waterman, unfortunately deceased and therefore unable to respond. However, David Evans reminds us with his respectful and informed disagreements with Oliver that we have by no means exhausted the depth and scope of consideration the subject deserves (as Oliver also acknowledges). Indeed, Evans himself has since the time of publication of the exchanges in 1972 continued to delve into the subject area: he is now convinced that the banjo is indeed of African derivation, but that the word "banjo" is derived from European names that returned to some areas in Africa in the nineteenth and twentieth centuries; additionally, he now believes that the "diddley bow" is derived from a one-stringed African instrument found primarily in Central Africa and not from an African musical bow. While Evans' *Folk Music in a Black Community* has not yet materialized, one can get a sense of Evans' views on this matter from the notes to *Afro-American Folk Music from Tate and Panola Counties, Mississippi*, AFS LP 167, sadly out of print.

Recommended Further Readings

Samuel Charters. *The Roots of the Blues: An African Search*. New York: Perigee, 1981.

Janheinz Jahn. *A History of Neo-African Literature*. New York: Grove, 1968.

Alan Merriam. "African Music." In *Continuity and Change in African Cultures*, eds. William R. Bascom and Melville J. Herskovits. Chicago: Phoenix Books, 1968.

Paul Oliver. *Savannah Syncopators: African Retentions in the Blues*. New York: Stein and Day, 1970.

Robert Palmer. *Deep Blues*. New York: Viking Press, 1981.

Winthrop Sargeant. *Jazz: Hot and Hybrid*. 1938. Rev. and Rpt. *Jazz: A History*. New York: McGraw Hill, 1964.

African Influence on the Music of the Americas

Richard Alan Waterman

THERE are two reasons why African musical elements have influenced the musical styles of the Americas.[1] In the first place, American Negro groups have remained relatively homogeneous with regard to culture patterns and remarkably so with respect to in-group solidarity. This has almost guaranteed the retention of any values not in conflict with the prevailing Euro-American culture pattern. Second, there is enough similarity between African and European music to permit musical syncretism. This has put some aspects of African musical style in the category of traditions not destined to be forced out of existence because of their deviation from accepted norms. The first factor has been dealt with adequately by Herskovits (115; 112; 118; 119; 120). The second, less well known because of the lack, until recently, of reliable data concerning the music of Africa, will be given consideration here.

In some respects, the western one-third of the Old World land mass is musically homogeneous, for it is set off from the other major musical areas by the extent of its reliance on the diatonic scale and by its use of harmony. Although the former appears sporadically elsewhere, as, for example, in China, it has not, except in the West, been used as the basis for musical development, and is to be distinguished sharply from the microtonal scalar system of the Indo-Arabic area. Harmony, on the other hand, appears in aboriginal music nowhere but in the western one-third of the Old World, where it is common in European folk music and African tribal music. Three points must be made here in amplification and clarification of this statement. In the first place, no reference is intended to the European school of literate music and musical theory; this has developed many aspects of music, and harmony in particular, to a point of complexity where it can scarcely be compared to either European folk music or African tribal music. Second, there exists a broad intrusive belt of Arabic and Arabic-influenced music which stretches across the middle of the western area, along both shores of the Mediterranean. Since the times of

Reprinted from Sol Tax, ed., *Acculturation in the Americas* (Chicago: University of Chicago Press, 1952), 207–18.

ancient history this alien musical outcropping has masked the fact of the previous existence of a continuous harmony-using bloc of cultures established earlier in the area.

The third point concerns the oft repeated assertion that Africans, except those who have been in contact with European music, use harmony only as the accidental result of polyphonic overlapping of leader and chorus phrases. This last fact merits closer examination, since it contradicts—by fiat, as it were—the evidence now available in many recordings of African music. It seems to have stemmed from certain preconceptions concerning the evolution of music which have proved inapplicable to the present case. The argument, in terms of these preconceptions, is simply that Africans had not developed enough culturally to be expected to have harmony. Given this bias, it is easy to see, in view of some factors immediately to be adduced, how an ethnomusicologist of a decade or two ago could have listened to African music, and even have transcribed African music, without ever hearing harmony used, even though harmony may actually have been present.

Let us first consider the nature of the machines used in gathering early recordings of African music. These necessarily were acoustical rather than electrical. A singer whose voice was being recorded had usually to be carefully placed in front of the horn. He had to sing loudly, and, even so, a deviation of any magnitude from the correct position might serve to put his voice out of collecting range. Since the usual field musicological task is looked upon simply as the collection of melodies, it is not difficult to comprehend how choral backgrounds, possibly harmonized, could elude the ear of the laboratory musicologist who heard only the recorded result, although he might be making use of the best equipment available at the time. Coupled to this consideration is the circumstance that most studies of African music were done by trained music analysts using phonographic materials provided by other, perhaps even "non-musical" researchers. Purely as a practical matter this division of labor between the collector in the field and the analyst in the laboratory, so unfortunate for the development of ethnomusicology as a branch of cultural anthropology, has been, until recently, a standard arrangement for the conducting of research in this discipline and is, of course, very effective in those rare cases in which true collaboration has been achieved between collector and analyst.

The fact that many African tribal styles actually do not use harmony to any great extent bolstered the accepted position. "Negro Africa" encompasses a number of peoples, and while, as will be seen presently, certain generalizations may be made concerning the musical style of the whole area, the great variety of styles actually present must never be lost sight of. The peoples of a large section of Dahomey, for example, manage to do almost entirely without harmony, while the Ashanti, in the neighboring West African territory of the Gold Coast, seem to employ at least two-part, and frequently three- and four-part, harmony for almost all of their music. It may be, therefore, that the notion of the absence of harmony in African music was connected initially with the fact that early samples came from non-harmonizing areas. Also, although this can by no means be used as a valid explanation of African harmony, it is true that the ubiquitous "overlapping call-and-response" pattern provides many instances of a sort of sporadic, although accidental, harmony when the beginning notes of the chorus refrain happen to harmonize with the simultaneously sounded terminal tones of the soloist's phrase.

That a hypothesis concerning the absence of harmony in African music could have been framed on the basis of early data presented, then, is completely understandable; how the hypothesis came to be accepted as fact and how it [illegible] to persist to this day are less readily understood. Yet we must realize that not only in ethnomusicology [illegible] an authoritatively stated, although invalid, generalization [illegible] inertia of its own. Nevertheless, facts, in the form of phonograph records, indicate that singing in harmony is common among African tribesmen. The presumption that the development of African music must of necessity be following the same evolutionary path blazed by European academic music is, furthermore, seriously undermined by recorded examples of the facile use by non-Europeanized African tribesmen of intervals considered extremely "modern" when encountered in European harmony.[2] African harmony, while it has remained simple, as has that of most European folk songs, nevertheless seems in some areas to have had certain striking autonomous developments.

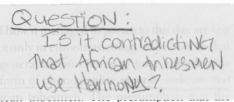

The presence of the same basic concept of scale and the use of harmony in both Europe and Africa have made easy and inevitable the many varieties of Euro-African musical syncretism to be observed in the New World. It is, for example, easy to understand how, to a member of an early American Negro group steeped in the value and behavior patterns of West African musical tradition, the European music which came to his attention must have appeared mainly as a source of new musical ideas to be worked out in terms of African concepts and techniques. Almost nothing in European folk music, to phrase the matter cautiously, is incompatible with African musical style, and much of the European material fits readily into the generalized African musical mold. An indicator of the fact that this is not true of any two styles of music taken at random is afforded by the rarity of examples of genuine syncretization between American Indian music and the music of either Europe or Africa.

Thus, in the United States as in other New World areas controlled by English-speaking Europeans, folk tunes and hymns stemming from the British Isles were often seized upon by African slaves and their descendants and, after suitable remodeling, adopted as American Negro tunes. The remodeling process was one of Africanization, and the tunes which emerged are best to be interpreted as European-inspired African music. In the Iberian-controlled areas of the New World, an additional factor facilitated the process of syncretization. The fact that the music of Spain and Portugal had already, over a period of several generations before the beginning of the slave trade with the Americas, been influenced by African musical traits imported along with West African slaves, was something that gave Euro-African musical syncretization in Latin America a head start, so to speak.

Both of the criteria offered above for the persistence of a tradition in an acculturative situation are thus seen to have been fulfilled in the case of the African musical style in the Americas. There has been sufficient density of Negro population, sufficient Negro group-consciousness, and sufficient homogeneity with respect to African musical values in most of the Negro areas of the New World to permit the transmission of these values to the young in consistent fashion. The sociological isolation of some of these Negro groups without relation to the actual proportions of African ancestry in the genealogies of members of the groups, as is the case in the United States, must not be overlooked as an important factor in maintaining relatively inviolate the African musical values in spite of a considerable infusion of non-African genetic strains. The ease with which many European musical traits could be incorporated into the African patterns simply permitted, through the processes of reinterpretation and syncretization, a retention of African musical formulae in bodies of New World Negro music which have become, if we start with African music, more and more European with each generation as the blending progressed.

This statement has been intended to show how African musical tradition, or at least, certain aspects of it, could persist in the New World. There would be no reason for the explanation, since such persistences of tradition are commonplace in acculturative situations, were it not for the fact that a sort of *academic* tradition has been in force which, placing emphasis on the many changes in the lives of the American Negroes brought about first by slavery, and later by the exigencies of life as a member of a minority underprivileged group, has systematically denied both the fact and the possibility of such persistence of [illegible].

This is not [illegible] American Negro music must be derived entirely from Europe or entirely [illegible]. Since the music actually is, for the most part, a blend of both African and [illegible] idioms, the answer to the question of derivation may well depend [illegible] approach to the problem. Thus, Negro spirituals have been pronounced by some scholars to be derived solely from Europe because they contain a great many Euro-American elements; the problem of the provenience of jazz, on the other hand, has been muddled by the proclamations of certain writers who, discerning Africanisms in that form of music, insist that jazz is purely African.

Attention thus far has been concentrated upon the aspects of African music which coincide with European; however, African music, obviously, is not European music. The European folk song is typically more complex harmonically and simpler rhythmically than African tribal song. Modulation from key to key, for example, is virtually unknown in African tribal music, while the consistent use of multiple meter—two or three time-signatures at once, as it were—is equally unknown in European songs. Melodic structure, however, seems to be at about the same level of complexity in both areas, although different forms are utilized.

The outstanding feature of African music which sets it most apart from that of Europe is the rhythm, a focal value which is implemented in a great number of ways. As Herskovits (114, p. 3) has written, "for the African, the important thing about rhythm is to have it, regardless of how it is produced." African rhythms have been spoken of (128, p. 61) as "incredible and incomprehensible to us." While this may be rejected as the counsel of defeat, it is undoubtedly true that the appreciation of African rhythms requires the development of a musical sense that, in the individual conditioned only to the norms of European music, usually lies somewhat dormant.

This may be spoken of as the *metronome sense.* Until it is developed, much of the aspect of African music most important to the African may well remain incomprehensible to the most careful investigator. From the point of view of the listener, it entails habits of conceiving any music as structured along a theoretical framework of beats regularly spaced in time and of co-operating in terms of overt or inhibited motor behavior with the pulses of this metric pattern whether or not the beats are expressed in actual melodic or percussion tones. Essentially, this simply means that African music, with few exceptions, is to be regarded as music for the dance, although the "dance" involved may be entirely a mental one. Since this metronome sense is of such basic importance, it is obvious that the music is conceived and executed in terms of it; it is assumed without question or consideration to be part of the perceptual equipment of both musicians and listeners and is, in the most complete way, taken for granted. When the beat is actually sounded, it serves as a confirmation of this subjective beat. And because it amounts to an unverbalized point of view concerning all music, this traditional value which differentiates African from "pure" European systems of musical appreciation is a typical example of the variety of subliminal culture pattern most immune to the pressures of an acculturative situation.

The metronome sense is not limited to the African; one variety of it is necessary in playing or listening to Hindu music, for example. But complete reliance on it, as a part of the standard musical equipment of every individual in making music, is an exclusively African musical trait. The metronome sense, in an extremely limited way, is also necessary in appreciating European music, particularly European social dance music and marching tunes. The rhythmic music of Europe, however, is so structured as to emphasize the very metric elements which African music is most likely to take for granted—the up-beat and the down-beat. The assumption by an African musician that his audience is supplying these fundamental beats permits him to elaborate his rhythms with these as a base, whereas the European tradition requires such close attention to their concrete expressions that rhythmic elaboration is limited for the most part to mere ornament. From the point of view of European music, African music introduces a new rhythmic dimension.

Additional features of African music which set it off markedly from that of Europe may be summarized as follows:

Dominance of percussion.—Most African music includes, and depends upon, percussion instruments. Indeed, most African musical instruments are of this type, including a bewildering array of drums, rattles, and gongs. These are the necessary implements for the peculiarly African elaboration of rhythmic and metric constellations. Melodic instruments, also, are utilized for their percussive values, as in the case of "thumb pianos," xylophones, and, for the last three centuries or so, the European guitar. Conversely, the gongs and drums frequently have melodic and harmonic importance. The percussive effect of hand-clapping, often in intricate rhythmic patterns, is also utilized constantly in African music.

Polymeter.—European rhythms are typically based on single metrical schemes, more or less elaborated according to the types of music the rhythms are used to reinforce. In European folk and popular music, particularly that used as accompaniment to the dance, the tempo is steady; in academic forms, the tempo may be varied greatly. African music, on the other hand—based, as we have seen, on the invariant or accelerated tempo consistent with the metronome sense—uses the interplay of two or more metrical frameworks as the primary material out of which the music is built. While the individual components may be quite simple, the combination is likely to sound to European-trained ears completely puzzling, particularly when, as often happens, rhythmic emphasis shifts back and forth from meter to meter. Anyone who cares to attempt to perform a $\frac{6}{8}$ beat with one hand, a $\frac{4}{4}$ beat with the other, and a $\frac{3}{4}$ tap with the toe of one foot will be convinced of the complexity, and will learn something about the character, of African multiple meter. This particular relationship of time signatures is a common pattern in African musical rhythm. The various rhythms are usually expressed by drums or other percussion instruments, but they need not be. Signs that these complex patterns pervade all of the African feeling for music are to be read in the accent patterns of melodies both instrumental and vocal and are likewise evident in the motor behavior of participants in African dance.

Off-beat phrasing of melodic accents.—From the African tradition of taking for granted the presence of a basic musical beat in the mind of the performer and auditor alike has stemmed not only the elaboration of meters just discussed, but also a quite different artistic technique completely dependent for its effect on the metronome sense. Syncopation, as utilized in European music, is in a way the simplest form of this technique, but in the absence of the metronome sense further development could hardly occur. In popular writings on the subject of jazz, the term "syncopation" has been used to characterize the technique as it appears in that form of music. However, in terms of total musical effect this label is felt to be misleading, and the more cumbersome but more general designation, offbeat phrasing of melodic accents, is preferred by the author.

In transcriptions of African music this pattern appears in the form of notes tied together across bar lines or across other main beats. Melodic tones, and particularly accented ones, occur between the sounded or implied beats of the measure with great frequency. The beat is, so to speak, temporarily suspended, i.e., delayed or advanced in melodic execution, sometimes for single notes (syncopation), sometimes for long series of notes. The displacement is by no means a random one, however, for the melodic notes not coinciding with the beat are invariably sounded, with great nicety, precisely on one of the points of either a duple or a triple division of the beat. Viewed a different way, this may be seen as a placement of tones *on* the beat of an implied meter at a tempo twice or thrice that of the controlling rhythm.

Certain psychological aspects of African off-beat phrasing must be considered if the pattern is to be fully understood. The maintenance of a subjective meter, in terms of the metronome sense, requires effort and, more particularly, a series of efforts regularly spaced in time. The regular recurrence of these "rhythmic awarenesses" involves the expectancy, at the moment of any beat, that the next beat will occur precisely at some succeeding moment determined by the tempo. Subjectively, the beat does occur. If it is reinforced by an objective stimulus in the form of a percussive or melodic tone, the metronome sense is reassured, and the effort involved in the subjective beat is masked by the effort of perceiving the objective pulse. If the objective beat is omitted, however, the co-operating auditor becomes very much aware of the subjective beat, which thus attains for him greatly increased significance. If the objective beat occurs ahead of time, the auditor, unprepared for it, perceives it and assigns to it the additional importance always accorded the unexpected, further reinforcing it with his subjective pulse which occurs at the "proper" time in terms of his experience. If the objective beat is delayed, the period of suspense between subjective and objective beats likewise increases the auditor's awareness of the rhythm. When the objective, audible beat occurs halfway between two subjective pulsations, as is frequently the case, both mechanisms operate to give the off-beat tone heightened significance.

On the other hand, it is apparent that if a whole tune were to be sung in such a way that each note occurred a half-beat ahead of a corresponding beat established by the subjective metronome on the basis of cues from, say, the initial beats of a percussion instrument, the subjective beats would sooner or later, depending on the degree of intransigence of the metronome sense of the auditor, come to be interpreted as off-beats, and hence would be realigned so as to coincide with the new beat pattern. In other words, complete "off-beating" has the same effect as complete lack of off-beat patterns; it is, in these terms, meaningless.

The off-beat phrasing of accents, then, must threaten, but never quite destroy, the orientation of the listener's subjective metronome. In practice, this means that a sufficient number of notes of varying degrees of importance in the structure of the melody must coincide with the auditor's rhythmic set to validate the gestalt through reinforcement of key points. A very few notes so placed will suffice for a listener whose metronome sense is highly developed, particularly since at least one percussion instrument is likely to reinforce the main beat. Occasions where melodic notes are on the beat, and percussion notes are off, are more trying to the metronome sense than the usual situation just sketched, and, of course, melodic notes may be in an off-beat relationship to one meter in such a way as to suggest even more complex relationships with other simultaneous meters. Theoretically, elaborations of the combination of polymeter with off-beat phrasing are almost endless. In practice, however, limits are set to this development by the fact that, regardless of conditioning, no musician's and no listener's metronome sense operates beyond a certain point of complexity. This point, however, is likely to be far beyond anything the European tradition would consider rhythmically intelligible.

Overlapping call-and-response patterns.—While antiphonal song-patterning, whereby a leader sings phrases which alternate with phrases sung by a chorus, is known all over the world, nowhere else is this form so important as in Africa, where almost all songs are constructed in this manner. A peculiarity of the African call-and-response pattern, found but infrequently elsewhere, is that the chorus phrase regularly commences while the soloist is still singing; the leader, on his part, begins his phrase before the chorus has finished. This phenomenon is quite simply explained in terms of the African musical tradition of the primacy of rhythm. The entrance of the solo or the chorus part on the proper beat of the measure is the important thing, not the effects attained through antiphony or polyphony. Examples of call-and-response music in which the solo part, for one reason or another, drops out for a time, indicate clearly that the chorus part, rhythmical and repetitive, is the mainstay of the songs and the one really inexorable component of their rhythmic structure. The leader, receiving solid rhythmic support from the metrically accurate, rolling repetition of phrases by the chorus, is free to embroider as he will.

The metronome sense, then, together with these four basic characteristics related to or derived from it, accounts for the major differences between tribal African and European folk and popular music. In attempting to trace the influence of African musical ideas on the music of the Americas, we must, therefore, pay particular attention to these features. The extension of purely rhythmic aspects of African musical style to Western Hemisphere music has already been discussed at some length. Certain additional musical and allied practices of that area may, however, be mentioned here, and the fact of their appearance in the Americas simply indicated. While, as has been mentioned, the African scale is diatonic like that of Europe, the tendency toward variable intonation of the third and seventh of the scale has occasionally been noted in West African music.[3] This is the "blues" scale. West African song often utilizes the device of contrapuntal duet, with or without an additional recurrent chorus phrase (250, Album II, record 6). This pattern is important in the religious singing of southern United States Negroes. The use of song as a device for social control and for the venting of aggression and the traditional contests of virtuosity in singing and playing are functioning elements of West African culture today, as they are of such musical styles as the Trinidad "calypso" in the New World. The counterclockwise circle dance, in which the dancers make up a part of the singing chorus, is common both in West Africa and in the New World, as is the custom of singing in falsetto. Finally, there is, in West Africa, little difference, in purely musical terms, between sacred and secular usage; this is mirrored in all the areas of Negro settlement in the Americas.

There are two aspects of the problem of African influence on the music of the Americas. One concerns the music of predominantly Negro populations, the other the spread of stylistic elements from American Negro music to the music of New World populations in general. Also, two distinct geographical areas—roughly, North American and Latin American—must be considered separately, since they have had different acculturation histories.

In the Negro population of Brazil all traits[4] of African music have been retained, and many songs are sung in West African languages.[5] Negro songs of Dutch Guiana exhibit all the listed traits of West African music; they are, however, sung in a creolized language compounded, for the most part, of English vocabulary and West African phonetics and grammar (119; 130). In Haiti, songs of the *Vodun* cult show all traits of African music, as do many secular songs (53; 52). In Jamaica, both sacred and secular music of the Negroes of the Port Morant district frequently show the five "basic" African traits.[6] Found here also is the use of a large African vocabulary, both in songs and in actual conversation. Negro music of the Island of Trinidad ranges from the religious songs of the Shango Cult of Port-of-Spain, conceived in purely African style, through the various urban secular styles, including the "calypso," in which all the basic African traits are to be observed, to the "reels," "quadrilles," "bongos," and "beles" of the rural districts, in which Europeans and African traits are commingled, although all the basic African traits are likely to appear (245). Most of the folk music of Puerto Rico is derived from Spain, although the style called "la bomba" is of purely African conception, while the popular urban Negro style, the *plena* (Puerto Rican equivalent of the calypso) sometimes shows all the African traits (246). Percussion instruments of African origin are used in connection with all the above styles.

In United States Negro musical styles, one of the main African components, polymeter, is usually absent except by implication, and there is a dearth of African-type musical instruments.[7] Metronomism, however, is present in all Negro sacred and secular styles, as is the importance of percussion (wherever percussion instruments or effects are not proscribed by circumstances) and the overlapping call-and-response pattern.

In modern American Negro spirituals and, to a greater degree, in the urban gospel hymns, percussion effects are stressed even in the absence of actual instruments, and the instruments (sometimes, but rarely, the pipe-organ, usually the piano, and frequently the guitar and tambourine) used are, in general, exploited to the full extent of their percussive possibilities (248). The overlapping call-and-response and the off-beat phrasing of melodic accents are important features of the religious music of the United States Negro, and a well-developed metronome sense is required for its appreciation.

It is evident, then, that in the regions mentioned, which span the habitat of the Negro in the Americas, music associated with Negroes is, in terms of the five dominant values listed, predominantly African. There are, even in the United States, cases of Negro songs with melodies almost identical to recorded African songs.[8] These identities must be laid to the fact that the songs have sprung from similar roots.

The music of these same areas which is *not* specifically identified with Negro populations likewise shows, in many instances, the same African traits. The diagnostic rhythm schemes of the Brazilian *samba* and the Cuban *rumba* and *conga*, to mention only three examples, are common in West African music. In general, most styles of popular dance music in these Latin American countries where the Negro population is at all dense have been strongly influenced by the basic African musical patterns listed, and many African musical instruments, such as drums, calabashes, etc., are used.

The areas referred to are those in which research has been done specifically from the point of view of African acculturation. There are undoubtedly many other instances of African musical influence in Latin America. For example, the Guatemalan "national instrument" is the *marimba*—an instrument certainly derived from Africa. In Mexico, especially in the region of the former slave port of Vera Cruz, African elements appear strongly in the rhythms of the folk music. The Argentine *maxixe*, to mention another example, probably can be considered as of partly African origin.

A major artistic product of the United States is the music called "jazz." Jazz is an intricate blend of musical idioms and has also had its own evolution as an art form. It is, of course, no one thing; yet any attempt to frame an all-inclusive definition points up the fact that those elements that mark off any kind of jazz from the rest of the popular music of the United States are precisely those we have cited as diagnostic of West African music.

For example, jazz depends, for its effect, largely on the metronome sense of its listeners and its players. Jazz terminology makes constant reference to this metronome sense. Musical terms like "rock" and "swing" express ideas of rhythm foreign to European folk tradition, and stem from African concepts, as does the extremely basic idea of the application of the word "hot" to musical rhythms. The development of a "feeling for the beat," so important in jazz musicianship, is neither more nor less than the development of the metronome sense.

The tremendous importance accorded to complex percussion patterns is another basic trait of African music to appear in jazz. An appreciable proportion of African dance music is entirely drum music; the tradition of long drum solos appears in all jazz styles, and, in the United States, only in the jazz styles.

The overlapping call-and-response pattern has, in jazz, been reworked in accordance with jazz instrumentation and orchestration. Typically, a soloist plays the call phrases as an improvised variation on the melody, while an appropriate section of instruments plays the chorus pattern, repeated with only those minimal changes forced by the changing harmonies, as a "riff." Most jazz band records contain examples of this use of the riff; since it is a pattern which gives a good deal of "rock" to the music, it is frequently reserved for the last, hottest chorus.

The off-beat phrasing of melodic accents is a stylistic trait which functions in jazz in unusually clear-cut fashion perhaps because of the absence of polymetric formations, which tend to make the off-beats equivocal. Syncopation has often been spoken of as an earmark of jazz melodies; of importance here is the fact that, in addition, jazz makes constant use of the more extended off-beat phrasing patterns. It is these, rather than syncopation per se, which give to the melodic line of jazz its characteristic impelling rhythmic quality.

In this short paper it has been possible to illustrate in only the most general way the character of African influences on the music of the Americas. To summarize: in areas (e.g., in Brazil, Haiti, and Cuba) where the official European religion permitted the syncretism of deities with the saints of the Church, African religious music has persisted almost unchanged, and African influence upon secular music has been strong. In Protestant areas where such syncretism has not been possible, the influence of African musical patterns on both religious and secular music has hinged upon a more extensive process of reinterpretation but is nonetheless considerable, in that fundamental characteristics of West African music have been retained.

In the case of the music of the Negro in the New World, we have an ideal situation for the study of musical change. We know, in general, the African side of the equation, although much field work must be done before specific tribal styles—the real raw data for our study—can be described. We also know the European side, and we are in a position to study the American results of musical acculturation. We also know enough about the general cultural contexts of the various American Negro musical styles to be able to assess both historical and contemporary factors bearing on change. Furthermore, among the less tangible aspects of culture, music is unique in that it can readily be quantified and submitted to rigid statistical analysis, although nothing of this sort has been attempted in this paper. The objective demonstration of the retention and reworking of West African tribal musical styles in the Americas, which seems likely to follow the collection of sufficient field data from specific African groups, may be expected to have relevance for the study of other cultural intangibles which, while not so easily subjected to quantitative treatment, are, like musical patterns, carried largely below the level of consciousness.

Notes

1. The writer gratefully acknowledges the aid of the Carnegie Corporation of New York in providing a field grant for ethnomusicological study among African-derived religious cults in Cuba during the summers of 1946 and 1948, from which stemmed many of the insights documented in this paper. He is even more deeply indebted to the Social Science Research Council of Northwestern University and to the Graduate School of that institution for their financial support over a period of years of a program of research which has resulted in the establishment of the Laboratory of Comparative Musicology and in most of the work in the field of Afro-American music which is summarized here.

2. Observe, for example, the use of parallel sounds in the choral music of the Babira of the Belgian Congo (23, side No. 2).

3. For a typical example of this, hear 250, Album I, song 5C.

4. "All traits" of African music, in the present list, must be taken to mean those basic traits discussed above as distinguishing tribal African from European folk music: the metronome sense, dominance of percussion, polymeter, off-beat phrasing, and overlapping call-and-response patterns.

5. See 121. Research now being conducted by A. P. Merriam, using a larger sample of Afro-Bahian cult music, confirms these findings (personal communication).

6. Recorded 1950, by Joseph G. Moore. To be deposited with the Laboratory of Comparative Musicology, Department of Anthropology, Northwestern University.

7. See, however, Courlander's convincing derivation of the United States Negro "tub" from the West African "earth bow" (54, p. 5).

8. Hear, for example, "Run Old Jeremiah" (150), and compare with "Bahutu Dance" (23). Also compare the "Mossi Chant" (250, Album I) with "Long John" (149).

Works Cited

23. "The Belgian Congo Records," *Denis Roosevelt Expedition Album.* New York: General Records, Inc.
52. Courlander, H. *Folk Music of Haiti,* Album No. 1407. New York: Ethnic Folkways Library.
53. ——. *Haiti Singing.* Chapel Hill: University of North Carolina Press, 1939.
54. ——. Pamphlet accompanying *Folk Music of Haiti,* Albums Nos. 1417 and 1418. New York: Ethnic Folkways Library.
112. Herskovits, Melville, J. *Life in a Haitian Valley.* New York: A. A. Knopf, 1937.
114. ——. "Music in West Africa." Pamphlet accompanying *Tribal, Folk, and Cafe Music of West Africa.* New York: Field Recordings, Inc.
115. ——. *The Myth of the Negro Past.* New York: Harper & Bros., 1941.
118. Herskovits, Melville J. and Frances S. *Rebel Destiny.* New York: McGraw-Hill Book Co., Inc. 1934.
110. ——. (eds.) *Suriname Folklore.* New York: Columbia University Press, 1936.
120. ——. *Trinidad Village.* New York: A. A. Knopf, 1947.
121. Herskovits, Melville J., and Waterman, R. A. "Musica de culto Afro-Bahiana," *Revista de estudios musicalos* (Mendoze, Argentina), I (1949), 65–127.
128. Jones, A. M. *African Music.* Livingstone, Northern Rhodesia: Rhodes-Livingstone Museum, 1949.
130. Kolinski, M. "Suriname Music." In Herskovits, M. J. and F. S. (eds.) *Suriname Folklore,* pp. 489–740. New York: Columbia University Press, 1936.
150. Lomax, John A. and Alan. "Run Old Jeremiah." In *Afro-American Spirituals, Work Songs, and Ballads* ("Library of Congress, Archive of American Folk Song," Album 3).
245. Waterman, R. A. "African Patterns in Trinidad Negro Music." Unpublished doctoral dissertation, Northwestern University, 1943.
246. ——. *Folk Music of Puerto Rico.* ("Library of Congress Archive of American Folk Song," Album XVII.) Washington, D.C.: Government Printing Office, 1947.
248. ——. "The Role of Spirituals and Gospel Hymns in a Chicago Negro Church," *Journal of the International Folk Music Conference* (London), III (1951).
250. *West African Folk, Tribal, and Cafe Music.* 2 albums. New York: Field Recordings, Inc., 1950.

From "Blues The Conflict of Cultures"

Janheinz Jahn

THE secular parallel to the jubilee and the spiritual is that music which is usually so completely misunderstood: the blues. 'A white song—black: that is, reduced to a simplified formula, blues.'[1] This is a widespread view. People also think that the *blue notes* and the modulation of tone exhaust the African part of the blues.[2] What is correct in all this is the fact that the blues did originate from the contact of African and European music. How the different contributions are divided, in what way these two very different styles affected one another, Dauer has described and determined. It is not the formula of the blues that is the true hallmark of blues but the sequence of voices, which is founded on the African antiphony. 'This consists in appeal and answer and explains the division of phrases in blues singing, as well as the function of the individual phrases. In the simplest case the phrase sequence runs A B and corresponds to the functions of an appeal and an answer. In the 12-beat blues, which have become classic, the sequence runs A A B, which corresponds to two appeals and one answer.'[3] Only in the blues the separate events of appeal by the first singer and answer by the chorus are 'consolidated into a single event, since they are all executed by a single voice'.[4] One song *in* the community becomes one song *before* the community, for the community is now only a listener. Instead of a chorus answering the singer, there are instruments accompanying the singing. In Africa the drums lead the singer's performance; one might say that the song accompanies the drums. In the blues this relation is reversed. First there is unaccompanied singing, then in the course of the development the instruments are added, but they are only accompaniment and the singing remains the most important part of the performance.

The texts of the blues follow the African narrative style almost entirely. They stem from the Afro-American ballads, which in turn continued the tradition of the African fable. 'In the fable', writes Senghor, 'the animal is seldom a totem; it is this or that one whom every one in the village knows well: the stupid or tyrannical or wise and good chief, the young man who makes reparation for injustice. Tales and fables are woven out of everyday occurrences. Yet it is not a question of anecdotes or of "material from life". The facts are

---

Reprinted from Janheinz Jahn, *Muntu: African Culture and the Western World* (London: Faber and Faber, 1961), 220–25. Reprinted by permission of Faber and Faber and Grove/Atlantic, Inc.

images and have paradigmatic value.'[5] The boll weevil ballad, which comes from Texas, may serve as an example.[6] The weevil is the arch enemy of the cotton planter.

Fahmah say to de weevil
'whut makes yore head so red',
weevil say to de fahmah
'it's a wonder ah ain't dead,
lookin' foh a home, lookin' for a home!'

Nigger say to de weevil,
'ah'll throw yo in de hot san'!'
Weevil say to de nigger
'ah'll stand it like a man,
ah'll have a home, ah'll have a home!'

Say de Capt'n to de Mistis
'what do yo think ob dat?
Dis Boll Weevil done make a nes'
inside my Sunday hat;
he will have a home, he'll have a home!'

The weevil, which bores into the bolls of cotton with its proboscis, is the plantation worker in his eternal search for a home. In the farmer's Sunday hat, his best piece of property, the weevil will have a home. Here again is the imperative future, which, in the form 'has made a nest', is set back into the perfect tense but means that the weevil *is to* make a nest there. It is the same technique that Césaire uses. The ballad is a song that invokes liberation; in the most harmless fable it conceals the call to rebel.

The old ballad was later turned into a blues song, for the two types fade imperceptibly into one another. In the Boll Weevil Blues the weevil then becomes the living symbol of liberation.[7] The blues cannot therefore be reduced to the formula: 'a white song—black'; for both textual and musical structure stem from African traditions.

Nor are the blues 'sad', although the legend of 'melancholy' blues has been influential for a century and for a couple of decades there have in fact been melancholy blues. In accordance with the common view we do indeed find in the *Negro Caravan* of 1941 the statement: 'In contrast to the spirituals, which were originally intended for group singing, the blues are sung by a single person. They express his feelings and ideas about his experience, but they do this so fundamentally, in an idiom so recognizable to his audience, that this emotion is shared as theirs.'[8] But this is the exact contrary of the real situation.

For the blues singer does not in fact express *his* personal experiences and transfer them to his audience; on the contrary, it is the experiences of the community that he is expressing, making himself its spokesman. Even when there is talk of loneliness, of the beloved who has run away, of the neglected wife, of nostalgia for the South, it is not the personal experience that is emphasized, but the typical experience of all those rejected by society in the Negro districts of the North. And even though indirectly, the note of rebellion is always heard too:

I'd rather drink muddy water, sleep in a hollow log,
dan to stay in dis town, treated like a dirty dog.[9]

The melancholy is a camouflage, the 'plaint' hides a *com*plaint.

If we read the text of the blues songs without prejudice and notice the double meaning, which all authors emphasize, we find them mocking, sarcastic, tragi-comic, tragic, dramatic and accusing, often crudely humorous—there is only one thing that they are only exceptionally, and then usually when they have been turned into a cabaret number, and that is—melancholy. Yet we read in the *Negro Caravan:* 'The mood is generally a sorrowful one; the word "blues" is part of the American vocabulary now as a synonym for melancholy, for unhappy moodiness.'[10] This widespread misinterpretation has various causes. The *blue notes* characteristic of the blues, which go back to the middle pitch of the West African tonal languages,[11] and have a modality between sharp and flat, sound sad to European ears. Besides, we are accustomed in Europe to interpret poetry and music psychologically as expressions of an individual soul. For African art, on the other hand, this means a confusion of means and meaning. Of the Afro-American *Work Songs,* which go back to the traditional form of communal work, and which are called *dokpwe* in Dahomey, *egbe* in Yoruba, *coumbite* in Haiti, *troca dia* in Brazil, and *gayap* in Trinidad, even Dauer writes: 'The basic law of the work song is to increase energy through music. Its effect consists in turning work into a kind of game or dance which in turn invokes an excitement that cannot be produced by pack mule work. This excitement increases energy and when reduced to a form that excludes all unnecessary movements itself becomes a driving force. The constant sequence of game and dance distracts the mind from the burdens of labour, the evenly rhythmic singing and playing becomes a (pretended) reality, work goes on automatically, and becomes subconscious.'[12] This interpretation of Dauer's correctly perceives the effects but not the causes. Song and dance do not have the purpose of lightening the work, but in song and dance Nommo is doing the real work, and conjuring up the latent forces of nature, while the work itself is only an addition. The meaning of the work lies in the song and dance; they are not a purposive means for the end of lightening the work, even though their influence has that effect. The song is not an aid to the work, but the work an aid to the song.

The same is true of the blues. The blues are sung, not because one finds oneself in a particular mood, but because one wants to put oneself into a certain mood. The song is the Nommo which does not reflect but creates the mood. And this mood is melancholy only from the romantic point of view current since the time of the abolitionists. The picture of the poor slave full of yearning, singing his sad song, corresponded to the mood awakened by Harriet Beecher Stowe with *Uncle Tom's Cabin.* Much as we may admire the sentiments of the abolitionists, we must not overlook the fact that they saw the slaves as alienated, helpless beings who were longing for freedom but ought not to rebel: enslaved by white men, they should also be set free by them. So they were drawn as patiently suffering lambs, helpless, pitiable and sad. Help and support was to be given the slaves, but from agitators one kept one's distance and tried to pacify them. This attitude was apparent as late as the beginning of this century in the generous help that was given to the pacifist Booker T. Washington, while every possible obstacle was put in the way of W. E. B. DuBois, who made rigorous demands.

The abolitionists opposed their picture of the sad slave with his melancholy songs to the picture of the willing, confident, happy slave which the slave owners habitually drew. For the latter, the song of the disenfranchized sounded by no means melancholy; they considered it the expression of a carefree and happy mood. But both pictures are distorted. Frederick Douglass, the runaway slave, writes in his autobiography the telling sentences: 'The remark is not infrequently made, that slaves are the most contented and happy labourers in the world. They dance and sing, and make all manner of joyful noises—so they do; but it is a great mistake to suppose them happy because they sing. The songs of the slave represent the sorrows, rather than the joys, of his heart. Slaves sing to *make* themselves happy rather than to express their happiness through singing.'[13] The blues do not arise from a mood, but produce one. Like every art form in African culture song too is an attitude which effects something. The spiritual produces God, the secularized blues produce a mood. Even there residual-African Nommo is still effective.

Notes

1. Joachim Ernst Berendt, *Blues* (Munich, 1957), 11.
2. Ibid., 12.
3. Alfons M. Dauer, *Knaurs Jazz-Lexikon* (Munich, 1957), 53.
4. Alfons M. Dauer, *Der Jazz, seine Ursprünge und seine Entwicklung* (Kassel, 1958), 74.
5. Léopold Sédar Senghor, "L'esprit de la civilisation ou les lois de la culture négro-africaine," *Présence Africaine* (Paris), 8–10 (1956): 60.
6. Dauer, *Der Jazz,* 146–47.
7. Ibid., 60.
8. Sterling A. Brown, Arthur P. Davis, and Ulysses Lee, *The Negro Caravan* (New York, 1941), 426.
9. Ibid., 429.
10. Ibid., 426.
11. Dauer, *Der Jazz,* 31.
12. Ibid., 53.
13. Douglas quoted in Brown, Davis, and Lee, *The Negro Caravan,* 726.

Song Structure and Social Structure

Alan Lomax

MUSIC-MAKING is one of the most strictly patterned forms of human behavior.[1] Its modes of communication are so limited that even a casual listener can distinguish quickly the best performers and identify the pieces in an idiom of whose technique and content he knows nothing. For many centuries and in many cultures, musical adepts have had at their disposal elaborate systems of notation and theory. The musicologists of our time have inherited this treasure of knowledge and have refined greatly their analytic tools. Thousands of volumes of accurately notated music exist, alongside of carefully wrought critical studies. Yet, it seems, none of us is much closer to understanding what music is and what it says than are the singers of primitive cultures. As one of America's leading musicologists remarked to me a year ago, "No one knows anything about melody." If melody, a possession of all human beings everywhere and at every stage of development, is a mystery, what of rhythm, harmony, and the superstructures erected with these three magic tools?

The suggestion of this paper is that ethnomusicology should turn aside, for a time, from the study of music in purely musical terms to a study of music in context, as a form of human behavior. In the first stages of such a study it is not necessary that all that is known and notable about music be accounted for. It would be a positive step forward to delineate the varying shapes of musical behavior and to begin to frame this behavior in its precise cultural setting. It should then be possible to discern the bonds between musical patterns and the socio-psychological traits available to the other humanistic disciplines.

As a working hypothesis, I propose the common-sense notion that music somehow expresses emotion; therefore, when a distinctive and consistent musical style lives in a culture or runs through several cultures, one can posit the existence of a distinctive set of emotional needs or drives that are somehow satisfied or evoked by this music. If such a musical style occurs with only a limited pattern of variation in the similar cultural setting and over a long period of time, one may assume that a stable expressive and emotional pattern has existed in group A in area B through time T. Thus we might look forward to a scientific musicology that could speak with some precision about formative emotional

Reprinted by permission from *Ethnology* 1, no. 4 (Oct. 1962): 425–51.

attitudes pervading cultures and operating through history. In this first stage of investigation we need not be concerned about the way that musical symbolism works, but only with a method that would locate sets of musical phenomena cross-culturally.

Until recently, the musical habits of mankind were not well enough known to make such a cross-cultural study possible. In the past twenty years, however, excellent field recordings from a wide sample of primitive and folk cultures have been published. We need no longer depend upon notations of music from exotic sources. Unlike the musicologists of the past, we need no longer evaluate the varied music of the peoples of the world from a perspective of the fine-art music of Western Europe, for we now have adequate comparative data and can examine them at leisure on their own terms.

In the summer of 1961 a Rockefeller grant enabled me, with my musicologist assistant, Victor Grauer, to assemble and to review approximately 400 sets of recordings and tapes from about 250 culture areas. Each selection was played over ultra-high-fidelity equipment through a pair of matched speakers, one for each listener, and was rated in a comparable manner. In this preliminary survey we could not, of course, completely control the size or the authenticity of the sample from all areas. Normally each culture was represented by from six to twenty selections on an LP recording, edited by the field recordist. We believe that, on the whole, these editor-collectors, most of whom were anthropologists or ethnomusicologists, chose representative materials for these LPs. Elsewhere I had to trust my own judgment, gained in a lifetime of field work and editing field tapes. In any case, our analytic technique—which was designed to look at gross traits rather than the detail of music—obviates this difficulty to a considerable extent. The method shows up stylistic pattern so quickly and in such bold relief that, even when a very large sample was available, we found it unnecessary to analyze more than two or three pieces; additional data usually confirmed the first observations.

Furthermore, we found that our descriptive method took care of the normally troublesome distinctions between the more or less "authentic" or "genuine" songs in the sample. As long as the material was recorded on the spot from native informants, even strongly acculturated music from an area conformed in most respects to the profiles established for conservative and traditional songs. For example, we found that "folk," banjo-accompanied, American mountain ballads differed in only two or three particulars from contemporary hillbilly songs; both could be classified legitimately as adhering to the same performance style, at least in terms of our level of analysis. Many similar experiences made us confident that, even when the sample of data from an area is small and acculturated, our method always tells us something important about the structure of the musical performance in that culture.

Cantometrics

This method is called *cantometrics*. Cantometrics is a system for rating a song performance in a series of qualitative judgments; one day it may be a way of using song as an indicator of social and psychological pattern in a culture. Cantometrics takes into account the phenomena described by European music notation—melody, rhythm, harmony, interval size, etc.—but it looks beyond these European basics at many other factors present in and (as far as we could tell by intensive listening) generic to the song style of other areas. These factors include the size and social structure of the music-making group; the location and role of leadership in the music-making group; the type and the degree of integration in the music-making group; the type and the degree of melodic, rhythmic, and vocal embellishment in a sung performance; and the qualities of the singing voice normally effected by the chosen singers in a culture. Since these features of a performance are judged by our system in a summary fashion, we also looked at the purely musical traits at a similar level. For example, rhythm was rated, not in terms of the precise meter that occurred in a selection, but in terms of levels of increasing complexity—from the simple one-beat rhythm, often found among Amerindians, to the free, almost meterless rhythms common to much Oriental singing. In addition, however, we looked at the type of rhythmic organization of both the singing and instrumental groups, here again rating the sample in terms of increasing levels of integration, from simple unison to complex counterpoint. Thus our rating system, for rhythm, quickly summarizes in four judgments much of the information that would be obtainable from painstaking notation and analysis of hundreds of examples by normal methods of music notation.

Cantometrics does not depend, except at one or two levels, upon formal musical analysis, but is limited, I believe, to those features of a sung performance which are available and important to a "normal listener" anywhere. Using the cantometrics system, a trained observer can make the same series of defined observations about any song that he hears, whether recorded or "live." These judgments are recorded in a series of 37 rating scales on a standard data sheet. Each one of these parameters or lines contains from three to thirteen points, each point being the locus of a proximate judgment in relation to the other points on the same line. The number of levels was limited to 37 by the size of the coding sheet, and the number of points on any line was limited by the thirteen punches available in a column on an IBM card. No more points were included on any line than we felt could be handled by an attentive listener.

These 37 lines, with 219 points, are set forth in a symbolic map on the right side of the coding sheet. The symbols, which are abbreviations for the distinctions made in each line, greatly facilitate learning and using the system. The listener records his judgments on the symbolic map and then transfers them to a number map on the left, which also serves as an IBM data sheet. Here the numbers are arranged and spaced so that they match the corresponding lines of symbols. With some practice, cantometrics enables a listener to describe a recorded song from anywhere in the world in a matter of minutes. The results of this notation may be compared and then averaged with material from the same culture, until, within a short working period, a master profile in numerical or linear form is ready for cross-cultural comparison.

The Coding Sheet

The cantometric coding book now ready for publication runs to more than 50 pages and thus can be only summarized here. Therefore, in what follows, each rating scale, which is fully defined in the coding book, is explained in the briefest terms. An exception is Line 1, with which this article is particularly concerned. Unless otherwise stated, Point 1 in each line stands for the nonoccurrence of a trait, and the line itself, reading from left to right, is a scale from nonoccurrence to maximal occurrence of a trait. Figure 1 reproduces a sample

Figure 1: Sample Cantometric Coding Sheet

CODE SHEET — The Musical Situation — Source: MEAD-SCHWARTZ TAPE 3 NO. 2

Group or Song: LAMENT | Language: MANUS | Location: MANUS, NEW GUINEA

Male Singer — Joseph Mataway

Parameter	Scale	Codes
1) Vocal Gp.	[2] 3 4 5 6 7 8 9 10 11 12 13	ø **L/N** L/NA -L L/N N/L L//N N//L L+N N+N L(N N(L N(N W̲
2) Orch. Relationship	[1] 2 3 5 6 8 9 12 13	**ø** /o /O O/ O //o //O (o (O
3) Orch. Gp.	[1] 2 3 4 5 6 7 8 9 10 11 12 13	**ø** L/N L/Na -L L/N N/L L/N N//L L+N N+N L(N N(L N(N
4) Vocal Org.	[4] 7 10 13	ø **M** U H P
5) Tonal Blend-V	[1] 4 7 10 13	**ø** b b̲ B B̲
6) Rhy. Blend - V	[1] 4 7 10 13	**ø** r r̲ R K̲
7) Orch. Org.	[1] 4 7 10 13	**ø** M U H P
8) Tonal Blend-O	[1] 4 7 10 13	**ø** b b̲ B B̲
9) Rhy. Blend - O	[1] 4 7 10 13	**ø** r r̲ R R̲
10) Words to Non.	[1] 4 7 10 13	**WO** wo wo-no wo-NO NO
11) Overall Rhy - V	[11] 13	ø R1 R- R-v R* R*v **Ri** Rpa
12) Grp. Rhy.-V	[1] 3 5 7 9 11 13	**ø** Ru RH RA Rp Rpm Rc
13) Overall Rhy-O	[1] 3 5 6 8 9 11 13	**ø** R1 R- R-v R* R*v Ri Rpa
14) Grp. Rhy.-O	[1] 3 5 7 9 11 13	**ø** Ru Rh Ra Rp Rpm Rc
15) Mel. Shape	[1] [9] 13	**A** T **U** D
16) Mel. Form	[10] 11 12 13	t+St*V St*v St* StV Stv StL*V L*vL **LV** Lv L C
17) Phrase Length	[1] 4 7 10 13	**P̲** P̲ P p- p
18) No. of Phrases	[13]	8+ 5/7 4/A 4/S 3/A 3/S 2/A **1/25**
19) Pos. of Final	[1] 4 9 11 13	**f** f̲ F F̲ F̲
20) Range	[7] 10 13	1-2 3-5 **5-8** 10+ 16+
21) Int. Width	[7] 10 13	ø w **w̲** W W̲
22) Pol. Type	[1] 3 6 8 10 13	**ø** DR Ic Pc H C
23) Embell.	[10] 13	E̲ E e̲ **e** ȩ
24) Tempo	[9] 11 13	t– t- t t̲ **T** T̲ T-
25) Volume	[4] 7 10 13	pp **p** N f ff
26) Rubato-V	[5] 9 13	))) **))**) ø
27) Rubato-O	[13]	)))))) **ø**
28) Gliss	[9] 13	(((((**(** ø
29) Melisma	[13]	M m **ø**
30) Tremulo	[7] 13	TR **tr** ø
31) Glottal Sh.	[13]	GL gl **ø**
32) Register	[7] 10 13	V-Hi Hi **Mid** Low V-Low
33) Vo. Width	[8] 10 13	V-NA NA Sp **Wi** V-Wi Yodel
34) Nasality	[4] 7 10 13	V-NAS **GT.** Intermit. Slight None
35) Raspiness	[4] 7 10 13	Ext **GT.** Intermit. Slight None
36) Accent	[10] 13	V.Force Fo Normal **Relaxed** V-Re
37) Conson.	[4] 7 10 13	V-Prec. **Pre.** No. Slur. V-Slur

cantometric coding sheet, coded for a lament recorded by Margaret Mead and Theodore Schwartz in Manus, New Guinea. A line-by-line explanation of the coding system follows.

(1) *Organization of the Vocal Group*, rated in terms of increasing group dominance and integration. This line asks the question: Is the performance a solo by a leader (L) with a passive audience (N) and the resultant situation that of the leader completely dominating the group (L over N), or is the group (N) in some way active in relation to the leader (L)? Point 2 indicates complete leader dominance (e.g., Orient, Western Europe). Points 3 and 4 represent other solo singing situations (e.g., Southern Spain). Points 5 and 6 denote simple unison singing in which leader and group sing the same material in the same way and in concert (e.g., Amerindian and many other primitive peoples). In 5 (L/N), the leader is dominant more than 50 per cent of the time, whereas the reverse relationship prevails in 6 (N/L). Point 7 represents the situation in which both L and N are active in singing the same melodic material, but one part slightly trails the other and often adds small melodic or rhythmic variations (e.g., Oriental choruses, Watusi). Point 8 (L+N) is noted when L sings a phrase and then N separately repeats it. Point 9 (N+N) is indicated when N sings a phrase and another part of the chorus (N) repeats it. Points 10, 11, and 12 denote what we term interlocked relationships, i.e., when a part of a singing group overlaps another or performs a supportive function for the other (e.g., Negro Africa). L(N, in 10, indicates an interlocked relationship between L and N in which L is dominant; N(L, in 11, indicates a similar relationship with N dominant; N(N, in 12, denotes a similar relationship between two groups. Point 13 (W) indicates complete interlocking (e.g., Pygmy hocketing style, European contrapuntal choir).
(2) *Relation of Orchestra to Singers*. Point 1 denotes absence of orchestra or accompaniment. Point 2 indicates a simple accompanying relation by one to three instruments; Point 3, the same with a larger orchestra; Point 4, the same with a dominant big orchestra. Point 5 indicates a big orchestra alone. Points 8 and 9 denote the trailing relationship with a small and a big orchestra; Points 12 and 13, the interlocked relationship with a small and a large orchestra.
(3) *Organization of the Orchestra*, rated in terms of increasing group dominance from left to right, as in Line 1.
(4) *Type of Vocal Organization*. Point 1: no singer. Point 2: monophony. Point 3: unison singing. Point 4: heterophony. Point 5: polyphony, i.e., any consistent use of part singing, no matter how simple.
(5) *Tonal Blend: Voices*. This line rates voice blending in the chorus from none to homogeneous to well integrated.
(6) *Rhythmic Blend: Voice*. This line rates the rhythmic integration of the chorus in five degrees, from poorly to well integrated.
(7) *Type of Orchestral Organization*. Rated as in Line 4.
(8) *Tonal Blend: Orchestra*. Rated as in Line 5.
(9) *Rhythmic Blend: Orchestra*. Rated as in Line 6.
(10) *Words to Nonsense*. This line rates the relative importance of meaningful words as against nonsense syllables (including vocal segregates) in a sung text. Point 1: words important and dominant. Point 2: words less important. Point 3: words with some nonsense. Point 4: nonsense more important than words. Point 5: nonsense only.
(11) *Over-all Rhythm of the Vocal Part*, rated in increasing degrees of metrical complexity. Point 3: one-beat rhythm. Point 5 and 6: simple meters such as $\frac{2}{4}$ or $\frac{3}{4}$. Points 8 and 9: complex meters such as $\frac{7}{8}$. Point 11: irregular meter. Point 13: no consistent meter.
(12) *Linking Rhythm of the Vocal Group*, rated in terms of increasingly complex integra-

tion. Point 3: unison. Point 5: heterophony. Point 7: accompanying rhythm. Point 9: polyrhythm. Point 11: Polymeter. Point 13: rhythmic counterpoint.
(13) *Over-all Rhythm of the Orchestra.* Rated as in Line 11.
(14) *Linking Rhythm of the Orchestra.* Rated as in Line 12.
(15) *Melodic Shape.* Point 1: arched. Point 2: terraced. Point 3: undulating. Point 4: descending.
(16) *Melodic Form*, rated from through-composed (1), through five increasingly simple types of strophe (2 to 6) and five increasingly simple types of litany (7 to 12), to Point 13, which represents the special type of litany typical of much Pygmy singing.
(17) *Phrase Length.* The length of the basic musical ideas which make up a melody is rated in five points, from extremely long to extremely short phrases. Complex strophes are generally composed of long phrases, litanies of short phrases.
(18) *Number of Phrases in a Melody*, rated from left to right in eight degrees, from eight or more phrases to one or two in each melodic section.
(19) *Position of the Final*, rated in five degrees from left to right, from the final on the lowest note to the final on the highest note of the scale used in a given tune.
(20) *Over-all Range*, rated in five degrees, from a second to two octaves or more.
(21) *Average Width of Intervals*, rated in five degrees, from dominance of narrow intervals (microtones) to dominance of wide intervals (fourths and fifths).
(22) *Type of Polyphony*, rated in six degrees of increasing complexity from none to counterpoint.
(23) *Embellishment.* The degree of melodic ornamentation is rated in five degrees from left to right, from highly ornamented to virtual absence of ornament.
(24) *Tempo*, rated in six degrees, from very slow to very fast. Point 9, the center point (walking pace), has about sixteen beats per minute. Point 13 was not used.
(25) *Volume of Singing*, rated in five degrees, from very soft to very loud.
(26) *Rubato: Voice.* The degree of rubato (rhythmic freedom) which affects the overall vocal rhythm (Line 11) is rated in four degrees from left to right, from very great to none.
(27) *Rubato: Orchestra.* Rated as in Line 26.
(28) *Glissando* (voice gliding between notes), rated in four degrees from left to right, from maximum to none.
(29) *Melisma* (two or more notes per syllable), rated in three degrees, from great to none.
(30) *Tremulo* (voice quavering), rated in three degrees, from great to none.
(31) *Glottal Shake.* Rated as in Line 30.
(32) *Register(s)* most commonly used, rated in five levels, from very high to very low.
(33) *Vocal Width* normally used by the singer, rated in five degrees, from very narrow and squeezed to very open and relaxed (the yodel).
(34) *Nasality.* The amount of nasalization characteristic of a singer is rated in five degrees, from very great to none.
(35) *Raspiness* (any type of harsh, throaty voice quality), rated in five degrees, from very great to none.
(36) *Accent.* The forcefulness of the singing attack is rated in five degrees, from very forceful to very relaxed.
(37) *Consonant Enunciation.* The precision of enunciation of sung consonants is rated in five degrees, from very precise to very slurred.

This coding system has its crudities and its areas of vagueness. Even so, I have been able to teach it to other students of folk music and have discovered to my delight that they concurred in most of the judgments Victor Grauer and I had arrived at separately. I do not know whether cantometrics will survive the examination of my colleagues for a short or a long time, but I can commend it in several respects. It produces consistent profiles when applied to the music of large culture areas that both anthropology and musicology tell us share a common cultural history. These profiles enable us to recognize and describe song performance structures for the Amerindians of North America, for Negro Africa, for Western European folk song, for the folk song of Eastern and Central Europe, for Mediterranean and Middle Eastern folk song, for the music of the high culture of the Orient, for Polynesia, and for perhaps a dozen other musical culture areas. These structures shape the music of very large areas and may be presumed to have had such formative influence for centuries, perhaps for millennia. Regional and tribal variations of appropriate dimensions are also exhibited by the coding sheets, and it seems likely that cantometrics can point up important differences as well as links between contiguous cultures. This paper, however, will concern itself only with contrasts between the profiles of large areas.

A final word of explanation is perhaps necessary for the way in which these large-area profiles were prepared. Normally the songs coded from any one area conformed to one, or at most three, profiles. Generally one of these was far more common than the rest. We presumed that this was the favorite mode of song performance in this area, and we brought all these matching profiles together into sets. Then we reviewed each number column and chose the most frequent number in each parameter. This list of numbers was then arranged on a master sheet, and a new profile was established, which became the master profile for the area. Random tests of this master profile indicated that it took care of the majority of song performances from its area. Deviations in subordinate profiles usually concerned minor matters which did not affect the over-all impression of stylistic unity.

Musical Acculturation

The usefulness of cantometrics is, perhaps, most quickly apparent in relation to the troubling problems of musical acculturation. The American folklore school, led by George Pullen Jackson (1943), studied the available musical scores and concluded that most so-called Negro melodies were variants of old European tunes. Africanists, such as Melville Herskovits (1941), pointed to the survival of African musical habits and institutions in the New World. A comparison of the cantometric profiles of song performance from Negro Africa and from a wide sampling of Afro-American groups provides the answer to this apparent paradox (see Figure 2).

In most respects the African and Afro-American performance profiles are identical and form a unique pair in our world sample. The social organization of the musical group, the degree of integration of the musical group, the layout of the rhythm, the levels of embellishment, and the voice quality sets conform to the same ratings in both Negro Africa and Negro communities in the New World. These paired profiles differ from each other principally at the level where Jackson discovered Western European influence, i.e., in Lines 16 and 17, which deal with melodic form and phrase length. The African profile codes 10 (simple litany) on Line 16 and 10 (short phrases) on Line 17. The Afro-American profile codes 2 to 12 on Line 16, which means that American Negroes sing every type of strophe as well as every type of litany; it also codes 7 and 10 (phrases of medium length as well as short phrases) on Line 17.

Figure 2: African and Afro-American Profiles (Left and Right, Respectively)

Parameter	African	Afro-American
1) Vocal Gp.	10 11 12 13	10 11 12 13
2) Orch. Relationship	12 13	12 13
3) Orch. Gp.	6 12 13	6 13
4) Vocal Org.	13	7 13
5) Tonal Blend-V	13	13
6) Rhy. Blend - V	13	13
7) Orch. Org.	13	13
8) Tonal Blend-O	13	13
9) Rhy. Blend - O	13	13
10) Words to Non.	7 10 13	4 7 10 13
11) Overall Rhy - V	6 8 9 11 13	6 8 9 11 13
12) Grp. Rhy.-V	3 5 7 9 11 13	1 3 5 7 9 11 13
13) Overall Rhy-O	6 8 9 11 13	6 8 9 11 13
14) Grp. Rhy.-O	11 13	3 11 13
15) Mel. Shape	13	13
16) Mel. Form	10 11 12 13	2 3 4 6 7 9 11 12 13
17) Phrase Length	10 13	7 10 13
18) No. of Phrases	13	13
19) Pos. of Final	1 4 9 11 13	1 4 9 11 13
20) Range	4 7 10 13	4 7 10 13
21) Int. Width	7 10 13	7 10 13
22) Pol. Type	8 10 13	6 8 10 13
23) Embell.	13	13
24) Tempo	9 11 13	9 11 13
25) Volume	10 13	10 13
26) Rubato-V	13	9 13
27) Rubato-O	13	13
28) Gliss	9 13	5 9 13
29) Melisma	13	13
30) Tremulo	13	13
31) Glottal Sh.	13	13
32) Register	7 10 13	7 10 13
33) Vo. Width	8 10 13	10 13
34) Nasality	7 10 13	7 10 13
35) Raspiness	7 10 13	7 10 13
36) Accent	4 7 10 13	7 10 13
37) Conson.	10 13	10 13

The cause for this shift of emphasis in the Afro-American profile seems clear. Perhaps the most prominent and powerful trait of Western European folk song is its attachment to the strophic melodic form, composed of phrases of medium length. It has exploited this trait pair (2 to 6 plus 7) to develop a body of melodies unmatched in the world for number and variety. It appears, then, that Negro singers, coming to the New World, were impressed by the European strophic form and added it to their musical resources, meanwhile keeping their own system more or less intact in other respects. As melody makers, they retained their interest in the litany, short-phrase form but learned how to use and to create melodies in the potent European style.

For another example of musical acculturation, we may look at modern Polynesian song. One of the most notable traits of old Polynesian music is the choral performance in perfect tonal and rhythmic unison of long and complex texts, where every syllable is clearly enunciated. In some areas, a rudimentary form of polyphony occurs: one of the voice parts rises in pitch and maintains this level while the chorus continues to sing at the original pitch, thus creating a simple drone harmony.

Shortly after contact with European explorers and missionaries, this older style was submerged by an acculturated choral style, which most Polynesians mastered. They astonished, delighted, and sometimes horrified European observers by choral performances in perfectly blended and often extremely banal Western European harmony. Indeed, a casually organized group of Polynesians could soon sing in the European harmonized style more skillfully than most Westerners. Recordings of these performances became popular hits in Europe and America, and today this Euro-Polynesian style is spreading into Indonesia, South Asia, and even aboriginal Australia.

The cantometric coding system provides a basis for understanding this historical development. In both Western Europe and Polynesia, text is of paramount importance. European singers, however, perform mostly in solo. Choral singing is rare in this area, and, when it occurs, it is badly integrated unison. In order to organize a polyphonic chorus, Western Europeans must be drilled to pronounce, attack, and accent each syllable together and in one manner. This ability to chant in perfect unison, which is a precondition for effective Western European harmonic singing, is a normal Polynesian culture trait. Ancient Polynesia had, as noted above, a leaning toward choral singing indicated by the presence of drone harmony, but it did not have a sophisticated harmonic system. Such a system was provided by the missionaries, eager for Polynesians to sing Christian hymns. European block harmony, when well executed, increases the tonal blend of a chorus to its maximum. Polynesians, concerned about voice blending, quickly adopted Western harmony as a part of their musical system and thus achieved maximal voice blending. In many other respects, however, the profiles of modern Polynesian song continue to conform to standards of the music of old Polynesia.

The stability of the profiles produced by the cantometric coding system is confirmed by a further discovery. I have said earlier that most folk and primitive cultures seem to erect their song structures on one or two or, at most, three models. Whatever the function of a song in a culture, it conforms to one of these models. Thus we have moved on beyond the crude analogies which functionalism has so far provided ethnomusicology—work songs, funeral laments, ballads, game songs, religious songs, love songs, and the like. On the whole, style, as a category, is superordinate over function, in song performance as in other patterns of culture. Therefore, the cantometric diagrams of song style, which represent the song-producing models in a culture, may stand for formative and emotional patterns that underlie whole sets of human institutions.

This extremely general statement must be qualified in one respect, but one that will be of special interest to ethnologists. Whenever a special profile is attached to a body of song with a special function, this exceptional phenomenon can often be explained by the survival, the adoption, or the recrudescence of an entire style in a culture for historical reasons. The Euro-Polynesian and Afro-American acculturated song styles are both pertinent instances of this process, but perhaps another, more general, example should be set forth.

In an earlier paper (Lomax 1960), it was suggested that an older choralizing, well-integrated singing style has survived in mountain areas, on islands, and, in general, on the fringes of Western Europe, largely submerged by the more modern and familiar solo-ballad style of folk song. Cantometric study has strongly confirmed and sharpened this hypothesis. We have found that, in those areas where people sing naturally in well blended choruses and sometimes in harmony, melodies tend to be in litany form, metrical pattern is more complex, melodic embellishment is less important, and voices are lower pitched, wider, more relaxed, less nasal, and raspy. In other words, the stylistic profile characteristic of this "Old European" area strongly resembles the model of simpler African song styles.

There are also choral-litany song types embedded in the repertoire of modern Western European folk song, notably the sea chanties of Britain, various types of work songs, children's game songs, and certain survivals of pagan ceremonial such as the Christmas and May carols of England. All of these song types integrate, strengthen, and direct group activity in various ways. With the exception of the children's games, however, all these functional song types seem to be survivals that are passing out along with the activities and the forms of social organization that supported them. In our society only the children know how to organize and dramatize their feelings in the ancient, collective fashion. That the need for such song types still exists among adult Westerners is evidenced by the recent popularity of highly charged, choral-litany song patterns, rooted in erotic dance forms and created by Afro-Americans. This summary exposition indicates how stylistic models maintain and renew themselves, by working hand-in-hand with history, to weaken or support functionally based song types.

Enough has been said to indicate the general nature and usefulness of the cantometric system. It looks at a level of musical activity which is highly patterned, resistant to change, and superordinate over function. The remainder of the paper will relate certain levels of song performance structure to social structure.

Pygmy-Bushman versus Western European Song Style

One of the universals of song performance seldom remarked upon by musicologists is the working organization of the musical group. There is a difference in kind between the main performance structure of Western European folk song, where a lone voice dominates a group of passive listeners (L over N), and the situation in which every member of a group participates, not only in the rhythm and the counterpoint of a performance, but in recreating the melody, as in the Pygmy hocketing style (W). Figure 3 compares the master profiles of Pygmy-Bushman music and Western European folk song—and exhibits their contrasts. A comparison of the structure of interpersonal relationships and of role-taking in the two societies shows the same order of contrast, strongly hinting that musical structure mirrors social structure or that, perhaps, both structures are a reflection of deeper patterning motives of which we are only dimly aware.

The general shape of Pygmy music must first be summarized. Colin Turnbull, who has done field work among the forest-dwelling Pygmies, discovered that they had concealed the very existence of their musical system from surrounding tribes for centuries. He told me that solo song does not exist among the Pygmies except in the form of lullabies; that their choral songs may be begun by anyone, no matter what his talent; that leadership, during the course of a song performance, shifts from an accomplished to a less accomplished singer with no apparent lessening of support from the whole group; and that the chief delight of the singers is to listen to the effect of group-produced counterpoint as it echoes through the dark cathedral of the jungle. This situation we code 13 (W) on Line 1 and 13 also on Lines 4, 5, 6, 16, 17, 18, and 22. At the bottom of the code, where we deal with register, timbre, and other voice qualities, it turns out that the Pygmy voice is generally low, lacking in nasality and rasp, relaxed, and slurred—13 in Lines 32, 33, 34, 35 and 37. This group sings with yodeling tone, which, in the estimation of laryngologists, is produced by the voice in its most relaxed state. When a singer yodels, all of the vocal dimensions, from the chords through the resonating chambers, are at their widest and largest. This extraordinary degree of vocal relaxation, which occurs rarely in the world as an over-all vocal style, seems to be a psycho-physiological set, which symbolizes openness, nonrepressiveness, and an unconstricted approach to the communication of emotion.

Our coding studies show that a high degree of choral integration is always linked with a relaxed and open manner of vocalizing. This connection is strikingly dramatized by the Pygmy-Bushman style. These stone-age hunters normally express themselves in a complex, perfectly blended, contrapuntal singing at a level of integration that a Western choir can achieve only after extensive rehearsal. Indeed, the Pygmy-Bushman profile represents the most extreme case of total focus on choral integration in our world sample, and in this sense it is unique among folk cultures.

The vocal empathy of the Pygmies seems to be matched by the cooperative style of their culture. All that Turnbull has told us about the Pygmies in his remarkable book and his many papers (Turnbull 1957, 1959, 1960a, 1960b, 1961) confirms this point. Normally the group never goes hungry. Their environment furnishes them what they need for food and shelter. The men hunt in groups, and the women gather in groups. A precise system of dividing food assures every individual of his exact share. There are no specific penalties for even the greatest crimes, such as incest, murder, or theft, nor do judges or law enforcement exist. The community expresses its vociferous dislike of the criminal, and he may be belabored and driven out of the group for a time, but soon he will be pitied and welcomed back among his people.

A Pygmy baby lives, literally, on his mother's body, his head positioned so that he can always take her breast, her voice constantly soothing him with a liquid-voiced lullaby. Children grow up in their own play community relatively unhampered by their parents. When a girl begins to menstruate, the whole tribe joins in rejoicing that a new potential mother is among them. Her joyful maturation ceremony concludes with marriage. Pygmy

Figure 3: Pygmy-Bushman and Western European Folk Song Profiles (Left and Right, Respectively)

Feature	Pygmy-Bushman (Left)	Western European (Right)
1) Vocal Gp.	13	2 3 4 5 6 7 8 9 10 11 12 13
2) Orch. Relationship	12 13	1 2 3 5 6 8 9 12 13
3) Orch. Gp.	1 11 12 13	1 2 3 4 5 6 7 8 9 10 11 12 13
4) Vocal Org.	13	4 7 10 13
5) Tonal Blend-V	13	1 4 7 10 13
6) Rhy. Blend - V	13	1 7 10 13
7) Orch. Org.	13	1 4 7 10 13
8) Tonal Blend-O	4 7 10 13	1 4 7 10 13
9) Rhy. Blend - O	13	1 4 7 10 13
10) Words to Non.	13	1 4 7 10 13
11) Overall Rhy - V	6 11 13	6 8 9 11 13
12) Grp. Rhy.-V	13	1 3 5 7 9 11 13
13) Overall Rhy-O	6 8 9 11 13	1 3 5 6 8 9 11 13
14) Grp. Rhy.-O	3 9 11 13	1 3 5 7 9 11 13
15) Mel. Shape	9 13	9 13
16) Mel. Form	13	6 7 8 9 10 11 12 13
17) Phrase Length	13	7 10 13
18) No. of Phrases	8 11 13	6 8 9 11 13
19) Pos. of Final	1 4 9 11 13	9 11 13
20) Range	13	7 10 13
21) Int. Width	13	7 10 13
22) Pol. Type	13	1 3 6 8 10 13
23) Embell.	10 13	10 13
24) Tempo	9 11 13	9 11 13
25) Volume	13	7 10 13
26) Rubato-V	13	9 13
27) Rubato-O	13	13
28) Gliss	1 5 9 13	9 13
29) Melisma	7 13	13
30) Tremulo	13	7 13
31) Glottal Sh.	13	13
32) Register	4 10 13	7 10 13
33) Vo. Width	13	6 8 10 13
34) Nasality	10 13	4 7 10 13
35) Raspiness	10 13	4 7 10 13
36) Accent	10 13	7 10 13
37) Conson.	13	4 7 10 13

men do not impose on their sons a painful puberty ceremony; in Pygmy terms, a boy becomes a man simply when he kills his first game. The Mbuti sometimes permit the Negro tribesmen with whom they live in symbiosis to put Pygmy adolescents through a rite of passage, but this is only one of many ways in which the Pygmies tactfully pretend to conform to the desires of their Negro neighbors in order to live at peace with them and to conceal the existence of their own forest culture. When the Negroes have gone back to their village, the Pygmy children are given the bull-roarer and the fetishes to play with, and the little hunters laugh together over the childish superstitions of their black masters. During the initiation ceremonies there is ritual whipping of the boys by the Negroes, but when this takes on a sadistic character the Pygmy fathers intervene.

The forest Pygmies do not share the magical beliefs of their Negro neighbors; indeed, the Pygmies look down on the Negroes because of their superstitious fears and their focus on evil. They have no myths and little formalized religious belief. Their only religious ceremonies occur in times of crisis, when they sing to wake the beneficent forest and to remind it to give them its usual protection. When the tribe gathers after the hunt, joy-filled dances and songs knit the group into a cohesive and fully expressive whole. In our code the Pygmy musical form emerges as a static expression of community joy sung in liquid, open-throated style.

I have dwelt upon this extreme, rare, and somehow utopian situation because it runs counter to most of the music we know and thus illuminates the rest of human musical activity in an extraordinary way. It points to the close bonds between forms of social and musical integration. The choruses of these hunting-gathering peoples sit in a circle, bodies touching, changing leaders, strongly group-dependent. Even their melodies are shared pleasures, just as are all tasks, all property, and all social responsibilities. The only parallel in our coding system is found at the peak of Western European contrapuntal writing, where again all the separate interests of a variegated musical community are subordinated to a desire to sing together with a united voice about universal human values.

Thus far we have assumed an identity between Bushman and Pygmy musical styles, and, indeed, this is what our profiles indicate. Perhaps no two peoples, so far separated in space (3,000 miles), living in such different environments (desert and jungle), and belonging to different racial and linguistic groups, share so many stylistic traits. Even after pointing out numerous musical idiosyncrasies, this cross-cultural mystery still disturbs the two researchers who have most closely examined it, Yvette Grimaud and Gilbert Rouget. Rouget (1956) speculates upon the possible influence of a common cultural heritage or similar environmental adaptation, then leaves the problem. It seems to me that he has neglected one important piece of evidence.

Solo songs are common among the Bushmen and rare, except in lullaby form, among the Pygmies. Otherwise, as far as cantometric analysis is concerned, the styles are, indeed, identical. Bushman males sing plaintive solo songs to the accompaniment of the mouth bow, which, like our blues, dwell upon loneliness and isolation. This sense of personal deprivation grows out of a special Bushman situation that does not exist among the Pygmies. Their harsh desert existence, beset by thirst and hunger, results in a scarcity of women. Thus, in order to have a mate, Bushman men often betroth themselves to infant girls. The result is long years of waiting for marriage and consummation, then a union with a capricious little girl who may be anxious to postpone the duties of a mother and a wife.

Meantime the Bushman men, battling for their group's existence in a barren waste, suffer the deprivations common to lonely males everywhere, and they voice this emotion in their solo plaints (Marshall 1959).

In all other important respects Pygmy and Bushman social and musical structures are extremely close. Both groups share; both are acephalous. Their hocketing, polyphonic, polyrhythmic, maximally blended style seems to mirror this system of closely integrated relationships. The Bushman solo "blues," the only major deviation from this pattern, thus suggests the influence of environment on an otherwise consistent social and musical structure. It does not matter whether this Bushman solo song style has been borrowed from a neighboring group. A musical structure stands for a social adjustment, for the fulfillment of a commonly felt emotional need, whether borrowed or not. There is no better proof of this hypothesis than this one divergence of Pygmy and Bushman musical structures.

For further evidence of the link between song structure and social structure we may look at the other extreme of the coding system—a leader dominating a passive audience (L over N)—the principal pattern of Western Europe folk song (see Figure 3, right). This profile shows only slight variation for most folk songs from Norway, Holland, the British Isles (apart from old Celtic areas of Wales, Cornwall, and the Hebrides), Western France, Central Spain, and colonial United States. Text is dominant and rhythm simple for three or four phrase strophes set in diatonic intervals, with an octave range and some degree of embellishment. Voices are from middle range to falsetto, with strong characterizers both of throat and nose and a clear enunciating pattern. The connection between voice type and the degree of integration in group song is reflected in unison singing with poor tonal blend and poor to moderate rhythmic coordination. We may think of the singing of a Rotarian meeting, a football crowd, a regiment on the march in World War II, or a pub group in Britain. Each of these situations is a gathering of extremely individualized specialists, each singing in his own normal tone of voice and uncompromisingly independent of others at the level of vocal empathy.

The familiar pattern in British and Kentucky ballad singing is for the singer to sit quietly with his hands passive in his lap as he sings; his eyes are closed, or he gazes unseeingly over the heads of his listeners. He tells his stories in simple strophes that permit a concentrated narrative pace and demand the full attention of his audience. Thus, during his song, the listeners must remain silent and physically passive. Any movement on their part would interfere with the story. Any distraction would break the ballad singer's spell. When the first singer has finished a number of such songs, another may take his place, and the same pattern is repeated.

The leading singer commands and dominates his listeners during his performance. His association with his audience is, in sociological terms, one of exclusive authority, a principal model for conduct in Western European culture (see Parsons 1949: 43, 140–147, 178–179, 286–295). When a doctor or a lawyer takes over a case, his authority is absolute for the duration of the relationship. The same unspoken pact joins boss and worker, priest and penitent, officer and soldier, parent and child. Dominance-subordination, with a deep sense of moral obligation, is the fundamental form of role-taking in the Protestant West. Our cooperative enterprises are organized in terms of an assemblage of experts, each one temporarily subordinating his separate, specialized, and exclusive function to an agreed-upon goal. Workers on belt lines cooperate in this way to produce automobiles for Ford or

Figure 4: The Oriental Bardic Profile: Near and Far East (Left and Right, Respectively)

Parameter	Near East (left)	Far East (right)
1) Vocal Gp.	2 3 4 5 6 7 8 9 10 11 12 13	2 3 4 5 6 7 8 9 10 11 12 13
2) Orch. Relationship	8 9 12 13	9 12 13
3) Orch. Gp.	7 8 9 10 11 12 13	6 7 8 9 10 11 12 13
4) Vocal Org.	4 7 10 13	4 7 10 13
5) Tonal Blend-V	1 4 7 10 13	1 4 7 10 13
6) Rhy. Blend - V	1 4 7 10 13	1 4 7 10 13
7) Orch. Org.	4 7 10 13	10 13
8) Tonal Blend-O	1 4 7 10 13	4 10 13
9) Rhy. Blend - O	1 4 7 10 13	10 13
10) Words to Non.	1 4 7 10 13	1 4 7 10 13
11) Overall Rhy - V	9 11 13	13
12) Grp. Rhy.-V	1 3 5 7 9 11 13	1 3 5 7 9 11 13
13) Overall Rhy-O	9 11 13	13
14) Grp. Rhy.-O	5 7 9 11 13	5 7 9 11 13
15) Mel. Shape	9 13	9 13
16) Mel. Form	1 2 3 4 5 6 7 8 9 10 11 12 13	1 2 3 4 5 6 7 8 9 10 11 12 13
17) Phrase Length	1 4 7 10 13	1 4 7 10 13
18) No. of Phrases	1 3 5 6 8 9 11 13	1 3 5 6 8 9 11 13
19) Pos. of Final	1 4 9 11 13	1 4 9 11 13
20) Range	4 10 13	4 10 13
21) Int. Width	4 7 10 13	4 7 10 13
22) Pol. Type	1 3 6 8 10 13	1 3 6 8 10 13
23) Embell.	1 4 7 10 13	1 4 7 10 13
24) Tempo	3 9 11 13	3 5 9 11 13
25) Volume	7 10 13	7 10 13
26) Rubato-V	1 5 9 13	1 5 9 13
27) Rubato-O	1 5 9 13	1 5 9 13
28) Gliss	1 5 9 13	5 9 13
29) Melisma	1 7 13	1 7 13
30) Tremulo	1 7 13	7 13
31) Glottal Sh.	13	1 7 13
32) Register	1 4 7 10 13	1 4 7 10 13
33) Vo. Width	1 3 6 8 10 13	1 3 6 8 10 13
34) Nasality	1 4 7 10 13	4 7 10 13
35) Raspiness	4 10 13	4 7 10 13
36) Accent	4 10 13	7 10 13
37) Conson.	4 10 13	7 10 13

bombers for Lockheed, just as instrumentalists combine to make the big symphonic sounds. Ultimately, this leader-follower pattern is rooted in the past, e.g., in the European concept of lifelong fealty to the king or the lord. Ignatius Loyola inculcated the same principle in his teaching of the Jesuits: "In the hands of my superior, I must be a soft wax, a thing . . . a corpse which has neither intelligence nor will."

This degree of compliance is precisely what the contemporary symphonic conductor demands and gets from his orchestra—and from his audience as well. In its role relationship the symphonic audience, quietly listening to a work of one of the masters spun out under the baton of the conductor (whose back is to his admirers), differs from the ballad audience only in its size. Even the most group-oriented and fully integrated Western music is produced by a collectivity, organized in a manner fundamentally different from that of the acephalous Pygmy chorus, where all parts are equal, where subordination does not exist, as it scarcely exists in the society itself.

A Western table of organization or a belt line or a symphony depends upon a series of clear and explicit commands, arranged in a clear pattern agreed upon in advance. Our Western European folk songs are arranged in the same fashion—a series of compact, clearly outlined strophes and stanzas, each of which bids the listener to view such-and-such an aspect of a sung tale in such-and-such an explicit fashion. While this series of explicit and well constructed packages of fantasy or fact is being delivered to the listeners, the leader-singer must not be interrupted. If he is, he will very likely refuse to sing any further. "If you know so much, sing it yourself," he will tell his rude listeners, much as a doctor might tell an anxious patient, "If you don't like my medical procedure, get another man."

According to Turnbull, a long Pygmy performance may, as a maximum, contain only enough text to make a normal four-line stanza. The rest of the phonating consists of hooted vocables or variations on one phrase of text. Tiring of this material, another singer is free to introduce another bit of text, which in its turn is torn apart into syllables and played with for a while in somewhat the manner of a child or a musing adult in our culture. Here language loses its cutting edge and becomes a toy in a delightful game with sounds. This contrast is noted in Line 10 of Figure 3, which deals with the relative importance of text as against nonsense syllables. Western Europe codes 1; Pygmies and Bushmen, 13.

The Bardic Style of the Orient

Having now described two styles which lie at the extremes of the cantometric system—one solo-unaccompanied and the other contrapuntal-hocketing—let us now consider three master codes that lie between these extremes and that show again how musical structures rise out of, or reveal, the general shape of their social contexts. First, there is the area which, for want of a better term, I call "bardic." Here solo performance is again dominant, but various levels of accompaniment support and reinforce the authority of the soloist-leader. Linking together several large subareas, this bardic style shapes most of the music of southern Europe and Moslem Africa, of the Near and Middle East, of the Far East, and indeed of most of Asia aside from certain tribal cultures.

A searching portrait of the societies which gave rise to the bardic tradition can be found in the analysis of the system of Oriental despotism by Karl Wittfogel (1957). Wittfogel argues that, wherever an agricultural system depends upon the construction and maintenance of a complex of great canals and dams, a despotic control of labor, land, political structure, justice, religion, and family life arises. All the great hydraulic empires—of Peru, of Mexico, of China, of Indonesia, of India, of Mesopotamia, of Egypt, of the Moslem world—conformed to the same over-all pattern. The center owned and controlled every person and all the means of production and power. Complete and blind obedience was the rule. The way to approach the throne was on the knees or the belly. Deviation was immediately and ruthlessly handled by capital punishment, imprisonment, confication, or torture. The ancient rulers of Mesopotamia asserted that they received their power from the god Enlil, who symbolized power and force. The ministry of justice in ancient China was known as the Ministry of Punishment. The Egyptian peasant who failed to deliver his quota of grain was beaten and thrown into a ditch. A court favorite could be executed or deprived of his perquisites at the whim of the emperor.

Wittfogel points out that this system results in a state of total loneliness for the top as well as the bottom of the society. The peasant or small official knows that no one will dare protect him if he disobeys; the king or the pharoah knows as well that he can trust no one with his confidence or, for that matter, with his life—neither his closest adviser nor the members of his family, and especially not his son and heir.

Depersonalized conformity to authoritarian tradition is the norm for such a society. Everywhere in the hydraulic world song styles shows an analogous set of traits. The singer learns to use his voice in a formalized way and then masters a complex set of rules for starting and improvising a theme, and he displays his talent by showing how far he can develop this theme without breaking the rules that apply. The growth of modal systems, with the elaborate set of beliefs and customs surrounding them, reminds one strongly of a society in which social stratification strictly limits the development and growth of each individual from birth to death. Above all there is one voice, expressive of doom and pain and anger, which speaks the varied moods of the center of power. It is a testimony to the noble spirit of the poets and musicians of the past that within this structure they created universes of plastic and plangent beauty.

The Oriental bard is a highly idiosyncratic solo singer, a master of subtly designed verse and of complex, shifting, and sometimes meterless rhythm. He performs highly complex strophes composed of many long phrases, with maximal ornamentation, vocal rubato, melisma, and tremulo, in a voice that is usually high or falsetto, narrow and squeezed—with maximal nasality, raspy, and often characterized by forcefully precise articulation. In places where a primitive type of feudalism still prevails, as in Mauretania and Afghanistan, bards are generally attached to a big or powerful chief and their duty is to celebrate the magnificence of their lords before their world. The bardic voice quality is generally tense, high, thin, feminine, and placatory. Sometimes it is harsh, guttural, and forceful, symbolizing ruthless power and unchecked anger. Its marked nasality, tremulo, and throbbing glottal shake and its quivering melodic ornaments speak of tears, of fear, of trembling submission. These vocal mannerisms are the norm among Eastern mystics, muzzein, and cantors—the bards of God—as well as among the epic singers and the composers of praise songs for the king.

King David, like the great singers of early high culture, probably sang in the bardic manner. This inference is strong, since the style still survives in the whole Orient today, reaching its apogee in the court music of Japan, Java, India, and Ethiopia. A profusion of musical flowers, representing a sort of conspicuous consumption of music, is everywhere pleasing to the ears of kings, and thus to the almighty, whatever his name or names. In the same way, the lover in the bardic area abases himself before his mistress, showering her with flowery compliments, telling her with trembling voice and lavishly ornamented melody that he is utterly her slave.

Thus the Oriental bard was a specialist and virtuoso of a high order. He was the product of long and rigorous training. He conformed to rigid and explicitly stated esthetic theories. In fact, it was in the bardic world that the fine arts of music and poetry arose, alongside of highly developed metrical and melodic systems. Here, too, instruments were refined and developed and complex orchestras established.

In his paeans of praise of the king or of God, the bard spoke for or about the all-powerful center, and it was important that these praise songs be as grand and impressive as possible. He extended this manner to all his productions. Normally he sang at length—in long phrases, long and complex strophes, often in through-composed style, characteristically in song or verse forms that lasted for hours and ran to thousands of lines. He also used his voice in a depersonalized manner, appropriate to the voice of the king, of the god, or of one of his ministers or supplicants. Generally the bard was unsupported by other voices; in an absolutely despotic situation, only one voice should be heard—the voice of the despot or his surrogate.

Thus group singing in the bardic area is at a minimum. Normally, when it occurs, it is unison with poor rhythmic or tonal blend, or it is heterophonic. One thinks here of the choirs of Ethiopia or Korea or the heterophonic style of the Watusi or the enforced unison of the royal chords of Dahomey. Yet the bard, like the king, needs support. He finds it in an elaborate accompanying style. The court orchestras of the Orient are generally large and play together heterophonically, that is, each instrument speaks the same melody but in its own variant, with many voices independently following the same line. Always, however, a high-pitched nasalized singer or an instrument with a similar timbre leads and dominates the orchestra.

An Amerindian Pattern

When Europeans first encountered Amerindian tribes, they could not understand how Indian society worked at all, for there were apparently no permanent authoritarian leaders. Walter Miller (1957) shows that American Indians and feudal Europeans followed two completely opposed concepts of authority. Europeans swore allegiance for life and carried out the commands of the representative of their king. Indians took orders from no one and bore allegiance to no one except on a temporary basis of personal choice. An Indian war party might be organized by a war chief if he were persuasive enough, but the braves who set out with him would desert if the enterprise encountered difficulties. A sizeable percentage of such enterprises ended in failure, and the participants straggled back to the village with no loss of face.

Among the Fox Indians, whom Miller particularly studied, each person had his own supernatural protector, whom he venerated when fortune smiled upon him but reviled in periods of bad luck. The permanent village chiefs had no direct authority; indeed, they were not much more than permanent presiding officers at a village council of equals.

Figure 5: Profile of North American Indian Song

Parameter	Scale
1) Vocal Gp.	6 7 8 9 10 11 12 13
2) Orch. Relationship	2 3 5 6 8 9 12 13
3) Orch. Gp.	6 7 8 9 10 11 12 13
4) Vocal Org.	7 10 13
5) Tonal Blend-V	7 10 13
6) Rhy. Blend - V	10 13
7) Orch. Org.	7 10 13
8) Tonal Blend-O	4 7 10 13
9) Rhy. Blend - O	10 13
10) Words to Non.	10 13
11) Overall Rhy - V	3 11 13
12) Grp. Rhy.-V	3 5 7 9 11 13
13) Overall Rhy-O	3 5 6 8 9 11 13
14) Grp. Rhy.-O	3 5 7 9 11 13
15) Mel. Shape	5 9 13
16) Mel. Form	1 2 3 4 5 6 7 8 9 10 11 12 13
17) Phrase Length	1 4 7 10 13
18) No. of Phrases	1 3 5 6 8 9 11 13
19) Pos. of Final	1 4 9 11 13
20) Range	4 10 13
21) Int. Width	10 13
22) Pol. Type	1 3 6 8 10 13
23) Embell.	7 10 13
24) Tempo	9 11 13
25) Volume	13
26) Rubato-V	13
27) Rubato-O	13
28) Gliss	5 13
29) Melisma	13
30) Tremulo	1 7 13
31) Glottal Sh.	1 7 13
32) Register	4 10 13
33) Vo. Width	3 10 13
34) Nasality	4 13
35) Raspiness	1 4 7 10 13
36) Accent	1 4 7 10 13
37) Conson.	10 13

Individuals were trained from childhood to venture self-reliantly into the wilderness. Collective activity was at a minimum, and, when it occurred, it was unforced, each individual participating, not upon command, but because he knew from tradition what he should do and how and when he should do it. Just as the individual Indian might ask for and obtain power directly from a supernatural source, so he might acquire a medicine song from the spirit world that would give him the power to heal or to lead a war party.

The shape of the American Indian musical group conforms to the pattern of role-taking briefly sketched above. The solo singer uses a chesty voice, wide rather than narrow, yet with strong characterizers of nasal resonance and throaty burr and with forceful accent—a voice which is expressive of a full-blown and unpressed masculinity or, perhaps better, of a strong bodily orientation. The major manner of Indian song performance, however, is that which we code as N/L—group superordinate over leader. The leader initiates the song but then is submerged in a chorus performing the same musical material in unison. This chorus links their bassy, resonant voices with moderate tonal blending (varying to well-integrated blend among the Iroquois and some Pueblo groups), but in precise rhythmic concert. Individual voices in these choruses can still be heard, and the effect is of a loosely knit but well coordinated group of individuals cooperating in relation to a common goal. Here, as with the Pygmies and in contrast with the West and the Orient, the importance of text is often minimized. Indian songs normally consist of a few phrases padded out by repetitions and vocal segregates, to form long strophes of complex structure, which the whole group knows how to perform.

Many Indian melodies may be described as through-composed, that is, basically open-ended, leaving the decision for extension and termination to a collective impulse. The strongest element in this situation is a dominant, one-beat rhythm that unites the group in a simple, highly physical re-enactment of their adventures on the hunt, on the war path, and in the supernatural world. Hardly anywhere in this system, except at this nonstratified rhythmic level, is the individual asked to conform either vocally or musically. The very style of conformity in group performances exhibits the principle of individualism.

The profile of Amerindian song remains remarkably constant throughout most of North America and many parts of South America. This consistency of style explains why Amerindian music has been so remarkably resistant to change and how it is possible for Indians to swap songs, as they frequently do, across linguistic and cultural barriers. Indeed, the solidity of this framework confirms a commonsense impression that there is an Amerindian music, distinct from other world musical systems and congruent with an over-all Amerindian culture pattern.

The Negro African Pattern

We have designated the working structure of West African song style as L/N. African music might be called interlocked antiphony. A leader initiates and a group responds, litany phrase by litany phrase, but the group does more than respond and overlap with the leader's part, and the leader usually does more than overlap with the chorus. Very frequently both L and N support and comment on the other part with murmurs, bits of chords, or snatches of musical laughter and with a complex pattern of counterrhythms from hands, feet, and orchestra, not to mention kinesic comment from the dancers. In the solo line, itself, a playful lead voice shifts from open, ringing tones to strong nasalization to powerful rasp, from falsetto coo to bass grunt. Indeed, without such exhibitions of vocal display, an African song leader is soon replaced by another.

Yet, despite the shifting vocal timbre of the African singer, the choruses blend their voices in striking tonal effects. Visible speech analysis shows how this is possible. Although rasp and nasalization are present in the harmonic pattern of the solo voice, they are controlled and precisely placed instead of being pervasive characteristics, as is the case with the vocal characterizers that Western European bardic and Amerindian voices handle. Also, the harmonics are well and widely distributed—signs of the well-tuned voice.

A leader and a chorus part are normally implied in Negro African song, whether or not the performance is solo, for both elements are essential to African song structure. The song leader never performs for long without complex counterbalancing comment by the instrumental or vocal chorus. Furthermore, our research indicates that the length of the leader's part varies roughly with the importance of tribal chiefs over against the tribal council. In more or less acephalous African tribes, song leaders usually perform against a constant background of choral singing. Where chieftainship is paramount, vocal solos are longer and more prominent.

This hypothesis is strengthened by our coding of the ceremonial music of the Kingdom of Dahomey and the court songs of the Watusi of Ruanda-Urundi. In Dahomey, long solos are again important; no polyphony is permitted and highly embellished chromatic passages, rare in Negro Africa but common in Oriental song, become prominent. Among the royal Watusi, highly embellished heterophonic singing, meterless rhythm, long bardic performances, and other traits link Watusi style with that of the hydraulic empires. It would be improper not to observe that, in both these cases, song functions as a support to a powerful ruling hierarchy rather than playing the role normal in most simpler African societies. Along the southern border of the Sahara, among peoples strongly influenced by the culture of Islam and in many tribes where powerful kingship systems dominate large nations, solo bardic singing of the type described previously is common. It is my conviction, however, based on examination of a number of cases, that bardic singing of a strongly Oriental type is not of significant importance except in those African societies where institutional patterns akin to despotic Oriental societies shape the whole social system.

This brief sketch of African song performance structure, as exhibited in the cantometric profile in Figure 2, matches in a remarkable way the gross structure of most African Negro societies (see Murdock 1959). An African normally belongs to several interlocked groups—to a tribe, then perhaps to a series of segmentary patrilineal kin groups, to one or more cult groups, to a work organization, to an age group, to a political faction, and so on. Each of these groups may have a different head, and in each of them an individual may achieve a varying degree of prominence in accordance with his talents and his status. Although the society is stratified, it is quite possible for a witty man with a highly developed sense of political maneuver to rise to the top of one or several of the organizations of which he is a member. If he is an hysteric, he may become a religious leader and prophet. This provides an exact analogy to the emergence of a talented individual in the African musical group. African music is full of spaces. The loose structure of this musical situation gives the individual dancer, drummer, or singer the leeway to exhibit his personality in a moment of virtuosic display. He will then be replaced, but later on he may preempt longer and more elaborate solo passages, thus establishing himself as a recognized and talented musical leader.

Since music is keyed to group integration in a wide variety of African activities, a strong musical personality may be or become a religious or political leader. Yet the very structure of African melodies stands in the way of the L over N dominance pattern, for African melody is litany and responsorial, made up of more or less equal contributions from solo and chorus, with the chorus part dominant more often than not. Thus, in Negro Africa, musical performance structure and social structure mirror one another, reinforce one another, and establish the special quality of both African music and African society—whether in Africa or in African enclaves in the New World.

The strong rhythmic bias of African music also represents this many-goaled, many-headed, group-oriented culture. African rhythm is usually anchored in a strongly accented two- or four-beat rhythm, but around and through this positive, thrusting, rhythmic unity plays a variety of contrasting counterrhythms on numbers of instruments that give voice to the diverse groups and personalities bound together in tribal unity. At any moment, one of these tangential rhythms can seize the imagination of the group and become dominant, just as in a West African cult ceremony an individual may be mounted by his cult deity and rise from obscurity to total group dominance for a period.

Nor does the Negro group discourage women from taking leading roles in singing, as do many primitive peoples. Here Negro society reflects the comparative importance and independence of women, recognized in other spheres by their ownership of land, their control of marketing activities, and their part in religious ritual.

Perhaps, too, the prominence of polygyny in Negro Africa (cf. Murdock 1959) finds its expression in African musical structure. African education and custom place great emphasis on sexual matters—on fertility, on potency, and on erotic skill. This focus of interest supports the system of polygynous marriage, where a man must be able to satisfy several wives and a woman must compete for the favor of her husband with a number of co-wives. African dance prepares and trains both sexes for strenuous love-making, and the swinging, off-beat, rhythmically climactic rhythms of Africa motivate and support this frankly erotic dance style. Yet not all African dancing is a dramatization of courtship and love-making, just as not all group rhythmic activity in Africa is dancing in the strict sense. Collective rhythmic activity runs like a bright thread through the web of African life and is, indeed, one of its organizing principles. Work is done, journeys are made, law cases are argued, myths and legends are told, social comment is made, religious rites are conducted to rhythms which can be danced and sung by leader and chorus in accordance with the main structures of African music. The result is that the whole of African culture is infused with the pleasurably erotic, community-based pattern of African song and dance style. The attractiveness of African music for all the world today may, indeed, lie in the fact that it is so practical, that it operates successfully in more of life's activities than any other musical system.

It is my hope that the preceding thumb-nail sketches have indicated the usefulness of the cantometric approach for both ethnomusicology and anthropology. Several viable concepts seem to be indicated by the research at this stage. First, that, as long as music is considered cross-culturally as a whole and in behavioral terms, it is possible to locate structure comparable to known culture patterns. Second, that these esthetic structures remain relatively stable through time and space. Third, that these stable structures correspond to and represent patterns of interpersonal relationship which are fundamental in the various forms of social organization. Fourth, that analysis of cantometric structures may provide a precise and illuminating way of looking at the cultural process itself. Fifth, that, since the cantometric coding system deals with expressive material which all societies provide spontaneously and unself-consciously, it may become a tool for characterizing and, in some sense, measuring group emotional patterns. Finally, the way may be open for us to make the all-important distinction, first discussed by Sapir (1922)—the intangible yet grave distinction that all human beings respond to—between spurious and genuine culture.

I should like to add one word about the troubling problem of esthetic level. The structures that appear in our coding system are basic to the acceptance of a musical performance in a cultural setting. Without the proper structure, a song is felt to be foreign, or unsuitable, or simply of no interest. The more closely a song conforms to the norm indicated by a given profile, the more acceptable and familiar it seems to be in its cultural setting, yet the beauty of a bit of music depends upon the way the performer and/or composer handle another and narrower level of patterns, which cantometrics is not equipped to examine.

This essay provides evidence that the principle messages of music concern a fairly limited and crude set of patterns; otherwise, they would not be so easily available to such a system. The art of music, however, lies in its capacity to repeat these main messages again and again in slightly disguised and subtly different ways. Here, at the level of musical conversation, we enter a limitless realm of nuance, where reinforcement never brings surfeit or fatigue, where the ear delights in playing with a scale of tiny differences, and the restatement of the familiar is not a command but an invitation to return home.

Note

1. The substance of this paper was read at the annual meeting of the Society of Ethnomusicology in Philadelphia, November 15, 1961. The research was sponsored by Columbia University and supported by the Rockefeller Foundation. Many of the ideas developed in the paper grew out of informal discussions with Professor Conrad Arensberg, under whose general direction the research was carried out.

Bibliography

Bargara, D. A. 1960. Psychiatric Aspects of Speech and Hearing. Springfield.

Herskovits, M. J. 1941. The Myth of the Negro Past. New York.

Jackson, G. P. 1943. White and Negro Spirituals. New York.

Lomax, A. 1959. Musical Style and Social Context. American Anthropologist 61: 927–954.

Marshall, E. 1959. The Harmless People. New York.

Miller, W. B. 1955. Two Concepts of Authority. American Anthropologist 57: 271–289.

Moses, P. J. 1954. The Voice of Neurosis. San Francisco.

Murdock, G. P. 1959. Africa: Its Peoples and Their Culture History. New York.

Parsons, T. 1949. Essays in Sociological Theory. Glencoe.

Rouget, G. 1956(?). Music of the Bushmen Compared to That of the Babinga Pygmies. Paris and Cambridge.

Sapir, E. 1922. Culture, Genuine and Spurious. American Journal of Sociology 29: 410–430.

Turnbull, C. M. 1957. Initiation among the Bambuti Pygmies of the Central Ituri. Journal of the Royal Anthropological Institute 87: 191–216.

—— 1959. Legends of the Bambuti. Journal of the Royal Anthropological Institute 89: 45–60.

—— 1960a. Field Work among the Bambuti Pygmies. Man 60: 36–40.

—— 1960b. Some Recent Developments in the Sociology of the Bambuti Pygmies. Transactions of the New York Academy of Sciences, ser. 2, 22: 267–274.

—— 1961. The Forest People. New York.

Wittfogel, K. A. 1957. Oriental Despotism. New Haven.

Record Bibliography

For an extensive list of selected records, see Lomax (1959). A wide range of material is available on Folkways Records and, in a more condensed form, on Columbia Records. A few representative long-playing records are cited below for each master profile.

Africa and American Negro

French Africa. Columbia Records KL 205.
British East Africa. Columbia Records SL 213.
Bulu Songs from the Cameroons. Folkways Records P 451.
The Topoke People of the Congo. Folkways Records FE 4503.
The Big Drum Dance of Carriacou. Folkways Records P 1011.
Folk Music of Jamaica. Folkways Records P 410.
Cult Music of Cuba. Folkways Records P 453.
Venezuela. Columbia Records KL 212.
Afro-Bahian Music from Brazil. Library of Congress Record 13.
The Roots of the Blues. Atlantic Records 1348.
Negro Prison Songs. Tradition Records 1020.
Afro-American Blues and Game Songs. Library of Congress Record 4.
Ray Charles at Newport. Atlantic Records 1289.

Pygmy and Bushman

The Pygmies of the Ituri Forest. Folkways Records FE 4457.
Music of the Bushman and Pygmy. Peabody Museum and Musée de l'Homme LD-9.

Western European Folk Song

France. Columbia Records KL 207.
England. Columbia Records KL 206.
Ireland. Columbia Records KL 204.
Scotland. Columbia Records KL 209.
Folk Music of Norway. Folkway Records FM 4008.
Anglo-American Ballads. Library of Congress Record 1.
Wolf River Songs. Folkway Records FM 4005.
Pete Steele. Folkways Records FS 3828.

Bardic

Wolof Music of Senegal. Folkways Records 4462.
Musique Maure. Musée de l'Homme Records.

Folk Music of Ethiopia. Folkways Records FE 4405.
Cante Flamenco. Westminster Records WAP 301.
Modern Greek Heroic Oral Poetry. Folkways Records 4468.
Arabic and Druse Music. Folkways Records P 480.
Music of the Russian Middle East. Folkways Records P 416.
Folk Music of the Mediterranean. Folkways Records P 501.
Folk Music of India. Folkways Records FE 4422.
Music of Indonesia. Folkways Records P 406.
Japan, the Ryukyus, Korea. Columbia Records KL 214.

American Indian

Eskimos of Hudson Bay. Folkways Records P 444.
Canada. Columbia Records KL 211.
Songs from the Iroquois Longhouse. Library of Congress Record 6.
Music of the Sioux and Navajo. Folkways Records FE 4401.
Music of the Indians of the Southwest. Folkways Records FE 4420.

African Influence on the Blues

Paul Oliver

I WAS delighted to learn that Lynn S. Summers had discussed with the ethnomusicologist Richard A. Waterman the subject of African influence on the blues, and some of the points that I had attempted to raise in *Savannah Syncopators,* but I must confess that when I finally had the opportunity to read the transcription of the interview I was very disappointed. My disappointment arose partly from the misrepresentation of the argument of my book by Lynn Summers, but mostly because Richard Waterman had so obviously not read it. Or at least, I cannot believe he would make some of the statements that he did make, either about the theories that I proposed or even about some aspects of African music if he *had* read the book.

As many *Living Blues* readers will doubtless have read the interview transcript but not *Savannah Syncopators* I feel it necessary to run over a few points at issue. But I would also like to emphasize certain basic pieces of evidence on which my argument rested, and I will do so very simply:

1) The slaves who were brought to the Americas came from Africa, and by far the majority of these were shipped from ports in West Africa. The regions now known as Angola and Congo played a not inconsiderable part, but East Africa, South Africa and other regions provided few of the slaves.

2) African rituals, drumming and cults have survived, often completely intact, in Haiti, Cuba, Trinidad, Dutch Guiana and particularly Brazil, as has been documented by Alfred Metraux et al. or most dramatically by Pierre Verger in *Dieux D'Afrique.*

3) These cults and rituals, drum patterns and drum types are rain forest West African in origin.

4) Most writers, especially Melville Herskovits, have emphasized the influence of rain forest cultures to the exclusion of all others.

5) No such survivals exist to any marked extent, with watered-down *voudun* excepted, in North America. African drumming has not been significant in North America, though the slaves reputedly came from the same regions.

Reprinted from *Living Blues* 8 (Spring 1972): 13–17. Used by permission of the author.

6) From earliest records, banjoes and fiddles have been associated with the music of black Americans. They are rare as rain forest instruments, and unknown among many of those cultures.

A number of questions arise from these facts:

1) Does the blues owe anything to Africa, and if so, which aspects of the blues? Blues, and much black folk music employs strings predominantly; is there evidence of string traditions in the areas from which slaves were obtained?

2) If links with African instrumentation can be found, is there evidence of the importation from those regions?

3) Blues is largely a solo instrumental music to accompany the solo voice; more rarely is it a group music, but even when there are two or more instrumentalists only one person sings. Is this a characteristic of any region?

4) Blues singers, and probably most black musicians in the past, play an ambivalent role in black society. Is this reflected in African custom?

5) Are there any other elements in African music that may be seen to have their parallels or links with blues?

6) Is there any other evidence to support or contradict these premises?

In an argument developed in a rather condensed and indigestible form over 112 pages, *Savannah Syncopators* offers some evidence that, I hope, suggests a re-appraisal of the subject is much overdue. This argument may be summarized as follows:

1) Behind the rain forest cultures of West Africa, further inland but sometimes less than 200 miles away, are savannah cultures which stretch in a broad swathe from the Senegambia to Niger 2000 miles to the east.

2) Drum cultures, and hence African characteristics of rhythm, exist in this region. But the essential difference with the rain forest is the prevalence throughout the savannah belt of string-dominated music.

3) Many of the stringed instruments, techniques employed and sounds produced, have their parallels in the blues.

4) A professional caste of musicians exists throughout the savannah regions and over an enormous territory—the *griots* or *jilli*. They are the source of both amusement and admiration, are low in caste and highly rewarded on occasion. They work solo, in pairs or in groups, and sing songs of praise, ridicule and other forms of social control or expressions of values. Their relationship to the role of blues singers in black America is very close.

5) In North America drumming was largely suppressed but the playing of strings was encouraged. Hence, *griot* musicians, members of Savannah tribes, had the advantage over rain forest musicians, and the elements of their culture were encouraged to survive.

6) *Griots* come from largely Islamized peoples, though in no way exclusively. Islam forbade sculpture and though sculptures in African forms survive in Brazil etc., only faint echoes appeared in the States.

7) There is much linguistic evidence to show links between the languages of Savannah peoples and black American slang and usage.

8) Other characteristics, physiological and genetic, support these contentions.

9) A re-examination of the few records of their capture and shipment by slaves reveals

that a Savannah origin was far from uncommon. Rain forest tribes would have profited most by the selling of people captured in the interior, rather than by the depletion of their own peoples, though the latter seems to have occurred in respect to South American slaves.

10) Some relationship may exist between *balafon* (xylophone) playing in Africa, and blues piano, although the *balafon* was never strongly represented in North America.

11) Musically, the elements of the blues, including blue notes, flatted thirds, sevenths, diatonic, heptatonic and pentatonic scales all exist extensively in string music of the savannah. Adaptation would present few problems to *griots* imported to the States.

12) As slaves, and the lowest or near lowest caste, *griots* would have been expendable among Savannah kingdoms and were probably represented in disproportionate numbers among captives.

I must apologize for so pedantically laying out these points but I hope that by doing so I shall have clarified my disagreement with some of the comments made by Dr. Waterman. However, I am perplexed by much of what he said which seems to me to confirm my contentions. Thus he states (page 31, *Living Blues* 6): "In fact the Ashanti . . . are almost unable to sing a song without harmony—one guy alone cannot sing," which only supports my contention that solo singing is often rare in such cultures. But the converse is not true: both solo singing (by *griots* for instance) and collective group singing while at work are characteristic of the savannah. The latter is *more* characteristic of the savannah as far as work songs are concerned, because savannah cultivation demands collective labor whereas rain forest farming (bananas, plantains, mangoes etc.) does not.

But let's consider Waterman's views on Islam. "If you hear something that sounds pretty Arabic, for instance, and you know you're in an area where Islam has just recently come in, then you should be suspicious of just how traditional the music is." Agreed, even if "Arabic" and "Islam" are by no means synonyms. However, how relevant is the remark? Islam had made deep inroads in West Africa long before the Europeans even touched its shores. The great Sundiate reigned as ruler of the Mande empire of Mali from 1230 to 1255, *four hundred* years before the slave trade to the Americas. Lynn Summers pointed out that I had argued that string instruments were predominant in the Savannah to which Waterman replied (not denying it): "That I think is partly related to the influences from the north that came in along with Islam. I don't think that the savannah music bears particular resemblance to blues." To which I can only reply that the influence could indeed be of Islam, though many Africanists involved in the Manding conference (to be held in London this July) do not think so but consider it to be indigenous to the savannah. But either way we are talking of centuries of adaptation; whatever the first slaves and their successors brought to America *was* their tradition, and was their music. As for the lack of a "particular resemblance" I would contest this and have issued a record to support my argument; but it seems incontestable that the links are stronger than are those of drum orchestras with blues.

Summers: "He (Oliver) also pointed out the *griot* as solo performer, in a way, is comparable to the solo blues performer." Waterman, in reply: "I don't think that follows because there are single singers in a great many places, it isn't all responsorial stuff *even* (my italics) down in Nigeria and Liberia. I thought he was probably talking about the *griots*, and the Wolof bunch, because they're the ones who have the plunkety-plunkety *balafon* playing. But the tone quality isn't like that of a blues singer, and the lyrics don't follow." And again, after discussing the *griots*, "I think there's just as much the roots of this blues stuff in the traditional African thing on the coast, as in Senegal and Gambia, which is where he's talking about" and he continues that he thinks my "hunch" is wrong.

But, Dr. Waterman, I am *not* just talking about the "Wolof bunch" or the plunkety-plunkety *balafon* playing either. Nor am I talking about Senegal and Gambia alone (which anyway, *are* on the coast, but the extreme western seaboard of West Africa). No, I am talking about Senegal, Gambia, Guinea, Mali, Upper Volta, northern Ivory Coast, Northern Ghana, Northern Nigeria, Niger and even Mauretania; I'm talking of a culture spread over a million square miles of Africa, which has much more in common in its tradition than plunkety-plunk sounds of *balafons*. In fact I made very little of the *balafon* tradition, just three pages, and could have made more. Certainly it is true that the xylophone, and lithophone, are found over a large part of Africa, but it seems unlikely that "it was a northern instrument to begin with." On the contrary, Father A. M. Jones has brought remarkable evidence to show that it is Oceanic in origin and brought across Africa by way of Madagascar. I find it hard to believe that Dr. Waterman is unaware of this.

The *balafon* is distributed widely in Africa, agreed, and this emphasizes the capacity of the instruments to persist over many centuries and long distances of transmission. But my point is not that the Savannah is the *only* influence or source, but that conditions both of slave importation and repression in the United States made it the predominant one. It doesn't negate the fact that there are strings to be found in the Congo, although I suspect that Congolese influences were to be heard more in Latin America—the passage was shorter, the controls after the early 19th century less strict. In fact, as I have said earlier, the elements of drumming and complex rhythm are to be found in the Savannah as well as the strings. To put it another way: If the rain forest and its drum culture was the *only* source of the slaves, could any possible connection with black folk music and blues in the United States be traced? If the Savannah, with its strings and drum cultures were the only source, could any possible connections with black folk music and blues be traced? The answer to the first question is surely "no" and to the second it is "yes." Yet Dr. Waterman, with no evidence at all to support his contention mentioned in the interview can say "I think you probably find more of the materials that went into the blues on the coast." To which one can only answer: "Which?"

Now the reply may be that this is covered in the long paragraph (pp. 31–32) which deals with overlapping chorus and responses and the possible origin of the "blues changes." It is too long to answer point by point, but I would like to question the *process* implied (while pausing to mention that this phenomenon is equally evident in the Savannah regions). "I suspect that in the alternation of these two chorus parts," said Waterman, "the second somehow got separated out by the guitar pickers. They could hear two versions of this second chord, a very complex chord, and began separating it into what became the V chord and into those parts of it which became the subdominant (IV) chord. I think this separation was what accounted for what we know as the blues changes."

It's an ingenious and interesting theory but what does it imply? That the guitar-pickers were somehow a separate group from the Africans whom they heard and attempted to translate on their guitars. In other words, it would fit a situation in which *white* guitarists had derived from African singers. But it also implies that the rain forest musicians had already made the transition from a drum culture to a string one—and surely there is no basis for this assumption. By what means, musical or physical, can drum music be translated into string terms, except simply rhythm? Isn't it far more logical that the relationship between string culture and song type already existed—as indeed it *did* in tribes, states and countries in a huge swathe beyond the rain forest?

This is a problem, to use designer's jargon, of a "poor fit." And this is what has perplexed me for so long. I had read all the literature which argued the influence of Africa on the Americas, from Richard Waterman's important, but not flawless paper, to Gunther Schuller's uncritical transcription of A. M. Jones's narrow researches (in drumming, not in *balafon* music which is another, and better, story). In fact I spent a chapter of *Savannah Syncopators* discussing these and other writings and my dissatisfaction with them. Before I went to West Africa I subscribed to the "parallel evolution" notion to which Lynn Summers has made glancing reference. I did so because of the poor fit of the theories; they applied to Central and South America but not to North America. Waterman made much of "hot rhythm" for instance, but I don't hear it in blues; whereas he made no mention of "swing" which seems an essential of both jazz and blues. But having the good fortune to spend quite some time in both the rain forest and Savannah regions I began to realize that the picture presented of African music was highly distorted and hampered by the authority of Melville Herskovits which was never questioned as to the origin of slaves. When I heard rhythm, swing, blue notes and string music in the savannah I began to recognize a far better fit of the evidence. Hence *Savannah Syncopators*. I was aware of course that what I was proposing upset many previously held notions, and that there is always resistance to theories that do this. Interestingly however, the opposition, such as it has been, comes from English and German-speaking sources. I believe this refers back to the Colonial experience. In West Africa this was for the British Nigeria, Ghana (Gold Coast), Sierra Leone and Gambia. But French authorities seem to have no difficulty, for their tradition of African experience included Senegal, Guinea, Mali, Upper Volta, Niger, Tchad, Ivory Coast and Dahomey which covers vast areas of both Savannah and rain forest; check with the map. Recently I discussed this with the eminent ethnomusicologists Guilbert Rouget at the Musee de L'Homme, and Charles Duvelle of Ortf/Ocora. Both were very responsive to the theory even though it did require the re-appraisal of many well established concepts. Duvell however had already commented on blue notes in Africa (which I quote pp. 94–95) in his sleeve notes to *Haute Volta* Ocora (F) Sor 10.

Which brings me to Lynn Summers's observation, totally unsupported by any data, that "There are no African retentions, as such, in the blues." (*Living Blues* 6, p. 31). Later (p. 33) he adds that "the final test, of course, would be to compare savannah music to blues." Which is what I have done on the record *Savannah Syncopators* on CBS 52799, issued in England but unfortunately not accepted by CBS in the United States. It includes my own field recordings and others from various sources. But listen to the Ocora recordings mentioned above, which are now available with much additional material on *Musique du Pays Lobi* Ocora OCR 51, and *Haute Volta* Ocora OCR 58. Or hear *Musique de Mali* on Disque B.A.M. LD5772, where incidentally, Serge Kochyne, who did the field recordings, notes "elle est sans doute l'origine du blues." But then Kochyne is French.

There is much else I would like to discuss arising from that interview where it affects the writing of LeRoi Jones and Alan Lomax as well as my own. But enough said. I would only appeal for careful consideration of the evidence I have tried to bring together and a re-examination of the problem which is unprejudiced, open-minded and accurate. Lynn Summers begins by quoting Buddy Guy as seeing no relation between African music and blues, but a check on the original text also shows that Guy states very clearly, "They never did give me the real true African music," that he kept on insisting that he wanted to hear it but that he hadn't had a chance to listen to the records and tapes of African music he had been given. So what kind of evidence is that? Again, the photograph of Dr. Waterman shows him playing the *mbira*, or *sansa*, with the note "this form of instrument is the basis of much sub-Saharan African music." The *basis* of it? Just *what* does that mean? "Paul Oliver's recent *Savannah Syncopators* is a must for would-be blues scholars," he writes. Now I'm not sure what that means either, but I think I can detect a would-be African scholar when I read one.

The problems raised are considerable for black studies, for jazz and blues history. I don't argue for a moment that the theories I've advanced are without flaws, that there isn't much evidence to be collected, heard and sifted. Perhaps in the end the old theories will be proven correct, though the evidence that has come to me from various sources since the publication of this modest "work-in-progress" book makes that ever more unlikely. Next year, 1973, I shall be on an extended field trip filming and recording in rain forest and savannah areas over a large part of West Africa, when I hope to be able to be in a better position to test the data I have collected so far. Meanwhile, I look forward to any serious comments, criticism and help, any references, recordings or texts that may throw further light on the subject.

Africa and the Blues

David Evans

IT IS good to see the issue of Afro-American folk music and its possible connections with African music debated once again after scholars for some decades had let the topic become virtually dormant. Paul Oliver's *Savannah Syncopators* (London, 1970, Studio Vista) is an important step in a new direction, and the comments on it by Dr. Richard Waterman, an earlier researcher of the subject are most welcome (*Living Blues* 6, pp. 30–36) as is the reply by Oliver (*Living Blues* 8, pp. 13–17). Due to the recent sad passing of Prof. Waterman, their exchange of views can not be continued. Therefore, I thought I would make a few comments on the views expressed in the two articles in the hope of mediating between them and possibly adding some useful information and suggestions.

It is a shame that the hectic circumstances of Prof. Waterman's interview (see *Living Blues* 7, p. 7) were not conducive to more carefully considered thought. Nevertheless, he makes a number of good points on the subject. (I will restrict my discussion here to the subject of African influences or "retentions" in the blues.) Basically he repeats the findings of earlier researchers. He sees blues as growing out of a combination of work songs and field hollers with a European musical influence. He sees the African influence on blues as general sub-Saharan rather than specifically from the Savannah region (still a vast geographical area) as Oliver proposes. Waterman agrees with Oliver that Savannah music emphasizes strings more than West Coast rain forest, which emphasizes drums, but, unlike Oliver, he doesn't think that this general distinction has much to do with the blues, which he believes partake equally of influence from both areas (p. 34). He points out that "the blues . . . is of U. S. coinage" (p. 36) and notes that songs of personal experience, the 12-bar AAB stanza structure, and the I-IV-V chord sequence, all common characteristics of the blues, are not characteristic of any kind of African music. I will not discuss his ideas as to how they might have developed in the U.S. out of African music, as I don't find them very enlightening. Nevertheless, with the exception of songs about personal experiences, which do occur, he is right in stating that these are not African characteristics. I will return to these problems after discussing Oliver's reply.

Reprinted from *Living Blues* 10 (Autumn 1972): 27–29. Used by permission of the author.

Basically Oliver has boiled down his book and answered criticisms from Waterman and others. He begins with six statements about the evidence for African carryovers in the New World, all of which are correct. He notes that the emphasis of previous scholars, especially Melville Herskovits, on the rain forest cultures as the sources for these carryovers has blinded us to other possibilities. In defense of Herskovits et al., however, it should be pointed out that when they were writing, the rain forest cultures were much better known in anthropological literature and were the sources of many Africanisms in South America and the West Indies. Herskovits' *The Myth of the Negro Past* (Boston, 1958, Beacon Press), originally published in 1941, is must reading for anyone interested in the general question of New World African cultural retentions. He devoted very little attention to music in the United States, however, apparently not being an expert in the subject. Actually the search by scholars for Africanisms in black music has mainly been concerned with spirituals, Louisiana Creole folk music, and jazz. Until the last few years very little notice was made of the blues, so that Oliver is really working in largely uncharted territory. He needlessly sets up the late Prof. Herskovits as a straw man blocking his expedition into the Savannah, something that I'm sure Herskovits never intended to do. Herskovits' evidence for the African tribal origins of American slaves (*Myth*, pp. 33–53), sketchy as it is, in no way denies a significant input of slaves from Senegal, Guinea, Sierre Leone, and the northern parts of the Ivory Coast, Ghana, and Nigeria, all within the Savannah region. But Herskovits also showed that large numbers of slaves were brought from the West Coast rain forest societies as well as from the Congo and Angola. Few records were kept, and our knowledge is unfortunately very incomplete on this subject, but we can probably say with reasonable certainty that slaves were brought to the U.S. in roughly equal numbers from these three regions—the Savannah, the coastal rain forest and Congo-Angola, with a much smaller component from East Africa and Madagascar.

But to return to Oliver. We find him concerned with the fact that blues and other forms of black folk music have always been dominated by stringed instruments, an important point which has been emphasized before but for a different purpose. Previous scholars have emphasized the suppression in the United States (unlike other parts of the New World) of African drumming, which was usually intimately associated with African religious and political systems. Overt expression of these African cultural institutions were likewise suppressed in the United States during slavery. From this one would be led to assume that the slaves turned to string instruments as more acceptable outlets for their musical expression. Instead, however, Oliver asks in a series of six questions whether in fact the string-dominated black folk music of America, especially the blues, may be derived from a culture area of Africa where stringed instruments also are dominant over drums. He would also like to find in this area a predominance of solo over choral vocal music and a social role for musicians which parallels that of black folk musicians in the United States, particularly bluesmen. He believes he has found this region in the Savannah.

Oliver develops his argument in twelve points, which I would like to examine in some detail in response to his printed request for comments, criticisms, and help (p. 17).

1 & 2) He states that drums were indeed played in the Savannah but that string music was prevalent there. This is generally true, but it should also be kept in mind that Savannah music contains oboes, horns, xylophones, and a number of types of other stringed instru-

ments, such as harps, which have no parallels in American black folk music. Also we must note that rain forest music contains many stringed instruments such as the pluriarc. A great variety of stringed instruments can also be found in the Congo, as anyone will realize from a quick glance at J. S. Laurenty, *Les Cordophones du Congo Belge et du Ruanda-Urundi* (Tervuren, 1960). And for much of East and South Africa we can make the statement, also made for the Savannah, that drums are dominated by other musical instruments. Surely the string music of these other regions, particularly, I think, of the Congo and Angola, deserves to be investigated along with that of the Savannah for possible influences on black music in America.

3) He notes that many of the instruments, techniques, and sounds of Savannah string music have parallels in the blues. This is quite true but it is also true to about an equal degree of the string music of the rest of Africa. The Savannah instruments which have their closest parallel in American black music are the banjo and fiddle. . . . But these very instruments are not primarily blues instruments but belong instead to an older American musical tradition with its beginnings in slavery. The blues has featured guitars, pianos, and harmonicas, all European instruments though not without parallels in Africa both in form and playing style. The problem then is to show how African instrumental techniques might have been adapted to these European instruments. In this regard Oliver has made some good suggestions in his book. He has, however, overlooked the musical bow, probably the most widespread African stringed instrument, found throughout the sub-Saharan part of the continent. It has persisted in the United States in two forms. In one it is played as a "mouth bow" with a repertoire mainly of fiddle tunes. Like the banjo, this instrument has even passed into white tradition, as Alan Lomax' Ozark recordings of Charles Everidge show. The other type has been adapted in America into a "diddley bow," which I have discussed at some length in an article, "Afro-American One-Stringed Instruments" (*Western Folklore* XXIX, 1970, pp. 229–245). I think that there can be no doubt that this African instrument and its Afro-American derivatives were responsible for the bottleneck guitar style, which is such a prominent feature of the folk blues. Yet the technique of stopping the string of the musical bow with a hard object is found throughout sub-Saharan Africa. The musical bow (*berimbau*) played in this style by black Brazilians has been traced to Angola!

4) Oliver compares the *griots*, a professional caste of musicians in the Savannah region, to blues singers. Before reading Oliver's book, I too was intrigued by the *griots* but because of their similarity to black folk musicians in general rather than simply to bluesmen. In my book, *Tommy Johnson* (London, 1971, Studio Vista, p. 108) I noted that black musicians in America and *griots* both travel frequently and stated that "both play mainly stringed instruments, are considered of low class and perhaps in league with the devil, yet can amass great wealth, are highly respected for their talents, and can be strong agents for social control or change through the lyrics of their songs." Of course, Oliver has developed most of these points at considerable length in his book. But it should be pointed out that not all bluesmen by any means fit this description. Also there are comparable figures in the coastal rain forest of Africa, the Congo, and East and South Africa—wandering minstrels who usually play stringed instruments, frequently social outcasts but not members of rigid castes. Finally, as Waterman pointed out (p. 34) there is no evidence that blues singers belonged to a caste like the *griots*. Blues singers usually come from the lower economic class, but so do most black people in this country, unfortunately. They do not have to

intermarry with other blues singers. Many blues singers may be considered disreputable by black churchgoers, but so are a whole host of other sinners who do not sing blues. All the blues singer has to do to clear his reputation is to join the church and lead a "Christian life," which, in fact, blues singers have continued to do by the score.

5) Since during slavery in the United States drumming was suppressed but stringed instrument playing encouraged, Oliver believes that *griots* would have had the advantage in becoming slave musicians here. This is quite true for those *griots* who played stringed instruments, but would it not be equally true for any African who played a stringed instrument? Nevertheless, the fact that fiddle and banjo were such important slave instruments and that they are equally important for *griots* does indicate a likely *griot* influence in slave music. But to show this influence in the blues, one must show how banjo and fiddle music developed into blues, not an easy task. I think that the main influence of the *griots* in America was in slave music (which probably survives best today in white tradition!) and in helping to shape the social role of black musicians, though not in terms of a caste structure. As for their contribution specifically to the blues, it certainly exists and is important, though I think it remains to be proven that it was any more important than the contributions from the music of the coastal rain forest or the Congo-Angola region. For me it still remains an open question.

6) Oliver notes that *griots* come from a largely Islamized population and that Islam forbade representational sculpture. Since African sculpture hardly exists at all in the United States, Oliver believes that these Islamized societies must have contributed heavily to the slave population of this country. He is partly right here but only to a point. In the first place, a number of Savannah cultures, such as the Bambara, Bobo, Dogon, and Senufo, have important sculptural traditions. In addition, much of Angola, East Africa, and South Africa is lacking in important sculptural traditions. Finally, there may be more evidence for African influences on sculpture in the United States than had been previously thought. Robert F. Thompson has compiled some impressive evidence in "African Influence on the Art of the United States" (in *Black Studies in the University*, ed. Armstead L. Robinson, Craig C. Foster, and Donald H. Ogilvie, New York, 1969, Bantam Books, pp. 128–177), where he states that the dominant African influence seems to come from the Congo-Angola region. William Ferris in "If You Ain't Got It in Your Head, You Can't Do It in Your Hand: James Thomas, Mississippi Delta Folk Sculptor" (*Studies in the Literary Imagination*, vol. 3, no. 1, Apr., 1970, pp. 89–107) reports on a man who makes clay skulls strongly reminiscent of African art. The sculptor is also a blues singer and guitarist!

7) The linguistic evidence which Oliver cites does indeed show a strong Savannah component, but most of the American evidence comes from the Gullah dialect of the Georgia and South Carolina coast and islands, which is not typical of the rest of the South and which is not in any case an area of much blues activity.

8) The physiological and genetic arguments are perhaps Oliver's weakest. The fact that many bluesmen bear "Savannah" physical features probably indicates nothing more than that they bear the proportion of those features comparable to the percentage of Savannah individuals in the total slave population of the United States, perhaps about thirty per cent. I see great pitfalls in pursuing this line of argument, as Oliver does. For one thing, as Oliver admits on pp. 92–93 of his book, Savannah physical features are by no means uniform but rather exhibit a range of variation comparable to that of, say, northern

Europe. Many of these features in America may also be the result of intermixture with whites and Indians, which was considerable during slavery. Such intermixture would have raised the percentage of genes in the "Negro" population responsible for features such as high cheekbones and straight noses, which Oliver finds characteristic of Savannah blacks.

9) Oliver states that rain forest tribes would have profited most by selling slaves from the inland (Savannah) tribes rather than depleting their own populations, but then he contradicts himself by saying that the latter does seem to have been the case in respect to South American slaves. Why should the United States then have had a different experience? Besides, an examination of African history in the eighteenth and nineteenth centuries reveals that the coastal rain forest states constantly fought among themselves and captured slaves in the campaigns for sale to European traders. There were some sixteen Yoruba city-states constantly at war with each other as well as with neighboring Igbo and Fon (Dahomean) peoples, for example. Undoubtedly the coastal tribes took slaves from wherever they could get them, including their coastal neighbors.

10) Oliver notes that the African *balafon* (xylophone) may have influenced blues piano, although the xylophone is only rarely cited in early accounts of black folk music in the United States. He adds later that the xylophone is found throughout sub-Saharan Africa. His suggestion may be right and is worth pursuing, though in view of the rarity of the xylophone in America except as a late introduction into jazz, other possibilities should also be investigated for the African influence (if any) on blues piano. Certainly the "thumb piano" (*sanza, mbira,* etc.) is a good candidate. But the problems with both xylophone and "thumb piano" are that they are played either with sticks or the two thumbs, while piano is played with the ten fingers of both hands. Perhaps we should search farther afield in African harps, lyres, and zithers, which are played with both hands usually and on which it is possible to set up contrasting bass and treble lines. Whichever way you look at it, blues piano is a tough problem.

11) Oliver states that the adaptation of Savannah music to the blues would not have been difficult. Unfortunately though, we don't yet know exactly how this was done, and the statement could probably be made for the string music of other African regions with equal validity. Only careful musical and textual analysis which considers all kinds of African music will settle this question.

12) Oliver states that as slaves or members of a low caste, *griots* would have been expendable to the overseas slave trade and therefore represented in disproportionately high numbers in the American slave population. But just the opposite reasoning could also be argued effectively. As skilled performers and entertainers, *griots* may have been deliberately kept back from the Europeans by powerful African leaders. A skillful *khalam* player would have been of no greater value to the captain of a slave ship than any other slave of strong physical stamina but could have been a valuable asset at a Mende court.

Although I have criticized all of Oliver's arguments, I don't mean to be totally negative about his research. He has called attention to the Savannah musical tradition which has been largely neglected by other Afro-American music scholars. This Savannah tradition may indeed prove to have been the predominant one in black music in the United States, but I think it is still an open question, especially as far as the blues is concerned. Certainly, as Oliver himself states, it is not the only African influence.

The subtitle of Oliver's book is "African Retentions in the Blues," and here, I think, lies the main problem in his work. We must always remember that the blues as a genre of music did not arise until around 1890 and did not become dominant in black folk music until around 1910–20. Most people would probably agree that the vocal part developed from the field holler to which various rhythmic and instrumental ideas were added. Quite early the twelve-bar AAB structure began to shape this genre. Whatever was the origin of these individual components, they were put together in the form we know as "blues" around 1890 and *in the United States.* Now at this time there were very few native Africans in the United States, and even those would have been almost all at least fifty years old. These are not the sort of people to go out and create a new musical genre. Instead it is far more likely that the inventors of the blues were second, third, fourth, etc. generation Africans who were already acculturated to whites, Indians, and especially each other. There are indeed African influences in the blues, but Lynn Summers, Waterman's interviewer, is correct when he states (p. 31) that "there are no African retentions, as such, in the blues," if by "retentions" we mean purely African instruments, lyrics, etc. The blues are instead distinctly Afro-American.

I think that the way to approach the problem of African influences on the blues is to begin with the origins of the blues in America and work backward. For instance, where does the field holler tradition come from? Is it African? And from what part of Africa? Did this vocal approach influence the instrumental approach of the blues? Were African techniques adapted to the European guitar, piano, and harmonica, and how were they adapted? What influence did black banjo and fiddle music have on the blues? And what is the African component in banjo and fiddle music? One must look at the full range of African and Afro-American music for possible answers to these questions. I hope to tackle some of these problems in a forthcoming book, *Folk Music in a Black Community,* though my findings will probably be at best steps in the direction toward answers to these questions. Meanwhile, Paul Oliver has made an important contribution in his *Savannah Syncopators,* and the results of his forthcoming field trip to Africa are to be awaited eagerly. I hope that he will devote equal attention to all parts of that continent which contributed musicians to the black population of the United States.

Echoes of the Jungle?

Paul Oliver

READERS of *Living Blues* may be already tired of the discussion concerning the possibility of African retentions in the blues; but it is an important subject on which there has been a lot of casual speculation but very little research. David Evans is one of the few who has been conducting research of his own on the subject and therefore I'm particularly glad that he was prompted to write his detailed analysis of my arguments and Richard A. Waterman's comments in LB #10. His points do need answering, and I suppose that any reply I may make may lead to other observations, so that readers will fear an endless debate on minutiae of African and Afro-American detail. So, apologies in advance. But if some are interested in following the matter further perhaps we can consider a few of the issues raised in David Evans' piece. Rather than continue with the inconclusive discussion on the Waterman interview to which he cannot, unhappily, reply, I will reply to the specific criticisms and comments on my own writing. David suggests that I have "needlessly set up the late Prof. Herskovits as a straw man blocking" my "expedition into the Savannah" It's an odd comment. He argues "in defense" of Herskovits, but I was in no way attacking him. My point was that Herskovits was limited in his frame of reference, as far as West Africa was concerned, beyond the rain forest and hence writers who depended on his conclusions for the basic data would have an unbalanced view. This is important because the writers who have devoted most attention to the problem of African origins (mainly from a jazz position) depended a great deal on Herskovits, as any reading of Ernest Borneman's *An Anthropologist Looks at Jazz*, Rudi Blesh's *Shining Trumpets*, Marshall Stearns' *The Story of Jazz* and to a lesser extent, Harold Courlander's *Negro Folk Music* must confirm. A profound re-think is necessary in my view, and this must question the dependability of the principal sources on which theories are built.

It is true to say that slaves were brought mainly from three areas. Evans has listed the first as "The Savannah" but it is essential to note that it is never so listed, but always as "the Senegal River." My point is that this, and many of the other sources can imply the Savannah, but Herskovits in his 1938 article "The Ancestry of the American Negro" (*American Scholar* Vol. VIII No. 1) specifically stated that the locale was "from the Senegal

Reprinted from *Living Blues* 13 (Summer 1973): 29–32. Used by permission of the author.

River in the north, around the Great Bend to the Guinea Coast, along the Bight of Benin and southwards beyond the Congo to the Portuguese territory of Angola. Relatively few slaves came from any great distance inland and most of them were brought from the narrow forested region that follows the coast at a depth from two to three hundred miles. The interior of the Congo" he added, by the way, "was apparently not an area of intensive slaving." In spite of David Evans' conviction that Herskovits did not exclude the Savannah, the above quotation from a much fuller argument on the theme shows that he did. In fact he poured scorn on what he termed "the thousand-mile theory." I attempted to produce a sampling of evidence which shows that this is not an accurate picture.

"Previous scholars have emphasized the suppression in the United States (unlike other parts of the New World) of African drumming," Evans continues, to account for the fact that the blues is dominated by stringed instruments. Mine was apparently a "different purpose." But here I must directly challenge him to produce *any* writing by *any* scholar which does this. To the best of my knowledge this point has only been made to account for the *beginnings of jazz in New Orleans,* the argument being succinctly made (for the first time, I think) in Robert Goffin's *Jazz: From the Congo to the Metropolitan* in 1943, and at greater length in Stearns' *Story of Jazz.* The argument has been that drumming, forbidden elsewhere in the Protestant dominated South, was permitted in the *laissez-faire* environment of New Orleans and its Congo Square, under the tolerant eyes of the French. There too *voudun* persisted and these were major factors in the formation of New Orleans jazz. That my interpretation of the fact of the suppression of drumming was to a different purpose is quite true, but the purpose was precisely that of showing how stringed instruments came to be dominant. It was one of the essential points that I was trying to make, but if unconsciously I was repeating what has been proposed earlier elsewhere I'm sorry; but I'd like to have the references. On the other hand I do recall outlining this theory to David Evans in a cafe off Red Lion Square in London four or five years ago—could he have subconsciously recalled this and assumed that it was a generally stated view of writers on the subject?

To turn now to the discussion on the 12 points from my article which David Evans debates.

1 & 2. Evans makes the point that the Savannah also includes oboes, horns, xylophones, etc., among its instruments, including harps (though the latter are more characteristic of the Angola-Congo region, and East Africa, surely?) Agreed, but I would take this as material for the researcher on jazz instrumentation. In fact I see this as strengthening of my argument, for the combination of horns and strings in West Africa of the Savannah region is far from uncommon. Recalling that Cable identified predominantly Savannah peoples in Congo Square, I feel jazz authorities too, should be looking to the Savannah. As for Angola-Congo—of course, in the interests of thorough research it should be examined with close scrutiny. But the Congo has been a romantic "source" of African slaves and their presumed legacy of music in jazz history, witness the very title of Goffin's book. In the critical centuries when the patterns of capturing, trading, "gentling" and working slaves were established, the Congo had little part to play in the British and American slave trade. As James Pope-Hennessy summarizes in his lengthy history of the Atlantic Slave Traders, *Sins of the Fathers,* the "gloomy littoral" of the "vast stretch of the Leeward Coast to the

north and south of the Congo River" whose "borders were not then defined, came to be loosely known as Angola, and, as far as the trade in slaves went, was in the seventeenth and eighteenth centuries virtually a Portuguese preserve. The slavers of other nations found Congolese Negroes difficult and expensive to buy, for the Portuguese monopoly was so complete that few slaves were likely to be available for random purchase." On the other hand, the Portuguese, who on the whole, as he makes clear, were more humanitarian than the slavers of other countries, shipped vast numbers to Brazil where elements of their Congolese (and also Yoruba-Benin) cultures survive still in very pure forms. Statistics as to the total shipment of slaves may therefore reveal a large proportion from the Congo—but relatively few went to North America.

3. Instruments and sounds of Savannah string music do have their parallels in the blues, as Evans acknowledges. He says the banjo is "not primarily a blues instrument," but I think this is not really the point. The point is that a continuity of string playing traditions can be clearly and unarguably demonstrated; from *khalam* to *bania* to banjo to, ultimately, guitar, the European instrument being adapted and used as it became available to blacks. On the other hand in no way can a continuity of instrumentation from drums through to guitar be demonstrated in any way whatsoever. David's own important paper on the musical bow highlights another continuity of tradition, and I think that the possibility of this as the origin of bottleneck style playing on a single-string instrument is very well made. But, as he says, it is found *throughout* sub-Saharan Africa—as indeed, is the xylophone—so that it comes as no surprise to find that Brazilian Negroes play in a manner traceable to the Congo, and North American Negroes play in a manner equally traceable to the Savannah.

4. Evans' comments on the *griots* and my observations on this culture seem too literal to me. The point I was making here is that a tradition of semi-professional commentators playing stringed instruments, considered shiftless and of low status and yet enjoying wide popularity and acclaim, existed in a widespread form in the savannah. That "blues singers do not have to intermarry with other blues singers" seems rather irrelevant, for *all* African marital customs and unions were suppressed by the slave owners as is exceptionally well documented. Perhaps the most interesting reflection on this is how much blues singers *do* marry in blues singing families, and how much they *do* beget blues singers. Consider the family connections of Lightnin' Hopkins from Texas Alexander to Clifton Chenier to get the pattern. Of course all blues singers do not fit the description; what is amazing, is that far more than a century after the end of the slave trade so many do.

5. Yes, indeed, it would be true for any African who played stringed instruments to have the opportunities over other musicians to develop their music in North America. This would undoubtedly apply to those Angolans who were in the United States. However, at the largest conference of its kind ever held, namely the Manding Conference in London in the summer of 1972, I had the opportunity to interview, hear and study the music of a great number of *griots* from Mali, Senegal, Gambia and elsewhere. One thing became plain—that after only a short while, all *griots* can play together, even though they may come from regions hundreds of miles apart. That this would give them a considerable edge over musicians who were outside their culture is obvious. To me, it was one of the clinching revelations of my study this last year. Furthermore, they play themes or narratives that are centuries old, so that the continuity of their tradition in West Africa is not in question.

6. On the subject of Islamised Africa and the prevalence of musical traditions and

sculptural ones, I can claim to have some specialized knowledge, having lectured on, collected and studied African sculpture at least as long as I have blues. Evans' comments on the face of it are quite correct; but full of half-truths. To take the peoples that he mentions; the Bambara are rather unique among the Mandingo peoples for having a sculpture tradition. (More than a third of the Bambara, in fact, do not make sculpture.) The Dogon are not a Manding people and do not have a *griot* tradition; their situation for centuries on the Bandiagera escarpment facing the Sahara protected them from the slavers and it is generally thought that they were little touched by the trade. This helped to keep their culture "pure" until recently, and this is why it has been the subject of study by French anthropologists like Marcel Griaule or Germaine Dieterlen for 40 years. The Bobo have two sculpture types only—they are considered one of the most genuinely primitive of African peoples—and are Gur-speaking and do not have a *griot* tradition. And so on. I don't wish to labor the point but my comments on this were not made without careful consideration of the facts. As far as the Bambara are concerned, this is another matter. I believe that the Bambara was one of the most important of the peoples to have been shipped in large numbers to the United States. There is good evidence to support this, including linguistic examples (like the source of the word *juke*). As an example of the kind of data that is emerging, I would instance the order for slaves made by William Dunbar, a Natchez, Miss., planter, to a Charleston trader in 1807. Dunbar specifically stated that "the negroes of the 'Iboa' nation were disliked in the Mississippi region and should, therefore, be excluded from the order. Preference was expressed for Africans of the Bornon, Houssa, Zanfara, Zegzeg, Kapina and Tombootoo tribes" (quoted from Charles S. Sydnor's *Slavery in Mississippi*, p. 141). Of those tribes that are identifiable the Iboa are the Ibo (eastern Nigeria, or 'Biafra'), the Bornon are the Bornu, the Hausa are the Houssa and one or two others (Kapina=Katsina?) came from the Savannah regions of Northern Nigeria, Niger and Upper Volta, while the Tombootoo were the Bambara of Mali.

Though the Bambara came in large numbers they were both a musical, *griot*-culture people and a sculpture-producing people, the sculptors being also blacksmiths. This means that though wood-carving was suppressed in North America with little of these skills surviving, slaves were employed as smiths on every plantation. Blacksmiths of low caste like the Bambara could use their skills on the much-photographed Georgia grave-markers and the like. The Senufo and Dogon also doubled as smiths and sculptors but this is not a characteristic of every West African tribe.

I am of course familiar with Robert F. Thompson's valuable work. I do feel that some of his conclusions are open to question on many grounds, while some of the data from which this work is being assembled needs checking. In 1972 I made a special visit to the Slave Mart Museum in Charleston to see examples of the exhibits that are being cited, but the abundant errors in attributions emphasized how carefully this subject has to be studied. At present I do not think cross-referential conclusions can be made between artifacts and blues in North America.

7. I feel that Evans has dismissed the matter of linguistic evidence too lightly in saying that "most of the American evidence comes from the Gullah dialect of the Georgia and South Carolina coast and islands." This may be true of Dr. Lorenzo Turner's work, which has been widely quoted, but Professor David Dalby's studies (which I quoted in *Savannah Syncopators*) both question Turner's methods and conclusions, and extend into all areas of

Black American words and language use. I have passed to him lists of essentially Negro usage in the blues and he has made careful comparisons with words of identical usage in African languages. I think I can say with confidence that three-quarters of the specifically Negro words known to blues collectors (from "doney" to "poontang") have a directly traceable Savannah origin, with almost exactly the same, or equivalent meanings. The most notable exception is "mamlish" which linguistically, I am informed, is in no way African. The sources used are largely Mississippi and Texas and are not Gullah. But Professor Dalby, who is Professor of African Languages at the School of Oriental and African Studies at London University and frequent visiting Professor at Bloomington, Indiana, is writing a book on the subject of African language retentions in the United States, so I will let the matter rest there. He was the organizer of the Manding Conference to which I referred above, and hence gave me the opportunities that I needed for further study of the music of the region.

8. Turning to the discussion of physiological and genetic arguments put forward in *Savannah Syncopators*, Evans argues that these are the weakest that I raised. Perhaps; I realized that they were the most contentious. However, like the issues he has himself raised, they all need investigating, pitfalls not-withstanding. I wouldn't argue that the kinds of genetic influence must be varied over centuries and with much miscegenation, which is why I feel that reference to geneticists who have done work in this area must be made. I'm not blind to the problem of intermixture of Indian and Negro blood—Mack McCormick and I have spent much of our many years of research on Texas blues on this very subject. It's not a subject to be dismissed lightly and I feel Evans is too summary in his disregard of its importance. Among the many geneticists working on the problems of genetic drift, the incidence of taste deficiency, the acquisition of new blood agglutinogens, the frequency of isoantibodies and segregants—and other issues which make of this aspect of genetics an exact science and not a mere matter of speculation, are Dr. Bentley Glass and Dr. C. C. Li. I cannot begin to summarize the many points at issue except to quote Dr. Glass's conclusion that the number of Negroes who have one American Indian ancestor over a few generations must obviously be very large, but that "the number of persons who claim to have at least one American Indian ancestor yields no clue whatsoever to the amount of gene flow from the Indian into the Negro population." In lay terms, however, it seems that the flow from Negro to Indian is much greater than from Indian to Negro; further, that Indian genetic influence is regressive. The effect in precise terms can be seen in the examples quoted by Evans of people who are clearly "Negro." In Mississippi and region, a very strong vein seems to be present in artists like Fred McDowell (OK, Tennessee, but near enough), Wade Walton or Scott Dunbar, all exhibiting characteristic Savannah features of high cheekbones, and straight noses. This Evans suggests could just as easily be the result of Indian mixed ancestry. However, if the genetic flow were Indian to produce these physiological characteristics one would expect to find straight hair of circular section. But these singers have all Negro "woolly" hair (or elliptical section) as do Savannah peoples. In fact they display strong features of the Fulani specifically, and my first encounter with the Fulani tribesmen so reminded me of Wade Walton that I was encouraged to explore this area of genetic flow, which I had been entirely skeptical about until that date.

9. The rain forest tribes certainly profited by selling slaves from the Savannah, and it is true that I raised the interesting problem of the South American slaves who came from the

eastern rain forest. Evans explains this by mentioning the internecine wars among the Yoruba—who supplied slaves for the Portuguese and later, the British, for South America and the West Indies. The study of the wars and changing fortunes of the empires of both the Savannah and the rain forest is a subject in itself: in the 18th century the rulers of the Bambara kingdoms in the central Savannah and the Hausa emirates of the eastern West African Savannah were the dominant peoples, only to be overthrown by the Fulani *jihad* of the early 19th century. The captives from these tremendous wars and changes of fortune of great tribes supplied coastal peoples with slaves from the north which the Ashanti, with no less than 18 slave forts along their coast, took full advantage of—and sold to the American slavers.

10. The African *balafon* or xylophone was clearly a direct influence on the music of Central and South America, where xylophones were introduced by the slaves and have been a dominant instrument ever since. I suggested that the potential xylophone players may have turned to the piano as being the most available similar instrument in North America. It's a long shot, for as Evans says, "blues piano is a tough problem." Playing the African xylophone requires considerable melodic, or melodic-rhythmic independence of left and right hands, which is why this seems to me to be a possibility. I have collected *sansas* or *mbiras* in West Africa and am firmly of the opinion that not only is the term "thumb piano" a misleading misnomer, but that there is just no connection between playing the hand instrument with two thumbs on five metal tongues and playing a piano of many keys with two hands. Agreed, we should turn to African stringed instruments perhaps, for the same kind of playing with two hands and contrasting bass and treble lines. Evans suggests "harps, lyres and zithers," but where do you get the most complex instruments of these kinds, and the greatest virtuosity of playing them? I'm sorry to have to state it again, but it is without question in Senegal, Gambia, Guinea and Mali, with the playing of the 19- and 21-string *seron* and *kore* by the *griots*.

11. I believe the transition from Savannah music to blues could not have been direct, for there are many other factors, including the adoption of European scales to a considerable extent, the use of European instruments and so on, and the time lag in the process which have to be taken in to consideration. I am merely saying that on the basis of the researches I have done to date, the music of the savannah provides the greatest number of lines of contact and parallels which would make it most likely. But comparison along musical analytical lines is obviously necessary; as far as textual analysis I have already done enough to find considerable evidence in support of this view, but this will have to await another day.

12. Finally Evans says that the *griots* could have been held back as they could "have been a valuable asset at a Mende court." (The Mende are a Mande people.) But this I think is a misunderstanding of caste in African Mande states. The *griots* are amusing, even admired, but are not *valued*. Like the smiths and the woodcarvers, whose work we rate as creative art, they are merely workmen of a kind going about a job of some value, but entirely replaceable, from the rest of the large caste. Being of the lowest castes they were expendable and could not have been protected at the expense of people of a higher caste. As a matter of fact, a skillful khalam player was of value to the captain of a slave ship, for in later decades of the trade captains often encouraged the musicians to play so that the slaves

could dance and by this means get some exercise and be a little healthier. But of course, this would not have been a factor in the purchase of slaves.

In conclusion Evans underlines the problems not of my work, as he says, but of the whole subject. I find myself agreeing that examination of the blues origins and working backwards with appropriate questions is a method; I thought that it was one that I had demonstrated, by showing that simple assumptions about the African origin of Afro-American music were untenable and could only be considered by a far more searching examination of both African and Afro-American characteristics, of which, as far as the African end was concerned, I hope I have made a contribution. There is much, much more to be done, and I feel sure that Evans' promised study of *Folk Music in a Black Community* will advance the study further. My further field trip was frustrated by political problems and is now unlikely to take place, so the job of devoting "equal attention to all parts of that continent which contributed musicians to the United States" will have to be passed on to someone else. I hope that whoever does succeed in doing this will be in a position to compare the evidence for Angola, the Bight of Benin, the West African coast and the Savannah regions. It had better be soon, and the funds needed for such research would seem only practical through a major anthropological research grant. Naturally I hope that the arguments for the Savannah origins of the musicians who influenced the Afro-American traditions in the United States will not be lightly dismissed, for they were not lightly made. But I am grateful to David Evans for having given careful and lengthy consideration of some of the points that I have raised, and look forward to further discussion on the subject. To those who feel that it is too esoteric to be a matter of concern I can only say that this was the attitude to blues as a whole not so very long ago. But time is running out for original research and an open mind is very much needed in the evaluation of all the evidence that is available, and that needs to be sought if we are to get any closer to the solution of the knottiest problem in blues study.

Works Cited

Blesh, Rudi. *Shining Trumpets: A History of Jazz.* Rev. ed. New York: Knopf, 1958.
Borneman, Ernest. *An Anthropologist Looks at Jazz.* New York: Jazz Music Books, 1946.
Courlander, Harold. *Negro Folk Music USA.* 1963. Reprint, New York: Columbia University Press, 1970.
Goffin, Robert. *Jazz from the Congo to the Metropolitan.* 1944. Reprint, New York: DaCapo, 1975.
Herskovits, Melville J. "The Ancestry of the American Negro." *American Scholar* 8, no. 1 (1938).
Oliver, Paul. *Savannah Syncopators.* London: Studio Vista, 1970.
Pope-Hennessy, James. *Sins of the Fathers.* New York: Knopf, 1968.
Stearns, Marshall. *The Story of Jazz.* New York: Oxford University Press, 1956.
Sydnor, Charles S. *Slavery in Mississippi.* New York: Appleton-Century, 1933.

2 Before and Alongside the Blues

EILEEN Southern notes in *The Music of Black Americans* the fact that "white observers had begun to notice differences between African-style music and European music as early as 1637" with regard to "concepts of sound, instruments, and the black folks' attitude toward making music" (152). However, given the interaction between African and European-derived cultures that took place in this country, however forced and inequitable it might have been, it was reasonable to expect that there could emerge an aesthetic and stylistic blend quite distinguishable from what had come before. What could not be anticipated or imagined was the astonishing variety of stunning new music that was generated by African Americans on American soil both before and around the time that blues was also being developed as a distinctive form in itself: work songs, field hollers, spirituals and jubilees, minstrel songs, ballads, game songs, ragtime, jazz, and even the rhythmic, heavily accented, antiphonal speech of the folk preacher's oral sermons.

Frederick Douglass, formerly enslaved in Maryland, produced in the 1845 version of his life the epitome of the genre known as the slave narrative. Douglass indicts slavery and the so-called Christian slaveholders for the cruelty, greed, and rapacity manifested on physical, psychological, and emotional levels that continue to resonate today. As Douglass wrestles with questions about his own identity that are symbolic of the enslaved person's dilemma in general, he pauses briefly to reflect upon the songs the slaves created and performed, discerning in them both the core sadness and exuberance that many commentators recognized in the blues that would begin to emerge two generations down the road. Douglass recognized the visceral power of the music to evoke strong passions and, though Douglass's narrative in general emphasized the centrality of literacy to emancipation, the songs that W. E. B. Du Bois later called "the Sorrow Songs" were finally beginning to garner appreciation for their valuable contributions to American culture.

In 1963 LeRoi Jones, an emerging avant-garde writer who was by his account in a transitional stage between his "Beat" and his Black Nationalist periods, published his seminal *Blues People,* which was, Langston Hughes asserted, "the first book on jazz by a Negro writer." As an early volume on jazz by an African American critic it provoked a great deal of interest and discussion. In reflecting theoretically on the origins of the blues, Jones takes a "socio-anthropological and musical" approach, examining the genesis of the music in this cultural matrix of African and American sociopolitical and aesthetic values. He links West African religious songs to postslavery music through the work song, which he sees as a secularized version of praise songs for the West African deities that had no counterparts in the religions of Protestant America that were forced upon the slaves. The circumlocution involved in creating a tradition that allowed slaves and former slaves to covertly continue a forbidden practice Jones identifies as part of the African tradition that carried over in various masking techniques implemented by African Americans to survive in America—exemplified by the blues lyric "you don't know my mind / When you see me laughin, I'm laughin to keep from cryin." Reviews for Jones's book were frequently enthusiastic, but not uniformly positive. Ralph Ellison lamented Jones's "straining for a note of militancy" (*Collected Essays* 279), his harsh criticism of the African American middle class, and doctrinaire approach that Ellison felt caused Jones to sacrifice his arguments to polemics. He disagreed most vehemently with Jones's assertion that "a slave cannot be a man" by countering that a slave musician was "a man who realized himself in the world of sound" (*Collected Essays* 284). Still, as Ellison and many others acknowledged, Jones brought some much needed social, anthropological, and historical discussion to the table with his important volume.

Paul Oliver, having written previously about the blues and its African origins, turned his attention in *Songsters and Saints* to the frequently ignored—especially by blues critics—folk and popular musical traditions that grew up before and alongside the blues and contributed to their formation and nature even as they co-existed with them. The focus of the selection included here on dance songs and routines drawn from the oral tradition and printed sources (fed back into the oral tradition) demonstrates how these elements were part of the repertoires of songsters (often erroneously thought of as exclusively blues performers) for whom blues were frequently only a fraction of a constellation of varied musical performances aimed at entertainment. His argument accentuates the artificiality of isolating blues from other musics, folk from popular culture, and oral from printed tradition, too strenuously and absolutely in the reconstruction of the formation of the blues.

Subtitled "Tradition and Creativity in the Folk Blues," David Evans's *Big Road Blues* considers the contributions that the community's musical legacy, the individual, and the commercial market make to the style, structure, and nature of the blues tradition. Based on his own extensive field work in Mississippi and grounded in his background as a folklorist, ethnomusicologist, and musician, the book focuses an extensive amount of time on the influence of blues great Tommy Johnson and his recording "Big Road Blues" had over a period of a half a century in the local Drew, Mississippi, tradition, in the state as a whole, and in the folk blues tradition in general. Evans' discussion of the origins of the blues form in field hollers and blues ballads draws admirably upon his scholarship, fieldwork, and speculation to provide an informative look at the emergence of the blues from what had come before it.

Recommended Further Readings

Ralph Ellison. *The Collected Essays of Ralph Ellison.* New York: Modern Library, 1995.

Dena J. Epstein. *Sinful Tunes and Spirituals.* Urbana: University of Illinois Press, 1977.

W. C. Handy. *Father of the Blues.* Ed. Arna Bontemps. 1941. Rpt. New York: Collier, 1970.

John Edward Hasse, ed. *Ragtime: Its History, Composers, and Music.* New York: Schirmer, 1985.

Bruce Jackson. *The Negro and His Folklore in Nineteenth-Century Periodicals.* Austin: University of Texas Press, 1967.

Lawrence Levine. *Black Culture and Black Consciousness.* Oxford: Oxford University Press, 1977.

Bruce Rosenberg. *The Art of the American Folk Preacher.* New York: Oxford University Press, 1970.

Eileen Southern. *The Music of Black Americans.* 3d ed. New York: W. W. Norton, 1997.

From *Narrative of the Life of Frederick Douglass, An American Slave, Written By Himself*

Frederick Douglass

THE slaves selected to go to the Great House Farm, for the monthly allowance for themselves and their fellow-slaves, were peculiarly enthusiastic. While on their way, they would make the dense old woods, for miles around, reverberate with their wild songs, revealing at once the highest joy and the deepest sadness. They would compose and sing as they went along, consulting neither time nor tune. The thought that came up, came out—if not in the word, in the sound;—and as frequently in the one as in the other. They would sometimes sing the most pathetic sentiment in the most rapturous tone, and the most rapturous sentiment in the most pathetic tone. Into all of their songs they would manage to weave something of the Great House Farm. Especially would they do this, when leaving home. They would then sing most exultingly the following words:—

> "I am going away to the Great House Farm!
> O, yea! O, yea! O!"

This they would sing, as a chorus, to words which to many would seem unmeaning jargon, but which, nevertheless, were full of meaning to themselves. I have sometimes thought that the mere hearing of those songs would do more to impress some minds with the horrible character of slavery, than the reading of whole volumes of philosophy on the subject could do.

I did not, when a slave, understand the deep meaning of those rude and apparently incoherent songs. I was myself within the circle; so that I neither saw nor heard as those without might see and hear. They told a tale of woe which was then altogether beyond my feeble comprehension; they were tones loud, long, and deep; they breathed the prayer and complaint of souls boiling over with the bitterest anguish. Every tone was a testimony against slavery, and a prayer to God for deliverance from chains. The hearing of those wild notes always depressed my spirit, and filled me with ineffable sadness. I have frequently found myself in tears while hearing them. The mere recurrence to those songs, even now, afflicts me; and while I am writing these lines, an expression of feeling has already found its

---

Reprinted from Frederick Douglass, *Narrative of the Life of Frederick Douglass, An American Slave, Written By Himself* (1845; reprint, New York: St. Martin's, 1993), 46–47.

way down my cheek. To those songs I trace my first glimmering conception of the dehumanizing character of slavery. I can never get rid of that conception. Those songs still follow me, to deepen my hatred of slavery, and quicken my sympathies for my brethren in bonds. If any one wishes to be impressed with the soul-killing effects of slavery, let him go to Colonel Lloyd's plantation, and, on allowance-day, place himself in the deep pine woods, and there let him, in silence, analyze the sounds that shall pass through the chambers of his soul,—and if he is not thus impressed, it will only be because "there is no flesh in his obdurate heart."

I have often been utterly astonished, since I came to the north, to find persons who could speak of the singing, among slaves, as evidence of their contentment and happiness. It is impossible to conceive of a greater mistake. Slaves sing most when they are most unhappy. The songs of the slave represent the sorrows of his heart; and he is relieved by them, only as an aching heart is relieved by its tears. At least, such is my experience. I have often sung to drown my sorrow, but seldom to express my happiness. Crying for joy, and singing for joy, were alike uncommon to me while in the jaws of slavery. The singing of a man cast away upon a desolate island might be as appropriately considered as evidence of contentment and happiness, as the singing of a slave; the songs of the one and of the other are prompted by the same emotion.

Slave and Post-Slave

LeRoi Jones

IT IS impossible to say simply, "Slavery created blues," and be done with it—or at least it seems almost impossible to make such a statement and sound intelligent saying it. Yet this kind of oversimplification has created a whole intellectual climate for the appreciation of blues in this country. Blues is *not,* nor was it ever meant to be, a strictly social phenomenon, but is primarily a verse form and secondarily a way of making music. By "strictly social phenomenon," I refer, of course to the din of nineteenth-century American social reform and European sociological concern.

Blues as a verse form has as much social reference as any poetry, except for the strict lyric, and that also is found in blues. Love, sex, tragedy in interpersonal relationships, death, travel, loneliness, etc., are all social phenomena. And perhaps these are the things which actually create a poetry, as things, or ideas: there can be no such thing as poetry (or blues) exclusive of the matter it proposes to be about.

Blues did begin in slavery, and it is from that "peculiar institution," as it was known euphemistically, that blues did find its particular form. And if slavery dictated certain aspects of blues form and content, so did the so-called Emancipation and its subsequent problems dictate the path blues would take.

One important result of the Emancipation was the decentralization of the Negro population. Even though there were about 500,000 Negro freedmen in the country at the time of the Emancipation, concentrated predominantly in cities like New York, Philadelphia, Boston, Albany, Newark, Pittsburgh, and in the border states, the major part of the Negro population lived in the South as slaves. The Emancipation, or at least the movement of the Union soldiers through the South and the subsequent departure of the plantation owners, produced an immediate movement among a great many Negroes. As soon as the Union Army approached, most of the slaves struck out to find themselves new places to live, or at least safer places. The great majority of ex-slaves remained in the South, but some left immediately for the West and North. And even the Negroes who remained in the South were more scattered than before, though, to be sure, there were Negro communities set up almost immediately.

Reprinted from LeRoi Jones, *Blues People* (New York: Morrow, 1963), 50–59.

The period of Reconstruction was a very chaotic period for the South and the North. It was especially confusing for the newly freed slaves. The establishment of black Reconstruction governments in some parts of the South and the cries in Congress by so-called Northern radicals (Thaddeus Stevens, John A. Griswold, and others) for "40 acres and a mule" for the freed slaves must have caused a great deal of optimism among the Negroes. But as W. A. Williams says in his book: "Coinciding with the south's lack of capital with which to regenerate and diversify its economy, and with the Negro's difficulty in finding employment at anything but agricultural labor . . . [the] northern businessmen's coalition consolidated the new economic slavery of tenant farming, sharecropping, and the planter store. Shackled to the cotton crop, the Negro (and his white counterpart) became perennial debtors to their new overseers. While it exaggerates the reality, there is a significant measure of truth in the idea that the Civil War gave more freedom—at least in the short run—to the white upper class of the south than it did to the slave. Both were liberated, but the one group far more effectively."[1]

However ineffectual Emancipation might have proven in its entirety, it did have a great deal of positive effect on the Negro. The black Reconstruction governments of the South, although hampered at every turn, managed to effect a few beneficial changes. The postbellum government of South Carolina, for instance, provided public schooling for *500 per cent* more children than the antebellum government had. These governments tried to institute some basic social and political reforms, but because for most of the Northern whites the Reconstruction had never been anything but a token proposition, and the actual transfer of political and economic power had never been intended, the Negroes were finally powerless. The Reconstruction governments fell because the Northern industrialists joined with the Southern planters to disenfranchise the Negro once again, fearful that a coalition of the poor and disenfranchised Southern whites, the disillusioned agrarian interests, and the newly freed Negroes, might prove too strong a threat to their design of gaining absolute political and economic control of the South. But the Reconstruction did give the Negro a certain feeling of autonomy and self-reliance that could never be fully eradicated even after the repressive segregation measures that followed the so-called "Redemption of the South" in 1876: ". . . the demagogues assumed leadership of the 'poor whites' and provided a solution of the class conflict among whites that offered no challenge to the political power and economic privileges of the industrialists and the planter class. The program, which made the Negro the scapegoat, contained the following provisions: (1) The Negro was completely disfranchised by all sorts of legal subterfuges, with the threat of force in the background; (2) the funds which were appropriated on a *per capita* basis for Negro school children were diverted to white schools; and (3) a legal system of segregation in all phases of public life was instituted. In order to justify this program, the demagogues, who were supported by the white propertied classes, engaged for twenty-five years in a campaign to prove that the Negro was sub-human, morally degenerate and intellectually incapable of being educated."[2]

It was during this period of legal subversion of the Negroes' rights as new citizens that such organizations as the Ku Klux Klan, Pale Faces, Men of Justice, Knights of the White Camelia, etc., appeared. These organizations, composed mostly of disenfranchised poor whites, but often inspired by the more well-to-do planter-merchant combine, sought to frighten Negroes into abandoning their newly won rights, particularly the right to vote, and in a great many cases these attempts succeeded.

There was, of course, a great deal of protest and resistance from Negroes, and especially the educated class of Negroes, but soon too many accepted the idea of segregation as the only way the Negro could continue to live in the white South. The Negro elite—professional men: doctors, lawyers, or small, financially ambitious merchants—soon were quite eager to promote the concept of "separate but equal." Thus in only about ten years after the Emancipation, there was already a great social reaction setting in. All the legal chicanery and physical suppression the South used to put the Negro back in his place was, in effect, aided and abetted by a great many so-called Negro leaders. For instance, after the North had more or less washed its hands of the whole "Southern dilemma," and it was a generally accepted idea that Negroes had ruined the Reconstruction simply because they were incapable of governing themselves, Booker T. Washington became prominent and influential because he accepted the idea of segregation as a solution to the race problem and because he advocated that Negroes learn trades rather than go into any of the more ambitious professions. W. A. Williams notes, "Coming from Booker T. Washington, who enjoyed entrée into the society of Standard Oil executives, railroad magnates, and Andrew Carnegie, the strategy was persuasive. Washington avowed his loyalty to laissez faire, took his stand in the south as a southerner, and accepted social inequality for the foreseeable future. Blocked by the power of the whites and told by their own spokesman that 'white leadership is preferable,' most Negroes followed. . . ."[3]

Thus the idea of the "separate but equal" society, with equality almost completely nonexistent, came into being—although, to be sure, there arose in the South a black bourgeoisie who oftentimes were better off financially than a great many of the poor white farmers they had to say "suh" to. However, they swallowed the socio-economic concepts of their white upper-class models whole. It is my idea that the Civil War and the Emancipation served to create for the first time among Negroes a separate meta-society, one whose members strove to emulate exactly the white society. The black Christian church was the preface to this society during slavery, but after slavery the relatively great amount of personal freedom was sufficient to insure, at least among the more opportunistic freedmen, the impetus necessary to create within the newly formed black communities a socio-economic structure based almost entirely on the social structure of the white man.

As a slave, the black man in America performed an integral function in the mainstream of white American society. One that was easy to ascertain, and almost as easy to provide for. Slavery was, most of all, a paternal institution. The slave was property just like the cows, fruit trees, or wagons. And he was handled in much the same way, with perhaps some small deference accorded him because after a while he began to understand what his white master was saying. All the minimal requirements necessary to sustain human life were provided for the slave by his owner; there was almost no need for any initiative or ambition. But with the release of the millions of black men to what was supposed to be the pursuit of happiness, the whole of American society, and particularly the Southern society, underwent a huge change. When the first attempts at a consolidation of the downtrodden Southerners, black and white, failed; and when the radical plans of men like Summer and Stevens to redistribute the land of the South among the freedmen, breaking up the large plantations and making small farms for both black and white, also failed; and the separateness of black and white in the South was insured by the repressive Redemption methods; for what was really the first time, Negroes became actually isolated from the mainstream of American society. The newly activated Jim Crow laws (Virginia's were not passed until 1901) and other social repressions served to separate the Negro more effectively from his former masters than ever before.

With the old paternalistic society of the South went the simple role of the Negro in the Western world. Now the Negro was asked to throw himself into what was certainly still an alien environment and to deal with that environment in the same manner as his newly found white "brother" had been doing for centuries.

What is so often forgotten in any discussion of the Negro's "place" in American society is the fact that it was only as a slave that he really had one. The post-slave society had no place for the black American, and if there were to be any area of the society where the Negro might have an integral function, that area would have to be one that he created for himself. The Jim Crow laws were the white South's attempts to limit the new citizen's presence and rights in the mainstream of the society, and they were extremely effective.

Also, for most of the ex-slaves, even the most banal of Western mores had to be relearned, as it were, from the point of view of the autonomous individual. For instance, the Negro had to realign himself with the concept of what a family is and of what it means to be working separately to keep oneself and/or one's family alive. The family had to be recognized again as a basic social unit, and the dominant image of the patriarchal society restored to full meaning. During slavery, one of the fundamental social breakdowns the Negro experienced was the disintegration of familial ties, especially the role of the man as the complete master of the familial unit. Under this disintegration, the role of the woman within the society became much less fixed. In West Africa there was a very definite division of labor. For the most part, women did the lighter work and the men, the heavier or more specialized. In agriculture, men did the preparing of the fields, and women tended to the actual growing and harvesting of the crops. But in America, the woman, like as not, worked alongside the man in the same fields. Here, as in other areas of the African captives' lives, the traditional order was broken down. The breakdown or disappearance of African mores and traditions in the New World proposed, paradoxically, a more egalitarian society among the slaves. Tribal and familial titles were gone in most cases, and the only hegemony that could be gotten by the slaves had to be extended by the white masters. Hence, Afro-American women, though raped and outraged by the slave South, usually assumed a status that was a good deal more "elevated" than the status of the average West African woman. And so it was that certain traditions that were usually given their impetus by the male members of an African community could, in the strange context of the slave and post-slave New World society, be developed equally by women, and in some cases could even be brought to their perfection by women. Blues, at a certain point of its development, was one of those traditions, as I will attempt to show later.

So the post-slave black society in America was a completely unique thing to the ex-slaves as well as to the rest of America. There was also such a thing as the "slave mentality," which had a large part in shaping the new black society. By "slave mentality" I mean what had been the most socially unfortunate psychic adjustments the slave had made during two hundred years of slavery. The very speed with which the white South dealt with the ex-slave's formal aspirations to complete freedom and social and economic autonomy can be attributed to the negative influence of the slave mentality upon the great mass of Negroes. Two hundred years of bending to the will of the white man had to leave its mark. And that mark was indelibly on the very foundations of the new separate black society.

Another aspect of the white society that the Negroes patterned their new meta-society upon was the idea of stations within the social order, a hierarchy relatively impossible before the formal end of slavery. Of course, there had been some differentiation even in the slave society. The house slave, as I mentioned before, certainly enjoyed a bit of hegemony, no matter how artificial, over the field Negro. Also, Negroes who managed to learn trades were held in somewhat high esteem by the rest of the slaves. And the church officials, when the Negroes finally embraced Christianity, enjoyed perhaps the greatest prestige of all during slavery. Still, even in those relatively rare cases where a Negro did enjoy some privilege or special position, he was still a slave, and the added privilege could hardly serve to make the institution of slavery enjoyable. After slavery, the stratification of the social order among Negroes was rapid. At the bottom of the new social ladder were the tenant farmers and migrant laborers, and at the other end were the ministers, storekeepers, and professional men. It was the latter who naturally came to be regarded as the leaders of the many Negro communities; usually they set the stance the new society would take. The emulation of white society proved to be not only a pattern for the new leaders, but an end in itself. Negroes who were highest in the social and economic hierarchy also became the most fanatic imitators of white society, while the great masses of Negroes were much slower in their attempts at complete imitation. This phenomenon caused a split in the psychical disposition of the Negro's temperament which certainly affected all areas of his life.

The developing middle class and the mainstream of black society found themselves headed two different ways. This disparity within the black community is of such importance that it cannot be overemphasized, and it became more and more pronounced as the Negro achieved more latitude and status in America. At its ugliest, this attitude was symbolized by the abandonment by a great many Negroes of the mores or customs they considered slave customs, or "too Negroid." Some black churches began to use as much of the white church music as they could. (My own church in Newark, New Jersey, a Baptist church, has almost no resemblance to the older, more traditional Negro Christian churches. The music, for instance, is usually limited to the less emotional white church music, and the choir usually sings Bach or Handel during Christmas and Easter. In response to some of its older "country" members, the church, which is headed by a minister who is the most respected Negro in Newark, has to *import* gospel groups, or singers having a more traditional "Negro church" sound.)

Robert A. Bone discusses a Negro author, Charles Chesnutt, who wrote a novel, *The Marrow of Tradition*, around the time a great many of the better class of Negroes were reacting against two hundred years of slavery by trying to abandon almost all their "Negro traits." Chesnutt's novel shows the kind of attitude that was adopted by some. The "hero" is a "refined Afro-American," a doctor, who is forced to share a Jim Crow car with dirty, boisterous, and drunken Negroes. He is revolted by these people, farm laborers, in the coach, and Chesnutt says, "These people were just as offensive to him as to the whites in the other end of the train."[4]

This kind of hideous attitude in a Negro (and most of the Negro novelists of the time were quite close to Chesnutt in their social attitudes) could only stem from an acceptance of the idea of the superiority of the white man, or at least the proposition that the Negro, somehow, must completely lose himself within the culture and social order of the ex-master. It is another aspect of the slave mentality.

Blues, too, or at that time the shouts, chants, hollers, which later took more lasting form as blues, received the same treatment from these "refined Afro-Americans." The Negro's music was the most impressive reminder for these people of slavery and of their less cultivated brothers. And it, too, was to be abandoned on the altar of assimilation and progress. During the time immediately after the Emancipation, this kind of thinking was limited to only a few Negroes; the growth to "maturity" of this finally anti-Negro attitude among Negroes comes a little later. It is sufficient to note here some of the reasons for its genesis.

The Negro, during those few years after the end of slavery, just before the exodus to the Northern cities, stood further away from the mainstream of American society than at any other time. It was also during these years that the Negro's music lost a great many of the more superficial forms it had borrowed from the white man, and the forms that we recognize now as blues began to appear. There were still black "ballit" singers who sang songs that used centuries-old classical Anglo-Saxon ballad forms and spirituals that were pure "lifts" from the Protestant hymnals. But in a few years after the Emancipation, the shouts, hollers, yells, spirituals, and ballits began to take shape as blues.

Notes

1. W. A. Williams, *The Contours of American History* (Cleveland: World, 1961).
2. E. Franklin Frazier, *The Black Bourgeoisie* (Glencoe, Ill.: Free Press, 1957), p. 18.
3. Williams, *Contours.*
4. Robert Bone, *The Negro Novel in America* (New Haven: Yale University Press, 1958), p. 18.

From "Primitive Blues and Primitive Jazz"

LeRoi Jones

A SLAVE cannot be a man. A man does not, or is not supposed to, work all of his life without recourse to the other areas of human existence. The emotional limitations that slavery must enforce are monstrous: the weight of his bondage makes impossible for the slave a great many alternatives into which the shabbiest of free men can project himself. There is not even a separate identity the ego can claim. "What are you going to be when you grow up?" "A slave."

The work song is a limited social possibility. The shouts and hollers were strident laments, more than anything. They were also chronicles, but of such a mean kind of existence that they could not assume the universality any lasting musical form must have. The work songs and later blues forms differ very profoundly not only in their form but in their lyrics and *intent.*

> Oh, Lawd, I'm tired, uuh
> Oh, Lawd, I'm tired, uuh
> Oh, Lawd, I'm tired, uuh
> Oh, Lawd, I'm tired, a dis mess.
>
> (*repeated*)

Primitive blues-singing actually came into being because of the Civil War, in one sense. The emancipation of the slaves proposed for them a normal human existence, a humanity impossible under slavery. Of course, even after slavery the average Negro's life in America was, using the more ebullient standards of the average American white man, a shabby, barren existence. But still this was the black man's first experience of time when he could be alone. The leisure that could be extracted from even the most desolate sharecropper's shack in Mississippi was a novelty, and it served as an important catalyst for the next form blues took.

Many Negroes who were sharecroppers, or who managed to purchase one of the tiny farms that dotted the less fertile lands of the South, worked in their fields alone or with their

Reprinted from LeRoi Jones, *Blues People* (New York: Morrow, 1963), 60–70.

families. The old shouts and hollers were still their accompaniment for the arduous work of clearing land, planting, or harvesting crops. But there was a solitude to this work that had never been present in the old slave times. The huge plantation fields had many slaves, and they sang together. On the smaller farms with fewer slaves where the older African forms died out quicker, the eight- and sixteen-bar "ballits," imitations of the songs of the white masters, were heard along with the shouts. Of course, there must have been lyrics to some of the songs that the slave could not wisely sing in front of his master. But the small farms and sharecroppers' plots produced not only what I think must have been a less self-conscious work song but a form of song or shout that did not necessarily have to be concerned with, or inspired by, *labor.* Each man had his own voice and his own way of shouting—his own life to sing about. The tenders of those thousands of small farms became almost identified by their individual shouts. "That's George Jones, down in Hartsville, shoutin' like that."

Along with this leisure there was also that personal freedom to conduct or ruin one's life as one saw fit. In the 1870's there were thousands of black migrant workers moving all through the South. There were also men who just moved around from place to place, not really migratory laborers, just footloose wanderers. There could come now to these ex-slaves a much fuller idea of what exactly America was. A slave on a Georgia plantation, unless he was sold or escaped, usually was born, grew to manhood, and died right in Georgia. To him, the whole of America would be Georgia, and it would have to conform strictly to what he had experienced. St. Louis, Houston, Shreveport, New Orleans, simply did not exist (and certainly not New York). But now for many Negroes there was a life of movement from farm to farm, or town to town. The limited social and emotional alternatives of the work song could no longer contain the growing experience of this country that Negroes began to respond to. Also, the entrance of Negroes into the more complicated social situation of self-reliance proposed multitudes of social and cultural problems that they never had to deal with as slaves. The music of the Negro began to reflect these social and cultural complexities and change.

Very early blues did not have the "classic" twelve-bar, three-line, AAB structure. For a while, as I mentioned before, blues-type songs utilized the structure of the early English ballad, and sometimes these songs were eight, ten, or sixteen bars. The shout as much as the African call-and-response singing dictated the form blues took. Blues issued directly out of the shout and, of course, the spiritual. The three-line structure of blues was a feature of the shout. The first two lines of the song were repeated, it would seem, while the singer was waiting for the next line to come. Or, as was characteristic of the hollers and shouts, the single line could be repeated again and again, either because the singer especially liked it, or because he could not think of another line. The repeated phrase also carries into instrumental jazz as the *riff.*

Another reason for the changes in musical form was the change of speech patterns among a great many Negroes. By now the language of America was mastered for casual use by most Negroes. While the work song or shout had only a few English words, or was composed of Africanized English words or some patois-like language that seemed more a separate language than an attempt at mastering English, early blues had already moved toward pure American lyrics (with the intent that the song be understood by other Americans). The endlessly repeated line of the shout or holler might also have been due to the relative paucity of American words the average field Negro possessed, the rhyme line being much more difficult to supply because of the actual limitation singing in American imposed. The lines came more easily as the language was mastered more completely. Blues was a kind of singing that utilized a language that was almost strictly American. It was not until the ex-slaves had mastered this language in whatever appropriation of it they made that blues began to be more evident than shouts and hollers.

The end of the almost exclusive hold of the Christian Church on the black man's leisure also resulted in a great many changes of emphasis in his music. The blues is formed out of the same social and musical fabric that the spiritual issued from, but with blues the social emphasis becomes more personal, the "Jordan" of the song much more intensely a *human* accomplishment. The end of slavery could be regarded as a Jordan, and not a metaphysical one either, although the analogy of the deliverance of the Jews and the Emancipation must have been much too cogent a point for proselytizing to be lost on the local black minister. There was a definite change of *direction* in the primitive blues. The metaphysical Jordan of life after death was beginning to be replaced by the more pragmatic Jordan of the American master: the Jordan of what the ex-slave could see vaguely as self-determination. Not that that idea or emotion hadn't been with the very first Africans who had been brought here; the difference was that the American Negro wanted some degree of self-determination where he was living. The desperation to return to Africa had begun to be replaced by another even more hopeless one. The Negro began to feel a desire to be more in this country, America, than chattel. "The sun's gonna shine in my back door someday!"

The leisure and movement allowed to Negroes after the Civil War helped to standardize the new blues form as well as spread the best verses that were made up. Although there were regional differences in the way blues began to be sung, there were also certain recurring, soon "classical," blues verses and techniques that turned up in a great many places simply because a man had been there from Georgia or Louisiana or South Carolina and shown the locals what his town or region produced.

But the thousands of black blues shouters and ballit singers who wandered throughout the South around the turn of the century moved from place to place not only because Negroes were allowed to travel after the Civil War, but because for a great many Negroes, emancipation meant a constant desperate search for employment (although there must also have been those people who, having been released from their bondage, set out at once to see what this country was really about). Not only the migratory workers who followed the crop harvests but the young men who wanted any kind of work had to tramp all over the South in search of it. It is also a strange note that once the Negroes were free, it was always the men who had the harder time finding work. Women could always find work as domestics wherever they were. But the black man who had done agricultural labor, as most Negroes had, found it difficult to find work because the impoverished whites of the South suddenly had to pay wages to their workers. The Negro had to have wages to live: for the first time he needed money and had to enter into the fierce struggle for economic security like any other poor man in this country. Again, even the economic status of the Negro after his freedom proposed new changes for his music. "I never had to have no money befo' / And now they want it everywhere I go." The content of blues verse had become much changed from the strictly extemporized lyrics of the shouts and hollers.

It seems possible to me that some kind of graph could be set up using samplings of

Negro music proper to whatever moment of the Negro's social history was selected, and that in each grouping of songs a certain frequency of reference could pretty well determine his social, economic, and psychological states at that particular period. From the neo-African slave chants through the primitive and classical blues to the scat-singing of the beboppers: all would show definite insistences of reference that would isolate each group from the others as a social entity. No slave song need speak about the slave's lack of money; no early Afro-American slave song would make reference to the Christian Church; almost no classical blues songs would, or could, make direct or *positive* mention of Africa. Each phase of the Negro's music issued directly from the dictates of his social and psychological environment. Hence the black man who began after slavery to eliminate as much of the Negro culture from his life as possible became by this very act a certain kind of *Negro*. And if this certain kind of Negro still endeavored to make music, albeit with the strict provision that this music not be a Negro music, he could still not escape the final "insult" of this music being evaluated socially, psychologically, and musically as a kind of *Negro* music. The movement of the Negro into a position where he would be able to escape even this separation from the white mainstream of America is a central theme of this book.

Even with the relative formalization of secular Negro music, blues was still an extremely personal music. There were the songs extolling the merits and adventures of heroes or heroic archetypes, John Henry, Stagger Lee, Dupree, etc., but even as the blues began to expand its references it still remained a kind of singing that told about the exploits of the singer. Heroic archetypes or cowardly archetypes were used to point up some part of the singer's life.

> In come a nigger named Billy Go-helf
> Coon was so mean was skeered of hisself;
> Loaded wid razors an' guns, so they say,
> Cause he killed a coon most every day.

And this intensely personal nature of blues-singing is also the result of what can be called the Negro's "American experience." African songs dealt, as did the songs of a great many of the preliterate or classical civilizations, with the exploits of the social unit, usually the tribe. There were songs about the gods, their works and lives, about nature and the elements, about the nature of a man's life on the earth and what he could expect after he died, but the insistence of blues verse on the life of the individual and his individual trials and successes on the earth is a manifestation of the whole Western concept of man's life, and it is a development that could only be found in an American black man's music. From the American black leader's acceptance of Adam Smith "laissez faire" social inferences to some less fortunate black man's relegation to a lonely patch of useless earth in South Carolina, the weight of Western tradition, or to make it more specific and local, the weight of just what social circumstance and accident came together to produce the America that the Negro was part of, had to make itself part of his life as well. The whole concept of the *solo*, of a man singing or playing by himself, was relatively unknown in West African music.

But if the blues was a music that developed because of the Negro's adaptation to, and adoption of, America, it was also a music that developed because of the Negro's peculiar position in this country. Early blues, as it came to differ from the shout and the Afro-Christian religious music, was also perhaps the most impressive expression of the Negro's individuality within the superstructure of American society. Even though its birth and growth seem connected finally to the general movement of the mass of black Americans into the central culture of the country, blues still went back for its impetus and emotional meaning to the individual, to his completely personal life and death. Because of this, blues could remain for a long time a very fresh and singular form of expression. Though certain techniques and verses came to be standardized among blues singers, the singing itself remained as arbitrary and personal as the shout. Each man sang a different blues: the Peatie Wheatstraw blues, the Blind Lemon blues, the Blind Willie Johnson blues, etc. The music remained that personal because it began with the performers themselves, and not with formalized notions of how it was to be performed. Early blues developed as a music to be sung for *pleasure*, a casual music, and that was its strength and its weakness.

> I don't want you to be no slave,
> I don't want you to work all day,
> I don't want you to be true,
> I just want to make love to you.

Since most Negroes before and after slavery were agricultural laborers, the corn songs and arwhoolies, the shouts and hollers, issued from one kind of work. Some of the work songs, for instance, use as their measure the grunt of a man pushing a heavy weight or the blow of a hammer against a stone to provide the metrical precision and rhythmical impetus behind the singer. ("Take this hammer, uh, / Take it to the captain, uh, / Take it to the captain, uh, / Tell him I'm gone.") Contemporary work songs, for example, songs recorded by Negro convicts working in the South—laying railroad ties, felling trees, breaking rocks, take their impetus from the work being done, and the form of the singing itself is dictated by the work. These workers for the most part do not sing blues. The labor is central to the song: not only is the recurring grunt or moan of these work songs some kind of metrical and rhythmical insistence, it is the very catalyst for the song. On one recent record, the Louisiana Folklore Society's, *Prison Worksongs* recorded in Angola, Louisiana, at the Louisiana State Penitentiary there, one song listed as *Take This Hammer* begins as that song, but lasts as that for only about three "bars" (three strokes of the hammer) and then wanders irresolutely into *Alberta, Berta*, several blues verses, and a few lines from a spiritual. The point is that the primitive blues was at once a more formal music since the three-line, twelve-bar song became rapidly standardized, and was also a more liberated music since there was literally *more* to sing about. In one's leisure one can begin to formalize a method of singing as well as find new things to sing about. (It is an interesting thought that perhaps all the music that Negroes in America have made might have been quite different if the work that they were brought here to do had been different. Suppose Negroes had been brought to this country to make vases or play basketball. How might the blues have developed then from the impetus of work songs geared to those occupations?)

Work songs and shouts were, of course, almost always *a capella*. It would have been extremely difficult for a man to pick cotton or shuck corn and play an instrument at the same time. For this reason pre-blues secular singing did not have the discipline or strict formality that a kind of singing employing instruments must have. But it is obvious from the very earliest form of the blues that instrumental accompaniment was beginning to be taken into consideration. The twelve-bar blues—the more or less final form of blues—is constructed so that each verse is of three lines, each line about four bars long. The words of the song usually occupy about one-half of each line, leaving a space of two bars for either a sung answer or an instrumental response.

It may seem strange that the formal blues should evolve *after* slavery, after so many years of bondage and exposure by the slaves to the larger Western cultural unit, into a form that is patently non-Western; the three-line verse form of the blues springs from no readily apparent Western source. But the use of instruments on a large scale was also something that happened after the Emancipation; the very possession of instruments, except those few made from African models, was rare in the early days of slavery. The stereotyped pictures that many of the apologists for the Southern way of life used as flyleaves for their numerous novels after the Civil War, depicting a happy-go-lucky black existentialist strumming merrily on his banjo while sitting on a bale of cotton, were, I'm sure, more romantic fiction than fact. The slave would hardly have had the time to sit on his master's bale of cotton during the work day, and the only instruments that were in common usage among the slaves were drums, rattles, tambourines, scrapers (the jawbone of a horse over which a piece of wood was scraped), and the like; even such an African instrument as the banjo was very scarce. The guitar was not commonly played by Negroes until much after the Civil War. An instrument like the harmonica grew in popularity among a great many Negroes simply because it took up almost no space and was so easy to carry around. But even the harmonica did not come into common use until after slavery, and certainly the possession and mastery of European instruments did not occur until much later.

When primitive or country blues did begin to be influenced by instruments, it was the guitar that had the most effect on the singers. And when the great masses of Negroes were just beginning to learn the instrument, the relatively simple chords of the country blues were probably what they learned. Conceivably, this also brought about another change: blues, a vocal music, was made to conform to an instrument's range. But, of course, the blues widened the range of the instrument, too. Blues guitar was not the same as classical or "legitimate" guitar: the strings had to make vocal sounds, to imitate the human voice and its eerie cacophonies. Perhaps the reason why the guitar was at once so popular was not only because it was much like the African instrument, the banjo (or *banjor*), but because it was an instrument that still permitted the performer to *sing*.

When the Negro finally did take up the brass instruments for strictly instrumental blues or jazz, the players still persisted in singing in the "breaks." This could be done easily in the blues tradition with the call-and-response form of blues. Even much later in the jazz tradition, not only were instruments made to sound like the human voice but a great many of the predominantly instrumental songs were still partially sung. The first great soloist of jazz, Louis Armstrong, was a formidable blues singer, as was the great jazz pianist Jelly Roll Morton. Both men sang blues almost as beautifully as they played their instruments.

The primitive blues was still very much a vocal music; the singers relied on the unpredictability and mobility of the human voice for their imaginative catalysts. But the growing use of European instruments such as brass and reeds almost precluded song, except as accompaniment or as an interlude. When Negroes began to master more and more "European" instruments and began to think musically in terms of their timbres, as opposed to, or in conjunction with, the voice, blues began to change, and the era of jazz was at hand.

Do the Bombashay

Dance Songs and Routines

Paul Oliver

A TALL man with proud features beneath his white skull cap, Joshua Barnes "Peg Leg" Howell was a familiar figure on Atlanta's Decatur Street. He played guitar and sang in a crackling, somewhat lugubrious voice, which was enlivened when he was joined by Eddie Anthony or another fiddler to play a stomping dance. Shot in the leg by an angry brother-in-law back in 1916, Howell was an amputee. The incident had ended his career on a farm and made it necessary for him to earn his living by his music. Born some eighty miles south-east of Atlanta in 1888, he had also worked in a fertilizer plant, made and sold moonshine liquor, and "just messed around town". Moving to Atlanta in 1923, he played on the street for coins outside Bailey's Theater. He was heard by the talent scout Dan Hornsby who arranged for him to record for Frank Walker of Columbia when the latter brought a field unit to Atlanta in November 1926 to record a number of preachers and religious artists. The small group of titles by Peg Leg Howell were the first they made of a rural black folk singer.[1]

His choice for his first song was probably unexpected: *Coal Man Blues* was hardly a conventional blues; it began as a ballad which described a railroad accident before slipping into the song of a street vendor hawking coal from his wagon:

> Let me tell you something that I seen,
> Coal man got run over by the 5.15;
> Cut off his arms and it crushed his ribs—
> Did the po' man die? No the po' man lives.
>   Hard coal, stovewood man,
>   Hard coal and the stovewood man.
>   I ain't got but a li'l bit left,
>   If ya don't come get it, gonna burn it myself.
>
> Sell it to the rich an' I sell it the po', (3)
> Sell it to the nice brown that's standin' at the do'.

Reprinted with permission of Cambridge University Press from Paul Oliver, *Songsters and Saints: Vocal Traditions on Race Records* (Cambridge: Cambridge University Press, 1984), 18–46, 292.

Furnish your wood, furnish your coal, (3)
Make you love me, doggone your soul.[2]

Among the other titles that Howell recorded on that date was *New Prison Blues* which he had picked up from a fellow convict in 1925 when he was serving time for selling bootleg liquor. When the unit came back in April the following year, Peg Leg was joined by his "Gang": Eddie Anthony sawing away at the fiddle placed high on his shoulder, and Henry Williams strumming guitar. Their pieces included a sixteen-bar song with suggestive "baker shop" lyrics, *Jelly Roll Blues*, which had been around for some years. Ferdinand "Jelly Roll" Morton had copyrighted a version in 1915, though he claimed to have composed it in 1905. The opening strains of *Original Jelly-Roll Blues* by Morton's Red Hot Peppers indicate that it was essentially the same theme as the one that Howell had heard "a fellow named Elijah Lawrence" sing.

Returning to Atlanta in the fall, the Columbia unit continued to visit twice a year until early in 1929. Over this period Howell recorded some thirty titles, of which all but two were issued in the Columbia 14000 Race Series. Many of these were of blues; some slow and lugubrious, like *Walking Blues,* or *Broke and Hungry Blues.* Many of Howell's blues verses dated back to the earliest stanzas noted by collectors: verses in *Rocks and Gravel Blues* and *Turtle Dove Blues* were noted by John A. Lomax in 1908 when he collected them from the Mississippi levee woman Dink as she was washing for the levee workers on the Brazos River in Texas.[3] Others he may have learned from a record, or they shared a common ancestry, like *Hobo Blues,* which was closely related to Charles Davenport's celebrated song and "showcase" piano piece, *Cow Cow Blues.* Sometimes he developed a blues-like theme from fragments of work song, or, as in the case of *Please Ma'am,* from the pleading of a rejected man. Perhaps the only blues to be recorded which was built from just one or two lines repeated in various forms, it suggested a field holler (or "over and over" as the repetitive field hand's songs were sometimes called) and bore out his simple statement: "I heard many of my songs around the country, I picked them up from nobody—no special person."[4] Its fragmentary lyrics echoed the words and sentiments of songs that had been in currency long before: *Oh My Babe, Take Me Back* and *Honey Won't You 'llow Me One More Chance.* Some of his songs were blues in name only; *Skin Game Blues* for example, which was a gambling song describing the fortunes of a player in the game of Georgia Skin:

Went out to the skin game last night,
Thought I'd have some fun,
Lost all the money that I had, baby,
Pawn my special gun,
  Had to pawn my special gun,
  Says I pawn my special gun, lovin' baby,
  Pawn my special gun.

  Says you better let the deal go down,
  Skin game comin' to a close
  And you better let the deal go down.

Says, gambled all over Missouri,
Gambled all through Spain, babe,

Police come to arrest me, babe,
And they did not know my name.
  And they did not know my name, (3)
  Better let the deal go down,[5] etc.

Skin Game was evidently a song which Howell had worked up from other sources; it related to old songs in both white and black traditions like *The Roving Gambler* and *The Coon-Can Game*, to which he had added a chorus based on the calls of the "pikers".

Certain of Howell's blues have been recognized as exceptional, and as an important figure in the Georgia tradition he has been included in every history of the blues: his *Low Down Rounder's Blues* has been quoted by Sackheim, Oakley and Titon in their various books. *Rolling Mill Blues* was one which I included in *Blues Fell This Morning*; there I related the closing of the mine to the closures of the Depression, but in fact the reference was much older. Howell's couplets began:

The rollin' mill, babe it done broke down,
Ain't shippin' no iron to town.

The longest train I ever seen
Run round Joe Brown's coal mine,

The engine was at the coal mine hill
And the captain never left town.

The train run off the track last night,
And it killed my lovin' Corinne.

Her head was found in the drivin' wheel
And her body have never been seen . . .[6]

The lyrics appear to have derived from a song cluster known to white singers, which included *In the Pines* and *The Longest Train*. After studying 160 versions of the song on record or in print, Judith McCulloh was of the opinion that the coal mine references were to those in Dade County, Georgia, owned by Governor Joseph Emerson Brown in the 1870s. The railroad accident with its gruesome image of the head found in the driver's wheel, but the body untraced, was fixed in the folk mind and, Judith McCulloh suggests, probably originated in the Reconstruction period.[7] Howell it seems, was synthesizing verses that had been in currency for over half a century. About half of his recordings were blues, excellent examples of the idiom that had developed in his maturity. But the other half of his recorded repertoire was a mixture of elements from many sources, which marked Peg Leg Howell as a typical songster of his generation.

As early as 1911 the collector Howard Odum noted in his epoch-making paper the terms used by black performers to describe themselves. "In general 'songster' is used to denote any Negro who regularly sings or makes songs; 'musicianer' applies often to the individual who claims to be expert with the banjo or fiddle" while the "music physicianer" was a traveler who was a combination of both. At almost the same time Will H. Thomas noted the term "songster"; seventy years later both "songster" and "musicianer" were still in use, though "music physicianer"—probably a medicine show term—had been discarded.[8]

As early as 1821 the term "songster" was being used for small songbooks of ballads, broadsides and popular songs. As Malcolm Laws noted "during the 19th Century hundreds or perhaps thousands of different songbooks were printed and sold throughout America. Most of them contained the word 'songster' in the title, sold for about a dime, and were of pocket size." *The Forget Me Not Songster, The Arkansas Traveler Songster* and the *Uncle True Songster* were typical. It is likely that the term was soon applied to those who sang their songs, while "musicianer" was used by extension.[9]

The good songster was expected to be a good musicianer too, when the need arose—which it did most frequently at country barbecues and dances; the kind of social function described in the background chatter between Peg Leg Howell and Jim Hill on *Chittlin' Supper* with its skilful mandolin imitation of a piano and its stumbling humor: "Bring me some of those ole best pan chittlin's in here. What do I care for expenses—uh? I'd soon as spend a dime as not—uh . . ."[10]

Songsters were entertainers, providing music for every kind of social occasion in the decades before phonographs and radio. They were receptive to a wide variety of songs and music; priding themselves on their range, versatility, and capacity to pick up a tune, they played not only for the black communities, but for whites too, when the opportunities arose. Whatever else the songster had to provide in the way of entertainment, he was always expected to sing and play for dances. This over-riding function bound many forms of black secular song together. Social songs, comic songs, the blues and ballads, minstrel tunes and popular ditties all had this in common, and whether it set the time for spirited lindy-hopping or for low-down, slow-dragging across a puncheon floor, the music of black secular song could almost always be made to serve this purpose. It was the regular beat that provided the pulse for the dance and the cross-rhythms of vocal and instrumental that inspired the shuffles, shimmies, hip-shakes and shoulder rolls.

Before much serious attention was paid to the songs of black Americans, their dances were the subject of white interest and mimicry. Charles Dickens, who visited "Almack's" cellar dive in the notorious Five Points district of New York in April 1842, was one of several writers who gave graphic descriptions of "a regular break-down". He saw "the corpulent black fiddler, and his friend who plays the tambourine, stamp upon the boarding of the small raised orchestra in which they sit, and play a lively measure" to which the young mulatto girls and their beaux responded. "A lively young negro who is the wit of the assembly, and the greatest dancer known" dashed in: "Instantly the fiddler grins, and goes at it tooth and nail; there is new energy in the tambourine" and the young black stepped: "single shuffle, double shuffle, cut and cross-cut; snapping his fingers, rolling his eyes, turning in his knees, presenting the backs of his legs in front, spinning about on his toes and heels like nothing but the man's fingers on the tambourine: dancing with two left legs, two right legs, two wooden legs, two wire legs—all sorts of legs and no legs . . ." and finishing by "leaping gloriously on the bar-counter and calling for something to drink".[11]

It is suggested by Hans Nathan in his detailed study of Dan Emmett and the origins of, as he decorously termed it, "Negro Minstrelsy", that the dancer Dickens saw was John Henry Lane, the celebrated "Juba"; he may have been, but there were many black dancers on whom the minstrels modelled their steps. They drew upon Scots and Irish sources too, and it is still arguable how much the "Ethiopian jigs" were derived from the Irish jigs, with their rapid footwork and almost motionless upper body and arms. As for the term "jig", it had a long history in Britain, where it had been used for the vigorous "capering" and satirical dances with songs and "rare discord of bells, pipes and tabors" since the late seventeenth century. Charles Read Baskervill concluded that "in spite of changing modes 'jig' remained an accepted term for dance song" through the seventeenth century.[12]

To what extent black capering and jigging were based on African steps remains questionable, though some West African dances have characteristics in common with early descriptions of American dancing. Violent dancing with shoulder and elbow snaps, and with the knees drawn up to the chin in swift, jerking movements is typical of the Ewe of the former Gold Coast (Ghana), for instance. White minstrel troupes drew inspiration from black rural dancing, and though many forms of dance must have had a short life there are some indications that others persisted. The dances of the slave quarters were a source of interest and amusement for whites.[13] Recalled one ex-slave, James Lucas, who was born in 1833: "us could dance about all night. De old-time fiddlers played fast music and us all clapped hands and tromped and swayed in time to de music, . . . Marster and Mistis laugh fit to kill at de capers us cut." Another ex-slave, James W. Smith, from Palestine, Texas recalled that "there am dancing and singing mostest every Saturday night. He had a little platform built for the jigging contests. Colored folks come from all around, to see who jig the best" and he described one man who "was the jiggingest fellow ever was . . . he could put the glass of water on his head and make his feet go like triphammers and sound like the snaredrum".[14]

For such dances the music was provided by fiddle, banjo and tambourine, or home-made instruments when better ones were not available. "Us take pieces of sheep's rib or cow's jaw or a piece of iron, with a old kettle, or a hollow gourd and some horsehairs to make a drum . . . they'd take the buffalo horn and scrape it out to make the flute. That sure be heard a long ways off. Then they'd take a mule's jawbone and rattle the stick across the teeth", Wash Wilson, another one-time slave, explained. As for the dances: "they wasn't no special name to them. There was cuttin' the pigeon wings—that was flippin' your arms and legs round and holdin' your neck stiff like a bird do. Then there was going to the east and going to the west—that was with partners and sometimes they got to kiss each other . . . And there was calling the figures and that meant that the fiddler would call the number and all the couples got to cut that number."[15]

These and numerous other testimonies of ex-slaves indicate that in the first half of the nineteenth century jigs and capers were a common feature of black dancing. If the slaves performed novelty dances imitating bird and animal movements, set dances, such as cotillions, were also danced by them, as they were by the families of their white owners. Black musicians played for both races, as Prince Johnson, from Clarksdale, Mississippi explained: "De same old fiddler played for us dat played for de white folks. And he sure could play. When he got dat old fiddle out you couldn't keep your foots still." The songs that accompanied the dances were often simple: "It goes sort of like dis: 'Turn your pardner round! Steal round de corner, 'cause dem Johnson gals is hard to beat! Just glance round and have a good time! Dem gals is hard to find!' " Robert Shepherd from Athens, Georgia, remembered.[16]

From the two thousand interviews in the *Slave Narrative Collection* of the Federal Writers' Project of the WPA, the vast, thirty-one volume collection of *The American Slave* compiled by George Rawick,[17] and the many other anthologies of slave narratives, a very full picture of music and dance in the ante-bellum years could, and should, be compiled. Unfortunately, no such comprehensive interviewing was conducted concerning black life in the Reconstruction, or indeed after, and detailed descriptions of their secular music during these periods are thin on the ground. In the interim a great many changes must have taken place in some elements of black dance and its related songs and music. Even so, several aspects appear to have persisted, among them the vigorous dancing with animal and bird-like movements, whirling arms and rapid footwork of the solo jigs. The instrumental music of fiddle and banjo continued, while the improvising of instruments from any suitable materials, from the jawbones and ribs of animals, to household utensils like the washtub, scrubbing board and stoneware jar remained common throughout the South.[18]

Black musicians still played for the white balls in the big plantation houses, and this too, remained a tradition throughout the century; others played in the barns or on the cornshucking grounds of the plantations and farms for the Saturday night frolics. They performed the tunes for the quadrilles and cotillions, set dances and barn dances of the white rural communities and from their simple platforms "called the sets". Their skill and timing was appreciated enough for them frequently to take precedence over white musicians, as many nineteenth-century illustrations indicate. Servants and hands who watched the white folks dancing were sometimes permitted to hold their own dances within the Big House, which meant that they had access both to the dances and to the music of the balls, and could copy them.[19]

Rural dance traditions of this kind die hard—they persisted to the 1940s all over the South and can still be witnessed in some areas. Fifty years ago they were customary. Among the recordings of "Old Time Fiddle Tunes" and other country music issued in the 1920s there were scores, even hundreds, of examples. White musicians like Fiddling John Carson, Riley Puckett, Gid Tanner and a great many others extensively recorded country dance music, but the records of a number of black musicians also captured something of the quality of the shared tradition. While these individual Race records do not illustrate all the instruments they employed, or the dance forms that they had performed, they do create a composite picture of the instrumental accompaniment to early dances, while the lyrics make connexions with early traditions. For example, Henry Thomas, who was a Texas guitarist born around 1880 and believed to be one of the oldest rural black singers on record, performed what was already, in his terms, an *Old Country Stomp*, singing couplets or single lines repeated:

> Get your partners, promenade,
> Promenade all around the town.
>
> Hop on, you started wrong,
> Take your partner, come on the train.
>
> I'm going away, I'm going away, (2)
>
> Miss Ginnie eat, Miss Ginnie talk,
> Miss Ginnie eat with knife and fork.
>
> Goodbye boys, fare you well, (2)
>
> I'm goin' back to Baltimore, (2)[20]

His guitar accompaniment was essentially rhythmic, but between the vocals he played the melody on the quills; apart from Big Boy Cleveland who recorded a single title, he was the only singer to record on this folk instrument. "In my childhood I saw many sorts of 'quills'. The quills were short reed pipes, closed at one end made from cane found in our Southern cane-brakes", wrote Thomas W. Talley in 1922. He differentiated between the five-note "little set" of quills and a "big set" with more reeds. "The reed pipes were made closed at one end by being so cut that the bottom of each was a node of the cane. These pipes were 'whittled' square with a jack knife and were then wedged into a wooden frame, and the player blew them with his mouth." It was an old tradition: George W. Cable wrote in 1886 of "the black lad, sauntering home at sunset behind a few cows that he has found near the edge of the canebrake whence he has also cut his three quills, blowing and hooting, over and over".[21] Henry Thomas played his quills between calling sets in a jaunty, shrill but clear melody. At one point he used a verse of ante-bellum date, once recalled as "jawbone eat, jawbone talk, jawbone eat with knife and fork" which was collected in Virginia and elsewhere, but which he now ascribed to "Aunt Ginnie".[22]

Another musician, Sam Jones, from Cincinnati, who styled himself "Stovepipe No. 1" was a "one-man band" who played guitar, harmonica (on a rack or neck-harness, as Thomas had probably played his quills) and a stovepipe into which he blew to produce a resonant and acceptable bass melodic line. He recorded in cities as far apart as St. Louis, Richmond (Indiana), New York and Atlanta but his themes, including those that were unissued, were rural and similar to white dance tunes. *Cripple Creek* and *Sourwood Mountain* were typical Appalachian songs, on which he called sets:

Me and my wife and a bob-tailed hound
Goin' away to Bagentown,
Me and my wife and bob-tailed hound
Take a lil ride and go to town,

he sang on *Cripple Creek*; and on *Sourwood Mountain*

I've got a gal on the Sourwood Mountain,
Swing your partners all the way round . . .

Raise hands [up], circle to the right,
Promenade all the way round . . .

His calls were similar on his recording of *Turkey In the Straw*:

Change hands up, circle to the right,
Promenade all the way round;
Swing the girl you love the best,
Please let mine alone . . .[23]

Turkey In the Straw was an old reel from Dan Emmett's Virginia Minstrels called *Old Zip Coon*. First published in the 1830s and probably performed as early as 1829 on the stage, it derived from Irish hornpipes. A century after its first performance it was recorded by Peg Leg Howell, with his companion Eddie Anthony on violin. Their *Turkey Buzzard Blues* was rough country music of the kind which may have inspired the imitations of the minstrel shows. Played in the black quarters it was, perhaps, too earthy for the white balls. Whereas Stovepipe No. 1 only called the sets, Howell and Anthony hollered the verses in rasping voices and played guitar and fiddle in a strongly syncopated fashion.

> Have you ever went fishin' on a bright summer's day,
> Standin' on the bank, see the little fishes play,
> Hands in your pockets, and your pockets in your pants,
> See the lil bittie fishes do the Hootchy-Kootchy dance.
>
> I had an ole hen, had a peg-leg,
> Fattest ole hen that ever laid an egg,
> Laid more eggs than the hen around the barn,
> Says "Another lil drink won't do me no harm".
>
> Sugar in the gourd, cain't get it out, (3)
> Way to get sugar—roll it all about.[24]

The Hootchy-Kootchy, or belly dance, had been introduced by the dancer "Little Egypt" at the Chicago Columbia Exposition, or World's Fair, in 1893 where her erotic movements created a sensation. *Sugar In the Gourd* was another song fragment that was known from the East Coast to west Texas. In these, as in other dance songs, an underlying vein of ribaldry was there to be found by those who had a mind to.

Play-parties, where immense gatherings of country folk came together for dancing and feasting, were a common feature of Southern rural entertainment, especially when the nights were short in the height of summer and in the cool of long evenings. In some regions, as in Mississippi in the 1870s and 1880s, huge picnics and barbecues, sometimes attracting thousands of blacks and their families to a single event, were held in the summer. Numerous bands provided music for the dancing that took place on platforms built for the purpose. Railroad companies offered excursions from Jackson to Vicksburg, Mississippi, sometimes with a riverboat trip to complete a circular tour. Music for dancing entertained the excursionists who crowded into the towns on the way. In 1880 the *Hinds County Gazette* questioned the right of any railroad to "pour fifteen hundred howling excursionists upon any peaceful community". Picnics continue in Mississippi still, if on a reduced scale.[25]

Singing and dancing that was most typical of the period was to be heard in the converted barns of rural settlements, and the grimy dance halls of black belt towns and waterfront dives. In a sharply, but sympathetically, observed article written in 1876, Lafcadio Hearn described the dance halls of the Cincinnati levee, where in one, "a well-dressed neatly-built mulatto picked the banjo, and a somewhat lighter colored musician led the music with a fiddle, which he played remarkably well and with great spirit". The dancing ranged from jigs with the customary water-glass on the head of the dancer, to a quadrille and an old Virginia reel. "The dancing became wild; men patted juba and shouted, the Negro women danced with the most fantastic grace . . . the musicians began to sing; the dancers joined in; and the dance terminated with a roar of song, stamping of feet, 'patting juba', shouting, laughing, reeling."[26]

Patting juba, or producing rhythms by beating the palms on the knees, hips, thighs, chest and other resonant parts of the body had been known since the earliest days of minstrelsy and continued as "pats" well into the present century. Combined with foot tapping they provided opportunities for participants, whether seated or dancing, to create complex cross-rhythms against the music of fiddle and banjo, and to introduce syncopated time into the performance.[27] Such syncopation was already evident in *Civil Rights Juba,* which was published as early as 1874, while *Rag Baby Jig,* included in the "Banjo Companion" of a decade later, hinted at the direction which black dance music and song was taking. It seems likely that the origins of piano ragtime lay in the dance music of the string instrumentalists of the 1880s. By 1885 the pioneer ragtime pianist Scott Joplin was living in St. Louis where he would have been able to hear folk instrumentalists performing for dances. Later, at the Chicago World's Columbian Exposition, he met Plunk Henry, a banjo player who had been born in the 1850s and who was, according to Rudi Blesh, one of the very early group in the Mississippi Valley who developed the rudiments of piano ragtime from banjo syncopation.[28]

None of the recordings of dance tunes mentioned so far were to banjo accompaniment; though banjo players made Race recordings, their instrument was already considered old-fashioned; the guitar was as popular in the twentieth century as the banjo had been in the nineteenth. Though Gus Cannon—Banjo Joe—played his *Madison Street Rag* in a percussive fashion which may reflect the style of the folk banjo rags from which the piano forms partly derived, the guitar rags of a performer like Blind Blake showed the superiority of the instrument for free-flowing dance rhythms. "Now we goin' to do the old country rock" he stated on *West Coast Blues*—which was certainly not a blues and more likely to have referred to the East Coast than to the West:

First thing we do—
Swing your partners—promenade—
See-saw to the right.

Swing that gal over there with the blue dress on,—an'
Bring her right on back to me.
If she starts to funny foolin'
Well its done got sweet to me . . .

He talked over the fast rag with its swinging, deft fingering, lazily commenting on his own prowess:

It's done got good to me,
It's good to the last drop,
Just like Maxwell House coffee—yes
Just boot that thing . . .[29]

Blind Blake, believed to have been born in Jacksonville, Florida in the mid-1890s, traveled extensively, singing in the streets and playing at work camps. He acquired a formidable technique and displayed it in many recordings of guitar ragtime, including *Wabash Rag, Sea Board Stomp, Hot Potatoes, South Bound Rag* and *Blind Arthur's Breakdown.* He also recorded *Dry Bone Shuffle,* a rag with an unknown player of the bones providing a clattering, brisk accompaniment.

Let's go, bones—Whip it bones,—do it a long time
Jus' like getting money from home,
That's the way I like it—
Play them bones boy—that way it's hot.
Play 'em boy—get'n good to me.
Let's have a bit of Charleston in it . . .[30]

commented Blind Blake. His rapid dance had breaks and suspensions of rhythm in which the dancer could hold a step or the bones could play a brief solo interlude. A folk rhythm instrument, the "bones" were popularized in the minstrel show as early as 1843 by Frank Brower of the Virginia Minstrels. Smoothly carved, slightly curved pieces of animal shin bone were held between the first and second, and second and third fingers so that they could be vibrated against each other. Wooden spoons and even fire-tongs were employed for this same purpose, on occasion.[31]

Spoken comments on the dance steps, sometimes interspersed with local or oblique asides appear frequently on guitar rags. William Moore, who claimed on his *Barbershop Rag* to be the "only barber in the world can shave you and give you music while he's doin' it", was a resident of Tappahannock, Essex County on the Rappahannock River in Virginia, where he moved from Georgia in 1904 at the age of eight. *Ragtime Crazy*, an old buck-and-wing dance theme was played to one of the melodies erroneously associated with the fandango and often called the "Spanish flang-dang" by country guitarists. Interrupting the flow with "stop-time" breaks, he invited the dancers to invent "crazy" steps:

. . . Come on Bubber, bump it up and down a little bit, sonny,
Yes Sir—Take those scroungers out of my face—
Give you a bottle of milk when you get home—
. . . now I'm goin to put it on while you take it off,
Take it slow and easy, Big Boy.
Look out Johnny, save a little bit of that corn.
Now let's go crazy folks, for a minute.
Step on it chillen—look foolish—
Cross-eyed and ev'rything—[32]

It seems likely that the guitar rags developed in the rural areas at much the same time as the pianists of Sedalia and St. Louis were developing piano ragtime. Both could have shared sources, but the guitar players may have derived their rags from the banjo and fiddle reels and dance tunes of the earlier generation when the new instrument became readily and cheaply accessible. The American firm of C. F. Martin originated the American-made guitar as early as 1833, but it was not primarily a folk musician's instrument until Orville Gibson began to manufacture for the popular market in 1894. Mail order guitars were soon made in competition; by 1908, Sears Roebuck were marketing a standard size guitar for only $1.89—inclusive of an extra set of strings, a capo, book of chords and a fingering chart. Several other models were available for less than five dollars. But it was Gibson and Martin's steel-strung guitars introduced in 1900 which were ideal for playing outdoors or at noisy dances. As the guitar notes could be sustained in a manner which was not possible on the banjo, with its short, staccato sounds, the guitar was particularly suited to the sliding and shuffle dance steps which were popularized in the 1890s.[33]

Ragtime, though viewed by the composers of piano rags as being a special and distinct music, was associated in the popular mind with a variety of song and music types of the day, from the "coon songs" which had their origins in the minstrel show, to the ragtime songs of vaudeville and concert hall and the instrumental music of the brass bands. Jim Reese Europe, C. Luckyeth Roberts and Will Marion Cook were among the prolific black composers whose instrumental and piano ragtime were closely related to the craze for cakewalks and two-steps. If they may not have been derived from the plantation jigging contests for the award of the cake, they certainly derived from the "walkarounds" and "cakewalks by the entire company" which were a concluding feature of many large minstrel shows. The strains of the ragtime compositions of trained musicians like Joplin, Tom Turpin and James Scott were probably based on the sets of the quadrilles, cotillions and other popular ball dances. Sousa's marches, the two-steps, cakewalks and quadrilles combined with the popular "coon" songs of the 1890s to stimulate a period of unprecedented excitement over new dances.[34] Some of these were still reflected in some degree in the songs of folk musicians thirty years later: Jim Jackson, for instance, whose markedly syncopated jig rhythm must have been close to the folk origins of the dances he mentioned on *Bye, Bye, Policeman:*

Now first thing honey is the Bombashay,
Oh turn right round, go the other way.
To the Worldly Fair, the Turkey Trot,
Oh, don't that girl think she's very hot?
She puts her hand on her head
And let's her mind rove on—
Stands way back, lookin' to stop—
Oh! She dance so nicely, and politely
She do the Pas-a-Ma-La . . .[35]

A guitar player born in Hernando, Mississippi, Jim Jackson spent most of his life there, on the road, or in Memphis. In performance his song was rural Southern in character but the words were directly from the original *Pas Ma La* by Ernest Hogan, published in 1895.

Fus yo' say, my niggah, Bombashay
Then turn 'round and go the other way
To the World's Fair and do the Turkey Trot,
Do not dat coon tink he look very hot?
  Hand upon yo' head, let your mind roll far,
  Back, back, back and look at the stars,
  Stand up rightly, dance it brightly
  That's the Pas Ma La.[36]

Possibly French Creole in origin, and known as La Pas Me Lé, the dance had been gently parodied by a black composer, Irving Jones, as the *Possumala Dance* a year earlier. In the mid-1890s it was widely popular.

The dreamy image of "put your hand on your head and let your mind roll on" persisted in the folk memory, to crop up in a number of songs, including Gus Cannon's *Walk Right In*—"sit right down, and honey, let your mind roll on". "Looking at the stars" and the three backward steps that accompanied the pose, gave an endearing and amusing effect to the dance, which continued to enjoy a fair measure of popularity for some fifteen years.

According to Max Hoffman's 1897 song, *Bom-ba-shay*, it was a "reg'la honalula dance" which incorporated the "possum a la", but which may have had some links with the impending annexation of Hawaii. In 1909 the Bombashay still appealed, if William Jerome's *That Spooney Dance* is an indication: "Oh that Spooney dance, oh that Cooney dance, Sweet lovin' Bombashay, just steals your heart away . . ." But only a year later Ed Rogers and Saul Aaronson were dismissing it in favor of the new dance *Alabama Bound*: "You may talk about your Salome dance and your Cubanola glide, your Pas'mala and your Bombashay have got to stand aside . . ." The Alabama Bound dance described in the song was one where the dancers were held close in the manner of the Bunny Hug and others of the new, and shocking, close-couple dances: "Come babe, look into my eyes, and roll them round and round; I'm feelin' oh so funny, won't you hug me honey, to dat Alabama Bound."[37] The back-arching abandonment of the Turkey Trot and the breast contact of the Grizzly Bear were erotic in their day and banned from the politer dance halls. As Jim Jackson lamented in another song:

> 'Cause when I woke up this morning she's gone . . .
> She made ma mad, I felt so sad,
> I would not tell you even the reason why;
> Oh, how she loved to dance that old Grizzly Bear
> I guess she's gone to Frisco to dance it there—
> 'Cause when I woke up this morning, she's gone,
> She's gone, gone, gone . . .[38]

In a period when the invention of new dances was an important part of popular culture, a professional song writer like Perry Bradford was quick to seize upon folk dances and to compose jazz songs with instructions on how to perform the dance. Songs such as *Ballin' the Jack*, by Chris Smith (1913) and *Walkin' the Dog* by Shelton Brooks, published four years later, were among the best known, but many others gave details of the new steps. Perry Bradford had seen a dance in Jacksonville, Florida which in 1907 he published as the *Jacksonville Rounder's Dance* "but people didn't like the title because 'rounder' meant pimp, so I wrote some new lyrics in 1919 and renamed it *The Original Black Bottom Dance*". Like his *Bullfrog Hop* of 1909 or *Messin' Around* of 1912 this gave instructions: "Hand on your hips and do the Mess Around, Break a leg until you're near the ground". Often in his songs he mentioned the titles of other dances that he had already published, doubtless with an eye to the sales of sheet music. The Black Bottom, the song stated, "started in Georgia and it went to France" which acknowledged both its origins and its rapid international appeal when cleaned up for the ballroom.[39] Though Smith's *Ballin' the Jack* was an exception, dance vocals seldom give instructions on *how* to dance in the songs, though they frequently exhorted the dancers to break into specific, named steps. In the folk tradition it seems, it was assumed that the steps themselves would be known. There are hints in *Georgia Rag* by Blind Willie McTell, that he was well aware visitors came to "Darktown" to pick up the dances. McTell was a highly accomplished performer on the twelve-string guitar; its resonance was ideal for the "dancing at house parties in Statesboro, in the smaller outlying towns like Register, Portal and Metter, and at farm houses out in the country" in rural Georgia where he played. He was attracted to Atlanta, as were many other rural musicians:

Down in Atlanta on Harris Street
That's where the boys and girls do meet,
Doin' that rag, that Georgia Rag

Out in the Alley, in the street
Every little kid, that you meet,
Doin' that rag, that Georgia Rag—(swing that Georgia Rag boy)
Buzz around like a bee,
Shake it like a ship over sea,
That wild rag, that crazy rag
Better known as the Georgia Rag.

Come all the way from Paris, France
Come to Atlanta to get a chance,
To do that Rag, that Georgia Rag

Peoples come from miles around
Get into Darktown t' break 'em down,
Doin' that rag, that Georgia Rag.[40]

Country musicians in and around Atlanta recorded a large number of dance tunes, suggesting that there may well have been some justification for the frequent linking of the name of a dance step and the state of Georgia in the title or lyrics of a song. Sinuous, often lascivious, undulating movements and thrusting of the hips had been known for years as the "bumps and grinds". One song, the *Georgia Grind* was published with music by Albert Grimble in 1913: a later version appeared in 1926 by pianist Jimmy Blythe. Blythe's composition was recorded by several singers and bands that year, including Louis Armstrong's Hot Five, and even Duke Ellington's Washingtonians—among the very first titles made by each of them, when their music still reflected an earthier origin. Henry Williams, a rough country guitarist and associate of Peg Leg Howell, recorded *Georgia Crawl* with fiddle player Eddie Anthony.

Run here papa—look at Sis
Out in the backyard jus' shakin like this—
Doin' the Georgia Crawl—ooh Georgia Crawl
We don't need nobody tryin' to do the Georgia Crawl.

Old Miss Sadie, old and grey
Did the Georgia Crawl till she died away,
Doin' the Georgia Crawl etc.[41]

An "Instrumental hit" called the *Georgia Crawl* had been published in 1912, and it could have been the dance on which Blythe based his tune. But Williams and Anthony might themselves have heard the Louis Armstrong record and based their "Crawl" on it; at least once one of the pair sings "Georgia Grind" rather than "Crawl". Another record, *Too Tight Blues*, by Peg Leg Howell and his Gang—which included Anthony and Williams—is one of the most successful at capturing the spirit of the country dance, with its marked swing, strumming guitars, scraped fiddle and spoken exchanges or shouted comments throughout the performance:

Grab your gal, fall in line,
While I play this rag o' mine.
Too Tight, this rag o' mine, (Listen boy—Yeah?)

Too tight, ain't cha 'shamed?
Too tight, shakin' that thing,
Too tight, this rag o' mine (no way of gettin' to it, boy)

and the singers urge the dancers and themselves on with

like Maxwell House coffee—Good to the last drop!—
Give 'em a little Charleston boy . . .[42]

But the dance had earlier been recorded by Blind Blake—well known in Georgia—with similar words; he recorded it again a year after Howell. The Maxwell House reference had also appeared on Blake's *West Coast Blues.* Certainly Howell was aware of popular recordings of the day: his *Peg Leg Stomp,* though played as a country dance, was based on *Bugle Call Rag,* which had been recorded by Red Nichols and His Five Pennies some months earlier. If there was plenty in the folk tradition to be milked by the composers it is also evident that rural musicians sometimes derived, if at one or two stages removed, from published and recorded dance tunes. It is by no means certain that all the dances referred to in the recordings of folk musicians, any more than those in sheet music, actually existed as separate steps. Another Atlanta guitarist, Robert Hicks who played for customers at a barbecue stand and was known as Barbecue Bob, sang of the "Scraunch". But it seems from his verses that it was a combination of other popular steps of the period:

Down in Dixie there's a dance that's new
Ain't much to it an' it's easy to do,
Called doin' that Scraunch,—oh doin' that Scraunch
Just wiggle and wooble it, honey when you do the Scraunch.

You wiggle and a-wooble it, an' you move it aroun'
Ball the jack and you go to town,
And does that Scraunch, etc.[43]

Subsequent verses follow a familiar form of describing a girl who's the "best in town", and the inevitable "grandmom and grandpapa at the age of eighty-three, they the best scraunchers you ever did see . . ."

Some dances had a relatively long life, and certain steps and movements were readily transposed to a variety of dance tunes which, in themselves, only enjoyed a brief vogue. The shimmy-shake, in which the shoulders, breasts, hips and knees of the dancer were shaken in a rippling movement may have first appeared on stage with the Hootchy-Kootchy. But it was popularized for white audiences and for dancers who were brave enough, by Gilda Gray, who slipped the straps of her chemise from her shoulders while dancing in a Western cabaret. "I'm shaking my shimmy, that's what I'm doing", she is reported to have explained, and such was the success of her dance that she wore a heavily sequinned chemise to show off her shakes.[44] Similarly, Ballin' the Jack, with its flexed legs, knees together movement left and right, followed by vigorous revolving or twisting, and the

Eagle Rock movement with extended arms and bird-like flapping, were also popular for a long time. Most celebrated of all the dances, and the one which appears to have typified the 1920s to generations afterwards, was the Charleston. Though it is questionable that it derives from "An Ashanti ancestor dance" as LeRoi Jones has hinted, it was undoubtedly current before 1905 when Noble Sissle learned it in Savannah, Georgia. Its back kicks, leg-shakes, crossed arms and knocked-kneed movements were spectacular and the dance gave the greatest opportunities for performers to "do the breakaway" and invent new steps to its jaunty rhythm.[45]

As a dance the Charleston encouraged competition. In country districts as well as in city dance-halls, dancers competed to win prizes and, perhaps more important to them, the admiration and envy of other dancers, as their parents had with the cakewalk and their sons and daughters were to do with the Lindy Hop. It also invited competition from the musicians, and *Charleston Contest* by Too Tight Henry seems to have been more of a demonstration of his own ability and a brag that might provoke a challenge, than a competition between dancers. "Too Tight" Henry Castle was born in Georgia in 1899 and traveled with both Blind Blake and the Texan Blind Lemon Jefferson. In Memphis he played with Jed Davenport and other musicians who must have respected his accomplishment. He spoke about his early life briefly in his two-part *Charleston Contest* recording, on which he played a twelve-string guitar and imitated the voice of an imaginary companion, "Chappie", who asked:

C. Say listen here Too Tight, they tell me you-all gonna have a Charleston Contest out your way tonight?
TT. Yeah boy, I heard 'em talkin' 'bout it.
C. Well, thing I want to know is, who is gonna play for 'em?
TT. Well, I heard them say they wanted to get ole Henry L. Castle to play, I guess that's me myself . . .

He invited "Chappie" to sit beside him and listen to his imitation on guitar of "that old hawg man bring that ole hawg he got down from his job".

C. Hey, boy, if you do that again I'm gonna have you run out of town.
TT. Yeah that's what they told me at the Mill when I keep on playing the Charleston— But you know one thing, Chappie, when I was a poor boy first started out playin' music, an' tried to travel from town to town and I didn't have any money . . .
C. What did you do, Too Tight?
TT. Oh well I'd go out to the freight yard and the first thing I saw lined out smokin' . . . and when she got out yonder on that long old lonesome freight I just could imagine if I had one of them ole browns of mine there to shake that thing with me—how we could keep time with that ole locomotive engine like so with this twelve-string guitar . . .

He continued by recalling "when I was a lil old boy comin' along I used to see ole mens playing the git-tar—and you know they said they could play a guitar, and keep time with the strings and beat the drum and never lose a note but . . . well, they didn't do anything but tap the strings occasionally and wear the piss out on the wood—but ole Too Tight never did on the steel . . ." He was apparently referring to the folk custom in which a second musician played an accompanying rhythm on the fingerboard with straws. Promising to Chappie that "you'll get a chance to see ole Sister Hooper shake that can of hers" he displayed his skill by referring to "that fool rag that mandoline he got" and imitating it on the guitar. Then he imitated the banjo player, "that ole feller doin' his Charleston now". Chappie asked,

C. I want to know how many you got in that string band you got over there?
TT. Oh well, ain't nobody but me, myself Henry L. Castle, ole Too Tight . . .
C. I don't care if you got you and your whole family, you sure is killin' me . . .

To each exchange Henry Castle swung into an exciting, if individualistic chorus or played a fast break, the equivalent of the dancer's "breakaway".[46]

In the breakaway dancers often devised new steps that briefly caught on with their contemporaries, establishing a "rage" or "craze" for a few weeks, or even months, before being superseded by another, more audacious or more fetching, step. Many of the dances noted by Marshall Stearns must have had their origins this way, and many that exist as name only and are otherwise undescribed in his work must have enjoyed a vogue that was briefer than that of the tunes to which they were danced.

"Say Pal," asked Papa Charlie Jackson on *Skoodle Um Skoo,* "do you know anything about that new dance they got over in town?" ("No I don't") "It's a dance they call Skoodle um skoo—let's go—

Now I know a lady, name of Sue, she like to know just what to do
Now sit right over there, sweet mama, I'm gonna tell you just what to do,
I'm gonna tell you just before you go . . .

You got to skoodle um skoo, oh' baby got to skoodle um skoo
Come on mama, got to skoodle um skoo, skoodle um, skoodle um skoo

and so on. "It's a wonderful dance . . ." he commented in an instrumental passage, but though there were several verses there was scarcely a hint of the steps. Jackson, who came from New Orleans, played banjo, which was already something of an anachronism. But he played so energetically at a brisk tempo and with a bright sound that he remained one of the most popular of the artists recording for Paramount. His banjo playing was probably the closest to that of the previous century that could be heard on disc. When the theme was recorded again in 1928, a year later, it was by the raucous Seth Richard, from Georgia, who played a twelve-string guitar and kazoo:

Aw skoodledum doo, oh baby, let's skoodledum doo
Come on mama, let's skoodledum doo, skoo-doo-doo,
  Mama, Mama, have you forgot
  The night I had you in the vacant lot?
Skoodledum doo—skoo doo-doo.[47]

Though the tune was the same, and the playing ideal for dancing, there was no mention of any dance in it. Like Blind Blake's more complex *Skeedle Loo Doo,* to which it was somewhat related, any specific steps associated with the tune appear to have been forgotten, though it was the kind of rag-based number which would have encouraged dancers to invent steps of their own.

On a number of recordings with strong dance music the vocal contributions were often minimal. The Kansas City team of Winston Holmes and Charlie Turner, who both played guitars on *Kansas City Dog Walk*, put their efforts into an exhilarating dance music, the rhythms of one offset by the sliding notes of the other. "I'm goin' down to the Yeller Front and walk the dog all night long . . .", commented Holmes, pointing out a woman on the floor: "she can strut" and concluding in the final ragtime choruses "all right, now . . . let's shut the windows, pull down the blinds . . . let's get messin' . . ." The strutting "walking the dog" had been a hit when danced by John Sublett, known professionally as Bubbles, of the Buck and Bubbles tap dance team; he claimed to have invented it in 1910 when he was eight years old. But it almost certainly started life as part of the plantation and minstrel show "walkarounds" in which the strutting steps to ragtime music were an invitation to display.[48]

Dancing was a release, an opportunity to vent emotions and to forget worries and pressures. Another guitar duet, Pink Anderson and Blind Simmie Dooley, who performed for picnics and country dances around Spartanburg, South Carolina implied this in a fast ragtime dance song, *Gonna Tip Out Tonight.* Sang Simmie Dooley in his hard nasal voice, to comments and encouragement by Anderson and against strong bass runs on the guitars:

Gee, I'm feelin' mighty lonesome,
Gee, I'm feelin' mighty homesome,
My gal quit me an' I don't know what ter do (what you do?)
She even tol' me from the start
If I go I would break her heart,
Every time I think about her, makes me feel so blue.
This mornin' I received a note (got a letter from her: I read it.)
And this is what the answer I wrote (what you say?)
"Go on gal, sing them blues to me
I'm sweet as any man can be,"
She even tol' me to ma face (what?)
That any ole rounder sure can take my place.
Say's "I'm gettin' tired of your lowdown ways,
I'm goin' back to my baby's days
Go on girl, honey you can't [change your] luck,
I'm gonna tip out tonight, I'm gonna strut my stuff,
I mean I'm gonna straw my stuff."[49]

Rural dances could be held in the open or in converted barns and warehouses; as the demand increased "jukes", or drinking and dancing parlors, were constructed in the rural regions. Often closed during the week they were open for dances on Friday and Saturday nights. Crude frame buildings clad in clapboard and roofed with corrugated iron, they were crowded to capacity. A bare table or a plank across barrels formed a bar; if they were lucky the guitarists were provided with stools. Often the function would be in a private house, with the meagre furniture pushed back to the walls and a big fire outside. "You can tell where the dances are to be held by the fires", wrote the black anthropologist Zora Neale Hurston, "Huge bonfires of faulty logs and slabs are lit outside the house in which the dances are held. The refreshments are parched peanuts, fried rabbit, fish, chicken and chitterlings. The only music is guitar music and the only dance is the ole square dance." As she recalled from her work in Florida, "one guitar was enough for a dance, to have two was considered excellent. Where two were playing one man played the lead and the other seconded him. The first player was 'picking' and the second 'framming', that is, playing chords while the lead carried the melody by dextrous finger-work. Sometimes a third player was added, and he played a tom-tom effect on the low strings."[50] Hezekiah Jenkins, with a guitar accompaniment that was rather less accomplished than those described by Zora Neale Hurston, conveyed the atmosphere of a similar function:

Went to a dance last Saturday night
And what I mean this dance was tight,
Given by a man named Lovey Joe
In a small room 'bout two by fo'.
And in this room they was thick as peas,
You could hardly tell the he's from the she's
And when the band began to play, I could hear them say,
"Oh, shout you cats, do it, stomp it, step you rats,
Shake your shimmy, break a leg,
Grab your gal and knock 'em dead,
Oh, do that thing!
Hey, hey, everybody sing."
They got so good they threw away they hats,
I could hear 'em hollerin' "Shout you cats!"
In came the cop 'bout half past fo'
I felt sure we was booked to go,
He said "everybody, fall in line!"
They kep' on dancin', paid him no mind.
A great big feller 'bout six foot tall,
Grabbed the cop and slammed him up 'gainst the wall,
The cop said "Buddy, everything Okay?" Listen to what I say—
"Oh, shout you cats, do it, stomp it, etc.[51]

Though the song was in a sense a stereotype, it was authentic enough to fit with the experience of his audience. Jukes were rough places, hot, noisy and dusty. In the excitement of the dance and the close proximity of the dancers jealousies were inflamed and tempers flared. Many musicians who played the jukes have spoken of nights that ended in violence, with the dances broken up by "the law". During the Prohibition era "bootleg" liquor was sold in the jukes, which often had additional rooms for gambling, or where local girls could "turn a trick" or two. As Sam Chatmon, one of the band who called themselves the Mississippi Shieks explained, his group would play in one room for a dance, while gambling was taking place in another. "Sometimes the law would come, and all of them was in there in the gambling room, they had to pay a fine. You'd spy more pistols laying on the floor when the law come in. You could just look anywhere and find a pistol or a big, long knife laying down on the floor, some of them stuck up under the heaters. You seen the houseman tell the law to come by to keep him from having a lot of trouble. Guys what got pistols on 'em, if the law come and take their pistols, they wouldn't have nothing to act with."[52]

Not all the dances and hops were wild ones, and not all the dancers armed. Nor, for that matter, were all the dances vigorous with kicking steps and flapping arms. Some were "glides" and "slides" with slower movements in which the dancers kept their feet close to the floor. At what stage such dances as these became popular is difficult to determine; perhaps because they were less spectacular than high-stepping versions of barn dances and the like, they seem not to have been noted by early observers. Or they were the dances that were labeled often as "lascivious", their body and leg contact offending nineteenth-century proprieties. The "slow drag", which has long been associated with the cluster of dances performed to the blues, appears to have been first identified in one of Scott Joplin's earlier compositions, *Sunflower Slow Drag,* published in 1901. On the Slow Drag, Marshall Stearns, historian of *Jazz Dance,* who described many dances of the period, was vague: referring to the "Congo" hip movements of the Slow Drag, which are otherwise unspecified, he grouped it with the "Snake Hips and other social dances of the Negro folk". These, the "Afro-American vernacular, that is the basic dances of the Negro as the Strut, Shuffle, Sand and Grind" receive scant description.[53]

In 1911, Scott Joplin wrote his three-act ragtime opera, *Treemonisha,* with its action set in 1884. It concluded with "A Real Slow Drag" by the entire company: "hop and skip, now do that slow,—do that slow drag". With the sheet music came directions on dancing the Slow Drag which "must begin on the first beat of each measure. When moving forward, drag the left foot; when moving backward, drag the right foot". Sideways movements to left or right were accompanied by dragging the opposite foot; "when prancing your steps must come on each beat of the measure. When marching and when sliding, your steps must come on the first and third beat of each measure." One was to hop and skip on the second beat and "double the schottische step to fit the slow music". It was an elaborate set of movements appropriate for a dance finale, but in the country dances it was less complicated. The cornet player Charlie Love was more succinct: "They did the Slow Drag all over Louisiana, couples would hang onto each other and just grind back and forth all night." He was talking about 1903, but it could have been 1953, or perhaps 1873.[54]

When the barber William Moore played his *Old Country Rock* it was as a slow drag rather than as the Eagle Rock. The rocking movement from side to side as the dancers shifted weight from the ball of one foot to that of the other set the pace of the music, with long notes squeezed on the strings encouraging the slides of the slow drag.

> Come on Bill, let's take 'em for an Old Country Rock,
> Let's go back down on the Rappahannock, down Tappahannock way . . .

He talked lazily over the guitar in a low voice with marked cadences:

> Rock me sister, rock me, Rock me till I sweat—
> Jump back folks and let your pappy rock—
> Pappy knows how—Chillen rock—
> Sister Ernestine, show your pappa how you rock,
> Mighty fine boys; rock it, rock it till the cows come home . . .

It was, he said, "too sad, I mean too sad for the public"; meaning that it was "happy" music in the use of slang inversions, such as "too bad" for "so good", which were current at the time.[55]

With the popularization of the blues, as both song form and dance, slow dragging became increasingly evident at black dances. The beat of the blues, and its frequent use of medium and slow tempos were ideally matched by the shuffle, rock and drag dances. They were also suited to cramped spaces, where "dancing on a dime" was a physical necessity. In the cities, in particular, where dances were often held in private premises and living rooms, slow drag blues were less noisy, and less of a threat to weak structures in timber framed tenements. Not that these were issues that were likely to have been given much consideration at "parlor socials" and "rent parties". Arranged in back rooms with local instrumentalists, especially pianists, to provide the entertainment, these events have been frequently described. The black poet Langston Hughes went to many "in small apartments where God knows who lived—because the guests seldom did—but where the piano would often be augmented by a guitar, or an old clarinet, or somebody with a pair of drums walking in off the street. And where awful bootleg whisky and good fried fish or steaming chitterlings were sold at very low prices. And the dancing and singing and impromptu entertaining went on until dawn came in at the windows." They were working-class functions, for attending which a small charge was made that would help pay the rent of the hostess; functions where he met "ladies' maids and truck drivers, laundryworkers and shoe shine boys, seamstresses and porters".[56]

William Moore recorded *Old Country Rock* and his other guitar rags for dancing with spoken commentaries like *Ragtime Crazy*, *Barbershop Rag* and *Raggin' the Blues*, in January 1928; later that year a number of recordings of similar type, but with spoken comments addressed to the dancers over a boogie woogie piano accompaniment, enjoyed a vogue. They were often modeled on Clarence Pine Top Smith's *Pine Top's Boogie Woogie*, and were recorded by pianists who sought to create the atmosphere of the rent party. Romeo (Iromeio) Nelson, Charles Avery and Speckled Red (Willie Perryman) were among them, but the number of pianists was legion. Sometimes one would emerge from the obscurity of Harlem or the Chicago South Side, to make a title or two—like Jim Clarke, whose only recorded item was *Fat Fanny Stomp*:

> . . . When I say 'Hold it!' this time, I want everybody to gully . . .
> Gut that thing, I mean gully,
> Hold it! Oh, gully . . . gully, gully low . . . gully like you live!
> Sister Fullbosom, you sure guttin' that thing . . .
> When I say hold it this time I want everybody to Sally Long
> Hold it!—Sally Long, Sally Long your fanny gal, Sally that thing,
> Shake your fat fanny—that's what I'm talkin' about . . .[57]

Though the Sally Long seems to have enjoyed a brief vogue in the late 1920s and is mentioned in several recordings, its name may have derived from the 1830s when William Whitlock and T. G. Booth sang of Sally King and Lucy Long in a dance song which included the lines "Take your time Miss Lucy Long, rock de cradle Lucy, take your time my dear". Other dances recur over many decades, those that were based on the actions of animals and birds being frequently revived by name, and in all probability in movements also. "Turkey Trot" was definitely used as a name to describe a dance in the 1850s while even *Scratchin' the Gravel*, which Perry Bradford mentioned in *The Bullfrog Hop* of 1909 and made into a dance-song (introduced, inevitably by "Slewfoot Jim") in 1917, had published as "Trike de toe and heel—cut de pigeon wing, scratch gravel, slap de foot—dat's just de ting" in *Sich a Gitting Up Stairs* in the 1830s.[58]

With house rent parties and boogie woogie, dances on Race records slip easily into the blues, bridged by the knowing, good-time music popularized as "Hokum". Of the many recordings, like Mozelle Alderson's *Tight Whoopee*, or Lil Johnson's *House Rent Scuffle*, *Come on Mama* by Georgia Tom and Hannah May (Jane Lucas) must serve to illustrate the persistence of traditional dance steps and striking imagery, and the teasing, challenging strutting of the dancer as she responded to the cheerful piano and guitar routine played by Tom Dorsey and Big Bill Broonzy:

> Come on mama, do that dance for me—
> Do the Mississippi Rub and the Mobile Bay,
> Turn right around and go the other way—
> Come on mama do that dance for me.
> Oh, do that dance, oh do that dance, } (2)
> Come on mama, do that dance for me.
>
> (See how you like this step—watch this shimmy I'm gonna shake—how do you like this mess around?)
>
> Put your hand on your hips, let your mind roll on
> Rather like you did the day you was born.
> Come on mama, do that dance for me,
> Do the Blacksnake Wiggle and the Possum Trot,
> Scratch the gravel in a vacant lot.
> Come on mama, do that dance for me,
> O, do that dance. etc.
>
> (the snake hips . . . what do you think about them?)
>
> Now there's an old sister about seventy years old,
> Don't know how to do it, she done got cold . . .
> Come on mama, do that dance for me.
> Now her hair turned grey, nose turned blue
> Some day this thing's gonna happen to you
> Come on mama, do that dance for me.
> Do that dance etc.[59]

Played and sung by a good 'musicianer', or 'songster', almost all black secular songs could be adapted to dancing, and they generally were. Those whose lyrics referred to the dance steps, or the functions where music was played, were clearly intended for dancing, but they are often no more suitable than many other pieces on which an experienced performer could draw. They do, however, contain phrases and references to specific dances that give clues as to their date or origin, and this helps in establishing the lineage of the tradition. Because the requirements for a good dance piece—a swinging rhythm and a beat that lightens the steps of the dancers—have not substantially changed since the early nineteenth century, there has been an identifiable continuity in the dance songs and routines that has not always been matched in other song types. The interplay between folk custom and published sheet music, and between the traditional and the new, which relates folk idiom to popular song has to be borne in mind when the sources of other items in the songsters' repertoires are pursued.

Notes

1. George Mitchell, "An Interview with Peg Leg Howell", Note to *The Legendary Peg Leg Howell,* Testament T-204.

2. Peg Leg Howell, vo, g, *Coal Man Blues,* Columbia 14194-D, Atlanta. November 8, 1926: see also Samuel Charters, *Sweet as the Showers of Rain,* New York: Oak Publications, 1973, pp. 108–9.

3. John A. Lomax, "Self-Pity in Negro Folk Song", *The Nation,* 105, July–December 1917, p. 14; see also Paul Oliver, *The Story of the Blues,* London: Barrie and Jenkins, 1969, p. 44.

4. Peg Leg Howell, vo, g, *Please Ma'am,* Columbia 14356-D, Atlanta, April 20, 1928; Mitchell, interview, *The Legendary Peg Leg Howell.*

5. Peg Leg Howell, vo, g, *Skin Game Blues,* Columbia 14473-D, Atlanta, November 9, 1927; see also, Paul Oliver, *Blues Fell This Morning: The Meaning of the Blues,* London: Cassell, 1960, p. 155.

6. Peg Leg Howell, vo, g, poss. Ollie Griffin, vln, *Rolling Mill Blues,* Columbia 14438-D, Atlanta, April 10, 1929; Oliver. *Story of the Blues,* p. 44.

7. Judith McCulloh, "In the Pines: The Melodic-Textual Identity of an American Lyric Folk-Song Cluster", Indiana University, unpublished Ph. D. Thesis, 1970; the complex interweaving of the songs, *The Longest Train, In The Pines, Reuben's Train, Train 45* and *900 Miles* is discussed in Norm Cohen, *Long Steel Rail: The Railroad in American Folk Song,* Urbana: University of Illinois Press, 1981, pp. 491–502, 503–17.

8. Howard Odum, "Folk-Song and Folk-Poetry as Found in the Secular Songs of the Southern Negroes", *Journal of American Folklore,* 24, 1911, pp. 258–9 [excerpt reprinted herein]; W. H. Thomas, *Some Current Folk Songs of the Negro and Their Economic Interpretation,* Austin, Folk-Lore Society of Texas, pamphlet 1, 1912, p. 5.

9. G. Malcolm Laws Jr., *American Balladry from British Broadsides,* Philadelphia: The American Folklore Society, 1957, pp. 47–9. For recent use of these terms see Mack McCormick, notes to Lance Lipscomb, *Texas Sharecropper and Songster,* Arhoolie F 1001, 1960; Little Brother Montgomery (1960) in Paul Oliver, *Conversation with the Blues,* London: Cassell, 1965, p. 62; Aaron Cleveland Sparks (1975, 1977) in Mike Rowe and Charlie O'Brien, "Well Them Two Sparks Brothers they been here and gone", *Blues Unlimited,* No. 144, Spring 1983.

10. Peg Leg Howell, vo, g, and Jim Hill, vo, mand, *Chittlin' Supper,* Columbia 14426-D, Atlanta, April 13, 1929.

11. Charles Dickens, *American Notes* (1850), London: Chapman and Hall, 1913, chap. 6.

12. Hans Nathan, *Dan Emmett and the Rise of Early Negro Minstrelsy,* Norman: University of Oklahoma Press, 1962, pp. 73, 83; Charles Read Baskervill, *The Elizabethan Jig and Related Song Drama,* New York: Dover Publications, Inc., 1965, p. 361.

13. C. K. Ladzekpo and Olly Wilson, "Basic Anlo-Ewe Dance Form" in 'Introduction to the Music of the Anlo-Ewe People of Ghana', unpub. MS, chap. 5. The suggestion that minstrel dancing was copied from blacks has been contested by San Dennison, "The Roots of Blackface Minstrel Music", paper given to the Symposium on *American Popular Music and Its Impact on World Culture,* Dartmouth College, May 13–15, 1983.

14. Norman R. Yetman, ed., *Life Under the "Peculiar Institution": Selections from the Slave Narrative Collection,* New York: Holt, Rinehart and Winston, 1970, p. 218; B. A. Botkin, ed., *Lay My Burden Down,* Chicago: University of Chicago Press, 1945, p. 56.

15. Dena J. Epstein, *Sinful Tunes and Spirituals: Black Folk Music to the Civil War,* Urbana: University of Illinois Press, 1977, pp. 53–4; Federal Writers' Project, *The Negro in Virginia,* New York: Hartings House, pp. 92–3.

16. Yetman, *Life Under the "Peculiar Institution",* pp. 190, 268.

17. George Rawick, ed., *The American Slave: A Composite Autobiography*, Westport, Conn.: Greenwood Press, 1972–78, see for example, *Mississippi Narratives*, Part 4, Jim Marlin, p. 1438, Harriet Miller, p. 1505, Glaccow Norwood, p. 1650.

18. Epstein, *Sinful Tunes and Spirituals*, pp. 139–60; Dena J. Epstein, "The Folk Banjo: A Documentary History", *Ethnomusicology*, Vol. 19, no. 5, September 1975, pp. 347–71; Harold Courlander, *Negro Folk Music U.S.A.*, New York: Columbia University Press, 1963.

19. Rawick, *The American Slave, Texas Narratives*, Part 3, John Crawford, p. 975.

20. Mack McCormick, *Henry Thomas*, album notes and transcriptions, Herwin 209, Glen Cove, N.Y., 1974. Henry Thomas (Ragtime Texas), vo, g, quills, *Old Country Stomp*, Vocalion 1230, Chicago, June 13, 1928. Compare it with the account of plantation dances by "Maum Katie, a very old Negro woman" in Henry C. Davis, "Negro Folk Lore in South Carolina", *Journal of American Folk-Lore*, July–September 1914, pp. 241–54.

21. Thomas W. Talley, *Negro Folk Rhymes*, New York: Macmillan Co., 1922, pp. 303–6; George W. Cable, "The Dance in Place Congo", *Century Magazine*, February 1886, reprinted in *Creoles and Cajuns*, New York: Doubleday and Company, Inc., 1959, p. 371. See also Epstein, *Sinful Tunes and Spirituals*, p. 145, for additional information on quills.

22. Dorothy Scarborough, *On the Trail of Negro Folk-Songs*, Cambridge, Mass.: Harvard University Press, 1925, pp. 102–4.

23. Stovepipe No. 1, vo, g, hca, stovepipe, *Cripple Creek and Sourwood Mountain*, Columbia 201-D, New York, August 20, 1924; *Turkey in the Straw*, Columbia 201-D, New York, August 20, 1924.

24. Nathan, *Dan Emmett*, pp. 174–5. Peg Leg Howell, vo, g, and Eddie Anthony, vo, vln, *Turkey Buzzard Blues*, Columbia 14382-D, Atlanta, October 30, 1928.

25. Vernon Lane Wharton, *The Negro in Mississippi 1865–1890* (1947), New York: Harper and Row, 1965, p. 270.

26. Lafcadio Hearn, "Levee Life", *Cincinnati Commercial*, March 17, 1876, reprinted in *The Selected Writings of Lafcadio Hearn*, ed. Henry Goodman, New York: Citadel Press, 1949, pp. 227, 228–9.

27. Epstein, *Sinful Tunes and Spirituals*, pp. 141–4.

28. Ann Charters, *The Ragtime Songbook*, New York: Oak Publications, 1965, pp. 19–21; Rudi Blesh and Harriet Janis, *They All Played Ragtime*, London: Sidgwick and Jackson, 1958, pp. 151–2.

29. Blind Blake, vo, g, *West Coast Blues*, Paramount 12387, Chicago, c. September 1926.

30. Blind Blake, vo, g, unk. bones, *Dry Bone Shuffle*, Paramount 12479, Chicago, c. May 1927.

31. Nathan, *Dan Emmett*, p. 127.

32. William Moore, vo, g, *Barbershop Rag*, Paramount 12613, Chicago, c. January 1928; *Ragtime Crazy*, Paramount 12648, Chicago, c. January 1928.

33. Tom and Mary Anne Evans, *Guitars: From the Renaissance to Rock*, London: Paddington Press, 1977, pp. 220–59.

34. Ann Charters, "Negro Folk Elements in Classic Ragtime", *Ethnomusicology*, Vol. 5, no. 3, September 1961, pp. 174–82; Edward A. Berlin, *Ragtime: A Musical and Cultural History*, Berkeley: University of California Press, 1980, part 1, pp. 1–56. Berlin gives extensive references on the "perceptions of ragtime", pp. 56–60.

35. Jim Jackson, vo, g, *Bye, Bye, Policeman*, Victor V38505, Memphis, September 7, 1928.

36. Ernest Hogan, *La Pas Ma La*, New York; M. Witmark and Sons, 1895.

37. Cannon's Jug Stompers, Gus Cannon, vo, bj, jug, acc. bj, vo, k, hca, *Walk Right In*, Victor V38611, Memphis, October 1, 1929; Max Hoffman, *Bom-Ba-Shay*, New York: M. Wit-

mark and Sons, 1897; William Jerome and Jean Schwurz, *That Spooney Dance*, New York: Jerome H. Remick and Co., 1909; Ed Rogers and Saul Aaronson, *Alabama Bound*, New York: M. Witmark and Sons, 1916.

38. Jim Jackson, vo, g, *This Mornin' She Was Gone*, Victor V38003, Memphis, August 27, 1928.

39. Marshall Stearns and Jean Stearns, *Jazz Dance: The Story of American Vernacular Dance*, London: Macmillan, 1968, 110–11.

40. David Evans, "Blind Willie McTell", *Atlanta Blues*, album notes to JEMF 106, p. 10. (Georgia Bill) Blind Willie McTell, vo, g, *Georgia Rag*, Okeh 8924, Atlanta, October 31, 1931.

41. Henry Williams, vo, g, and Eddie Anthony, vo, vln, *Georgia Crawl*, Columbia 14328-D, Atlanta, April 19, 1928.

42. Peg Leg Howell, vo, g, and His Gang, *Too Tight Blues*, Columbia 14298-D, Atlanta, November 1, 1927.

43. Barbecue Bob, vo, g, *Doin' the Scraunch*, Columbia 14591-D, Atlanta, December 5, 1930.

44. Stearns, *Jazz Dance*, p. 105; Sylvia Dannett and Frank Rachel, *Down Memory Lane*, New York: Greenberg, 1954, p. 94.

45. LeRoi Jones, *Blues People*, p. 17 [excerpt reprinted herein]; Stearns, *Jazz Dance*, p. 112.

46. Jim O'Neal and Steve LaVere, "Too Tight Henry" in *Living Blues*, No. 34, 1977. Too Tight Henry, vo, g, *Charleston Contest*, Columbia 14374-D, Atlanta, October 27, 1928.

47. (Papa) Charlie Jackson, vo, bj, *Skoodle Um Skoo*, Paramount 12501, Chicago, c. July 1927; Seth Richard, vo, g, *Skoodeldum Doo*, Columbia 14325-D, New York, May 15, 1928.

48. Winston Holmes, vo, and Charlie Turner, g, *Kansas City Dog Walk*, Paramount 12815, Richmond, Ind., June 21, 1929. Stearns, *Jazz Dance*, p. 213.

49. Pink Anderson, vo, g, and Simmie Dooley, vo, g, k, *Gonna Tip Out Tonight*, Columbia 14336-D, Atlanta, April 14, 1928.

50. Paul Oliver, *Juke Joint Blues*, Sleeve note for Blues Classics, BC 23, 1970, reprinted in *Blues Off the Record: Thirty Years of Blues Commentary*, Turnbridge Wells: Midas Books, 1984; Zora Neale Hurston, *Mules and Men*, Philadelphia: Lippincott, 1935, p. 66; Zora Neale Hurston, in *Negro*, ed. Nancy Cunard, London: Nancy Cunard, 1934.

51. Hazekiah Jenkins (sic), vo, g, *Shout You Cats*, Columbia 14585-D, New York, January 16, 1931.

52. Margaret McKee and Fred Chisenhall, *Beale Black and Blue*, Baton Rouge: Louisiana State University Press, 1981, p. 184.

53. Stearns, *Jazz Dance*, p. 13.

54. Scott Joplin, *Treemonisha—Opera in 3 Acts*, St. Louis and New York: Scott Joplin Music Company, 1911; Stearns, *Jazz Dance*, p. 21.

55. William Moore, vo, g, *Old Country Rock*, Paramount 12761, Chicago, c. January 1928.

56. Oliver, *Blues Fell This Morning*, pp. 163–5; Oliver, *The Story of the Blues*, pp. 83–4; Langston Hughes and Arna Bontemps, eds., *The Book of Negro Folklore*, New York: Dodd, Mead, and Co., 1958, 596–600.

57. Jim Clarke, vo, p, *Fat Fanny Stomp*, Vocalion 1536, Chicago, December 1929.

58. Nathan, *Dan Emmett*, pp. 130–1; 88–91; 72.

59. Georgia Tom, vo, p, and Hannah May, vo, acc. g, *Come On Mama*, Oriole 8033, New York, September 16, 1930.

3. From "Folk and Popular Blues"

David Evans

Origins of the Blues Form

IN THE preceding discussion of early blues, the field blues or field holler has often been mentioned. Many of the early writers did not distinguish between these songs and instrumentally accompanied blues. It is obvious that the two are closely related. The relationship would seem to be that the hollers have served as a major source for the creation of the blues. Most blues writers are agreed on this point.[1] Though many hollers are wordless or textually very simple and repetitious, their melodic and thematic characteristics are generally in accord with those of the blues. The main difference is that the field hollers are much freer and more embellished melodically and rhythmically, probably because their form is not restricted by an instrumental accompaniment.

Many of the texts and tunes printed by Charles Peabody, Gates Thomas, John Lomax, and Mary Wheeler were actually hollers or unaccompanied field blues. There is considerable evidence that the holler was sung by blacks during slavery.[2] One of its earliest appearances in print was in a journal kept by Frances Anne Kemble on a coastal Georgia plantation in 1839. She wrote the following about a slave song that she overheard:

> To one, an extremely pretty, plaintive, and original air, there was but one line, which was repeated with a sort of wailing chorus—
>
> "Oh! my massa told me, there's no grass in Georgia."
>
> Upon inquiring the meaning of which, I was told it was supposed to be the lamentation of a slave from one of the more northerly states, Virginia or Carolina, where the labor of hoeing the weeds, or grass as they call it, is not nearly so severe as here, in the rice and cotton lands of Georgia.[3]

Kemble could easily have been describing an unaccompanied version of one of Odum's "one-verse songs."

Reprinted from David Evans, *Big Road Blues: Tradition and Creativity in the Folk Blues* (Berkeley: University of California Press, 1982), 41–48. Used by permission of the author.

The singing of hollers did not end with Abolition but lingered on wherever blacks continued in agricultural work and other heavy labor, such as among the river roustabouts. Johann Tonsor, writing on black singing from Louisville, Kentucky, in 1892, mentioned hearing "a distant chorus, rising and falling in unearthly, plaintive cadences, like the moaning of the wind or the cry of a lost spirit."[4] Tonsor observed the singing of a note that was "neither A nor yet A flat, but between the two,"[5] in other words, a blue note. Tonsor stated that this was probably an African trait. He noted also, as did John Lomax some years later, that women would sing while working. He stated, "It is quite a common thing for the negro women to improvise words and music while they are at work, a sort of Wagnerian 'melos,' or endless melody, as it were. I have often heard them drone softly thus all through the live-long, bright summer day."[6] Tonsor must have been hearing the kind of singing which, within a few years, would be transformed into the blues.

Hollers have continued over the years to provide words, melodies, and much of its general vocal freedom to blues singing. They have even entered the southern white folksinging tradition as part of a general pattern of borrowing from black music over the years.[7] Hollers are not encountered so often today simply because much agricultural and other heavy work has become mechanized. A black tractor driver could not hear himself holler over the noise of the motor, nor would a man driving home from work in an automobile, rather than riding a mule, be likely to feel the urge to holler. Levees are no longer built by hand labor. One has to go deep into the country or to some of the archaic southern prison farms to hear hollering today.

Folk blues singers themselves tend to attribute the origin of blues singing to the field hollers. Eddie "Son" House, a Mississippi blues singer, says:

> People wonder a lot about where the blues came from. Well, when I was coming up, people did more singing in the fields than they did anywhere else. Time they got to the field, they'd start singing some kind of old song. Tell his ol' mule, "Giddup there!," and he'd go off behind the mule, start plowing and start a song. Sang to the mule or anybody. Didn't make any difference. We'd call them old corn songs, old long meter songs. They'd make it sound good, too. You could hear them half-a-mile off, they'd be singing so loud. Especially just before sundown. They sure would go a long ways. Then they called themselves, "got the blues." That's what they called the blues. Them old long meter songs. You'd hear them talking and one would say, "You know ol' so-and-so really can sing the blues!" They didn't use any instruments. Just natural voice. They could make them rhyme, though, just like the blues do now, but it would just be longer meter. Holler longer before they say the word. They'd sing about their girl friend or about almost anything—mule—anything. They'd make a song out of it just to be hollering.[8]

By "long meter," House means that words were drawn out and highly ornamented, as in the singing of "long meter" hymns in black Baptist and Methodist churches, songs which are also unaccompanied by any instrument.

Booker White, also from Mississippi, attributed the origin of the blues to men in the country relaxing after a hard day's work:

> That's where the blues start from, back across them fields, you know, under them old trees, under them old log houses, you know. Guys will sit there at night—the moon was

> shining—and drink, you know. . . . It didn't start in now city, now. Don't never get that wrong. It started right behind one of them mules or one of them log houses, one of them log camps or the levee camp. That's where the blues sprung from. I know what I'm talking about.[9]

Jack Owens, a farmer and a blues singer, described how he still composes blues in the original manner:

> See, you just be out in the fields. Sometimes you strike a little tune, something like that, and it come to you. Something like that. Then you come back and strike your box [i.e., guitar] and start to hum it on your box. When you know anything, you got a little tune. That's the way I do all the time. . . . And when I get the tune with my voice and the box, I got it. . . . It's kind of hard to do, I'll tell you, but I does it.[10]

This very process of transition from field holler to accompanied blues is demonstrated by Othar Turner, also a Mississippi farmer, in a song that he calls "just the old cornfield blues."[11] Turner's text is highly repetitious, and in both an unaccompanied version of the song and one accompanied by the guitar he sings the same kind of long, strident, highly ornamented, descending lines. The only important musical difference between the two versions is that when he accompanies himself, he leaves spaces between the sung lines for his simple, highly percussive, guitar playing. His song must be close to the sound of the first accompanied blues.

The more rhythmic group labor songs, also a very old form with African antecedents, have had some influence on the blues. Samuel Charters, for example, shows how the first line of Ishmon Bracey's "Saturday Blues" (Victor 21349) is like that of a typical group worksong.[12] In addition, most of these worksongs make use of blue notes. The common twelve-bar AAB blues pattern, however, is not normally performed by a work group, and in any case the blues are normally sung by only a single voice. The influence of group worksongs on the blues, therefore, could be of only secondary importance, compared to that of the solo field holler.

Some writers have also tried to make a case for the influence of spirituals on the blues.[13] Indeed, as we have just noted, blues singer Son House compared his "corn songs" to "long meter" hymns. There is a similar degree of emotional depth in the best blues and spiritual singing, but the actual influence of the spirituals on blues could have been of only the most general sort. Many blacks have their first singing experiences in church, and in this sense the singing of spirituals could have stylistically affected some blues singing. But such stylistic features would be those that characterize black vocal music in general. There is very little actual similarity between the blues and church songs in respect to stanza patterns, melodies, or lyrics. Almost all of the spirituals are in couplet or quatrain form, and the older ones were normally sung by groups rather than solo.

Alan Lomax has proposed that four-line southern white mountain songs, like "Careless Love," provided the mold into which the hollers were poured in order to form the blues.[14] This suggestion might explain the origins of four-line AAAA and AAAB blues through a tailoring of the loose field hollers to the fixed eight-bar and sixteen-bar patterns of white folksong. The particular song "Careless Love," however, was not likely to have been a model for the blues, since its second line usually ends on the major second of the scale, a characteristic rarely found in blues melodies. Furthermore, we cannot be certain whether "Careless Love" is of white or black origin, as it is known in both traditions.

In our search for immediate antecedents of the blues form, we should essentially be seeking an accompaniment pattern for the blues vocal. Most four-line white mountain songs were probably sung unaccompanied around the turn of the century. Furthermore, most blues approximate the three-line, twelve-bar AAB pattern. The loose field hollers by themselves do not provide a form or pattern for most blues but instead serve more as raw material for the blues. Therefore, I find Paul Oliver's suggestion the most plausible, that the field holler vocal was combined with one of the common harmonic accompaniment patterns of the blues ballad.[15] Blues ballads are narrative folksongs that tell a story in a very loose, subjective manner and tend to "celebrate" events rather than relate them chronologically and objectively in the manner of other American folk ballads. Most of the blues ballads whose subjects can be dated would appear to have been composed between 1890 and 1910, although some, like "John Henry," refer to earlier events.[16] They have been sung, quite often with instrumental accompaniment, by both black and white singers, and the original composers of most are unknown. A great many of them have twelve-bar stanza patterns with three vocal lines and the standard chord progression of blues accompaniment. The vocal lines consist of a rhymed couplet and a one-line refrain. The same refrain is repeated in each stanza. Typical blues ballads that often fit this pattern are "Frankie and Albert," "Delia," "Railroad Bill," "Stagolee," "The Boll Weevil," and "McKinley's Gone" ("White House Blues"). Mississippi John Hurt's recording of "Frankie" could be taken as an example of this pattern.[17] Hurt was born in Teoc, Mississippi, in 1892 and spent most of his life in nearby Avalon as a farm worker.[18] His 1928 recording of this piece is probably typical of the way it was performed around 1910 and earlier.

The harmonic pattern of the accompaniment to this piece can be seen to be basically the same as that of a typical twelve-bar blues. Hurt extends the IV chord into the seventh measure and in some stanzas cuts short the twelfth measure to begin a new stanza or instrumental chorus, but these are typical of the variation one finds in twelve-bar patterns and should cause no concern. There are, however, some major differences from the typical blues stanza pattern that we discussed earlier. One difference is the extremely fast tempo of the piece. Hurt begins at ♩ = 208 and by the end has accelerated to ♩ = 230. This is about twice as fast as an average blues tempo, though it is fairly typical of accompaniments to blues ballads using this pattern. Another difference is that Hurt's piece has very short breaks of only a quarter rest after the first and second vocal lines, while most blues have over a measure of rest. In Hurt's song, as in most other blues ballads using this pattern, these two lines are each slightly over three measures in length. Blues vocal lines, however, are usually only slightly over two measures in length. In fact, Hurt's first two lines use a different meter from that of the blues. They are simply a very loose form of the meter typical of Anglo-American balladry, a quatrain that alternates lines of four and three iambic feet. If we were to write Hurt's two lines in this ballad meter, they would look like this:

(◡) – |◡ – |◡ – | (◡) – |
Frankie was a good girl,

(◡)–|(◡) –|◡ –
Ev' ry bod y know.
◡ –|◡ –|◡ –|(◡) –|
She paid a hundred dollars
◡ –|◡ ◡ –| ◡ – |
For Albert's one suit of clothes.

Hurt's third line is the refrain, which is repeated in every stanza with only slight variation. It is in a typical blues metrical pattern with a caesura in the middle, something not found in the first two lines.

Hurt's pattern, as noted earlier, is typical of a number of well-known blues ballads. It must have been adapted to the nonnarrative blues in the following way. First, the tempo was slowed down considerably. This was done because new types of couple and individual dances, which required slower tempos, were replacing the older square dances and others with called figures. Quite likely the twelve-bar AB-refrain pattern of the blues ballad was played at the slower tempo by string bands and guitarists as an instrumental piece for dancing. Then people began adding singing derived from the field hollers. With the slower tempo it became possible to take longer breaks after the first two vocal lines and let the instruments respond to the singing. The result was the blues.

If such was the case, we should expect to find transitional pieces exemplifying this process, and we do. Howard W. Odum, for instance, prints a number of texts of lyric songs, evidently blues, with an AB-refrain pattern.[19] These demonstrate the change from narrative to lyric, still using the blues ballad stanza pattern. There are, as well, a few narrative ballads that have been cast into an AAA or AAB blues stanza pattern with instrumental breaks after each line. Probably the best known of these is "Joe Turner," a song about a penal officer, actually named Joe Turney, who transported convicts in Tennessee between 1892 and 1896.[20] Many musicians call the song a "blues," even though it has a narrative thread. From the standpoint of its stanza structure it is, of course, a blues, yet its narrative text makes it a blues ballad. Some of the early singers of this piece may have been uncomfortable with the longer breaks at the ends of the first and second lines, for there is a tendency in some performances to fill these in with a vocal phrase such as "Oh, Lordy." Handy prints a version, set to a typical twelve-bar blues chord progression, containing the following stanza:

> He come wid fo'ty links of chain, Oh Lawdy.
> Come wid fo'ty links of chain, Oh Lawdy.
> Got my man and gone.[21]

Several early blues texts also display this trait at the ends of lines.[22]

Lucius Smith, a Mississippi banjo player born in 1892, who began playing around 1902, describes "Joe Turner" as the origin of all blues. Smith uses a twelve-bar pattern with stanzas that are sometimes AAB and sometimes AAA. After the first line he usually sings, "Oh Lord," thus filling out the space at the end. Smith says that Joe Turner was a handcuffed prisoner who escaped from a moving train. Of the song's beginning, around 1900, he says:

> That's old "Joe Turner" when it first came in, maybe seventy years ago. . . . All these blues come from "Joe Turner" more or less. . . . "Tell me Joe Turner done come" [a line from the song]. . . . See, when "Joe Turner" first come in, it wasn't in the blues way. And they changed it to the blues, all, you see.[23]

Lucius Smith played for many years in Sid Hemphill's string band, a group that performed mainly older reels and blues ballads for set dancing. He vividly recalls the slowing of the tempo in the music when the blues arrived on the scene and the accompanying change in the dancing and audience behavior. Here he describes the difference between the two forms of music:

> Blues is, I'd say, a whole lots of difference. It's owing to the dances, new dancing. Now the blues is swinging dancing, like double together, you know. . . . That done ruined the country. The blues done ruined the country. . . . It just make 'em go off at random, I'd say, frolicing, random, you see. More folks have got killed since they start playing the blues than ever been. It's just a, you know, just a out of order piece. Now such as "Walking in the Parlor" and all them other old pieces, that's dancing on a set, . . . calling figures, promenade, swing your right partner, all that, you know, object partner, you see. But the "Memphis Blues" and all that, it done brought about a whole lots of it, you know, I'd say, trouble. They started that "Memphis." That's these young folks. Started that "Memphis." Hear 'em say, "Oh, do it once for me!" Done started a mess then. You see it. You see it. I done told you. Makes a racket, you know, with young folks, you see. But that other dancing, it didn't have time to make no racket, 'cause you got to pick up your foots and go. I'll tell you. But all that old stuff is but eternity, the blues, you know. Yonder got all in the church houses and everything. It's just something kind of out of order like, you know. Oh, it done got everywhere, the blues. It done got everywhere. . . . It's just kind of, you know, old drunkards, you know, frolicing. . . . Now we have been in places, you know, and somebody would ask Sid Hemphill maybe to play a waltz. And they in there playing, hollering and singing the blues across him. You see, well, this brings about eternity, that blues does. Sometimes he had to close down. "I can't play. They singing something else, you know." See, I just call it a racket. The blues ain't nothing but a racket. A whole lot of drunk folks, you know, don't care for nothing, and they just bring eternity, the blues do. Heap of folks love to hear it, but it just brings eternity. A lot of trouble while that stuff going on, you know. Oh, I don't care. Don't none of it bother me, 'cause I ain't no racket man. It don't bother me, but it's just a racket thing. It get all in your home, tear up the church house, everything. The blues do. You hear 'em hollering, "Play the 'Memphis Blues'." They gonna start something. You can't do nothing with 'em. Get a little drink in 'em, and that's just trouble. It's just a racket, you know.[24]

Smith is a conservative, and his views are representative of the preblues generation. His is the complaint of every older generation in America against the music of the young. The blues have not proven as socially disruptive as Smith claims, but they can be considered as representative of a new social outlook. Certainly the lyrics of the blues display, in general, a greater seriousness and awareness of the world than did the older secular dance songs of the nineteenth century with their emphasis on humor, animal activities, and slave life. The blues also represented a greater spirit of individualism in the black community. They were often performed by self-accompanied individuals, in contrast to the older music performed by aggregations like Sid Hemphill's four-piece string band. The individual and couple dancing done "at random" to the blues could also be considered a model of greater individualism among blacks, in contrast to the square dance, a model of a more cohesive, cooperative community. Finally, the blues were sung in the first person, while much of the older music was sung in the third person about animals or folk heroes of the black community.

Notes

1. Samuel Charters, *The Bluesmen* (New York, 1967), pp. 27–28; Paul Oliver, *The Story of the Blues* (London, 1969), pp. 17–25; Harry Oster, *Living Country Blues* (Detroit, 1969), pp. 11–13; Richard Middleton, *Pop Music and the Blues* (London, 1972), pp. 55–61; John A. and Alan Lomax, *Folk Song U.S.A.* (New York, 1966), p. 70; Alan Lomax, *The Folk Songs of North America* (Garden City, N.Y., 1960), p. 573. Bruce Cook unaccountably minimizes the obvious importance of field hollers in *Listen to the Blues* (New York, 1973), pp. 55–56.

2. Harold Courlander, *Negro Folk Music U.S.A.* (New York, 1963), pp. 80–88; Dena J. Epstein, *Sinful Tunes and Spiritual* (Urbana, 1977), 161–183.

3. Frances Anne Kemble, *Journal of a Residence on a Georgian Plantation in 1838–1839* (New York, 1863), pp. 128–129.

4. Johann Tonsor, "Negro Music," *Music*, 3 (1892–93), 119–120.

5. Ibid., p. 120.

6. Ibid., pp. 120–121.

7. Ray B. Browne, "Some Notes on the Southern 'Holler'," *Journal of American Folklore*, 67 (1954), 73–77; Ray B. Browne, "The Alabama 'Holler' and Street Cries," *Journal of American Folklore*, 70 (1957), 363; Peter T. Bartis, "An Examination of the Holler in North Carolina White Tradition," *Southern Folklore Quarterly*, 39 (1975), 209–218; Mark Wilson, notes to *Hollerin'* Rounder 0071, 12" LP.

8. Son House, "I Can Make My Own Songs," *Sing Out!*, 15, No. 3 (July 1965), 45. For a recording of one of House's own hollers with Fiddlin' Joe Martin see "Camp Hollers" on *Negro Blues and Hollers*, AFS L59, 12" LP.

9. David Evans, "Booker White," in *Nothing But the Blues*, ed. Mike Leadbitter (London, 1971), p. 255.

10. Jack Owens, Bentonia, Miss., Sept. 1, 1970. Recorded by David Evans.

11. Othar Turner, "Black Woman." Senatobia, Miss., Mar. 22, 1969. Recorded by David Evans. Issued on *Afro-American Folk Music from Tate and Panola Counties, Mississippi*, AFS L67, 12" LP.

12. Charters, *The Bluesmen*, pp. 27–28. See also Cook, pp. 56–58. For a detailed study of group and individual worksongs see Bruce Jackson, *Wake Up Dead Man: Afro-American Worksongs from Texas Prisons* (Cambridge, Mass., 1972).

13. Ernest Borneman, "Black Light and White Shadow: Notes for a History of American Negro Music," *Jazzforschung*, 2 (1970), 55; Cook, p. 56.

14. Lomax, *The Folk Songs of North America*, pp. 574–575.

15. Oliver, *The Story of the Blues*, pp. 22–25. See also Cook, pp. 58–60; and Abbe Niles in W. C. Handy, *Blues, An Anthology* (New York, 1972), pp. 17–20.

16. Most of the best known blues ballads are indexed in G. Malcolm Laws, Jr., *Native American Balladry*, rev. ed. (Philadelphia, 1964), pp. 245–256, 275–276.

17. The guitar part is discussed and transcribed in tablature notation in Donald Garwood, *Masters of Instrumental Blues Guitar* (New York, 1968), pp. 47–49; and Stefan Grossman, *The Country Blues Guitar* (New York, 1968), pp. 44–47.

18. For more information on Hurt see Lawrence Cohn, "Mississippi John Hurt," *Sing Out!*, 14, No. 5 (Nov. 1964), 16–21; and George W. Kay, "Mississippi John Hurt," *Jazz Journal*, 17, No. 2 (Feb. 1964), 24–26.

19. Howard W. Odum, "Folk-Song and Folk-Poetry as Found in the Secular Songs of the Southern Negroes," *Journal of American Folklore*, 24 (1911), nos. 18, 20, 22, 23, 25, 39, 62, 69, 91, and 101. [Excerpt reprinted herein.]

20. Archie Green, *Only a Miner: Studies in Recorded Coal-Mining Songs* (Urbana, Ill., 1972), pp. 195–196. For versions of the song see Howard W. Odum, p. 351 (no. 54, AAA pattern) [excerpt reprinted herein]; Handy, *Blues, An Anthology*, pp. 17–20, 210 (AAB pattern); William Broonzy, *Big Bill Blues*, rev. ed. (New York, 1964), pp. 53–59 (AAA pattern).

21. Handy, *Blues, An Anthology*, p. 19. See also Louis Ford and the Son Sims Four, "Joe Turner," on *Muddy Waters: Down on Stovall's Plantation*, Testament T-2210, 12" LP.

22. Howard W. Odum, p. 282 (no. 32) [excerpt reprinted herein]; Handy, *Blues, An Anthology*, p. 61; Mary Wheeler, *Steamboatin' Days* (Baton Rouge, 1944), pp. 29, 49–51, 53, 81.

23. Lucius Smith, Sardis, Miss., Aug. 1, 1973. Recorded by David and Cheryl Evans. Abbe Niles in Handy, *Blues, An Anthology*, p. 210, suggested that "Joe Turner" might have been the prototype of all blues. Broonzy, pp. 53–54, set the date of its composition in 1890.

24. Lucius Smith, Sardis, Miss., June 27, 1971. Recorded by David and Cheryl Evans. For recordings by Smith and Sid Hemphill's band, including a blues ballad in an AB-refrain pattern, "The Carrier Line," see *Afro-American Folk Music from Tate and Panola Counties, Mississippi*, AFS L67, 12" LP. For a similar view by another performer of Smith's generation that the blues began as a slow dance music, see Mack McCormick, "Mance Lipscomb, Texas Sharecropper and Songster," in *American Folk Music Occasional, No. 1*, ed. Chris Strachwitz (Berkeley, 1964), pp. 63–64.

3 Folklore and the Blues

PREVIOUSLY dubbed "popular antiquities" and now sometimes termed "folklife" in recognition of nonverbal elements that also form part of traditional culture, folklore has been an important field of endeavor in documenting the blues tradition. The founding of the American Folklore Society in January 1888 at Harvard University, in part a response to the increasing interest in capturing for posterity a way of life that was disappearing in the face of encroaching industrialization and urbanization—an impulse that also gave impetus to the local color and realistic movements in literature—was a precipitous event in our nation's cultural history that helped lead to some of the earliest extant examples of and comments about the blues. Although some early twentieth-century American folklorists tended to have a rather romanticized view of "the folk" and could be bound in some ways by the prejudices of their times, still their efforts in the field at collecting and preserving folk traditions provided lyrics, themes, and stanza patterns in embryonic form, the material collected before the issuance of blues sheet music in 1912 and phonograph records in 1920 uninfluenced by commercial blues efforts.

The selection included here by the folklorist and sociologist Howard W. Odum is one of the most significant of the early articles on the blues. Drawn from his own fieldwork collected between 1905 and 1908 primarily in Newton County, Georgia, and Lafayette County, Mississippi, the article provides important discussions of the performers—"musicianers," "music physicianers," and "songsters" whose performed material included folk songs of African American origin and popular songs sometimes altered to suit the needs and purpose of the performers—in addition to classifications and transcriptions of their lyrics, a number of which will be familiar to the blues fan through subsequent commercial recordings.

Guy B. Johnson, writing in 1927, sounds an early lament, echoed throughout the years, regarding the commercialization of the folk tradition that caused "the production of blues" to be "like the production of Fords or of Ivory Soap." It is worth mentioning that the "folk" tradition is not always as free of popular and commercial aspects as some people would like to believe. Such a conception springs from a sometimes romantic notion of the "folk" being insulated from the corruptions of the mainstream market and existing in an artistic world of their own, but it ignores some of the actualities as they have been exposed, for example, in Paul Oliver's *Songsters and Saints*, which examines in part how popular songs and sheet music entered and influenced "folk" performers. Johnson's main focus, however, is the exploration of sexual double-entendres in popular recordings, carried over into these popular songs from the "vulgarities" of the folk tradition. (Sterling Brown lamented the "belt line" production of blues and the diminution of the folk's Rabelaisian humor into prurient smut in three separate essays: "The Blues as Folk Poetry" published in 1930, and "Negro Folk Expression" and "The Blues," published in 1952 and 1953.) Although Johnson explains a number of points for the uninitiated, some references, such as to the lyric "I got your bath water on" (or just "got your water on") are not really satisfactorily explored, particularly since recordings such as the Memphis Jug Band's "Papa's Got Your Bath Water On" appear to have more violent than sexual overtones.

Alan Lomax and his father, John A. Lomax, were the most important folklore collectors of the 1930s and 1940s, beginning their folklore collecting trips for the Archive of Folk Song (established in 1928 with Robert W. Gordon as its initial archivist) in 1933. Among the artists recorded by the Lomaxes were Leadbelly, W. C. Handy, Jelly Roll Morton, and a host of lesser-known but often fascinating blues performers. The piece included here, published in 1948 in *Common Ground*, a quarterly magazine that was published by the Common Council for American Unity, is at least partially fictionalized, since the recordings from which it was drawn were made at the Decca Studios in New York City on a Sunday in 1947. Still, Lomax often accurately transcribes the interview tapes (currently available on *Blues in the Mississippi Night*, Rykodisc 90155), and though he shrouds his interview session in an artificially conjured atmosphere of danger and racism and characterizes one of the performers, Sib (Sonny Boy Williamson), using stereotypical language, he presents a powerful portrait of three African American bluesmen—the other two are Big Bill Broonzy and Memphis Slim—speaking frankly about their encounters with racism, their lives as African Americans, and the ways their art reflects their experiences and temperaments.

The contributions by Dennis Jarrett and John Barnie were both published in *Southern Folklore Quarterly* in 1978 in an issue devoted to the blues that also included David Evans's "Fieldwork with Blues Singers: The Unintentionally Induced Natural Context." Jarrett proposes that the singer-composer creates a fictional self he terms "the bluesman" (a term that unfortunately does not account for women performers), which allows the singer to perform communally rather than personally, accounting in part for the coexistence of despair and hope so common in the blues. This view is a direct challenge to the notion that blues are purely autobiographical, first-person songs, though of course the performers can be describing experiences that might happen to them or have happened to people who they see as being like them in some crucial way. As B. B. King stated, "I've seen many people hurt, homes broken, people killed, people talked about, so today I sing about it" (see Michael Haralambos, "Soul Music and Blues"). Jarrett defines this blues self as a "generic personality" or "traditional person" whose personality is encoded in lexical and psychological conditions and reflected in the use of common words, phrases, and stanzas in blues songs. Jarrett's piece places the blues performer squarely in the oral-formulaic tradition which, as outlined by Milman Parry in *The Making of Homeric Verse* and Albert Lord in *The Singer of Tales,* posits that the singer of epic verse in a preliterate society creates songs in the act of performance with the extensive assistance of formulas, "a group of words which is regularly employed under the same metrical conditions to express a given essential idea"—adaptable units rather than mere cliches. Barnie, however, cautions that the blues, though in accentual meter of 4–6 stresses per line with a strong medial caesura, is looser and therefore distinguishable from Old English verse and the Jugoslav epic that was Parry's focus. Additionally, since the blues are often neither epic nor narrative—important conditions for the oral-formulaic concept—Barnie views the repetitions of common words and phrases in the blues as formulaic, but not necessarily formulas themselves.

As these selections demonstrate, folklorists have been collecting blues material and confronting important ontological issues from very near its inception, and they continue to collect and take methodical, careful, and conflicting looks at the material to this day, by which time some have been willing to pronounce the blues dead as a folk genre. One's understanding depends upon how one defines folklore, and upon how extensively—and where—one is willing to look for what is there. Of course, not everyone has the same definition of folklore, or an exalted idea of folk materials. In response to the view that the folk musician is the most valid, authentic blues artist, little sullied by sophisticated commercialism, and a creative force and wellspring of more refined art, Albert Murray argues in *Stomping the Blues* that the folk musician is conservative, conventional, imitative, derivative, unimaginative, and naive. Murray seems to be seeking to correct what he sees as the erroneous notion that the stylistic innovations and refinements of professional jazz musicians necessarily dilute the blues, producing artificiality, pretension, and affectation. Of course, he is right that those qualities are not inevitable by-products of the encounters between professional jazz performers and the blues. Many of his own favorite blues performers would be labeled jazz performers (or blues-influenced jazz performers) by blues aficionados and folklorists, suggesting that definitions of what the blues are and do, and what they sound like, do not correspond and pointing up how labeling and categorizations can sometimes inhibit appreciation and exclude worthy talents from adequate consideration (one might make this same argument with regard to white blues performers—see the discussion in the "Blues as Influence" section). Murray's blues musicians frequently bring fresh, meaningful ideas to the blues tradition—Duke Ellington is Murray's prime example, indeed a man who responded creatively and passionately to the blues. However, to some commentators Murray's characterization of folk blues performers places him just this side of contempt for them, undervaluing the abilities and important contributions of folk blues performers (see Paul Garon's review of Murray's book in *Living Blues* 31 [March-April 1977]). Clearly many people have experienced passionate responses to, have been inspired by, the artists labeled folk blues performers—far too many to have been merely delusional victims of their own romantic notions of "the folk." Nonetheless, a revisionist challenge such as Murray's can compel us to reevaluate our positions, scrutinizing our assumptions and the assumptions of those who have gone before us in an effort to gain a more comprehensive and complex view of the blues. If we find ourselves listening to more blues, reading and re-reading other commentary, and reflecting on the differences between what we hear and read, then we have done something of value.

Recommended Further Readings

Sterling Brown. "The Blues." *Phylon* 13 (1952): 286–92.

——. The Blues As Folk Poetry." In *Folk-Say I.* Ed. B. A. Botkin. Norman: University of Oklahoma Press, 1930.

——. "Negro Folk Expression: Spirituals, Seculars, Ballads, and Work Songs." *Phylon* 14 (1953): 45–61.

Harold Courlander. *Negro Folk Music U.S.A.* New York: Columbia University Press, 1970.

David Evans. "Folk, Commercial, and Folkloristic Aesthetics in the Blues." *Jazzforschung* 5 (1973): 11–32.

Lawrence Gellert. "Notes." *Negro Songs of Protest.* Rpt. Rounder LP 4004.

——. "Preface." *Me and My Captain (Chain Gangs).* New York: Hours Press, 1939.

Michael Haralambos. "Soul Music and Blues: Their Meaning and Relevance in Northern United States Black Ghettoes." In *Afro-American Anthropology,* ed. Norman Whitten and John F. Szwed. New York: Free Press, 1970.

Zora Neale Hurston. *Mules and Men.* 1935. Rpt. Bloomington: Indiana University Press, 1978.

Alan Lomax. *The Land Where the Blues Began.* New York: Pantheon, 1993.

Albert Murray. *Stomping the Blues.* New York: Da Capo, 1976.

Howard W. Odum and Guy B. Johnson. *Negro Workaday Songs.* Chapel Hill: University of North Carolina Press, 1926.

Dorothy Scarborough. *On the Trail of Negro Folk Songs.* 1925. Rpt. Hatboro, Pa.: Folklore Association, 1963.

W. Prescott Webb and Floyd Canada. "Notes on Folk-lore of Texas." *Journal of American Folklore* 28 (1915): 291–96.

Folk-Song and Folk-Poetry as Found in the Secular Songs of the Southern Negroes

Howard W. Odum

AN EXAMINATION of the first twenty volumes of the *Journal of American Folk-Lore*, and a study of the published folk-songs of the Southern negroes, reveal a large amount of valuable material for the student of folk-songs and ballads. Investigation of the field indicates a still larger supply of songs as yet not collected or published. Unfortunately the collection of these songs has been permitted to lapse within recent years, although there is no indication that even a majority have been collected. In fact, the supply seems almost inexhaustible, and the present-day negro folk-songs appear to be no less distinctive than formerly. It is hoped that special efforts will be made by as many persons as possible to contribute to the negro department of American folk-lore as many of the songs of the Southern negroes as can be obtained. That they are most valuable to the student of sociology and anthropology, as well as to the student of literature and the ballad, will scarcely be doubted.

Two distinct classes of folk-songs have been, and are, current among the Southern negroes,—the religious songs, or "spirituals;" and the social or secular songs. An examination of the principal collections of negro songs shows that emphasis has been placed heretofore upon the religious songs, although the secular songs appear to be equally as interesting and valuable. My study of negro folk-songs included originally the religious and secular songs of the Southern negroes; analysis of their content; a discussion of the mental imagery, style and habit, reflected in them; and the word-vocabulary of the collection of songs. The religious songs have already been published in the *American Journal of Religious Psychology and Education* (vol. iii, pp. 265–365). In order to bring this paper within the scope and limits of the *Journal of American Folk-Lore*, it has been necessary to omit the introductory discussion of the songs, for the most part, and to omit entirely the vocabulary and discussion of the mental imagery, style and habits, of the negro singers. In this paper, therefore, only the secular songs are given, which in turn are divided into two classes,—the general social songs, and work songs and phrases.

To understand to the best advantage the songs which follow, it is necessary to define the

Reprinted from *Journal of American Folklore* 24 (July–Sept. 1911): 255–94. Used by permission of the American Folklore Society. Not for further reproduction.

usage of the word "folk-song" as applied in this paper, to show how current negro songs arise and become common property, to note their variations, and to observe some of the occasions upon which they are sung. Each of these aspects of the Southern negro's songs is interdependent upon the others; the meaning of the folk-songs is emphasized by the explanations of their origin and variations; the singing of the songs by many individuals on many occasions emphasizes the difficulty of confining any song to a given locality or to a single form; and the value of the song is increased as it passes through the several stages.

The songs in this collection are "negro folk-songs," in that they have had their origin and growth among the negroes, or have been adapted so completely that they have become the common songs of the negroes. They are "folk-poetry which, from whatever source and for whatever reason, has passed into the possession of the folk, the common people, so completely that each singer or reciter feels the piece to be his own."[1] Each singer alters or sings the song according to his own thoughts and feelings. How exactly this applies to the negro songs may be seen from the explanations which follow, and from the study and comparison of the different songs. It is not necessary, therefore, in order to classify the songs as negro songs, to attempt to trace each song to its origin or to attempt to determine how much is original and how much borrowed. Clearly many of the songs are adapted forms of well-known songs or ballads; others, which in all probability had their origin among the negroes, resemble very strongly the songs of other people; while still others combine in a striking way original features with the borrowed. In any case, the song, when it has become the common distinctive property of the negroes, must be classed with negro folk-songs. Variations of negro folk-songs among themselves may be cited as an illustration of this fact. Likewise there is abundant material for comparing with well-known folk-songs or ballads of other origins. One may note, for instance, the striking similarity between the mountain-song—

> "She broke the heart of many poor fellows,
> But she won't break this of mine"—

and the negro song "Kelly's Love," the chorus of which is,

> "You broke de heart o' many a girl,
> But you never will break dis heart o' mine."

Or, again, compare the version of the Western ballad, "Casey Jones,"—which begins,

> "Come, all you rounders, for I want you to hear
> The story told of an engineer.
> Casey Jones was the rounder's name,
> A heavy right-wheeler of mighty fame,"—

with the negro song, "Casey Jones," which begins,

> "Casey Jones was an engineer,
> Told his fireman not to fear,
> All he wanted was boiler hot,
> Run into Canton 'bout four 'clock,"

and, having recited in a single stanza the story of his death, passes on to love affairs, and ends,

> "Wimmins in Kansas all dressed in red,
> Got de news dat Casey was dead;
> De wimmins in Jackson all dressed in black,
> Said, in fact, he was a cracker-jack."

Thus Canton and Jackson, Mississippi, are localized; in "Joseph Mica" similar versions are found, and localized in Atlanta and other cities,—

> "All he want is water 'n coal,
> Poke his head out, see drivers roll;"

and the entire story of the engineer's death is told in the verse,

> "Good ole engineer, but daid an' gone."

In the same way comparisons may be made with "Jesse James," "Eddy Jones," "Joe Turner," "Brady," "Stagolee," of the hero-songs; "Won't you marry me?" "Miss Lizzie, won't you marry me?" "The Angel Band," and others similar to some of the short Scottish ballads and song-games of American children; and "I got mine," "When she roll dem Two White Eyes," "Ain't goin' be no Rine," and many others adapted from the popular "coon-songs;" together with scores of rhymes, riddles, and conundrums. In any case, the songs with the accompanying music have become the property of the negroes, in their present rendition, regardless of their sources or usage elsewhere.

In the same way that it is not possible to learn the exact origin of the folk-songs, or to determine how much is original and how much traditional, it is not possible to classify negro songs according to the exact locality or localities from which they come. The extent to which they become common property, and the scope of their circulation, will be explained in subsequent discussions of the songs. The best that can be done, therefore, is to classify the songs according to the locality *from which they were collected,* and to give the different versions of the same song as they are found in different localities. The majority of the songs collected from Lafayette County, Mississippi, were also heard in Newton County, Georgia; and a large number of the songs heard in Mississippi and Georgia were also heard in Tennessee (Sumner County). From many inquiries the conclusion seems warranted that the majority of the one hundred and ten songs or fragments here reported are current in southern Georgia, southern Mississippi, parts of Tennessee, and the Carolinas and Virginia. It may well be hoped that other collections of negro songs will be made, and that similarities and differences in these songs may be pointed out in other localities, as well as new songs collected. The large number of "one-verse songs" and "heave-a-hora's" were collected with the other songs, and are representative of the negro song in the making.

In studying the negro's songs, three important aids to their interpretation should be kept in mind,—first, facts relating to the manner of singing, and the occasions upon which they are sung; second, the general classes of negro songs, and the kinds of songs within each class; and, third, the subject-matter, methods of composition, and the processes through which the songs commonly pass in their growth and development. The majority of songs current among the negroes are often sung without the accompaniment of an instrument. The usual songs of the day, songs of laborers, of children, and many general care-free songs, together with some of the songs of the evening, are not accompanied. In general, the majority of the songs of the evening are accompanied by the "box" or fiddle when large or small groups are gathered together for gayety; when a lonely negro sits on his doorstep or by the fireside, playing and singing; when couples stay late at night with their love-songs and jollity; when groups gather after church to sing the lighter melodies; when the "musicianers," "music physicianers," and "songsters" gather to render music for special occasions, such as church and private "socials," dances, and other forms of social gatherings. Special instances in which a few negroes play and sing for the whites serve to bring out the combined features of restrained song and the music of the instrument. The old-time negro with his "box" (a fiddle or guitar), ever ready to entertain the "white folks" and thus be entertained himself, is less often observed than formerly. The majority of younger negroes must be well paid for their music. In the smaller towns, such negroes not infrequently organize a small "ochestra," and learn to play and sing the new songs. They often render acceptable music, and are engaged by the whites for serenades or for occasions of minor importance. They do not, however, sing the negro folk-songs.

Of special importance as makers and mediums for negro folk-songs are the "music physicianers," "musicianers," and "songsters." These terms may be synonymous, or they may denote persons of different habits. In general, "songster" is used to denote any negro who regularly sings or makes songs; "musicianer" applies often to the individual who claims to be expert with the banjo or fiddle; while "music physicianer" is used to denote more nearly a person who is accustomed to travel from place to place, and who possesses a combination of these qualities; or each or all of the terms may be applied loosely to any person who sings or plays an instruments. A group of small boys or young men, when gathered together and wrought up to a high degree of abandon, appear to be able to sing an unlimited number of common songs. Perhaps the "music physicianer" knows the "moest songs." With a prized "box," perhaps his only property, such a negro may wander from town to town, from section to section, loafing in general, and working only when compelled to do so, gathering new songs and singing the old ones. Negroes of this type may be called professionals, since their life of wandering is facilitated by the practice of singing. Through their influence, songs are easily carried from place to place. There are other "music physicianers" whose fields of activity are only local. In almost every community such individuals may be found, and from them many songs can be obtained. From them and from promiscuous individuals, a "musicianer" may be influenced to obtain songs new to himself, which he, in turn, will render to the collector. Finally, a group of young negroes, treated to a "bait" of watermelons or to a hearty meal, make excellent "songsters" in the rendering of the folk-songs. In addition to these special cases, it is a constant source of surprise to the observer to learn how many songs the average negro knows; and they may be heard during work hours, or, in some cases, by request.

The great mass of negro songs may be divided into three general classes, the last of which constitutes the folk-songs as commonly used,—first, the modern "coon-songs" and the newest popular songs of the day; second, such songs greatly modified and adapted partially by the negroes; and, third, songs originating with the negroes or adapted so completely as to become common folk-songs. The first class of songs is heard more frequently by the whites. All manner of "rag-times," "coon-songs," and the latest "hits," replace the simpler negro melodies. Young negroes pride themselves on the number of such songs they can sing, at the same time that they resent a request to sing the older melodies. Very small boys and girls sing the difficult airs of the new songs with surprising skill, until one wonders when and how they learned so many words and tunes. The second class of songs easily arises from the singing of popular songs, varied through constant singing or through misunderstanding of the original versions. These songs appear to be typical of the process of song-making, and indicate the facility of the negroes in producing their own songs from material of any sort. The third class of negro songs is made up of the "folk-songs" proper; and while the variations of the songs of the first and second classes would constitute an interesting study, they are in reality not negro songs. Accordingly, only those that have become completely adapted are given in this collection. In all of these the characteristic music and manner prevail, and the principal characteristics may be enumerated simply. The music may be reduced to a few combinations. The harmonies are made up mostly of minor keys, without reference to studied combinations or movement toward related keys. There is much repetition in both words and music. The song and chorus are adapted to an apparent mood or feeling. Verses are sung in the order in which they occur to the singer, or as they please the fancy. The great majority of the songs are made up of repetitions, but they do not tire the singers or the hearers. The negro song often begins with one conception of a theme, and ends with another entirely foreign to the first, after passing through various other themes. This may be explained by the fact that when the negro begins to sing, he loves to continue, and often passes from one song to another without pausing. In time he mingles the two or more songs. Most of the groups and "socials," and especially the dance, require continuous music for a longer period of time than the average song will last. It thus happens that the negro could sing the great majority of his songs to a single tune, if the necessity called for it; although it is likely that the last part of his melody would scarcely be recognizable as that with which he began. In words, as in music, variation seems unlimited. As is pointed out subsequently, and as was true in the case of the religious songs, there is no consistency in the use of dialect. Perhaps there is less consistency in the social songs than elsewhere. It is common for the negro to mingle every kind of song into one, or to transpose the one from its usual place or origin to any other position. Thus "coon-songs," "rag-times," "knife-songs," "devil-songs," "corn-songs," "work-songs,"—all alike may become love-songs or dancing "breakdowns." The original names given to such songs serve to distinguish them in the mind of the negro, rather than to indicate their separateness. However, the distinctions are often made clearly enough for a definition of what the negro means to be made.

The "musicianer" will play many "rag-times," which he carefully names, and calls off with pride. Usually they are not accompanied by words, but are represented on the fiddle or guitar. When he is through with these, he will offer to play and sing "some song." This he does to precisely the same music as the "rag-time." With the words, it is a song; without the words, it is a "rag-time," in which case the negro puts more life into the music. Likewise the "knife-song" is by origin instrumental only, but it is regularly associated with several songs of many verses. Its name is derived from the act of running the back of a knife along the strings of the instrument, thus making it "sing" and "talk" with skill. Instead of the knife, negroes often carry a piece of bone, polished and smooth, which they slip over a finger, and alternate between picking the strings and rubbing them. This gives a combination of fiddle and guitar. The bone may also serve as a good-luck omen. The knife, however, is more commonly used. The "musicianer" places his knife by the side of the instrument while he picks the strings and sings. He can easily take it up and use it at the proper time without interrupting the harmony. In this way the instrument can be made to "sing," "talk," "cuss," and supplement in general the voice and the ringing of the fiddle or the tinkling of the guitar. It is undoubtedly one of the negro's best productions, and defies musical notation to give it full expression.

The "train-song" derives its name from its imitation of the running train. The most popular name for it is "The Fast Train." The negro's fondness for trains and railroad life has been observed. In the railroad-songs that follow, the extent to which the train appeals to the negro may be seen. In no way is this spirit better portrayed than in the train-songs, which picture to the vivid imagination the rapidly-moving train. This imitation is done by the rapid running of the fingers along the strings, and by the playing of successive chords with a regularity that makes a sound similar to that of the moving train. The train is made to whistle by a prolonged and consecutive striking of the strings, while the bell rings with the striking of a single string. As the negroes imagine themselves observing the train, or riding, the fervor of the occasion is increased; and when "she blows for the station," the exclamations may be heard, "Lawd, God, she's a-runnin' now!" or, "Sho' God railroadin'!" with others of a similar nature. The train "pulls out" from the station, passes the road-crossings, goes up grade, down grade, blows for the crossing, blows for smaller stations, blows for the operators at the stations, rings the bell for crossings and for stopping the train; this train meets the "express" and the mail-train, blows for the side-track, rings the bell; the mail-train in turn whistles, rings the bell, passes; both bells ring, and they continue on their run; the wheels are heard rolling on the track and crossing the joints in the rails. If the song is instrumental only, the man at the guitar announces the several stages of the run. If the song is one of words, such as the railroad-songs cited subsequently, the words are made to heighten the imagination, and between the stanzas there is ample time to picture the train and its occupants.

I. General Social Songs

A study of the social songs current among the Southern negroes shows that they have arisen from every-day life, and that they portray many of the common traits and social tendencies. The majority may be said to have sprung up within comparatively recent years. For the subject-matter of his songs, the negro has drawn freely upon his favorite themes; and the growth and development of his songs have been spontaneous and natural. The singers are often conscious that they are singing folk-songs, and they attempt to pose as the authors; others give interesting stories to show how they learned the songs; while many negroes are averse to singing or collecting such songs for those desiring them. The accounts given by negroes concerning the origin and authorship of their songs, while most interesting, are quite misleading, for the most part. One negro affirmed that he had heard a song "played by a white lady in New York," and that, from hearing it there, he had learned to reproduce the music on his guitar and sing the song to accompany it. Another affirmed that he got the same song from a neighboring town, and that he had been forced to pay dearly for it (therefore he should be rewarded accordingly). The song was one of the widest known of the negro songs. So, too, negro singers may often purposely mislead the investigator by misquoting the song, or by giving verses which they have got from books or papers, or heard from "coon-songs." Many negroes maintain that they are the original authors of the songs they sing, and they are able to give apparent good evidence to substantiate the statement. Even if one were inclined to accept such testimony, it would be a difficult matter to select the author from a number who thus claim to have composed the song. This is well illustrated by the young negro who wished to call out his name before each song which he was singing into the grapho-phone. "Song composed by Will Smith of Chattanooga, Tennessee," he would cry out, then begin his song; for, he maintained, these songs would be sung all over the world, and he deserved the credit for them. His varied song furnished excellent material for getting the characteristic notation of the music. Once or twice he hesitated before giving his name as the author, and several times said he guessed that the song was composed by some other person whose name he wished to give. This person was a "partner rounder" of his acquaintance; and when told that the origin of a song which he was singing was not that which he gave, but was well known, he begged to have his name taken away, adding that he only meant to say, "Song sung by Will Smith." This may be cited as an illustration of the difficulty of getting at the origin of a song through the negroes. In no case could the general testimony be accepted for any purpose other than to give an insight into the negro's own conception of the possible origin of songs.

The negroes have many songs which they call "one-verse songs." By this they mean a single line, repeated again and again, constituting the entire song. Usually the line is repeated with regularity, so that it makes a stanza of two, four, or six lines, sometimes three and five. In such cases the last repetition adds some word or exclamation, as "oh," "my," "yes," "well," "and," "so," and others. The great majority of negro songs which are current now are "one-verse songs," and almost all have arisen and developed along the one-verse method. A close examination of the songs that follow in subsequent pages will show the processes. In this way the origin of song is simple and natural. Any word may lead to a phrase which itself becomes a one-verse song, and naturally calls for a rhyme and additional verses. A negro is driving a delivery-wagon; the weather is cold, and the wind is blowing with a drizzling rain. He pulls his coat around him, and says, "The wind sho' do blow." Not having any special song which he wishes to sing at the moment, he sings these words and others: "Sho' God is cold dis mornin'," "Ain't goin' to rain no mo'," "Goin' where chilly win' don't blow." In the same way he sings whatever happens to be foremost in his mind. Perhaps it is, "I bin workin' so long—hungry as I kin be;" "Where in de worl' you bin?" "I'm goin' 'way some day;" "Jus' keep a knockin' at yo' do';" "Had a mighty good time las' night;" or as many others as there are common scenes in the negro's life. The examples given in the list of one-verse songs will serve to illustrate further this common origin of many of the negro songs. In the same general way the prose or monotone songs have arisen. The negro often talks to himself; his singing is simply a musical "thinking out loud." His monologues uttered in a monotone manner lead to song. Perhaps he will talk to himself a while, then sing the same words that he has been uttering. Pleased with this effect, he may then introduce his chant into a group. Such a song is given farther on.

1. Dony Got a Hole in de Wall

"A girl was luvin' a coon," so the story goes, "an' she thought he did not go to see any other girl; she found out he did, an' she made a hole in the wall of her house so she could watch an' see did her lover go to see any other coon. Her luvin' man found this out an' it made him laugh; an' he wus sorry, too." Thus is given the origin of a bit of song. The lover makes a song, and says,—

> "Dony got a hole in de wall,
> Dony got a hole in de wall,
> Dony got a hole in de wall,
> Oh, my Dony got a hole in de wall.
> "Baby weahs a number fo' shoe,
> Baby weahs a number fo' shoe,
> Baby weahs a number fo' shoe,
> Oh, my baby weahs a number fo' shoe."

In this way the negro makes a story back of the song. If it is a lover's song, he tells of a particular man and his woman. If it is Railroad Bill, he tells when and where he lived and what he did, then sings the song. If it is another "bully boy," the same is true. If the song be that of the wanderer, he tells of the adventures; if it is of a murder, he narrates the story of arrest and trial. A study of the songs reveals the immense possibilities for stories back of the song. No song is enjoyed so much as when the singer has told his story before singing it. In theory at least, then, the negro song is based on incident; in practice it develops through the common events of negro life. Indeed, one may accept the statement that many of their songs are actually derived from story; but there may be as many variations to the song and story as there are negroes who sing it.

Individuals among the negroes take pride in making secular songs, as they do in claiming the composition of religious songs. Enough has been said to indicate this habit. But undoubtedly the negro has a consciousness of power or ability to create new songs when he wishes to do so. This very feeling enables him to make his boasts true. Most negroes are bright in composing songs of some kind. Besides being led to it by their own assertions, they enjoy it. It matters little what the theme is, the song will be forthcoming and the tune applied. Nor would one suspect that the song was a new one, were it not for its unfinished lines and the lack of characteristic folk-song qualities. In the examples here given it will be seen that the lines do not have the finished form of the older songs. In time they too may become good folk-songs.

2. Mule-Song

The negroes have much to say about the mule in their work, and have much to do with him in actual life. Their songs also contain references to him. A mixture of parts of song added to experience and imagination produced the following "mule-song:"

> "I went up Zion Hill this mornin' on a wagon,
> I went on a wagon up Zion's Hill this mornin',
> The durn ole mule stop right still this mornin', this mornin', so soon.

"I got out an' went 'round to his head this mornin',
I got out an' went 'round to his head this mornin',
The durn ole mule was standin' there dead, this mornin', so soon.

"Yes, I hollow at the mule, an' the mule would not gee, this mornin',
Yes, I hollow at the mule, an' the mule would not gee,
An' I hit him across the head with the single-tree, so soon."

The negro expected that his song would be a humorous one, as indeed it is. Such songs lack the rhyme and more regular measures, and employ words at random to fill out the lines.

3. The Negro and His Mule

In the following song the same characteristics may be observed:

"Say, look here, Jane!
Don't you want to take a ride?"—
"Well, I doan care if I do."
So he hitch up his mule an' started out.

Well, it's whoa, mule, git up an' down,
Till I say whoa-er, mule.

Well it's git up an' down
Jus' fas' as you can,
Fer I goin' to buy you
All of de oats an' bran.

An' it's whoa-er mule, git up an' down,
Till I say whoa-er mule:
Ain't he a mule, Miss Jane—'m—huh.

4. Poor John

In the next song may be observed a peculiarly mixed imagery. Quite a number of phrases are borrowed from other songs, but the arrangement is new. "Poor John" is a common character with the negro; stabbing and running are common accomplishments with the criminal. The other scenes, losing his hat, falling down the steps, the cry of murder, and the policemen, all appeal to the imagery of the negro. He sings, with a combination of vaudeville rhyme,—

"Yes, he caught poor John with his hawk-tail coat,
An' he stab him to the fat;
He ran the race an' he run so fas',
Till he bust his beaver hat.

"Poor John fell down them winding steps,
Till he could not fall no further;
An' the girls all holler murder;
Go tell all policemen on this beat to see,
Can't they catch that coon.

"'What coon am you talkin' about?'
'The coon that stab po' John;
I'm goin', I'm goin', to the shuckin' o' de corn,
I'm goin' jus' sho's you born.'"

5. At the Ball

An adopted form of an old song, "Won't you marry me," but equally as true in its representative features, is the song "At the Ball." Here the rhyming effort is clearly felt, and the picture is definitely portrayed. The negro's idea of courtship may here be hinted at, as it has been in many of the songs that follow.

Yes, there's going to be a ball,
At the negro hall;
Ain't you goin'?
Lizzie will be there,
Yes, with all her airs;
Don't you want to see the strolling?

Ha, ha, Miss Lizzie, don't you want to marry me—marry me!
I will be as good to you as anybody—anybod-e-e,
If you'll only marry me.

Yes, I goin' to the negro hall,
Have a good time, that's all,
For they tell me Miss Lizzie will be there;
An' you bet yo' life,
I goin' win her for my wife,
An' take her home to-night.

Well, Miss Lizzie could not consent,
She didn't know what he meant,
By askin' her to marry him;
Well, Miss Lizzie couldn't consent,
She didn't know what he meant,
By askin' her to marry him.

So he got down on his knees,
"O Miss Lizzie, if you please,
Say that you will marry me;
An' I'll give you every cent,
If I git you to consent,
If you'll only marry me."

6. When He Gits Old—Old an' Gray

There are apparently a good many sayings current among the negroes about the whites. Few of these, however, are heard by any save the negroes themselves. Likewise the songs of this nature would scarcely be sung where the whites could hear them. Two of these are here given. The first is a reply to the accusation that the negroes are nothing more than apes or monkeys. As the story goes, it is likely that the song originated with a bright negro's retort behind the back of a white who had called him an ape. "That's all right," said the negro in the proverbial phrase; but

When he gits old,
old and gray,
When he gits old,
old and gray,
Then white folks looks like monkeys,
When dey gits old, old an' gray.

It is needless to say that the song struck a responsive note as well as appealed to the negro as a very bright song for the occasion. In fact, it must be admitted to be a good rejoinder. The subtle and sulky manner in which it is sung is a powerful comment on the negro's growing sense of race feeling. Whether there are other verses to this comment on the aged whites has not been ascertained.

7. Ain't It Hard to Be a Nigger

The second song which is now well known is composed of two popular rhymes about the negro and the white man, together with other verses composed to make an agreeable song and to make suitable rhymes and combinations. The effort to make a complete song is easily felt as one reads the words. The tune may be one that the singer happens to think of; it matters little which he chooses. The theme "Ain't it Hard?" is one that is common in negro life and song. He sings,—

"Ain't it hard, ain't it hard,
Ain't it hard to be a nigger, nigger, nigger?
Ain't it hard, ain't it hard,
For you can't git yo' money when it's due.

"Well, it make no difference,
How you make out yo' time;
White man sho' bring a
Nigger out behin'.

"Nigger an' white man
Playin' seven-ups;
Nigger win de money—
Skeered to pick 'em up.

"If a nigger git 'rested,
An' can't pay his fine,
They sho' send him out
To the county gang.

"A nigger went to a white man,
An' asked him for work;
White man told nigger,
'Yes, git out o' yo' shirt.'

"Nigger got out o' his shirt
An' went to work;
When pay-day come,
White man say he ain't work 'nuf.

"If you work all the week,
An' work all the time,
White man sho' to bring
Nigger out behin'."

The above song illustrates the method of making song out of rhymes, fragments, sayings, and improvised rhymes. The song as heard in its present form was collected in Newton County, Georgia. In a negro school in Mississippi, at a Friday afternoon "speaking," one of the children recited for a "speech" the stanza "Nigger an' white man playin' seven-ups," etc., exactly as it occurs in the song. The stanza ending "white man sho' bring nigger out behin"' incorporates the exact sentiment of an old ex-slave who maintained that in slavery and out of slavery the white man always brought the nigger out behind. So also it is a most common saying among the negroes that "if nigger git 'rested, he sho' be sent to gang." The other two stanzas are clearly made to order in the effort to make song and rhyme. However, this mixed assortment of verses and sentiments made a most attractive song when sung to a common tune.

Just as in the religious songs many verses are composed with the avowed intention of contributing a song, so in the secular songs original "poems" are turned into songs. One thrifty teacher wrote verses on the sinking of the "Maine," to be sung to the tune of "John Brown's Body," etc.; another, called "Hog-killin' Time," to be sung to the tune of "The Old Oaken Bucket." While such songs do not ordinarily become standard folk-songs, they illustrate the ease with which any sort of song may arise and become current. Thus the "songster" closes his description of a day's ploughing in the hot month of June:

"Dem skeeters dey callin' me cousin,
Dem gnats dey calls me frien',
Dem stingin' flies is buzzin',
Dis nigger done gone in."

Enough has been pointed out to show something of the environment of the negro songs. Further explanations and analysis must be made in connection with the songs themselves. It was pointed out that the negro's religious songs did not lend themselves to exact classification. The social songs can be classified with no more exactness than can the spirituals. The best that can be done is to arrange the songs according to a partial analysis of the subject-matter; but any such classification must be considered entirely flexible, just as, for instance, work-songs may be sung on occasions where no work is done, and just as any popular song may be adapted to become a work-song. Themes are freely mingled; verses, disjointed and inconsequential, are sung to many tunes and variations. Repetition of words and thought is thus most common. Each song may consist of a number of themes, which in turn are sung to other songs of other subject-matter. Thus it happens that it matters little what the song is called, provided it is given its proper setting. In the songs that follow, not infrequently a song is reported as having only three or four stanzas, whereas stanzas already reported are included by the singer until his song is as long as desired. The effort is made to avoid as much repetition as possible, and at the same time to report the songs in such a way as to do justice to the characteristic qualities of the song. Hence stanzas that have been given in one song will generally be omitted in others in which they are found. The dialect is that of the average singing; for the negro, in his social and secular songs, even more than in his religious songs, uses no consistent speech. The language is neither that of the whites nor that of the blacks, but a freely mingled and varied usage of dialect and common speech. Colloquialisms are frequent. The omission of pronouns and connectives, assyndeton in its freest usage, mark many negro verses, while the insertion of interjections and senseless phrases go to the other extreme. Such peculiarities may be best noted when the songs are studied. In the songs that follow, the words of the chorus are italicized. It should be remembered that in addition to beginning and ending the song with the regular chorus, each stanza is followed by the same chorus, thus doubling the length of the song.

Perhaps no person is sung more among the negroes than the homeless and friendless wanderer, with his disappointments in love and adventure; but here the negro sings of woman, and the desire for pity and love, as the accompanying feelings of the wanderer. These references must be added to those songs of the next division which tell of woman, sweetheart, and love. In no phases of negro life do the negro's self-feeling and self-pity manifest themselves more than in the plaintive appeals of the wandering negro. With his characteristic manner, he appeals to both whites and blacks for pity and assistance. As the tramp invents many ingenuous stories in order to arouse the pity of those whom he meets; as the cook tells of many misfortunes in the family, thinking thus to secure more provisions,—so these songs portray the feelings of the negro vagrant. He especially appeals to his women friends, and thus moves them to pity him. His appeals to their sympathy are usually effective; and the negro thus gets shelter, food, and attention. The wandering "songster" takes great pride in thus singing with skill some of his favorite songs; then he can boast of his achievements as "a bad man" with his "box." As he wanders from negro community to community, he finds lodging and solace. So the negroes at home take up the songs, and sing them to their companions, this constituting perhaps the most effective method of courtship. In these songs the roving, rambling thoughts of the negro are well brought out by the quick shifting of scenes; so his rambling and unsteady habits are depicted with unerring though unconscious skill.

8. Po' Boy Long Way from Home

In the following song, which is sometimes sung with the knife instrumental music described elsewhere, each stanza consists of a single line repeated three times.

|: I'm po' boy 'long way from home, :|
Oh, I'm po' boy 'long way from home.

|: I wish a 'scushion train would run, :|
Carry me back where I cum frum.

|: Come here, babe, an' sit on yo' papa's knee. :|

|: You brought me here an' let 'em throw me down. :|

|: I ain't got a frien' in dis town. :|

|: I'm out in de wide worl' alone. :|

|: If you mistreat me, you sho' will see it again. :|

My mother daid an' my father gone astray,
You never miss yo' mother till she done gone away.

|: Come 'way to Georgia, babe, to git in a home. :|

No need, O babe! try to throw me down,
A po' little boy jus' come to town.

I wish that ole engeneer wus dead,
Brought me 'way from my home.

Central gi' me long-distance phone,
Talk to my babe all night long.

If I die in State of Alabam',
Send my papa great long telegram.

In the same way the following "one-verse" songs are added:

|: Shake hands an' tell yo' babe good-by. :|

Bad luck in de family sho' God fell on me.
Have you got lucky, babe, an' then got broke?
I'm goin' 'way, comin' back some day.
Good ole boy, jus' ain't treated right.
I'm Tennessee raise, Georgia bohn.
I'm Georgia bohn, Alabama rais'.

9. On a Hog

Very much like the above song is "On a Hog," which means the condition of a "broke ho-bo" or tramp. By "broke" he means that usual state of being without money, or place to sleep, or food to eat. The song, like the above one, consists of lines repeated, without a chorus. There is little sense or connection in the words and verses. It represents the characteristic blending of all kinds of words to make some sort of song. At the same time its verses are classics in negro song.

|: Come 'way to Georgia to git on a hog, :| (*three times*)
Lord, come 'way to Georgia to git on a hog.

|: If you will go, babe, please don't go now, :|

|: But heave-a-hora, heave-a-hora, babe, heave! :|

|: I didn't come here to be nobody's dog. :|

|: I jest come here to stay a little while. :|

|: Well, I ain't goin' in Georgia long. :|

And with characteristic rhyme-making, a negro, after he had finished the few verses that he knew, began adding others. Said he,

"I didn't come here to be nobody's dog,
Jes' come here to git off'n dat hog."

10. Frisco Rag-Time

Even more disjointed and senseless is the song called, for convenience at the moment, "Frisco Rag-Time," "K. C.," or any other railroad name that happens to be desired. The song may be sung by man or woman or by both. It is expected that the viewpoint of man be indicated in the use of woman as the object, and woman's viewpoint be indicated in the reference to man. Such is sometimes the case; but usually the negro sings the song through, shifting from time to time from man to woman without so much as noticing the incongruity of meaning. In the verses which follow the scenes will be portrayed with clear vision by the negro singer.

|: Got up in the mornin', couldn't keep from cryin', :| (*three times*)
Thinkin' 'bout that brown-skin man o' mine.

|: Yonder comes that lovin' man o' mine, :| (*three times*)
Comin' to pay his baby's fine.

|: Well, I begged the jedge to low' my baby's fine, :| (*three times*)
Said de jedge done fine her, clerk done wrote it down.

|: Couldn't pay dat fine, so taken her to de jail. :| (*three times*)

|: So she laid in jail back to de wall, :| (*three times*)
Dis brown-skin man cause of it all.

|: No need babe tryin' to throw me down, :| (*three times*)
Cause I'm po' boy jus' come to town.

|: But if you don't want me, please don't dog me 'round, :| (*three times*)
Give me this money, sho' will leave this town.

|: Ain't no use tryin' to send me 'roun', :| (*three times*)
I got plenty money to pay my fine.

It will be observed that the last-named verses are practically the same as those given in other songs, and have no connection with the theme with which the song was begun; yet they formed an integral part of the song. In the same way single lines repeated four times are sung at length, although one would need to search diligently for the connection of meaning.

If you don't find me here, come to Larkey's dance.
If you don't find me there, come to ole Birmingham.
Ain't goin' to be in jungles long.
Yonder comes that easy-goin' man o' mine.
Ain't Jedge Briles a hard ole man!

"Jedge Briles" is only a local name given to Judge Broyles of Atlanta. His reputation is widely known among the negroes of Georgia. Instead of this name are often inserted the names of local characters, which serve to add concreteness to the song. So instead of Birmingham, the negro may sing Atlanta, Chattanooga, or any other city that ranks as a favorite among the negroes. Besides the feeling of the wayward wanderer, the scenes of court and jail are here pictured. Another division of song will group these scenes together. The difficulty of any sort of accurate classification of such a song is apparent. In addition to the words of the wandering man, this song gives also an insight into the reckless traits of the negro woman, which are clearly pictured in many of the negro love-songs.

11. Look'd down de Road

Mixed in just the same way, and covering a number of themes, utterly without sense-connection, the following song might well be a continuation of those just given. It is sung, however, to a different tune, and should be ranked as a separate song. Its form is not unlike that already cited,—repetition of a single line twice, or, in rare instances, a rhymed couplet.

Look'd down de road jes' far as I could see,
Well, the band did play "Nearer, my God, to Thee."

|: I got the blues, but too damn mean to cry. :|

Now when you git a dollar, you got a frien'
Will stick to you through thick an' thin.

I didn't come here fer to steal nobody's find.
I didn't jes' come here to serve my time.

I ask jailer, "Captain, how can I sleep?"
All 'round my bedside Police S. creeps.

The jailer said, "Let me tell you what's best:
Go 'way back in yo' dark cell an' take yo' rest."

If my kind man quit me, my main man throw me down;
I goin' run to de river, jump overboard 'n' drown.

Here, again, the local policeman is always spoken of as creeping around the bedside. It makes an interesting comparison to note the contrast between the police and the angels of the old wish-rhyme. Various versions of the above stanzas are given, some of which are far from elegant. So in the last stanza the negroes sing, "If my *good* man quit me, my *main* man throw me down." Profanity is inserted in the songs in proportion as the singer is accustomed to use it, or as the occasion demands or permits its use.

12. If I Die in Arkansas

Ridiculous and amusing in its pathos, "If I die in Arkansas" is typical and representative. It is quite impressive when sung with feeling. The negro gets a kind of satisfaction in believing that he is utterly forlorn, yet begs to be delivered from such a condition. He sings,—

"If I die in Arkansa',
Oh, if I die in Arkansa',
If I die in Arkansa',
Des ship my body to my mother-in-law.

|: "If my mother refuse me, ship it to my pa. :|

|: "If my papa refuse me, ship it to my girl. :|

"If my girl refuse me, shove me into de sea,
Where de fishes an' de whales make a fuss over me."

And then, after this wonderful rhyme and sentiment, the singer merges into plaintive appeal, and sings further,—

|: "Pore ole boy, long ways from home, :|
Out in dis wide worl' alone."

Suppose he should die! Suppose he has no friends! How he pities himself! Indeed, he is a forlorn being, and his emotions might well be wrought up.

13. Got No Where to Lay My Weary Head

Another song, also called "Po' Boy 'way from Home," repeats much the same sentiment; and besides many verses of other songs, the singer adds,—

|: "I want to see do my baby know right from wrong, O babe! :|

|: "Well, I got no where to lay my weary head, O babe! :|

|: "Well, a rock was my pillar las' night, O girl!" :|

Thus repetition makes a long song of a short one.

14. Baby, You Sho' Lookin' Warm

So in the next song, "Baby, You sho' lookin' Warm," three lines are alike, while the fourth varies only by an exclamation. This, too, is an appeal to the "baby" or sweetheart for pity and admission into the house.

|: Baby, you sho' lookin' warm, :| (*three times*)
O my babe! you sho' lookin' warm.

|: Baby, I'm feelin' so tired, :| (*three times*)
O my babe! I'm feelin' so tired.

|: Got no whar' to lay my weary head, :| (*three times*)
O my babe! got no whar' to lay my weary head.

|: Sometimes I'm fallin' to my face, :| (*three times*)
O my babe! sometimes I'm fallin' to my face.

I'm goin' whar' de water drinks like wine. (*as before*)

Gwine whar' I never been befo'. (*as before*)

Baby, I love the clothes you wear. (*as before*)

Whar' in de worl' my baby gone? (*as before*)

Gone away never come back no more. (*as before*)

15. Take Your Time

"Take your Time" represents the negro in a more tranquil and independent state of mind. It matters little what the circumstances may be, he does not care: there's no hurry, so "take your time." And these circumstances are varied enough: from the home to the court he is rambling aimlessly about.

Baby, baby, didn't you say,
You'd work for me both night and day?
Take your time, take your time.

Baby, baby, don't you know
I can git a girl anywhere I go?
Take yo' time, take yo' time.

Baby, baby, can't you see
How my girl git away from me?
Take yo' time, take yo' time.

Went down country see my frien',
In come yaller dog burnin' the win',
Take yo' time, take yo' time.

'Tain't but the one thing grieve my mind:
Goin' 'way, babe, an' leave you behin',
Take yo' time, take yo' time.

Carried me 'roun' to de court-house do',
Place wher' I never had been befo',
Take yo' time, take yo' time.

Jedge an' jury all in de stan',
Great big law-books in dere han',
Take yo' time, take yo' time.

Went up town 'bout four o'clock,
Rapt on door, an' door was locked,
Take yo' time, take yo' time.

I'm goin' back to de sunny South,
Where sun shines on my honey's house,
Take yo' time, take yo' time.

16. 'Tain't Nobody's Bizness but My Own

Jingling rhymes are sought at the sacrifice of meaning and the sense of the song. Rhymes are thus more easily remembered. If the sentiment of the subject of the song appeals to a negro, he may take it and make his own rhymes, departing from the original version. The frequent omission of words, and the mixing of dialect and modern slang, usually result. " 'Tain't Nobody's Bizness but my Own" represents the more reckless temperament of the wanderer.

Baby, you ought-a tole me,
Six months before you roll me,
I'd had some other place to go,
'Tain't nobody's bizness but my own.

Sometimes my baby gets boozy,
An' foolish 'bout her head,
An' I can't rule her,
'Tain't nobody's bizness but my own.

I'm goin' to happy Hollow,
Where I can make a dollar,
'Tain't nobody's bizness but my own.

I want to see my Hanner
Turn tricks in my manner,
'Tain't nobody's bizness but my own.

Don't care if I don't make a dollar,
So I wear my shirt an' collar,
'Tain't nobody's bizness but my own.

17. I'm Going 'Way

The swaggering tramp decides to leave the town, as indeed he is often doing; but he expects to come back again. He looks forward to the adventures of the trip with pleasure, not with fear, although he knows he must ride the rods, go without victuals, and sleep where he may. He sings,—

"I'm goin' 'way, comin' back some day,
I'm goin' 'way, comin' back some day,
I'm just from the country, come to town—
A Zoo-loo-shaker from my head on down.
If I git drunk, who's goin' ter carry me home?
Brown-skin woman, she's chocolate to de bone."

18. O Babe!

Thus he visualizes and grows boisterous. He begins again the life of the "rounder," whose adventures are sung in other songs. In anticipation of his future adventures, the negro continues,—

"Late every evenin' 'bout half pas' three,
I hire smart coon to read the news to me.
O babe, O my babe, O my babe!

"O babe, O babe, O my babe! take a one on me,
An' my padhna', too, that's the way sports do,
O babe, O my babe, O my babe!

"Well you talk 'bout one thing, you talk 'bout another,
But 'f you talk 'bout me, gwine talk 'bout yo' mother.
O babe, O my babe, O my babe!

19. Sweet Tennessee

But this is not all the easy times he is going to have. To be sure, he will not work: he will have his own way, where the "water drinks like wine," and where the "wimmins" are "stuck" on him. He bids farewell.

"Come an' go to sweet Tennessee,
Where de money grows on trees,
Where the rounders do as they please, babe!
Come an' go to sweet Tennessee.

"Come an' go to sweet Tennessee,
Where the wimmins all live at ease,
Where the rounders do as they please, babe!
Come an' go to sweet Tennessee.

"Come an' go to sweet Tennessee,
Where the wimmins do as they please,
Where the money grows on trees, babe!
Come an' go to sweet Tennessee."

As woman occupies a prominent place in the songs of the wanderer, so woman and sweetheart occupy the most prominent part in the majority of negro social songs. The negro's conception of woman as seen in his songs has been observed. There are few exalted opinions of woman, little permanent love for sweetheart, or strong and pure love emotions. Woman and sensual love, physical characteristics and actions and jealousy, are predominant. The singer is not different from the wanderer who figured as the hero in the class of songs just given. Woman here is not unlike woman there. The negro sings,—

20. I Ain't Bother Yet

I got a woman an' sweetheart, too,
If woman don't love me, sweetheart do,
Yet, I ain't bother yet, I ain't bother yet.

Honey babe, I can't see
How my money got away from me,
Yet I ain't bother yet, ain't bother yet.

Or the woman sings in retort to the husband who thus sings, and who does not support her properly, or has failed to please her in some trifle,

I got a husband, a sweetheart, too,
  Ain't goin' to rain no mo',
Husband don't love me, sweetheart do,
  Ain't goin' to rain no mo'.

21. I'm on My Last Go-Round

But the negro lover sometimes gets more or less despondent, after which he assures himself that he does not care. The theme of rejected love is strong, but the sorrow lasts only a short time. While this feeling lasts, however, the lover, in his jealousy, will do many things for his sweetheart, and often is unwilling to be out of her presence. Sometimes he is determined.

|: It's no use you sendin' no word, :|
  It's no use you sendin' or writin' no letter,
  I'm comin' home pay-day.

|: I'm on my last go-round, :| (*three times*)
  God knows Albirdie won't write to me.

|: There's mo' pretty girls 'an one, :|
  Swing an' clang an' don't git lost,
  There's mo' pretty girls 'an one.

22. Learn Me to Let All Women Alone

The negro is constantly singing that woman will get him into trouble; and such is the case. In a large per cent. of his quarrels and fights the cause of the trouble is the "woman in the case." It is she who gets his money and makes him do all manner of trifling things to please her fancy. He then claims that she will turn from him as soon as she has got all he has. Such is, in fact, true. It is not surprising to hear the song "Learn me to let all Women alone" as the expression of a disgruntled laborer.

One was a boy, an' one was a girl;
If I ever specs to see 'em again,
I'll see 'em in de other worl':
Learn me to let all women alone.

All I hope in this bright worl',
If I love anybody, don't let it be a girl:
Learn me to let all women alone.

Firs' girl I love, she gi' me her right han',
She's quit me in de wrong fer anoder man:
Learn me to let all women alone.

Woman is a good thing, an' a bad thing too,
They quit in the wrong an' start out bran'-new:
Learn me to let all women alone.

I got up early nex' mornin', to meet fo' day train,
Goin' up the railroad to find me a man:
Learn me to let all women alone.

23. O My Babe! Won't You Come Home

The negro sings, "I don't know what I'll do! Oh, I don't know what I'll do!" "Oh, I'll take time to bundle up my clothes! Oh, I'll take time to bundle up my clothes," and he is off; but he is soon involved again, and sings his promiscuous allegiance.

"I love my babe and wouldn't put her out of doors,
I'd love to see her kill a kid wid fohty-dollar suit o' clothes,
O my babe! won't you come home?

"Some people give you nickel, some give you dime;
I ain't goin' give you frazzlin' thing, you ain't no girl o' mine.
O my babe! won't you come home?

"Remember, babe, remember givin' me yo' han';
When you come to marry, I may be yo' man.
O my babe! won't you come home?

"Went to the sea, sea look so wide,
Thought about my babe, hung my head an' cried.
O my babe! won't you come home?"

24. Make Me a Palat on de Flo'

Perhaps the lover is again turned out of doors, and pines around the house. He studies up various means to regain the affections of his lady-love, but finds it difficult. "That's all right, treat me mean, treat me wrong, babe. Fare you well forever mo', how would you like to have a luvin' girl turn you out o' doors?" he sings, and pretends to leave. But true to the negro proverb, "Nigger ain't gone ever time he say good-by:" he returns again to sing,—

"Make me a palat on de flo',
Make it in de kitchen behin' de do'.

"Oh, don't turn good man from yo' do',
May be a frien', babe, you don't know.

"Oh, look down dat lonesome lan',
Made me a palat on de flo'.

"Oh, de reason I love Sarah Jane,
Made me a palat on de flo'."

In another strain the lover sings promiscuously,—

"O Jane! love me lak you useter,
O Jane! chew me lak you useter,
Ev'y time I figger, my heart gits bigger,
Sorry, sorry, can't be yo' piper any mo'."

So, too, he sings "Ev'y time I dodge her, my heart gits larger."

25. Can't Be Your Turtle Any Mo'

Somewhat like it is the song "Can't be your Turtle any mo'," localized to apply to Atlanta, Memphis, or other specific places.

Goin' to Atlanta, goin' to ride de rod,
Goin' to leave my babe in de hands o' God,
Sorry, sorry, can't be your turtle any mo'.

Goin' up town, goin' hurry right back,
Honey got sumpin' I certainly lak',
Sorry, sorry, can't be yo' warbler any mo'.

26. No More Good Time

While there is much repetition in thought in the songs of woman and sweetheart, they are very true to actual life, and depict with accuracy the common scenes and speeches of the negroes. The morals of the negro are also reflected. Some of his ideals of love and "a good time" are indicated. "No More Good Time" tells of a common scene.

No more good time, woman, like we used to have,
Police knockin' woman at my back do'.

Meet me at the depot, bring my dirty clothes,
Meet me at depot, woman, when the train comes down;

For I goin' back to leave you, ain't comin' back no mo';
You treated me so dirty, ain't comin' back no mo'.

I got a little black woman, honey, an' her name's Mary Lou,
She treat me better, baby, heap better than you.

The negro adds much zest and fun to his song when he introduces local characters. In the above line it is "Police Johnson, woman, knockin' at de do'," or in other localities it is the name of the most dreaded officer. The negroes sing these and laugh heartily, boasting now and then of fortunate escapes.

27. Diamon' Joe

Very much like the above in general tone, but sung by a woman, "Diamon' Joe" typifies the usual custom common in every negro community. It is a love-song.

Diamon' Joe, you better come an' git me:
Don't you see my man done quit?
Diamon' Joe com'n git me.

Diamon' Joe he had a wife, they parted every night;
When the weather it got cool,
Ole Joe he come back to that black gal.

But time come to pass,
When old Joe quit his last,
An' he never went to see her any mo'.

28. Baby, What Have I Done?

"Baby, what have I done?" introduces the various scenes of negro love-life. The same wail of "knockin' at de do" ' is heard again and again,—a hint at infidelity, which is so often sung in the next few songs. The simple life and simple thought appear primitive. What if this poetry means as much to him as any other? No other ideals would satisfy him, or even appeal to him.

Late las' night an' night befo',
Heard such a knockin' at my do',
Jumped up in stockin' feet, skipped across the flo',
Baby, don't never knock at my do' no mo'.

|: *Oh me, oh my! baby, what have I done?* :|

Where were you las' Saturday night,
When I lay sick in my bed?
You down town wid some other ole girl,
Wasn't here to hold my head.

|: Ain't it hard to love an' not be loved? :| (*four times*)

Other verses of one long line are divided into two short lines or repeated each four times to make the stanza. The art of negro singing is brought out best in his repetition.

It's ninety-six miles from Birmingham
I tramped it day by day.

It's fifteen cents' wuth o' morphine,
A dollar's all I crave.

I didn't bring nuthin' in this bright worl',
Nuthin' I'll carry away.

I laid my head in bar-room do',
Ain't goin' to get drunk no mo'.

Han' me down my grip-sack,
An' all my ole dirty clothes.

If my baby ask for me,
Tell her I boun' to go.

29. Things Ain't Same, Babe, Since I Went 'Way

Both men and women appear changeable in their affections. A husband and wife may quarrel the first of the week, separate, vow that they will never speak again; the latter part of the week may find them as loving as ever. This does not happen one week, but many times. A negro man will often give his entire week's or month's wages in order to pacify his wife who has threatened to go live with some other man. She in turn spends the money, and begins to quarrel again. In the same way the wife may often beg to be received back after she has left him; she is often received, sometimes with a beating, sometimes not at all. A typical appeal of these characters is sung:

Things ain't same, babe, since I went 'way,
Now I return, please let me stay;
I'm sorry I lef' you in this worl' alone,
I'm on my way, babe, I'm comin' home.

30. Baby, Let Me Bring My Clothes Back Home

Another appeal of the husband to his wife is a little more forceful. It is the present moment that counts with the average negro: he will easily promise to do anything to get out of an emergency or to get into favor. So the negro often makes promises of fidelity, if only he will be given another chance. The picture of the big, brawny negro thus whining before his "woman's" door is an amusing one. It is, however, characteristic in its adaptation of the "coon" song into a negro song:

The burly coon, you know,
He packed his clothes to go,
Well, he come back las' night,
His wife said, "Honey, I'm tired o' coon,
I goin' to pass for white."

But the coon got mad,
He's 'bliged to play bad,
Because his color was black;
O my lovin' baby! don't you make me go;
I git a job, if you let me, sho'.

I'll wuk both night an' day,
An' let you draw my pay;
Baby, let me bring my clothes back home!
When you kill chicken, save me the bone;
When you bag beer, give me the foam.

I'll work both night an' day,
An' let you draw the pay;
Baby, let me bring my clothes back home;
When she make them strange remarks,
He look surprise—goin' roll them white eyes,
Goin' cry, baby, don't make me go!

31. Long and Tall an' Chocolate to the Bone

One of the most common descriptions, and one of the most complimentary to the negro woman, as found in negro songs, is "chocolate to the bone." The negro often makes trouble for the meddler in his home. Here arises many of the capital crimes of the negroes. Jealousy runs riot among both men and women. In the following song a hint is given of the boasting spirit of the negro:

Well, I'm goin' to buy me a little railroad of my own,
Ain't goin' to let nobody ride but the chocolate to the bone.

Well, I goin' to buy me a hotel of my own,
Ain't goin' to let nobody eat but the chocolate to the bone.

|: *She's long an' tall an' chocolate to the bone,* :|

Well, I goin' to start a little *graveyard* of my own,
If you don't, ole nigger, let my woman alone.

She's long an' tall an' chocolate to the bone,
She make you married man, then leave yo' home.

32. Goin' Back to Sweet Memphis, Tennessee

In much the same way, now the woman, now the man, sings back at each other. In the first stanza of the song "Yo' Man," the woman is supposed to be talking; the man often sings the song, however, as he does all of them. It is also interpreted to be the words of one man to his wife, and also of one woman to another. The song is well mixed.

|: Well, if that's yo' man, you'd better buy a lock an' key, O babe! :|
An' stop yo' man from runnin' after me-e-e.

|: *Well, I goin' back to sweet Memphis, Tennessee, O babe!* :|
Where de good-lookin' wimmins take on over me—make a fuss over me.

Now, a good-lookin' man can git a home anywaher' he go,
The reason why is, the wimmins tell me so.

She change a dollar an' give me a lovin' dime,
I'll see her when her trouble like mine.

33. Started to Leave

The sense of humor is very marked in many of the verses sung by the negroes. The commonplace, matter-of-fact statement in the following song is noticeable. Says the negro, "Yes,"

"I'm goin' 'way, goin' 'way,
Goin' sleep under the trees till weather gits warmer,
Well, me an' my baby can't agree,
Oh, that's the reason I'm goin' to leave."

But, as in other cases, the negro does not stay long. Perhaps it is too cold under the trees for him; perhaps the song has it all wrong, anyway. But the negro again sings,—

"Well, I started to leave, an' got 'way down the track,
Got to thinkin' bout my woman, come runnin' back, O babe!

"She have got a bad man, an' he's as bad as hell, I know,
For ev'body, sho' God, tell me so.

"I thought I'd tell you what yo' nigger woman'll do,
She have another man an' play sick on you."

34. I Couldn't Git In

Thus, although the singer begins, as he often does, with the better thoughts of the woman, he ends with the usual abuse and distrust. This spirit of infidelity is unfortunately common among the negroes. With some it is a matter of no concern, for what does it matter to them? with others it is a matter of anger and revenge; while still others are jealously troubled about it. What has already been touched upon in the songs given may be shown further in "I couldn't git in."

Lawd, I went to my woman's do',
Jus' lak I bin goin' befo':
"I got my all-night trick, baby,
An' you can't git in."

"Come back 'bout half pas' fo',
If I'm done, I'll open de do', (or let you know)
Got my all-night trick, baby,
An' you can't git in."

I keep a rappin' on my woman's do',
Lak I never had been dere befo';
She got a midnight creeper dere,
An' I couldn't git in.

"Buddy, you oughter to do lak me,
Git a good woman, let the cheap ones be,
Fur dey always got a midnight creeper,
An' you can't come in.

"Buddy, stop an' let me tell you
What yo' woman'll do;
She have 'nuther man in, play sick on you,
She got all-night creeper, Buddy,
An' you can't git in.

"You go home; well, she layin' in bed,
With red rag tied all 'round her head;
She done had fo'-day creeper in here,
Dat's de reason you couldn't git in."

In the same way other verses are sung: "Keep a knockin', can't come in, I got company an' you can't come in," or "You can't come in dis do'."

35. What, Stirrin' Babe

The singer uses the common slang "fallin' den" for his bed. As he has sung of his love and jealousies, so he sings of varied affection and infidelity, but with little serious regret.

"Went up town 'bout four o'clock,
What, stirrin' babe, stirrin' babe?
When I got there, door was locked:
What stir'd babe, what stir'd babe?

"Went to de window an' den peeped in:
What, stirrin' babe, stirrin' babe?
Somebody in my fallin' den—
What, stirrin' babe, stirrin' babe?"

The woman tells the "creeper" that he had best be watchful while he is about her house. At the same time, besides his general rowdyism, he is perhaps eating all the provisions in the house. She sings,—

|: Don't you let my honey catch you here—:| (*three times*)
He'll kill you dead jus' sho's you born.

36. Hop Right

It will thus be seen that the songs of the most characteristic type are far from elegant. Nor are they dignified in theme or expression. They will appear to the cultured reader a bit repulsive, to say the least. They go beyond the interesting point to the trite and repulsive themes. Nor can a great many of the common songs that are too inelegant to include be given at all. But these are folk-songs current among the negroes, and as such are powerful comment upon the special characteristics of the group. A few of the shorter themes thus sung will illustrate further.

|: Hop right, goin' to see my baby Lou, :|
Goin' to walk an' talk wid my honey,
Goin' to hug an' kiss my honey,
Hop right, my baby!

The negro does not mind that his comment may be undignified, or that it may be injurious to personal feelings or race opinion. Sings he,—

"I wouldn't have yellow gal,
Tell you de reason why:
Her neck so long, 'fraid she never die.

"I wouldn't have a black gal,
Tell you de reason why:
Her hair so kinky, she break every comb I buy."

37. If You Want to Go A Courtin'

More original and satisfying in sentiment and rhyme and sensuous pictures is the following:

If you want to go a courtin', I sho' you where to go,
Right down yonder in de house below.

Clothes all dirty an' ain't got no broom,
Ole dirty clothes all hangin' in de room.

Ask'd me to table, thought I'd take a seat,
First thing I saw was big chunk o' meat.

Big as my head, hard as a maul,
Ash-cake, corn-bread, bran an' all.

38. If You Want to Marry

Another that sounds like some of the songs used in children's games in the Colonial days is "Marry Me." The song has come to be thought a negro song, but is apparently a form of the old rhymes, "If you will marry, marry, marry; If you will marry me," or "For I want to marry, marry, marry you;" "Soldier, will you marry me?" The negro sings,—

"If you want to marry, come an' marry me-e-e,
Silk an' satin you shall wear, but trouble you shall see-e-e.

"If you want to marry, marry the sailor's daughter,
Put her in a coffee-pot and sen' her 'cross the water.

"I marry black gal, she was black, you know,
For when I went to see her, she look like a crow-ow,
She look like a crow-ow-ow."

39. Honey, Take a One on Me

A variation of the well-known little song, "Honey, take a One on Me," has a great number of verses that have become popular, and are undoubtedly negro verses. Most of these, however, are not suitable for publication. An idea may be given of the song.

Comin' down State Street, comin' down Main,
Lookin' for de woman dat use cocaine,
Honey, take a one on me!

Goin' down Peter Street, comin' down Main,
Lookin' for de woman ain't got no man,
Honey, take a one on me!

40. Don't Hit That Woman

One other illustration may be given, to show this mental attitude toward a woman:

Don't hit that woman, I tell you why:
Well, she got heart-trouble an' I scared she die.

That shot got her, how do you know?
For my woman she told me so.

Now, if you hit that woman, I tell you fine,
She will give you trouble all the time.

41. I Love That Man

More serious and of much better sentiment is the lover's song, ordinarily sung as the appeal of a woman.

|: I love that man, O God! I do,
I love him till the day he die; :|

|: If I thought that he didn't love me,
I'd eat morphine an' die. :|

: If I had listened to what mamma said,
I wouldn't a been here to-day; :|

: But bein' so young, I throwed
That young body o' mine away. :|

|: Look down po' lonesome road,
Hacks all dead in line. :|

: Some give nickel, some give dime,
To bury dis po' body o' mine. :|

42. Kelly's Love

In "Kelly's Love" the note of disappointed love is sounded:

|: *Love, Kelly's love,* :| (*three times*)
You broke de heart o' many a girl,
You never break dis heart o' mine.

|: When I wo' my aprons low, :| (*three times*)
Couldn't keep you from my do'.

|: Now I weahs my aprons high, :| (*three times*)
Sca'cely ever see you passin' by.

|: Now I weahs my aprons to my chin, :| (*three times*)
You pass my do', but can't come in.

|: See what Kelly's love have done. :| (*three times*)
See what Kelly's love have done.

|: If I had listened to what my mamma said, :| (*three times*)
I would a been at home in mamma's bed.

43. My Love for You Is All I Knew

Nearer the simple longing of a sincere affection is the chorus "Farewell." This conception has been found in the common mixed song that is current:

|: My love for you is all I knew, :| (*three times*)
Hope I will see you again.

|: Farewell, my darling, farewell! :| (*three times*)
Hope I will see you again.

44. Thought I Heard That K. C.

The negro grows imaginative when he thinks of things absent. In his religious song it is Heaven and the angels that bring forth his best expressions. He is an idealist, and utopianism is perhaps only the childlike imagery of fairy fancies. So in his social songs he tells of the good times he has had and is going to have. He does not sing so much of the present: he sings of dangers he has escaped. In the same way he longs to see his sweetheart while he is away from her. Says he, "My honey might be far from home; ask central to gi' me long-distance phone."

Thought I heard that K. C. whistle blow,
Blow lak she never blow befo'.

How long has Frisco train been gone?
Dat's train carried my baby home.

Look down de Southern road an' cry,
Babe, look down de Southern road an' cry.

45. Sweet, Forget Me Not

The negro looks longingly for the train and the time when he will have money enough to go back "home." Pay-day will come, and for a time he will be happy. Sometimes he thinks of all good times in the future. Sometimes, however, he sings plaintively that they are gone.

|: O girl, O girl! what have I done?
Sweet, forget me not. :| (*three times*)

I've got a girl dat's on de way,
Sweet, forget me not.

Times ain't like dey use ter be,
Sweet, forget me not.

Times have been, won't be no more,
Sweet, forget me not.

Nowhere is the negro more characteristic than in his wanton and reckless moods. Nothing pleases this type of negro fancy more than deeds of bravado and notoriety. He loves to tell of them and hear them recited. He is apparently at his best on such occasions. His self-feeling in its positive state is given gratification, and his vivid imagination easily makes him the hero of the hour. The feeling of rowdyism is thus encouraged. The notorious character is thus sung as the hero of the race: his deeds are marvelled at. Perhaps he is the most interesting figure within the whole field of activities. Certainly he is a distinct character, and has a tremendous influence upon the conduct of his people. He is admired by young and old; and those who do not approve of his deeds or example marvel at his powers.

46. Stagolee

"Stagolee" must have been a wonderful fellow! though not so much dreaded as "Railroad Bill" and some others. Here the negro sings in his best vein.

Stagolee, Stagolee, what's dat in yo' grip?
Nothin' but my Sunday clothes, I'm goin' to take a trip,
O dat man, bad man, Stagolee done come.

Stagolee, Stagolee, where you been so long?
I been out on de battle fiel' shootin' an' havin' fun,
O dat man, bad man, Stagolee done come.

Stagolee was a bully man, an' ev'y body knowed,
When dey seed Stagolee comin', to give Stagolee de road,
O dat man, bad man, Stagolee done come.

The refrain "*O dat man, bad man, Stagolee done come*" is sung at the end of each stanza, and adds much to the charm of the song, giving characteristic thought to the words, and rhythmical swing to the music. The singer continues his narration, adding the refrain to each stanza,—

Stagolee started out, he give his wife his han',
"Good-by, darlin', I'm goin' to kill a man."

Stagolee killed a man an' laid him on de flo',
What's dat he kill him wid? Dat same ole fohty-fo'.

Stagolee killed a man an' laid him on his side,
What's dat he kill him wid? Dat same ole fohty-five.

Out of house an' down de street Stagolee did run,
In his hand he held a great big smokin' gun.

Stagolee, Stagolee, I'll tell you what I'll do,
If you'll git me out'n dis trouble I'll do as much for you.

Ain't it a pity, ain't it a shame?
Stagolee was shot, but he don't want no name.

Stagolee, Stagolee, look what you done done,
Killed de best ole citerzen; now you'll hav' to be hung.

Stagolee cried to de jury an' to de judge: Please don't take my life,
I have only three little children an' one little lovin' wife,
O dat man, bad man, Stagolee done come.

47. Stagolee

The above version is more usually sung in Mississippi, Louisiana, and Tennessee, though it is known in Alabama and Georgia, besides being sung by the negro vagrants all

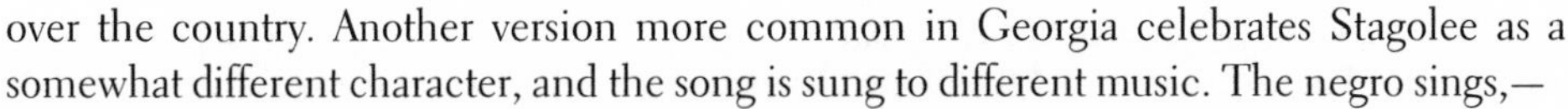

over the country. Another version more common in Georgia celebrates Stagolee as a somewhat different character, and the song is sung to different music. The negro sings,—

I got up one mornin' jes' 'bout four o'clock;
Stagolee an' big bully done have one finish' fight:
What 'bout? All 'bout dat raw-hide Stetson hat.

Stagolee shot Bully; Bully fell down on de flo',
Bully cry out: "Dat fohty-fo' hurts me so."
Stagolee done killed dat Bully now.

Sent for de wagon, wagon didn't come,
Loaded down wid pistols an' all dat gatlin' gun,
Stagolee done kill dat Bully now.

Some giv' a nickel, some giv' a dime,
I didn't give a red copper cent, 'cause he's no friend o' mine,
Stagolee done kill dat Bully now.

Carried po' Bully to cemetary, people standin' 'round,
When preacher say Amen, lay po' body down,
Stagolee done kill dat Bully now.

Fohty dollah coffin, eighty dollah hack,
Carried po' man to cemetary but failed to bring him back,
Ev'y body been dodgin' Stagolee.

The scenes of Stagolee's activities are representative of this type of negro life. From the home to the cemetery he has gone the road of many a negro. Sometimes the man killed is at a picnic or public gathering, sometimes elsewhere. The scenes of the burial, with its customs, are but a part of the life: hence they are portrayed with equal diligence.

48. Railroad Bill

But Stagolee has his equal, if not his superior, in the admiration of the negro. "Railroad Bill" has had a wonderful career in song and story. The negro adds his part, and surpasses any other in his portrayal of this hero of the track. One must take all the versions of the song in order to appreciate fully the ideal of such a character. In the first song that follows, the reader will note that after the theme is once in the mouth of the singer, it matters little what the song is. The effort is to sing something about "Bill," and to make this conform to the general idea; and at the same time it must rhyme. Here is the song, and a wonderful picture it is:

Some one went home an' tole my wife
All about—well, my pas' life,
It was that bad Railroad Bill.

Railroad Bill, Railroad Bill,
He never work, an' he never will,
Well, it's that bad Railroad Bill.

Railroad Bill so mean an' so bad,
Till he tuk ev'ything that farmer had,
It's that bad Railroad Bill.

I'm goin' home an' tell my wife,
Railroad Bill try to take my life,
It's that bad Railroad Bill.

Railroad Bill so desp'rate an' so bad,
He take ev'ything po' womens had,
An' it's that bad Railroad Bill.

49. It's That Bad Railroad Bill

With all these crimes to his credit, it is high time that some one was going after Railroad Bill. The singer starts on his journey as quickly as he can, but has to make many trips.

I went down on Number One,
Railroad Bill had jus' begun.
It's lookin' for Railroad Bill.

I come up on Number Two,
Railroad Bill had jus' got through,
It's that bad Railroad Bill.

I caught Number Three and went back down the road,
Railroad Bill was marchin' to an' fro.
It's that bad Railroad Bill.

An' jus' as I caught that Number Fo',
Somebody shot at me wid a fohty-fo'.
It's that bad Railroad Bill.

I went back on Number Five,
Goin' to bring him back, dead or alive.
Lookin' for Railroad Bill.

When I come up on Number Six,
All the peoples had done got sick,
Lookin' for Railroad Bill.

When I went down on Number Seven,
All the peoples wish'd they's in heaven,
A-lookin' for Railroad Bill.

I come back on Number Eight,
The folks say I was a minit too late,
It's lookin' for Railroad Bill.

When I come back on Number Nine,
Folks say, "You're just in time
To catch that Railroad Bill."

When I got my men, they amounted to ten,
An' that's when I run po' Railroad Bill in,
An' that was last of po' Railroad Bill.

50. It's Lookin' for Railroad Bill

But that was *not* the last of Railroad Bill; for the singer had only imagined that he was the hero to "down him." Railroad Bill soon appears again, and now he is worse than before. The next version differs only slightly from the foregoing one. One must remember that the chorus line follows each couplet, and the contrast in meaning makes a most interesting song.

Railroad Bill mighty bad man,
Shoot dem lights out o' de brakeman's han',
It's lookin' fer Railroad Bill.

Railroad Bill mighty bad man,
Shoot the lamps all off the stan',
An' it's lookin' for Railroad Bill.

First on table, nex' on wall,
Ole corn whiskey cause of it all,
It's lookin' fer Railroad Bill.

Ole McMillan had a special train,
When he got there wus a shower of rain,
Wus lookin' fer Railroad Bill.

Ev'ybody tole him he better turn back,
Railroad Bill wus goin' down track,
An' it's lookin' fer Railroad Bill.

Well, the policemen all dressed in blue,
Comin' down sidewalk two by two,
Wus lookin' fer Railroad Bill.

Railroad Bill had no wife,
Always lookin' fer somebody's life,
An' it's lookin' fer Railroad Bill.

Railroad Bill was the worst ole coon,
Killed McMillan by de light o' de moon,
It's lookin' fer Railroad Bill.

Ole Culpepper went up on Number Five,
Goin' bring him back, dead or alive,
Wus lookin' fer Railroad Bill.

Standin' on corner didn't mean no harm,
Policeman grab me by my arm,
Wus lookin' fer Railroad Bill.

The negroes sing different forms of these verses, as they are suggested at the moment; so they add others or omit parts. Also are sung:

MacMillan had a special train,
When he got there, it was spring.

Two policemen all dressed in blue
Come down street in two an' two.

Railroad Bill led a mighty bad life,
Always after some other man's wife.

Railroad Bill went out Wes',
Thought he had dem cowboys bes'.

Railroad Bill mighty bad man,
Kill McGruder by de light o' the moon.

51. Right on Desperado Bill

It is not surprising that a song so popular as "Railroad Bill" should find its way into others of similar type. Another version of the same song has a separate chorus, to be sung after each stanza. This chorus, of which there are two forms, adds recklessness to the theme. Another achievement is given the desperado; and he combines gambling, criminal tendencies, and his general immorality, in one. The following version is somewhat mixed, but is known as "Railroad Bill:"

Railroad Bill was mighty sport,
Shot all buttons off high sheriff's coat,
Den hollered, "*Right on desperado Bill!*"
Lose, lose—I don't keer,
If I win, let me win lak' a man,
If I lose all my money,
I'll be gamblin' for my honey,
Ev'y man ought to know when he lose.

Lose, lose, I don't keer,
If I win, let me win lak' a man,
Lost fohty-one dollars tryin' to win a dime,
Ev'y man plays in tough luck some time.

Honey babe, honey babe, where have you been so long?
I ain't been happy since you been gone,
Dat's all right, dat's all right, honey babe.

Honey babe, honey babe, bring me de broom,
De lices an' chinches 'bout to take my room,
O my baby, baby, honey, chile!

Honey babe, honey babe, what in de worl' is dat?
Got on tan shoes an' black silk hat,
Honey babe, give it all to me.

Talk 'bout yo' five an' ten dollar bill,
Ain't no Bill like ole desperado Bill,
Says, Right on desperado Bill.

Railroad Bill went out west,
Met ole Jesse James, thought he had him best,
But Jesse laid ole Railroad Bill.

Honey babe, honey babe, can't you never hear?
I wants a nuther nickel to git a glass o' beer,
Dat's all right, honey babe, dat's all right.

Some of the verses just given are far from elegant; others still less elegant must be omitted. Some conception of popular standards of conduct and dress, social life and the home, may be gained from the song, in addition to the now familiar character of "Railroad Bill."

52. Lookin' for That Bully of This Town

In most communities there is one or more notorious characters among the negroes. Often these are widely known throughout the State, and they are familiar names to the police. Sometimes they are known for the most part to the negroes. Such characters, noted for their rowdyism and recklessness, sometimes with a criminal record, are usually called "bullies." To be sure, "Stagolee," "Railroad Bill," "Eddy Jones," and the others, were "bullies," but they were special cases. The song "I'm lookin' for the Bully of this Town" represents a more general condition. It is rich in portrayals of negro life and thought.

Monday I was 'rested, Tuesday I was fined,
Sent to chain gang, done serve my time,
Still I'm lookin' for that bully of this town.

The bully, the bully, the bully can't be found,
If I fin' that bully, goin' to lay his body down,
I'm lookin' for that bully of this town.

The police up town they're all scared,
But if I fin' that bully, I goin' to lay his body 'way,
For I'm lookin' for that bully of this town.

I'm goin' down on Peter Street;
If I fin' that bully, will be bloody meet,
For I'm lookin' for that bully of this town.

I went down town the other day,
I ask ev'ybody did that bully come this way,
I wus lookin' fer that bully of this town.

Oh, the gov'ner of this State offer'd one hundred dollars reward,
To any body's arrested that bully boy,
I sho' lookin' for dat bully of this town.

Well, I found that bully on a Friday night,
I told that bully I's gwine to take his life,
I found dat bully of this town.

I pull out my gun an' begin to fire,
I shot that bully right through the eye,
An' I kill that bully of this town.

Now all the wimmins come to town all dressed in red,
When they heard that bully boy was dead,
An' it was the last of that bully of this town.

What a picture the song gives of the bully and his pursuer! The boasting braggart sees himself the hero of the whole community, but chiefly among the women. He is better than the police: they will even thank him for his valor. The governor will give him his reward. Everybody he meets he asks about the bully boy, and takes on a new swagger. What satisfaction he gets from it! Perhaps he too will be a bully. The scene of the shooting, the reaching for the pistol, and the "laying-down" of the bully's body,—these offer unalloyed satisfaction to the singer. Every word becomes pregnant with new meaning and feeling; and invariably he must remember that his deeds are lauded, and he is the hero among the "wimmins" from the country round about. His picture would never be complete without this. Altogether it is a great song, and defies a superior picture.

53. Eddy Jones

Other notorious characters are sung with the same satisfaction. The characteristic pleasure and oblivion of the time accompany the singing. While at work, one may sing the words, whistle the tunes, and visualize the picture, thus getting a richer field of vision. When alone, the negro gets much satisfaction out of songs like those here given. Likewise such songs are sung in groups, at which times the singers talk and laugh, jeer one another, and retort, thus varying the song. "Eddy Jones" seems very similar in character to "Stagolee."

Slow train run thru' Arkansas,
   Carryin' Eddy Jones.

Eddy died with a special in his hand,
   Eddy Jones, Eddy Jones.

Eddy Jones call for the coolin'-board,
   Lawdy, lawdy, lawd!

Eddy Jones look'd 'round an' said,
"Man that kill'd me won't have no luck."

Ain't it sad 'bout po' Eddy bein' dead?
Eddy Jones was let down in his grave.

What did Eddy say before he died?
He said, "Nearer, my God, to Thee."

Eddy's mother she weeped a day,
Lawdy, Eddy Jones, Eddy Jones!

The singer turns to the "ladies," if they be present, and sings,—

You want me to do like Eddy Jones?
You mus' want me to lay down an' die for you.

Note

1. Dr. John Meier, quoted by Professor H. M. Belden, *Journal of American Folk-Lore*, vol. xxiv, p. 3.

Double Meaning in the Popular Negro Blues

Guy B. Johnson

THOSE who are acquainted with the popular blues songs[1] of to-day, especially with what are known as the "race blues," have doubtless often had occasion to suspect that these songs are not always what they seem. A little research into Negro vulgar expressions and the origin of the blues will show such a suspicion to be well founded. After a long acquaintance with Negroes and Negro songs, the writer feels that there is no doubt of the presence of double meanings of a sex nature in the blues, and he wishes to present certain data in relation to that subject.

The blues, arising originally from the common Negro folk, have been widely exploited as a form of popular song. The word "blues" has such a market value to-day that song writers and composers of dance music attach it to many pieces which have no resemblance whatever to the original Negro article. In so far as one may speak of the original blues, they may be thought of as the wail of the despondent Negro lover. All peoples have their lonesome songs, but there was something naïve, something different in the Negro's melancholy songs which set them apart and marked them for preservation. Once they were introduced to the public,[2] they became nationally popular. At first they were interpreted by Negroes who had grown up with them, so to speak. But the exploitation of this kind of song has become so profitable that practically every writer of popular songs has tried his hand at it. Many of the best sellers to-day are written by white men.

Indeed, the production of blues to-day is like the production of Fords or of Ivory Soap. Since the phonograph holds the center of the stage at present as far as the distribution of songs is concerned, it is the phonograph record companies that produce most of the blues. Several of the major phonograph companies maintain "race record" departments, employ Negro artists, and make special efforts to cultivate the Negro trade. The 1925 general catalogues of the three largest producers of "race records" listed a total of 1,330 titles, of which 1,160 or 87 per cent were secular and therefore blues according to the regular Negro usage of the word to-day. The total sales of blues records by these three companies alone last year were around six million records. While the majority of these went to

Reprinted from *Journal of Abnormal and Social Psychology* 22, no. 1 (April–June 1927): 12–20.

Negroes, there was a tremendous sale to white people. Thus it is evident that the blues as they are issued on phonograph records at present are no small item in the social life of the country. It is these popular blues that we shall now examine.

Needless to say, the double meanings in the blues are of a sexual nature. Not that other types of double meanings are not found in Negro songs,[3] but merely that such as are present in the blues would almost inevitably be of sexual significance because the blues deal with the man-woman relation.

We may divide the double meanings into two general groups:

1. those meanings pertaining specifically to the sex organs and
2. those relating to the sex act or to some other aspect of sex life.

Of course, it is understood that this division is merely one of convenience in presentation and that the two classes of meanings frequently coincide.

Relatively few symbols for the sex organs are found in the blues, but these few are worked to the utmost. By far the most common of these terms is *jelly roll.* As used by the lower class Negro it stands for the vagina, or for the female genitalia in general, and sometimes for sexual intercourse. Doubtless it is the only word which many Negroes have to designate the female organs. Its use among Negroes of the lower class is so extensive that few will deny its meaning when they encounter it in the blues. Yet, because of its decent meaning, it passes fairly well in popular song society, being used occasionally even in white songs. The following lines from popular phonograph blues will illustrate the usage of jelly roll in these songs:

> I ain't gonna give nobody none o' this jelly roll.
>
> Nobody in town can bake sweet jelly roll like mine.
>
> Your jelly roll is good.

Of course, respectable persons are supposed to get the impression that something to eat is meant. But no Negro laborer contends that jelly roll means something to eat when he sings stanzas like the following:

> I don't know but I've been tol',
> Angels in heaven do the sweet jelly roll.
>
> Dupree was a bandit,
> He was brave an' bol',
> He stole that diamon' ring
> For some of Betty's jelly roll.

Another term for the female organs is *cabbage.* While not as common as jelly roll, it is used to such an extent that its lower meaning is readily recognized by the ordinary Negro when he hears it in a song. The line, "Anybody here want to try my cabbage", illustrates the use of this symbol in the blues. Other symbols are *keyhole* and *bread.* The former is found infrequently, but the latter, sometimes found as *cookie* and *cake,* is almost as common as jelly roll in everyday Negro slang. A Negro youth, wishing to express superlatively his estimate of his sweetheart's sexual equipment, often refers to it as *angel-food cake.* The old

Negro song, *Short'nin' Bread,* had a vulgar meaning, and even when recorded in its supposedly innocent versions retains an undercurrent of sexual meaning:

Two little niggers layin' in bed,
One turned over to the other an' said,
"My baby loves short'nin', short'nin' bread,
My baby loves short'nin' bread."

Symbols for the male organs are more difficult to find. There are numerous references to "thing" and "it", but these are usually descriptive of the sex act itself rather than the male organ. In fact, it is doubtful if there is a clear-cut example of male symbolism in the blues. This is probably due to the fact that Negro vulgarisms for the male organs are not suited to double usage, that is, they are not easily clothed with conventional meanings which would give them safe passage into respectable circles.

Expressions carrying double meanings relating to the act of cohabitation are much more numerous in the blues than are symbols for the sex organs. Many persons will be surprised, no doubt, to learn that the word *jazz* deserves to head this list. Used both as a verb and as a noun to denote the sex act, it has long been common vulgarity among Negroes in the South, and it is very likely from this usage that the term "jazz music" was derived.[4] It is almost unbelievable that such vulgarity could become so respectable, but it is true nevertheless. Of course, much of the use of the word jazz in popular songs is without vulgar intent, but the fact remains that its original connotation was indecent and that several million people are aware of its original meaning. In such lines as

I got the jazz-me blues,
I want a jazzy kiss,
Those jazzin' babies blues,

the word retains its vulgar meaning.

Strange to say, the majority of the expressions in the blues relating to the sex act are sung from the point of view of woman and are mostly concerned with the quality of the movements made by the male during coitus. The following expressions are frequent. They are presented with brief explanatory comments.

"My man rocks me with one steady roll." Here the woman boasts of the steady movement with which her man executes the act. Numerous vulgar versions of this song have been in vogue in the Negro underworld for several years, and their kinship with the phonograph version is indisputable. In the phonograph piece the song is stuffed with pointless rigamarole between the frequent repetitions of the refrain line, "My man rocks me with one steady roll." The following folk stanzas collected by the writer not long ago show the line of thought in the undeleted versions:

Looked at the clock, clock struck one,
Come on, daddy, let's have some fun.

Looked at the clock, clock struck two,
Believe to my soul you ain't half through.

Looked at the clock, clock struck three,
Believe to my soul, you gonna kill poor me.

Looked at the clock, clock struck four,
If the bed breaks down we'll finish on the floor.

My daddy rocks me with one steady roll,
Dere ain't no slippin' when he once takes hold.

"Do it a long time, papa." Here the vulgar meaning is obscured by the usual means. One is led to believe that "do it" refers to something innocuous like kissing or dancing. But the sex meaning is too plain to be hidden so easily. The woman wants her partner to prolong coitus.

"Daddy, ease it to me." Here the woman requests the man to perform the act in an "easy" way. This way of speaking has considerable currency among both whites and Negroes of the lower classes. "Play me slow" has the same connotation.

"Easy rider." This apt expression is used to describe a man whose movements in coitus are easy and satisfying. It is frequently met both in Negro folk songs and in formal songs. "I wonder where my easy rider's gone," is a sort of by-word with Southern Negroes. There is an interesting circumstance connected with this expression which throws light upon the question of how vulgar meanings get over into art songs from folk songs. W. C. Handy, mentioned above as the author of the first popular blues, noticed the widespread use of "easy rider" as well as the existence of various folk songs based on that theme. He wrote a song *Yellow Dog Blues*, in which he used the phrase. In this song there is a race horse and a jockey (sic!) involved. The jockey deserts his horse, goes back South, and the horse wonders "where my easy rider's gone". If one judged the song on its own merits alone, Handy's efforts seemed to fall flat. But the song had symbolic meanings which were rooted deep in folk sources, and such popularity as it enjoyed among Negroes was doubtless derived from the fact that to them it was an old friend in disguise.

"Shake it", "shake that thing", etc.[5] Such expressions are very frequent in the blues. Ostensibly they refer to dancing, but they are really Negro vulgar expressions relating to coitus. Here is a stanza from a recent popular piece:

Why, there's old Uncle Jack,
The jelly-roll king,
Got a hump on his back
From shakin' that thing,
Yet he still shakes that thing.
For an ole man how he can shake that thing!
An' he never gets tired o' tellin' young folks how to shake that thing.

The type of double meaning most frequently found in the blues is not one which hinges upon a particular word or phrase, but one which depends upon the general content of an expression. The following lines are good examples of this kind of double meaning:

"I got what it takes to bring you back." Most students of Negro folk song have come across one or more vulgar versions of this theme. The expression forms the refrain of a popular blues of the same name. It is sung from the point of view of woman, and in its darker meaning it refers to the woman's sexual attractions as something which will eventually bring back the straying lover.

"Mama's got something I know you want." This is similar to the above expression. Even in its whitewashed form its meaning is clear, but it probably passes because it contains no specifically indecent words. Following is the concluding stanza of the popular song:

> Mama's got something sho' gonna surprise you,
> Mama's got something gonna hypnotize you,
> Mama's got something I know you want.

"I'm busy and you can't come in." The kinship of the popular song of this name with the folk song of similar name is indisputable. The writer has several variations of the latter. Usually the woman is represented as being sexually engaged with a man, so that she refuses to let her other "daddy" come in. The latter sings, in one of the semi-vulgar versions:[6]

> Lawd, I went to my woman's do'
> Jes' lak I been doin' befo';
> She says, "I got my all-night trick, baby,
> An' you can't git in.
>
> "Come back 'bout half pas' fo',
> If I'm done I'll open de do',
> Got my all-night trick, baby,
> An' you can't git in."

"I got your bath water on." Here the original meaning was related to the sexually stimulating effect of a warm bath. Like so many other blues, it "gets by" because the song contains no words which are vulgar *per se*.

Additional lines from the popular blues in which this undercurrent of vulgarity runs are as follows:

> It's right here for you; if you don't get it, 'tain't no fault of mine.
> I'm gonna see you when your troubles are just like mine.
> If I let you get away with it once, you'll do it all the time.
> You've got what I've been looking for.
> How can I get it when you keep on snatching it back?
> Put it where I can get it.
> If you don't give me what I want, I'm gonna get it somewhere else.

Lest the reader bring the charge that the writer is merely reading suggestive meanings into the blues, the writer will present certain lines of reasoning which substantiate his claims.

First, there is the circumstance already mentioned, namely, the fact of the presence of the above expressions in their vulgar meanings among the common Negro folk. Anyone who is at all acquainted with Negroes of the laboring class knows this to be true. Furthermore, several prominent Negro leaders who grew up in the South have readily admitted to the writer the existence of these vulgarities and have vouched for the reality of double meanings in the blues. Some of these folk expressions were not indecent in their intention, for they were in ordinary and semi-respectable usage among Negroes. Especially was this true of the terms for various parts of the body, such as penis, vagina, anus, rectum, etc., for many Negroes—and whites, too, for that matter—knew no terms for these parts other than the vulgar ones.

Next we may consider the origins of Negro popular songs in general. Naturally the everyday songs of the Negro adventurer and roustabout abounded in suggestiveness and indecency. Houses of prostitution, gambling dens, and other resorts, especially in the cities along the Mississippi, were the clearing houses for such songs. Some of these songs of the Negro underworld have made the ascent to the realm of decency. In the lowest type of cabarets they can be heard in their original versions. Passing on up through the various grades of cabarets and vaudeville shows, they lose objectionable words and phrases here and there until they finally become either decent or indecent, as you will. Then song writers, white and black, adopt them and alter them just enough to "get by".

W. C. Handy, who, as stated above, published the first song under the title of blues, spoke as follows in a conference with Dorothy Scarborough: "Each one of my blues is based on some old Negro song of the South. . . . I can tell you the exact song I used as a basis for any one of my blues."[7]

James Weldon Johnson, one of the most prominent Negro leaders and authors of to-day, has written as follows of the origins of Negro ragtime songs:

> The earliest ragtime songs, like Topsy, "jes' grew." Some of these earliest songs were taken down by white men, the words slightly altered or changed, and published under the names of the arrangers. . . .
>
> Later there came along a number of colored men who were able to transcribe the old songs and write original ones. I was, about that time, writing words to music for the music show stage in New York. I was collaborating with my brother and the late Bob Cole. I remember that we appropriated about the last one of the old "jes' grew" songs. It was a song which had been sung for years all through the South. The words were unprintable, but the tune was irresistible, and belonged to nobody. We took it, rewrote the verses, telling an entirely different story from the original, left the chorus as it was, and published the song. . . . The song was, "Oh, Didn't He Ramble!"[8]

There is every reason to suppose that this process of borrowing from unprintable folk songs has continued to operate. Indeed, the process is singularly accelerated to-day by the situation in the phonograph record business. Nearly all of the leading blues artists are persons who grew up in ordinary Negro society in the South. Their acquaintance with a great many Negro vulgar songs and expressions can be taken for granted. Furthermore, their employers encourage them to make their own blues. What more natural than that they should draw upon their old songs? The writer has frequently met the remark, after repeating the words of some late blues to a Negro laborer, "Why, I've known a song like that for ten years—except mine wouldn't do to put on a record."

The writers of the blues have been fortunate in their materials in several respects. Some of the Negro's terms for the sex organ were not known extensively outside of the lower strata of Negro society, therefore the writers found it easy to smuggle them into their songs and to invest them with passably respectable meanings. Furthermore, as regards the songs whose indecent meanings are not dependent upon words but upon general interpretation, they had little difficulty, for in such cases there is always the better or proper meaning. One takes his choice. In still other cases the authors could retain the folk phrases and change the contents of the songs. Handy's *Yellow Dog Blues*, mentioned above, is a case in point. The following might also be cited, a stanza from an old folk song:

Thirty days in jail
With my back turned to the wall;
"Look here, Mr. Jailer,
Put another gal in my stall."

This was originally sung by the *man*, and it had an actual basis in the custom which some jailers followed of locking Negro men and women in the same cell. Now comes a popular song based on the folk theme, but of course it is sung from the point of view of the woman!

There is one other phenomenon which might be mentioned as tending to substantiate the foregoing statement concerning the origin of some of the blues. Negro churchmen and educators almost without exception oppose vigorously the singing of blues. They are attempting to attach a stigma to the blues, and in so doing they often brand every song which is not a spiritual as something to be sung no longer by respectable Negroes. In their opposition to blues and other popular secular pieces there is an implicit recognition of the undercurrent of vulgarity which runs through many of these songs.

The writer is not passing upon the question of the good or bad of the state of affairs which he has described. Neither is he touching upon the subject of double meanings in white popular songs. Double meaning in secular song is after all nothing new. Folk song students know that many standard folk songs have come up out of the slime. But it is doubtful if any group ever has carried its ordinary vulgarities over into respectable song life so completely and successfully as the American Negro. And the ease with which the Negro has put this thing over leads one to suspect that the white man, too, enjoys seeing "the other meaning".

Notes

1. For information on the blues as a type of Negro song, see Odum and Johnson, *Negro Workaday Songs* (Chapel Hill: University of North Carolina Press, 1926), chap. II; Scarborough, *On the Trail of Negro Folk-Songs* (Cambridge: Harvard University Press, 1925), chap. X; and Handy, *Blues: An Anthology* rev. ed. (1926; New York: Macmillan, 1972). The use of the term "blues" has become very loose. In fact, many Southern Negroes distinguish just two classes of colored songs to-day: spirituals and blues. In the present article the writer would not restrict the meaning of "blues" to those songs bearing blues titles but would let it include the majority of popular Negro secular songs of to-day.

2. The first piece to appear in print under the name of blues was *Memphis Blues*, 1910, by a Negro, W. C. Handy. Handy's works are nearly all based on folk themes.

3. There are, for example, many hidden references to the white man in the Negro's songs. This is an interesting field of research in which little has been done.

4. Jazz music originated in Negro pleasure houses—"jazz houses", as they are sometimes called by Negroes. The writer would like to add one more to the list of rather asinine theories on the origin of the term jazz. It is his opinion that the word was suggested by Negro preachers in their tirades on the wicked woman, Jezebel.

5. A note on "shake the shimmy" may be of interest here. Chemise is pronounced "shimmy" by most Negroes and a great many whites in the South. In its original meaning it described the effect produced when a woman made a movement or did a dance step which caused her breasts to shake. This caused her "shimmy" to shake. The expression could easily have been a Negro household usage before it got into the dance halls.

6. See Odum and Johnson, *The Negro and His Songs* (1925; rpt. Hatboro, PA: Folklore Associates, 1964), pp. 189–90.

7. Scarborough, *On the Trail of Negro Folk-Songs*, p. 265. See also the introduction to W. C. Handy's *Blues: An Anthology*.

8. Johnson, *The Book of American Negro Poetry* (New York: Harcourt, Brace, 1922), pp. xi–xii.

I Got the Blues

Alan Lomax

I got the blues,
But I'm too damn mean to cry . . .

THE last chord sounded on Leroy's guitar, the last blues of the evening.

"Well," Natchez told me, "I reckon now you got an idea about the blues around Memphis."

"I reckon I have," I said.

"Yeah, that *po*lice in Memphis had *you* singin' the blues," he chuckled. About that time the hard-faced man who ran the honkey-tonk blew out the lamp. Old Natchez picked up the nearly empty gin bottle, Leroy and Sib grabbed the guitars, and the four of us walked out into the two o'clock dark. It was black out there. You could feel the Delta night rubbing itself against your cheek.

We sat down on the front step and smoked. The stars hung just above our heads, like fireflies caught in the dark tangle of the night. I felt good. Sib, Leroy, and Natchez had been singing for several hours, and every blues had been like another drink of raw gin. The brights and shadows of their blues reflected the wonderful and hateful land of the South that had produced all of us. We were warmed with the undeniable vitality and humanity that the blues carry beneath their melancholy.

I wasn't sure exactly where I was and I didn't much care. The man who owned the little country tonk was named Hamp, they told me. This was Hamp's place, somewhere out in the Arkansas blackland across the river from Memphis. It was a one-room shanty store that doubled as a country bar room at night, a place where the people who made the cotton in this fat land came to dance and gamble and commit a bit of friendly mayhem. Tonight it had been a refuge for the three blues musicians and myself—"where *no*body gonna bother us," they said. "No laws or nothin'."

We had needed a hole to hide in. When we had come racing across the river bridge from Memphis into this dark plain, we had had the feeling that we were pursued, that we would like to keep on going right out of this world. We were running away from the

Reprinted from *Common Ground* 8 (Summer 1948): 38–52.

Memphis police and their attitudes about human relations. Not that we had committed a crime; we had just forgotten, temporarily, that we were in the South.

I had hit Beale Street in Memphis about the first cool of the evening, and, as usual, had begun to poke around for folk singers. A Negro bartender told me I wasn't allowed in any of the Beale Street joints because of a new segregation ordinance. So I paraded Beale Street until I heard the music I wanted coming from a barber shop. Natchez and Leroy were playing their boxes to Sib's harmonica-blowing. When they had collected their tips, we sat down together in a vacant lot to talk blues, but a dribble-chinned Memphis cop interrupted our libations and harshly ordered us to move on. "We don't want no Washington Yankee foolin' around niggertown," he said. "If you like this nigger music, take it back North with you. We don't like it down here in the South."

With the cop pacing behind us, our feet dragged in a chain-gang walk up Beale Street. We piled into my car and headed out of town, and, by what was said, I knew that the Memphis cop had made these blues singers my friends. They tried to make a joke of the whole incident, but in the pauses between laughs Leroy kept saying, "Man, just as soon as I can rake and scrape money together, I'm gonna leave this country and they ain't never gonna see me down here again."

At Hamp's place we solaced ourselves with gin and with hours of the blues. Child of this fertile Delta land, voice of the voiceless black masses, the blues crept into the back windows of America maybe forty years ago and since then has colored the whole of American popular music. Hill-billy singers, hot jazz blowers, crooners like Crosby, cowboy yodelers—all these have learned from the native folk blues. Now the blues is a big, lonesome wind blowing around the world. Now the whole world can feel, uncoiling in its ear, this somber music of the Mississippi. And yet no one had ever thought to ask the makers of these songs—these ragged meister-singers—why they sang.

Now we sat together in the Delta night, smoking and saying little. Here was Natchez, who had helped to birth the blues forty years ago in this same Delta country. Here was young Leroy, making the blues for his own time. Finally here was Sib, the buffoon of the blues, who, like all fools, expressed in apish gestures the sorrows of life.

I turned to Natchez. You couldn't tell how old he was by looking at him. You just knew that he was old and strong, like the big live-oaks in these bottoms. "Natchez," I said, "tell me why you sing the blues."

There was a pause in which the insects and little animals of the night joined together in the sound that is the earth breathing in its sleep. Then Natchez began in his grave and hesitant way.

"Some people say that the blues is—a cow wantin' to see her calf, but I don't say it like that. I say it's a man that's got a good woman that turns him down. Like when you sing—

> If you see my milk cow, tell her to hurry home,
> 'Cause I ain't had no lovin' since she been gone . . .

Things like that happen, you know. You want to see your lovin' babe, you want to see her bad, and she be gone. That gives you the blues:

> I woke up this mornin' just about an hour before day,
> Reached and grabbed the pillow where my baby used to lay. . . ."

Natchez paused and looked at Sib, the stutterer—Sib, the slightly addled one. On Sib's dark brow a frown was eternally in conflict with the clownish grin that twitched the corners of his mouth. No one could sing Sib's blues because they were a complete expression of Sib—his stammering speech, his wild and idiot humors, his untrammelled fancy. Natchez, who treated him like a child, would yet sit back and play for an hour while Sib indulged in rhymes and stanzas which no other singer could ever invent. "So what do you think about it, Sib?" said Natchez softly. "You must have some reason why you have the blues."

Sib began to speak in his plaintive way, the words tumbling out of him in a rush as if he were afraid someone might interrupt him at any moment. "I'll tell you, Natchez, it really worries me to think I had a sweet little girl named Annie Belle. You know, we used to go to school together and grew along up together. So I wanted to love her and I axed her mother for her and she turnt me down. That cause me to sing the blues:

> Good mornin', little school girl,
> Good mornin', little school girl,
> May I go home wid you?
> May I go home wid you?
> You can tell your mama and your papa
> That Sib's a little school boy, too. . . .

"Her parents thought I wasn't the right boy for Annie Belle. They turnt me down, and then I just got to thinkin' and that started me to drinkin' and from that I got the blues."

Truly, they have sung ten thousand blues verses about lack of love. Open the big book of the blues and you will find all the bitterness, all the frustration, all the anger, and all the heartbreak that accompany love when people live precariously in the slums.

Sib went on spurting words, but Natchez interrupted him by directing the question to Leroy. "Now what do you think about the blues situation, old Leroy?"

"Tell you, Natchez, the blues have hope me a lot. Yes, sir, the blues will help a man. When I has trouble, when I'm feelin' low down and disgusted and can't be satisfied, you know how it is sometimes—

> I woke up this mornin' with the blues all round my bed,
> Went to eat my breakfast, had blues all in my bread. . . .

Then singin' a blues like that is the onliest thing to ease my situation."

But Natchez wasn't satisfied. "Yeah, you feel better. The blues helps a man to explain his feelin's, but why do he feel blue in the first place?"

"Here's my thought on it," Sib came busting in. "We er-uh colored people have had so *much* trouble, but we's a people that tries to be happy anyway, you ever notice that? Because we never had so much, we tries to make the best of life. We don't have nothin', but we try to be jolly anyway; we don't let nothin' worry us too much. You take them old-fashioned country suppers." (As Sib talked, you could see him smacking his lips over the barbecued ribs and the field-ripe watermelons he had eaten.) "I thought I was a rich man when I'd go there with a dollar in my pocket. I never was used to much anyway, you understand? Always had to work."

He paused, and the puzzled and angry frown triumphed over the happy-go-lucky grin that twitched at his lips. "One year we cleaned up a whole big bottom where the willows was thick. The mud was so heavy I many times stalled four mules to a wagon down there. We'd work and clean up a bottom in the winter so we could plant it next summer. And I think this. You work hard all the year and you expectin' your money once a year, and, when that year wind up, you don't get nothin'; then you get the idea that 'I ain't doin' no good no way an' what's the use of livin'?' You know? You'll have all them funny thoughts like that."

Natchez, softly, "Sho, sho."

"And that gives you the blues, the po' man's heart disease. I remember I used to sing the blues down in that old black bottom—

> I could hear my name,
> My black name, a-ringin'
> All up an' down the line.
> I could hear my name,
> My black name, a-ringin'
> All up an' down the line.
> Now I don't believe I'm doin' nothin'
> But gradually throwin' away my time. . . ."

Sib put his harmonica to his lips and began to play. It was hardly music. It was a compound of shrieks and squeals and moans, like a farm in a tornado, where the cries of terror from the animals and the human beings are mixed with the noise of splitting planks and cracking timbers, and all are swallowed up in the howl of the storm. The words and phrases burst out in spasms through the harmonica as if Sib had learned to sing through the metal reeds because he was unable to express his feelings adequately in his own throat. Presently Natchez and Leroy joined Sib, underscoring his harmonica with their two guitars, until the song had run out in him. In the silence that followed, they chuckled quietly together. "That's the blues, man. That's purely it."

"You see what I mean about the blues expressin' a man's feelin', Natchez?" said Leroy.

"Yeah," Natchez replied. "It looks like the blues gits started thataway—when a man is goin' down some country road, whistlin' and singin' to himself somethin' or another like—

> Hey, I feel like hollerin' and I feel like cryin',
> Hey, I feel like hollerin' and I feel like cryin'.
> I'm here today, Lawd, but tomorrow I'll be gone,
> I'm here today, Lawd, but tomorrow I'll be gone.

He don't play no instrument or nothin'. He just hollers about what's worryin' him."

"They the *jump-up* blues," added Leroy. "They just *jump* up in your mind when you be down in trouble. Like those little numbers like they have over in *Tenn*-essee." And Leroy began to sing in his rich baritone—

> "Well, have you ever been to Nashville,
> Well, have you ever been to Nashville,
> Have you ever been to Nashville,
> O Lawdy, to the Nashville pen?
> Boys, if you don't stop stealin',
> Boys, if you don't stop stealin',
> Boys, if you don't stop stealin',
> O buddy, you'll go back again. . . .

That's what I mean about the heart part. You singin' the way you feel from the heart."

"That's *right*, man," from Sib.

"Nobody could play behind them jumped-up blues," said Natchez, "because they ain't got no music to 'em. They ain't never been wrote down and won't never be, and I reckon all blues originated from just such stuff as that."

Out of the lonesome field hollers, out of the chain-gang chants, out of the full-throated choruses of the road builders, the clearers of swamps, the lifters and the toters—out of the biting irony, the power and savage strength and anger of work-songs—sprang the blues. Here was music with its tap root in African singing—Africa, the continent of communal work, the preeminent continent of the work-song. The work-song flowered under slavery and put forth its thorns after reconstruction. Forty-odd years ago singers like Natchez began to set these old cadences "to music," making their banjos, their guitars, and their pianos sound the work-gang chorus. Thus the old work-songs, given a regular harmonic form, became dance music in the unstable and uncertain world of the southern Negro worker. Here, from the experience of Leroy and Natchez, had come confirmation for my own notions about the origin of the blues.

"You sing about things you want to do or things you want to know or—" Leroy continued—"things that really have happened to you."

"And," Natchez added, "some people that haven't had no hardship, they don't know how it is with the poor man that has had hardships and still has them."

"Yeah, classics and stuff like that," said Leroy, lumping musicians who played written music with all the secure and wealthy and privileged people in the world. "People like that don't know what the blues is."

"Naw, they couldn't play the blues if they wanted," Sib said with great scorn.

"What I mean," explained Leroy, "it takes a man who *had* the blues to really *play* the blues. Yeah, you got to be *blue* to sing the blues, and that's the truth:

> I was down in the bottom with the mud up to my knees,
> I was workin' for my baby, she was so hard to please.
>
> I worked all the summer, Lord, and all the fall,
> Went home to take my Christmas, good pardner, in my overalls. . . ."

Natchez scrooched up on the step and spat far into the night. He could spit like a muleskinner. His voice rang now with authority.

"Let's come to a showdown now. Just where did the blues originate from? I'm thinkin' they didn't start in the North—in Chicago or New York or Pennsylvania."

"Naw, man, they started in the South," from Sib.

"From slavery, I'm thinkin'," Leroy muttered, half to himself.

"All right, then what we really want to know is why and how come a man in the South *have* the blues. Now I've worked on levee camps, in road camps, and in extra gangs on the railroad and everywhere. I've heard guys singin'—'Mm-mp' this and 'Mm-mp' that—and they was really expressin' their feelings from their heart the only way they knowed how.

"I've knowed guys that wanted to cuss out the boss and was afraid to go up to his face and tell him what they wanted to tell him. And I've heered a guy sing those things to the boss when he were out behind a wagon, hookin' up the horses. He'd make out like a horse stepped on his foot and he'd say, 'Get off my foot, goddamit!'—saying just what he wanted to say to his boss, only talkin' to the horse—'You got no business doin' me like that! Get offa my foot!' "

"That's just my idea, Natchez," Leroy broke in. "The blues is mostly revenge. You want to say something (and you know how we was situated so we couldn't say or do a lot of things we wanted to), and so you sing it. Like a friend of mine. He was workin' down on a railroad section gang a long time ago. I don't remember when it was. Anyhow, this friend of mine looked at the boss lyin' up in the shade sleepin' while him an' his buddies was out there shakin' those ties. He wanted to say something about it, but he couldn't you know. So that give him the blues and he sung a little number about—

> Ratty, ratty section,
> Ratty, ratty crew,
> The captain's gettin' ratty, boys,
> I b'lieve I'm gonna rat some, too.

Meanin' that he was signifying and getting his revenge through songs."

"And he didn't quit because he didn't know where he gonna find his next job," Natchez added.

"Yeah, and maybe he had one of those jobs you *couldn't* quit." Leroy chuckled.

"What you mean? Sumpin' like a chain gang?" Sib asked.

"Naw, I mean one of the jobs only way you could quit was to run off," said Leroy.

"Man, how they gonna hold you?" from Sib, querulously.

"They hold you just like this, Sib, boy. You didn't have no payday on them jobs. They give you an allowance in the commissary store for you an' yo' woman. You draw on that allowance, so much a week, and after it was up, that's all you git. Most boys didn't know how to read and write and figger and so they charge them what they wants, like twenty-five dollars for a side of side meat. And you gonna stay there till you paid for that meat, Sib, maybe gettin' twenty-five cents a day wages. When you take a notion to leave, they tell you, 'Well, you owe us four hundred dollars.' "

"Four hundred dollars! Aw, be quiet, man." Sib started to laugh his mad and infectious laugh.

"I said four hundred dollars," Leroy cut in. "Just for eatin' and sleepin'."

Natchez took up the story. "Suppose you be workin' a team of mules and one git his leg broke and have to be killed? That's your mule, then! Yessir, that dead mule is one you bought and you gonna work right on that job till you pay for him or slip off some way."

"Whyn't you say somethin' about it?" Sib inquired plaintively.

"Say something about it and you might go just like that mule," Natchez said seriously. "All odds are against you, even your own people."

"That's right," agreed Leroy. "The white man don't all the time do those things. It's some of your own people at times will do those dirty deeds because they're told to do them, and they do what they're told."

Treat a group of people as if they had no right to dignity, allow these people no security, make them bend their knees and bow their heads, and some of them will conform to slavery in their souls. Perhaps these so-called "Uncle Toms" are the most grievous result of the slavery system.

Natchez interrupted my reflections. "Looky here. Leroy. Did you ever work for the Loran brothers?"

"You mean those guys that built all these levees up and down the river from Memphis? Sho, man, I've worked for the bigges' part of the Loran family—Mister Isum Loran, Mister Bill Loran, Mister Charley Loran—all them. I think them Lorans are something like the Rockefeller family. When a kid is born, *he* Loran junior. They got Loran the second, Loran the third, Loran the fourth. They always been and they is now—Loran brothers—some of them big business mens in towns, some of them running extry gangs and levee camps and road camps. And *they* were peoples wouldn't allow a man to quit unless they got tired of him and drove him away."

"That's right," Leroy chucked. "And you remember how the boys used to sing—

> I axed Mister Charley—
> What time of day:
> He looked at me,
> Threw his watch away.
>
> I axed Mister Charley
> Just to give me one dime.
> 'Go on, old nigger,
> You a dime behind!'
>
> I axed Mister Charley
> Just to give me my time.
> 'Go on, old nigger,
> You're time behind!' . . ."

I had heard this levee camp blues from one end of the South to the other. It was the epic of the muleskinner, the man who did the dirt-moving jobs before the bulldozer was developed, the Negro who, working his big mule-drawn scoop, piled up the levees, graded the roads, and dug the canals of the South. This muleskinning blues has thousands of verses, attached to the mournfulest wailing tune in the world, a tune I never was able to sing myself until they put me on K.P. in the Army, and the mess sergeant began to look like a levee camp boss looks to a muleskinner.

All the way from the Brazos bottoms of Texas to the tidewater country of Virginia I had heard Negro muleskinners chant their complaint against Mister Charley but, although I had asked a score of singers, I had never found one who could identify him. I grinned with excitement. Maybe here, under the knee of one of the Loran brothers' levees, I had at last discovered the identity of my elusive Mister Charley.

I asked my second question of the evening. "Who is this 'Mister Charley'?"

"Mister Charley Loran," Natchez immediately responded.

"What sort of a man is he?" I asked.

"Well," Leroy drawled, "now I couldn't hardly describe him to you. You know, it's hard for a colored man to talk like a white man anyhow." (Leroy was talking for my benefit now. He had been reminded there was a white man listening there in the dark. He began to rib me gently.) "Mister Charley was one of them *real* Southerners; had a voice that would scare you to death whenever he'd come out with all that crap of his. Always in his shirt sleeves, I don't care how early in the mornin' and how cold it was."

"Night or day." Natchez began to chuckle with him. "Didn't make no difference to Mister Charley what time it was."

"Don't care how early he'd get up, *you* gonna get up, too. He'd holler—

> Big bell call you, little bell warn you,
> If you don't come now, I'm gonna break in on you. . . .

And he *meant* it."

"Sho he did," laughed Natchez. "He the man originated the old-time eight-hour shift down here. Know what I mean? Eight hours in the morning and eight more in the afternoon."

Sib kept adding eight to eight and getting sixteen and going off into peal after peal of high whinnying laughter. In this shared laughter I felt the three had again accepted me. I asked another question.

"I'd always heard of this Mister Charley in the song as 'the mercy man.' Is *he* the same as Charley Loran?"

"Naw, man, that's Mister Charley *Hulen,* the best friend we had down in this part of the country, really a friend to our people. He was the man we all run to when somebody mistreated us," Natchez told me.

"Otherwise known as 'the mercy man,'" Leroy added. "Now I remember an incident about Charley Hulen happen in Hughes, Arkansas. It's hard to believe it, but I know it for a fact. They had a Negro there name Bolden, run a honkey-tonk and had a lot of property. In fact the sheriff of the county lived in one of Bolden's houses. But he wouldn't pay Bolden no rent, just stayed there and gave Bolden a whuppin' every time Bolden asked him for his money."

"That's what he did," said Natchez, listening, seeing it, feeling it in his guts.

"So this Bolden happen to be, as they say, one of Charley Hulen's niggers. He finally got up nerve to go tell Mister Charley what was goin' on. So Charley Hulen tells the *po*lice, say, 'Saturday evenin' at one o'clock, meet me. I'm killin' you or you kill me.' And that's what happen. He met that sheriff that Saturday and told him, 'I come to kill you. You been messin' with one of my niggers.'

"The *po*lice started after his gun and Charley Hulen shot him through the heart. So they pulled that *po*lice over out the street, and let the honkey-tonk roll on." Softly, seeing it, wondering about it, he repeated, "Yeah, man, let the old honkey-tonk roll *right* on."

"Toughest places I *ever* seen," said Natchez, "were some of them honkey-tonks, call them barrel-houses, in Charley Loran's camps. Negroes all be in there gamblin', you know, and some of them short guys couldn't quite reach up to the crap table—and I've seed them pull a dead man up there and stand on him."

"Yeah, stand on 'em. I've seed that," Leroy said.

But Natchez had more to tell. "Down in them barrel-houses in Loran's levee camps I've seen them stand on a dead man and shoot craps all night long; and I've heard Loran come around and say, 'If you boys keep out the grave, I'll keep you out the jail.' Yeah, and I've heard him say, 'Kill a nigger, hire another. But kill a mule and I'll have to *buy* another.'"

"That's just what he believed, Natchez," Leroy said, in anger and at the same time with curious pride. "Peoples like him had another word, too. On those camps, when the fellows were wore down from carrying logs or doing some kind of heavy work, the bosses used to say, '*Burn out, burn up. Fall out, fall dead!*' That was the best you could do. You had to work yourself to death or you proved that you were a good man, that's all."

"Main thing about it is that some of those people down there didn't think a Negro ever get *tired!*" Natchez' ordinarily quiet voice broke with a sound that was half sob, half growl. "They'd work him—work him till he couldn't work, see! You couldn't *tell* 'em you was tired."

"Why couldn't you?" I asked.

"They'd crack you 'cross the head with a stick or maybe kill you. One of those things. You just had to keep on workin' whether you was tired or not. From what they call 'can to can't.' That mean you start to work when you just can see—early in the mornin'—and work right on till you can't see no more at night."

"Only man ever helped us about our work was Charley Hulen, the mercy man," said Leroy. "He used to come out and say, 'Those fellows are tired; give 'em some rest.' Ain't he the man, Natchez, cut them sixteen hours a day down to eight?"

"Right in this section he was," Natchez replied.

"How did he do it?" I asked.

"Why, he and his son, Little Charley, just didn't like the way things was going on, so they just come in and taken over, that's all. Otherwise they was the baddest men down through this part of the country. Both of them was ex-cowboys from Texas and sharp-shooters. Could shoot like nobody's business. So after they taken over, that made it a lot better. And it's still better today."

"You mean the people were just scared of old man Hulen and his boy?" I asked.

"That's right," Leroy said. "I'll tell you how bad they was scared. You know they put up a law in Arkansas—no *hitchhikin'*. It made it kinda tough on a fellow to move around and change jobs if he wanted to. So, one afternoon I were hitchhikin' a ride to Little Rock and a fellow by the name of Mister Gotch stopped in his car. He were one of the baddest mens down in this country."

"He was so bad he was scared of hissef," Natchez chuckled.

"So Mister Gotch say to me, 'What you doin' hitchhikin', boy?' Called me 'boy.'

"I say, 'I'm tryin' to get home to work.'

"He say, 'Well, who do you work *for?*'

"I tell him"—Leroy imitated the mild and insinuating way he made his reply—" 'I work for Mister Charley Hulen.' You know what that man told me? He say, 'Come on, I'll take you there!' "

Sib, Natchez, and Leroy threw back their heads and laughed, laughed quietly and long, as if they shared some old joke, burdened with irony, but bearable out of long acquaintance. "Any other time. . . . Or if you'd worked for another man. . . . Or if you hadn't been workin'. . . . You'd got a whuppin'. . . . Or went to jail or the farm and worked for no pay. . . . That's it, worked for no pay!" came bursting out between chuckles. "But, since I worked for Mister Charley Hulen, Mister Gotch taken me to his place. Scared to bother me, because I was one of Mister Charley's mens," Leroy went on.

"One of his *niggers!*"

"Yeah. So Mister Gotch took me in his car. Even gave me a drink!"

Natchez, shaking his head in wonder, chuckled. "They'll do that, too."

"You know, Leroy," Natchez said, "you and I worked in all kind of camps—levee camps, road camps, rock quarries and all—but what I want to get at is—how we lived in those places? I mean in tents and eatin' scrap food other people had refused, such as old bags of beans and stuff they couldn't sell."

Leroy, beginning to howl with laughter over the old and painful joke he recalled, interrupted, "And they had a name for it in the camp I was in—

> La-la-loo!
> If you don't like it,
> He do!"

Natchez, chuckling with him, "Yeah, but you'll *like* it!"

"Unh-hunh, you might not like it when you first get there, but you'll like it before you leave." Leroy was still laughing.

Natchez went on, forcing us to savor the dirt, see the hoggish way the men had to live. "They'd just go out in those big truck gardens and pull up greens by the sackful, take 'em down to some lake or creek, sort of shake 'em off in the water, and cook 'em, roots, stalk, and all, in one of them big fifty-two gallon pots."

Leroy, beginning to laugh his big laugh again, broke in. "And if you found a worm in your greens and say, 'Captain, I found a worm here,' he'd say, 'What the hell you expect for nothing?' "

Natchez and Sib burst out in great yells of laughter, as Leroy hurried on to top his own story: "And then some fellow over 'long the table would holler, 'Gimme that piece of meat!' "

"Yeah, I've heard that—'Gimme that piece of meat! Don't throw it away!' " Natchez gasped out between the gusts of laughter that were shaking his whole body. Sib couldn't sit still any longer; his laughter was riding him too hard. He went staggering off down the dark path, beating his arms in the air, squealing and guffawing like a wild animal.

When we had recovered from this healing laughter, Leroy added thoughtfully, "Those guys seemed to get a kick out of the whole thing."

"Well, in them times what did you know? What did you know?" Natchez asked the night and the stars.

> "Ham and eggs, pork and beans,
> I would-a ate more, but the cook wasn't clean."

"Did you ever see those guys they called 'table-walkers'?" Natchez went on.

"Yeah, many times," said Leroy.

"I mean one of these guys had made up his mind he didn't care whether he died or no; was just tired of the way he'd been living and the kind of food he'd been eating. He'd snatch out his .45 revolver, get up on one end of the mess table and walk it, what I mean, walk right down the whole length, tromping his big dirty feets in everybody's plates, grabbin' up your food."

"Those guys were what you might call 'tough peoples,' " Leroy said respectfully.

"Yeah, 'cause they know they gonna get a whuppin' from the boss," Natchez agreed.

"He may have that .45, that so-called tough guy," Leroy went on, "but, when the white man come, *he'll* whup him with that .45 right on his hip. White man won't have no gun or nothin'. Just come in and say, 'Lay down there, fellow; I'm gonna whup you.' " Leroy spoke quietly, with bitter, weary irony. "So this tough guy gonna lay right down and the white man would kick the gun out of his scabbard and give him a whuppin'." There was a pause. We could all see the big, black figure cowering on the earth and the white man standing over him with a stick, beating him as he might a chicken-killing hound. After a moment, almost in a whisper, Leroy continued, "After this table-walker get his whuppin', he'd pick up that big pistol he toted and go on back to work.

> Well, you kicked and stomped and beat me,
> And you called that fun, and you called that fun.
>
> If I catch you in my home town,
> Gonna make you run, gonna make you run. . . ."

"Yeah," Natchez said. "Then maybe this guy that took the beating would come out there on the job and kill one of his buddies. I've seen that many times."

"If you were a good worker, you could kill anybody down there," Leroy added.

"What you mean is—" Natchez rapped this out—"you could kill anybody down there as long as you kill a *Negro!*"

"Any *Negro.*" Leroy's voice was flat and painstakingly logical, as if he were reading the rules out of a book. "If you could work better than him and you were sorry! But don't go killin' a good worker!"

"That's right," said Natchez. "You could kill anybody you want in those days, if you could work better than him.

> Stagolee, he went a-walkin' in that red-hot broilin' sun;
> He said, 'Bring me my big pistol, I wants my forty-one.'
>
> Stagolee, he went a-walkin' with his .40 gun in his hand;
> He said, 'I feel mistreated this mornin', I could kill most any man.' "

The small hot breeze of midnight had died away and the dawn wind had not yet begun to stir. The night wrapped around us a choking black blanket of stillness and quiet. The quiet voices of Natchez and Leroy moved on with the sureness and strength of the great river that had given them birth.

They were both entertainers. They had made their way safely and even pleasantly through their violent world, their guitars slung around their necks—like talismans. Wearing these talismans, they had entered into all the secret places of this land, had moved safely through its most dangerous jungles, past all its killers, who, seeing their talismans, had smiled upon them. They lived the magic life of fools. (Remember the hard drawling voice—"I got a nigger on my place that can keep you laughin' all day. I don't know where he gets all the stories he tells and them songs of his. Reckon he makes them up, nigger-like. And sing! Sing like a mockin' bird. You ought to hear him. You'd split your sides.") Now these buffoons with their clear artist's vision were making a picture of their world, a terrifying picture of which they were not at all afraid. They were at home with it.

"You know, Natchez," said Leroy, "we had a *few* Negroes around here that wasn't *afraid* of white people. They actually talked back to them. People like that they called 'crazy'—'crazy niggers.' I wonder why do they call them crazy and bad because they speak up for their rights?"

"They afraid they might *ruin* the other Negroes, make *them* crazy enough to talk back," said Natchez. "I had a crazy uncle and they hung him. My uncle was a man that, if he worked, he wanted his pay. And he could figger as good as a white man. Fact of the matter, he had a better education than some of them and they would go to him for advice."

Leroy chuckled. "Um-hum, a lot of the white peoples down here are about as dumb as we are."

"Anyhow," Natchez went on, "this is how they found out my uncle was really a crazy nigger. One day his white boss come to his house and told him, say, 'Sam, I want you to git that woman of yours out of the house and put her to work.' Say, 'It's no woman on this plantation sits up in the shade and don't work but Mizz Anne.'

"An' my uncle say, 'Well, who is Mizz Anne?'

"The white man tell him, 'Mizz Anne is my wife.'

"My uncle say, 'Well, I'm sorry, Mister Crowther, but my wife is named Anne, too, and *she* sets up in the shade and *she* don't come out in the field and work!'

"The man say, 'She *got* to come out there.'

"My uncle look at him. 'There's one Mizz Anne that's a *Negro* and *she* ain't gonna work in the field.'

"The white man jumps off his horse and my uncle whipped him and run him *and* his horse off his place." Natchez went on in a flat and weary voice to finish his story. "So the white man rode to town and he got him a gang and come back after my uncle. My uncle shot four or five of them, but they finally caught him and hung him. So that's the story of *him!* Yeah, that's the story of my crazy uncle."

"Lynched him," Sib muttered.

"Fifty or sixty of them come out there and killed him." Natchez began to speak with mounting rage. "That was on account of him trying to protect his own *wife*. Because he didn't want his own *wife* to work out on the farm when she had a new baby there at the house an' was expecting another one pretty soon!

"I've seed this happen, too. One boy I know was likin' the same girl a white man was likin'. The white man told the colored boy not to marry the colored girl, because *he* wanted her for hisself. The boy told him he loved the girl and was going to marry her, so the white guy say, 'You can't git no license here!'

"Well, the boy and girl ran off to another town and they got married and then come back home. The white fellow asked if they was really married and they told him they were. Now this girl figger if she showed him the license he would leave her go. She showed him the license, so they went and got her husband and killed him. Then they come back and got her—she was in a fam'ly way—and they killed her. Then they went and killed the boy's daddy and they killed his mother, and then, one of the brothers, *he* tried to fight and they killed *him*. So they killed twelve in that one family. That family was named Belcher, and all this happened at a place they call Longdale, Arkansas, way out in the woods from Goulds, Arkansas."

Without any more feeling than one would recall a storm or a flood or any other past disaster, Leroy commented, "Yeah, I heard of that, heard all about it."

"It was no protection at all that the poor peoples got in places like that back in those days," Natchez went on with calm anger. "You try to fight back, then it's not just you they gonna get. It's anybody in your family. Like if I have three brothers and do something and they can't catch me, they'll catch the brothers."

"It don't matter to them—just anybody in the family," Leroy said.

"*You* might do things and get away. But why do something or another and get your whole family kilt? You know what I mean?"

"I know it!"

"That's what they got on you, see?"

"Yeah, that's what they got on you," observed Natchez. "And if your family have a girl *they* like, you might's well's to let them *have* her, because if you don't, they liable to do something outrageous. When they see a Negro woman they like, they *gonna* have her, if they want her, especially down here.

> If I feel tomorrow, like I feel today,
> If I feel tomorrow, like I feel today,
> Stand right here and look a thousand miles away.
>
> I'm goin' to the river, set down on the ground;
> I'm goin' to the river, set down on the ground;
> When the blues overtake me, I'll jump overboard and drown.
>
> I feel my hell a-risin', a-risin' every day;
> I feel my hell a-risin', a-risin' every day;
> Someday it'll bust this levee and wash the whole wide world away. . . ."

"You know, they's another kind of Negro the white man call *bad*," Natchez went on. "A bad *seed*, a seed that ruins the rest of the Negroes, by opening their eyes and telling them things they don't know."

"Otherwise he is a *smart* Negro," Leroy chuckled.

"Yeah," said Natchez. "He would git the Chicago Defender, for an instance, and bring it down here and read it to the Negroes."

"Speakin' of the Chicago Defender," Leroy interrupted, "I were in a place once they called Marigold, Mississippi. They had a restaurant there and in the back they had a room with a peephole in the door. I thought it was a crap game goin' on back there and I went back to see. Fact of the business, I were kind of stranded and I wanted to shoot some craps and make me a stake, if I could.

"And you know what they were doin' back there? They were readin' the Chicago Defender and had a lookout man on the door. If a white man had come in the restaurant, they'd stick the Defender in the stove. Burn it up. And start playin' checkers." Leroy laughed. "That's the way they had to smuggle the Defender down there. Now if they'd caught this fellow that *brought* the Defender, they'd have called him a bad nigger."

"Might-a killed him."

"Yeah. He was the kind they call a *really* bad Negro—a man that has the nerve to smuggle the Defender into Mississippi where they don't even allow the paper to be put off the train."

The Chicago Defender has more than a hundred thousand circulation among Negro readers. It is far from radical. It prints news about Negro life, much that does not appear in the non-Negro press.

"That's what makes the Negro so *tetchious* till today," Natchez said. "He have been denied in so many places until if a gang of guys is, for an instance, standing in some certain place and they say to them *all,* 'You fellas, git back and don't stand there,' the Negroes in the crowd figger they're pointin' straight to *them.* A lot of times they don't mean that. They really mean they don't want *nobody* standin' there, but the Negro thinks, straight off, they referrin' to him because he's black."

Sib had been listening to his two older friends for a long time. He had had no experience of the deeps of the South—the work camps, the prison farms, the wild life of the river that they had known. He was a boy right off the farm, whose half-mad genius on his Woolworth harmonica was gradually leading him out into the world.

But Sib knew how it was to feel "black and tetchious."

"Well, boys, I'll tell you what happen to me. My mother, she bought a mule from er-uh Captain Jack, who was the boss of the county farm at my home. It was a nice mule. But, by me bein' young—you know how young boys are?—I rode this mule down, run him, you understand. After all, Captain Jack didn't have nothin' to say. He'd done sold the mule to my mother. And this mule finally got mired up in the bottom."

"You say married? Is that the mule you married?"

"Naw, naw, mired, mired up in the mud."

"That *must* be the mule you bought the hat for," Leroy cracked, and all three men burst into guffaws of country laughter, while Sib kept stuttering his story.

"Naw, it ain't! Now listen! Just this old mule got mired up and *died* down there in the bottom."

"I understand."

"Yeah. So er-uh Captain Jack, he told my mother that he was just crazy to git his hands on that stuttering fool of hers. Which was me. Said he was gonna do me just like I did the mule. Get me out there on the gang and—"

"I understand," said Natchez, now grave.

"And my mother had to just scuffle to keep me offa that gang. Ever' little move I'd make, he was watchin' me. And, after all, he done *sold* the mule and she done *paid* him. But he say I killed the mule and—"

Natchez interrupted sharply. "You see the main point is that word they have down here—'Kill a nigger, hire another one. Kill a mule, buy another one.' All these things, everything we've talked about, all these blues and everything, come under that one word. Fact of the business, back not long ago, a Negro didn't mean no more to a white man *than* a mule."

"Didn't mean as much," said Leroy.

"A black man," Natchez went on, "to what they looked at, was just a *black face.* I knew a man (they call him Mister White) had a plantation about fifty or sixty miles square and he didn't even want a Negro to come *through* his place. The government highway ran through his land, you know? What they call a pike, a main highway where everybody had to go, but he built a special road, ran all around his place, and when you got there it was a sign said 'NEGRO TURN.' You had to turn off the highway and go all around his plantation."

"I knew him, knew him well," Leroy muttered.

"And this Mister White had all white fences around his place. The trees, he painted them white as high as he could reach. All his cattle, his sheeps, goats, hogs, cows, mules, hosses, and everything on his place was white. Anytime one of his animals have a black calf or a black goat—whatsomever it was—Mister White give it to the niggers. Even down to the chickens. He had all white chickens, too. And when a chicken would hatch off some black chickens, he'd say, 'Take those chickens out and find a nigger and give 'em to him. Get rid of 'em. I won't have no nigger chickens on this plantation!' "

"I've seed all that, too," said Leroy. "And you know the time a Negro and a white man was standin' by a railroad crossin'? They was talkin', you know. The white man was tellin' the Negro what he wanted him to do. So along come another Negro drivin' a wagon with a white mule hitched to it. Well, the railin' was kinda high at this crossin' and the wheels got caught and the wagon stopped. This Negro who was drivin' begin to holler at that mule. 'Get up!' he says. 'Get along there.'

"So the white man holler up there and asked him, say, 'Hey you, don't you know that's a *white* mule you talkin' to?'

" 'Yassuh, boss,' the Negro tell him. 'Get up, *Mister* mule!' "

Natchez and Leroy began to guffaw, and, after a moment, when he got the point of the joke, Sib's laughter burst over him in torrents. Again he went staggering down the path, howling with glee and beating his arms helplessly in the air. So we all laughed together in the early morning breeze, blowing the blues out of our lungs and hearts in gusts of wild laughter.

"And how about that Prince Albert tobacco?" gasped Natchez, when he could speak again.

"I've heard of that," said Leroy.

"You know you couldn't go into one of these here little country stores and say, 'Gimme a can of Prince Albert'? Not with that white man on the can."

"What would you say?"

"Gimme a can of *Mister* Prince Albert!"

We were caught up in the gales of squalling laughter that racked Sib, until we must have looked like a party of madmen capering there in the dawn under the lee of the levee. We were howling down the absurdity, the perversity, and the madness that grips the land on which we stood, a beautiful and fecund land, rich in food and genius and good living and song, yet turned into a sort of purgatory by fear.

Now for an instant we understood each other. Now in this moment of laughter, the thongs and the chains, the harsh customs of dominance, the stupefying and brutalizing lies of race had lost their fallacious dignity, but only for an instant. The magic night had gone. Back in Memphis our night's friendship and understanding would vanish like this morning's mist under the pitiless southern sun. The blues would begin again their eternal rhythm, their eternal ironic comment:

> The blues jumped a rabbit, run him a solid mile,
> When the blues overtaken him, he hollered like a baby child. . . .

"Yeah," said Natchez, his face showing somberly now in the hard light of the July morning, "that's the way things go down around these little southern places—enough to give anybody the blues."

The Singer and the Bluesman

Formulations of Personality in the Lyrics of the Blues

Dennis Jarrett

AS MANY observers have noticed, the blues song, despite its basis in a traditional vocabulary and method, is associated with the single performer who is also its composer. Sometimes a singer will more or less memorize his song, delivering an essentially identical text each time he sings it. Other times, combining traditional and original materials, a singer will improvise a song which, unless it is recorded, is lost as an entity. Harry Oster, for example, speaks of Willie B. Thomas as singing lyrics which "took shape spontaneously as he was singing," and adds: "Later, although he was aware that he had produced an excellent song, he could not repeat it, but had to listen to the tape recording to find out what he had sung."[1] Yet once a song is established, either in fixed-phrase form or as a somewhat variable collocation of stanzas, it tends to remain the property of one performer. Referring to a number the white guitarist Johnny Winter had recorded, blues singer Lightning Hopkins told his audience at a Berkeley concert, "I'm the onliest man on God's earth who wrote that song."

Because of its association with an individual singer, and because of its basically autobiographical, first-person format, it is tempting to assume that a given lyric is the realistic account of one man's experience. But although the blues is widely recognized as "the truth," many blues singers acknowledge that their productions are not strictly personal. Michael Haralambos quotes Albert King, for instance, as saying ". . . I wouldn't be here today if it all happened to me," and Bobby Bland, who remarks: "More or less I'm telling my own story, because if you don't know about it, you can't sing about it. But I didn't have a real hard time actually. It was just the environment and growing up with the music."[2]

The blues is a genre whose conventions are always very much in evidence; and clearly the presentation of a kind of fictional self—whom I will call the *bluesman*—as distinct from the singer-composer, is one of them. This notion of the blues persona has received little critical attention, yet as a generic feature of the blues it is of real importance. The "meaning of the blues" must be embodied in the bluesman; he comes across as an autobiographer. It is precisely through the agency of the bluesman, or the singer in the song, that the

Reprinted from *Southern Folklore Quarterly* 42, no. 1 (1978): 31–37.

individual artist is able so successfully to sing communally rather than personally. It is only in the supreme artificiality of the bluesman that such familiar contradictories as despair and hopefulness, and complaint and pleasure, can be sustained. I will argue that the creation of a bigger-than-life personality is essentially formulaic, that the bluesman is encoded in lexical and psychological traditions which contribute to the genre.

Like other oral literatures, the blues is fully meaningful only in the context of performance. The bluesman embodies concerns he shares with his audience, and it is in an antiphonal relationship with his listeners that he makes himself known. Many conventions of performance add to his credibility; his physical movements, gestures, tone, facial expressions and reactions to audience feedback all participate in both the entertainment value and the efficacy of his presentation. Furthermore, though the blues artist purports to be telling us about himself, he does so within the highly stylized, contrived context of music—a means of expression which exaggerates the element of artifice and correspondingly militates against "realism." We are constantly reminded by the music that we are listening more to a contrivance than a confession. But although musical performance and lyrics are separable only in analysis, I want in this paper to concentrate specifically on the rhetoric with which the bluesman expresses himself, and to suggest that his personality is effectively contained within it.

In his provocative essay "Oral Sermons and Oral Narrative,"[3] Bruce Rosenberg seriously questions the usefulness of the term "formula," noting that it has been used carelessly and vaguely, and that except in the case of actual lexical features we would do well to avoid the term. He is also critical of the term "system," arguing that so-called systems by which oral composers improvise are simply the same systems underlying universal competence in language. Thus, he suggests, it is misleading to imagine that oral composers have in mind formulas which they are able to modify according to the occasion. What they do have, says Rosenberg (and this distinguishes them from the rest of us), is skill: "The oral performer has ability, not thousands of formulas."[4] As evidence of this, Rosenberg cites the case of a preacher who was able without breaking stride to create a metrically intact apology for his faulty biblical reference. Clearly the apology was not formulaic; yet it became part of the fabric of the preacher's sermon. Observing that "All grammatical utterances are formulaic," Rosenberg maintains that to identify oral narrative composition as formulaic (analogous to grammatical competence) does not advance our understanding of the process. He concludes: "If we must speak of oral formulas, we would do well to restrict our discussion and definition to lexical features . . ."[5]

Surely Rosenberg is correct in identifying the folk preacher as skillful and in noting, as he later does, that folk performers do not think of their productions as being systematically composed. But it seems to me that the process of association—which Rosenberg posits as the basis of improvisation—is itself formulaic and that a skill model is not inconsistent with one in which formulaic guidelines function to keep the performer within his genre. We cannot stretch the Lord-Parry understanding of a formula to explain traditions which, like the blues, are not narrative. But we require some terminology which will identify a process of composition which proceeds largely according to prescription and guideline. The analogy with linguistic competence (which is universal) does not seem nearly as appropriate as the analogy with jazz improvisation, which requires skill but which is supported and informed by somewhat variable formulas. The jazz soloist makes choices as he plays, but the choices occur within the framework of a chord structure, a rhythm, a scale, and what might be called a stylistic structure. The sound he makes is recognizably jazz.

I want to suggest that the blues singer (probably to a much greater extent than the folk preacher) relies on lexical formulas which can be varied somewhat without losing their identity, and that in using them the singer assents to a given personality. I want further to suggest that the process by which a singer extends himself beyond fixed lexical features of his tradition and continues to create an image, a self-image, is equally formulaic.

Several writers have shown that blues lyrics frequently include oral-formulaic phrases and stanzas. As David Evans remarks in an essay on blues composition, many singers "rely on a vast body of traditional formulaic lines and stanzas for composing their blues."[6] Prefabricated blues components, which include single, exclamatory words as well as longer statements, are available to the composer for use in a unique arrangement or in combination with original lyrics. Tried and tested, such elements maximize the quality of a song, providing familiar touchstones for the audience. But in addition, they are inevitably characteristic of the self—the bluesman—who utters them. Such formulas provide the singer with his generic personality, epitomizing the persona of the bluesman at his best. Many single words (e.g., "satisfy," "pacify," "ease," "ramble," "worried") are used often as constituent elements in blues lines. And phrases such as "lose a happy home," "ease my worried mind," "good morning, blues," and "my good gal," are found in combination with various complementary possibilities. The complete line, ending with a word which will rhyme with either a preceding or capping line, is the most common verbal formula in the bluesman's repertory. Examples are: "Mama told me, papa told me too," "I'm gonna pack my suitcase, make my getaway," "I was not sick, just dissatisfied," and "Sometimes I think I lover her then again I think I don't." And the singer has at his disposal such ready-made stanzas, allowing for a variable repetition of the first line, as these: "You never miss your water till your well runs dry / Never miss your baby till she say goodbye," and "See me coming raise your window high / See me leaving hang your head and cry."

The singer who uses traditional first-person rhetoric becomes, *ipso facto,* a traditional person. Verbal formulas sustain him in the presentation of a blues self. Revealed by his own words, the bluesman typically expresses those qualities Harry Oster describes as the surface of the blues: ". . . frustration, anger, aggressiveness, sadness, oppression, hunger, sickness, the pangs of the cuckold, the restlessness of the wanderer."[7] As Oster points out, while these disturbances comprise the surface of blues lyrics, the function of the bluesman is to transform complaint into affirmation. This accomplishment involves, predominantly, the *tone* of the bluesman, i.e., his attitude toward his situation. This tone is built into his oral-formulaic tradition.

Perhaps the most salient tonal feature of the bluesman is his verbal stylization. Like a master dozens players, the bluesman is recognized and admired for his facility with language. He describes sorrow and complains about his life not as a downtrodden victim but as a virtuoso, undermining and transforming his complaint by the use of a device which is basically ironic: the epigram. Abrahams notes of his taletellers that ". . . all noncasual discourse seemed to gravitate toward rhyme or clever turn of phrase."[8] Likewise, and obviously drawing on an Afro-American tradition which informs several genres of verbal performance, the bluesman comes across as a Man of Words. He is able to address melancholy playfully: "Honey you so beautiful you know you gonna die some day / All I want's a little lovin' before you pass away." And even abject sorrow with no sexual referent may be approached and lessened through stylization: "Rather be in the river floating like a log / Than be here in Mississippi treated like a dog." "You don't believe I'm sinking look what a hole I'm in." Guaranteed by a formulaic vocabulary, the articulateness of the bluesman is unmistakably a sign of personal power and an instrument with which to confront the blues.

In addition to pre-fabricated formulas which are more or less complete units for the singer to provide with a context, the genre offers many formulas which are incomplete. These too perform the function of establishing tone. The singer may fill in the blank with a traditional or an original expression. The following are examples of incomplete formulas: "The blues ain't nothin' but ——;" "Honey, let me be your —— until your —— comes;" "I don't mind dying but ——;" "Sometimes I think —— then again I think ——;" "I'll stick closer to you than ——;" "When you see me coming ——;" "Caused a man like me to ——." Like lexically complete formulas, such set-ups guide the singer toward and emphasize verbal facility.

But possibly even more significant than these partial formulas are certain generic guidelines which aid the singer in his creation of a bluesman. It is possible to create a blues song without recourse to fixed-phrase formulas. Assuming that the audience can still recognize such a production as the blues, then on what basis does that recognition occur? The answer, I think, is that the singer is able to originate not just a musical structure but a rhetoric which conforms in terms of content and tone to the expectations of the blues audience. The singer Roosevelt Sykes, for example, performs a song with the following chorus:

> Wasn't I lucky when I got my time
> Oh wasn't I lucky, lord, when I got my time
> You know my partner got a hundred, yeah and I got ninety nine.

These lines, as far as I can ascertain, are original with Sykes, yet they are unmistakably typical of their genre. Formally, the blues stanza, a formula, is employed; but Sykes sings not as a disconsolate prison inmate, but as the bluesman personified when he makes an epigrammatic, sarcastic joke out of his misfortune. This line of rhetoric is continued during a portion of the song where the singing is interrupted by talk:

> He said now look here, son, when you do the ninety-nine years you come back, you be a good boy. I said, judge, how in the world can I do ninety-nine years and then come back and be a good boy? And if I don't be a *dead* boy I'll be a *old* boy because there's natural born rollin' down on that river line . . .[9]

The irony of being "lucky" is exposed here with a pointed question to the judge. But it is replaced by another, mocking sarcasm, based on the word "boy." Improvising as the bluesman by adopting a stylized ironic frame of reference, Sykes subsumes a personal situation to the requirements of a larger personality.

Original, non-traditional blues lyrics then, are composed so as to resemble those which are the common property of singers. They may be patterned with reference to what I have called an incomplete formula, or they may be lexically original. In either case, the tone of the bluesman operates as a kind of guideline. A common device exhibiting great stylization is the propensity for exploiting a metaphor in almost every detail. Thus, in addition to the standard line "If you don't want my peaches please don't shake my tree," one finds such extended versions of the peach image as Blind Lemon Jefferson employs in his song "Peach Orchard Mama," including "... you swore that / no one picked your fruit but me / I found three kid men / shaking down your peach-a-tree," and the lines "... I work in your orchard," "I hate to see your peach-a-tree fall," and "let me keep your orchard clean."[10] The extended metaphor is a device which helps direct the process of composition; it is a tool the singer has at his disposal.

Other formulas which are elements in the blues oral-formulaic tradition include impersonating the blues, locating it in a place (by the bed, in the kitchen, etc.), doubling up on a metaphor ("she got ways like the devil / and hair like a Indian squaw"), and such situational frameworks as talking to a train engineer or depot agent, making a long distance call, and waking up in the morning. The singer who begins to compose a blues song, then, has many touchstones to rely upon, and the ultimate character of his song is inevitably traditional in many more ways than just the obvious use of a certain chord pattern or a stanza form or a fixed phrase.

Although as Paul Oliver has shown the content of the blues is remarkably wide-ranging, incorporating specific work situations and even homosexual jealousy, the stance of the bluesman is much more confined. In addition to being stylish, epigrammatic and ironic, the bluesman may be moralizing and didactic ("you got to reap just what you sow"), bragging and "bad" ("I started to kill my woman till she lay down 'cross the bed") and self-pitying ("I wouldn't hurt so bad but it hurts my tongue to talk").[11] He is very much given to exaggeration of the sort which demands the recognition that he is a fictional rather than a real person. As such, he can function openly as a projection of the fantasies of his audience. The bluesman who speaks the traditional words "I'm gonna beat my woman until I'm satisfied," which present him as extravagantly "bad," is indistinguishable from the bluesman whose utterance is non-traditional: "I'm gonna take you down / by the riverside / tie your hands / tie your hands / tie your feet / push you in the water till the bubbles roll up . . ."[12] Both statements are essentially formulaic and characteristic of the Man of Words who sings them.

In one mood, the bluesman can threaten to buy some bulldogs to guard his woman against her natural inclination to cheat on him, and in another he can tell his lover: "You oughta buy you a bulldog / to watch us while we sleep / So he can see your husband / if he makes a 'fo day creep." These voices, like so many others in the blues which can be turned on suddenly, or faded in and out at will, do not ask to be taken literally. In his irony and duplicity, the bluesman manages to describe the full complexity of his sorrows and to ease them gracefully and entertainingly. He freely allows himself whatever inconsistencies he needs (and feels) to sing the blues and to transcend it. When he begins to sing, using a language which is heavily based on an oral tradition, he sings with a personality which is not his alone, but which is also, inevitably, an element in the blues tradition, contained in his language and in his way of composing. He does not sing the same songs other bluesmen perform, but his lyrics and theirs are from the same mold.

Notes

1. Harry Oster, "The Blues as a Genre," *Genre* 2 (1969), p. 268.
2. Michael Haralambos, *Right On: From Blues to Soul in Black America* (New York: 1975), pp. 57–58.

3. Bruce A. Rosenberg, "Oral Sermons and Oral Narrative," *Folklore Genres*, ed. Dan Ben-Amos (Austin and London: University of Texas Press, 1975).

4. Ibid., p. 97.

5. Ibid., p. 100.

6. David Evans, "Techniques of Blues Composition among Black Folksingers," *Journal of American Folklore* 87 (1974), 245.

7. Oster, p. 273.

8. Roger D. Abrahams, *Deep Down in the Jungle: Negro Narrative Folklore from the Streets of Philadelphia* (New York: 1964), p. 92.

9. I am indebted to Venitia Terrell for this transcription.

10. Eric Sackheim, *The Blues Line* (New York: Grossman, 1970), p. 78 transcription.

11. I have dealt more extensively with the stances of the bluesman in "The Poetry of the Blues," Diss., University of California, Berkeley, 1972.

12. John Lombardi, "John Lee Bad Like Jesse James," *Rolling Stone* (March 4, 1971), p. 18.

Oral Formulas in the Country Blues

John Barnie

ANYONE listening to a number of country blues songs will have noticed that they share certain basic linguistic and thematic features. Most noticeably, half-lines, lines, and stanzas will be found to recur in the songs of a great many singers. These may be modified, sometimes radically so, but they bear a recognizable relationship to lines and stanzas in other songs within the tradition. A similar correspondence exists at the thematic level, since the country blues singer develops a comparatively limited range of themes. Yet it is rare to find one singer reproducing *exactly* the blues of another. A close relationship exists between many blues, but it is not that of a copy (even an imperfectly remembered one) to its original.

An explanation for these features may be sought in the theory of oral-formulaic composition, first propounded by the American classical scholars Milman Parry and A. B. Lord in relation to the Homeric poems and Jugoslav folk epics.[1] The results of their research have received a wide currency in recent years, and the theory has been applied with varying degrees of success to such diverse material as Old English alliterative poetry and black American chanted sermons.[2] Its relevance to the blues, however, is only now being appreciated by scholars in the field; and unfortunately, with the exception of Jeff Titon's exposition in *Early Downhome Blues* and the important research-in-progress of Michael Taft,[3] most attempts to apply the Parry-Lord thesis in this area have been far from satisfactory.

William Ferris, Jr., for example, refers to the theory in *Blues from the Delta*, but fails to take into account the difficulties caused by the lyric rather than narrative structure of the blues.[4] Likewise, John Fahey, in his study of blues singer Charley Patton, alludes to Parry and Lord's thesis, but is confused as to the nature and significance of formulas in Patton's blues. He identifies formulaic lines which he refers to as "traditional commonplaces," but goes on to assert that, "In no case does the use of a particular commonplace play an integral or even especially important part in one of Patton's texts."[5] Yet in a later characterization of his blues Fahey claims that they are "an extreme case of oral-formulaic creativity in which the singer, if he does not (and Patton probably did not) actually make up the stanzas at the time of the performance, simply selects stanzas and verses at random from a large storehouse of them in his mind."[6] Unfortunately, Fahey never defines exactly what he means by a formula in the blues.

The uncertainties and contradictions in these two studies are indicative, I think, of some of the problems involved in adapting the oral-formulaic theory to the blues. For while it is clear that the country blues singers were working within a tradition similar to that described by Parry and Lord, there are fundamental differences which must also be taken into account. The most important of these relates to genre. Parry and Lord developed their ideas from the study of Jugoslav folk epic: poetry which is essentially narrative, sometimes extending into thousands of lines. The blues, on the other hand, is lyric insofar as it can be equated with any Western poetic genre. It is a crucial difference, which I will return to later.

Briefly, the Parry-Lord thesis is that the singer of epic verse in a pre-literate society creates his songs in the act of performance, largely, though not exclusively, with the aid of an extensive repertoire of formulas: a formula being in Parry's definition, "a group of words which is regularly employed under the same metrical conditions to express a given essential idea."[7] The oral poet is able to draw on a large store of such formulas, some of which will be common to the tradition as a whole, others limited to a group of related singers, and yet others unique to the songs of a particular singer. Such formulas should not be thought of as clichés, for as Lord has pointed out, they are "capable of change and are indeed frequently highly productive of other and new formulas."[8] Nor does a formula necessarily involve word-for-word repetition. Elements in a given formula may vary, providing they meet the demands of metre and the "given essential idea." Extensive variation, however, results in the formation of a "formulaic system" which is defined by Parry as: "a group of phrases which have the same metrical value and which are enough alike in thought and words to leave no doubt that the poet who used them knew them not only as single formulas, but also as formulas of a certain type."[9]

In applying this concept to the blues, one is at once confronted with a problem of definition: what is the basic metrical unit of the blues and hence the basic unit of the formula? With most work in recent years concentrating on the stanza as a unit of *meaning*, it is a problem which has received little attention.

Several writers have emphasized the non-narrative structure of the country blues, which consists typically of a series of discrete stanzas which may collectively evoke a particular mood or experience.[10] Such stanzas correspond more or less to the "themes" of oral epic poetry, defined by Lord as "the repeated incidents and descriptive passages in the songs."[11] To this extent therefore, William Ferris, Jr. is right to argue that "any relevant study of the blues must focus its attention on the verse (sic) as the basic unit."[12] It is misleading however to claim, as he does in the same sentence, that "the verse [stanza] is the only textual unit which remains structurally intact." For while a singer *may* adopt a stanza wholesale, he is more likely to borrow lines and in particular half-lines which he recombines into stanzas of his own. At one level, therefore, it is the line and half-line which should be considered the basic "textual unit" of the blues, and upon which any discussion of oral formulas must concentrate.[13]

I would suggest that the metre of such lines is accentual, based on a comparatively free patterning of stressed (´), half-stressed (`), and unstressed (ʌ) syllables.[14] Certain normative features are discernible however. Usually a metrical line will consist of 4 to 6 stresses, with most singers I have analysed showing a preference for 5 or 6.[15] It is divided by a caesura, with a tendency towards an equal distribution of stressed syllables if the line is composed of 6 stresses, and towards a 2/3 ratio in a 5-stress line. Half-stress is quite common, while unstressed syllables, though in theory unlimited, rarely exceed 3 to 5 in any given line. Thus, for example:

> Júdge pléase dôn't kìll mé | Î wón't bê bád nô móre.[16]

It should be noted that the caesura is often heavily emphasised in performance, since it serves the dual function of breath pause and formula boundary.

An accentual structure of this kind centers on the distribution of stressed and, to a lesser extent, half-stressed syllables; while unstressed syllables may vary in number without necessarily affecting the basic metre of a given half-line. Superficially, this structure is reminiscent of the accentual verse of the Anglo-Saxons, much of which is oral-formulaic in origin.[17] One major difference, however, is that in Old English verse a *particular* stress pattern forms an integral part of any given formula from which little or no variation is permissible. But in the blues, for a number of reasons, it is not possible to define the metrical basis of the formula (or indeed its verbal components) so precisely. An example will make this clear.

A widely disseminated formula is based on the "given essential idea" of the singer's *going away*. With few exceptions, it is a formula of the first half-line of verse one (1^a), and is sufficiently generalised to allow a range of formulas or non-formulaic phrases in the second half-line (1^b). In the examples I have collected, however, there are four apparent "variants" of this formula which need to be considered.

The simplest consists of a bare statement of the "given essential idea" which may be shortened by the omission of the personal pronoun and auxillary verb, as in:

> Î'm góin' âwáy
> Góin' âwáy.[18]

It will be noticed that in both examples, accent is placed on the two key words "goin"' and "away," and although there are exceptions to be discussed later, metrical stress usually reinforces the key words of the formula in this way.[19]

Most singers expand the half-line, however, by the addition of tags placed either at the beginning or the end of the formula proper, or both. As is well known, tags such as "Lord," "mama" and "honey" are ubiquitous in the blues, so much so that they are frequently ignored by scholars who do not always transcribe them when establishing texts. This is regrettable, for tags often serve the dual function of heightening the dramatic element in a blues and (I would suggest) of satisfying the singer's innate preference for a particular pattern of stresses within the half-line. They are far from being mere ornamentation.

For example, the *I am going away* formula is most frequently used with reference to a woman whom the singer has decided to leave. The insertion of "baby," "honey" or "mama" after the formula addresses the singer's words directly to the woman, emphasizing her personal involvement in the stanza. It also provides the singer with the possibility of a 2½ or 3 stress half-line which is the commonest of the metrical variants open to him:

Î'm góin' âwáy bábŷ
Î'm góin' âwày bábe.[20]

More rarely, the singer *may* retain the 2 stress pattern by emphasizing the concluding tag at the expense of the initial stress on "goin'." The second syllable of "away," however, always receives stress or, very occasionally, half-stress:

Î'm gôin' âwáy mámâ
Î'm gôin' âwáy bábŷ.[21]

A third variant involves the addition of a tag such as "says," "well," "and" or "Lord" before the formula (examples 22–30). With the exception of "Lord," however, these are almost always unstressed and so do not affect the given stress pattern of the formula. They seem to serve an introductory function, allowing the singer to signal a new stanza by a prefatory interjection which is often omitted in the second verse (examples 24–6, 29, 30, 33, 34). "Lord," on the other hand, always receives half-stress and occasionally stress: an indication of its relative importance as an intensifier of the singer's intention as expressed in the formula (examples 30–2, 35).

As one might expect, the largest single group (examples 31–42) contains initial and concluding tags, since this allows the singer to fulfill all the conditions noted above: the preference for a half-line of 3 or 2½ stresses; the desire to heighten the content of the formula dramatically; and the need to mark off the first verse of a new stanza with an interjection.[22]

A related function of tags should also be noted. It is a direct result of the unusual structure of the three-line blues stanza, in which the second line is essentially a repetition of the first. Through the addition or subtraction of tags, the singer is able to modify the stress pattern of the line, thus providing a degree of variation in a potentially monotonous verbal repetition.[23]

However, while the stress pattern may be altered by the introduction of tags, it can be argued, I think, that the "given essential idea" is not. There is a significant difference, for example, between "I'm goin' away *mama*" and "I'm goin' away *to leave you*" (examples 43–5). In the latter, the singer has modified the formula to such an extent that it must be considered a different formula within the larger system based on the idea of going away. In the first example, however, "mama" represents so slight a modification to the main idea of the formula that the singer may choose to delete it in the second, repeated line. "I'm goin' away" and "I'm goin' away mama" clearly represents minor variations of a single formula, although the metrical pattern is not the same. In this respect, oral formulas in the blues are quite distinct from those in Old English verse or Jugoslav folk epic, where the formula is integrated with a particular and largely inflexible metrical unit. It should be noted however that significant limits are placed on the singer's use of stressed tags by the prevalence in the blues of a half-line or two or three stresses, two of which *generally* correspond with the key words of the formula.

In the examples I have collected, four major themes are developed in line 1^b. These are concerned with: (1) the duration of the singer's absence, (2) his motive for leaving, (3) the real or imagined reaction of his woman, and (4) the assertion that he is leaving *soon*. A larger sample would undoubtedly reveal others. They are expressed through a variety of formulas and non-formulaic phrases, although a glance at the appendix makes it quite clear that formulas predominate.[24]

Four blues songs in the sample incidentally confirm that the singers worked with half-line units when composing their blues in performance. In the examples below, the singer uses the *I am going away* formula in two separate stanzas, followed in each case by a different formula in 1^b:

A st.3 Wêll Î'm góin' âwáy mámâ | wón't bê baćk tîll Fáll
st.7 Sâys Î'm góin' âwáy | máke it̂ lónesôme hére

B st.2 Ì'm góin' âwáy | bábŷ an̂d it̂ wón't bê lóng
st.6 Lórd Î'm góin' âwáy | hónêy hôw cán Î stáy?

C st.1 Sàid I'm̂ góin' âwáy mámâ | wéar yôu óff mŷ mínd
st.2 Sàid I'm̂ góin' âwáy bábŷ | cátch t̂he Hóllŷwoòd líne

D st.5 Sâys I'm̂ góin' âwày mámâ | bábŷ dón't yòu cŕy
st.7 Sàys I'm̂ góin' âwày mámâ | Î am̂ góin' tô stáy.[25]

In C it should be noted that the singer substitutes what appears to be a non-formulaic half-line in st.2, 1^b. Thematically however it is closely related to the formulaic system based on the idea of catching a specified train or riding a specified line.

As I will suggest, a singer may show a preference in his blues for a particular collocation of formulas in 1^a and 1^b, but it is clear that the tradition as a whole provides a wide range of formulas for 1^b which the more inventive singer may vary at will.

An important but so far unresolved problem relating to oral-formulaic composition in the blues, concerns those factors which influence a singer's choice and juxtaposition of formulas. It is beyond the scope of this paper to discuss the problem in detail; it would seem, however, that rhyme words play an important part in determining the progression of formulas within a stanza. This becomes evident when a singer either makes a mistake or deviates for some other reason from the more usual collocations of rhymed formulas. As an example, one may take the following stanza from "Court Street Blues" by Stovepipe No. 1:

Góin' âwáy | aín't cômîn' báck t̂íll Fáll
I'm̂ góin' âwáy | aín't cômîn' báck nô móre
Wêll t̂he blúes ôvêrtáke mê | Î aín't cômîn' báck nô móre.

1^a and 1^b represent a familiar collocation of formulas. In the second line, however, the singer substitutes the closely related formula *ain't comin' back no more.*[26] This places him in a dilemma, since the formula he sang in 1^b is almost always associated with *won't be back at all* in 3^b, with its logical progression underpinned by the rhyme on "Fall" and "all." Conversely, the formula in 2^b is normally associated with the *hang crepe on your door* formula in 3^b, with which it shares the rhyme on "more" and "door."[27] Unable to resolve his dilemma, Stovepipe No. 1 compromises weakly by repeating *ain't comin' back no more* in 3^b, even though this formula is most often reserved for lines 1 and 2.

It is perhaps not possible to talk with certainty of a "mistake" on the singer's part here, although he was certainty aware of the Fall/all progression which he uses in st. 4. But the unusual substitution in 2^b highlights the way in which rhyme words act as a determining factor in the collocation of formulas, helping to ensure the inner logic and narrative consistency of the stanza. Through his inattention to the progression of rhyme words, Stovepipe No. 1 has sacrificed both.

A detailed study of similar stanzas in which the singer either makes a mistake or deviates radically from the more usual collocations, could add to our understanding of the process of oral-formulaic composition in the blues.

In this paper, in common with Michael Taft and Jeff Titon, I have taken the half-line as the basis of oral-formulaic composition in the blues. But there are complicating factors which Parry and Lord did not encounter in their study of Jugoslav epic poetry and which arise from the lyric as opposed to the epic structure of the blues. Even in the most favourable 'field' conditions, a blues song never achieves the length of an oral epic, and narrative complexity is essentially alien to the tradition. As Ferris, Jr. and others have observed, the thematic unit of the blues is a discrete three-line stanza. It is hardly surprising therefore that a singer will often find one coupling of half-line formulas particularly to his liking, with the result that in *his* songs the two formulas invariably appear linked together. In many instances the positioning of the caesura makes it clear that the singer is thinking from the beginning in terms of a completed line and not half-lines. For example:

> Cryin' Lord I wonder will I | ever get back home.
> Some people say the | Green River blues ain't bad.[28]

Where the singer is composing through the medium of half-line formulas, the caesura acts as a formula and syntax boundary. Here however, the singers ignore syntax in the positioning of the caesura: a certain indication that they are thinking in terms of a *line* unit rather than basic half-line formulas.

Similarly, there are many stanzas which tend towards a set form. A singer who begins with "The sun's gonna shine in my back door some day" will almost invariably conclude with "The wind's gonna rise, blow my blues away." It should be noted, however, that the formulaic basis of such stanzas does allow an inventive singer to substitute other half-line formulas for the more conventional collocation.

No doubt the widespread dissemination of blues via gramophone records hastened this process of ossification; but it is probably inherent in the lyric structure of the blues itself, which makes it easy and natural for memorable lines and stanzas to achieve a set form. Many of these still retain the aura of the formulas from which they undoubtedly derived, but although they may be considered "formulaic" they are not themselves formulas. Perhaps the closest analogy is with similar lines and stanzas in ballad tradition; and indeed, one difference between blues singers and Jugoslav epic singers is that the former usually include a range of other secular and religious songs in their repertoires which, unlike their blues, have been learnt by heart. Composing and singing within an oral-formulaic tradition *and* something approaching a literary song tradition must have hastened the process whereby the blues lost its pure oral-formulaic character—if indeed it ever had one.

Appendix

Note: with the exceptions of examples no. 32 and 42 (available on a Library of Congress LP), all records indicated in parentheses are 10″ 78s.

1. Big Boy Cleveland, "Goin' to Leave You Blues" (Gennett 6108, 1927), st. 2.
Î'm góin' âwáy | tô wéar yòu óff m̂y mínd (3)
Keep me worried bothered all the time.

2. Elizabeth Johnson, "Sobbin' Woman Blues" (OKeh 8789, 1928), st. 8.
Î'm góin' âwáy | jùst tô wéar yôu óff m̂y mínd
Góin' âwáy | tô wéar yòu óff m̂y mínd (2)
Keeps me worried bothered all the time.

3. Papa Charlie Jackson, "Ash Tray Blues" (Paramount 12660, 1928), st. 8.
Î'm góin' âwáy | wón't bê lóng
You look for me I'll be gone. . .

4. Lottie Beaman, "Going Away Blues" (Brunswick 7147, 1929), st. 1.
Î'm góin' âwáy | ît wón't bê lóng
I know you'll miss me even singing this lonesome song
Î'm góin' âwáy | ît wón't bê lóng
And then you'll know you must have done me wrong.

5. Charlie Kyle, "Kyle's Worried Blues" (Victor 21707, 1928), st. 2.
I'm̂ góin' âwáy | báby̑ an̂d ît wón't bê lóng (2)
You mistreated me and I'm gonna lay my hat at home.

6. Henry Thomas, "Don't Leave Me Here" (Vocalion 1443, 1929), st. 6.
I'm̂ góin' âwáy | an̂d ît wón't bè lóng
Just [ ] you train lovin' baby I'm Alabama bound.

7. Charley Patton, "Down the Dirt Road Blues" (Paramount 12854, 1929), st. 1.
Î'm gôin' âwáy | tó thê ón̂e Î knów (2)
I'm worried now but I won't be worried long.

8. Charley Patton, "Green River Blues" (Paramount 12972, 1929), st. 7.
I'm̂ gôin' âwáy | gónnâ máke ìt lónesôme hére
I'm̂ gôin' âwáy báby̑ | tô máke ìt lónesôme hére
Yês I'm góin' âwáy | tô máke ìt lónesôme hére.

9. Blind Lemon Jefferson, "Struck Sorrow Blues" (Paramount 12541, 1927), st. 1.
Î'm góin' âwáy | hónêy dón't yòu wánt tô gó?
Î'm góin' âwáy báby̑ | dón't yoù wánt tô gó?
I'm goin' to stop at a place I haven't never been before.

10. Stovepipe No. 1, "Court Street Blues" (OKeh 8514, 1927), st. 1.
Góin' âwáy | aín't cômin̂' báck tíll Fáll
Î'm góin' âwáy | aín't cômin̂' báck nô móre
Well the blues overtake me I ain't comin' back no more.

11. Blind Blake, "Doing a Stretch" (Paramount 12810, 1929), st. 7.
Góin' âwáy | hòw háppy̑ Í wíll bé
If I know you still love me . . .

12. Charley Patton, "Circle Round the Moon" (Paramount 13040, 1929), st. 4.
I'm goin' away make it lonesome here (2)
I'm goin' away babe to make it lonesome here.
(Note: I have not heard this song. The text is taken from Fahey, *Charley Patton*, p. 107.)

13. Tom Dickson, "Happy Blues" (OKeh 8590, 1928), st. 6.
I'm̀ góin' âwáy bábŷ | sée whât yóu gôin' dó
I'm góin' âwáy bábŷ | sée whât yóu goîn' dó
I done all I could can't get along with you.

14. Furry Lewis, "Big Chief Blues" (Vocalion 1133, 1927), st. 1.
Î'm gôin' âwáy bábŷ | táke mê sév'n lòng mońths tô ríde (2)
January February March April May June July.

15. Charley Patton, "When Your Way Gets Dark" (Paramount 12998, 1929), st. 6.
Î'm gôin' âwáy bábŷ | (dón't yôu wánt tô gó?) *spoken*
Î'm gôin' âwáy bábŷ | dón't yôu wánt tô gó?

16. Charley Patton, "Devil Sent the Rain Blues" (Paramount 13040, 1929), st. 6.
Î'm gôin' âwáy mámâ | dón't yôu wánt tô gó?
Î'm gôin' âwáy mámâ | dón't yôu wánt tô . . . (2)

17. Henry Thomas, "Bull Doze Blues" (Vocalion 1230, 1928), st. 1.
Î'm góin' âwáy bábe ańd ît wón't bê lóng
Î'm góin' âwáy | ańd ît wón't bê lóng
Î'm góin' âwáy ańd ît wón't bê lóng.

18. Blind Lemon Jefferson, "Lonesome House Blues" (Paramount 12593, 1927), st. 2.
Î'm gôin' âwáy mámâ | jûst tô wéar yôu óff m̂y mínd
Î'm gôin' âwáy prèttŷ mámâ | jûst tô wéar yôu óff m̂y mínd
Gonna find a lady in Chicago murder is gonna be my crime.

19. Roosevelt Sykes, "Single Tree Blues" (Paramount 12827, 1929), st. 4.
Góin' âwáy mámâ | cómiñg hére nô móre
Góin' âwáy bábŷ | cómiñg hére nô móre
You know you sure is mean you thrown my trunk out-door.

20. Walter Taylor, "Thirty-Eight and Plus" (Gennett 7157, 1930), st. 6.
Góin' âwáy prèttŷ mámâ | wón't bê báck tíll Fáll
If I don't get back then I won't be back at all.

21. Hi Henry Brown, "Skin Man" (Vocalion 1692, 1932), st. 3.
Well it's skins oh skins | skin skin skin skin
Well it's skins it's skins | skin skin skin
I'm̀ gôin' âwáy ôld skín bût I'm | cóm̀in báck âgáin.

22. Henry Thomas, "Don't Leave Me Here," st. 5.
Sâys I'm̀ gòin' âwáy | ánd ît wón't bê lóng
Just as sure as the train leaves out of the yard
She's Alabama bound.

23. Lewis Black, "Rock Island Blues" (Columbia 14429-D, 1927), st. 7.
Said mmm-well-mm-well-well I'm | máke ít lónesôme hére
Sâys Î'm góin' âwáy | máke ît lónesôme hére
Sâys Î'm góin' âwáy mámà máke ît lónesôme hére.

24. Lonnie Coleman, "Old Rock Island Blues" (Columbia 14440-D, 1929), st. 5.
Wêll Î'm góin' âwáy | aîn't cómîn hére nô móre
Î'm góin' âwáy | aîn't cómîn' hére nô móre
[ ] hang crepe on your door.

25. Tommy Johnson, "Bye-Bye Blues" (Victor 21409, 1928), st. 3.
    Wêll I'm̀ góin' âwáy | wón't bê báck tîll Fáll
    I'm góin' âwáy Lórd | bábŷ wón't bê báck tîll Fáll
    If I meet my good gal then baby won't be back at all.

26. Otto Virgial, "Little Girl in Rome" (Bluebird B6213, 1935), st. 3.
    Wêll Î'm góin' wáy-âwáy tô | wéar yôu óff m̂y mínd
    'Cause you keep me worryin' bothered all the time
    Î'm gòin' wáy-âwáy tô | wéar yôu óff m̂y mind.

27. Papa Charlie Jackson, "Shave Em Dry" (Paramount 12264, 1925), st. 3.
    Nòw Î'm góin' âwáy | tô wéar yôu óff mŷ mínd
    You keep me broke and hungry mama all the time . . .

28. Kid Cole, "Hey Hey Mama Blues" (Vocalion 1186, 1928), st. 5.
    Añd Î'm góin' âwáy | â-prèttŷ mámâ cŕyin' ít wón't bê lóng
    Añd Î'm góin' âwáy | prèttŷ mámâ crýin' ít wón't bê lóng (2)
    Get your typewriter mama and type the [ ] days I'm gone.

29. Kid Cole, "Hard Hearted Mama Blues" (Vocalion 1187, 1928), st. 7.
    Añd Î'm góin' âwáy | líttle bábŷ crýin' ít wón't bê lóng
      Lórd ît wón't bê lóng
    Î'm góin' âwáy | líttle bábŷ crýin' ít wón't bê lóng
    Said take your bible pretty mama and read the days your daddy's gone.

30. Charlie Kyle, "Kyle's Worried Blues," st. 6.
    Lórd Î'm góin' âwáy | hónêy hôw cán Î stáy?
    I'm̀ góin' âwáy | hónêy hôw cán Î stáy?
    I can't be downhearted mistreated this-away.

31. Papa Charlie Jackson, "The Faking Blues" (Paramount 12281, 1925), st. 4.
    Lórd Î'm gôin' âwáy mámâ | b'líeve mé ít aín't nô stáll (2)
    'Cause I can get more women than a passenger train can haul.

32. Son House, "Low Down Dirty Dog Blues" (Lib. Congress AAFS L-59, 1942), st. 4.
    Mmmm Lòrd Î'm góin' âwáy bábŷ | I'ḿ gôin' stày â gréat lóng tíme
    Ohhhhhh | Î sày Î'm gôin' stáy â gréat lóng tíme
    You know I ain't comin' back now honey oooh-babe until you change your mind.

33. Jabo Williams, "Fat Mama Blues" (Paramount 13130, 1932), st. 5.
    Sâys Î'm góin' âwày mámâ | bábŷ dón't yòu cŕy
    Î'm góin' âw`
    ay mámâ | dón't yòu cŕy Lòrd
    Î'm góin' âwày mámâ | plèase dón't yòu cŕy
    Î'm góin' âwày mámâ | bábŷ dón't yòu cŕy
    I will be back by and by.

34. Jabo Williams, "Fat Mama Blues," st. 7.
    Sàys Î'm góin' âwày mámâ | Î âm góin' tô stáy
    Î âm góin' âwày mámâ | góin' tô stáy Lòrd
    Î'm góin' âwày mámâ | góin' tô stáy
    Them big legs baby gonna keep me away
    Them big legs goin' keep me away.

35. Cannon's Jug Stompers "Springdale Blues" (Victor 21351, 1928), st. 1.
Sàid Î'm góin' âwáy mámâ | wéar yôu óff mŷ mínd
Lòrd Î'm góin' âwáy mámâ | wéar yôu óff mŷ mínd
You keep me worried and bothered baby lordy all the time.

36. Cannon's Jug Stompers, "Springdale Blues," st. 2.
Sàid Î'm góin' âwáy bábŷ | cátch tĥe Hóllŷwòod líne
Sàid Î'm góin' oût hére nòw | cátch tĥe Hóllŷwòod líne . . .

37. Kid Cole, "Sixth Street Moan" (Vocalion 1186, 1928), st. 4.
Ând Î'm góin' âwáy mámâ | bábŷ swéar ît wón't bê lóng
—Oh doany don't you want to go along?—
Ând Î'm góin' âwáy brównsk`
in | hónêy ît wón't bê lóng
And I swear you goin' miss your Kid Cole baby baby when I'm gone.

38. Lewis Black, "Rock Island Blues," st. 3.
Wêll Î'm góin' âwáy mámâ | wón't bê báck tíll Fáll
Sâys Î'm góin' âwáy mámà | wón't bê báck tíll Fáll
And if I get kind of lucky won't be back at all.

39. Mooch Richardson, "T and T Blues" (OKeh 8554, 1928), st. 4.
Wêll Î'm gòin' âwáy brównskìn | Î aìn't gônnâ côme bâck hêre bêfôre nèxt Fáll
Wêll Î'm gòin' âwáy brównskìn Í | áin't cômîng bâck hêre bêfôre nèxt Fáll
If I don't get no good brown I ain't comin' back in this town at all.

40. Skip James, "Cyprus Grove Blues" (Paramount 13088, 1931), st. 2.
Wèll Î'm góin' âwáy nòw | góin' âwáy tô stáy (2)
That'll be alright pretty mama you gonna need my help some day.

41. Tommy Johnson, "Maggie Campbell Blues" (Victor 21409, 1928), st. 4.
Wêll Î'm góin' âwáy Lórd | wón't bê báck tíll Fáll | wón't bê | báck tíll Fáll
Wêll Î'm góin' âwáy Lórd | wón't bê báck tíll Fáll
And if I meet my good gal mama won't be back at all.

42. Son House, "Special Rider Blues" (Lib. Congress AAFS L-59, 1942), st. 1.
Wêll Î'm góin' âwáy hónêy | Î wón't bê báck nô móre
When I leave this time I'm goin' hang crepe on your door.

43. Roosevelt Sykes, "As True As I've Been to You" (Victor 23286, 1931), st. 4.
Î'm gôin' âwáy tô leáve yóu | Î knòw tĥe mén wíll bè glád íf Î dó (2)
Because as long as I'm round here they can't get a fair break at you.

44. Curley Weaver, "Oh Lawdy Mama" (Champion 50077, 1935), st. 8.
Gòin' âwáy t'leáve yòu | crýin' wôn't máke mê stáy
—Oh lawdy mama great God almighty—
Gòin' âwáy t'leáve yòu | crýin' wôn't máke mê stáy
I may be back in June baby may be back in first of May.

45. Furry Lewis, "Mr. Furry's Blues" (Vocalion 1115, 1927), st. 5.
Some of these mornings baby listen to what I say (2)
Î'm góin' âwáy tô léave yòu | ít wíll bê tôo láte tô práy.

46. Blind Lemon Jefferson, "Broke and Hungry" (Paramount 12443, 1926), st. 3.
You miss me woman why count the days I'm gone

You miss me woman count the days I'm gone
I'm góin' âwáy tô búild mè â | ráilròad ôf mỳ ówn.

47. Lewis Black, "Gravel Camp Blues" (Columbia 14291-D, 1927), st. 1.
. . . . góin' oùt ón thê cúe
Sâid Î'm gòin' âwáy tômór' mámâ | góin' oût ón t̀he cúe
And if I find anything comin' back after you.

48. Frank Stokes, "What's the Matter Blues" (Victor V38531, 1928), st. 3.
An̂d Î'm góin' dòwn tówn | gònnâ stày rôund thére tîll Fáll
An̂d Î'm góin' dòwn tówn gónnâ stáy roûnd thére tîll Fáll
Don't get the gal I want I don't want no girls at all.

Notes

1. See A. B. Lord, *The Singer of Tales* (1960, rpt. New York: Atheneum, 1968). Parry's pioneering studies are collected in *The Making of Homeric Verse,* ed. A. Parry (Oxford: Oxford University Press, 1971).

2. For the latter see Bruce A. Rosenberg, *The Art of the American Folk Preacher* (New York: Oxford, 1970).

3. See Jeff Titon, *Early Downhome Blues: A Musical and Cultural Analysis* (Urbana: University of Illinois Press, 1977), ch. 5. [Excerpt reprinted herein.] I am most grateful to Titon and Taft for generously allowing me to read their work in typescript and for their detailed criticism of an earlier draft of this paper.

4. *Blues from the Delta* (London: Studio Vista, 1970), pp. 34ff.

5. *Charley Patton* (London: Studio Vista, 1970), pp. 58ff.

6. Ibid., p. 65. Paul Oliver, *Screening the Blues* (London: Cassell, 1968), p. 18 observes: "Often a single line rather than a verse reappears in numerous contexts; sometimes even a single phrase. Maverick lines that move from blues to blues are given new rhymes and new meaning by their juxtaposition with other ideas, while they retain the quality of surprise." He is describing, without apparently being fully aware of it, the process of oral-formulaic composition.

7. M. Parry, "Studies in the Epic Technique of the Oral Verse-Making," in *The Making of Homeric Verse,* p. 272.

8. *The Singer of Tales,* p. 4.

9. Parry, "Studies," p. 275.

10. See, e.g., William Ferris Jr., *Blues from the Delta* (London: Studio Vista, 1971), pp. 34, 36; Oliver, *Screening the Blues,* pp. 17ff.

11. *The Singer of Tales,* p. 4.

12. Ferris Jr., *Blues from the Delta,* p. 34. He is presumably using "verse" here in the sense of "stanza" rather than "metrical line" since on p. 36 he writes: "The stanzas . . . are the fundamental unit of black song, and it is through their study rather than through patterns of narrative development that black song style can be understood." Cf. Samuel Charters, *The Poetry of the Blues* (New York: Oak, 1963), p. 14 who makes the same claim. [Excerpts reprinted herein.].

13. Michael Taft, "I WOKE UP THIS MORNING: A Transformational-Generative Approach to the Formulaic Structure of Blues Lyrics" (Unpubl. paper delivered at the annual meeting of the American Folklore Society, Austin, Texas, 1972), and Titon, *Early Downhome Blues,* ch. 5, demonstrate this clearly. Ferris Jr., *Blues from the Delta,* pp. 34ff. and 58 has asserted that formulas are closely related to tunes. This is based on his assumption that the unit of the formula is the stanza. The argument seems to me invalid however if the basic unit of the

formula is the half-line. Formulas such as *I woke up this mornings* and *I'm going away* are too widely distributed within the blues tradition to be discussed meaningfully in the context of tune patterns.

14. The blues are certainly not composed in iambic pentameters as Oliver casually remarks in *Screening the Blues*, p. 18.

15. It should be noted that the distinction between stress and half-stress is at times a difficult one, and is bound to be arbitrary to some extent.

16. Barefoot Bill, "Bad Boy" (Columbia 14526-D, 1930), st. 2. For an extended use of unstressed syllables see appendix, example 39, 1^b.

17. For a convenient description see T. A. Shippey, *Old English Verse* (London: Hutchinson, 1972), pp. 101ff. and, on the oral-formulaic theory, pp. 89ff.

18. Big Boy Cleveland, "Goin' to Leave You Blues," st. 2; Stovepipe No. 1, "Court Street Blues," st. 1. See also examples 1–12 in the appendix.

19. In a written communication, Titon has suggested to me that the demands of the tune may sometimes cause the singer to "wrench stress away from a normally accented syllable and place it on a normally unaccented syllable." Whether or not one agrees with this depends on one's definition of the essential components of stress in language; but if Titon is correct, its relevance to the metrics of oral formulas in the blues is obvious. The problem is a complex one however, beyond the scope of this paper, and I would refer the reader to Titon's account of the phenomenon in *Early Downhome Blues*. [Excerpt reprinted herein.]

20. Tom Dixon, "Happy Blues," st. 6; Henry Thomas, "Bull Doze Blues," st. 1. See also examples 13–20 and 31–42.

21. Blind Lemon Jefferson, "Lonesome House Blues," st. 2; Charley Patton, "When Your Way Gets Dark," st. 6. See also examples 14 and 16. This is a metrical variant favored by Patton, which may explain his unusual adoption of a single stress half-line in "Down the Dirt Road Blues" (example 7). This is extremely rare. In the vast majority of cases, two stresses represent an obligatory basis for the formula.

22. Examples 43–47 represent different formulas within the larger system based on the general idea of going away. 43–46 are interesting in that the basic idea is expanded to include an account of the singer's motive in leaving: something which is normally expressed in 1^b.

23. I am aware of course that there are other ways in which the singer may do this.

24. (1) *won't be back till Fall* 10, 20, 25, 38, 39, 41, 48; *coming here no more* 19, 24, 42; *going to stay* 34, 40; *possible non-formulaic phrases* 14, 21, 32. (2) *wear you off my mind* 1, 2, 18, 26, 27, 35; *make it lonesome here* 8, 12, 23; *possible non-formulaic phrases* 7, 11, 36, 46, 47. (3) *don't you want to go?* 9, 15, 16; *possible non-formulaic phrases* 30, 31, 33, 44, 45. (4) *won't be long* 3, 4, 5, 17, 22, 28, 29, 37.

25. A. Lewis Black, "Rock Island Blues," B. Charlie Kyle, "Kyle's Worried Blues," C. Cannon's Jug Stompers, "Springdale Blues," D. Jabo Williams, "Fat Mama Blues."

26. Cf. examples 19, 24, and 42.

27. Fall/all 20, 25, 38, 39, 41 (cf. 48). More/door 24, 42 (cf. 19).

28. Tommy Johnson, "Cool Drink of Water Blues" (Victor 21279, 1928), st. 2; Charley Patton, "Green River Blues" (Paramount 12972, 1929), st. 4.

4 The Blues and Religion

He said, "If I catch you playin the devil's music again, I'm gonna take that bull whip and beat you almost to death with it." . . . I was beatin out some boogie woogie when the old man come. God dog! The old man threw me down and started beatin me so bad with that bull whip.

BIG JOE Duskin's anecdote is not an isolated narrative among blues performers, although it is among the most shockingly brutal, evoking as it does an instrument of torture commonly associated with slavery. Throughout the history of the blues, many Christians have considered it "the Devil's music," not only a worldly strain, but a music of the underworld: immoral not only in its acceptance and portrayal of alcohol and other drugs, violence, promiscuity, and familial irresponsibility but also in its tempting its listeners to taste of the forbidden fruit by drawing them to barrelhouses, juke joints, whorehouses, and bars where the blues were commonly performed and such illicit activities are likely to take place. There are, in truth, blues songs that detail the interference of the "blues life" with the Christian one, such as Son House's "Preachin' the Blues"—"Oh, I lay in my room, I bowed down to pray / Say the blues came along and they drove my spirit away"—and Wright Holmes's "Alley Blues," where the singer bows to pray but winds up asking, "If you got any brownskin women in heaven would you please to send Wright Holmes one?" And that line of demarcation between the blues and Christian sacred music is crossed regularly in the songs of Leola Manning, whose "He Fans Me" mixes a salacious hokum phrase with devotion to God in a conceit as audacious as those of John Donne, as well as in the sanctified-barrelhouse piano stylings of Arizona Dranes, the guitar playing of Sister Rosetta Tharpe, and the songs of Wynona Carr.

However, not all blues songs embrace those subjects and values, nor do all blues singers. There are blues songs that celebrate a mate and/or espouse commitment; detail the evils of alcohol, drugs, and violence; lament the fact that a singer had not listened to what his or her mother said; and express concern and responsibility for the family. Not only that, but blues performers so frequently invoke the names of God or Jesus (or the Lord) in blues songs that one wonders whether such invocation is merely an empty habit learned in childhood days proven hard to break, a blasphemous cry of exasperation devoid of serious religious connotation, a deliberate rejection of or challenge to the power and authority of the Christian God, or a serious reflection of the spiritual universe of a person caught with one foot in the street and one in the sanctuary, struggling to walk a straight and satisfying path in this world.

In this section, Langston Hughes registers matter-of-factly his first experience with censorship, apparently unexpected, as he is directed by a preacher not to read his blues poems in the preacher's pulpit. This was neither Hughes's first nor last dispute with the forces of religion, but it does reveal on the one hand Hughes's sense that his blues were entirely appropriate in the sanctuary, reflecting as they did of the lives and spirit of many lower-class African Americans who recognized that they lived in a world with secular realities and problems, and on the other the preacher's determination to keep his congregation focused on the God at hand.

Charles Keil presents us with a related discussion regarding the role of the blues artist in relation to the role of the African American preacher. Focusing on the transition from blues singer to minister and the motivations behind it, through interviews and analysis Keil highlights the ways that the blues singer's former vocation can in fact outfit him singularly well for his new calling, even as he retains certain blues performance devices. Rod Gruver extends consideration of the relationship by identifying the blues as a secular religion, an existentialist one in which self-reliant blues prophets liberated themselves from conventional organized religion, celebrating and mythologizing their sexuality, and generating a unified world view out of their creative insights. African American theologian James H. Cone subsequently asserted that the blues, because they help actuate a move toward unity by evoking a manner of divine spirit, are in fact theological, confronting not God but the mundane actualities of existence. The blues, then, are "secular spirituals," embracing both body, especially sexuality, and spirit in their quest for the wholeness of human life. (See also Larry Neal's essay in the section "Literature, Criticism, and the Blues" for his take on the relationship between the blues and the church).

Gruver and Cone have radically altered the critical approach to the relationship between blues and religious music, asking listeners to reconsider their preconceptions about blues as an irreligious art form. Paul Garon's *Blues and the Poetic Spirit* was also a startling revolutionary volley when it was published in 1975, and remained so upon reissue in 1998. Placing blues performers in the context of a surrealist view of the creative artist and drawing upon Freudian psychology and Marxist political thought, Garon depicts the blues artist as a heroic primitive struggling against the harshly repressive forces of the church, an embodiment of a smothering social system. The blues performer, reveling in the role of religion's adversary, embraces evil as all truly great revolutionary artists do, firing off startling tropes at the bulwarks of Christianity. While some commentators have seen Garon's criticism of religion as excessive and his view of the blues artist as a noble primitive romantic (see David Whiteis's review in *Living Blues* 139 [May/June 1998]), Garon certainly takes the blues poet seriously, providing a number of provocative ideas with which to wrestle. Jon Michael Spencer, in *Blues and Evil,* has provided more recently what he has dubbed a theomusicological discussion of the subject. He sees the blues as a theological discourse that explores the existence and meaning of evil, not a tradition devoid of spiritual values nor one in which the blues singer is allied with the devil against the forces of Christianity. As with all works that spark controversy, it is also worth the time to read reviews and rebuttals such as Paul Garon's review in *Living Blues* 113 (February 1994) in order to ensure a considered response.

Perhaps the singer Etta James drives most directly to the heart of the issue when she reports in a story by Mark Greilsamer in the October 1998 issue of *Blues Revue,* "Someone once told me that everything I sing has got the spirit of gospel and the feeling of the blues." And the gospel singer Thomas A. Dorsey, formerly blues performer Georgia Tom, carries the idea further:

> Blues is as important to a person feeling bad as "Nearer My God to Thee." I'm not talking about popularity; I'm talking about inside the individual. The moan gets into a person where there is some secret down there that they didn't bring out. See this stuff to come out is in you. When you cry out, that is something down there that should have come out a long time ago. Whether it's blues or gospel, there is a vehicle that comes along maybe to take it away or push it away. A man or woman singing the blues in the church will cry out, "Holy, holy, holy."

Just a little bit of consolation for a weary mind.

Recommended Further Readings

Julio Finn. *The Bluesman.* New York: Interlink, 1992.
Michael W. Harris. *The Rise of Gospel Blues: The Music of Thomas Andrew Dorsey in the Urban Church.* New York: Oxford University Press, 1992.
Robert Sacre, ed. *Saints and Sinners.* Liege, Belgium: Societe Liegeoise de Musicologie, 1996.
Jon Michael Spencer. *Blues and Evil.* Knoxville: University of Tennessee Press, 1993.

From "My Adventures as a Social Poet"

Langston Hughes

MY ADVENTURES as a social poet began in a colored church in Atlantic City shortly after my first book, *The Weary Blues*, was published in 1926. I had been invited to come down to the shore from Lincoln University where I was a student, to give a program of my poems in the church. During the course of my program I read several of my poems in the form of the Negro folk songs, including some blues poems about hard luck and hard work. As I read I noticed a deacon approach the pulpit with a note which he placed on the rostrum beside me, but I did not stop to open the note until I had finished and had acknowledged the applause of a cordial audience. The note read, "Do not read any more blues in my pulpit." It was signed by the minister. That was my first experience with censorship.

Reprinted from *Phylon* 8, no. 3 (1947): 206. Reprinted by permission of Harold Ober Associates, Incorporated.

From "Role and Response"

Charles Keil

IN THIS chapter I shall attempt to bind together some of the analytic strands left dangling in the preceding descriptive sections by viewing the blues artist and his audience from a somewhat more theoretical perspective. Since there are little data but my own to draw upon, and since a unified socio-cultural theory of music has only just begun to take shape, this analysis is of necessity fragmented, disjointed, and incomplete.

The role of blues artist holds particular interest for the anthropologist in at least two respects. In spite of the fact that blues singing is ostensibly a secular, even profane, form of expression, the role is intimately related to sacred roles in the Negro community. Second, the role is all-encompassing in nature, either assimilating or overshadowing all other roles an adult male may normally be expected to fulfill.

As professions, blues singing and preaching seem to be closely linked in both the rural or small-town setting and in the urban ghettos. We have already noted some of the stylistic common denominators that underlie the performance of both roles, and it is clear that the experiences which prepare one for adequately fulfilling either role overlap extensively. Participation in the musical life of the church and intimate knowledge of and passionate living within the Negro reality provide both the mold and the raw materials for blues lyrics and sermons. This observation is further strengthened by the not uncommon occurrence of the same person's fulfilling both roles at different phases of his life. The pattern remains essentially unbroken when the rural Negro migrates to the urban centers. The number of important male roles which are possible in the city increases; these two roles, however, remain completely contained within Negro culture. A person must go to a white university (for that matter, any university is white) in order to become a doctor or lawyer, but no such contact with white middle-class culture is essential to the aspiring bluesman or preacher. If anything, such contact would tend to decrease the authenticity of such roles, granting that they could be possible at all under such circumstances. For a bluesman like Ray Charles who does reap considerable financial rewards from a white audience, the connection with this particular audience segment is rather inessential to the role. Charles manages to retain

Reprinted from Charles Keil, *Urban Blues* (Chicago: University of Chicago Press, 1966), 143–48.

his cultural identity even when singing a hillbilly song with chorus and string section accompaniment; further, Negro listeners tend to ignore these more commercial efforts in favor of his more representative work. In most other instances to date, whenever the audience for a male singer shifts from black to predominantly white, the blues role ceases to apply as far as the Negro audience is concerned. Another point of interest is that whereas in the rural Sou [illegible] men, sharing all the traditional socic [illegible] e urban context the emergence of p [illegible] eling but decidedly strong blues sing [illegible]

Evidence for [illegible] entiful. Some of the best-known blin [illegible] n and the currently popular folk artis [illegible] bluesmen but have always been will [illegible] elf and are still best known for their [illegible] l earn his way as a bluesman one w [illegible] he "stop straddling the fence."[2] "Be [illegible] ore ready cash and excitement on th [illegible] gia Tom gave up a promising blues [illegible] illness, to devote himself to the pro [illegible] orsey is the leading writer and publis [illegible]

J. B. Lenoir (I [illegible] Mississippi, "used to play nothin' bu [illegible] ching and church affairs. J. B. himself has given up the fast world "to follow the Lord," although he keeps his hand in by occasionally recording a number for Chess Records. He regards his own talents and those of other prominent bluesmen as God-given gifts, as when describing Jr. Parker as "blessed to blow harp" (harmonica), and hence feels that every blues artist should be true to his talent and to its spiritual source. It is on the basis of these criteria that he judges the current crop of bluesmen: B. B. King is true to himself and therefore his soul; Bobby Bland doesn't play an instrument, sometimes follows commercial trends, and therefore isn't as good a singer as he might be. Lenoir doesn't label blues "devil music" as many in the church do, but feels that all valid music has a sacred source (his best lyrics come to him in dreams) and a singer strays from this source at the risk of losing his soul. Many of the other singers I have interviewed share this same general point of view.

Concerning the transition from a blues role to a ministerial one, there are two significant stories that a number of singers have told me: the first concerning Gatemouth Moore, the second, Little Richard. Gatemouth, at the peak of his popularity, was playing an engagement at the Club DeLisa, one of Chicago's leading blues rooms during the 1940's.[4] One night, in the midst of a rocking blues rendition, he brought the proceedings to an abrupt halt, sang a chorus of *Shine On Me,* announced his retirement, and "he just up and walked off the stand." The Reverend Dwight Moore served his apprenticeship with Reverend Cobbs, and has been preaching the gospel in Chicago ever since.[5] He is fondly remembered and much respected by all the bluesmen I've interviewed. Little Richard was one of the first well-known cry singers, and his pioneering work earned for him a considerable amount of money. He also renounced the stage to become a religious leader, but was less successful than he had anticipated. His recordings of spirituals didn't sell too well, he ran out of capital before he could set up a functioning church, and so he tried to make a comeback in the entertainment world. The consensus among bluesmen and blues lovers at large is that once an entertainer returns to the fold he should stay there. "If he had the money," said one well-known blues singer, "he should have set up a nice little church and recreation center and he would have been set, although with these college educated pastors comin' along, it's tough to set up anything but a storefront these days."

Similarly, Little Jr. Parker speaks of the switch from blues to preaching: "I know why they stop singing the blues—their conscience troubles them. But why anyone starts again I can't figure out. Myself, I promised God that in eight more years, whether I'm popular or not, I'm going to show my appreciation and devote myself to his service, 'cause he made it possible for all the other people to dig me." The transition, then, from a blues role to a preacher's position can normally be made only once.

There is a strong prodigal-son pattern here: a set of related concepts or common understandings that allow a man to move from a most decidedly secular role to the sacred role without a strain or hitch. First of all, in the Negro community few expect a young man to be saintly—in fact many mothers inculcate a particularly strong sex-role identity in their little boys of the stud, rogue, lady-killer type. John Lee Hooker states it neatly in one of his blues soliloquies as he tells of his parents' reaction to his incipient blues career: Father disapproved, but Mama said, "It's in him, and it's got to come out." It is understood and expected that every boy will sow some wild oats—something's wrong with him if he doesn't—and his wild period will not be held against him in later years. The Negro woman's concept of the no-good man (sexually desirable but domestically intolerable—good lover but bad provider), as reported by Esther Newton,[6] closely parallels the defining expectations most fans verbalize when considering the blues singer's role or what Nadel might call the role's "halo effect."[7] The converse concept of the good man is severely restricted in its application—some women claim there is no such creature—but clearly the preacher as an ideal type at least offers an approximation or model of what a good man might be like: steady, reliable, above the sexual strife (in theory though not often in fact)—a man of God after all. Bluesman and preacher may be considered Negro prototypes of the no-good and good man respectively.

It should be obvious that a reformed bluesman is not only an acceptable preacher, but may even have an advantage over his fellow clerics. I would suggest that the most exciting, attractive, and charismatic preachers are often those who have been big sinners in their prime. To absolve sins successfully, you may find it helpful to have been a transgressor yourself once upon a time. The prodigal returned to the fold is living evidence of God's power to redeem and is better qualified than most to lead the flock. He knows what life is all about.[8]

The transition, then, from blues role to preacher role is unidirectional but peculiarly appropriate and smooth for anyone who cares to make the shift. Gatemouth Moore's "call" must be respected; Little Richard is ostensibly a backslider of the worst order.

There is a firm economic foundation to this transitional pattern. It is possible to get rich quick in the blues or rhythm-and-blues field; a few hit records in succession, a corresponding boost in personal appearance fees, and a singer can find himself on easy street. Usually a blues artist builds a following over a period of years, and his popularity is not likely to vanish as suddenly as that of some teen-age idol. Nevertheless, there invariably comes a point when the financial returns no longer compensate for the tremendous amount of time and energy spent in singing the blues, and the smaller (perhaps) but steadier income of the collection plate looks very appealing. Some bluesmen persist in their prodigal ways—"I love the life I live, and I live the life I love"—until drink, a bit of violence, or the infirmities of old age bring their careers to a close. Most, however, return to the church and settle down to a day job of some kind, often for familial as well as economic reasons.

Notes

1. Through the years a number of the better Negro churches in Chicago have developed into family empires. The patriarch's children serve in administrative capacities, relatives start branches of the church in other neighborhoods, members of the congregation marry into the hierarchy, a son may take over the ministry upon his father's death, and so forth. In short, a "church family" can present a picture that is just the opposite of a "matrifocal complex."

2. *Big Bill Blues: William Broonzy's Story as Told to Yannick Bruynoghe* (London, 1955).

3. George Robinson Ricks, "Religious Music of the United States Negro" (Ph.D. Dissertation, Northwestern University, 1959).

4. As I write, the Club DeLisa has just reopened and is now called The Club E. Rodney Jones and other WVON regulars are prompting the revival and have mustered an impressive array of talent, including a chorus line, to insure its success.

5. Reverend Cobbs is the well-known leader of the largest Spiritual church in Chicago. His philosophy exalts life and tolerates "sin" as part of the natural order of things. "This is one church," says Moore, "where high livin' is not frowned on." All men partake of the spirit, and people "from all walks of life" (including all the less legitimate walks) are welcome to join the congregation. Reverend Moore, resplendent in the robes of a Catholic cardinal, teaches his version of this gospel of acceptance at "Wesley Chapel," next to the Maxwell street "flea market." But he still spends a few months of each year making appearances at Spiritual churches all over the country. "I've always been nervous in one place; I like to *go*, even if it's just across the street."

6. "Men, Women, and Status in the Negro Family" (Master's Thesis, University of Chicago, 1964).

7. S. F. Nadel, *The Theory of Social Structure* (Glencoe, Ill., 1957), p. 26.

8. Reverend Moore states: "Experience is my big advantage, like Paul, but he was on the scene before, now I'm here. You see, I don't *need* to handle money—went through a quarter of a million in a few fast years. I don't *need* to sin any more because I've been around, traveled all over, had all the women, cars, clothes any man could want . . . so there was nothin' left for me to do but live right. It's the one thing I hadn't done up til my conversion in '48."

The Blues as a Secular Religion

Rod Gruver

Part One

THERE is still much that needs to be done with the larger meaning of blues, with its full significance as a form of art, a modern mythology and a secular religion. Paul Oliver has studied the social and economic backgrounds of blues; Peter Welding, the lives and recordings of many of the singers; Charles Keil, the functions of the blues singer as a cultural hero; and LeRoi Jones, the important historical sources of blues. And while each has performed a valuable service in relating blues to the culture of its birth, none has been able to lift blues out of its status as a folk art. All tend to see it more or less as, to use the words of Paul Oliver, 'a direct expression of its immediate environment.' Thus no one yet has been able to see blues as poetry, defined by the literary critic R. P. Blackmur as 'life at the remove of form and idea.'

There is justification, however, for looking at blues as poetry; for it is truly a creative expression, related to its environment, yes, but going beyond it also in giving form and idea to it and in creating a vision to take its place. Freed by the license of art from any necessity to reproduce what already exists, blues poetry moves and has its being in a realm of its own—like the imaginary geometries created by theoretical mathematicians or the sunflowers painted by Van Gogh. These imaginary creations of art and science are not useless illusions but prized possessions, a valuable resource, because they teach us to see larger and finer than we saw before.

In *Blues People* Le Roi Jones claims that only with the advent of bop in the forties was the Negro able to look critically at white America; only then was he able to see himself as an integral person apart from its '"meaningless" social order.' He says:

> '*Cool* meant non-participation; *soul* means a "new" establishment. It is an attempt to reverse the social roles within the society by re-defining the canons of value . . . White is then not "right," as the old blues had it, but a liability, since the culture of white precludes the possession of Negro "soul".' (219)

Reprinted from *Blues World* 29 (April 1970): 3–6; 30 (May 1970): 4–7; 31 (June 1970): 5–7; 32 (July 1970): 7–9. Originally published in *Down Beat*'s "Music '70" and used by permission of *Down Beat*.

But Jones is wrong about 'the old blues'. The individual song he refers to is Big Bill Broonzy's 'Black, Brown, and White', which includes the line, 'If you're white, you're all right'. Big Bill, however, did not want that line to be taken literally. He hoped instead to show how foolish the idea was just by giving it a clear and direct statement. In reply to such misreadings as Jones's, Big Bill said: 'That song doesn't tell the Negro to get back, but just about where and who tells them to get back. . . . I, Big Bill don't like to get back, I'm a blues singer and I sing about it.'

Considered collectively, 'the old blues' had already redefined America's canons of value long before bop was ready to blow a call for a new social order. 'The reversal of social roles', 'non-participation', 're-defining the canons of value', and especially, the vision of a 'new establishment'—all this began much earlier than the forties with the advent of bop. It began with the origin of the blues, which marked the beginning of a new day in America. That day is still dawning but seems to be getting lighter now at a much faster pace; the process has been speeded up with the re-discovery of blues by rock singers. What they are finding in 'the old blues' is a fascinating part of their protest against traditional ways, old dogmas that seemed to have out-lived their usefulness.

In *Understanding Media* Marshall McLuhan tries to lift blues out of its folk art traditions by claiming it was part of a large movement that arose to express a nostalgic yearning for organic unity. In his view, blues laments an Edenic wholeness that was lost after the invention of mechanized printing. 'The poets and painters and musicians of the later nineteenth century all insist,' he says, 'on a sort of metaphysical melancholy as latent in the great industrial world of the metropolis'. (243) The frustrations of the period were symbolized by Cyrano de Bergerac, the classical figure of frustrated love. 'This weird image of Cyrano, the unloved, the unlovable lover, was caught up,' says McLuhan, in the phonograph cult of the blues'. (243)

McLuhan is right, of course, in sensing that blues is more than a folk art related only to its 'immediate environment'. But his claim that blues derives its sadness solely out of the loss of organic wholeness, that it laments only the crushing power of mechanized machinery, is still far from the truth. For his idea also forces blues into playing the part of a passive victim; thus he too denies its function as an agent for revolutionary change, as a force for re-defining America's canons of value. Charles Keil in *Urban Blues* shows that man is not a passive victim of a mechanized society by claiming that '. . . instances of man over machine (in jazz and blues) could be listed on page after page'. (176)

Though the victories cited are relatively minor, behind each is an attitude that recognizes the supremacy of the organic, of man as the measure, not the machine. But organic man, man the irrepressible, wins a major victory in the blue note itself; for the blue note is a symbol of man's refusal to give up his unpredictable orneryness, his inalienable right to be himself and nobody else's. For there is in the blue note and the improvisations based upon it a freeing of the spirit that gives full play to the creative imagination.

> 'Anytime a person can play the blues,' says Jimmy Rushing, 'he has a soul and that gives him a sort of lift to play anything he wants to play. The blues are a sort of base, like the foundation to a building, because anytime you get into trouble, you curve the blues down and get out of it.'

But blues has also been used to help solve more than just musical problems, for the blues poets also used its lyrics to help release America from the moral prison of its Puritan ethos. Blues, then, shows man not as a victim of the machine but as triumphant over it; and it provides, in addition, a symbol of his success in winning that victory. Thus blues differs from such dramas of the early 20's as *The Adding Machine* and *R.U.R.*, which show man as McLuhan found him—reduced to the pathetic roles of zeros and robots, dehumanized victims of a mechanized society.

But if blues goes beyond its immediate environment in showing man triumphant over a linear, mechanistic society, there is a history behind it that must be studied in any attempt to determine its full meaning. For blues could not have been written if its poets had not lived through a period of toil and trouble, had not suffered the throes of rejecting a long-accepted cultural stance. For blues is religious poetry that arose to express what James Joyce in the person of Stephen Dedalus swore to express for the Irish nation: Its uncreated conscience. The creators of blues were poets and prophets, visionaries announcing the advent of a new day, heralding with their blues the emerging of the lower class Negro. The newly awakened prophets of the lower class Negro arose to revenge themselves against white America and the blacks who had accepted its Puritan ethos. These black prophets emerged to forge in the smithies of their prophetic souls, to transform in the crucible of the blues, a new social-religious order of their own. They gave us in their blues a new world in the making, a world not yet here but coming.

Part Two

There have been other poets than those of the blues who have created new religion out of their poems of love. . . . The poetry of the blues also became a religion, and it too was historically determined.

Although Negro slaves were taken from intensely religious cultures where religion was an integral part of their daily life, they were forced to abandon their religious ways as soon as they were placed on Southern farms. Slave owners prohibited slaves from worshipping their gods because they feared it might lead to a nostalgic wish to return home or to an endless series of revolts. And at first slave owners also denied their slaves access to the local Christian religion; for they had rationalized the purchase and working of slaves by thinking of them as less than human, as animals without souls to save. Thus owners of slaves did not dare to offend their God by permitting slaves to worship Him.

But zealous missionaries succeeded finally in converting some of the house slaves, reasoning against objections that, if brought into the flock, even these black slaves might reflect the greater glory of God. And when, in comparison to those not converted, Christianized slaves became more docile, less eager to go home or revolt, slave owners looked upon the conversion of slaves with less distaste and began to encourage it. But the converted slaves were given a carefully edited version of Christianity.

In *Blues People* Le Roi Jones says:

> Christianity, as it was given to the slaves . . . was to be used strictly as a code of conduct which would enable its devotees to participate in an afterlife; it was from its very inception . . . a slave ethic. It acted as a great pacifier and palliative. . . . (38)

By insisting that life on earth was a vale of tears, a trial to test us all for a greater glory beyond the grave, Christianity gave those who could believe it an enormous capacity to endure. Christian slaves could believe that if they endured the thorns of slavery without protest, accepted all its heart-aches and pains in joyous surrender, they would be more ready to walk the glory road.

Before Emancipation this other-worldly Christian ethic was virtually all that slaves were permitted to know. Working from sunup to sunset, they had almost no access whatever to the idea that life here on earth had any value or that it could be improved. 'During the time of slavery,' Jones says, 'the black churches had almost no competition for the Negro's time.' (48) And to show their appreciation for the gift of Christianity, the officials of the black churches echoed white sentiment by condemning 'all dem hedun ways' of the secular Negro and by calling 'sinful' all the "fiddle songs," "devil songs," and "jig tunes" ' that the secular Negro sang and played. (49)

Collectors of Negro folk music after the Civil War were mystified by 'the paucity of secular songs'. They found little to collect outside of the religious anthems approved by the black churches, for the secular songs—all the devil's music—had been driven underground. Thus the black churches had unwittingly created a poetic vacuum that was destined to be filled soon by the capacity of the secular Negro to create music and song.

By forcing all the devil's music underground, the black churches forced the songs first to cohere and then to harden into a gem of beautiful brilliance. What emerged from the process was a song so fine, a music so inevitably appealing, that no power now could drive it away. The song was the blues, and by singing of the joys and the sorrows, the good and the bad, of life on earth, it opposed itself to the thoughts and feelings expressed in the spirituals. And because blues saluted life on earth as opposed to life after death, it also signaled the arrival of a new man, a man who differed from the one who sang the spirituals. For with the blues secular man had once more emerged out of a religious culture based on supernatural values. And like the others before him, this secular man also based his life on values his unaided reason found by itself.

When the first boat load of African slaves landed on American shores in 1619, the West was already enjoying the fruits of the Renaissance, drawing benefits from the idea that reason unaided by light from above could lead to a fuller and better life. White slave owners, however, denied those benefits to their slaves. But in one of the finer ironies of history, three hundred years later descendants of those same slaves had a renaissance of their own. They created a renaissance in the words of their blues which, like the poems, plays and essays of the first Renaissance, saluted the idea that life was not a mere trial but of value itself.

But if blues arose to balance the supernaturalism of black Christianity, blues also emerged to oppose the imitation of white society by the black middle class. Emerging out of the movement from farms to cities after Emancipation, the black middle class 'strove to emulate exactly the white society'. (Jones, 58). But what it found to emulate was the life satirized by Mark Twain in *The Gilded Age* and later by Sinclair Lewis in *Babbitt*—a life dominated by greedy materialism, flagrant business dishonesty and a mindless struggle to plunder the planet. Having aligned itself with a bigoted class of white Philistines, the black middle class also turned its back on all expressions and customs it considered 'too Negroid'—as had the officials of the black churches. They too condemned the devil songs of the lower class Negro, fearing greatly the process of guilt by association and the lash of white society. It came to believe 'that the best way to survive in America would be to *disappear* completely, leaving no trace at all that there had ever been an Africa, or a slavery, or even, finally, a black man' (Jones 124).

But the black middle class never succeeded in disappearing completely; nor did it succeed in becoming an accepted member of the society it strove to emulate. Thus the class found itself on the razor's edge of having rejected its own past and of being rejected in turn by those it wished to join. Jones says of their dilemma:

> 'The moral-religious tradition of the black middle class is a weird mixture of opportunism and fear. It is a tradition that is capable of reducing any human conceit or natural dignity to the barest form of social outrage.' (127)

Lower class Negroes, the lowly field hands of slavery day, were only marginally connected to the black churches and were excluded entirely from the black middle class. They were the last Negro group to accept Christianity, which on the plantations had moved from house to yard to field. When one of them became a member of a black church, he was usually among the least devout of its believers. From this class came the 'backsliders', those who joined only to slide back into non-belief and the 'heduns', those who never joined. The most devout members, on the other hand, were usually those of the black middle class. They were devout because their emulation of white society had the effect of forcing them to swallow whole its dedication to the Puritan ethos, that uneasy combination of finance and religion. The members of the black churches and the black middle class were alike in attempting to gain white acceptance by looking down upon the lower class Negro and by condemning his 'Negroid' ways and his devil music.

Of this cultural split between middle and lower class Negroes on the one hand and between religious and secular Negroes on the other, Jones says: 'Of course, the poor and unlettered (all lower class Negroes) were the last to respond to the gift (the Puritan ethos) but the strivers after America, the neophytes of the black middle class, responded as quickly as they could.' (126) Having turned themselves as 'white' as they could by accepting the Puritan ethos of the white society, the members of the black churches and the black middle class 'tried always to dictate that self, the image of a whiter Negro, to the poorer, blacker Negroes'. (130)

Thus the lower class Negro found himself alienated from all classes and all beliefs: he stood all alone in an alien land. The alliance against him was tight and complete. He had no place to go and no one to turn to. He had no country, no home, no ideology and no art to call his own. History had forced upon him the awful realization that, if the black man wanted to have a home of his own in America, he would have to create it himself out of elements of his own culture.

Part Three

The task of tearing down to prepare for the job of building a-new is accomplished in the blues by satirizing the values of the Puritan ethos, the religion so much admired by both the black churches and the black middle class. The lower class blues poets took their revenge against those above them by turning their beliefs upside down, by looking around and finding something better to put in their place. There are, for example, constant references to the colour 'black', which was so much despised by the black middle class. 'I'm the Black Ace', brags a singer by the same name. 'I'm the boss card in your hand'. And when black is disparaged, which it sometimes is, the poet may only be putting the middle class on. The blues poets also insist that no other love can compare with the love that comes either before or outside of marriage. 'A married woman's the best woman ever born', sings Red Nelson in 'Sweetest Woman Ever Born'. And there is a continuous flouting of such middle class Puritan virtues as thrift, hard work, prayer and continence—the whole process of preparing for heaven.

In 'Harlem Blues' Little Son Willis sings: 'I know blues singers don't go to heaven 'cause Gabriel bars them out (x2). But all the good ones go to Harlem and help the angels beat it out'. In 'Talking, Preaching' Leadbelly offers a view of heaven as a pleasant place with pretty girls, good food and lots of old friends and relatives to talk to. The first stanza reads:

> There's a lot of pretty girls up in heaven.
> That's gonna make everybody want to go to heaven.
> Going up there to see the pretty girls.

In an interview with Pete Welding the Reverend Robert Wilkins, a former blues singer-turned-preacher, gave a clear statement of the antagonism between blues and spirituals:

> Now, the difference between blues and spiritual songs . . . You can only sing one and not the other. Only one at a time that man can serve. . . . See, your body is the temple of the spirit of God, and it ain't but one spirit can dwell in that body at a time. That is the good spirit or the evil spirit. And that's spirituals or blues. Blues are songs of the evil spirit.

But these anti-Christian sentiments are only the negative aspects of blues, its clear recognition that tearing down must precede building a-new. There are positive things in the blues, too, a modern mythology, for example, with different levels of interpretation and a new religion to take the place of the one it opposed.

The attempt of blues singers to remold America's canons of value is remarkably similar to Wagner's effort to breathe new life into the German middle class. His opera *Tristan and Isolde* is a reversal of Germany's Puritan ethos, an attempt to re-awaken Nordic sensuality by celebrating passion as the one value that measures all others. Francis Fergusson in *The Idea of a Theater* says: 'Wagner's opera shows concretely what is eternally human and eternally comprehensive in life—i.e. passion as the one reality in our experience.' (89) Thus both Wagner and the blues poet are alike in celebrating passion as the value of values, the one good beyond all others. 'I even kill a man about my boogie', warns one blues singer. By their celebrating of passion to the exclusion of all other values, both Wagner and the blues poet rejected the values of middle class respectability and of Puritan morality. That the passionate love in the blues and in Wagner's *Tristan* leads to neither emotional satisfaction nor lasting relationships can be explained by looking more closely at their main purpose. The main purpose of each was to stimulate dormant desires— not to satisfy them vicariously by picturing happy marriages. They wanted to re-awaken sleeping passions and then, by leaving them unsatisfied, to force their fulfillment outside the world of art.

To explain 'the desperate and gloomy eroticism' and the close-to-suicidal longings that many object to in *Tristan,* Fergusson relies on the ideas of the French philosopher Henri Bergson who claims that whenever the visions of mystics and artists envisage a new world, their work takes on a morbid cast. The melancholy is caused by the emotional disturbance involved in passing from what is static, closed and habitual to what is dynamic, open and new. Bergson says:

> The images and emotions that arise out of such changes indicate that the disturbance is a systematic re-arrangement looking forward to a new equilibrium: the image is the symbol of what is being prepared and the emotion is a concentration of the soul in the expectation of a transformation.' (Fergusson, 83)

But I think Bergson's idea applies equally well to the melancholy evident in the blues, which, like the suicidal longings in *Tristan,* is also suffered in 'the expectation of a transformation'. However, the poet musicians of the blues took the morbid effect inherent in mystic visions, in any attempt to envisage a new world, and made it into a sound that uplifts and cleanses the soul, leaving it serenely peaceful. Paradoxically, the blues poets changed the effect of the emotional disturbance—a morbid or melancholy sound—into one of the chief appeals of their poetic opera.

That blues has various religious functions is not a new idea. Charles Keil, for example, shows how both blues singers and preachers perform remarkably similar services. He says:

> Blues singers and preachers both provide models and orientations, both give public expression to deeply felt private emotions, both promote catharsis—the blues singer through dance, the preacher through trance; both increase feelings of solidarity, boost morale, strengthen the consensus. (164)

Keil has performed a valuable service in pointing out these functional similarities and in noting elsewhere that 'Blues singing is . . . intimately related to sacred roles in the Negro community.' (143) But while the functions Keil lists can be called religious, they neither exhaust nor define the nature of religion; for the functions listed can also be performed by good athletes, exceptional dancers and a popular singer like Frank Sinatra. To get at the religion of the blues one must analyze its meaning, find out what it says on other levels than the literal. For sacred roles can only be played by those who provide resurrection, reconciliation, reunion, regeneration, at-onement. Religion is the power that overcomes the separation of man from nature from others and from himself; by joining opposites it shows the essential oneness of nature's manifold appearance and assures the stable flow of all processes. And, of course, religion must also provide an external power to worship, some human faculty projected outward, as a god or principle, that men will honor and seek to enact. The power of blues to renew and resurrect, to breathe new life into what has withered or become old, can be seen in what the Negro songwriter Reece D'Pree said once about the blues: 'The blues', he told friends one evening, 'the blues regenerates a man'.

Part Four

In *Language and Myth* the German philosopher Ernst Cassirer contrasts logical, discursive thinking, which expands concepts into an ever-widening series of relationships, with that of myth-making. 'The mental view (of the latter) is not widened,' he says, 'but compressed; it is distilled into a single point. Only by the process of distillation is the particular essence found and extracted which is to bear the special accent of "significance".' (90). These distillations become 'significant' in a religious sense if they evoke feelings of awe, wonder and delight—as in the blues where behaviour is compressed into the single point of sex. The function of these awe-inspiring distillations is to divide the sacred from the profane. 'By this process of division the object of religious worship may really be said to be brought into existence, and the realm in which it moves to be first established.' (66) For the creation of a sacred area is 'the prerequisite for any definite divinities whatever' because in the realm of the sacred 'The Self feels steeped . . . in a mythico-religious atmosphere . . . ; it takes only a spark, a touch, to create a god or a demon out of this charged atmosphere'. (72).

Blues poets made a religion of their blues by distilling behavior into the single point of sex, by creating a sacred realm of charged atmosphere conducive for the appearance of Men and Women, the gods of the blues. By creating a song-type with Woman as one of its chief characters, blues poets created a mythology that unifies opposites and offers a new religious orientation. Woman has been nearly forgotten in the Christian doctrine of a male-dominated trinity. The Christian fathers blamed woman for the sensual depravity that helped to wreck ancient Rome, and her infamous deed in the Garden of Eden has not been forgotten yet. Her place was taken by the Virgin Mary whose sexless pregnancy devalued not only sex but woman's proper role in child bearing and rearing. Under Christianity her sexual appeal became a pagan snare, her essential humanity, a heathen delusion. There were paternally oriented societies before Christianity that devalued the female role. However, Christianity seems to be the external expression of social male-female conflict. The female devaluation may be an escape valve for this unresolved tension. What Christianity feared was her power to absorb man's attention, to turn him away from God, who alone was considered worth attending to.

The Christian fear of woman is evident in a medieval couplet by Cardinal Hugues de St. Cher: 'Woman pollutes the body, drains the resources, kills the soul, uproots the strength, blinds the eye, and embitters the voice'. The Cardinal's hatred of woman contrasts sharply with Sonny Boy Williamson's exaltation of her and the good she does: 'Every time she starts to lovin' she brings eyesight to the blind'. Sonny Boy's Woman not only brings eyesight to the blind, but she makes the dumb talk, the deaf to hear and the lame to walk. So in Sonny Boy's blues Woman has become a more than mortal female, she has become a god. She is, and so are all the Women in the blues, a manifestation of pagan Woman, a symbol of those qualities in nature that have always been felt to be feminine. But there is evidence in the blues also for the apotheosis of Man. What else but a god is a 'king bee', a man with 'a stinger as long as my right arm', a 'rattle-snakin' daddy', who 'rattles all the time', a man who 'can boogie all night long'?

The ancients divided the world into male and female halves, and the myths of their amorous unions and spiteful divisions '. . . typify with accuracy that astounds the whole nature, the inalterable nature, of the two forces (positive and negative) that create life'. All else, continues folklorist Elisabeth Goldsmith, 'pales before the absorbing interest that is excited by the heartbreaking differences, the intermittent struggles for supremacy, for understanding, for reconciliation, for peace that is the history of this diametrically opposed yet passionately loving pair'.

The motives behind the stories of these two gods are those of all religions: to overcome the loneliness and anxiety of separateness and to provide gods for man to worship and adore. Their behavior symbolized the basic polarity of penetration and reception, of the polarity, as Erich Fromm has said, 'of earth and rain, of the river and the ocean, of night and day, of darkness and light, of matter and spirit'. Thus the 'passionately loving pair' symbolized the essential unity of nature; together they represent the mysterious generative force man has called the *élan vital* and libido.

In the stories told about them Man symbolized the positive, powerful, energizing, orderly, active and intense aspects of nature. He was the sun or the sky, and his color was red. Woman symbolized the negative, chaotic, diffuse, passive aspects. She was the moon and the earth, and her color was blue. (The coincidence is worth noting that a modern mythology that deifies Woman is known as 'the blues'. 'Her color has become the name of her song'. Without these two gods in constant relationship, Elisabeth Goldsmith says, 'man forgets the sublime and awe-inspiring need of equilibrium'. In the blues Man and Woman serve the same function as they did in the myths of the past—they are gods to remind us of 'the awe-inspiring need of equilibrium', the need to come to terms with the eternally opposite. The importance of this need is the subject of an editorial in *Saturday Review* by the English philosopher L. L. Whyte, who says in 'Man's Task: A Union of Opposites': 'When man not merely knows but experiences in his emotional nature that the union of contrasts is his destiny, he is saved, no matter how hideous his history and despite the vast indifference of the older generation. A new generation that rejoices in the union of contrasts must take over and make itself heard'.

The religion of the blues, as interpreted here, has been shown to be anti-puritan on its negative side and on its positive side, a vision of a new religion. Its poetry speaks of a world that is dynamic, open and new, a mythological realm with two gods who symbolize the basic unity of all oppositions—natural, sexual, social, and racial. Blues, then, is a reaching out towards a mature self-reliance, towards an independence of spirit. It is an attempt to replace the immature dependence that organized religion has all too often tended to foster. As James Baldwin has said: 'It is not too much to say that whoever wishes to become a truly moral human being . . . must first divorce himself from all the prohibitions, crimes, and hypocrisies of the Christian church. If the concept of God has any validity or any use, it can only be to make us larger, freer and more loving'. And that is the central message and purpose of the blues, its reason for being: 'to make us larger, freer and more loving'.

Man	vs. Woman
↳ Positive	↳ –
↳ Sun	↳ moon
↳ powerful	↳ color: blue

The Blues

A Secular Spiritual

James H. Cone

What did I do
To be so black
And blue?

THEOLOGICALLY, there is more to be said about the music of black people than what was revealed in the black spirituals. To be sure, a significant number of black people were confident that the God of Israel was involved in black history, liberating them from slavery and oppression. But not all blacks could accept the divine promises of the Bible as a satisfactory answer to the contradictions of black existence. They refused to adopt a God-centered perspective as the solution to the problem of black suffering. Instead, they sang, "Got the blues, and too dam' mean to cry."

The blues depict the "secular" dimension of black experience. They are "worldly" songs which tell us about love and sex, and about that other "mule kickin' in my stall." They tell us about the "Black Cat's Bones," "a Mojo hand," and "dese backbitin' womens tryin' fo' to steal my man." The blues are about black life and the sheer earth and gut capacity to survive in an extreme situation of oppression.

I wrote these blues, gonna sing 'em as I please,
I wrote these blues, gonna sing 'em as I please,
I'm the only one like the way I'm singin' 'em,
I'll swear to goodness ain't no one else to please.

The Rise of the Blues

The exact date of the origin of the blues is difficult to determine. Most experts agree that they probably began to take form in the late nineteenth century.[1] But the spirit and mood of the blues have roots stretching back into slavery days and even to Africa. As with the

Reprinted from James H. Cone, *The Spirituals and the Blues: An Interpretation* (New York: Seabury Press, 1972; reprint, New York: Orbis Books, 1991), 97–127. Used by permission of Orbis Books.

spirituals, the Africanism of the blues is related to the *functional* character of West African music. And this is one of the essential ingredients of black music which distinguishes it from Western music and connects it with its African heritage. "The fact that American Negro music, like the African, is at the core of daily life explains the immemorial African quality of all Negro *folk* music in this country, if not of the Negro in exile everywhere."[2]

Black music, then, is not an artistic creation for its own sake; rather it tells us about the *feeling* and *thinking* of African people, and the kinds of mental adjustments they had to make in order to survive in an alien land. For example, the work songs were a means of heightening energy, converting labor into dances and games, and providing emotional excitement in an otherwise unbearable situation. The emphasis was on free, continuous, creative energy as produced in song.[3] A similar functional character applied to the slave seculars, ballads, spirituals, as well as the blues.

Slavery is the historical background out of which the blues were created. From a theological perspective, the blues are closely related to the "slave seculars." The "secular" songs of slavery were "non-religious," occasionally anti-religious, and were often called "devil songs" by religious folk. The "seculars" expressed the skepticism of black slaves who found it difficult to take seriously anything suggesting the religious faith of white preachers. Sterling Brown reported:

> Bible stories, especially the creation, the fall of Man, and the flood, were spoofed, 'Reign, Master Jesus, reign' became 'Rain Masser, rain hard! Rain flour and lard, and a big hog head, Down in my back yard.' After couplets of nonsense and ribaldry, slaves sang with their fingers crossed, or hopeless in defeat: 'Po' mourner, you shall be free, when de good Lord set you free.'[4]

While seculars were not strictly atheistic as defined by modern Western philosophy, they nonetheless uncover the difficulties black people encountered when they attempted to relate white Christian categories to their situation of oppression.

The blues reflect the same existential tension. Taking form sometime after the Emancipation and Reconstruction, they invited black people to embrace the reality and truth of black experience. They express the "laments of folk Negroes over hard luck, 'careless' or unrequited love, broken family life, or general dissatisfaction with a cold and trouble-filled world."[5] And implied in the blues is a stubborn refusal to go beyond the existential problem and substitute otherworldly answers. It is not that the blues reject God; rather, they *ignore* him by embracing the joys and sorrows of life, such as those of a man's relationship with his woman, a woman with her man.

> Ef you don't want me, baby, ain't got to carry no stall.
> I can get mo' women than a passenger train can haul.
>
> Gonna build me a scaffold, I'm gonna hang myself.
> Cain't get the man I love, don't want no body else.

Because the blues ignore the "religious" concerns of the church, many interpreters of black music make a sharp distinction between the blues and the spirituals. John W. Work's treatment is representative:

> The blues differ radically from the spirituals. . . . The spirituals are intensely religious, and the blues are just as intensely worldly. The spirituals sing of heaven, and of the fervent hope that after death the singer may enjoy the celestial joys to be found there. The blues singer has no interest in heaven, and not much hope in earth—a thoroughly disillusioned individual. The spirituals were created in the church; the blues sprang from everyday life.[6]

Unfortunately, it is true that many black church people at first condemned the blues as vulgar and indecent. But that was because they did not understand them rightly. If the blues are viewed in the proper perspective, it is clear that their mood is very similar to the ethos of the spirituals. Indeed, I contend that the blues and the spirituals flow from the same bedrock of experience, and neither is an adequate interpretation of black life without the commentary of the other. "The blues issued directly out of . . . the spiritual."[7] They express and formalize a mood already present in the spirituals. For example, the spirituals,

> Nobody knows the trouble I've seen;
>
> I'm rollin' through an unfriendly world;
>
> I'm a-trouble in the mind;
>
> Sometimes I feel like a motherless child;
>
> Sometimes I hangs my head and cries;

anticipated the "worried blues." That was why Leadbelly (Huddie Ledbetter) said: "Blues was composed up by the Negro people when they was under slavery. They was worried."[8]

The blues are "secular spirituals."[9] They are *secular* in the sense that they confine their attention solely to the immediate and affirm the bodily expression of black soul, including its sexual manifestations. They are *spirituals* because they are impelled by the same search for the truth of black experience.

Yet despite the fact that the blues and the spirituals partake of the same Black Essence, there are important differences between them. The spirituals are *slave* songs, and they deal with historical realities that are pre-Civil War. They were created and sung by the group. The blues, while having some pre-Civil War roots, are essentially post-Civil War in consciousness. They reflect experiences that issued from Emancipation, the Reconstruction Period, and segregation laws. "The blues was conceived," writes LeRoi Jones, "by freedmen and ex-slaves—if not as a result of a personal or intellectual experience, at least as an emotional confirmation of, and reaction to, the way in which most Negroes were still forced to exist in the United States."[10] Also, in contrast to the group singing of the spirituals, the blues are intensely personal and individualistic.

Historically and theologically, the blues express conditions associated with the "burden of freedom." However, freedom in the blues is not simply the "existential freedom" defined by modern philosophy. Philosophical existentialism speaks of freedom in the context of absurdity and about the inability to reconcile the "strangeness of the world" with one's perception of human existence. But absurdity in the blues is factual, not conceptual. The blues, while not denying that the world was strange, described its strangeness in more concrete and vivid terms. Freedom took on historical specificity when contrasted with legal servitude. It meant that simple alternatives, which whites took for granted, became momentous options for newly "free" black slaves. It meant getting married, drinking gin, praising God—and expressing these historical possibilities in song.

The Emancipation decentralized the black population, and the Reconstruction gave black people a certain feeling of autonomy and self-reliance that they had not experienced during slavery. For the first time, many black people were free to move from town to town and from farm to farm, without being restricted by slave codes and patrollers. They had leisure and the freedom to be alone and to reflect. But these options also revealed new limitations. To be sure, blacks had free time, but they also needed money for food and shelter.

> I never had to have no money befo',
> And now they want it everywhere I go.

The Hayes Compromise of 1877 led to the withdrawal of federal troops from the South and ended the hopes of black people becoming authentic participants in the political processes of America. In 1883 the United States Supreme Court declared the Civil Rights Act of 1875 as unconstitutional; and in 1896 it upheld the doctrine of "separate but equal" (Plessy vs. Ferguson), giving legal sanction to the dehumanizing aspects of white supremacy. By the end of the nineteenth century, the political disfranchisement of black people was complete. White people could still do to black people what they willed, just as in slavery days. This was the situation that created the blues. As LeRoi Jones put it:

> The Negro could not ever become white and that was his strength; at some point, always, he could not participate in the dominant tenor of the white man's culture. It was at this juncture that he had to make use of other resources, whether African, subcultural, or hermetic. And it was this boundary, this no man's land, that provided the logic and beauty of his music.[11]

During slavery the social movement of black people was limited, and the church served as the primary social unit for black expression. After the Civil War, the social mobility of blacks increased, and the church became only one of several places where blacks could meet and talk about the problems of black existence. Other "priests" of the community began to emerge alongside of the preachers and deacons; and other songs were sung in addition to the spirituals. The "new priests" of the black community were the blues men and women; and their songs were the blues. Like the preacher in the church, they proclaimed the Word of black existence, depicting its joy and sorrow, love and hate, and the awesome burden of being "free" in a racist society when one is black.

> Oh, Ahm tired a dis mess,
> Oh, yes, Ahm tired a dis mess.

Toward a Definition of the Blues

What is the precise meaning of the blues? And how is that meaning related to the experience of the black community? These questions are not easy to answer, because the blues do not deal with abstract ideas that can be analyzed from the perspective of "objective reason." They are not propositional truths *about* the black experience. Rather they are the essential ingredients that define the *essence* of the black experience. And to understand them, it is necessary to view the blues as a *state of mind in relation to the Truth of the black experience*. This is what blues man Henry Townsend, of St. Louis, has in mind when he says: "When I sing the blues I sing the truth."[12]

The blues and Truth are one reality of the black experience. The blues are that "true feeling," says Henry Townsend.[13] Or as Furry Lewis of Memphis puts it: "All the blues, you can say, is true."[14] The blues are true because they combine art and life, poetry and experience, the symbolic and the real. They are an artistic response to the chaos of life. And to sing the blues, it is necessary to experience the historical realities that created them. In the words of Memphis Willie B.: "A blues is about something that's real. It is about what a man feels when his wife leaves him, or about some disappointment that happens to him that he can't do anything about. That's why none of these young boys can really sing the blues. They don't know about the things that go into a blues."[15]

The thing that goes into the blues is the experience of being black in a white racist society. It is that peculiar feeling that makes you know that there is something seriously wrong with the society, even though you may not possess the intellectual or political power to do anything about it. No black person can escape the blues, because the blues are an inherent part of black existence in America. To be black is to be blue. Leadbelly is right: "All Negroes like the blues . . . because they was born with the blues."[16] This truth is expressed in the lyrics:

If de blues was whiskey,
I'd stay drunk all de time.

If de blues was money,
I'd be a millioneer.

For many people, a blues song is about sex or a lonely woman longing for her rambling man. However, the blues are more than that. To be sure, the blues involve sex and what that means for human bodily expression, but on a much deeper level.

De blues ain't nothin'
But a poor man's heart disease.

The blues express a black perspective on the incongruity of life and the attempt to achieve meaning in a situation fraught with contradictions. As Aunt Molly Jackson of Kentucky put it: "The blues are made by working people . . . when they have a lot of problems to solve about their work, when their wages are low and they don't have no way to exist hardly and they don't know which way to turn and what to do."[17] Blind Lemon Jefferson expresses a similar feeling in song:

I stood on the corner, and I almost bust my head,
I stood on the corner, almost bust my head,
I couldn't earn me enough money to buy me a loaf of bread.

The blues experience always is an encounter with life, its trials and tribulations, its bruises and abuses—but not without benefit of the melody and rhythm of song.

When a woman takes de blues,
She tucks her head and cries.
But when a man catches the blues,
He catches er freight and rides.

Through song a new dimension is created and the individual is transported to another level of experience. Blues music is music of the black soul, the music of the black psyche renewing itself for living and being.

People, I've stood these blues 'bout as
long as I can.
I walked all night with these blues, we
both joined hand in hand.
And they travelled my heart through,
just like a natural man.

The blues are an expression of fortitude in the face of a broken existence. They emphasize the will to be, despite non-being as symbolized in racism and hate.

Lord, going to sleep now for mama just got bad news,
Lord, going to sleep now for mama just got bad news,
To try to dream away my troubles, counting the blues.

The blues are a state of mind that affirms the essential worth of black humanity, even though white people attempted to define blacks as animals. The blues tells us about a people who refused to accept the absurdity of white society. Black people rebelled artistically, and affirmed through ritual, pattern, and form that they were human beings. "You never seen a mule sing, have you?" asked Big Bill (William Lee Conley) Broonzy.

The affirmation of self in the blues is the emphasis that connects them theologically with the spirituals. Like the spirituals, the blues affirm the somebodiness of black people, and they preserve the worth of black humanity through ritual and drama. The blues are a transformation of black life through the sheer power of song. They symbolize the solidarity, the attitudes, and the identity of the black community and thus create the emotional forms of reference for endurance and esthetic appreciation. In this sense, the blues are that stoic feeling that recognizes the painfulness of the present but refuses to surrender to its historical contradictions.

The blues tell us how black people affirmed their existence and refused to be destroyed by the oppressive environment; how, despite white definitions to the contrary, they defined their own somebodiness and realized that America was not their true home.

Ain't it hard to stumble,
When you got no place to fall?
In this whole wide world,
I ain't got no place at all.

The blues feeling was not just a temporary "bad mood" that would soon pass away. The blues have to do with the structure and meaning of existence itself. Black people were asking questions about the nature of being and non-being, life and death. They knew that something was wrong; people were not created to be defined by others. And neither was it meant for a woman to be separated from her man. And Clara Smith pleads for a prescription for "de mean ole blues."

> All day long I'm worried;
> All day long I'm blue;
> I'm so awfully lonesome,
> I doan know what to do.
>
> So I ask yo', Doctor,
> See if you can fin'
> Somethin' in yo' satchel
> To pacify my min'.
>
> Doctor! Doctor!
> Write me a prescription fo' dih blues.
> De mean ole blues.

Because the blues are rooted in the black perception of existence, they are historical. They focus on concrete events of everyday existence. When asked about the origin of the blues, Son House of Mississippi replied:

> All I can say is that when I was a boy we always was singin' in the fields. Not real singin', you know, just hollerin'. But we made up our songs about things that was happenin' to us at the time, and I think that's where the blues started.[18]

Historical experience, as interpreted by the black community, is the key to an understanding of the blues. Black people accepted the dictum: Truth is experience, and experience is the Truth. If it is lived and encountered, then it is real. There is no attempt in the blues to make philosophical distinctions between divine and human truth. That is why many blues people reject the contention that the blues are vulgar or dirty. As Henry Townsend puts it: "If I sing the blues and tell the truth, what have I done? What have I committed? I haven't lied."[19]

The blues tell us about the strength of black people to survive, to endure, and to shape existence while living in the midst of oppressive contradictions. They also tell us about the joy and sweetness of love.

> Hey mama! Hey girl!
> Don't you hear me calling you?
> You're so sweet, so sweet,
> My baby, so sweet.
>
> Say I love you baby, love her to the bone.
> I hate to see my sweet sugar go home.
> She's so sweet, so sweet,
> My little woman, so sweet.
>
> See my baby coming, don't get so smart.
> I'll cut you just a little above your heart.
> She's so sweet, so sweet,
> My little woman, so sweet.

The blues also deal with the agony of love. The blues woman is the priestess and prophet of the people. She verbalizes the emotion for herself and the audience, articulating the stresses and strains of human relationships.

My man left this morning, just about half past four.
My man left this morning, just about half past four.
He left a note on the pillow saying he couldn't use me no more.

I grabbed my pillow, turned over in my bed.
I grabbed my pillow, turned over in my bed.
I cried about my daddy until my cheeks turned cherry red.

It's awful hard to take it, it was such a bitter pill.
It's awful hard to take it, it was such a bitter pill.
If the blues don't kill me that man's meanness will.

The blues are not abstract; they are concrete. They are intense and direct responses to the reality of black experience. They tell us about floods, pneumonia, and the train. The train was a symbol of escape from the harsh reality of the present. It was the freedom to move; and many blacks "got on board," expressing their liberated being.

Some day ah'm gonna lay down dis heavy load,
Gonna grab me a train,
Gonna clam aboh'd.

Gonna go up No'th,
Gonna ease mah pain,
Yessuh, Lord, gonna catch dat train.

Every aspect of black life was exemplified in the blues. There are blues about prisons, highways, and the St. Louis storm.

The shack where we was livin', she reeled and rock but never fell—Lord have mercy!
The shack where we was livin', she reeled and rock but never fell—Lord have mercy!
How that cyclone started, nobody but the Lord can tell.

The blues dealt with TB and other forms of sickness. They focused on guns, highways, the Greyhound buses, and the boll weevil. The boll weevil was that little black bug that invaded Texas over fifty years ago, and destroyed more than a billion dollars in cotton. It was nearly indestructible. Though black people were the chief victims, they also admired it for its power of endurance. Like Brer Rabbit in black folklore, the weevil was the symbol of the small defeating the rich and mighty.

The Boll Weevil is a little black bug
Come from Mexico, they say,
He come to try the Texas soil,
Just lookin' for a place to stay;
Just lookin' for a home,
Just lookin' for a home.

The farmer took the Boll Weevil
And put him in the hot sand;
The Weevil say "This is mighty hot,
But I'll stand it like a man
For it is my home,
This'll be my home."

Boll Weevil say to the doctor,
"You can throw out all your pills;
When I get through with the farmer,
He won't pay no doctor bills:
Won't have no home,
He won't have no home."

Merchant got half the cotton,
Boll Weevil got the rest;
Didn't leave the poor farmer's wife
But one old cotton dress,
And it's full of holes,
Yes, it's full of holes.

The blues were living reality. They are a sad feeling and also a joyous mood. They are bitter but also sweet. They are funny and not so funny. The blues are not evil per se; rather they represent that sad feeling when a woman's man leaves or joy when he returns. They are part of that structure of reality in which human beings are condemned to live. And because the black person had to live in the midst of a broken existence, the reality of the blues was stark and real.

Well, the blues ain't nothin'
But a workingman feelin' bad.
Well, it's one of the worst old feelin's
That any poor man's ever had.

The personification of the blues feeling and experience is most revealing: to black folk he is no shadow, but a person whose presence is inescapable.

I worry all day, I worry all night,
Everytime my man comes home he wants to fuss and fight.
When I pick up the paper to try to read the news,
Just when I'm satisfied, yonder comes the blues.

This blues person is no stranger, but somebody every black knows well. For "When I got up this mornin', [the] Blues [was] walking round my bed; I went to eat my breakfast, the blues was in my bread." And I said:

Good mornin', blues,
Blues, how do you do?
Yes, blues, how do you do?
I'm doing all right,
Good mornin', how are you?

The Blues and Black Suffering

The origin and definition of the blues cannot be understood independent of the suffering that black people endured in the context of white racism and hate. Therefore, the question that gave shape and purpose to the blues was: How could black people keep themselves together, preserving a measure of their cultural being, and not lose their physical lives? Responding to the significance of that question for the black community, blues people sang:

> Times is so tough, can't even get a dime,
> Yes times is so tough, can't even get a dime,
> Times don't get better, I'm going to lose my mind.

The blues tell us about black people's attempt to carve out a significant existence in a very trying situation. The purpose of the blues is to give structure to black existence in a context where color means rejection and humiliation.

Suffering and its relation to blackness is inseparable from the meaning of the blues. Without pain and suffering, and what that meant for black people in Mississippi, Tennessee, and Arkansas, there would have been no blues. The blue mood means sorrow, frustration, despair, and black people's attempt to take these existential realities upon themselves and not lose their sanity. The blues are not art for art's sake, music for music's sake. They are a way of life, a life-style of the black community; and they came into being to give expression to black identity and the will for survival. Thus to seek to understand the blues apart from the suffering that created them is to misinterpret them and distort the very creativity that defines them. This is what Clarence Williams, a New York publisher who has written many blues, meant when he said:

> Why, I'd never have written blues if I had been white. You don't study to write the blues, you *feel* them. It's the mood you're in—sometimes it's a rainy day . . . just like the time I lay for hours in a swamp in Louisiana. Spanish moss dripping everywhere . . . White men were looking for me with guns—I wasn't scared, just sorry I didn't have a gun. I began to hum a tune—a little sighing kinda tune—you know like this. . . . 'Jes as blue as a tree—an old willow tree—nobody 'round here, jes nobody but me.'[20]

It is impossible to sing the blues or listen to their authentic presentation without recognizing that they belong to a particular community. They were created in the midst of the black struggle for being. And because the blues are an expression of that struggle, they are inseparable from blackness and trouble. That is why Henry Townsend says that the distinctive quality of the good blues singer is "Trouble . . . that's right. That's the one word solution. Trouble. You know you can only express a true feeling if you're sincere about it. You can only express what happened to you."[21]

The trouble that makes the blues is not just the particular difficulties of an individual blues singer. It involves much more than that. The trouble of the blues refers to the history of a people, and the kinds of difficulties they encountered in their struggle for existence. As John Lee Hooker puts it:

> When I sing the blues . . . it's not . . . that I had the hardships that a lot of people had throughout the South and other cities throughout the country, but I do know what they went through . . . it's not only what happened to you—it's what happened to your foreparents and other people. And that's what makes the blues.[22]

The blues, as Charley Patton sang about them, are a "*Mean Black Moan.*" They recognize that there is something wrong with this world, something absurd about the way that white people treat black people. The blues singer articulates this mood, and thus provides a degree of transcendence over the troubles of this world. When the blues caught the absurdity of black existence in white America and vividly and artistically expressed it in word and suitable music, it afforded black people a certain distance from their immediate trouble and allowed them to see and feel it artistically, thereby offering them a certain liberating catharsis. That black people could transcend trouble without ignoring it means that they were not destroyed by it.

But the questions can be asked: How could black people endure the stresses and strains of segregation and lynchings and not lose their sanity? If the blues were, as LeRoi Jones said, the result of thought,[23] what do they tell us about black people's reflections on their pain and sorrow? What is the explanation of black suffering in the blues? It is important to observe that the blues, like the spirituals, were not written or sung for the purpose of answering the "problem of evil." They merely describe the reality of black suffering without seeking to devise philosophical solutions for the problem of absurdity. In this sense, the blues are *existential*; that is, they assume that reality inheres in historical existence and not in abstract essence. That is why there is much emphasis on the concrete restrictions placed on the black community, and why color is a dominant theme of the blues.

> Now, if you're white
> You're all right,
> If you're brown,
> Stick aroun'
> But if you're black
> Git back! Git back! Git back!

The blues do not speak about abstract Man but about particular men and women who encounter the trials and tribulations of human existence. They tell us about that "po' boy long way from home" and about "de freight train . . . sixteen coaches long." The blues are about "goin' up North, where they say—money grows on trees," but "I don't give a doggone, if my black soul leaves." They are about love and sex and the pain of human relationships. They are also about death.

> You know I got my suitcase and took on down the road,
> Uumh, took on down the road,
> But when I got there, she was laying on the cooling bo'd.

The response to suffering in the blues is, however, different from what we saw earlier in the spirituals. According to the spirituals, blacks of slavery could endure oppression because they believed that the God of Israel would eventually set them free. The spirituals do not reflect the problem of theodicy since black people did not identify God as being responsible for their slavery. Instead, their concern was for God not to leave them alone in a world full of trouble. The blues people, however, sing as if God is irrelevant, and their task is to deal with trouble without special reference to Jesus Christ. This is not atheism; rather, it is believing that *transcendence* will only be meaningful when it is made real in and through the limits of historical experience. The achievement of being is an entirely historical reality, grounded and defined within the context of the community's experience.

The blues people believe that it is only through the acceptance of the real as disclosed in concrete human affairs that a community can attain authentic existence.

While the blues reject an "objective transcendence," they do not reject "historical transcendence." Insofar as the blues affirm the somebodiness of black people, they are transcendent reflections on black humanity. Through the sheer power of melody and rhythm of song, black people transcended historical restrictions and affirmed a black being not made with hands. They refused to accept white rules and regulations as the definition of their community. To be sure, they cried, "I got the blues an' can't keep from cryin'." They were hurt, and they were bruised. But through the sharing of their troubles with each other, black people were able to move to another level of human existence and *be*, in spite of the non-being of the white community. That is why they could sing:

> I got the world in a jug,
> The stopper in my hand.

The important contribution of the blues is their affirmation of black humanity in the face of immediate absurdity. Although blacks were beaten and shot, they refused to allow their perception of black humanity to be reduced to the sum total of their brutalization. They transcended the restrictions of history by affirming that perception of black humanity revealed in and through the historical struggle for being.

The Blues and Sex

Because we know that we have survived, that we have not been destroyed, and that we are more than the stripes on our backs, we can sing as a way of celebrating our being. Indeed, for black people, existence is a form of celebration. It is joy, love, and sex. It is hugging, kissing, and feeling. People cannot love physically and spiritually (the two cannot be separated!) until they have been up against the edge of life, experiencing the hurt and pain of existence. They cannot appreciate the feel and touch of life nor express the beauty of giving themselves to each other in community, in love, and in sex until they know and experience the brokenness of existence as disclosed in human oppression. People who have not been oppressed physically cannot know the power inherent in bodily expressions of love. That is why white Western culture makes a sharp distinction between the spirit and the body, the divine and the human, the sacred and the secular. White oppressors do not know how to come to terms with the essential *spiritual* function of the human body. But for black people the body is sacred, and they know how to use it in the expression of love.

Most interpreters agree that the dominant and most expressive theme in the blues is sex. Whatever else is said about them, the blues cannot be understood if this important theme is omitted. As blues man Furry Lewis puts it: "The blues come from a woman wanting to see her man, and a man wanting to see his woman." Or, as Henry Townsend says: "You know, that's the major thing in life. Please believe me. What you love the best is what can hurt you the most." Ma Rainey also puts it well:

> People have different blues and think they're mighty sad,
> But blues about a man the worst I ever had . . .

And another says:

You know my woman left me,
Left me cold in hand.
I wouldn't hate it so bad,
But she left with another man.

The blues are the songs of men and women who have been hurt and disappointed and who feel the confusion and isolation of human love.

'Gwine lay my head right on de railroad track,
'Gwine lay my head right on de railroad track,
Cause my baby, she won't take me back.

The blue mood is about black men and women—their lament, grief, and disillusionment. In a world where a people possess little that is their own, human relationships are placed at a high premium. The love between men and women becomes immediate and real. Black people live in that kind of world; and they express the pain of separation and loneliness.

Did you ever wake up in the morning, find your man had gone?
Did you ever wake up in the morning, find your man had gone?
You will wring your hands, you will cry the whole day long.

But the blues were not just sad feelings about separation, the loss of a man or woman. There was also humor about sexuality.

Good lookin' woman make a bull dog break his chain,
Good lookin' woman make a bull dog break his chain,
Good lookin' woman make a snail catch a passenger train.

Yaller gal make a preacher lay his Bible down,
Yaller gal make a preacher lay his Bible down,
Good lookin' high brown make him run from town to town.

Good lookin' woman make a mule kick his stable down,
Good lookin' woman make a mule kick his stable down,
Good lookin' woman make a rabbit move his family to town.

Woman without a man like a ship without a sail,
Woman without a man like a ship without a sail,
Ship without a sail like a dog without a tail.

There is seriousness, too, when a man appeals to his woman to make up her mind.

If you didn't want me girlie what made you say you do,
If you didn't want me girlie what made you say you do,
Take your time little girl, nobody's rushin' you.

The blues are honest music. They describe every aspect of a woman's feelings about a man, and what a man thinks about a woman. Through the blues, black people express their views about infidelity and sex. The blues woman said:

> You can cheat on me, you can steal on me, you can fool me all along.
> You can cheat on me, you can steal on me, you can fool me all along.
> All I ask you daddy, please don't let me catch you wrong.

And her man answered:

> I'm a hard-working man and, baby, I don't mind dying,
> I'm a hard-working man and, baby, I don't mind dying,
> I catch you cheating on me, then, baby, you don't mind dying.

It has been the vivid description of sex that caused many church people to reject the blues as vulgar or dirty. The Christian tradition has always been ambiguous about sexual intercourse, holding it to be divinely ordained yet the paradigm of rebellious passion. Perhaps this accounts for the absence of sex in the black spirituals and other black church music. But most blacks only verbalized the distinction between the "sacred" and "profane" and found themselves unable to follow white Christianity's rejection of the body. And those who did not experience the free acceptance of sexual love on Saturday nights, expressed it indirectly on Sunday mornings through song and sermon.

In the blues there is an open acceptance of sexual love, and it is described in most vivid terms: "She moves it just right," "I'm going to have it now," "It hurts me so good," "Do it a long time," "Warm it up to me," "Drive it down," "Slow driving."

> Peach Orchard Mama, you swore nobod'd pick your fruit but me,
> Peach Orchard Mama, you swore nobod'd pick your fruit but me,
> I found three kid men shaking down your peaches free.

What are we to make of such blatant descriptions of sexual love? Theologically, the blues reject the Greek distinction between the soul and the body, the physical and the spiritual. They tell us that there is no wholeness without sex, no authentic love without the feel and touch of the physical body. The blues affirm the authenticity of sex as the bodily expression of black soul.

The blues are not profane in any negative sense and neither are they immoral. They deal with the truth of human existence and the kinds of difficulties black people experience trying to hold themselves together. They tell us about their strengths and weaknesses, their joys and sorrows, their love and hate. And because they expressed their most intimate and precious feelings openly, they were able to survive as a community amid very difficult circumstances. They sang together, prayed together, and slept together. It was sometimes sweet and sometimes bitter; but they could make it because they tried; they "kept on pushing" looking for that new black humanity.

White people obviously cannot understand the love that black people have for each other. People who enslave humanity cannot understand the meaning of human freedom; freedom comes only to those who strive for it in the context of the community of the enslaved. People who destroy physical bodies with guns, whips, and napalm cannot know the power of physical love. Only those who have been hurt can appreciate the warmth of love that proceeds when persons touch, feel, and embrace each other. The blues are openness to feeling and the emotions of physical love.

The Blues and Social Protest

Much has been said about the absence of social protest in the blues.[24] As Samuel Charters put it: "The blues do not try to express an attitude toward the separateness of Negro life in America. Protest is only a small thread in the blues."[25] There is some truth in Charters' observation. The blues do not *openly* condemn white society, and there is little *direct* complaint *to* white people about the injustice of segregation. But my difficulty with Charters' interpretation and others like it is the implied and often stated conclusion that the absence of open attack upon white society means that black people accepted their oppressed condition. As Paul Oliver openly states: "That the number of protest blues is small is in part the result of the Negro's acceptance of the stereotypes that have been cut for him."[26]

Assuming from the absence of open protest that black people internalized the values of white society and thus accepted the injustice committed against them reminds us of a similar view held regarding the spirituals. Since I have already made my objection to that kind of interpretation, there is no need to rehearse it here. It is enough to observe that white recorders and interpreters should know that blues men and women would have to be very naïve to couch the blues in white categories of protest. Moreover, if they did, they would not likely sing them in recording studios! Deception was present not only during slavery but is still with us today, and it will continue to exist as long as there are white people in power who define law and order according to white supremacy and black inferiority. This simple fact seems to have been overlooked by even the most sensitive white interpreters of the blues.

In order to understand the black reaction to the social restrictions on the black community as reflected in the blues, it is necessary to view the blues from the perspective of black people's attempt to survive in a very hostile white society. The blues are not political treatises, and neither are they radical statements on social revolution. (It is safe to assume that blues people did not read Karl Marx.) The blues are statements *of* and *for* black people who are condemned to live in an extreme situation of oppression without any political leverage for defining their existence. The blues attempt to deal with the question: How can we black people survive in a world of white racism and hate? This question defines the sociological and theological background for an interpretation of the blues.

> Feeling tomorrow, like I feel today,
> If I feel tomorrow, like I feel today,
> I'll pack my suitcase, make my get away.

Consider the blues "Another Man Done Gone," which was created by Vera Hall, "a peaceloving cook and washerwoman and a pillar of the choir in her Baptist Church."[27] This blues is about chains, bloodhounds, prisons, and the need to escape the harsh realities of inhumanity. "It is enigmatic, full of silent spaces, speaking of the night and of a man slippin' by in the night." Then "you see his face, you know him, but at the same time you put him out of your mind, so that when the white man asks after him, you can say: 'I didn't know his name, I don't know where he's gone.' "[28] This song is a moving description of the blues feeling. It is not romantic about politics, nor is it evidence that black people accepted white rules and regulations as a definition of their being. This song is about the *togetherness* of the black community in view of the county farm and the chains.

Another man done gone,
Another man done gone,
From the county farm
Another man done gone.

I didn't know his name,
I didn't know his name,
I didn't know his name,
I didn't know his name.

He had a long chain on,
He had a long chain on,
He had a long chain on,
He had a long chain on.

He killed another man,
He killed another man,
He killed another man,
He killed another man.

I don't know where he's gone,
I don't know where he's gone,
I don't know where he's gone,
I don't know where he's gone.

Radical social protest assumes that the victimizers of human beings have a conscience and that the victims have the political leverage to publicize societal wrongs committed against them. But black people had little evidence that white people had a conscience and thus could hear their cries and moans. And they certainly did not possess the needed social and political power to verbalize the injustice of white people against the black community. What were black people to do when the slightest expression of social resentment could mean death? Without political freedom or the means of achieving it, many blacks turned to the blues for identity and survival. As Ralph Ellison has put it: "For the art—the blues, the spirituals, the jazz, the dance—was what we had in place of freedom."[29] The blues were techniques of survival and expressions of courage. They tell us about the contradictions that black people experienced and what they did to overcome them.

They say we are the Lawd's children, I don't say that ain't true,
They say we are the Lawd's children, I don't say that ain't true,
But if we are the same like each other, ooh, well, well, why do they treat me like they do?

I want to live on children, children, I would like to see,
I want to live on children, children, I would like to see,
What will become of us, ooh, well, by nineteen and fifty-three.

Some of the Good Lawd's children, some of them ain't no good,
Some of the Good Lawd's children, some of them ain't no good,
Some of them are the devil, ooh, well, well, and won't help you if they could.

Some of the Good Lawd's children kneel upon their knees and pray,
Some of the Good Lawd's children kneel upon their knees and pray,
You serve the devil in the night, ooh, well, and serve the Lawd in the day.

Black people were not oblivious to the fact of "Colored Only" and "White Only" signs on toilets, water fountains, and restaurants. They knew about friends and relatives who were beaten or lynched. They experienced the quiet nights of waiting for a brother or a father to come home and not knowing whether he had been permanently detained by a white mob looking for entertainment. They did not sing about it much, at least not directly. But the experience was present in the mood and style of the blues. The despair and loneliness were there, and the "tears came rolling down."

I'm awful lonesome, all alone and blue,
I'm awful lonesome, all alone and blue,
Ain't got no body to tell my troubles to.

The political significance of the blues is not very impressive to those who have not experienced black servitude. Neither is it impressive to persons who are fascinated by modern theories of political revolution. But for black people who *live* the blues, who experience and share that history with their black fathers and mothers, the blues are examples of Black Power and the courage to affirm black being. Ellison is right:

> Any people who could endure all that brutalization and keep together, who could undergo such dismemberment and resuscitate itself, and endure until it could take the initiative in achieving its own freedom is obviously more than the sum of its brutalization. Seen in this perspective, theirs has been one of the great triumphs of the human spirit in modern times, in fact, in the history of the world.[30]

The Blues and Hope

Related to black suffering and the transcendent affirmation of being is the idea of the future, the not-yet of black existence. The question is: How are the blues related to the hope and future of the black community? It is a commonly held opinion that there is no hope in the blues. Taking their clue from the "non-religious" perspective of the songs and the political disfranchisement of black people, some critics say that these songs represent black people's acceptance of their oppressed condition. According to this interpretation, the blues represent complete despair and utter hopelessness.

I think this interpretation needs to be re-evaluated in the light of the blues themselves and the cultural environment that created them. It is true that hopelessness is an authentic aspect of the blues' experience, and despair is a central theme in the blues. It was not possible for black people to experience the disappointment of post-Civil War America and not know the meaning of despair. Like the spirituals, the blues are not romantic; they do not camouflage the reality of social oppression. Oppression is real, and it often appears to the black community that there is little that can be done about it. It is this feeling of helplessness that produces the blues. The blues are that mood which owes its origins to powerlessness in the face of trouble.

Sometimes I feel like nothin', somethin' th'owed away,
Sometimes I feel like nothin', somethin' th'owed away,
Then I get my guitar and play the blues all day.

Money's all gone, I'm so far from home,
Money's all gone, I'm so far from home,
I just sit here and cry and moan.

The despair is real, not imagined. It is clear that the blues singer is searching for a reason to live, for purpose and meaning in existence. And the external realities of oppression seem to have gotten the best of him. And he lifts up his voice again:

Ninety-nine years so jumpin' long,
To be here rollin' and cain' go home.

Don't yo go worrin' about forty [the years of the prison sentence]
Cause in five years you'll be dead.

If you don't believe my buddy's dead,
Just look at that hole in my buddy's head.

Great gawdamighty, folks feelin' bad,
Lost everything they ever had.

On the basis of these verses alone, it would be foolish to discount the presence of despair and hopelessness in the blues. But it is important to point out that despair is not the whole picture. For underneath the despair there is also a firm hope in the possibility of black people's survival despite their extreme situation of oppression. That is why blacks also sing: "Times is bad, but dey won't be bad always." Why? Because times "gotta get better 'cause dey cain't get w'us."

The hope of the blues is grounded in the historical reality of the black experience. The blues express a belief that one day things will not be like what they are today. This is why buses, railways, and trains are important images in the blues. Each symbolizes motion and the possibility of leaving the harsh realities of an oppressive environment. "Ef ah kin jes grab me a handfulla freight train—ah'll be set." The blues emphasize movement, the possibility of changing the present reality of suffering.

I'd rather drink muddy water, sleep in a hollow log,
Dan to stay in this town, treated like a dirty dog.

Sitting here wondering would a matchbox hold my clothes,
I ain't got so many, and I got so far to go.

I'm got a mind to ramble, a mind for to leave this town.

The blues are a lived experience, an encounter with the contradictions of American society but a refusal to be conquered by it. They are despair only in the sense that there is no attempt to cover up reality. The blues recognize that black people have been hurt and scared by the brutalities of white society. But there is also hope in what Richard Wright calls the "endemic capacity to live."[31] This hope provided the strength to survive, and also an openness to the intensity of life's pains without being destroyed by them. This is why Lonnie Johnson could sing:

> People is raisin' 'bout hard times, tell me what it's all about,
> People is hollerin' 'bout hard times, tell me what's it all about,
> Hard times don't worry me, I was broke when it first started out.
>
> Friends, it could be worser, you don't seem to understand,
> Friends, it could be worser, you don't seem to understand,
> Some is cryin' with a sack of gold under each arm and a loaf of bread in each hand.
>
> People ravin' 'bout hard times, I don't know why they should,
> People ravin' 'bout hard times, I don't know why they should;
> If some people was like me, they didn't have no money when times was good.

While the blues recognized poverty:

> Pocketbook was empty,
> My heart was full of pain

Yet black people did not let such sociological realities define the status of their being:

> When you lose your money,
> don't lose your mind.

In order to affirm being, a people must create forms for the expression of being and project it with images that reflect their perceptions of reality. They must take the structure of reality and subject it to the conditions of life—its pain, sorrow, and joy. That black people could sing the blues, describing their sorrows and joys, meant that they were able to affirm an authentic hope in the essential worth of black humanity.

> My burden's so heavy, I can't hardly see,
> Seems like everybody is down on me,
> An' that's all right, I don't worry, oh, there will be a better day.

The better day is not naïve optimism. It is simply the will to be.

Unlike the spirituals, the hope of the blues is not located in the concept of heaven. "One cannot continually ride in chariots to God when the impact of slavery is so ever present and real."[32] The blues ground black hope firmly in history and do not plead for life after death. Even in death, there is no retreat from the willingness to accept the consequences of life. The bluesman only made one simple request:

> Well, there's one kind favor I ask of you,
> One kind favor I ask of you,
> Lord, there's one kind favor I ask of you,
> Please see that my grave is kept clean.

In sum, when the blues people are "standin' here looking one thousand miles away," they are looking for a home that is earthly *and* eschatological. Home would always be more than a plot of land, more than a lover, family and friends—though it would include these.

Home would be the unrestricted affirmation of self and the will to protect self from those who would destroy self. It would be self-reliance and self-respect. In short, home could only be freedom, and the will to create a new world for the people I love.

> Well, I'm going to buy me a little railroad of my own,
> Well, I'm going to buy me a little railroad *all* my *own,*
> Ain't going to let nobody ride but the chocolate-to-the-bone.

Notes

1. See LeRoi Jones, *Blues People* (New York: William Morrow and Company, 1963) [excerpts reprinted herein]; Alain Locke, *The Negro and His Music* and *Negro Art: Past and Present* (New York: Arno Press, 1969); Charles Keil, *Urban Blues* (Chicago: The University of Chicago Press, 1966) [excerpts reprinted herein]; Phyl Garland, *The Sound of Soul* (Chicago: Henry Regnery Co., 1969); Harold Courlander, *Negro Folk Music U.S.A.* (New York: Columbia University Press, 1963); Eileen Southern, *The Music of Black Americans* (New York: W. W. Norton, 1971); Rudi Blesh, *Shining Trumpets* (New York: Alfred Knopf, 1946); Paul Oliver, *The Meaning of the Blues* (New York: Collier Books, 1963) and *The Story of the Blues* (Philadelphia: Chilton Book Co., 1969); Samuel Charters, *The Bluesmen* (New York: Oak Publications, 1967) and *The Poetry of the Blues* (New York: Avon, 1963) [excerpts reprinted herein]; Russell Ames, *The Story of American Folk Song* (New York: Grosset and Dunlap, 1960); and John A. and Alan Lomax, *Folk Song U.S.A.* (New York: Meredith Press, 1947). The list of commentators on the blues could be extended but these are some of the important studies. For the lyrics, Oliver's *The Meaning of the Blues,* Charters' *Poetry of the Blues* and Sterling Brown's "The Blues" in *The Negro Caravan,* ed. Sterling Brown, Arthur P. Davis, and Ulysses Lee (New York: Dryden Press, 1941) and his "Blues" in Langston Hughes and Arna Bontemps, *Book of Negro Folklore* (New York: Dodd Mead, 1958) are most useful.
2. Blesh, *Shining Trumpets,* p. 47.
3. Blesh, p. 48.
4. Brown, "Negro Folk Expression" in A. Meier and E. Rudwick, *The Making of Black America,* New York: Atheneum, 1969, p. 215.
5. Brown in *Negro Caravan,* p. 426.
6. John W. Work, *American Negro Songs and Spirituals* (New York: Bonanza Books, 1940), p. 28.
7. Jones, *Blues People,* p. 62.
8. Cited in Russell Ames, *American Folk Song,* p. 262.
9. I am indebted to C. Eric Lincoln of Union Theological Seminary for this phrase.
10. Jones, *Blues People,* p. 142.
11. Jones, p. 80.
12. Cited in Charters, *Poetry of the Blues,* p. 58.
13. Cited in Charters, p. 17.
14. Cited in Charters.
15. Cited in Charters, p. 18.
16. Cited in Arnold Shaw, *The World of Soul* (New York: Coronet Communications, 1971), p. 31.
17. Cited in Ames, *American Folk Song,* p. 252.
18. Cited in Shaw, *World of Soul,* p. 38.
19. Cited in Paul Oliver, *The Blues Tradition* (New York: Oak Publications, 1970), p. 47.

20. Cited in E. Simms Campbell, "Blues," in Frederic Ramsey, Jr. (ed.), *Jazzmen* (New York: Harcourt Brace, and Co., 1939), pp. 110–111.

21. Cited in Charters, *Poetry of the Blues*, p. 18.

22. Cited in Tony Russell, *Blacks, Whites and Blues* (New York: Stein and Day, 1970), p. 77.

23. See Jones, *Blues People*, pp. 152, 153.

24. See Oliver, *Meaning of the Blues*; Charters, *Poetry of the Blues*.

25. Charters, p. 12.

26. Oliver, p. 322.

27. John and Alan Lomax, *Folk Song U.S.A.*, p. 376.

28. Lomax, p. 377.

29. Ralph Ellison, *Shadow and Act* (New York: Signet Book, 1964), p. 247.

30. Ellison, "A Very Stern Discipline," *Harpers* (March, 1967), p. 84.

31. Richard Wright, "Forward," in Paul Oliver, *The Meaning of the Blues*, p. 9.

32. E. Simms Campbell, "Blues," in *Jazzmen*, ed. Frederick Ramsey, Jr., and Charles Edward Smith (New York: Harcourt Brace Jovanovich, 1939), p. 104.

The Police and the Church

Paul Garon

> The police are the absolute enemy.
>
> Charles Baudelaire

> Give us stones, brilliant stones, to drive off the infamous priests.
>
> André Breton

MARCUSE (1970) has suggested that 'the cornerstone of psychoanalysis is the concept that social controls emerge in the struggle between instinctual and social needs . . .' (53). We can see the emergence of such controls if we study the blues singers' reactions to two crucial instruments of repression: the police and the church. So often have these two institutions worked hand in hand toward the structuring of repressive categories within the mind as well as within society as a whole, that it becomes thematically necessary to discuss them together under one heading.

The antipathy of the police for the black working class (indeed, the working class as a whole) and vice versa is common knowledge. The police can be defined, in fact, as highly specialised defenders of existing property relations. Freud's most basic theories of super-ego formation, in simplified form (identification with parents, etc.) have passed into general acceptance. While the parents are expected to exert control over the child's behaviour, the identificatory processes of super-ego formation are expected to result in an internalisation of parental control. But civilisation provides its own methods of control in case the process of internalisation of parental authority meets with partial failure.

The connection between father, super-ego and police, well enough known not to need proof here, is evidenced by the fact that one is often replaced by the other. In some songs the police might appear in a benevolent-advisory capacity:

> I heard somebody call me, it was the policeman on
> his beat. (x2)

Reprinted from "Imagination, Instincts, and Reality," in Paul Garon, *Blues and the Poetic Spirit* (London: Eddison Press Ltd., 1975), 130–36. Used by permission of the author.

Well, well, now, he just wanted to tell me, oooh, well, well,
  that I was driving on the wrong side of the street.

(Peetie Wheatstraw, *Crazy with the Blues*)

But the role of the police, socially roughly analogous to the super-ego's role in controlling the individual's unconscious impulses, is to control *absolutely* the deepest desires and impulses of humanity. Implicit in this analogy, of course, is the connection between the working class (*contra* the police) and the id (*contra* the super-ego). The working class represents basic desires and needs, the police represent the control of these desires and needs. The control exerted by the police is senseless and merciless:

Oh, they accused me of forgery and I can't write my name.

(Texas Alexander, *Levee Camp Moan Blues*)

Standing on the corner, talking with my brown. (x2)
Up step the policeman, take both of us down.

(Julius Daniels, *My Mamma Was a Sailor*)

It is clear to the singer that the policeman's role is not simply to restore 'order' in the conventional societal sense. In a highly revealing 'slip of the tongue'—of the sort on which psychoanalysis has thrown considerable light—the mayor of Chicago remarked during police atrocities against demonstrators in 1968: 'The policeman is not there to create disorder; he is there to *preserve* disorder.' Above all the police are hired to maintain *repression*, even in the most strictly psychoanalytic sense. In the following verse by Sleepy John Estes, the intervention of the police (the 'chief') in the second line is prefaced only by an intriguing image of sexuality, and it can only be sexuality (in this verse) that elicits the association of the police (control).

I want to play marbles on my baby's marble ground. (x2)
I won't be worried with the chief, I'm gonna move out on the
  edge of town.

(The Delta Boys, *You Shouldn't Do That*)

Our analogy makes clear how the police, as representatives of the super-ego and, earlier, the father, become associated with the repressive control of sexuality, and of course, aggression:

Well, I poisoned my man, I put it in his drinking . . .
Now, I'm in jail, and I can't keep from thinking,
I poisoned my man, I put it in his drinking cup.
Well, it's easy to go to jail, but, Lord, they sent me up.

Bloodhounds, bloodhounds, bloodhounds is on my trail. (x2)
They want to take me back to that cold, cold, lonesome jail.

Well, I know I done wrong, but he kicked me and he blacked my . . .
I done it in a passion, I thought it was the fashion,
I know I done wrong, but he kicked me and blacked my eyes.
But if the bloodhounds ever catch me in the electric chair
  I'll die.

(Victoria Spivey, *Blood Hound Blues*)

Our discussion also makes clear how, in one sense, the working class is analogous to the unconscious or, structurally, the id. Freedom from repression, and liberation of the unconscious, is analogous to the liberation of the working class. Yet there is still more to be gained in a further application of psychoanalytic theory. Through the resolution of the oedipus complex, the young boy abandons his mother as sexual object—just as in many cases the process may not be a clear-cut example of dissolution or abandonment, the erotic as well as the hostile attachments to the father are subject to any number of instinctual fates: sublimation, repression, displacement, projection, etc. Freud (1927b) has shown how these defences contribute integrally to the construction and maintenance of religion. 'Thus [the child] fears [the father] no less than it longs for him and admires him. The indications of this ambivalence in the attitude toward the father are deeply imprinted in every religion . . .' (24). Just as the Devil, historically, represented the repressed (*Minutes* 1909, no. 66), in modern society, these harsher aspects of the super-ego's role are delegated to the police. The church assumes the more benevolent aspects for itself, but nonetheless remains a repressive force—in essence, in practice, in totality.

Religion has always been an agency of repression, concerning itself chiefly with the inhibition of aggression and desire, and the maintenance of guilt. It is Friedrich Nietzsche who said: 'You say you believe in the necessity of religion. Be sincere! You believe in the necessity of the police!' The black church, in attempting to incorporate the more 'civilising' aspects of Christianity, has served the purposes of the ruling class by attempting to crush the spirit of revolt, replacing it with the doctrine of accommodation. Yet within the complex of psychodynamic factors that contribute to religious belief and its perpetuation, there runs the 'private dialectic' of the church: hypocrisy.

> If you want to hear a preacher cuss, bake the bread, sweet
> mama, and save him the crust. (x2)
>
> Preacher in the pulpit, bible in his hand, sister in corner,
> crying, 'There's my man.' (x2)
>
> Preacher come to your house, you ask him to rest his hat,
> Next thing he want to know, 'Sister, where's your husband
> at?' (x2)
>
> 'Come in here, elder, shut my door, I want you to preach the
> same text you did night before.' (x2)
>
> See that preacher walking down the street, he's fixing to mess
> with every sister he meet. (x2)
>
> Preacher, preacher, you nice and kind, I better not catch you
> at that house of mine. (x2)

(Hi Henry Brown, *Preacher Blues*)

More than one singer depicted the stereotypical deceitfulness of the black preacher (Frank Stokes, the Mississippi Sheiks, etc.), one of the best being Joe McCoy in *Preachers Blues.*

Some folks say a preacher won't steal, but I caught three in
my cornfield,
One had a yellow, one had a brown, looked over the mill and one
was getting down.
Now some folks say a preacher won't steal,
But he'll do more stealing than I get regular meals.

I went to my house about half-past ten,
Looked on my bed where that preacher had been.
Now some folks say, etc.

He will eat your chicken, he will eat your pie,
He will eat your wife out on the sly.
Now some folks say, etc.

I been trying so hard, to save my life,
Just to keep that preacher from my wife.
Now some folks say, etc.

Refusing to be placated by Christianity's offer of a posthumous reward, the blues singer demands more earthly gratification.

Take me out of this bottom before the high water rise. (x2)
You know I ain't no Christian (preacher?), and I don't wanna
be baptised.

I cried, Lord, my father, Lord, eh, kingdom come. (x2)
Send me back my woman, then 'thy will be done.'

(Texas Alexander, *Justice Blues*)

In making this demand, the singer pursues the only historical reality that can offer gratification, that reality which lies outside the reality principle, but within the pleasure principle, that reality which *corresponds* to the true needs of humanity. Within such a framework, the church appears ludicrous and out of place.

You know I went to church last night and they called on
po' Lightnin' to preach. (x2)
I said, 'I ain't got time, Galveston beach is over there, I'm
going down on the Galveston beach.'

(Lightinin' Hopkins, *Get Off My Toe*)

My mother told me, 'Son, don't forget to pray.'
I fell down on my knees, I forget just what to say,
I said, 'Baaa-by.'

(Lightnin' Hopkins, *Baby*)

Some critics, notably Oliver (1968), have suggested that the blues singers' treatment of religious themes is really quite tempered and conservative. Let us admit that there is much of radical import that is not treated in the blues; but only by carefully tracing certain themes, their development and their interconnections, does the thread of revolt which runs through the blues become properly illuminated. It is clear that this has not been Oliver's purpose, but a few words must be said about the position he espouses. As we said earlier, a study of the poetic quality of the blues is not enhanced by the drawing up of a poetic balance sheet. Similarly, our discussion of the nature of revolt and more particularly of 'the dialectic of negativity as the moving and generating principle' (Marx 1844: 177) as they appear in the blues does not rest for its proof (as if any were needed) on the construction of a 'revolutionary' balance sheet.

When Oliver suggests that in dealing with the repressive forces of the church the blues singer relies on 'well worn phrases', he is undermining the dynamic nature of the whole process of negation. Having established itself in a poetic context, the appearance of 'well worn phrases' in the blues must be viewed as an extremely poor gauge on which to base one's evaluations. It remains to be seen how 'well worn' a phrase must become for it to be worthless; certainly the negating power of the simple 'no' has lost none of its vitality throughout the centuries.

What Oliver fails to emphasise is that the very process of 'negative thinking' is, in this case, fundamentally poetic. When he points out that the blues singer unoriginally concentrates his disparagement on the preacher rather than the church, thus following an older minstrel theme, he misses the point. The blues singer does not, of course, worry over the finer points of theology; I think it can safely be said that nothing is further from the thoughts of Victoria Spivey and J. B. Hutto than the contrived interpretations of Saint Augustine's *De Civitae Dei* which so troubled the medieval scholastics. The blues critique, emphatically materialist, is directed not against heavenly abstractions (God, Jesus, the Holy Ghost) but against the hypocrisy and pretension of the pompous self-appointed 'representatives' of God on earth. Nothing would be more false, however, than to suggest that the blues is therefore not opposed to religion as such, but only to this or that organised religious institution, or (still worse) to suggest that the blues itself is some sort of 'secular religion' (sic). The entire spirit of the blues is antithetical to this cheap and sentimental agnostic reformism. The blues does not intervene on the theological plane with the obsolete tools of rationalism or in the name of some empty 'humanism'. On the contrary, it enters the fray wholeheartedly *on the side of Evil.* The 'Devil's music' is the denunciation of everything religion stands for and the glorification of everything religion condemns. The blues singer could say, as the black surrealist poet Aimé Césaire (1939) said in his *Return to My Native Land,* speaking for all those of African descent throughout the world, 'I have assassinated God with my laziness with my words with my gestures with my obscene songs' (76). The blues is uncompromisingly atheistic. It has no interest in the systems of divine reward and punishment: it holds out for 'paradise now'.

This 'evil' aspect of the blues is wholly in keeping with the course of all authentic poetry. As William Blake said in his *Marriage of Heaven and Hell,* 'The reason Milton wrote in fetters when he wrote of Angels and God, and at liberty when of Devils and Hell, is because he was a true Poet and of the Devil's party without knowing it.' More than one blues singer could be said to have made a pact with the Devil. The great Peetie Wheatstraw, drawing on a long tradition of Negro folklore (especially the saga of John the Conqueror) proclaimed himself the Devil's Son-in-Law and the High Sheriff from Hell. In Robert Johnson's *Me and the Devil* we find the line: 'Hello, Satan, I believe it's time to go.'

And Julia Moody in her *Mad Mama's Blues* (quoted elsewhere in these pages) said of herself: 'I'm the Devil in disguise, got murder in my eyes.'

Works Cited

Césaire, Aimé. 1939. *Return to My Native Land.* [New ed., with preface by André Breton.] Présence Africaine, Paris, 1917.

Freud, Sigmund. 1927b. *The Future of an Illusion. Standard Edition* XXI. (Hogarth Press, London, 1961), 5–56.

Marcuse, Herbert. 1970. *Five Lectures.* Beacon Press, Boston, 1970.

Marx, Karl. 1844. *Economic and Philosophic Manuscripts of 1844.* International Publishers, New York, 1964; Lawrence & Wishart, London, 1970.

Minutes. 1909. *Minutes of the Vienna Psychoanalytic Society,* ed. H. Nunberg & E. Federn. Volume II (1908–10), Session 66, 117–24. [Reprinted by International Universities Press, New York, 1967.]

Oliver, Paul. 1968. *Screening the Blues.* Cassell & Co Ltd, London, 1968; Oak Publications, New York, 1970 [retitled *Aspects of the Blues Tradition*].

5 Style

IT SHOULD be as easy as breathing to sound like yourself, but it is, in fact, one of the most difficult—and one of the most crucial—elements of blues performance. Difficult because to sound like yourself you have to know who you are, including how you are similar to and different from others, or at least be on a singular and courageous journey on the way to discovering and establishing an individual voice in a world that frequently expects—even demands—uniformity.

In his selection reprinted from *Living Blues Magazine*, Lawrence Hoffman provides a succinct, comprehensive, and authoritative discussion of an instrument of primary importance to the blues, the harmonica. Its widespread employment in blues performances seems to stem in part from its easy portability, relative inexpensiveness, and, perhaps most important, its ability to express the nuances of emotion in the melismatic human voice. Including attention to historical development, stylistic origins in the African and African American tradition, subtleties of technique, and an outline of major practitioners, Hoffman's article is an ideal introduction to an instrument that is central to the sound of the blues.

Few blues singers have exerted such a distinctive and dominant influence as its first superstar stylist, Bessie Smith, who could take even inferior lyrics and mediocre sidemen and raise them to the highest levels of performance. Fortunately, Smith frequently used strong material and excellent accompanists, which raised her performances to even greater heights, as on her legendary session with Louis Armstrong that produced the definitive version of W. C. Handy's landmark "St. Louis Blues," which Langston Hughes designated in the *Chicago Defender* of

November 28, 1942, as "the greatest American song written in our time." Indeed, there were over 150 recordings of the song by jazz and blues artists prior to 1942. Describing the artistry of these two performers is a challenge undertaken by Edward Brooks with seriousness and insight. Brooks's characterization of the songs and performances and the rapport between these two great artists is a valuable companion to the music.

Unfortunately, the artistry of the country blues musician has not always received the close and careful analysis that it deserves. It is particularly fortunate, then, that Stephen Calt and Gayle Wardlow turned their attention to the life and music of Charlie Patton, a seminal Mississippi Delta blues performer whose music evidenced a complexity and genius that mark him as one of our century's most accomplished and influential blues musicians. Significant for his own recordings as well as his influence on such performers as Son House, Willie Brown, Tommy Johnson, Bukka White, and Howlin Wolf, Patton's recorded masterpieces such as "Pony Blues" and "High Water Everywhere" demonstrate his power and artistry, and the discussion here of "Pony Blues" is, while systematic and technical, also illuminating to the general reader in its demonstration of Patton's prodigious creativity and technique. Some critics have responded that the authors sometimes build up Patton with the unnecessary disparagement of other worthy performers, and that their claims for Patton are excessive, but whether that is true or not, their analysis of Patton's performance in the context of his career and the blues tradition is detailed and convincing.

One of the most dynamic and influential of all blues stylists is B. B. King, a brilliant singer and guitarist whose vision, technique, and passion coalesced into a style that informs much contemporary blues performance and has practically become a musical and cultural matrix for those wishing to generate new directions in popular electric guitar music. This section from Jerry Richardson's exemplary doctoral dissertation confirms King's pedigree as a master guitarist by minutely examining the sources and characteristics of his style and analyzing how he successfully executes his ideas on recorded examples of his work. By placing King in the context of both rural and urban blues performers as well as jazz guitarists such as Charlie Christian and Django Reinhardt, Richardson demonstrates how King, and the blues, draw on disparate elements that are transmuted by individual genius and technical exertion into a stylistic triumph.

Recommended Further Readings

Humphrey Lyttelton. *The Best of Jazz.* New York: Taplinger, 1979.
Albert Murray. *Stomping the Blues.* New York: Da Capo, 1976.

The Blues Harp, Parts One and Two

Lawrence Hoffman

Part I

THE harmonica has secured an enduring place in American music and a very special and central place in the blues.

Its history, as related in *A Brief History of the Harmonica*, distributed by the Hohner Company, and in *America's Harp*, an article by Michael Licht, is as follows. The harmonica, or mouth harp, is one of the family of free reed instruments—those which create a tone by the vibration of reeds which do not strike the frame to which they are attached. This free-reed concept led to the development of the Sheng (sublime voice), said to be invented in 3,000 BC by the Chinese empress Nyn-Kwa, and brought by a traveler to Western Europe in the seventeenth century. The Sheng is the earliest expression of the principle later applied to such instruments as the concertina and harmonica.

The prototype of the instrument in its present state was invented in 1821 by Christian Friedrich Ludwig Buschmann, a 16-year-old German clockmaker who put 15 pitch pipes together, and called it a "mund-eaoline" (mouth-harp). Another clockmaker, Christian Messner, learned how to make the instrument and sold them on the side to other clockmakers.

In 1857, at 24 years of age, Matthias Hohner bought one and decided to produce it commercially, making 650 of them the first year.

He was made the mayor of his home town of Trossingen which soon became the harmonica capital of the world. In 1932 his sons founded the State Music College of Trossingen, where harmonica, accordion, piano, and violin are still taught today. This school has graduated 3,000 harmonica players certified to teach the instrument.

Sometime before the outbreak of the Civil War, Hohner sent a few harmonicas to cousins who had emigrated to the United States, and they found the instrument to be extremely popular there. During the Civil War many soldiers on both sides had one and, along with peddlers and immigrants, helped spread the instrument throughout the country.

Reprinted from *Living Blues* 99 (Sept.–Oct. 1991): 24–31; 100 (Nov.–Dec. 1991): 43–48. Used by permission of the author.

By the end of the century, America was purchasing more than half of the ten million instruments being manufactured in Germany every year. The Marine Band harmonica, still widely popular today, was introduced in 1896 when it sold for 50¢. The harmonica was well on its way to becoming the most popular instrument in America's history.

The first steps towards blues stylings on the harmonica must have resulted from attempts at what the nineteenth century classical musician might have termed "programmatic music"—that is, music that attempted to paint a sound-picture. The unique sound potential of the harmonica enabled the more clever players to imitate many of the sounds that surrounded them everyday.

Trains, for example, have inspired musicians of all eras. Arthur Honneger, the Swiss composer, created an orchestral train in his *Pacific 231,* while Duke Ellington created one for his orchestra in the *Happy Go Lucky Local.* The *Orange Blossom Special* is a standard showcase tune for country fiddlers and banjo pickers, while *Honky Tonk Train Blues* by Meade Lux Lewis remains one of the most famous of all boogie-woogie piano compositions. Singer/guitarist Bukka White got on track with his famous *Panama Limited* which he performed in bottleneck style.

In the hands of a master, however, the harmonica creates the most vivid portrait of all, due to its capacities for tone-bending and chordal rhythm. Some of the first recorded and best examples available on record are Palmer McAbee's *Railroad Piece,* Freeman Stowers' *Railroad Blues,* and Deford Bailey's *Dixie Flyer Blues.* Of the many Library of Congress field recordings of train tunes, examples by Ace Johnson and Richard Amerson are extraordinary. Countless numbers of harmonica players must have been expert at imitating trains, but the vast majority of them were never recorded either by folklorists or commercial record companies.

Trains were not the only subjects of these folk tone-poems, however. There were "mama blues," in which the harmonica imitated a baby calling out "mama" or "I want my mama;" "fox chases" that depicted these ritualistic events step-by-step, complete with vocal yelps and descriptive interjections; vignettes of escaped convicts being hunted down by the dogs, as well as pure barnyard scenes with animal sounds of all varieties fill the harmonica repertory—some with uncanny realism.

The connection between this rural impressionism and the origin of what we recognize as blues-harp style lies in the way the instrument is constructed and played. The ten-hole diatonic harmonica, the most common of the blues harmonicas, produces a major chord in the key of the harmonica when the holes are blown, and a dominant ninth chord in that same key when the holes are drawn. And, to put it simply, the lower part of the instrument is easier to manipulate when drawn, the upper when blown. That is, when each of the four lowest holes is drawn in a deflected manner, the tone bends and the pitch slides lower; and, when each of the highest four holes is blown in a deflected manner the pitch will also slide lower.

In addition to this, the players discovered that although each harmonica was pitched in a specific key, wherein the tonic or central pitch was located on the number one hole blow, it could be used effectively for other keys by using a different sound hole—blow or draw—as the tonic. Each key created a very different effect or mode that could be used for the purpose of varying the color. These alternative playing modes have become known as positions, of which there are four: straight harp or first position (C harp plays in the key of C); cross-harp or second position (C harp plays in key of G); third position (C harp plays in key of D); and fourth position (C harp plays in key of E). Other positions are used—but far less frequently.

Because the players found the lowest registers to be the most expressive, especially for the purposes of mimicry, they found themselves favoring the lowest holes drawn; especially #2, which became the central tone, or tonic. This meant that they were blowing their C harp in the key of G—a perfect fifth higher than the actual key of the harp. This position produced cross-harp style, or second position.

First position, also known as straight-harp, consists of playing in the actual key of the harmonica, where the lowest hole (#1) when blown becomes tonic, and we play the C harp in the key of C. In this position the expressive high register is exploited. The most well-known master of this position is Jimmy Reed. Straight harp is also used by harmonica players to improvise over ragtime changes and for more folk-style melodies. That familiar, low, wailing sound, however, is an almost certain indication of cross-harp style.

Third position is achieved by making the lowest or first hole draw the tonic or central pitch; the C harp is played in the key of D. Little Walter is a master of third position and used it for a number of his instrumentals. The hallmark of third position is a very unusual and jazzy minor thirteenth chord with added eleventh that is produced when the holes are drawn. This sound is unforgettable.

Most rarely, a fourth position can be achieved by making the #2 hole blow the tonic; that is, playing our C harp in key of E.

To the beginner this must be confusing, as it must have been for the first players who discovered these positions as well as for their guitar or piano-playing partners. There is a great example on record of a guitar and harmonica seemingly trying to get into the same key, as the guitar player was playing in the actual key of the harp while the harp player was playing in second position. Not until the very end of the tune were they finally in the same key. (*Just It, Harmonicas Unlimited,* DLP 503/504)

Harmonica players of classical and jazz music, however, obtain different keys and foreign tones to the key by using a chromatic harmonica rather than a diatonic one. A chromatic harp has a button on the side that when pushed raises the pitch of every blown or drawn tone one half-step. Larry Adler and John Sebastian, Sr., are two modern-day classic masters, while Toots Thielemans is probably the greatest jazz and pop player well-known today. Blues players use the chromatic mostly in second or third position, in the same manner as the diatonic, to achieve a deep chordal timbre impossible to get on the smaller diatonic model. Bending is tougher, though, on the more sturdy chromatic type. Blues artists have been known to use two or more harps on the same tune—and, conversely, to use the same key harp for tunes pitched in different keys. Obviously, the players' talent, taste, and creativity are tested here.

The harmonica was for many reasons a very natural choice for the Southern African Americans in the developmental stages of the blues. It was small, inexpensive, durable, portable, and easy for the beginner to approach. Musically, it provided a modern and convenient substitute for the quills, an instrument made of three bound pieces of cane; and it was cheaper and easier to play than the violin—whose place in blues the harmonica usurped. In addition, it had the ability to mimic everything from the human voice to trains, animals, and whistling, as well as the Cajun concertina, and the sophisticated stylings of the jazz-age clarinet and cornet.

One could get a tremendous variety of tone color, attack, vibrato, tremolo, and glissando, not to mention effects made by manipulating the hand used to cup the harmonica. Moreover, it provided three definite registers, was equally expressive chordally and melodically, and covered the entire dynamic range from a whisper to a shout—quite an arsenal for the size and money.

There must have been an enormous number of African Americans playing the harmonica by the turn of the century, but not until 1924 do we get our first harmonica blues on record. Johnny Watson, known as Daddy Stovepipe, recorded *Sundown Blues* that year—demonstrating a sort of melodic/folky sound using straight or first position harp for fills and solos around his vocals. If various written accounts are true of this amazing performer, born in 1867, we find him touring with the Rabbit Foot Minstrels in the early 1900s, playing for tips in Mexico during the Depression, with zydeco bands in Texas by the end of the '30s, and on Chicago's Maxwell Street from the early '40s until his death in 1963.

Among the very finest players who recorded in or before 1930 were Robert Cooksey, Chuck Darling, and Blues Birdhead. Cooksey was a master of the vaudeville sound which he executed in a unique, virtuosic style. He recorded often with his partner Bobby Leecan through the '20s and '30s. Chuck Darling was a ragtime virtuoso whose complex lines wove effortlessly through all registers. James Simons, known also as Blues Birdhead or Harmonica Tim, is perhaps the best example of how the diatonic harp functioned as a jazz instrument in the early days of that music. His phrasing and timbre are a cross between those of Louis Armstrong and Johnny Dodds, vintage 1928. It is amazing to hear such an advanced jazz concept executed so perfectly on this instrument, and one wonders how it could be that this master recorded only once.

The very first wailing, cross-harp style player to record solo seems to have been the Alabaman, Jaybird Coleman, who made some 20 sides between 1927 and 1930. In his style we hear vestiges of the field holler and work song which were building blocks of the blues; and, through his music, we get an unadulterated and impassioned sense of the meaning of the blues in the South during the '20s. Jaybird entertained the troops during World War I, after which he toured the South with Big Joe Williams as part of the Rabbit Foot Minstrels show. He also toured with the Birmingham Jug Band, but seems to have spent a great deal of his time playing locally in the Birmingham/Bessemer, Alabama, region until he moved to West Memphis in 1949, the year before his death. Jaybird brought his unmistakable style to a large number of major Southern cities, inspiring and influencing many of the harp players of his era. It is perhaps one of blues' greatest ironies that he was managed in 1929 by the Ku Klux Klan.

The seeds of the modern day blues harp that reached fruition in the golden era of mid-'50s Chicago were sown in the American musical mecca of Memphis, Tennessee. That city, which has played such a crucial role in almost every genre of indigenous American music, boasted the simultaneous presences of Noah Lewis, Jaybird Coleman, Will Shade, Jed Davenport, Hammie Nixon, John Lee Williamson, and Walter Horton all—off and on—between the years 1925 and 1930. It must have been a boiling pot of musical ideas as these musicians, some of them not more than children at the time, played on the streets, in Handy Park, in clubs, with jug and jazz bands, and as solo attractions.

As reported in *Memphis Blues and Jug Bands*, by Bengt Olsson, jug bands probably started in Louisville and were active there from around 1915. By the early '30s there were at least six bands in Memphis. The two standout examples were the Memphis Jug Band with Will Shade on harp, and Gus Cannon's Jug Stompers with Noah Lewis on harp.

Noah Lewis was discovered in Ripley, Tennessee, by guitar and banjo player Gus Cannon; and it is said that his harmonica playing was unparalleled at the time. As many masters of the day, he was able to play two harps at one time—one with his nose. His style is unique and could be said to represent a consummation of the early chordal-melodic technique being practiced in the South for many years. His playing displays a wealth of ideas, always executed to perfection. His recordings show him to be equally at home as part of a duo, a larger ensemble, or as a solo. Unfortunately, no recordings seem to be available by the older musicians from whom he learned.

Will Shade, before founding the Memphis Jug Band in 1925, played with Furry Lewis and various medicine shows. After touring with the Memphis Jug Band, he joined the Ma Rainey show in Indiana in 1931, and later recorded under his own name in Chicago as well as with Little Buddy Doyle. Probably his most memorable tune is *Jug Band Waltz* which he recorded with the Memphis Jug Band in 1928. His unique style is in the same general mold as Noah Lewis, but his tone is darker and often he is more melodic.

Jed Davenport, on the other hand, had a distinctively wilder sound than his two contemporaries, often using a "flutter-tongue" technique that lent a metallic edge to his lines. Being flashy and dynamic, he was among the most exciting players of his time. He also recorded with Memphis Minnie, and with some local Memphis jazz bands in the early '30s, and played on the streets of Memphis off and on through the '60s. There can be no doubt that these three players represented the models of excellence for all aspiring bluesmen fortunate enough to have heard them.

If we were to search for one talent that linked this wonderful chordal-melodic style to the horn-style pioneered in the 1930s, we might find Hammie Nixon, who actually learned from Noah Lewis and taught John Lee "Sonny Boy" Williamson.

Hammie Nixon was the perfect musical counterpart for the traditional blues guitarist/singer. He had a great talent for filling the sound while never covering it. Perhaps this expertise defeated a possible career as a leader, for he was always the sideman. He became known for his work with Little Buddy Doyle, Son Bonds, Yank Rachell, and especially with Sleepy John Estes, with whom he shared a partnership lasting over 50 years. It could be that Hammie recognized his niche, as did others, and that his career was perfectly suited to his talent. He had a unique sense of how to blow lines behind the singer's verses as sort of an obligatto trumpet, spinning a fragile, contrapuntal web that surrounded and enhanced the overall sound.

Before Nixon joined Sleepy John Estes, Noah Lewis was Estes' partner, and Nixon learned much by hearing and watching the master at work. Through the '20s and '30s he practiced his trade on the streets and at parties and picnics, finding just the right riff or chordal touch to complement each song. According to David Evans (notes to High Water LP1003), Nixon played often in Brownsville, Tennessee, a town that boasted a rich musical life for the blues musician throughout the '30s. There was much work available for a good player, and many travelled there to take advantage of the opportunities—among them Rice Miller (Sonny Boy Williamson II), Big Joe Williams, and John Lee Williamson (Sonny Boy Williamson I). It was perhaps in Brownsville that the next link of the chain was forged, as John Lee Williamson absorbed the style of Hammie Nixon, leaning more heavily on the melodic side, discarding much of the chordal work, and redoing this rural mix into a concept which he was to pioneer in Chicago in just a few years—a concept that was to shape the blues harp style into what it is a half century later.

It is necessary to digress at this point to consider the work of two very special and exceptional virtuosi: Deford Bailey, and his disciple, Sonny Terry.

Although there were many fine harp players active between the wars, the most influential and widely known was unquestionably Deford Bailey, the Harmonica Wizard. As told by Bengt Olsson in his May–June 1975 *Living Blues* article, "The Grand Ole Opry's Deford Bailey," Bailey's story is as unique as any in all of music. In spite of his color, he was a featured performer in the Grand Ole Opry, playing in 48 out of 52 Opry broadcasts—twice as many as any other performer. Between 1925 and 1941, Bailey was heard every Saturday night playing virtuosic train tunes, blues, and all sorts of harmonica showcase instrumentals, inspiring players around the country—white and black. Although there was more than just a touch of the backwoods influence in Deford's playing (he was self-taught and learned as a child by imitating all of the animal and train sounds that he knew), his style was polished to the point of utter perfection—each original tune unique, each a gem. In addition to his astounding appearances on the Opry, Bailey was also the focus of the first major recording project in Nashville, Tennessee; and, during the years 1927–28 he recorded 11 tunes that were to set the standard for harmonica display pieces in recorded American blues.

Sonny Terry was 11 years younger than Deford Bailey and was one of his innumerable admirers. Using the fox chases, train tunes, and original blues instrumentals as models, the younger player formed a basis for a personal style that would become world famous.

He began as a young child playing buck dances in his native Georgia, and then moved to the streets of North Carolina. He later toured as soloist with Doc Bizell's Medicine Show, before teaming with Blind Boy Fuller in 1934. His career breakthrough occurred when the great American producer John Hammond engaged him in New York City to participate in the From Spirituals to Swing concert in 1938 at Carnegie Hall.

In 1939 he met Brownie McGhee and there began one of the most famous musical partnerships in all of blues or, for that matter, all of American music. During the next 45 years Sonny Terry and Brownie McGhee played concerts, clubs, and festivals. They appeared on radio, television, and motion pictures, making countless recordings together with other players, and as solo performers.

Sonny Terry was a tremendously influential player of brilliance whose career and talent could rival almost any other player in the history of blues. He was the finest exponent of the rural, chordal-rhythmic style characterized by whoops and hollers and driving chordal work. The vocal and harp work are so closely knit that one can hardly tell where one starts and the other takes over. He commands a wide variety of tone color and vibrato and an impeccable sense of timing—all of which combine to make his work instantly identifiable and among the very best examples of this style of blues harp.

Prior to 1925, players were learning primarily by imitating the sounds of their surroundings, from older musicians who played in their area, by the instrumental styles heard on recordings, and from the music heard in the traveling shows such as the Rabbit Foot Minstrels.

However, when Deford Bailey began his radio career in Nashville he initiated an entirely new channel through which musicians would be influenced. James Cotton remembers, for example, that Rice Miller (Sonny Boy Williamson II) would talk of hearing Deford Bailey on the radio. In the early '50s in Memphis, Cotton was able to hear blues on radio from noon until well into the night. And, in fact, he first became seriously interested in the harmonica after hearing Sonny Boy Williamson II on KFFA radio in the mid-'40s.

These beginnings of blues on radio, along with the dissemination of race records featuring contemporary harp styles, and the subsequent invention of the juke box—all in conjunction with the snowballing effects of the first great migration of African Americans to the north, (as detailed by Mike Rowe in his *Chicago Blues: The City and the Music*), created an environment conducive to the assimilation of all existing styles of the blues harp. The stage was set for the next plateau of growth for the instrument, as it soon would be participating on equal terms with the more urban piano and guitar stylings—and, later, with the full rhythm sections of the bands of the northern cities—especially Chicago.

Perhaps the finest Southern harp player to become an integral part of the modern professional Chicago blues scene was William "Jazz" Gillum, who traveled from Greenwood, Mississippi, to Chicago in 1923, beginning an active career that was to last until his death in 1966. He recorded more than 100 tunes on the Bluebird and Victor labels between 1934 and 1950, using some of the finest sidemen in Chicago including Big Bill Broonzy, Blind John Davis, and Ransom Knowling.

Gillum was at his best in a folksy or ragtime situation when he used the high end of the harmonica in first position (straight harp). Although he was not in the same class as Blues Birdhead or Chuck Darling, he was a respectable singer and player who, nonetheless, enjoyed great success.

Gillum's influence, or lack of it, on the younger players, must be evaluated against the backdrop of the Chicago blues world of the 1920s and 1930s. The Jazz Age placed blues in a collateral position; and, as a result, jazzmen playing in the contemporary ragtime vein were often engaged for blues sessions. The great Ma Rainey, for example, recorded with Tampa Red on some occasions and with jazz bands on others. As with many instrumentalists of the day, these classic blues singers can properly be regarded as belonging to either genre.

Players such as the legendary guitarist/singer Blind Blake found Chicago jazz to be a natural extension of their syncopated East Coast style. Blake often recorded with jazz horn players and singers; and, although it is brilliant work, it is not strictly blues. A real dichotomy of style exists in the work of guitarist/singer/pianist Lonnie Johnson who was perhaps the only bluesman who could hold his own with the greatest jazzman of the day, Louis Armstrong, while still functioning as a bluesman on other occasions. Some other startling combinations were downhome Mississippi bluesmen Ishman Bracey and Tommy Johnson, both of whom were recorded with clarinetist Ernest "Kid" Michall of the Nehi Boys.

Because the vast majority of bluesmen lacked either the skill or inclination to play in the demanding contemporary jazz style, some resorted to a sort of comic—or "hokum" style—replete with nonsense lyrics, kazoos (sometimes called jazzhorns), washboards, and catchy choruses occurring over the same repetitive set of ragtime chord changes. They sounded like jug bands minus jug and soul, and their function was simply to entertain. Although a few exceptionally talented artists such as Tampa Red were able to transcend this limited style, most, including Jazz Gillum, were not. His limitations were most obvious when he played in a "downhome" style using second position (cross-harp), and he seems to have had very little effect—if any—on the subsequent blues harp players in Chicago.

This entertainment-oriented strain of early urban blues in Chicago is documented excellently in Mike Rowe's aforementioned classic. He points out that "the urban blues were altogether more sophisticated—lighter in texture with the emotional power turned down and the beat turned up." And that "It was probably a reaction to the trauma of the Depression years that the emphasis was more on entertainment." In addition, he describes a scene controlled almost entirely by Lester Melrose, a white businessman who recorded almost every bluesman of note in Chicago. Big Bill Broonzy, Tampa Red, Jazz Gillum, Big Joe Williams, Memphis Minnie, Lonnie Johnson, and John Lee "Sonny Boy" Williamson, among others, formed a remarkable reservoir of talent used over and over again in various combinations throughout the '30s and '40s on the Bluebird label as fodder for innumerable blues hits based on the proven "formula." Although this is a one-sided look at the entrepreneur, it paints a vivid portrait of the same old sound issuing from Chicago during these years.

In spite of the application of this assembly-line production technique, certain talents were of such magnitude that they seemed to jump out of their prescribed setting. One such talent was John Lee "Sonny Boy" Williamson from Jackson, Tennessee—the father of the modern blues harp style. John Lee Williamson's role in the evolution of the style can be compared to that of jazz pianist Earl Hines, who is credited with developing the "trumpet-style" right hand; or, later, to pianist Bud Powell who expressed the bop style concepts of Charlie Parker and Dizzy Gillespie through his right-hand work. Like these two great pianists, Williamson created a strongly melodic potential for an instrument bound most to a chordal or subordinate role. He transformed the harp into a dynamic lead voice.

Williamson, the original Sonny Boy, played straight and cross-harp styles, ragtime type tunes, and straight blues—all with enormous conviction and great style. His vocals were equally impressive, employing expressive vibrato and changing timbre. He used formula-like fills and cadence figures to frame his lines, and switched freely from a chordally dominated style to a predominantly single-note style—with all possible gradations between these two stylistic poles. He used sustained tones, short repeated notes and five-six note motives with great intelligence and care and might well have been the first harp player to construct solos consistently in this manner.

One truly amazing characteristic of Williamson's music is that in it, one hears not only the past (shades of Noah Lewis and Hammie Nixon are always present), but also the future. One hears some of the architecture of Little Walter, the vocal and instrumental phrasing of Sonny Boy II (Rice Miller), and the tone of Big Walter Horton—all virtually implied by the older musician's vocal and instrumental innovations. In addition, Williamson was the first of a long and distinguished modern line of accomplished singer/harp players who performed their own tunes.

He began his recording career in Chicago in 1937 with a series of records that featured him fronting his own group and performing as a sideman with Big Joe Williams. He was enormously popular and successful but, tragically, was murdered one night in 1948 while walking home from a performance at the Plantation Club in Chicago. His career must be regarded as one of the most significant phases in the development of blues harp style.

Certain contemporary factors converged to exert a tremendous influence on blues music during the '40s. Perhaps the most significant of these was the so-called Petrillo Ban of 1942. Because James C. Petrillo, president of the Musicians Union, saw recordings and juke boxes as dire threats to the livelihood of musicians, he banned all union members from recording. "This and the strict rationing of shellac" (used for record production), recounts Paul Oliver in his *The Story of the Blues*, "effectively stopped the recording of blues." This two-year ban served to take blues out of the studio and into the clubs and streets where it was infused with new life.

In addition, another peak migration period of blacks to the north was creating a bigger audience for blues; and a grassroots talent-search by the new independent label-owners in Chicago was providing encouragement and work for the younger players.

Part II

From the mid-'40s there collected in Chicago a nucleus of harp players whose work, based at least partially on that of John Lee Williamson, constituted a new style that gained more and more definition as the strictures of the Melrose empire loosened and independent record labels began to appear. Maxwell Street served as the perfect breeding ground for these avant-gardists who jammed there regularly, exchanging ideas and strutting their stuff. In addition, the South Side was dotted with small clubs that seemed to unite the black community, serving as both a sweet reminder of the good side of what many of them had left behind, as well as a musical signpost towards the future. Although the lines of development that these Chicago-based artists were pursuing were very different from the directions being taken by the players based in the South, Junior Wells refuses to think of it as a "city style." Wells is quoted as saying: "We had a country sound, but we also were getting into a different type thing. I wouldn't call it a city-type thing, I would just say we had learned some new riffs to put into the thing and it was more of an up-tempo sound. We were listening to different type records."

It was in Chicago that the Brownsville, Helena, and Memphis styles coalesced into what is now regarded as the modern blues harp style and sound. So definitive are its markings, so powerful its effect, that almost one half-a-century later, it has changed hardly at all. Perhaps there is no reason for it to change. Of the many fine harp players practicing today it would be difficult to find many who did not get the basis of their style from players who were fully mature in the '50s.

Snooky Pryor, born in Lambert, Mississippi, moved permanently to Chicago in 1945, and was one of the first of these pioneers to record the new post-war Chicago sound. At his best, he is magnificent, displaying a perfect balance of chordal and melodic style. Using a tenor-range sound, he is capable of contrasting a beautifully smooth tone with a rough-edged complement. From a stylistic/historical point of view, one hears in his work the influence of all the major players of the day. He was greatly influenced by his favorite player Rice Miller (Sonny Boy Williamson II) whom he heard on KFFA radio, as well as by the original Sonny Boy, John Lee Williamson, with whom he sat in regularly. An astonishing track, *Boogie*, recorded in 1947/48, reveals the note-for-note opening motif of *Juke*, the masterpiece recorded by Little Walter in 1952. We will perhaps never know who first developed this classic line, or if, in fact, it was a cliché used by many harp players at the time. Snooky is in great form at the time of this writing—still playing in the style he helped create in the late '40s.

"I had admired the original Sonny Boy, Rice Miller, Big Walter . . . but when I met Little Walter, then it was an entirely different thing to me. Walter was the best—to me—that I had heard. The different things that he could do on the harmonica was an entirely different thing from what everyone else was doing. John Lee had the blues-type thing—Walter had the blues, but he had that up-tempo type stuff also . . . it was the execution that he was getting out of the harmonica." This Junior Wells quotation echoes that of Louis Myers, Walter's guitar player of many years: "All of them cats come along and try to play after John Lee died—but Little Walter was more important than all those cats. He was the best after John Lee . . . was none of them as good as Walter . . . and none of them that have come after [are as good]. He was the best in Chicago . . . the baddest." Lester Davenport, a veteran harp player on the Chicago scene since 1944 who recorded with Bo Diddley, says: "I would say that Little Walter was the greatest and most influential that ever played."

Marion "Little Walter" Jacobs was born in Louisiana in 1930. At 12 he was working the small clubs and streets of New Orleans, at 14 he played on Sonny Boy Williamson II's "King Biscuit Time" on KFFA, at 15 he was in East St. Louis, Illinois, and St. Louis, Missouri—and, at 16 he was in Chicago on Maxwell Street. In 1947 he recorded for Ora-Nelle records and a year later was with Muddy Waters. During the next few years he toured and recorded with the Muddy Waters band and frequently recorded as a sideman with others. His breakthrough occurred with *Juke*, recorded for the Checker label in 1952. As soon as he realized that he had a hit, he left Waters' band to pursue a solo career, backed by the Aces, a band that was at the time fronted by Junior Wells. The band consisted of Louis Myers on guitar, his brother Dave Myers on bass, and Fred Below on drums—arguably the finest band that ever played. Walter's reputation grew throughout the country as well as England and Europe. He was recognized by some of the superstar rock groups of the '60s, and recorded as late as 1968, the year he died a violent death.

Little Walter is considered by many peers, harp-playing disciples, blues scholars, and serious fans to be the greatest blues harp player who ever lived. A great musician, songwriter, harmonica player, bandleader—a genius. And, as many productive geniuses, his influences were many and varied. Honeyboy Edwards recalls Walter speaking of the profound effect on him by the musicians he heard in Louisiana as a child. Walter's third-position work, in fact, sounds sometimes like a Cajun concertina. Big Walter spoke of how he taught Walter in Memphis (Edwards introduced them in the '40s). Louis Myers remembers Walter hanging around John Lee Williamson—and how the older player took him under his wing. "John Lee liked Walter because he was young. He was a kid trying to learn," recalls Myers (who remembers this well because Robert Myers, Louis' brother, was playing gigs with John Lee Williamson at this time). On the other hand, Mike Rowe, in his *Chicago Blues: The City and the Music*, tells of Walter playing "all kinds of music" (probably waltzes, pop tunes, and polkas) "until he came under the influence of Big Bill

Broonzy and Tampa Red." In addition, Willie Cobbs, Honeyboy Edwards, and Junior Wells all relate stories of Walter learning licks from the jazz horn players of the day—especially Louis Jordan and Bullmoose Jackson. Given the broad range of his style and the marked originality of his concept, it is entirely believable that Walter absorbed all of these influences—that he was learning from everything musical that appealed to him—and that he was capable of assimilating all of this into an original style.

In considering Walter's style, one must admire how masterfully he was able to use every existing technique of blues harp-playing, and how easily he was able to shape each of them to his own expressive purpose. He used a rainbow of tone color and sometimes exploited that one facet for a solo (*Mean Old World*). His chordal work is fascinating, especially during his beautiful excursions into the dark chordal regions of the chromatic harp or 12-hole diatonic, particularly in third position (*Lights Out*). His "bent" tones are extremely effective, because he was capable both of controlled glissandi (slidings) at any speed (*Blue Midnight*) or of merely jumping to the bent tone with perfect intonation at any point in the phrase. His trills, bent or natural, were executed at varying speeds; his numerous types of vibrato; his shifts of tone color; his Monk-ish gift for playing slightly off the beat (introduction to *I Don't Play*); his jazz-oriented phrasing and overall concept (even Sonny Rollins would have been proud of inserting *A Tisket A Tasket*, and then sequencing it in the very next phrase as Walter did in *Crazy Legs*)—all of these techniques would have amounted to merely great virtuosity in the hands of a lesser artist. In addition, as a composer and soloist, perhaps Walter's greatest gift was his ability to perfectly balance his lines. He was always the master architect—creating original designs of consummate symmetry.

Walter was equally as creative and virtuosic in a supportive role, never disturbing the solo lines or integrity of the tune. Of the many songs he recorded as a sideman in the Muddy Waters band, *Forty Days and Forty Nights* and *I'm Ready* serve as fine examples of Walter's extraordinary talent in this capacity. In addition to making great tunes even greater, he was also able to make very ordinary ones such as Muddy's *Young Fashioned Ways* positively jump out of their grooves with his use of cross-rhythms and jazzy off-the-beat accents. Clearly, he was not challenged by Muddy's material then and, in fact, was not touring with him at the time—only recording with him at Chess' request.

Among Walter's many contributions to blues music in general, and to harmonica-playing specifically, one must acknowledge as paramount his elevating the amplified harp style to state-of-the-art status. One hears the gradual development in style from the acoustic work in *Louisiana Blues* to the modern amplified masterpiece, *Juke*. There are various accounts of John Lee Williamson, Rice Miller, Snooky Pryor, Big Walter Horton, and Little Walter being the first to cup the harp against a microphone, thereby completely altering the timbral attack and over-all playing style. One might conclude that this technique was a natural and gradual result of trying to be heard over a rhythm section that grew bigger and louder from the late '40s on.

Like T-Bone Walker and Charlie Parker, Walter redefined for all time the role of his instrument and set standards of excellence that will perhaps never be surpassed.

While the blues was being revolutionized in the northern cities, a complimentary strain was being nurtured and developed by players who remained active in the South throughout the '40s and '50s. The central figure of this activity—Rice Miller or Sonny Boy Williamson II—was perhaps every bit as great and influential as Walter in his own way.

As enigmatic as any character in the blues pantheon, Rice Miller would not divulge his real name or date of birth, although Paul Oliver in his notes to Arhoolie CD310 fixes his birthplace as Glendora, Mississippi; and the year as either 1894 or 1899. [Research of government documents by *Living Blues* has revealed that Sonny Boy Williamson was born in 1910. This information was also confirmed by Williamson's surviving relatives.]

Sonny Boy II's musical achievement is sometimes overshadowed by the enormous humanity, sense of humor, and personality that pervades his work. One of the greatest blues lyricists that ever lived, he recorded relatively few instrumentals and gave equal time to both his highly expressive vocals and his harp-blowing, using both of these talents to underscore the humor, irony, and pathos that infuse his musical poems.

It is important to note that Sonny Boy Williamson was a born entertainer, and that his style was honed for the live, improvisational playing of the juke joints; and, starting regularly in 1941, the live radio broadcasts from KFFA in Helena, Arkansas. He was 40 years old when he made his first records for the Trumpet label in Jackson, Mississippi. Although there are some gems such as *Mighty Long Time*, some of these early recordings are perhaps too loose to qualify as classics. When he began recording with Chess in Chicago, the change in both producers and sidemen helped to tighten the arrangements and make the tunes more memorable. Talents such as Robert Lockwood, Jr., Otis Spann, Lafayette Leake, and Fred Below helped Williamson turn out lasting works—Chicago classics such as *Help Me, Trust My Baby, Nine Below Zero, Cross My Heart*, and many others.

Although he may have lifted the basics of his style from his namesake at some time or another, Rice Miller represents a wholly original style that is the modern epitome of the "downhome blues." He lacks none of the technique that other more "modern" players had. His use of vibrato, sustained tones, trills, glissandi, varying timbral shades, sense of symmetry, along with his impeccable timing, were uniquely developed for his personal, expressive needs. If Walter was abstract perfection, Sonny Boy II was pure natural exuberance.

Rice Miller had many admirers who were greatly influenced by his style. In addition, though, he had a few who were his actual pupils, learning techniques directly from him. Among the first and most famous of these was Chester Burnett, known as the Howlin' Wolf. Williamson and Wolf teamed up and toured the jukes of Tennessee, Arkansas, and Mississippi. Wolf was in no way the virtuosic harp-blower that his teacher was, although he was truly a great bluesman. His playing—expressive and dynamic—was used to create fills and solos around his imposing vocals, and add even more punch and character to his now-classic original tunes.

While Little Walter was in Chicago presiding over the new urban developments, and Sonny Boy II was in Arkansas bringing the rural style into the '50s, there was a very important group of players ruling by committee in Memphis, Tennessee. Once again, this city was to serve as a focal point for the development of the blues in general and of the harp in specific. Howlin' Wolf, both Walters, both Sonny Boys, Jed Davenport, Jaybird Coleman, Sammy Lewis, Junior Parker, James Cotton—all of this talent was in and around Memphis at some time during the late '40s and early '50s. Appearing on radio, in clubs and on the streets and parks, some of these players were to begin their recording career there under the direction of Sam Phillips. Two very influential players who seemed to be always on the move between Chicago, Memphis, and points South were Big Walter Horton and Forrest City Joe Pugh.

"Big Walter was always in and out—a hard person to keep up with . . . always on the move," relates Junior Wells. Walter Horton was associated with almost all of the great blues scenes since he reputedly recorded as a child with the Memphis Jug Band in 1927. He claimed to have toured with the Ma Rainey Show in Indiana as well as with various bands in the South before settling for a brief time in Memphis in 1935. In 1940 he was on Chicago's Maxwell Street, and seemed to move between there and Memphis off and on from the 1940s to the '60s, playing and recording with many of the great bluesmen of the day including Muddy Waters, Jimmy Rogers, Robert Nighthawk, Howlin' Wolf, and Johnny Shines.

Although he never achieved much fame or fortune for his work, certain masterpieces such as *Easy, Little Walter's Boogie, Cotton Patch Hotfoot,* and *Walkin' By Myself* (recorded as sideman with the Jimmy Rogers band) assure him a place among the very best players in history.

Sometimes called Mr. Tone, Big Walter played with as rich and deep a color as anyone. He also used various types and speeds of vibrato, trills, and glissandi that he employed with great imagination and flair. His playing bears the shades of Hammie Nixon, Will Shade, and even Jed Davenport; yet he delivers his sculptured lines with such swing that one finds believable his claim to have taught Little Walter.

If Walter Horton's output is uneven in quality it is because his career was interrupted by various bouts with sickness. In addition, he seemed to be teamed often with incompetent or unprepared sidemen and producers who ruined more than just a few of his best efforts. Big Walter, who represents a middle ground between the downhome and uptempo styles, was an exceptionally gifted and personal player, who had an enormous influence on postwar blues harp style.

The enigmatic Forrest City Joe Pugh seems to have been a man of many parts. From his recordings, he seems little more than an expert imitator of John Lee Williamson; yet, Junior Wells remembers that he had a far deeper tone than Sonny Boy I: "I thought Forrest City Joe was great—but he didn't make it. I admired everything he did because he had such a deep, deep tone. He had a really, really deep tone . . . and notin' and shakin' the harp." James Cotton used to hear Forrest City play piano while playing harp on a rack, and added that "Forrest City was a boogie-woogie man. First time Big Walter ever heard boogie on the harp was from Forrest City Joe. He was his own man . . . independent. He had his own style and he influenced me quite a bit. During the late '40s and early '50s, I used to love to hear him play—he used to tell us about Chicago 'cause he'd been there and back. He was very, *very* good." Lester Davenport says: "He was great . . . I'd put him in the same category as Big Walter. He did a lot of things with the harmonica that other players didn't do. I only remember hearing him outside, playing by himself on the street—never in a club." It is very unfortunate that Joe Pugh died at age 34.

Jimmy Reed began his harp-playing career in the early '50s, recording as a sideman with John Brim, John Lee Hooker, and Eddie Taylor. Often these early recordings showcase his cross-harp style; however, he became a superstar due to his high-end playing in first position over the lay-back shuffle rhythms and fine second guitar work provided by his childhood friend and long-time partner, Eddie Taylor.

Although many of his harp-blowing peers in Chicago did not recognize him as a major talent at first, he was an enormous influence in Louisiana where he affected the work of an entire school of young players such as Silas Hogan, Lazy Lester, Louisiana Red, and the future star Slim Harpo. Reed continued to tour until his death in 1976.

James Cotton and Junior Wells, born within a year of each other, are both brilliant musicians whose careers have intertwined for more than 50 years. Each of their styles, once extremely derivative, have become highly personal ones that are still evolving.

Cotton began imitating trains on the harmonica at age six. Three years later he ran away from home to learn from Rice Miller whom he heard on KFFA radio. A few years later he had taken over Williamson's band when the older master had gone to Jackson, Mississippi, to record. Cotton recorded with Howlin' Wolf in 1952, and two years later recorded the classic *Cotton Crop Blues* for Sun Records in Memphis. When he joined the Muddy Waters band after 1955, he was forced to play in a more urban style in order to fill the shoes of Walter, Junior, and George Smith—all of whom had preceded him. Since then he has toured and recorded with his own groups, being one of the few authentic bluesmen still working full time and one of the greatest harp players alive.

Junior Wells was influenced by all the major players of the day; and, in fact, recorded tributes to Rice Miller and Little Walter. His debt to John Lee Williamson is obvious in his recording of a number of the original Sonny Boy tunes including *Hoodoo Man Blues* and *Cut That Out.*

Wells was influenced mostly, however, by Little Walter's "up tempo" sound and remembers being taken to meet him one day in the late '40s when Walter and Waters were playing the Ebony Lounge. Walter let Junior sit in and use his microphone and amplifier. Afterwards, Walter asked him if he played the saxophone. Junior said "Nah" and Walter said "Good, you'll be alright—you got the same ideas about doin' things that I have." About five years later, Wells was to replace Walter in the Muddy Waters band, before going out on his own. Well's country feel is tempered a great deal by the swing style pioneered by Walter, leaving him with a very dynamic and individual approach to the instrument. He and Cotton are probably the two greatest authentic players alive and working.

Sources

February, 1991: quotations from James Cotton, Lester Davenport, Honeyboy Edwards, Louis Myers, and Junior Wells taken from personal interviews with the author.

R. M. W. Dixon and J. Godrich, *Blues and Gospel Records 1902–1943*

David Evans, notes to *Tappin' That Thing*, High Water LP1003

Sheldon Harris, *Blues Who's Who*

Mike Leadbitter and Neil Slaven, *Blues Records 1943 to 1970*, Volume One

Michael Licht, "Harmonica Magic: Virtuoso Display in American Folk Music," *Ethnomusicology*, Vol. XXIV, no. 2, May 1980

Paul Oliver, *The Story of the Blues*

Bengt Olsson, *Memphis Blues*

"The Grand Ole Opry's Deford Bailey," *Living Blues*, May–June 1975, no. 21

Mike Rowe, *Chicago Blues: The City and the Music*

Discography

The complete recordings of El Watson, Palmer McAbee, Freeman Stowers, Blues Birdhead and Alfred Lewis; *Great Harp Players* (1927–30); Matchbox/MSE209

Deford Bailey and D. H. Bert Bilbro. Complete recordings; *Harmonica Showcase* (1927–31); Matchbox/MSE218

Daddy Stovepipe, William McCoy, others; *Harmonicas Unlimited (1924–49)*; Document/ DLP503/504

Chuck Darling, Leecan and Cooksey, Jaybird Coleman, Alfred Lewis, Deford Bailey, others; *Harmonica Blues*; Yazoo/1053

Complete recordings of Jaybird Coleman, others; *Alabama Harmonica Kings (1927–30)*; Wolf/WSE127

Noah Lewis w/Cannon's Jug Stompers; *The Complete Works 1927–30*; Yazoo 1082/3

Will Shade/Memphis Jug Band; *The Memphis Jug Band*; Yazoo/1067

Noah Lewis and Jed Davenport (complete recordings); *Memphis Harmonica Kings* (1929–30); Matchbox/MSE213

Hammie Nixon; *Sleepy John Estes, Down South Blues (1935–40)*; MCA/1339; *"The Delta Boys", Son Bonds with Sleepy John Estes and Hammie Nixon*; Wolf/WSE129

Jimmy Reed; *The Best of Jimmy Reed*; Telstar/TSD3502

Sonny Terry; *Sonny Terry (1938–55)*; Document/DLP536

Jazz Gillum; *Me and My Buddy*; Contact/BT2013

John Lee "Sonny Boy" Williamson; *Throw a Boogie Woogie*, RCA/9599-2-R; vol. 1. Blues Classics/BC3; vol. 2. Blues Classics/BC20; vol. 3. Blues Classics/BC24

Snooky Pryor; *Snooky Pryor*; Flyright/FLY CD20

Little Walter; *The Best of Little Walter*, vol. 1 MCA/CHD9192; vol. 2 MCA/CHD9292

Sonny Boy Williamson II; *King Biscuit Time*, Arhoolie/CD310; *Clownin' with the World*, Trumpet/AA-700; *The Real Folk Blues*, MCA/CHD9272; *More Real Folk Blues*, MCA/ CHD9277

Big Walter Horton; *Mouth Harp Maestro*, ACE/CHD252; *An Offer You Can't Refuse*, Red Lightnin'/008

Howlin' Wolf; *Moanin' in the Moonlight*; MCA/CHD5908

James Cotton; *Chicago/The Blues/Today*, Vanguard/VMD79217; *High Compression*, Alligator/4737; *From Cotton with Verve*, Black Magic/9009

Junior Wells; *Messin' with the Kid*, Flyright/FLY CD03; *Hoodoo Man Blues*, Delmark/DD-612; *Blues Hits Big Town*, Delmark/DEL 640

Lowdown Memphis Harmonica Jam (1950–55); Nighthawk/103

Take a Greyhound Bus and Ride; Moonshine/BLP117

Baton Rouge Harmonica; Flyright/FLY614

Blow-by-Blow; Sundown/CG709-01

Suckin' and Blowin'; Sundown/CG709-03

Low Blows; Rooster Blues/R7610

Rural Blues; Matchbox/MB904

A *Taste of Harp*; Moonshine/BLP102

Chicago Kings of the Harmonica; Flyright/FLY567

Chicago Blues Harmonica; Flyright/FLY CD11

January, 1925

Edward Brooks

THE *St. Louis Blues* on which Bessie and Fred Longshaw are joined by Louis Armstrong was cut on 14th January, 1925 at a session which marks the start of the most important phase in her early career. The artistic level of her work with Armstrong, whilst being not entirely without flaw, easily transcends all that has gone before. The tune was not new, having been published by W. C. Handy in 1914 but during those three minutes in 1925 she and Louis made it the definitive version. We are fortunate that this should have happened as Bessie was reputed to have preferred accompaniment from less flamboyant performers and to have initially disapproved of Armstrong's presence: Armstrong himself later said he preferred his recordings with Maggie Jones, (a singer of far less talent). Perhaps it was this conflict which enabled them to produce some of the best music either of them was to put on record. The most important thing about this piece is the perfect rapport between Louis's open cornet and Bessie's voice; in transcribing the vocal line from single-note piano approximation, I found myself constantly continuing with the cornet response after a phrase by Bessie had finished, so homogeneous were the two lines.[1] Confirmation of this rapport is found in the low number of takes required to produce each acceptable master. Out of nine titles on which they were both present, not one was completely rejected and two was the maximum number of takes per title needed. Five first takes were released including this one. (It is true that a third attempt at *Nashville Woman's Blues* was cut in May, 1925 but both this and the second take were released under the same Columbia record number.) This is a much better average than at her sessions with other musicians.[2]

Handy's composition, never an authentic blues in the first place, has been further modified for this performance. Here, a one-bar introduction by cornet and harmonium leads into two choruses of twelve-bar blues followed by a 16 bar verse; the piece is completed by another twelve-bar blues chorus. In the original the verse comes at the beginning and here Louis Armstrong makes a brief reference to this with his long held B♭ first note—

Reprinted from Edward Brooks, *The Bessie Smith Companion: A Critical and Detailed Appreciation of the Recordings* 2d ed. (Oxford, England: Bayou Press, 1989), 67–71. Used by permission of Bayou Press.

B♭ being not only the fifth of the scale of the choruses (E♭) but the (minor) third of the scale of the verse (the relative minor, G minor). The verse is in tango time (derived from the habanera) a deliberate move by Handy to make his composition more commercial. The words about deserted love, at this distance in time at least and perhaps because of familiarity, sound reasonably authentic, at least in the twelve-bar sections. Like much of Handy's work, this piece has elements taken from the common-stock[3] synthesised by him into a whole for publication. He was the leader of a brass and concert band and also a trumpet player. Whilst some of his later recordings feature well-known jazz names, his early releases and his own trumpet work reveal a ragtime-like stiffness rather than jazz fluidity. His title, 'The Father of the Blues', is certainly a misnomer and he has even less to do with jazz. It is fair to point out however that this was not a title which he sought himself, and whatever his performing shortcomings, his compositions form ideal vehicles for jazz interpretation. In *The St. Louis Blues,* Handy's own instrument is revealed in the choice of melodic line at the start of each of the twelve-bar choruses—it is based upon the fourth, fifth and sixth pitches in the harmonic series of an E♭ fundamental. A phrase, which once the correct harmonic series has been located (by valve depression), can be played by lip pressure alone.

Bessie's penchant for unorthodox pauses, regrouping melodic lines into new, more imaginative patterns, is well displayed in this performance as pointed out by Humphrey Lyttelton.[4] Blue notes abound—her treatment of 'sun' in the first chorus is exceptional even by her standards; on the flat-third (G♭) of the key, she moves above and below the note in perfect control, as if testing the limits of the pitch, outside of which it is called something else.

Louis Armstrong, at twenty-four, was not yet widely known to the general public but he had already won respect amongst musicians who were beginning to use his phrases in their own work (and not only trumpeters and cornettists). Two years later he was to reach the peak of his innovatory powers and become the foremost influence in jazz, his ideas affecting the music down to the present day. But in January, 1925, the Hot Fives were ten months in the future and the even better Hot Sevens, over two years away. In spite of this he had obviously made sufficient mark upon the jazz world to cause Bessie some uneasiness.

To adapt C. Northcote Parkinson's Law, melody expands so as to fill the time available for its completion. This is often true with Armstrong and to a lesser extent, Bessie Smith. Bessie however at twenty-nine, had a fully mature style which was not to develop very much more during the rest of her career. In her faster pieces it has been noticeable that the only way she could cope with the melody was by cutting ornaments to the bone. In slower pieces she certainly allows them to flower but she rarely seeks innovation for its own sake. Armstrong however, was still a year or two away from his peak and with his immense energy was pushing against boundaries in every direction; he would often suggest the harmony and even the antiphony to his melodic line. Whereas Bessie found tempos around ♩ = 84 and below[5] just right for the full display of her art, Armstrong, used to the faster tempos of instrumental pieces, found time heavy on his hands. In his performances with Bessie Smith the slow pace was sometimes too much of a temptation and his elaborations could lead to the brink of chaos. In the last chorus for instance, he courts disaster in his ambitious phrase following Bessie's 'just as blue as I can be'. Bessie was fairly clear as to the limitations of her art but Armstrong either could not, or would not recognise boundaries, at least until 1929.[6] Certainly then, enthusiasm led him into occasional errors of judgement but it is this enthusiasm which made him greater than all other jazz musicians of this time, only Earl Hines (piano) approaching the lofty realms he inhabited. *The St. Louis Blues* at once makes all this clear. His choice of notes, timing, and most obvious of all, his timbre, are quite unique. This latter feature in particular, is full of swinging life—with vibrato alone he can often produce a surging drive. His dynamic approach, whilst perhaps not quite so unique, is still exceptional; he proves that even at this early stage of his career when his technique was relatively untamed, it is not all forte dynamics and brilliance—often it will subside to provide a quiet, rich harmony behind the voice. And on these sides with Bessie, his technique whilst formidable, is still basically within the New Orleans tradition. Later, as his skill developed, he was to be a considerable contributor to the downfall of that seminal style.

There is not much to be said about Longshaw's harmonium except, as Humphrey Lyttelton points out, 'its sound has become woven into the very atmosphere of the piece'.[7] With a cornet and voice as rhythmically aware as those of Armstrong and Bessie Smith, Longshaw needs only to produce the harmony, which he does competently. Because of the limitation of the instrument (the delay between key-pressure and resulting sound), he is not able to produce a vestige of rhythmic drive.

However, in spite of the drawbacks of the somewhat artificial construction, the out of place harmonium and the acoustic recording,[8] the result is still a small masterpiece, the listener's awareness being heightened by the sheer beauty of conception.

Notes

1. Humphrey Lyttleton has also noticed the extraordinary rapport between the vocal and cornet lines. 'The Best of Jazz' (New York: Taplinger, 1979), p. 77.

2. Presumably also, a growing refinement in recording techniques made this possible.

3. Blesh, in 'Shining Trumpets' (New York: Knopf, 1946), p. 146, identifies its origin except for the tango section, as *Jogo Blues*.

4. 'The Best of Jazz', pp. 61–85. Lyttleton's chapter on Bessie Smith provides an interesting analysis of this performance. And Winthrop Sargeant in 'Jazz, Hot and Hybrid' (New York: E. P. Dutton, 1946), pp. 181–82, gives a detailed comparison between Handy's published first line and Bessie's metamorphosis.

5. The tempo here is ♩ = 70.

6. In 1929, Louis Armstrong made a deliberate decision to reduce the innovatory aspect of his work and produce a more commercially acceptable product. As will be seen, Bessie Smith who did not change her style, began to find her career on the slide about this time whereas Armstrong went on to new fame.

7. 'The Best of Jazz', p. 76.

8. Bessie Smith cut her last acoustic recording at this session. From May 5, 1925, she was electrically recorded.

From "The Greening of the Delta Blues"

Stephen Calt and Gayle Dean Wardlow

"CHARLIE PATTON, he had about two-three pieces everybody loved . . . white and colored," Ernest Brown recalled. Though we do not know what these pieces were, it is certain that *Pony Blues*, a piece played in the E position and sung in F#, was one of them. *Pony Blues* would be as closely identified with Patton's career as *Some Of These Days* was with Sophie Tucker: it was the one song that people who heard Patton readily recalled decades afterwards. It became one of his three pet vocal themes, along with *Maggie* and *Banty Rooster.* While Patton concocted ambitious rearrangements of the former songs, he never succeeded in giving *Pony* a striking instrumental facelift, or spinning out a recorded revision that equalled the original.

Pony Blues remains such an appealing song that it could have made the blues career of anyone who invented it. Its fourteen bar title verse had the kind of insinuating melody that makes for a song hit or standard. Except for its keynote phrase endings, the placid melody of its title verse was altogether untypical of blues. Its four notes employed major intervals (the keynote, major third, major fifth, and major sixth) that eliminated the tonal ambiguity of most blues. The prominence of the dominant in all three phrases further removed it from conventional blues melody, which would often lack a dominant in its first two phrases. Instead of treating the dominant as a ceiling tone (in the fashion of *Maggie*), Patton made it a true melody note by sandwiching it between the higher sixth and lower third. While many blues melodies sound forced, *Pony Blues* began with three complementary phrases, so closely intertwined as to constitute a single basic phrase with variations.

Whereas the first half of the initial phrase ascends during its first three beats, the last part of the phrase inverts its note sequence for four beats (descending from the major sixth to the dominant, the major third, and keynote). The second phrase begins with the same ascent, but instead of hovering at the major sixth on the sixth beat, it repeats the closing cadence of the previous phrase. The third line resumes the melody of the first six beats, and then toys with its three lowest tones for its closing measure.

Patton's remarkable phrasing and rhythmic presentation of *Pony Blues* made it far

---

Reprinted from Stephen Calt and Gayle Dean Wardlow, *King of the Delta Blues: The Life and Music of Charlie Patton* (Newton, N.J.: Rock Chapel Press, 1988), 98–100. Used by permission.

superior to the ordinary ditty, and converted what would otherwise have been a memorable melody into a masterpiece. Over the first two phrases of the title verse, he held the final word (which began on the tenth beat) for six beats while playing a guitar figure. This hold created a symmetrical effect, since the opening phrase snippet of the tune ("Hitch up my pony") had also consisted of six beats. The final word of the stanza was held for two full measures—a feat never duplicated on a blues recording.

The vocal accenting of *Pony Blues* was the most complicated of any dance blues song. The unique vocal accenting of the title verse involved a tug of war between a 1-2 scheme and a legato singing style involving sustained notes that displaced expected stresses. As in *Screamin' And Hollerin'*, the vocal had a weak sixth beat that Patton fortified by penetrating his singing with instrumentation. In this instance, he created a complementary rhythm with a non-melodic seven beat mosaic, beginning with a bass tonic note on the second beat followed by three beats of damped and bent treble notes. A three beat variation of this phrase began on the sixth beat:

Vocal Beats: 1-2-3-4-5-6-7-8-9-10
Guitar Beats: 1-2-3-4-1-2-3
b t t t b t t

(b = bass)
(t = treble)

Patton seems to have been the only blues musician who was able to think in terms of such dual rhythm patterns.

By using short instrumental figures Patton not only filled in every vocal beat (except the opening one, and the fifth beat of the final phrase), but was able to attain a variety of tones and instrumental accepting patterns. The bass and treble interplay that formed Patton's accompaniment punctuations was extremely exotic within the realm of blues-playing. His rhythmic punctuations would have sounded unintelligible without the presence of the vocal line they were grafted onto. In this respect the arrangement given *Pony Blues* was musically ancestral to present day "soul" and disco songs, where percussive phrase snippets abound. The same is not true of Patton's recorded versions of *Maggie*: most of his guitar work on these songs is phrased in single measure blocks. Generally, Patton used a heavy bass to amplify his basic 1-2 vocal beat. His accompaniment was so full that his playing almost had the effect of two guitars: a bass percussionist and a lead guitarist who mimicked accents and embroidered the melody with treble work.

By the time Patton recorded *Pony Blues* in 1929, it must have undergone considerable refining and evolution. The three vocal tunes its six verses contained (each bearing a distinctive phrasing pattern and accompaniment features) marked a level of melodic ambition that was otherwise unknown in the sphere of blues dance music. It involved seven melodic strands; the reiteration of the same line (A") in each couplet gave its strains a cohesiveness not found in medley presentation:

verse one	AA'A"
verse two	BCA"
verse three	BCA"
verse four	DEA"

verse five	BCA"
verse six	DEA"

The vocal variations introduced unexpected dynamic alterations that contributed an air of drama to the song. In the first variant, a 13 bar stanza, Patton shouted at full voice, dropping to a lowered volume in delivering the second phrase (C). In the second variant, a 16½ bar stanza, he inverted this sequence. In accompanying this variant Patton used the technique he had fostered on *Maggie*: a repeating single measure riff (based on a IV^7 chord) began on the second beat and was extended for two measures beyond the tenth beat. His rhythmic presentation of the first variant was uniquely creative: after singing a ten beat line with a 1-2 accent, Patton strummed a half-measure fill and launched the second phrase with an implied, unaccented IV^7 chord played for a single beat. His first measure of singing then took a *1*-2 rhythm pattern; thanks to the accenting of the instrumentalized beat that preceded it, the new vocal pattern did not transform the accenting of the song itself.

Because of its dramatic nuances and percussive orientation, *Pony Blues* demanded an inspired performance, and Patton's recording of the piece in 1929 could not have been exceeded even by himself for inspired musicianship. Patton's timing is wondrous to behold, and he handles his instrument like a toy, producing percussive and tonal contrasts by choking strings for split seconds, muting individual bass notes, and tapping his guitar percussively during the V^7 section over the third and fourth beats of the final vocal phrase. Jazz guitarist Woody Mann terms *Pony Blues* "the most perfect blues recording ever made," and it is certainly one whose magic cannot be indicated by analysis. It was obviously a song that was very dear to Patton, for he played it with sheer love.

B. B. King

Analysis of the Artist's Evolving Guitar Technique

Jerry Richardson

B. B. KING is the world's preeminent electric blues guitarist. His style has influenced guitarists and contemporary rock stars throughout the world. It is the purpose of this article to examine the development of King's guitar technique from his earliest recordings up through the 1980s.

The development of B. B. King's guitar technique has been gradual yet continuous and deliberate. In fact, the artist has always been motivated toward self-improvement, which accounts for his great penchant for listening to a variety of musical styles. His early reluctance to use his instrument as an accompanying medium, borne out in his statement: "I've never been able to actually accompany myself with chords like a guitarist would do,"[1] has only served to increase his capacity for inventiveness and creativity in effecting single string solos. It can be shown that King's guitar technique has advanced over the years with respect to dexterity, facility and the gradual acquisition and development of certain idiomatic or stylistic devices such as hand slides or hand-position shifts, note embellishments, tremolos, and pull-offs.

B. B. King had not developed an impressive guitar technique by the time he did his first recording session for the Bullet label in 1949. In these earliest recordings (four altogether), King can be seen as a crude unrefined soloist relying on a limited set of skills. He adhered to a single guitar position and played only descending blues scales. These early recording sessions displayed loose arrangements without much continuity or direction, always staying close to the key of C major, the tonality used on his first four sides.

B. B. King played two separate sessions for Bullet in 1949, one in July and one in November. In the July session he recorded "Miss Martha King" (Bullet 309) and "When Your Baby Packs Up and Goes" (Bullet 309), both uptempo, boogie-woogie jump tunes. His only solo work on both songs was confined to the introduction, which in the former was manifested by two short descending blues scales and a brief statement of a "T-Bone" Walker-derived motif (Figure 1). In fact, this motif was to become one of King's signature "licks" during his early style development and is still identifiable in a few cases in more recent examples.

Reprinted from *American Music Research Center Journal* 6 (1996): 89–107 and from *B. B. King Companion* (New York: Schirmer Books, 1997), 182–97. Used by permission of the author.

Figure 1. "Miss Martha King"

He begins the introduction to "When Your Baby Packs Up and Goes" with the same descending scale, only differing from the former in his contracting the eighth-note triplet to the quarter-eighth figure . In both previously mentioned songs we find short solo choruses by the tenor saxophonist and the trombonist. Novice guitar improvisers often confine themselves to a single key and a single position. King was no exception in both Bullet sessions.

On the November 1949 session, King recorded two sides, a fast boogie-woogie entitled "Take a Swing With Me" (Bullet 315) and a slower twelve-bar blues called "Got the Blues" (Bullet 315). In both renditions very little guitar is heard. In fact, one has to listen carefully to detect a few disjointed guitar responses to several vocal lines. Thus we can conclude that in these earliest King sessions the artist possessed minimal dexterity for soloing, limiting himself to several memorized blues scale patterns in one position (at the eighth fret) and a "lick" or motif borrowed from his idol, Aaron "T-Bone" Walker.

On entering the modest studio of Sam Phillips in the early part of 1950, it appears that B. B. King had made some strides as a soloist. Prior to his sessions for Phillips in the early 1950s, King apparently devoted much of his time to practice and to the scrutiny of his guitar idols. Many of his early recordings for Phillips reflect the strong influence from "T-Bone" Walker once again; in fact, they are almost imitations. This influence can be detected by comparing Walker's solo in "I Got a Break Baby" (Capitol 10033, 1942) with B. B. King's "Questionnaire Blues" (KST 539) recorded in January, 1951 (Figures 2 and 3).

It is also interesting to note that in a few of his early sessions for Phillips, King functions merely as a blues vocalist, as is evidenced by the overlapping guitar lines. The side musicians in these sessions consisted of several young Memphis jazz players, including Phineas Newborn on piano, Hank Crawford on tenor saxophone, and apparently Calvin Newborn on lead guitar. Upon first hearing "B. B. Boogie" (RPM 304), one might mistakenly attribute the guitar solo to B. B. King himself (no clear documentation of the sidemen's identities could be found). However, given the fact that King's solo development had not reached the inventiveness and jazz-like quality demonstrated in this rendition

Signs Used in Transcriptions

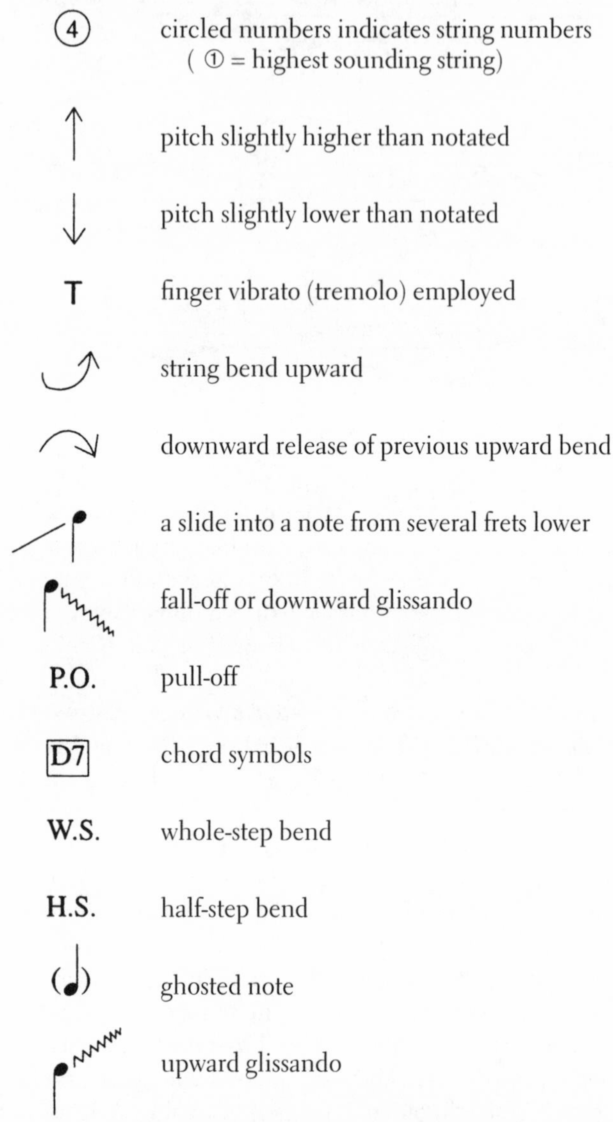

elsewhere, the guitarist most likely to have been capable of it was Phineas' brother Calvin, who played on several of King's early sessions (Figure 4).

One of the first stylistic elements incorporated into B. B. King's developing technique was his repetition of the same pitch played consecutively on adjacent strings. Probably used as a means to achieve tonal contrast, this same technique was utilized by "T-Bone" Walker, as well as by many rockabilly guitarists. It is effected by playing a given note on a higher string, then immediately sliding on the next lower adjacent string up to the same pitch. It is also a reliable method of going from a lower to a higher position. This gesture is evident in

Figure 2. "T-Bone" Walker, "I Got a Break Baby"

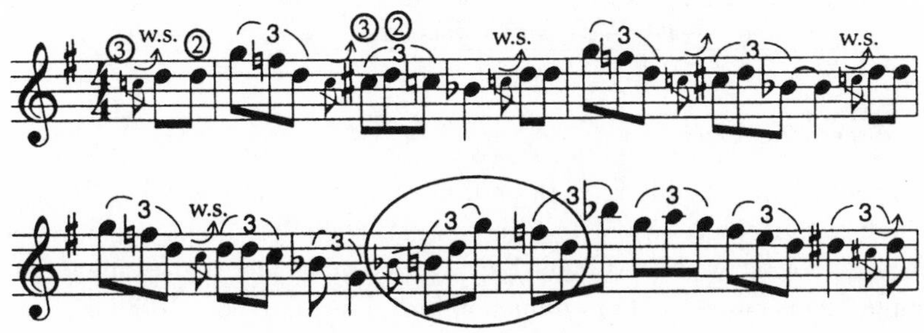

Figure 3. B. B. King, "Questionnaire Blues"

Figure 4. Calvin Newborn [?], "B. B. Boogie"

many of King's recordings of the early 1950s. A case in point can be found in the ninth bar of his improvised guitar solo in "She Don't Love Me No More" (RPM 348, 1952), (Figure 5).

Figure 5. "She Don't Love Me No More"

Another example can be detected in his first national hit, "Three O'Clock Blues" (RPM 339), which was released in 1951 (Figure 6).

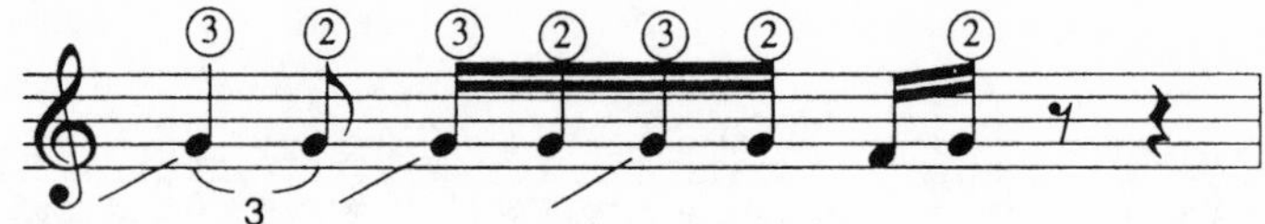

Figure 6. "Three O'Clock Blues"

Significantly both repetitions occur on the dominant harmony and in the same measure of this twelve-bar blues song. This repetitive note-sliding technique can be found in "T-Bone" Walker's solos as well as in Chuck Berry's guitar solos of the mid- to late 1950s. A typical example occurs in the latter's introduction to "Johnny B. Goode" (Chess 1691, 1958). King has continued to use this technique throughout his career, although not in the same manner as has been already demonstrated. In the mid-1950s and later he contracted the technique into one single repetition. King's guitar solo in "Boogie Rock" (RPM P435), a 1955 instrumental, illustrates the point, in both the second and seventh measures (Figure 7).

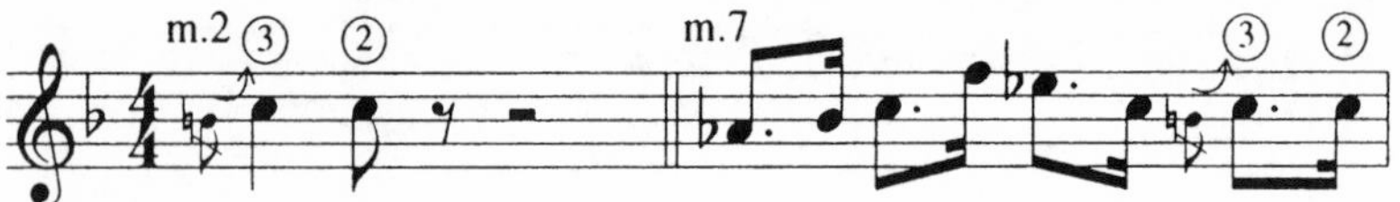

Figure 7. "Boogie Rock"

As can be seen in the preceding examples, King bends up to the first note on a lower string, then plays the same note on the adjacent higher string (Figure 8).

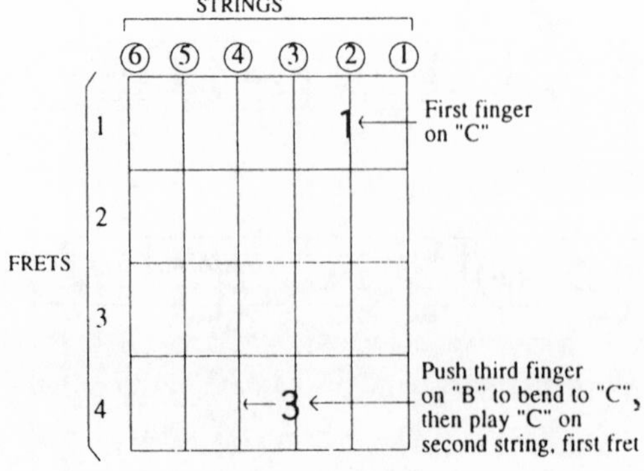

Figure 8. Method of executing mm. 2 and 7 of "Boogie Rock."

This same technique is employed in "Gambler's Blues" (BL 6001, reissued later on MCA 27010 and ABC 509, 1965) in m. 8 of King's guitar introduction (Figure 9).

Figure 9. "Gambler's Blues"

Other examples can be found in "Don't Answer The Door" (ABC 10856, 1966) and in "Sweet Little Angel" (ABC 509, 1965). Slides like these not only gave King a tonal contrast but also helped him extend his range on the instrument. In the mid- to late 1950s, B. B. King confined his soloing range to one or two close positions, only occasionally moving into distant positions, and then with some uncertainty and uneasiness. In listening to King's second twelve-bar solo chorus in "Days of Old" (Kent 307, 1958/59), one can detect a certain amount of apprehension and awkwardness in his attempt to go from the fourth position to the sixteenth fret to play an A-flat. To do this, he slides on the first string to the sixteenth fret. He barely executes the note intended, and that in a muddled fashion; then he quickly returns to the fourth position where he regains his security. Through the 1960s, with much practice, King became more proficient in moving into and out of various positions on his guitar. The results are evident in his live recording, "My Mood" (Bluesway 6031, 1969), an instrumental using the same chord progression as Claude Gray's "Night Life" (Decca, 1968). In his second solo chorus he is able to go from the seventh to the fourteenth position (Figure 10) within four measures, a procedure which takes considerable dexterity.

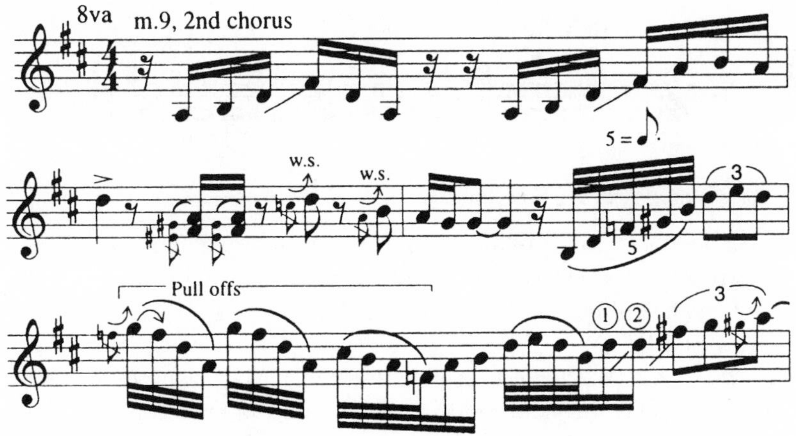

Figure 10. "My Mood"

A technique which gradually appears in King's guitar solos in the mid-fifties is his use of grace-notes, embellishments, turns, and mordants. This technique stems from his initial listening to Lonnie Johnson and later to such jazz guitarists as Charlie Christian, Django Reinhardt, and Bill Jennings, who played guitar in Louis Jordan's Tympani Five. An early example of such embellishment can be heard in m. 5 of a recording previously mentioned,

"Boogie Rock" (RPM 435) (Figure 11). His models can be observed in Lonnie Johnson's "Stompin' 'Em Along Slow" (OKEH 8558, 1928) in m. 6 of the third chorus and again in mm. 8 and 9 (Figure 12).

Figure 11. "Boogie Rock"

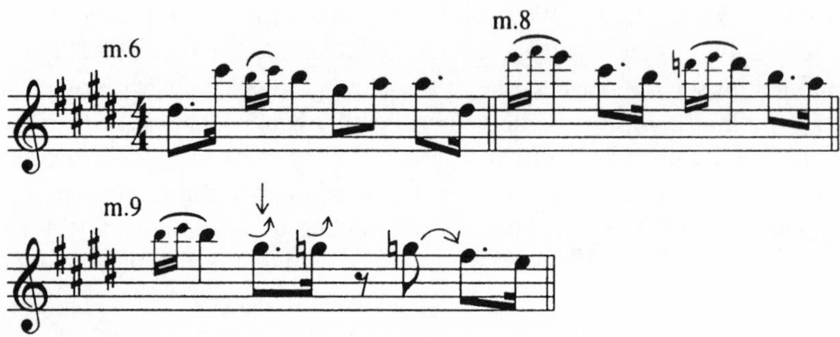

Figure 12. Lonnie Johnson, "Stompin' 'Em Along Slow"

One of B. B. King's favorite jump bands of the 1940s was Louis Jordan's Tympani Five whose song "Salt Pork, West Virginia" (Decca 18761, 1946) left a strong impression on him.[2] In Bill Jennings' guitar solo one can hear a similar embellishment at the end of m. 10 of this twelve-bar blues (Figure 13).

Figure 13. Bill Jennings, "Salt Port, West Virginia"

This example is a rhythmic retrograde of the embellishment found in King's "Boogie Rock." However, it can also be compared with King's "Days of Old" (Kent 307, 1958/59). King's entire solo here is based on a similar embellishment figure occurring in mm. 4, 6, 10 and 12 (Figure 14).

During the time B. B. King was living in Indianola, Mississippi, in the mid-1940s, a close friend, Willie Dotson, on home leave from the army in France, brought him several of Django Reinhardt's records from Paris.[3] King was immediately intrigued with the Gypsy guitarist's innovative technique and mode of phrasing. It is obvious that B. B. King absorbed some of these techniques, especially those involved with note bending and the use of embellishments (Figure 15).

B. B. King was also impressed with Charlie Christian's style, having first heard him on a moviola located at Jones' Night Spot in Indianola.[4] It is difficult to trace details of

Figure 14. "Days of Old"

Figure 15. Django Reinhardt, "Djangology"

Christian's style in King's solos, especially through brief ornaments. However, in the tune "Wholly Cats" (Columbia, CL 642) the jazz guitarist employs an embellishing figure in the sixth bar of his second solo break which resembles several of King's (Figure 16).

Figure 16. Charlie Christian, "Wholly Cats"

It must be pointed out that considerable practice over a period of time is required to effect a good grasp of embellishment technique on any instrument. Embellishments such as mordants present more complex problems of execution on the guitar because of the need to use a pull-off technique in order to sound the upper neighboring tone before returning to the original note.

King's use of embellishing notes diminished somewhat after the 1950s, at which time a noticeable development of other techniques became apparent, especially the refinement of his left-hand finger tremolo. King fancied the bottleneck style of Delta blues guitarists, notably that of his cousin Bukka White. But he was not sure how to transfer White's idiomatic vibrato sound to his own instrument. In fact, it took him nearly a decade to fully develop the technique, which appears to have entered his guitar improvisations between 1958 and 1960. In "Days of Old" (Figure 14), a slight amount of tremolo is utilized on notes held longer than a beat, but the frequency of oscillation is much slower compared to his solos of the mid-1960s where his tremolo speed is increased considerably. In his guitar solo choruses found in "Please Love Me" (Kent 336, 1960) and "Crying Won't Help You" (Kent 336, 1960) we see this tremolo development manifested both in the speed and in the frequency of usage. His employment of the technique is fully developed in his solos found in "Sweet Little Angel" (1965) and "Gambler's Blues" (1967), both on the album *B. B. King: Back in the Alley* (ABCD 878), (Figure 17 and Figure 18).

Figure 17. "Sweet Little Angel"

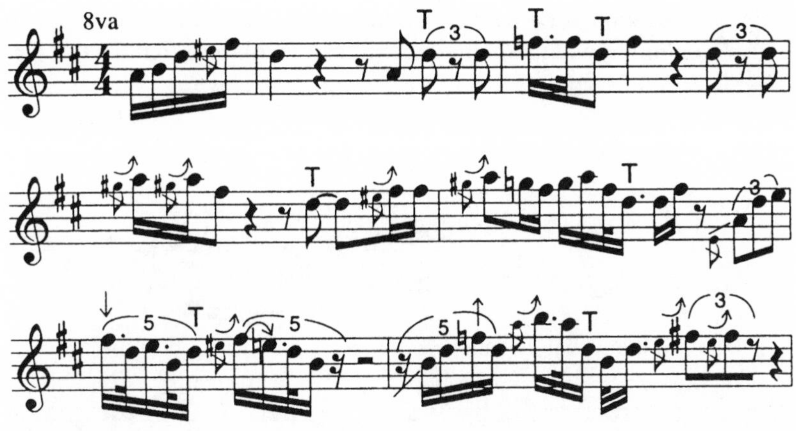

Figure 18. "Gambler's Blues"

It is significant that both of these songs are slower in tempo than the previously mentioned "Please Love Me." In general King more frequently uses the tremolo technique in slower twelve-bar tunes, although even in a faster shuffle tune like "Paying the Cost to Be the Boss" (BL 61015, 1967), we find King's tremolo employed on most quarter notes and notes of longer duration (Figure 19).

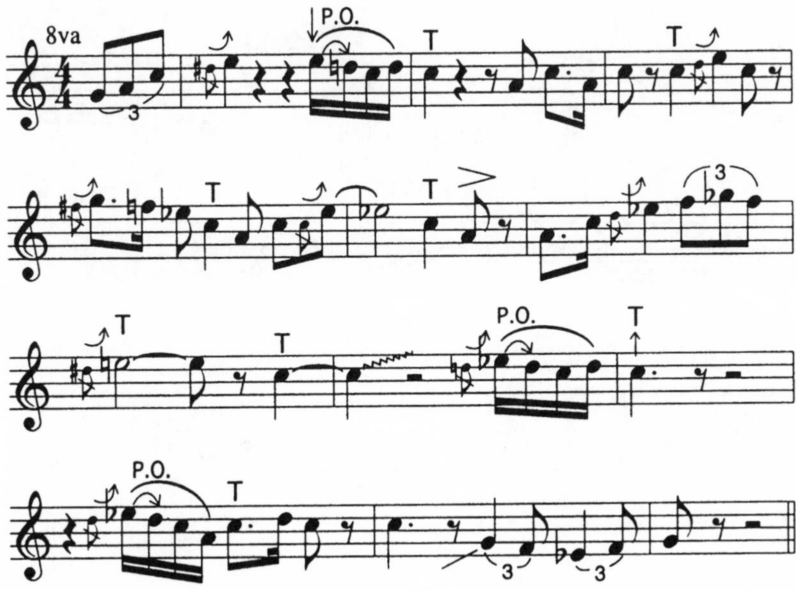

Figure 19. "Paying the Cost to Be the Boss"

B. B. King executed his fully developed tremolos with the utmost speed and agility, a feat he accomplished by lifting his left thumb completely off the back of the neck while fanning his index finger as fast as possible. Most jazz guitarists play their vibrato with the thumb supported behind the neck using slower motion. The fanning technique of B. B. King is both revolutionary and unique. The continuation of King's tremolo technique into the 1980s is illustrated in Figure 20.

Figure 20. "Broken Heart" (MCA-5413, 1983)

Still another device that B. B. King employs, though in moderation, is the pull-off, a technique usually reserved for jazz guitarists and some folk blues players. There are two types of pull-off, the single string pull-off and the chord pull-off. The former can be diatonic or chromatic. It is played by initially putting down from two to four left-hand fingers on a single string on consecutive frets (Figure 21).

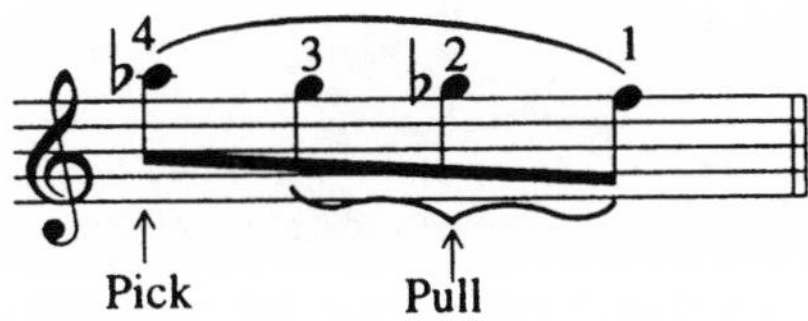

Figure 21. The single string pull-off

The highest note is sounded with the pick and the remaining notes are sounded consecutively by pulling (plucking) off the remaining fingers. The second type is played by placing three or four fingers on a given chord position and beginning with the lowest note (lowest string), playing each string consecutively, picking in one direction, and lifting each finger from the chord position after playing each note. This gives the aural illusion—to the uninitiated listener—of a virtuosic picking technique (Figure 22).

Figure 22. The chord pull-off

Both types are very difficult to master. B. B. King plays the second type only from a lower string to a higher, whereas some jazz guitarists like Barney Kessel or George Benson (both of whom King acknowledges and respects) will play from a higher to a lower string. This technique necessitates putting the chord fingers down and then immediately releasing them after they have been played, a device requiring extreme dexterity and diligent practice. B. B. King incorporated the single string pull-off into his solos early in his career. In the song "Bad Luck" (RPM 468), recorded in 1956, he employs a repeated pull-off riff starting on the flat seventh of the tonic D (Figure 23).

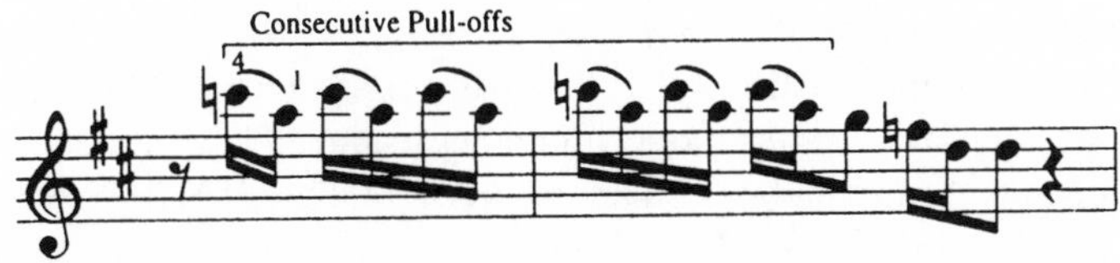

Figure 23. "Bad Luck"

In another song, entitled "Time to Say Goodbye" (Kent 327, 1958/59), he employs a pull-off on the third beat of the seventh bar of his eight-bar solo (Figure 24).

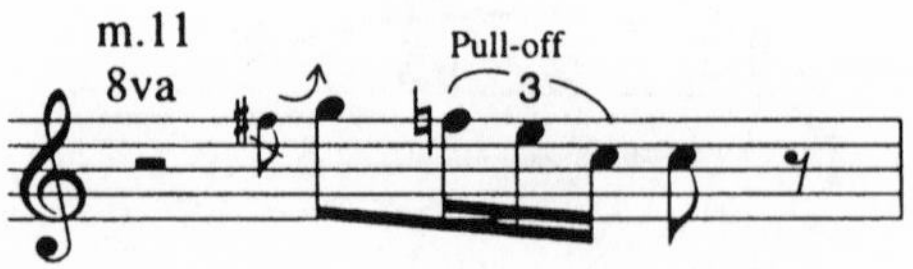

Figure 24. "Time to Say Goodbye"

In his introductory solo to the song "Sweet Sixteen" (Kent 330, 1960), he employs several repeated pull-offs in a single bar (m. 2) (Figure 25).

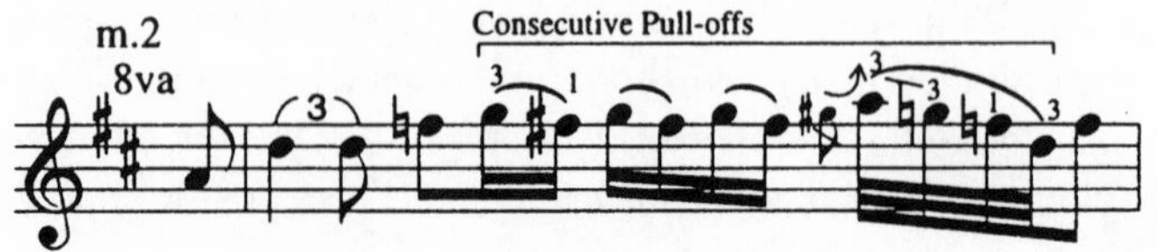

Figure 25. "Sweet Sixteen"

King also uses pull-offs effectively in the same song in his guitar responses to his vocal lines.

B. B. King employs the chord type pull-off less often because it is more difficult to play and perhaps too jazz-like to use very well in a blues framework. A representative example of this type can most easily be distinguished in "Gambler's Blues" (Bluesway 6001, 1967), (Figure 26).

Figure 26. "Gambler's Blues"

This pull-off riff sounds very virtuosic and impressive, occurring on the second half of the fourth beat.

In a later album, entitled *Live and Well* (Bluesway 6031, 1969), King plays a three-chorus introduction to "Sweet Little Angel," where he displays an exceptionally high number of pull-offs, mainly of the first type. However, in the eighth and ninth bars of the first solo chorus he employs both types (Figure 27).

In this solo, King sounds amazingly like the Gypsy master Django Reinhardt by straying from his normal blues style, adding more chromaticism and creative jazz-like lyrical lines.

Pull-offs are also exemplified in his later recordings: "Three O'Clock Blues" from his album *Together For the First Time* (DHL 6-50190, 1976), "Don't You Lie to Me" on *King Size* (ABC 977, 1977), and in "Big Boss Man" from *Six Silver Strings* (MCA 2675, 1985).

A technique which King begins to employ in the late 1970s is his use of octaves. This technique generally consists of strumming three adjacent strings but muting the middle one. B. B. King's usage of this technique is somewhat limited, as was also the case with the pull-off technique. King often employs this technique toward the end of a solo passage.

It has been established that King is an eclectic guitarist drawing on many sources in

Figure 27. "Sweet Little Angel"

forming his style and technique. He has no doubt incorporated nuances into his playing technique through his constant listening to other musicians over the course of his career. His octave technique was probably derived through his listening initially to Django Reinhardt and jazz guitarists like Wes Montgomery, whose solos were completely based on octave playing, and to George Benson, who has continued that same tradition in many of his solo choruses.

B. B. King's octave technique is first evident in his album *King Size* (ABC-977, 1977) on a song entitled "I Just Want to Make Love to You." He builds his guitar solo around the rhythmic motif for an extended period of repetitions. The entire song is a funky type of tune based on an A-flat seventh chord endlessly repeated. His solo consists of playing many melodic riffs based on this rhythmic motif. His octave usage begins at measure four and is stated several times using the rhythm mentioned above. In ending the song and his solo he alters the above octave riff by adding the dominant seventh of the chordal harmony—a G-flat directly below the tonic note A-flat.

B. B. King continues his octave technique up to the present time. In his song "The Victim" from the album *There Must Be a Better World Somewhere* (MCA-27034, 1981) he ends his twelve-bar blues solo with an octave figure, the last note falling off into a glissando. In the song "Broken Heart" from the album *Blues 'N Jazz* (MCA-5413, 1983) King employs a similar octave technique at the end of the tenth bar of his twelve-bar solo in almost the same manner as the preceding example. One can also find octave usage in B. B. King's album *Six Silver Strings* (MCA-5616, 1985). In the song "Big Boss Man" he plays octaves at measures 10 and 11 and again at measures 21 and 22. This is an interesting song in that the harmonic scheme is similar to Michael Jackson's "Billy Jean" (Epic 03509, 1982). King's song utilizes the repeated chord formula Ami - Bmi C6 - Bmi which repeats every two measures. On the same album, in a twelve-bar blues-rock tune entitled "My Lucille" King plays an octave figure in his second solo chorus at measure 10, glissing off the final octave B-flat.

Another technique, which is characteristic and fundamental to all blues guitarists and employed in a rather unique way by B. B. King, is that of string bending. In the first place, King's string bending technique is unusual in that it developed out of his insecurity and inability early in his career to hit accurately notes outside a given position on the instrument. This insecurity necessitated finding a compensatory approach. He found that by hitting the note a fret lower and bending up to it a half step he could sound bluesy and at the same time gain a sense of security in his soloing. King explains his unparalleled technique this way:

> —I'd never heard anybody do it the way I do it. My reason was that my ears don't always hear like they should. I'm always afraid that I might miss a note if I try to hit it right on the head, so if I hit down and slide (or bend) up to it, my ears tell me when I get there. But also it's more like violin or a voice; you just gliss up to it.[5]

Any B. B. King guitar solo is rife with this technique, although it has become more intense and more dramatic as his style has developed.

During the early stages of his style development he mixed glissandos and string bending proportionately, obviously because of the insecurity he alluded to earlier. One can notice this mixture of sliding and string bending in his early hit "Three O'Clock Blues" (RPM-339, 1951) in measures three through six.

In later solos King favors his tremolo and string bending technique over sliding as he has become more accurate in going in and out of positions. For example, in the song "My Lucille" (MCA-5616, 1985), King's solo displays a string-bending and tremolo technique which out-weighs any other technical or idiomatic devices. Besides being initially influenced by "T-Bone" Walker and other Delta guitarists, King also acknowledges saxophonist Louis Jordan as having given him the inclination to stretch notes up or down a half step.

In string or note bending King often plays these notes sharp or flat, especially if he is going to play the note twice, which occurs when he is returning to the original note a half-step lower. Often, when he bends up and holds a note out, his intonation tends to fluctuate. When changing from a minor third to a major third he may play the major third flat.

Development of Motifs in Guitar Solos

Charles Sawyer contends that B. B. King uses no more than two signature motifs in his guitar improvisations.[6] However, upon making a thorough perusal of his improvised guitar solos spanning his entire career, one finds at least three pervasive motifs which comprise a sort of musical grammar unique to King's guitar style. In analyzing these melodic fragments one can see a kind of evolution and style development of the guitarist in this respect.

In the beginning, King is somewhat confined to a very limited "bag" of motifs, ostensibly because of his inexperience as a soloist. We can see, though, in his development a gradual inclination either to vary or discontinue some of these melodic fragments in favor of others. However, it can be noticed that now, when performing songs from his earlier repertoire, he reverts back to some of his earlier motifs. The reason perhaps is that his older audience expects to hear a validation of their former conception of B. B. King and the artist obviously recognizes this and is very comfortable with his earlier repertoire himself. This also seems to be the case with other professional entertainers who do this as a means of continuing their identity and uniqueness.

One of the first motifs significant to B. B. King's style development can be compared to a similar motif of "T-Bone" Walker, as heard in King's "She Don't Move Me No More" (US 7788, 1949–50) and "T-Bone" Walker's "I Got A Break Baby." "T-Bone" Walker was the first and foremost contributor to B. B. King's melodic style development. This same signature motif can be found in many of King's guitar solos throughout the 1950s. He also employed the motif in his guitar responses to his vocal lines during the same time span. B. B. King hasn't abandoned this motif entirely, as it is found in his guitar solo in "Broken Heart" (MCA 5413, 1983) at measure 8. It is nonetheless rare to hear him employ it now.

A second motif which King himself invented and began employing in the mid-1960s is a triplet figure beginning on the fifth of the chord going up a whole step and leaping to the tonic note. It then ascends to the third, descending to either the tonic or the fifth on the first measure. Charles Sawyer briefly discusses this motif in his biography of the bluesman but without documentation of its occurrence.[7]

King generally reserves this triplet motif for introductions to slow 12-bar blues songs, although there are occasional exceptions where he will employ a four-note variation on a faster song like "Gambler's Blues" (MCA 27010, 1966). In his hit song "Paying the Cost to Be the Boss," an up-tempo blues, he remains on the third of the tonic chord on measure one which resolves to the tonic notes on measure two. In the introductory solo to "Gambler's Blues" King repeats a variation of this motif two times with several permutations. He begins the motif by sliding up to the sixth "B." Then, skipping to the tonic "D" and on to the second "E," he arrives as usual to the third, this time a minor third. King continues the use of this basic motif up to the present time, especially when playing older hits in live performances. In his live album, *B. B. King and Bobby Bland: Together For the First Time* (MCA 2 4160, 1974), he utilizes the motif to introduce his classic "Three O'Clock Blues."

In observing the artist perform an engagement in Memphis, Tennessee, in 1985, this author witnessed usages of this same motif to introduce "Lucille" and "Paying the Cost to Be the Boss."

A third motif employed consistently in B. B. King's guitar solos is one which begins on a note bent up a half step to the lowered seventh of the tonic chord. The motif is most often played against the I^7 harmony although it may fit any of the three chords employed in a traditional 12-bar blues framework. In the song "The Victim" (MCA 27034, 1981) King begins the motif on the fourth bar of this 12-bar blues. The underlying harmony at this point is a I^7 ready to move to a IV^7 at measure five.

The basic motif itself can be analyzed in several ways. It is fundamentally a descending A-minor pentatonic scale starting on "G," or it could be seen as an implied "A" blues scale without the flatted fifth E flat. A jazz musician might see the motif or "lick" as part of a dominant seventh (Mixolydian) scale or arpeggio. We might also say that it is a tonic minor seventh motif pitted against the underlying secondary dominant harmony. The C natural gives it the bluesy dissonant effect. King employs this motif characteristically at times just before a chord change to IV^7 to create tension and climactic building. Therefore, it is seen as a building device to arrive at the second "A" section or the "B" section of the typical three part blues form—AAB. This motif is first evident in King's solos around the mid-1960s. He uses it very effectively in his second solo chorus in the song "Worry, Worry" (*B. B. King: Live at the Regal*, MCA 27006, 1964). He employs the motif here repeatedly as a building device in the first four measures to arrive at the IV^7 at the fifth measure.

As can be seen, he alters the motif slightly on the third repetition at measure three. The harmony does briefly change to the IV^7 chord at measure two, but this is a common variation from the traditional harmony I - I - I - 17 for the first four measures.

In the second improvised chorus from his introduction to "Gambler's Blues" (MCA 27010, 1966), he essentially employs the motif in the same manner preceding the IV^7 chord change at measure five. He continues this same modus operandi in his second chorus of "Sweet Sixteen" (MCS 27074, 1971).

In his solo in "Three O'Clock Blues" (MCA2 4160, 1974) he again plays the motif several times, first at the end of the third measure, which seems premature to set up the IV^7 chord on measure, and then again at the end of the sixth bar to announce the arrival of the I^7 (tonic 7) again in measures seven and eight. We notice at this point that King deliberately ends up on an F sharp to coincide with the tonic "D" chord at measure seven. In the song "Don't You Lie to Me" (ABC 977, 1977) he employs the motif in the same manner to arrive at the I^7 coming up in measure seven.

B. B. King also uses this motif outside the traditional 12-bar blues framework in tunes like "My Lucille" and "Big Boss Man" from his latest album *Six Silver Strings* (MCA 5616, 1985). His solo chorus in the former is built around a harmonic progression based on suspended $I^7 + 4$ (sus 4) chords. He employs the motif twice in his solo chorus, both times on a B-flat (sus 4) harmony just before a subsequent B flat 7 harmonic change. The motif, however, is played identically in both cases.

King's song "Big Boss Man" (MCA 5616, 1985) is essentially a 12-bar blues with a double-time feel, making the overall form 24 bars. It also has a moving harmonic structure within each bar thus making the song rather unusual. The underlying harmony is taken from Michael Jackson's "Billy Jean" (Epic 03509, 1982), which was immensely popular. This progression gives King a new slant on his otherwise sometimes monotonous three-chord blues framework. This borrowed harmonic accompaniment or formula is utilized only on measures that would regularly employ a tonic harmony in a traditional 12-bar blues. Again, predictably, King plays the motif in the measure preceding the change to the IV^7 harmony (minor). In this case, it occurs on the eighth measure because the song has a double-time feel.

In his song "Broken Heart" (MCA 5413, 1983), a regular 12-bar blues, he digresses slightly from his normal usage in employing the motif. It is permutated rhythmically, on the second measure, and again on the fourth. As usual King utilizes the motif for dynamic contrast and expression in building his solo. This motif can be seen as an intrinsic part of B. B. King's musical grammar, unequivocally defining his style. We can see that he has continued its usage up to the present time and almost always in the same harmonic context.

Motifs Developed in Guitar Responses

One of the main style characteristics of blues artists is the instrumental response following their vocal lines, especially in the 12-bar blues format. Examples of these responses can be found throughout the recorded history of the blues, from the early recordings of Louis Armstrong, Bessie Smith, Blind Lemon Jefferson, the Delta blues singers, and right up through to the post World War II urban bluesmen like Muddy Waters, "T-Bone" Walker, and Howlin' Wolf. Of course, B. B. King is no exception. Historically instrumental responses have taken the following directions: (1) orchestral accompaniment providing the responses (Bessie Smith and other female blues singers), (2) soloists in the background playing responses, (3) the blues singer himself providing the response. B. B. King has incorporated all three types, but for the majority of his recordings he chooses to play his own, especially in smaller group contexts.

King considers his guitar responses very important in communicating the totality of his thoughts. He asserts that these short melodic fragments following his vocal lines are merely a continuation of his vocal statements. He confirms this in stating, "When the serious part comes after the melodic (vocal) line leaves the lips, then the serious part starts on the guitar."[8]

In other words, we might perceive his vocal lines as being punctuated by short series of notes that could be seen as musical statements serving to enhance his vocal statements.

An interesting phenomenon unique to King's style, which can be observed occurring simultaneously with his guitar responses, is his facial expressions. He denotes these as taking the place of his strumming:

> —then I'm hearing, after I stop singing, the guitar. I am singing through the guitar (by means of the guitar response). Then my facial expression (which he has observed on video tape) and all that is like the tempo of the strumming on the guitar that goes along with the melodic line on the guitar.[9]

As was mentioned in an earlier chapter, one of the main incentives for King to develop responses on the guitar came out of his own insecurity as an accompanist. He had the choice of becoming a blues singer like Bobby Bland or Joe Williams, who rely on their backup groups to play their responses, or to utilize his guitar in creating his own responses. King's guitar responses have also come to define the artist and his unique style.

These responses have basically taken on the same motivic shapes as his extended improvisations, though over the course of his career they have developed into shorter motifs limited to tonic clarification or emphasis.

His earlier responses consisted of longer melodic fragments paralleling and limited to those found in his improvised solos. For example, in the song "She Don't Move Me No More" (US 7788, 1949–1950) he employs a similar melodic fragment to one found in his 12-bar solos during the same tune.

As we follow the development of King's guitar responses during the 1950's, we find that they continue to be almost identical to the motifs observed in his extended solos. In comparing several motifs found in his guitar solo in "Three O'Clock Blues" (RPM 339, 1951) with his guitar responses in the same song, we see an amazing similarity. In examining a recording of the same song made almost 25 years later we see that King draws on a mixture of earlier motifs while developing newer ones.

Depending on the makeup of his accompanying group, King may play his own responses, or he may play them against a riffing ensemble background. He may also simply choose to have his back-up soloists play the responses entirely. In several early songs he chose to play his own responses for a few verses. Then in succeeding verses his sidemen took over. His 1950 recording, "Questionnaire Blues" (KST 9011, 1951), is a prime example. Many times King will play responses in a free-for-all context, everyone competing for the spotlight. This occurs in early songs like "My Own Fault Darlin'" (RPM 335, 1950) and "B. B.'s Blues" (RPM-323, 1950). He still follows this trend in many of his live recordings where he is not confined to a strict time factor. Such albums as *Live at the Regal* (MCA-27006, 1964), *B. B. King: Live and Well* (Bluesway-6031, 1969), and *Blues Is King* (BL-6001, 1966), are exemplary. A specific example of the bluesman playing responses against a riffing ensemble background is found in his recording "I've Got a Right to Love My Baby" (Kent-333, 1960). This piece is also an excellent illustration of King's usage of earlier motifs in his guitar responses.

During the 1960s B. B. King continued to play several identifiable signature motifs in his guitar responses. This is clearly demonstrated in his song "Wee Baby Blues" (MCA 2-4124, 1966). These responses occur consecutively. The first follows the textual line—"It was early one Monday morning, I was on my way to school." The second response, a pull-off, is employed at the end of the vocal phrase "and that was the Monday morning that I broke my teacher's rule."

In the late 1960s, B. B. King's responses began to take the shape of several shorter fragments accentuating the tonic note of the key, sometimes isolated or followed by longer melodic fragments. This trend can be seen in examining his responses from approximately 1968 up to the present time. In the song "Having My Say" (MCA 2-4124, 1968) his response begins with a statement of the tonic note "C," which is an upward bend, followed in the succeeding measure by a short melodic fragment, both defining the tonal center. The next response beings with a similar "C," also bent upward, then followed by a longer melodic fragment. In another of King's songs from the same time period, "Worried Dream" (MCA 2-4124), his first response is a concise motif beginning on the tonic note with E-flat, F, and G to follow, thus alluding to the C-minor tonality. The ensuing response consists of a typical statement of the tonic note "C," an upward bend, followed by a longer melodic fragment.

By the early 1970s, King's responses continued to become shorter and compressed, mostly beginning on the tonic and only occasionally followed by longer melodic fragments. In his song "Sweet Sixteen" (MCA-27074, 1971) his first response begins with a tonic statement on "D" accented. The rest of the response diminishes in sound, seeming to imply a lesser significance.

From the mid-1970's to the present time we see a trend toward very short motifs, usually employing the tonic note on a fast "trill" (vibrato). These are often followed by notes of a shorter rhythmical value, which usually include the third or the sixth note of the key. In the song "Don't Answer the Door" (MCA2-4160, 1974) we find two consecutive responses, each concise and going to the third or the sixth note of the key. One finds a similar usage in "Never Make a Move Too Soon" (MCA-27011, 1978). The first response consists of a long "trilled" note followed by the sixth of the key, a shorter one. The second response is simply a trilled tonic G note. Most of King's other response motifs since 1978 have been limited to a range of a fifth. Exceptions to this can be found in motifs originating on the flatted seventh of the key. In the song "Heed My Warning" (MCA 5413, 1983) we see the use of the dominant seventh motif as well as the shorter "trilled" tonic motif. Other examples of King's usage of flatted seventh motifs occur in several of his songs on a more recent album, *Six Silver Strings* (MCA 5616, 1985). In the second response in the song "The Midnight Hour" he bends up to the flatted seventh, B-flat, then bends up to third, "E," finally sounding the tonic more "C" with a finger vibrato (trill). In the song "My Guitar Sings the Blues" (MCA 5616, 1985) a more typical flatted seventh motif is executed in the second response. This can be compared to measure two of his 12-bar solo in "Broken Heart" (MCA 5413, 1983).

Through developing numerous motifs during his career, B. B. King has been able to become more of a spontaneous improviser, possibly playing more from his "head" rather than contriving his solos or responses in a more predictable manner as manifested in his earlier works. It often takes many years of on-the-job experience to develop the expertise in conceiving and inventing musical lines spontaneously. King has begun to approach this ideal in the span of approximately 35 years.

The Relationship of King's Guitar Responses to His Vocal Lines

It has already been pointed out that B. B. King perceives his guitar lines as a continuation of his vocal phrases. It is apparent, however, that King's vocal phrases are more closely related to his vocal sources as represented in the works of Roy Brown, Wynonie Harris, Joe Williams, and Louis Jordan, to name a few. Many of King's vocals have not been original manifestations, although to be certain he has affixed his own individual stamp on each song. His first commercial success came with "3 O'Clock Blues" (RPM 339, 1951) recorded two years earlier by Lowell Fulson, its composer. "Every Day I Have the Blues" (RPM 421, 1955) was recorded earlier by Joe Williams, Lowell Fulson, and Memphis Slim. "Sweet Sixteen" (Kent 330, 1960) came from Joe Turner via Walter Davis, and "Sweet Little Angel" (Kent 340, 1960), one of King's most identifiable hits, had been previously recorded by Tampa Red and later by Robert Nighthawk. B. B. King's greatest hit, "The Thrill Is Gone" (BL-61032, 1970), was recorded earlier by Roy Hawkins.

King's guitar ideas, on the other hand, do not draw so specifically from a particular recording but more from a set "bag" or reservoir of licks, melodic fragments, or preconceived melodic lines—sort of a defined repertoire. In other words, King's instrumental improvisations as well as his guitar responses are somewhat set and predictable in an ad lib context. Earlier recordings of several vocalists serve as sources for songs, not for arrangements. His guitar responses thus can be seen as internal refrains, an instrumental extension of the vocal text drawn from a previously mentioned readily available collection of musical material.

B. B. King's Jazz Guitar Style

To be certain, King's overwhelming style characteristics place him in the blues idiom. However, it must be pointed out that on rare occasions his guitar sound and use of certain idiomatic devices may have momentarily positioned him in the realm of a jazz guitar style. King performs most of the time in a three-chord 12-bar blues framework. To be sure he has recorded with a plethora of jazz musicians, whose influence has had a substantial impact on his musical thinking. Nevertheless, he has confined his playing to the B. B. King blues style for the most part. This can be confirmed in listening to such jazz session albums as *King Size* (ABC-977, 1977), *There Must Be a Better World Somewhere* (MCA-5162, 1981), and *Blues 'N Jazz* (MCA-5413, 1983). Therefore, King's jazz guitar style has only been evident on a few live performance recordings and at his after-hours jam sessions. It is on these rare occasions that we may hear a jazzier guitar style emanate from the veteran bluesman. He obviously feels most at home performing in his own blues context, even when other musicians may take liberties. He always puts his audience first, desirous to play what they want to hear, not wanting to betray their image of who B. B. King is:

> —but what makes identity, what makes a person be themself, is being what they are continually, as far as I am concerned,—There are certain licks that you are going to hit because that is me. I have to do that. That is kind of like trying to talk to you—you say the cliches or something to try to get my point over. I think the same way when I am on stage. To me I am carrying on a rapport with my audience—in other words, I am trying to say something so to identify to me—I feel like I am on stage with long rubber arms with a dancing partner which is the audience, and I like to be able to reach.[10]

It is easy to see why King is reluctant to change his image and the blues-infected style he is most noted for.

What then distinguishes King's blues style from his jazz style? King's jazz style evolved very slowly to be sure. He began by inserting jazzy nuances and "licks" into his pervasive blues style, therefore, on occasion offering a unique or peculiar sound.

King began to acquire a few jazz guitar techniques in the early 1960s. This is evident in his recording of "Mr. Pawnbroker" (Crown 5188, 1960). In this rendition he transcends the blues idiom by incorporating a pull-off into his more lyrically conceived jazz sounding solo and at the same time using fewer bluesy effects. Even his vocal lines hint more towards a Joe Williams sound rife with jazzy embellishment.

While "Mr. Pawnbroker" demonstrates King's growing awareness and predisposition for utilizing a few jazz guitar sounds, we do not hear a more fully developed jazzy guitar inclination until his album *Live and Well* (Bluesway 6031) produced in 1969. A most exemplary jazz-conceived solo occurs in King's introduction to "Sweet Little Angel," where he displays a phenomenal use of jazz guitar technique and novel devices in a few of his guitar lines. He begins his solo with a signature motif in measures one and two, continuing to play in a typical King blues style up to the third measure. At this point he slides into several double-stopped notes on beat two. Sliding into thirds is more common in the jazz guitar idiom, as evidenced in the solos of Barney Kessel, Kenny Burrell, and a host of other jazz guitarists. In measure five King sets up a jazzy sound by his employment of stark chromaticism and by his grace note usage. In measure six he portrays a jazz-like style in his slide to F sharp on beat three and in his glissando and pull-off on beat four. However, his inadeptness in fitting notes to the implied harmonic background stands out at this same point as he implies a "D" harmony against the G7 accompaniment. A common fault of amateur jazz soloists is to improvise ahead of an upcoming harmonic change. This is the case on beats three and four of measure six where King creates ambiguity and dissonance erroneously and prematurely. King gets back on track in measures seven and eight with his tasteful usage of note sliding and embellishment. The zenith of his jazz-like digression occurs in measures nine and ten. He begins measure nine with a flashy jazz pull-off on beat one. On beats two and three his tasty A7 scale, with its chromatic passing tone, compliments the implied harmony at that point. On beat four he again prematurely sets up the forthcoming IV harmony by playing an E minor chord arpeggio. However, these notes tend to sound consonant because they are really an extension of the present A7 harmony, thus making the end result an A9 sound. This can be seen as purely accidental, as King would not have purposely created this tension. In measure ten he continues his jazz sound by playing a G-major-seven arpeggio on the first beat, which is syncopated, then completes the measure emphasizing the sixth of the G chord - E. In measure eleven he brings us back home to the blues with his string bends from a minor to a major third.

This rendition shows us that King has purposely listened to jazz guitarists and other jazz instrumentalists in a quest to diversify his style, and while he is capable of showing some expertise in this remote area, his inexperience as an improviser is apparent. It also shows us that King is reluctant to perform in his jazz style except in a relaxed context.

As has been the case with many jazz aspirants, B. B. King showed great curiosity and interest in Charlie Christian's jazz guitar style. During King's formative years, which encompassed the mid-1940s, the only jazz guitarists of any notoriety were Charlie Christian, Django Reinhardt, and to a lesser degree, Bill Jennings. These as well as later guitarists motivated King to practice major and minor scales and some arpeggios at various times in his development. However, one of King's greatest attractions was for the diminished harmonies of Charlie Christian. This attraction is borne out in King's own statement:

> —Charlie Christian was really known for what we call diminished chords, and, man, he could break them up so pretty.[11]

As has been previously demonstrated, most of King's studio recordings are devoid of the jazz guitar style alluded to in his live recordings or performances. In these few rare instances, King's knowledge and use of altered scales is apparent. This occurred specifically in his instrumental ballad "My Mood" (Bluesway 6031, 1969) from the album *Live and Well.* King demonstrated a style influence from both Charlie Christian, with his use of diminished runs, and Django Reinhardt with his use of embellishments and phrasing. This ballad is in a 32-bar A-A-B-A form with cycle-of-fourth harmonies resembling Claude Gray's early tune "Night Life" (Decca, 1968). King has followed this chord formula in many of his ballad songs throughout his career.

A sampling of this genre of ballads can be found in the following B. B. King repertory: "I'll Survive" (CST-195, 1958), "I'm King" (CST-195, 1958), "How Long How Long Blues" (MCA-2-4124, 1981), "There Must Be a Better World Somewhere" (MCA-5162, 1981). It is interesting that in these examples King never plays the guitar but functions solely as a vocalist. The probable reason for this is that the harmonic scheme does not lend itself to a downhome bluesy style but rather more to a jazzy popular vocal style. Since all of these are studio recordings, King chooses to focus on his lyrical vocal style rather than to risk making mistakes in his attempt to improvise over the more diverse harmonies. "My Mood," on the other hand, is the perfect vehicle for B. B. King to demonstrate his limited prowess in the jazz style he is moderately familiar with. He is also situated in a more relaxed atmosphere—the club or concert setting.

Up to the present time jazz musicians have enjoyed improvising to tunes which either change chords in every measure or every other measure, giving them the opportunity to play a diversity of scales, arpeggios and idiomatic motifs. This type of improvising occurred in small group settings beginning with bebop in the 1940's and continuing in the "Cool" era of the mid to late 1950's. The tunes played would be standards drawn from the 1930's and 1940's such as "I Got Rhythm," "Sweet Georgia Brown," and "Stardust." In the 1950's and 1960's jazz musicians liked to improvise to tunes like "Misty," "Satin Doll," "Early Autumn" and "Girl from Ipanema." All of these tunes have a harmonic scheme focusing on a cycle of fourth chord progressions. This same kind of progression is found in measures 4–8 in the "A" sections of "Night Life." Here each successive chord moves up by a fourth -B7-E7-A7-D.

"My Mood" demonstrates King's inventiveness and use of jazzy nuances, such as note sliding, pull-offs, embellishments, and glissandos. In several cases he uses altered chord scales, never distinguishable in any of his studio recordings.

B. B. King begins his second eight-bar solo chorus (the A section repeated) with several slides which serve to get to a higher position while exhibiting both a jazzy and bluesy effect. In measure 2 he employs double stopped thirds, which he slides into twice. On the upbeats of "three" and "four" he plays the melody slightly altered by whole step note bends which are uncharacteristic of his straight blues solos. He also hints at the melody on the first two beats of bar 3. However, on the third and fourth beat King surprises us with a premature G sharp diminished seventh run, as the organist does not sound the harmony until the beginning of the following measure. As we have seen before, this is not out of line with King's thinking or background. Fortunately, his diminished seventh run doesn't sound too bad with the exception of the G-sharp which is dissonant with the accompanying G-natural. Finally arriving at measure 4 he plays a series of G-sharp diminished seventh chord pull-offs which are very jazzlike, fully complimenting the underlying harmony at that point. Then, at measure 5, King returns to a bluesy feel with half-step note bends to several F-sharps and an A-natural. He brings us back to a jazzy style in measure 6 with a glissando from "E" down to "A," a technique he reserves mostly for his jazz style. On beat "three" of the same measure we are once more surprised at his rare end employment of an augmented run against a dominant harmony. On beat "four" he returns again to a more bluesy effect by bending up and back on the eighth notes which move toward the tonic harmony in measure 7. In bar 8 he adequately sets up the subdominant harmony of the forthcoming "B" section by playing a tonic-7 (D7) scale lick which includes several chromatic triplet figures on the upbeat of "two" and on the down-beat of "three."

In the ensuing "B" section (refrain) he returns to his typical blues style with a riffing horn section in the background. In this section he does nothing extraordinary. However, in the final "A" section he again reminds us of Charlie Christian with his descending G-sharp diminished seventh melodic structure, the first three notes bent upward in measure 4.

Finally, we can conjecture that B. B. King sees himself primarily as a blues guitarist with a diversity of musical interests, and an occasional inclination to get away from a strict three-chord blues framework. He accomplishes this by showing off his somewhat limited jazz technique in situations where he feels most relaxed—the live performing context. We must keep in mind that his 300-plus nights-per-year performing schedule allows him at least some flexibility to perform in other style mediums.

As evidenced, B. B. King is not an expert jazz soloist, but he does exhibit enough knowledge and technique to impress the average blues enthusiast and is perhaps poor enough to sow the seeds of doubt in the minds of a few schooled jazz musicians or jazz critics.

In summary, B. B. King has gradually incorporated a variety of technical devices—some original—into his playing style. These advances in technique have served to distinguish him as a unique soloist capable of improvising in an electric blues guitar style and occasionally in a more jazzy mode of expression. Thus, over the period of his entire career he has become a consummate soloist drawing upon a reservoir of predetermined motifs and melodic fragments, enabling him to appear as a spontaneous and creative musician.

Chronology of B. B. King's Developing Guitar Style

1935 Receives instruction on guitar from Archie Fair.
1943 Plays and sings on Indianola street corners (frailing style).
1945 Absorbs note bending & embellishment techniques from recordings of C. Christian & D. Reinhardt. Scrutinizes T-Bone Walker's guitar style. Copies Walker's melodic motifs.
1946 Lives with cousin Bukka White who tutors him on guitar.
1949 Begins recording career. Begins note sliding technique.
1950 Introduces repeated notes on adjacent strings.
1951 Records "Three O'Clock Blues," his first hit.
1955 Two-note repetitions employed (first note bent up, second note repeated on higher adjacent string). Range confined to close positions.
1956 Pull-off technique first employed.
1958 Tremolo technique first discernible.
1960 Jazz guitar style begins to emerge.
1964 Range expanded to higher playing positions. Introduces triplet motif in introductions. First employment of descending Dom 7 motifs. Tremolo technique fully developed.
1968 Begins to employ shorter response motifs following vocal lines.
1969 Mature jazz guitar style. Diminished 7th runs first discernible in recordings.

1977 Octave technique first employed.
1985 Use of novel chord progressions (montunos).

Table of Recordings Cited

Date	Label/Number	Performer	Album/Song Title
1928	OKEH 8558	Lonnie Johnson	"Stompin' 'Em Along Slow"
[c. 1940]	CL 642	Charlie Christian	"Wholly Cats"
1942	Capitol 10033	"T-Bone" Walker	"I Got a Break Baby"
1946	Decca 18761	Louis Jordan's Tympani Five	"Salt Pork, West Virginia"
1949	Bullet 309	B. B. King	"Miss Martha King" "When Your Baby Packs Up and Goes"
1949	Bullet 315	B. B. King	"Take a Swing With Me" "Got the Blues"
1950/51	RPM 304	B. B. King	"B. B. Boogie"
1951	KST 539	B. B. King	"Questionnaire Blues"
1951	RPM 339	B. B. King	"Three O'Clock Blues"
1952	RPM 348	B. B. King	"She Don't Love Me No More"
1955	RPM 435	B. B. King	"Boogie Rock"
1956	RPM 468	B. B. King	"Bad Luck"
1958	Chess 1691	Chuck Berry	"Johnny B. Goode"
1958/59	Kent 307	B. B. King	"Days of Old"
1958/59	Kent 327	B. B. King	"Time to Say Goodbye"
1960	Kent 330	B. B. King	"Sweet Sixteen"
1960	Kent 336	B. B. King	"Please Love Me" "Crying Won't Help You"
1965	ABC 509	B. B. King	*Live At The Regal* "Sweet Little Angel"
1966	ABC 10856	B. B. King	"Don't Answer the Door"
1967	BL 6001	B. B. King	*Blues Is King* "Gambler's Blues"
1967	BL 61015	B. B. King	"Paying the Cost to Be the Boss"
1968	Decca	Claude Gray	"Night Life"
1969	Bluesway 6031	B. B. King	*Live and Well* "My Mood"
1972	ABCD 878	B. B. King	*B. B. King: Back in the Alley* "Gambler's Blues" "Sweet Little Angel"
1976	DHL 6-50190	B. B. King	*Together For the First Time* "Three O'Clock Blues"
1977	ABC 977	B. B. King	*King Size* "Don't You Lie to Me"
1979	Camden QJ-25221	Django Reinhardt	"Djangology"
1985	MCA 2675	B. B. King	*Six Silver Strings* "Big Boss Man"

Notes

1. B. B. King, interview with author, 7 June 1986.
2. Charles Sawyer, *The Arrival of B. B. King: The Authorized Biography* (New York: Doubleday, 1980), 23.
3. Ibid., 157.
4. Ibid., 53.
5. Tom Wheeler, "B. B. King," *Guitar Player Magazine*, September 1980, p. 64.
6. Sawyer, p. 172.
7. Ibid.
8. B. B. King, interview with author.
9. Ibid.
10. Ibid.
11. Ibid.

6 Performance

A KEY determinant of both style and subject matter during a blues performance can be the audience's interaction with the artist. There are clearly a number of elements of the blues that are antiphonal, inherited, it is likely, from the frequent characteristic call-and-response nature of African music, and keyed in, of course, to communal organization and practice. There is the interplay between voice and instrument, where frequently an instrument picks up where the vocal leaves off or pauses to echo, punctuate, or dialogue with the voice; the repetition of the A line and the response of the B line in an AAB stanza (played out variously in other stanzaic patterns); and the special interchange that frequently takes place between artist and audience in performance, where performance depends upon and may even be completed by the contributions of the crowd. Such a relationship extends beyond what contemporary reader-response critics suggest about the reader's relationship to a written text: that the text doesn't produce meaning itself, but causes the reader to produce meaning in interaction with the text.

The blues go beyond this interaction in the sense that the audience can be part of the performance, literally changing what the performer produces through a variety of responses. And the responses of the crowd can be oral, some affirmative word or phrase, a sudden swish like the air racing from a safety valve. They can be physical, exultant, upraised arms testifying to the truth of the matter, or a sensuous switch of the hips; they can be visceral or spiritual, evidenced by the roar of the crowd at the first hint of wordless moans, soaring falsettos, and string-teasing vibratos that seem to touch so many where they live; or they can be physical and communal at once, in the rush to the dance floor to participate in the communal fertility rites.

All of these and more may catch the attention of the performers, who may comment on them verbally or musically, making a lyric or perhaps a whole song out of them on the spot or, artistic sap rising, raise the performance to a higher level, energized artistically and physically by their collaborators. As Sterling Brown points out in his brilliant blues poem "Ma Rainey," it is clear that performer and audience draw on each other for inspiration, for sustenance, mean more to each other than the price of a ticket or the crackling noise from a gramophone horn.

An arts patron/novelist/photographer/literary executor/assistant music critic for the *New York Times*, and press agent and party-thrower supreme of the Harlem Renaissance, Carl Van Vechten provides one of the earliest glimpses of the vaudeville blues singer in performance before a crowd of her admiring African American masses. Calling Bessie Smith "the true folk-spirit of the race" who "sings Blues as they are understood and admired by the coloured masses," Van Vechten reveals himself not to be immune to the primitivism that was rampant in some quarters during the Harlem Renaissance, especially in his comments about "African beats" and "strange rites" and his characterization of Bessie Smith as an "elemental conjure woman" with a voice that "sounded as if it had been developed at the sources of the Nile." Still, Van Vechten was an important admirer of Bessie Smith, Clara Smith, and Ethel Waters. He once invited Bessie Smith to sing at his salon for a gathering of wealthy cultural notables, with what was reported to have been successful artistic (though disastrous social) results. Like many others, he recognized the power of such singers to mesmerize audiences in live performance.

Teacher, critic, and poet Sterling Brown had a great deal to say about the blues during his distinguished career (see the recommended readings in the folklore section—though as Brown himself pointed out, he was not a folklorist). However, his deepest, most concise, and most beautiful words were in his poetry, particularly his heartfelt portrayal of the reciprocal relationship enjoyed by the performer Ma Rainey (whom Brown had met), her audience, and the poet in his poem "Ma Rainey." Brown's sense of place, anticipation, performance, meaning, and inspiration capture the experience where it lives and resonates most meaningfully, in the exchange of inspiration and strength and support and emotion liberated in the heat of performance and its aftermath. Through a skillful use of language, stanza patterns, antiphonal voices, and communal spirit, Brown created a blues poem unsurpassed in brilliance, and one that forcefully demonstrated the kinship between the blues singer, the "common" folks, and the literary artist. (See also Houston Baker's discussion of the poem in *Modernism and the Harlem Renaissance.*) Certainly those interested in the blues, African American folklore, and literature would do well to pick up a copy of *The Collected Poems of Sterling A. Brown* (Evanston: Tri-Quarterly Books, 1996) and pay special attention to his marvelous "Strange Legacies," "Southern Road," "Odyssey of Big Boy," and "When de Saints Go Ma'ching Home," the latter dedicated to Big Boy Davis, an itinerant singer-guitarist whose two extant recordings have been issued on Document CDs 5575 and 5601.

Langston Hughes made no secret of his love for African American vernacular music. In fact, he made it a central part of his artistic aesthetic reflected in his myriad of artistic activities—poetry, short stories, plays, novels, autobiographies, song lyrics, libretti, and the like. He recognized the attempts of those in the commercial marketplace to appropriate the blues—"You done taken my blues and gone" he wrote in "Note on Commercial Theater" before asserting how we was going to take them back—and he did his best to claim and reclaim them over and over again in his remarkable body of work. "Happy New Year! with Memphis Minnie" is an evocative piece revolving around a 1942 performance by the great Memphis Minnie, one of the blues world's most powerful and distinctive singers and guitarists. Hughes emphasizes how the blues beautifully and accurately reflect the hard times of the lives of the singer and audience, while the economic benefits come primarily to the bar owners, who are neither audience participants nor familiar with the nuances of African American life or music. And in his comment that Minnie weaves the details of African American existence "into runs and trills and deep steady chords that come through the amplifier like Negro heartbeats mixed with iron and steel," he comes close to capturing the technique, power, and endurance of Memphis Minnie's music, the blues.

The liner notes to the Ruth Brown Skye LP *black is brown and brown is beautiful,* as related to Mort Goode by WIGO disk jockey Herb Lance and Brown herself, present a remarkable portrait of the racism faced by an African American woman traveling the rhythm and blues circuit in the 1950s and 1960s. With a clipped cadence that captures the frustration and outrage at the jim crowing and casual and gratuitous violence and humiliation, the notes emphasize the attempt of the performer to lead a life of dignity and integrity and artistry in a world permeated with demeaning indignities. As the notes move from one nightmare to another, it becomes apparent that Brown does not sing the blues easily, does not come by her artistic intensity casually. And the shame of American racism and the remarkable triumph of the African American spirit are set off in forceful, resounding relief.

One of the most important and influential researchers and writers and editors of the blues field was Mike Leadbitter, a British aficionado who from his editor's chair at *Blues Unlimited Magazine* and on his field trips and other forays into the realm of African American music demonstrated a deep and abiding love for the blues when most whites virtually ignored it. As a champion of the music he loved, Leadbitter employed his considerable writing skills in the service of blues performers both famous and obscure, never more evocatively than in his liner notes to the first Flyright LP, Flyright 3501, by the brilliant but underappreciated Juke Boy Bonner. In the piece, Leadbitter captures through acute observation of the details and nuances of an appearance by Bonner at a Houston club something of the joy, wistfulness, frustration, anger, dedication, and hopefulness that is reflected in Bonner's music, mingling personal, social, and musical observations with the crack of pool balls, good-natured set-em-ups of appreciative bar patrons, and the threat of violence palpable in the heavy night air of Houston's blues bars.

That threat of violence is the subject of the excerpt from folklorist Barry Lee Pearson's book *Sounds So Good to Me*, which skillfully weaves together field interviews to present blues performers' takes on a variety of issues. Whether personal, intentional, or indiscriminate, violence is a fact of life that many performers experience in bars and clubs, with jealous partners being the primary culprits. Many bluesmen attempt to avoid such clubs or, as Albert Washington once related to me, simply drop down behind instruments or amplifiers—in Albert's case an electric piano—and keep the music going so as not to draw additional attention to the altercation. Pianist Lonnie Bennet tells the story of how he had two of his fingers shot nearly all the way off in a bar where he was playing, only later to plead with surgeons who planned to amputate them to sew them back on because he needed them to play the piano. One does not wish to overemphasize the place of violence in the milieu of a blues performer, but it would be a mistake for anyone to ignore it. It is one of the conditions under which the performer must work, and with which the performer must learn to cope, in order to continue to ply the trade of musician in the sometimes warm, sometimes volatile world of the neighborhood bars and joints where the blues have been so frequently played.

This section would not be complete without Charles Keil's marvelous description and discussion of a performance in front of an African American audience by the incredible Bobby "Blue" Bland. Bland is not only a master singer but a master showman as well, not flashy and extroverted, but subtle and sincere as he stages and acts out his blues dramas with the form, depth, and sincerity of a preacher in front of his flock. (Indeed, this selection would have fit in the "Religion and the Blues" section as well.) Cooperation, solidarity, catharsis—Keil sees Bland's performance as a synthesis of these elements through the singer's own charisma and artistry, and leave us with a strong sense of how effective and meaningful a blues performance can be.

Recommended Further Readings

Chris Albertson. *Bessie*. 1972. Rpt. New York: Scarborough Books, 1982.

Glen Alyn. *I Say Me for a Parable*. New York: Da Capo, 1994.

Paul Oliver. *Conversation with the Blues*. 1965. Rpt. Cambridge: Cambridge University Press, 1997.

Negro "Blues" Singers

An Appreciation of Three Coloured Artists Who Excel in an Unusual and Native Medium

Carl Van Vechten

Editor's note:—New York is celebrated for its transitory fads. For whole seasons its mood is dominated by one popular figure or another, or by a racial influence. We have had Chaliapin winters, Moscow Art Theatre winters, Jeritza winters, Jazz winters, Russian winters, and Spanish winters. During the current season, indubitably, the Negro is in the ascendancy. Harlem cabarets are more popular than ever. Everybody is trying to dance the Charleston or to sing Spirituals, and volumes of arrangements of these folksongs drop from the press faster than one can keep count of them. Since September, at least four white fiction writers have published novels dealing with the Negro, while several novels and books of poems by coloured writers are announced. Paul Robeson, Florence Mills, Taylor Gordon and Rosamond Johnson, Roland Hayes, and Bill Robinson are all successful on the stage or concert platform. Soon, doubtless, the homely Negro songs of lovesickness known as the Blues, will be better known and appreciated by white audiences.

A TRIP to Newark is a career, and so I was forced to rise from the dinner table on Thanksgiving night shortly after eight o'clock if I wished to hear Bessie Smith sing at the Orpheum Theatre in that New Jersey City at a quarter of ten. I rose with eagerness, however, and so did my guests. Bessie Smith, the "Queen of the Blues," whose records sell into figures that compete with the circulation of the *Saturday Evening Post,* was to sing in Newark and Bessie Smith, who makes long tours of the South where her rich voice reaches the ears of the race from which she sprang, had not been heard in the vicinity of New York, save through the horn of the phonograph, for over a year.

The signs and tokens were favourable. When we gave directions to the white taxicab driver at Park Place, he demanded, "Going to hear Bessie Smith?" "Yes," we replied. "No good trying," he assured us. "You can't get in. They've been hanging on the chandeliers all the week." Nevertheless, we persevered, spurred on perhaps by a promise on the part of the

Reprinted from *Vanity Fair* 26, no. 1 (1926): 67, 106, 108. Used by permission of Condé Nast Publications, Inc.

management that a box would be reserved for us. We arrived, however, to discover that this promise had not been kept. It had been impossible to hold the box: the crowd was too great. "Day jes' nacherly eased into dat box," one of the ushers explained insouciantly. However, Leigh Whipper, the enterprising manager of the theatre, eased them out again.

Once seated, we looked out over a vast sea of happy black faces—two comedians were exchanging jokes on the stage. There was not a mulatto or high yellow visible among these people who were shouting merriment or approval after every ribald line. Where did they all come from? In Harlem the Negroes are many colors, shading to white, but these were all chocolate browns and "blues." Never before had I seen such an audience save at a typical Negro camp-meeting in the far South.

The comedians were off. The lights were lowered. A new placard, reading BESSIE SMITH, appeared in the frames at either side of the proscenium. As the curtain lifted, a jazz band, against a background of plum-coloured hangings, held the full stage. The saxophone began to moan; the drummer tossed his sticks. One was transported involuntarily, inevitably, to a Harlem carbaret. Presently, the band struck up a slower and still more mournful strain. The hangings parted and a great brown woman emerged—she was the size of Fay Templeton in her Weber and Fields days, and she was even garbed similarly, in a rose satin dress, spangled with sequins, which swept away from her trim ankles. Her face was beautiful, with the rich, ripe beauty of southern darkness, a deep bronze brown, like her bare arms.

She walked slowly to the footlights.

Then, to the accompaniment of the wailing, muted brasses, the monotonous African beat of the drum, the dromedary glide of the pianist's fingers over the responsive keys, she began her strange rites in a voice full of shoutin' and moanin' and prayin' and sufferin', a wild, rough Ethiopian voice, harsh and volcanic, released between rouged lips and the whitest of teeth, the singer swaying slightly to the rhythm.

> "Yo' treated me wrong;
> I treated yo' right;
> I wo'k fo' yo' full day an' night.
>
> Yo' brag to women
> I was yo' fool,
> So den I got dose sobbin' h'ahted Blues."

And now, inspired partly by the lines, partly by the stumbling strain of the accompaniment, partly by the power and magnetic personality of this elemental conjure woman and her plangent African voice, quivering with pain and passion, which sounded as if it had been developed at the sources of the Nile, the crowd burst into hysterical shrieks of sorrow and lamentation. Amens rent the air. Little nervous giggles, like the shivering of venetian glass, shocked the nerves.

> "It's true I loves yo', but I won't take mistreatments any mo'."

"Dat's right," a girl cried out from under our box.

> "All I wants is yo' pitcher in a frame;
> All I wants is yo' pitcher in a frame;
> When yo' gone I kin see yo' jes' duh same."

"Oh, Lawdy! Lawdy!" The girl beneath us shook with convulsive sobbing.

"I'se gwine to staht walkin' cause
  I got a wooden pah o' shoes;
Gwine to staht walkin' cause I got
  a wooden pah o' shoes;
Gwine keep on walkin' till I lose
  dese sobbin' h'ahted Blues."

The singer disappeared, and with her her magic. The spell broken, the audience relaxed and began to chatter. The band played a gayer tune.

Once again, Bessie Smith came out, now clad in a clinging garment fashioned of beads of silver steel. More than ever she was like an African empress, more than ever like a conjure woman.

"I'm gwineter sing dose mean ornery cussed *Wo'khouse Blues*," she shouted.

"Everybody's cryin' de wo'khouse
  Blues all day,
    All 'long,
    All 'long . . ."

A deep sigh from the gallery.

"Been wo'kin' so hard—thirty days
  is long,
    long, long,
    long, long . . ."

The spell once more was weaving its subtle sorcery, the perversely complicated spell of African voodoo, the fragrance of china-berry blossoms, the glimmer of the silver fleece of the cotton field under the full moon, the spell of sorrow: misery, poverty, and the horror of jail.

"I gotta leab heah,
Gotta git duh nex' train home . . .

Way up dere, way up on a long lonesome road;
Duh wo'khouse ez up on a long lonesome road . . .

Daddy used ter be mine, but look who'se got him now;
Daddy used ter be mine, but look who'se got him now;
Ef yo' took him keep him, he don't mean no good nohow."

II

If Bessie Smith is crude and primitive, she represents the true folk-spirit of the race. She sings Blues as they are understood and admired by the coloured masses. Of the artists who have communicated the Blues to the more sophisticated Negro and white public, I think Ethel Waters is the best. In fact, to my mind, as an artist, Miss Waters is superior to any other woman stage singer of her race.

She refines her comedy, refines her pathos, refines even her obscenities. She is such an expert mistress of her effects that she is obliged to expend very little effort to get over a line, a song, or even a dance. She is a natural comedienne and not one of the kind that has to work hard. She is not known as a dancer, but she is able, by a single movement of her body to outline for her public the suggestion of an entire dance. In her singing she exercises the same subtle skill. Some of her songs she croons; she never shouts. Her methods are precisely opposed to those of the crude coon shouter, to those of the authentic Blues singer, and yet, not for once, does she lose the veridical Negro atmosphere. Her voice and her gestures are essentially Negro, but they have been thought out and restrained, not prettified, but stylized. Ethel Waters can be languorous or emotional or gay, according to the mood of her song, but she is always the artistic interpreter of the many-talented race of which she is such a conspicuous member.

III

When we listen to Clara Smith we are vouchsafed another manifestation of the genius of the Negro for touching the heart through music. Like Bessie Smith—they are not sisters despite the fact that once, I believe, they appeared in a sister-act in vaudeville—Clara is a crude purveyor of the pseudo-folksongs of her race. She employs, however, more nuances of expression than Bessie. Her voice flutters agonizingly between tones. Music critics would say that she sings off the key. What she really does, of course, is to sing quarter tones. Thus she is justifiably billed as the "World's greatest moaner". She appears to be more of an artist than Bessie, but I suspect that this apparent artistry is spontaneous and uncalculated.

As she comes upon the stage through folds of electric blue hangings at the back, she is wrapped in a black evening cloak bordered with white fur. She does not advance, but hesitates, turning her face in profile. The pianist is playing the characteristic strain of the Blues. Clara begins to sing:

"All day long I'm worried;
All day long I'm blue;
I'm so awfully lonesome,
I don' know what to do;
So I ask yo', doctor,
See if yo' kin fin'
Somethin' in yo' satchel
To pacify my min'.

Doctor! Doctor!

(Her tones become poignantly pathetic; tears roll down her cheeks.)

Write me a prescription fo' duh Blues
Duh mean ole Blues."

(Her voice dies away in a mournful wail of pain and she buries her head in the curtains.)

Clara Smith's tones uncannily take on the colour of the saxophone; again of the clarinet. Her voice is powerful or melancholy, by turn. It tears the blood from one's heart. One learns from her that the Negro's cry to a cruel Cupid is as moving and elemental, as is his cry to God, as expressed in the Spirituals.

- They come 2 hear Ma from everywhere

- She's an inspiration

Ma Rainey

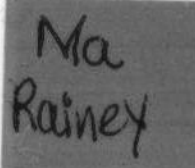

Sterling Brown

I

When Ma Rainey
Comes to town,
Folks from anyplace
Miles aroun',
From Cape Girardeau,
Poplar Bluff,
Flocks in to hear
Ma do her stuff;
Comes flivverin' in,
Or ridin' mules,
Or packed in trains,
Picknickin' fools. . . .
That's what it's like,
Fo' miles on down,
To New Orleans delta
An' Mobile town,
When Ma hits
Anywheres aroun'.

II

Dey comes to hear Ma Rainey from de little river settlements,
From blackbottom cornrows and from lumber camps;
Dey stumble in de hall, jes a-laughin' an' a-cacklin',
Cheerin' lak roarin' water, lak wind in river swamps.

An' some jokers keeps deir laughs a-goin' in de crowded aisles,
An' some folks sits dere waitin' wid deir aches an' miseries,
Till Ma comes out before dem, a-smilin' gold-toofed smiles
An' Long Boy ripples minors on de black an' yellow keys.

III

O Ma Rainey,
Sing yo' song;
Now you's back
Whah you belong,
Git way inside us,
Keep us strong. . . .
O Ma Rainey,
Li'l an' low;
Sing us 'bout de hard luck
Roun' our do';
Sing us 'bout de lonesome road
We mus' go. . . .

IV

I talked to a fellow, an' the fellow say,
"She jes' catch hold of us, somekindaway.
She sang Backwater Blues one day:
'It rained fo' days an' de skies was dark as night,
Trouble taken place in de lowlands at night.

Thundered an' lightened an' the storm begin to roll
Thousan's of people ain't got no place to go.

'Den I went an' stood upon some high ol' lonesome hill,
An' looked down on the place where I used to live.'

An' den de folks, dey natchally bowed dey heads an' cried,
Bowed dey heavy heads, shet dey moufs up tight an' cried,
An' Ma lef' de stage, an' followed some de folks outside."

Dere wasn't much more de fellow say:
She jes' gits hold of us dataway.

Happy New Year! with Memphis Minnie

Langston Hughes

Music at Year's End

MEMPHIS Minnie sits on top of the icebox at the 230 Club in Chicago and beats out blues on an electric guitar. A little dung-colored drummer who chews gum in tempo accompanies her, as the year's end—1942—flickers to nothing, and goes out like a melted candle.

Midnight. The electric guitar is very loud, science having magnified all its softness away. Memphis Minnie sings through a microphone and her voice—hard and strong anyhow for a little woman's—is made harder and stronger by scientific sound. The singing, the electric guitar, and the drums are so hard and so loud, amplified as they are by General Electric on top of the icebox, that sometimes the voice, the words, and the melody get lost under their noise, leaving only the rhythm to come through clear. The rhythm fills the 230 Club with a deep and dusky heartbeat that overrides all modern amplification. The rhythm is as old as Memphis Minnie's most remote ancestor.

Memphis Minnie's feet in her high-heeled shoes keep time to the music of her electric guitar. Her thin legs move like musical pistons. She is a slender, light-brown woman who looks like an old-maid school teacher with a sly sense of humor. She wears glasses that fail to hide her bright bird-like eyes. She dresses neatly and sits straight in her chair perched on top of the refrigerator where the beer is kept. Before she plays she cocks her head on one side like a bird, glances from her place on the box to the crowded bar below, frowns quizzically, and looks more than ever like a colored lady teacher in a neat Southern school about to say, "Children, the lesson is on page 14 today, paragraph 2."

Beating Out the Blues

But Memphis Minnie says nothing of the sort. Instead she grabs the microphone and yells, "Hey, now!" Then she hits a few deep chords at random, leans forward ever so slightly over

---

Chicago Defender, January 9, 1943. Reprinted in *Living Blues* 19 (1975): 7.

her guitar, bows her head and begins to beat out a good old steady down-home rhythm on the strings—a rhythm so contagious that often it makes the crowd holler out loud.

Then Minnie smiles. Her gold teeth flash for a split second. Her ear-rings tremble. Her left hand with dark red nails moves up and down the strings of the guitar's neck. Her right hand with the dice ring on it picks out the tune, throbs out the rhythm, beats out the blues.

Then, through the smoke and racket of the noisy Chicago bar float Louisiana bayous, muddy old swamps, Mississippi dust and sun, cotton fields, lonesome roads, train whistles in the night, mosquitoes at dawn and the Rural Free Delivery that never brings the right letter. All these things cry through the strings on Memphis Minnie's electric guitar, amplified to machine proportions—a musical version of electric welders plus a rolling mill.

Big rough old Delta cities, float in the smoke, too. Also border cities, Northern cities, Relief, W.P.A., Muscle Shoals, the jooks. "Has Anybody Seen My Pigmeat On The Line," "See-See Rider," St. Louis, Antoine Street, Willow Run, folks on the move who leave and don't care. The hand with the dice-ring picks out music like this. Music with so much in it folks remember that sometimes it makes them holler out loud.

Folks Have Jobs

It was last year, 1941, that the war broke out, wasn't it? Before that there wasn't no defense work much. And the President hadn't told the factory bosses that they had to hire colored. Before that it was W.P.A. and Relief. It was 1939 and 1935 and 1932 and 1928 and years that you don't remember when your clothes got shabby and the insurance lapsed. Now, it's 1942—and different. Folks have jobs. Money's circulating again. Relatives are in the Army with big insurance if they die.

Memphis Minnie, at year's end, picks up those nuances and tunes them into the strings of her guitar, weaves them into runs and trills and deep steady chords that come through the amplifiers like Negro heartbeats mixed with iron and steel. The way Memphis Minnie swings it sometimes makes folks snap their fingers, women get up and move their bodies, men holler "Yes!" When they do, Minnie smiles.

But the men who run the place—they are not Negroes—never smile. They never snap their fingers, clap their hands, or move in time to the music. They just stand at the licker counter and ring up sales on the cash register. At this year's end the sales are better than they used to be. But Memphis Minnie's music is harder than the coins that roll across the counter. Does that mean she understands? Or is it just science that makes the guitar strings so hard and so loud?

Liner Notes to *black is brown and brown is beautiful*

Mort Goode

IN THE dark days they beat up on her soul from Harlem to Dixie. What for? Why, just for being black.

Ruth Brown paid her dues. It's the frizzly-haired truth. I ain't going into the whole pedigree, but there ain't no cause to lie or jive you or sweet-talk.

Folks who ain't suffered much can't appreciate it. Race-prejudiced dogs barked at her. Snarled. Nipped. Lickered-up honkies teased her, bad-mouthed her at gigs. When she was small they bugged her with put downs that took her mind. Those jail-house mothers did it all.

Ruth picked up on it. The Jim Crowing. The heavy sadness. Keeping her place. Getting somewhere. Recognition. Star. Miss Rhythm. They were messing with her all the time but she was getting along climbing on the side of nowhere.

She had it all together when the R & B scene turned on. She jumped in with her hat in her hand and turned it on. Musicians knew real well. She was saying something.

It seeped into her and oozes out. So when she sings, what comes out is what she feels. No more. No less. But what she feels is all of it. You know it, baby. She has a kinda "it-gets-down-to-where-you-live" thing. In my life there ain't been many that had such natural sounds.

In the beginning whitey didn't know what she was singing about. Then some few stray cats latched on to her and what she was saying. And more folks heard her and listened and dug. Then came the hit records and the name in lights and the one-night stands.

But let's go back a minute. She comes out of the South. Portsmouth, Virginia and grew up before and during the World War II. Her father was the choir director in church. She got her musical beginning there. Lavozier Lamar heard her, taught her the first pop tunes. (He's still teaching talented young ones. Now he is the Director in the Y.M.C.A. in Newark, N.J.) Her father didn't like it. She was the first of 8 kids. So she started to sneak gigs at Army bases and U.S.O.'s. She worked the lunch counter at the Portsmouth U.S.O. and did shows at Langley Field and Camp Lejeune. Her mother said it was okay and cooled her dad.

Name performers heard her. Redd Foxx. Bette Roche. Ruth was moving. To Petersburg

---

Reprinted from Notes to *black is brown and brown is beautiful,* as told to Mort Goode by "Cousin Herb" Lance and Ruth Brown (Skye LP SK-13, 1969).

and Moe Barney's Theatre. To Detroit and the Frolics Show Bar. Chico Alvarez of Stan Kenton's Band caught her, told Lucky Millinder about her. She joined Lucky. She was 16 then. The war was slowed down. Jimmy Nottingham, Bernie Peacock and Al Grey were with the band. They looked after her, kept her straight. But she riled up Lucky one night in Washington and she was fired. Stranded.

Otis Mosely introduced her to Blanche Calloway, who put her to work singing at the Crystal Cavern. The bread was $30.00 a week. But folks were hearing her, talking about her. Willis Conover dropped in one night. He called Atlantic Records, which was just starting. They told her to come up to New York.

Blanche got her booked into the Apollo on a bill with Dizzy Gillespie. The word was out on Ruth by then. The word was good. But she had no wardrobe. She bought 4 gowns at the Salvation Army and headed North. On the drive up there was a bad accident. It laid her up for months. It was part of the dues.

The hit records started with "So Long" and "Teardrops In My Eyes" and "Oh, What A Dream" and "Mama, You Treat Your Daughter Mean." Herb Lance knows about "Mama." He wrote it with Johnny Wallace (Coley's brother) and was at Atlantic when Ruth cut it. Hal Jackson shook the tambourines. The effect had something. It became part of Ruth's act. She had to join the Union to play it.

Ruth was in on the start of the whole R & B scene. She was beating the story out of her own life. The hurt in her soul was coming through. It leaped. It jumped and hollered and shouted. It reached out and took your mind.

She was a star. Miss Rhythm in lights. The big gigs began. The one-night stands. Travelling in her own Cadillac with her own band down South. It was the early '50s.

Yeah! The one-night stands and riding thru' the land of muck, the bottom and segregation and honky-tonks and red-necks and the Man. Dressing in sheds and outhouses by candlelight. In Gulfport, Miss. she tried to use the white facilities at a gas station. The man was gonna beat up on her. The salty man and that motherin' klan. She-e-e-t! Ruth Brown was payin' her dues . . . by the installment plan.

In Knoxville, Tenn. at Chillowee Park Ruth tried to hang her gowns in a dressing room on the white level. A big, part-time cop ate her out. "You black New York bitch. Dress with the other niggers downstairs!" Ruth bit back. The man pulled a pistol. Amos Millburn [sic], with Ruth then, pulled the man off. It started a riot. Ruth hasn't played Knoxville since.

In Bradentown, Florida. They stopped on the highway at an orange-juice stand for refreshments. She and her group were travelling in her Caddie. Her manager, Nick Zale, white, was driving. Ruth was asleep with her head resting on his shoulder. There was noise. And cussing. "Get up, you bitch!" She opened her eyes and was staring into a .12-gauge shotgun held by a red-neck. The local sheriff rode them to the city limits and told them to keep moving.

In Macon, Georgia they were doing a show at the Municipal Auditorium. The Caddie sedan with RB insignia and plates was parked outside. When Ruth got back to the car there was red paint on the seats and flour in the gas-tank. Southern hospitality.

In Birmingham, Alabama, Ruth was the first act to follow that Nat Cole riot there. She had to do two shows. One for whites. One for the blacks. The klan marched around the theatre every minute.

In Opalocka, Florida, Ruth and her group had to stay on the road all night and sit. They were out of gas. The white cracker wouldn't sell them any because she couldn't explain the Caddie and how she came by it good enough to satisfy him.

In Meridian, Miss., they stopped for gas. Charlie Brown was with her then. So was his 80-year-old grandfather. (Ruth can't remember why.) She got out to use the facilities. The owner pointed up the road to the woods and said: "Use that, nigger, but don't let the troopers see yo' ass turned up to the light or they'll shoot it off." An argument started. The law came in an open truck. Ruth isn't sure yet why they got away. She does know Charlie's grandpa took the troopers aside and talked and talked. She doesn't know what he said or did.

In New Orleans. Ruth headlined with Billy Eckstine and the Count Basie Band. The orchestra floor had 2,500 seats. 500 whites filled all the front rows. There were no blacks. The rest of the orchestra was empty. The blacks were all crowded at the rear of the stage so that they would have seen only the backs of the entertainers. When Billy came out to start the show and saw that, he put up his hand. The band turned their stands around so they faced the blacks. Their backs were turned to the whites in the audience. Ruth and Billy and the Count did the whole show just like that.

In Gulfport, Miss. again. Joe Louis was traveling with Ruth. She got out for a drink at a gas station. The cracker screamed at her. When Joe stepped out to see what went on, the cracker recognized him and shut his own mouth. Quick. Apologized. And fixed a special pitcher of water.

Maybe some of it is passé, gone, finished. Maybe you don't hear: "Hey, bitch, what are you doing in this neighborhood?" as often. Maybe it's getting better.

But the hurt in her soul ain't ever gonna be all gone. It's all there. She's got it all together as good as any ever can and puts more into a song than most people can ever know. She's got no gimmicks. No gyrations. No gestures. She's pure.

Listen to what she does to "Yesterday." It's never been done like this. Real gospel. An R & B Ballad. The truth. And get on to "Miss Brown's Blues." It's more than 7 minutes of the baddest feeling that'll make you feel you lived.

Yeah, man! She had her ass kicked good. Look at these photos. The living is clear. Ruth Brown has been paying her dues. Hear what she's saying. You know it's the truth.

Juke Boy's Blues

Mike Leadbitter

IT IS early evening in Houston. The sun is setting and the air is still. On the corner of Pease, just across the railway tracks from Dowling stands the dejected looking 'Family Inn', looking out on a vista of dusty, dirty roads and listless groups of men and women watching small, grubby children at play. Saturday night is beginning and soon more people will emerge from the tumbledown, wooden houses neighbouring the Inn to set out for the earnest business of drinking, loving, quarrelling and often fighting. Whether their money is from work or from the Welfare, it will be spent this night trying to ease away the sordid reality of Ghetto life. Inside the Inn the huge freezer is full of canned Jax, Schlitz and Pearl beer; the morose houseman, S.P., and his wife sit at one of the rough tables surrounding the pool table, and wait.

Darkness is creeping when Juke Boy Bonner parks his station wagon on the corner and staggers in with his electric guitar and amplifier. In spite of the intense humidity he is neatly dressed and managing to look clean and fresh. The first of the customers have arrived and the balls on the pool table are clicking gently. Friends turn to greet the resident musician and are answered with a quick smile and a grateful 'yes' to the offer of a beer. He is a lean and light skinned man with handsome regular features. His voice is quiet as he speaks to friends whilst settling himself in the space provided by the door. By 8 o'clock his equipment is set up and the guitar is tuned to satisfaction. It is time for him to put down his beer bottle and begin entertaining anyone who cares to listen.

As the first few notes of the harmonica and guitar ring out in unison, faces begin to look up. One suddenly feels that Saturday Night has now really started. People begin to speak loudly and shout for more beer, while the balls on the pool table now connect with violent cracks. Juke Boy has finished a short instrumental warm up, and swallowing a mouthful of beer waits for requests. It is still too early and he begins by playing numbers of his own choice. 'Can't Hardly Keep From Crying' and 'Got No Place To Run' show his mood. His stomach is bothering him and signs of strain show round his eyes. His voice is full of frustration and bitterness, and the harmonica seems alive as it blends with his voice. For a

---

Reprinted from *Blues Unlimited* 111 (Dec.–Jan. 1974–1975): 6. Used by permission of Mrs. R. E. Leadbitter.

moment he has lost himself, and with a grin turns to 'I Live Where The Action Is'. As the solid beat, accentuated by his stomping feet, reaches the ears, broad smiles are in evidence. 'Real Quiet Fellow' follows with its Franklie Lee Sims overtones and a drunk begins a slow, solo dance on the floor, carefully watching his feet as they shuffle in complex patterns.

Darkness has settled and the light from the Inn calls to the crowds outside. The wire door bangs frequently and soon the bluesman is surrounded by a jostling throng. The beer is flowing freely and paper cups appear on the tables destined to be filled from concealed wine and whisky bottles. Despite the loud laughter and shouted conversations, Bonner's heavily amplified equipment can still be heard with ease. More people are shuffling on the splintered wooden floor, and the pool players curse as someone collides against the table. Requests pour in. 'Dust My Broom', 'Man Or Mouse', 'Meet Me In The Bottom', 'You Don't Have To Go', 'Things I Used To Do', 'Nine Below Zero'. No one calls for Juke Boy's own songs for they have never seen or heard his records, so he picks out the blues favourites and cleverly turns them around to suit himself. Still pleased, the askers bring over beer to help their man oil his throat and begin again.

As the night wears on, one wonders how many songs he knows and can play. He has sung twenty, or is it thirty by now. Perhaps it's more, as it is now 11 o'clock. Bonner is really tired and the effects of drink are showing on the faces around him. He slows the pace and sings 'Movin' Back To The Country' to please those dissatisfied with city life. 'Can't Let Your Troubles Get You Down' to console everyone including himself, and 'Why Do You Treat Me Like You Do' for all the mistreated 'lovers' who have come in alone. Suddenly a girl walks in and sits next to Juke Boy. They smile at each other, and he seems very happy to see her. He bursts into 'Goin' Crazy 'Bout You' whilst voices shout advice and encouragement.

Midnight! Only one more hour to go. The crowd's attitude has changed. Many are beginning to stagger home and others argue or sit quietly looking at their beer. Will S.P. fire his pistol tonight? As you sit watching it is easy to appreciate that at this moment someone close by is being shot or cut (the usual aftermath of Houston's big night). Juke Boy is singing 'I Wonder If You Know How It Is', and follows with 'Bad Breaks'. The old bitterness is rising again as he thinks of lost chances and broken promises. His thoughts turn to Europe where his only real fans seem to be and how he has no chance to meet them. 'Blues, Blues, Blues' is the finale at 12.55. Five minutes later he wearily packs his guitar away, and with his girl friend's help gets his equipment into the wagon. With a final and tired smile he leaves into the morning, knowing that tomorrow night at the same time he will have to go through it all over again. The fifteen dollars he has in his pocket is small consolation.

From "Big Bobby Blue Bland on Stage"

Charles Keil

ON STAGE, Bobby stresses his dependability and then calls on the Bland Dolls to assist him in a number or two. The three girls strut out in flesh-fitting sheath dresses and group themselves tightly around the microphone at the other side of the stage. At the same time they heighten Bobby's image as the ladies' man they offer definite visual pleasure to the men in the audience. The best-known song that Bland and his Dolls do together gets directly to the core of a fundamental problem in the Negro community: the instability of the conjugal bond. *Yield Not to Temptation* is church music, and recognized as such by all present. Bobby plays the preacher role, the girls represent a choir, and the audience is the participating congregation. But the problem being symbolized is as usual, completely personal. The touring blues singer is invariably separated from his wife or sweetheart during most of the year; will she be true while he is away, and can he withstand the temptations that his many female admirers present as he travels from town to town? The conflict—the temptation—cuts both ways; although the conflict is practically universal in Negro ghetto life, the blues singer, by the very nature of his profession, is exposed to this difficult situation to a greater extent and with greater intensity. Before discussing its implications, I shall examine the lyric itself and the interplay between soloist, singing group, band, and audience.

Yield Not to Temptation begins with a rocking medium-tempo rhythm by the drummer and a figure repeated over and over again in unison by electric bass, piano, and electric guitar. The rest of the band sets up an intricate off-beat hand clapping pattern that is quickly picked up by members of the audience who are familiar with the rhythm from church services they have attended since childhood. (If it is a Saturday night, some in the audience will be participating in the same way Sunday morning.) In the following, chorus parts are in parentheses and other features are in brackets.

[rhythm section introduction and hand clapping]
Yield not
To temptation

Reprinted from Charles Keil, *Urban Blues* (Chicago: University of Chicago Press, 1966), 134–42.

Oh, my love
While I'm away.

Don't you know (ooooo—girls hold chords softly in background)
You got to be strong (ooooooo)
Leave all the other guys alone (ooooooo)
One bright sunny day (ooooooo)
I'll be back home to stay (ooooooo)

Yield not (yield not)
To temptation
And let no one
Lead you astray (yield not)

So many times (so many times) [trumpets in unison with girls throughout]
You're gonna be lonely (but yield not)
So many times (so many times)
You're gonna be blue (but yield not)
But yield not (yield not to temptation) [some women in the audience sing along]
Yield not (yield not to temptation)
Oh, yield not (yield not to temptation)
Yield not (yield not to temptation)

Don't you know (ooooooo)
You got to be strong (etc.)
Leave all the other guys alone
One bright sunny day
Oh, I'll be back home to stay
Yield not (yield not)
To temptation (yield not) ooooooh-aah!
[tenor saxophone solo, spoken encouragement to soloist from Bland]

Don't you know (ooooooo)
You gotta be strong
Leave all the other guys alone
One bright sunny day
I'll be back home to stay.
Yield not (yield not)
To temptation (yield not)
(Yield not to temptation)
(Yield not to temptation)
(Yield not to temptation)

I got to know
[the verse is repeated by the Bland Dolls with every measure twelve more times while Bland shouts his lines in and around the responses]
I said I want to know
And I gotta know
Without a doubt
You got nobody

Takin' you out
I want to know
Ooooooh, baby,
I want to know
I said I got to know
One of these days
I want to know, baby
I just got to know, baby [band begins to fade out and girls march off stage still singing]
I got to know [Bland waves goodby].

Bobby is "moralizing" and preaching not from any superior vantage point but out of empathy. The command "Thou shalt not commit adultery" is there, but it is also a plea, a request, even a hope or prayer that the relationship will not fall apart as it has so many times before. Bland's repeated shouts of "I want to know," "I got to know" at the end have a feeling of helpless desperation. The chorus can be seen as supporting and reinforcing the protagonist in his frenzied call for loyalty, or it could also be interpreted as giving a counter-commandment—women asking their men to be faithful. This latter interpretation accurately reflects the matrifocal pattern of so many lower-class Negro families. At the same time that the basic male-female conflict is musically symbolized in the dialogue between Bland and the girls, their overlapping call-response patterns intertwined with the intricate band and audience accompaniment form a carefully planned and extremely effective aesthetic unity. The sight and sound of a common problem being acted out, talked out, and worked out on stage promote catharsis, and the fact that all present are participating in the solution creates solidarity. The constant repetition of phrases and driving intensity of the rhythm reflect the redundant patterns of ghetto life and all the persistent anguish that goes with it. As the song comes to an end and the girls go off stage, Bobby Blue Bland has the audience in the palm of his hand. Whatever distance has existed between artist and audience to this point has been all but eliminated. Bland and his listeners are one unit.

As if to emphasize this fact beyond all shadow of a doubt, Bland concludes his show with two pieces that chronicle the vicissitudes of the Negro week. *Yield Not to Temptation* serves as an excellent example of a musical style mirroring life style. In Bland's treatment of *Stormy Monday* and *That's the Way Love Is* the musical mirror is dispensed with and the Bland organization presents a distillation of reality itself.

Stormy Monday is a blues with a long history. T-Bone Walker first made it famous, but the lyric goes back to blues prehistory for its source material, to work songs and spirituals, to the literal facts of day-to-day post-slavery existence. The fact that the lyric is more powerful and popular today than ever speaks for itself—unfortunately. Bland handles the words slowly, deliberately, and with humility. The accompaniment consists simply of piano, bass, drums, and electric guitar; the guitar plays all the countermelodies and solos. There are no frills or flourishes here; the simple words tell a story that every member of the audience knows by heart.

They call it stormy Monday
But Tuesday's just as bad.
(repeated)

They call it stormy Monday
But Tuesday's just as bad.

Wednesday's worse
Lord, and Thursday's oh, so sad.

The eagle flies on Friday,
And Saturday I go out to play

Yes . . . the eagle flies on Friday
And Saturday I go out to play.

Sunday I go to church
And I kneel down 'n' pray.
. . . And this is what I say, baby (spoken).

Bobby kneels on the stage as he delivers this line and then talks to the audience. People shout encouragement and words of understanding as he bows his head.

Lord have mercy,
Lord, have mercy on me.
You know I cried, Lord, have mercy (shouted)
Lord, have mercy on me (whisper).

You know I'm trying, trying to find my baby,
Won't somebody please send her home to me . . . Yeah (spoken).

Bobby gets up, walks over to the guitarist and praises him as he bends over his instrument to extract the long-drawn-out whining phrases that are as much a part of the song as the lyrics. Suddenly the guitarist doubles the tempo and repeats a particularly funky phrase a few times accompanied by "oohs," "aahs," and "yeahs" from the audience. Bland says, "Play it one more time, brother," and the guitarist takes another chorus, finishing with the same double-time figure while Bland shakes his head in wonderment. Bland puts his hand on the guitarist's shoulder and beckons to the audience for applause, making a comment like "Ain't that the truth?" A third and even better chorus by the guitarist follows, and Bland wanders slowly around the stage, head cocked to one side, making clear his appreciation with a "yeah" between phrases. At the end of the chorus he turns abruptly to the audience and cries with all his might:

Well, I cried, Lord, have mercy
  (women wail in the audience)
Lord, have mercy on me (whisper).
I said I cried, Lord, have mercy,
Lord, have mercy on me.

You know I'm trying, trying to find my baby,
Whooa . . . send her home to me.

It should be noted here that Bland makes a special point of his dependencies during these final selections. Unlike most blues singers, who are instrumentalists capable of supplying their own melodic counterpoint, Bobby plays no instrument, though he once tried to learn guitar and is now interested in the tenor sax. This deficiency forces him to rely heavily on soloists within the band. He turns this liability into an advantage, however, when he acknowledges his debt and works with his solo countervoice; he thereby makes a show of teamwork, cooperation, and respect for another that enhances the binding-together mood of his performance.

This feeling of solidarity is further strengthened with the reappearance of Al Braggs and Vi Campbell for the final selection of the evening. Bobby is a big man and not exactly graceful; so it is difficult for him to enact his lyrics in the manner of, say, Chuck Berry, who often dances as he sings and plays guitar. In *That's the Way Love Is* (and in some other numbers as well) Al Braggs choreographs the lyrics, and Bland works with him in the same way that he cooperates with soloists in the band. Because the lyrics of this song are so similar to those of *Stormy Monday* it is not often that they are used in tandem to climax a performance. Usually one or the other brings the show to an end.

Monday's so good;
Tuesday's so cruel,
One day you're sooo happy now,
The next day you're in tears.

So you take it where you find it,
Or leave it like it is.
That's the way it's always been.
That's the way love is.

Wednesday's all right
But Thursday's all wrong
One day, you are with your baby,
The next it's all gone.

So you take it where you find it,
Or leave it like it is.
That's the way it's always been,
That's the way love is.
(band interlude)

While the band plays, Al Braggs and two of the Bland Dolls enter from the wings doing a little dance step. They dance up to and around the microphone. At the end of each of Bland's lines they shout, "That's the way it is!" then do circular steps in different directions; their bodies wheel, and the three heads converge at the microphone at the exact instant when the vocal response is called for. This separation-and-reunification pattern is repeated during the next few verses.

Friday you'll beg her, Saturday she'll plead,
One day she'll say she loves you,
The next day she might leave.

So you take it where you find it,
Or leave it like it is.

That's the way it's always been,
That's the way love is.

It seems so fair sometimes
But that's the way love is
It makes you want to cry . . .
But that's the way love is.

I know you don't know what I'm talkin' about, baby,
Because I don't believe you ever been in love,
But that's the way love is.

Braggs breaks away from the microphone at this point and begins to inch across the stage on one foot in time with the music. The audience applauds, and Bland holds out a hand to Braggs, who is slowly but surely propelling himself to center stage. Bland goes on singing, "I see you comin'," "You're doin' all right," "Don't stop now, baby," "You're lookin' good." Each time he is answered by the girls with "That's the way it is." Finally, Braggs reaches out his hand, achieves his goal, and falls exhausted into Bobby's arms as the curtain closes and Bobby sings,

That's the way it's always been,
That's the way love is.

It is difficult to imagine a more simple and direct way of dramatizing solidarity and the basic idea that we're all in this thing together. It is interesting that *all* the instances of direct unification and cooperation are man to man—Bland in relation to Al Braggs and vis-à-vis various soloists in the band. These ritualistic acts certainly have an aesthetic *raison d'être:* Bobby needs these choreographic and instrumental extensions of himself to round out his image as the complete blues artist and unifying force. But there are probably other reasons for these displays of brotherhood. Obviously, if a woman were to be united with Bland before the world, it would tarnish his reputation as a man for all women; but it is more important, I think, that he be perceived by the Negro community at large as a man among men, or, better still, as a leader among men. Braggs' final pilgrimage across the stage and the feeling of mutual respect that Bland creates with his supporting soloists contribute to this effect. The more Bobby initiates and integrates successful teamwork on stage, the easier it is for men to identify with him, the greater his sex appeal for women, and the higher his status within the lower-class Negro community as a whole. The "lower-class" label may be misleading here, however, since Bland fans tend to have middle-class aspirations, and in a sense Bland's success and his appeal are functions of each other.

In the foregoing description, the familiar concepts of charisma, catharsis, and solidarity have been illustrated in passing but are of central concern. Bland's performance represents a dramatic synthesis of these forces as they are welded together in the more potent aesthetic patterns of Negro culture. In the following chapter, these concepts and others will be applied to an analysis of the role of the blues artist, the responses of his audience, and the emergent soul movement.

From "Wasn't only my songs, they got my music too"

Barry Lee Pearson

HE JUST drank himself to death. Well, it's mostly a habit. They just get to running with those types of people, you know, drinking, and they always drinking. Somebody buying them a drink and they don't know how to turn it down."[1]

Besides the bottle, the bluesman also copes with physical violence—although the two are often related. But here too, stereotype and reality merge. According to popular opinion, the blues artists' world includes nightly murders and fights, and in the real world artists have traditionally played tough clubs where audiences worked hard at blowing off steam. But tales of violence are somewhat exaggerated—or in any event represent unusual working conditions. Still, musicians tell of dangerous clubs, "buckets of blood," and of witnessing shootings, cuttings, and other mayhem. Although they avoid working such places—if they can—they know most people are interested in violence, that fights or murder make a good story. And since they have experienced or witnessed violence, they have a story to tell.[2]

The bluesman, stage center, is capable of being either hero or scapegoat. For an audience or an individual turned evil and ugly, there is no more convenient victim, and the musician knows this. It only takes one crazy drunk or jealous husband to end it all, and while a few bluesmen are fighters, most prefer to be thought of as lovers. Both can be dangerous.

The intentional violence directed toward the musician can be attributed to his visibility and attractiveness. Simply being in the spotlight can be dangerous, because others may envy your position. Byther Smith illustrates the problem and how the performer learns to cool down dangerous customers:

"He come up to me and says, 'You think you are really something because you up there playing that guitar,' he says, 'and you got every woman in here looking at you.' He says, 'You think you're something don't you?' I said, 'No. I'm not as much as you because you're more than I am because you had money to pay to come in and see me.' I says, 'I didn't have no money.' So I had to think of something to tell him to make him feel that he was as much as

---

Reprinted from *"Sounds So Good to Me": The Bluesman's Story*, by Barry Lee Pearson (Philadelphia: University of Pennsylvania Press, 1984), 101–4.

I was, you know. Because I told him, I said, 'I'm not as much as you are because you had the money to come in, to pay and to spend.' I said, 'I don't have no money to spend.' I said, 'That's why I'm working here, because I don't have anything!'"[3]

The bluesman improvises on and off the bandstand.

No matter how well the bluesman learns to cope with tavern patrons or how fast he can jump out the window, he most fears being the unintentional victim because there's nothing he can do to prevent it. Unintentional violence is quite literally out of control. James Thomas points out the problem of random violence in a southern club:

"Well, it's dangerous now in these nightclubs. It's like you in a big nightclub and they get to shooting, you don't never know which way that bullet's going. Cause plenty people done got killed—wasn't shooting at this person, but kill somebody else. There was a man in the country killed a man, killed two men, but one of them he wasn't intending to kill."[4]

Otis Rush parallels this statement in the Chicago context:

"It's very, very, very hard. It's dangerous. Cause anybody can start a fight and get it. Hey, a bullet don't care who it hits, or a chair or a brick, or something, you know—

"Yeah, well, there's a lot of places I won't play because of, uh, peoples are so evil now today. There's a lot of confusion all over. I try to pick up a few places I won't be running into that, cause I'd rather play my guitar. I don't want to fight."[5]

How does the artist counteract so much "evil" and "confusion" without allowing it to consume him? Otis Rush tries to keep away from the dangerous clubs, in a sense taking the music out of the volatile atmosphere in which it developed.

For Byther Smith the fear of being shot by accident almost came true:

"I was playing with Ricky Allen. We was out of Joliet one night, playing out there, and they got to fighting in that place. They got to fighting in that place, and man, I have never been so scared in my life.

"And it didn't scare me at first, but when I got ready to take my equipment down and looked at my guitar—I had a red fender guitar like this one I have over at T's [Theresa's]. They had about three shots, and one guy or two guys had got shot. I heard em say that three of them had got shot, but I know they shot three or four times in that place and one bullet went in.

"A boy was playing organ—you know how they got that great big Hammond organ speaker—I'm standing up there and I was leaning up against that organ, just playing. I was just playing and a bullet hit up above my head up there. But I thought this was the man playing the organ, hit down on the organ. I never even opened by eyes. I was just standing up there. I heard the guns shoot, but I thought they was shooting just cause it's New Year's night, you know. And I thought there was some people in there shooting fireworks and things. And all of a sudden I heard them screaming and hollering, 'He shot him. He shot him. He shot him.' And I decided I better get down behind my amplifier.

"I chose to duck, and when I pulled my guitar off—I don't know when the bullet hit the guitar, honest to God I don't. I jumped on behind this speaker cabinet for the organ, I laid down behind there. Peoples running all up on that bandstand going down to the basement and hid.

"When we got ready to take down that night and I was looking at my guitar and I saw this busted, you know, the wood busted. After looking at it, and the corner, right where the guitar come right down across this part of it, of your body, there's a bullet from about a twenty-five automatic was stuck in that guitar.

"And on my way home that night I got to thinking. Supposing that went on through there, and maybe he'd missed the guitar and got me. And I was driving around, I got so nervous like that. I pulled over to the side and stopped. And the highway patrolman pulled up behind me there and a state trooper asked me, 'What's wrong?' And I told him, I says, 'I didn't mean to park here.' He says, 'You'll have to go.' I said, 'I'll go, but you have to give me a minute to get myself together.' I says, 'I just got off of work and guy got to shooting and people got killed up there, got shot, and I got to thinking about it. I'd like to show you my guitar, how close I come to the bullet hitting me.' He said, 'Okay, sit there until you get yourself together.' I said, 'I'll be all right,' I says, 'but right now I just can't drive.'

"So he pulled out there in front of me, went on. But then I was just like that, and the more I got to thinking about it, you know, just pressed down on me like that. It was really bad."[6]

While tales of violence tend to be blown out of proportion, the working artist who must go on stage night after night cannot afford to forget about it. Otis Rush has paid his dues:

"Yeah, it is dangerous. Very, very much so. Cause there's been so many fights. Hey, you up there playing music, right? What the hell do you know about what's happening out there, somebody fixing to blow somebody's brains out, you know. I've seen it happen in so many places I've played. Somebody lay out dead in front of the bandstand. I've seen it several, several times. I say several, six or seven times saw people get killed."[7]

Sometimes the bluesman feels a premonition, as Byther Smith did, a sense of danger in the atmosphere of a place:

"There used to be a place over here on Lake Street. I went there and I worked a couple of times and I refused to go back the next time. And I called the man up and told him to get somebody else to play because I couldn't stand the atmosphere of the place.

"It used to be a place out on Roosevelt Road they used to call 'the Bucket of Blood.'[8] I went there one night, hooked up my equipment, and I just got to looking around and I took down my equipment and walked out. Now, I had to pay a fine because I had signed a contract.

"Now, I had to pay a fine. I had to pay twenty-two dollars that night for leaving. I went there and hooked up my guitar and tuned up with everybody, and I got to looking around there and it just look like death was in that place. And I told the man, 'Man,' I says, 'look, I ain't playing.' I says, 'I'm not going to play here.' And I never did go back to that club. I never have been back in there no more. Never did."[9]

Notes

1. J. T. Adams, at his home, Indianapolis, Indiana, March 1976.

2. Actually, fights in blues clubs are quite infrequent. In Chicago some clubs are in tough neighborhoods, but generally once inside a blues club you won't get into trouble if you behave yourself.

3. Byther Smith, at his house, Chicago, Illinois, May 1974.
4. James Thomas, at my home, Bloomington, Indiana, March 1973.
5. Otis Rush, Wise Fools, Chicago, Illinois, December 1973.
6. Byther Smith, 1974.
7. Otis Rush, 1973.
8. The traditional name "The Bucket of Blood" has been applied to a number of rough taverns, but it is tied especially to Chicago. James Thomas spoke of a friend who he said got killed in Chicago: "He was up there about three or four months, and he got killed, place called 'The Bucket of Blood' in Chicago. You heard of it, 'The Bucket of Blood'?"
9. Byther Smith, 1974.

7 Racism and Social Protest

"NIGGER and the white man playin seven up," runs the rhyme, "nigger played a seven, scared to pick it up." A simple game of chance, a recreation, but with one tragic rule that overrides all others: if you are African American, you must not win. It is dangerous, even deadly, to win, and you must negotiate a victory so as to seem that you have won without winning (we think of the dilemma of Trueblood in Ellison's *Invisible Man*, who had to move without moving), the seemingly dispassionate, almost joyless demeanor of Joe Louis in victory being a prominent example. Often, what seems to be true on the surface reflects neither the reality of the situation nor the desire or intentions of those involved.

Over the years, commentators on the blues have debated how much social protest is present in the blues. On the one hand, those who see the blues as relatively silent or passive in the area of social protest point out that (1) the blues is primarily a music intended for entertainment, to accompany dancing, for example, and does not, therefore, aim at delivering social commentary; (2) the lyrics are, in fact, primarily about love relationships between men and women (and sometimes people of the same sex), not about racism or injustice; (3) there are other African American musical forms that more directly—even if metaphorically—state social concerns and confront issues, such as spirituals, jazz, soul, folk tales, and toasts; and (4) blues singers have not tended to be in the forefront of the civil rights movement, as some other people from the entertainment industry have been. Conversely, those who see a strong strain of social protest in the blues counter that (1) even though songs are recreational or for entertainment value, that does not preclude the strong African and African American tradition of songs of social allusion and commentary from operating; (2) in fact, even though lyrics are frequently about love relationships, an African American tradition of masking (which includes such works as Paul Laurence Dunbar's "We Wear the Mask," the blues lyric "you don't know my mind / when you see me laughin I'm laughin to keep from cryin," and the anecdote included in "I Got the Blues" in this volume regarding the fabricating of an opportunity to yell at a mule in order to vent frustration over mistreatment) may conceal under the surface of the lyrics other concerns or dilemmas. For example, Paul Oliver and Angela Davis have suggested that spousal mistreatment may be a metaphor for social mistreatment; (3) just because other forms seem to have confronted social issues more directly, that does not mean that they are absent in the blues, since different forms with different demands, settings, and purposes may generate different strategies of expression; and (4) even if it is true that blues singers have not been visibly in the forefront of expressing social concerns—which may be because they have not frequently had the clout to gain such a forum—critics such as Larry Neal and Amiri Baraka have emphasized the revolutionary nature of the blues embedded in the artistry itself, which has delivered a subtle but powerful social commentary whatever the songs may seem to be about.

The carefully crafted tunes of singer-pianist Eddie Boyd are among the mournful joys of postwar blues recording, especially his classics "Five Long Years" and "Third Degree." However, the preamble to Boyd's recording career, unfortunately sidetracked by disputes with recording executives, was marked by the racism and prejudice all too common in the lives of African Americans. In Part I of his interview with *Living Blues* co-founders Jim and Amy O'Neal, Boyd speaks bitterly and defiantly of his experiences as a black man subjugated to the order and violence of unscrupulous whites, and of his efforts to live a life of dignity and independence, self-identification and self-determination.

Many students of the blues who began familiarizing themselves with the blues in the late 1950s and early 1960s through the popularizing agent of the folk boom received some of their first serious discussion of the genre from Samuel Charters in such works as *The Country Blues* and *The Poetry of the Blues.* In the latter work, Charters took up the subject of protest in the blues with a chapter-opening volley that has been much challenged subsequently: "There is little social protest in the blues." Differentiating between complaint and protest—a distinction recently challenged by Angela Y. Davis in *Blues Legacies and Black Feminism*—Charters enumerates a number of individual complaints as expressed in blues lyrics, but argues that a larger social element is lacking in the songs, that complaints are primarily personal, and that songs about relationship difficulties predominate. In *Early Downhome Blues*, Jeff Titon also takes up the subject of the relative paucity of overt social protest in blues songs and addresses the question of whether covert protest in the form of blues portraying aggression occur as the result of the sublimation of racial frustrations and anger, but he rejects the notion as a negative rather than positive role for the blues singer, since it allows racial hostilities and injustices to continue by diverting attention away from the racial problems. It seems likely that the question of whether blues singers consciously encoded racial protest beneath the surface of their song lyrics or expressed such issues unconsciously in their songs—or whether the songs simply did not have anything to do with social protest—will of course not be definitively answered, but there are sufficient diverse pieces of evidence, interpreted in conflicting ways, to keep us wondering about this issue for a long time.

For some examples of blues songs that feature socially relevant/protest material, the reader should listen to the following recordings:

J. B. Lenoir. *Vietnam Blues*. Evidence CD 26068.
Various Artists. *Defiance Blues*. House of Blues CD 51416-13402-4.
Various Artists. *Hard Times*. Rounder LP 4007.
Various Artists. *News and the Blues*. Columbia CD CK 46217.
Various Artists. *Roosevelt's Blues*. Agram CD 2017.
Josh White. *Complete Recorded Works in Chronological Order Vol. 4*. Document DOCD 5405.
——. *Free and Equal Blues*. Smithsonian-Folkways CD 40081.

Recommended Further Readings

Tad Jones. "Separate but Equal." *Living Blues* 77: 24–28.
Margaret McKee and Fred Chisenhall. *Beale Black and Blue*. Baton Rouge: Louisiana State University Press, 1981.

From "Living Blues Interview: Eddie Boyd"

Jim and Amy O'Neal

EDDIE BOYD: When I first started trying to play music, I first started to play harmonica, and I didn't like harmonica because it seemed like it was such poor excuse for a musician to me in those days, you know. So then I tried playing guitar and I could learn to play two melodies. And I played a lot of gigs playing guitar, but I wasn't really playing nothing, though. But I used to could holler real loud and I would play tunes, you know, like I'd start off, I'd play this one real fast, and then the next one a little bit slower, playing the same thing and singing different words. And a little slower and a little slower until it come to be a slow drag, you dig? But the people went for it, because the market wasn't so full of entertainment then.

Living Blues: Was this in Clarksdale?

EB: No, that was after I had went to Memphis. When I first started trying to play the harmonica, I was in Mississippi. Not in Clarksdale, though, it was out on the plantation when I came up. Out at Stovall. I was born on another little farm joining Stovall called Frank Moore's farm, up on Coahoma County. But my grandfather, my mother's father, raised me, and he was living on Stovall. I stayed there from the time I was, oh, I guess three months old till I was 14 years old, and I left home at that time.

LB: Then you went to Memphis?

EB: Yeah. I went to Memphis and we stayed there a little while, and I left there and went to Blytheville, Ark., and then back to Memphis. And that's where I stayed and that's where I got started out of, really, there on Beale Street.

LB: So you never lived in Clarksdale?

EB: I lived there a short while. But that wasn't the place for me. I mean, I couldn't see myself getting no place.

LB: Were there other musicians on Stovall's then that you knew?

EB: Yeah, it was a fellow named Louis Ford and a piano player named Lit Fraction. He didn't live there all the time but he would come and go. He was a fine piano player. I mean

Reprinted from *Living Blues* 35 (Nov.–Dec. 1977): 12–15. Used by permission of the authors.

he wasn't just a blues artist, he was a real good musician, 'cause he made his living mostly playing for white people in those days.

LB: Did he have a group?

EB: No, he played solo.

LB: Louis Ford recorded some with Muddy, didn't he, when the Library of Congress came through there?

EB: Yeah, but I was gone at that time. I heard about that. I think at that time I was in Chicago.

LB: Did you know Muddy Waters back then?

EB: Oh, yes. The first day I went to school, Muddy and I went to school the same day and we was going to school together until I left home and we would play together mostly every day, and fight every day! I'm about two years older than Muddy, but Muddy in those days was a real strong guy. He really could whip me but I mean I never did accept that for real, you know. We'd still fight. But we couldn't stay away from each other, though. We loved each other but that just was a habit of kids, you know.

LB: Were you playing music together?

EB: Oh, we played a little bit together here in Chicago a few times. But my style and Muddy's style doesn't really blend, you know. I'm not criticizing him, now. But there's plenty people have different styles, they can be in the same field, but I mean if you have any originality, you're bound to sound different from the other person.

LB: Did you learn harmonica or guitar from anybody, any of those musicians around there?

EB: Guitar? No, I picked that up by listening to Memphis Minnie on records. What I could play was something similar to what she was doing. I wasn't really playing, I admit that. I liked guitar but I never could halfway master the instrument. I don't master no piano, but I mean I'm comfortable, you know.

LB: Did you know Memphis Minnie then?

EB: Yeah, I knew her. I played a few gigs with her in Chicago after I moved to Chicago.

LB: Were you playing with different people when you were playing guitar? Did you have a little band or were you playing by yourself?

EB: No, always alone. I wouldn't even accept playing with nobody with the guitar 'cause I was playing so wrong so many times until I knew I would have thrown the other people off, you know. But I had sense enough to know that. I wasn't like some people, was playing wrong and didn't know it. But I mean it was a matter of existing and not meeting that ding-dong, if you know what I mean. That's that bell on the plantation.

LB: Where were you playing?

EB: Well, it used to be a cat had a joint at Hernando, Miss. He used to come up and get me on weekends and I would go right back on a Saturday and I would work Saturday and Sunday and the first part of Sunday night down at his joint. So he'd pay me about $4 and my food, and that was enough to keep me and my mother, too, till I opened next week, you know. Well, that was during the Depression time. I used to work on Beale Street seven nights a week for $7 a week and I started playing when it started to getting dark. I didn't work by no clock. When the people started coming in the joint, I started playing, and I'd play to the next morning sometime until 9:00 the next morning. I never got tired. I enjoyed that.

LB: Were you playing piano—

EB: Yeah, I was playing piano then.

LB: At the time you moved to Memphis, had you already started playing piano?

EB: Yeah. Well, I started trying to play the little time I was in Blytheville, Ark. But in Memphis where I kind of called myself got in the know a little bit. But first in Memphis I was working with a guy named Willie Hurd who was a drummer. He always kept a pretty good little group. And he was well known. He was a good hustler, you know. He had a car and everything. So he would find those gigs in Arkansas and different places for those colored people, and you *had* to be able to sing and he couldn't sing and none of those musicians could sing. But I could play a little piano and sing a whole lot, so I mean I would fake a lot, but I was always singing all right, you know. So that's how I got known to the musicians in Memphis. Then after I played there on Beale Street a while solo, then I formed me a little group.

LB: Who did you have in your first band?

EB: The first time I had a cat names Sims played drums and Alex Atkins. He died here in Chicago—used to play with Memphis Slim. Well, at that time he was playing clarinet only. I had drums, clarinet and piano. To me that sounded like a 20-piece orchestra for me, you know. There were some great days.

LB: What kind of material were you doing?

EB: Oh, I was doing all of Roosevelt Sykes' tunes and playing some of Count Basie's tunes and faking a whole lot of Fats Waller tunes. I was a great faker in those days. Once I had a trumpet. I took the trumpet and took the mouthpiece off and then I put a kazoo into that. That was down in Memphis. And a friend of mine, he died too, his name was Snook Anderson. He was a real wonderful guitar player and piano player. So when there wasn't a piano in the place, he played guitar and I played the trumpet. And those country people really thought I was playing trumpet, you know. I'd watch Louis Armstrong, Cootie Williams, and all those cats. They would come down there sometimes and play one of those white theaters in Memphis, and we watched them from up in the buzzard roost, you dig? Once in a while they would play a colored theater on Beale Street there, the Palace. But we'd see 'em a lot of times when they didn't play there because we would go to those segregated theaters and go up in the buzzard roost and watch the musicians. I'd watch how those cats finger that trumpet, you know, and I would do all of that, and it would knock those people out. Well, I could holler real loud, and I was hollering through that kazoo, and wow! They thought I was a terrible trumpet player. And I couldn't play one note really if I were playing a trumpet!

LB: Who else did you have in your band then? Were there other people that worked with you after that?

EB: Oh, yeah, after I got started I mean I used various musicians. I really can't think of all of those guys' names because it was changing so fast, you know. If the gig I had didn't pay, if he could make 50¢ more with somebody else and he had agreed to work with me, well, he just said, "Well, look, man, I can make a half more, so I'm going with blah-blah, you know." And I'd have to get some other cat. It wasn't often in those days that I had no set group. Mostly I was playing solo. And that's the way a whole lot of musicians was working then, if they played piano. And the piano players was the men who kept jobs the most.

LB: So there were a lot of piano players along Beale Street?

EB: Oh yeah, man.

LB: Remember some of 'em?

EB: Yeah, there was P.R. Gibson, Hatcher, Van Hook, and one piano player who I always admired named Struction. I done forgot what his real name was. [Bill Johnson.] But he's still living. And there was another cat named Booker T. they called Slopjar. He was a heck of a piano player in those days. But I think I heard that he hasn't improved any from those days from back there, and he stopped playing. I think he plays for church now, a little bit. And there was one cat was born with seven fingers. I think it was three on his left hand and four on his right hand. But he wasn't handicapped at all. His name was Jack Slack. I never heard a cat could make no beautifuler sound that that cat. I used to follow him up and down the street before I learned how to play, and just go to those joints and *look* at this cat play. Man, he could play more with those seven fingers so *easy*, much better than a whole lot of cats, I mean, who's supposed to be good piano players, that had all their fingers.

LB: Who were the piano players that influenced you the most?

EB: Roosevelt Sykes and Leroy Carr. Those were the men whose music used to ring in my ears so much till I tried to stop it and I couldn't. I'd go to bed, the last thing I'd hear when I'm dozing off to sleep and when I wake up the next morning. I wouldn't be humming that song, I mean out, but I was always singing it inside and hearing that piano that they played. Always.

LB: Was Roosevelt playing in Memphis then?

EB: Well, sometime he would come. He'd never stay in no one place too much, especially down there. I think he stayed in St. Louis more regularly than any other city, in those days.

LB: How about Leroy Carr? Did you ever see him?

EB: I never saw him in person. But he was really one of the men who really gassed me, man. Singing and playing.

LB: What was it like in Blytheville when you were there?

EB: Well, it wasn't too much going on in the city, but it was a whole lot of joints then throughout southern America, you know. On those plantations, because they had a system. A big plantation would have maybe two boarding houses for people who were not sharecroppers. For what they called drifters. People just work a little and leave, you know, so it was always a boarding house to keep those people, and they would give some man the privilege to run the boarding house. He'd feed and sleep those people, and then they'd give him the privilege to sell whiskey on that plantation. And then he was protected by the owner of the plantation because he was keeping labor for the big boss, you know. And I used to play at a lot of those boarding houses. I did a whole lot of that up and down 61 Highway, like from Wilson, Ark., up to Catron, Mo. That used to be my beat. I'd watch the cotton harvest, I would start off like in Erin(?), Tenn., where they start to gathering strawberries. And then when that harvest was over for strawberries, it'd be time to chop cotton. So I'd make it on to Arkansas. 'Cause it lasted longer and it was more joints there. And so I always liked to be in Missouri, though, in the fall of the year. 'Cause it wasn't *so* racist. I mean, you know, I had a lot of trouble in those Southern states, 'cause I was always trying to be a musician. I didn't have no interest in nothing else. And in those days, man, a white man down there didn't see you being nothing but a farmer, you know what I mean.

And so I would have a lot of trouble in those small towns, 'cause I couldn't hide. I could hide on a Saturday night or whenever it was payday, you know. But when all those people were strung out across those cotton fields and I'm sitting up there in one of those boarding houses, you know, they would always be asking me who do I work for and why ain't I chopping cotton or plowing or whatever it might be it happened the people were doing. So I would always have to get going. That's why I went to Missouri, because if you were playing at a boarding house, I mean, they'd consider you having a job. They didn't try to make me go out in the field. But Arkansas and Mississippi—man, they would tell you, "Boy, we ain't lookin' for no damn piano thumpers. We lookin' for somebody to chop cotton or plow." And they wasn't joking. You do it or get going, or they would beat you to death.

LB: So you had to chop cotton?

EB: No, I had to *leave*. If I wanted to chop cotton, I would have stayed on Stovall's plantation. I got sick of that farming, man, soon as I was 11 years old. When I got to know a little bit about mathematics and I found out, when my grandfather would clear at the end of the year 12 or $1800, man, we had worked for 35 to 52¢ a day, all of us. That's all you got. But you get it in a lump sum, it seemed like a whole lot, you understand. But it didn't to me. I didn't like that hot sun and plowing that slow mule. That kind of obligation was too much for me. I just was born with that type of mentality. I had a lot of trouble with those plantation owners.

LB: Were there any rough experiences that you had?

EB: Oh, man, I had a lot of bad experiences in America. Before I was 23 years old there was three times they plotted in Arkansas and Mississippi to mob me.

LB: White people did?

EB: Sure, it wasn't no other kind gonna do that, man. Yeah, just because I was no "good nigger," you know. If a white man hired me to work for him, many times I had to work for them for a short while, you know. But I didn't tell him I was gonna work for him two weeks. I'd just work till I make a payday and get me some money to catch a bus and ride where I'm going. I never hoboed. I would hitchhike, 'cause that wasn't against the law. But if they catch you on a freight train or something, then they would put you in jail. Then the big white man who owns the county fair, he come and pay your fine, then you go there and work for him a year, you understand. So I never let them catch me hoboing. I paid my fare. That's why if I get stranded someplace, I'd take that job, whatever it was doing, and work for this big boss man, make a payday. And a lot of times I have worked up to one day of the payday, and then he come and tell me I wasn't working fast enough, and "Hey, nigger, you keep up with them other niggers out there. When you see me coming, you must put some speed in you . . ." Those are not the words he was really using, you know, I mean, I'll hold back the profanity. But he could talk to you real cruel, man. I told him, "Listen, when I came here to work, I told you my name and I'm no nigger. I call you Mr. George, or whatever his name may be, you know, and I'm not grown, so I know you're not gonna call me mister if I was 50 years old. But I would like for you to call me by my name. I'm no nigger and I'm no Negro. I'm a black man and you're a white man and I respect you, that I know how the system goes. But don't get that idea that you're gonna whip me, 'cause I told you I didn't want you to curse me and you don't drive me, 'cause I'm not a prisoner." And many times, man, when I would tell him that, some of 'em had enough nerve to try to get off that horse to whip me. One, I hit in the back with a hay fork, man. I did, 'cause he would have killed me if I let him get off that horse. And I had to go across a bayou that was full of those cottonmouth moccasins and full of thorns. I didn't even step on a pebble, man. And in the middle of it—I can't swim today—the water was over my head. I just walked on through it. I don't even remember holding my breath. That's why when people tell me there's no God, I don't like to talk to people like that. 'Cause He saved me through all of that, man. You know what a poison lamp eel is? That's a type of snake. Well, that slough was full of those things, man. I never seen nothing. And made it to the levee. This was up the road from West Memphis, Ark. And I walked down that levee to that Harry Ames Bridge and walked across. And I was nothing but a 17-year-old boy. They really didn't pay me any attention. I was all muddy and wet, but that was nothing. You see a thousand other little blackies like that, you know. So that's how I got back to Memphis without getting killed. And this bad chief of police from West Memphis, Ark., called Cuff, he was such a cruel white man. Man, he have kicked babies out of pregnant women's stomachs right there in West Memphis, Ark. He came that night, him and four other men, looking for me at my mother's and her husband's shack where they were living there on a sawmill job. He ripped my mother's mattress up looking for me, in that one-room shack. I was such a small boy until he thought I could have been hiding in there. And I were already in Memphis then.

Another time, I was trying to work for a white man for about three months to get me a car to meet the harvest. Me and my first wife, Georgia Mae. This was at Senatobia, Miss. When I hired to him, I knew he had that habit of whipping black men. But I've never been whipped by no white man. It have been some jumped on me but God give me the strength to whip him. Because I didn't have that fear and when I fight him, that's make him have more fear than he would have if he were fighting you, you know. This man came out, I was working for him. I was cutting some bushes. And so he came standing over me and the wind was blowing from him to me, and he had the TB. He smelled *so* bad, you know, and I figured that I'm swallowing his germs. He says, "God damn it, you been foolin' around." I said, "Listen, when you were trying to hire me, I told you, I'm no boy, I proved that I am a man, 'cause my wife is cooking for you. I'm no boy, that's No. 1, and if I was, I'm not your boy. Black as I am, I don't have a drop of white blood in me, so you have no right to try to whip me, you understand." And he said, "Well, don't, listen here, you must remember I'm a white man." I said, "I wouldn't give a damn about that. I knew that when I were hiring to you. I'm a human being like you, man, and I'm not a prisoner. I don't owe you anything. I'm working for you." So he was afraid to touch me. And when he went on back in the house, I just give it up. Well, OK, I guess the cat's all right, you know, he's not gonna bother me no more. And man, soon as the sun started sinking, just some instinct came out of the blue and told me to leave. We left, and do you know, about 11:00 that night I was in Memphis, 'cause I found a colored man who I could trust to take me to Senatobia to catch the train to go to Memphis. He went in the drug store and bought the tickets for us, and we sit in his car behind the warehouse where they unload all the freight, until the train conductor had blowed that whistle the third time. Not the first or second did I go out. 'Cause when he blow the third time, the door's gonna close and the train's gonna take off. But the man had went in and put our suitcases on the train so we didn't have nothing to do but step on. It only took a hour and 39 minutes to go to Memphis. And by 11:00, I guess I had took a bath and was in the bed at my mother's house. Leon Price was the guy I was working with, and his brother was named Ray. Then they had a little old chief of police of Senatobia named John. Deep racist people as you ever could see, man. They called him out to join them. So if they get a chance to catch me and kill me, why, the law was with them, you understand. And they rode around that night looking for me all over the vicinity, man, about a 40-mile square—that's about 160 miles. They even went to Georgia Mae's grandfather's house and asked about me. They got in Ray's pickup truck and roamed those fields.

There was another time that from out of the blue came that warning to leave, man. They would have *killed* me, man, 'cause they were always beating some black man to death down there. I went through terrible experiences here in this country, man. Just because I didn't buck dance and scratch behind my head when I'm looking at a white man. If a white man talked to me, he didn't want you to look him in his eye. But this was the act of a whole lot of black cats: "yessir, well, um, yessir," and he never looked in that man's eye. But when I looked at him, that make him angry. But if I was working for him, I must look at him to understand what he's trying to tell me to do. I've seen cats, man, when the man go to tell him to do something, he start to running to do something before he understand what he's supposed to do, you know. And when I didn't act like that, man, wow, I was some kind of outcast. Many times he told me, "You better leave here, nigger, 'cause you're a bad influence for the good niggers." I said, "Thank you very much. I'm on my way." But he would be expecting me to say something else so he would have a chance to shoot me. 'Cause he wasn't gonna whip me, you know. So if I didn't let him whip me, then he would kill me, and it was really just like I would take a fly swatter and kill a fly, you know. It meant no more than that. Especially for me.

LB: You must have been thinking about moving North. When did you start thinking about moving North?

EB: Well, after I was in Memphis, then after I was married and I had been following those cotton harvests and I had got a little confidence in myself as being a musician, you know. That I *was* some kind of musician. Then I heard that the market was open in Chicago and I heard that it wasn't so racist up here. Really and truly, if you compare those days with the worst racism in Chicago, I mean it seemed like it was none. 'Cause he doesn't know what it was, man, for a black person in the South. I mean with my type of mentality. Some people, it was all right, you know, because they just really thought, "Well, if he's a white man, he's supposed to have that much authority over me." But I always seen people as people, you know. I respect a black man or a white man just equal if he respect me. And if he didn't, I always used to hate rich white men 'cause they'd want you to bow to them. But his money didn't make me bow, 'cause he wasn't gonna give me any of it, you know what I mean. It just only made me look humble to him for nothing. But I thought of coming to Chicago where I could get away from some of that racism and where I would have an opportunity to, well, do something with my talent. And no matter where I roam, I forget that I was born in Mississippi unless'n the question comes up, because this really seems like home. Chicago. The most enjoyment I ever had out of life in America was in Chicago. It wasn't peaches and cream, man, but it was a hell of a lot better than down there where I was born.

LB: Did you ever do any broadcasting on the radio down South?

EB: No, I never did.

LB: Did you have any opportunities to record?

EB: Down South? In those days? No. There's only a very few people did. 'Cause it was a lot of artists coming to Chicago to record. Some hoboed their way up here to record. They wasn't getting a lot of money out of it, but I mean they was doing what I was trying to do. I was trying to get my name on records so I figured that would help me to make a living.

LB: How often would you play for white audiences down South?

EB: Oh, I have played for white audiences a lot when I first started out. When I'd play with those groups, I used to play a lot of popular tunes. That wasn't really what I wanted to play, but I couldn't play no blues all night for no white people in those days, like today, you know. 'Cause you know how they used to be, man. They called that race music and niggerism and all that kind of stuff, so you'd have to play what they liked. I used to sing a lot of western tunes—I wasn't playing 'em, because they didn't ever know the difference. 'Cause it was understood that I was the singer, so I didn't try to tell those musicians that I could play perfect. But I could stay within the key and somewhere around the melody and then they must cover up for me, you know. And that's the way I made it. The tempo and the melody, that's all the people were listening to. They didn't know whether I was playing the right chords or anything like that. Once in a while I was playing the right one. But more often I wasn't. But nobody heard that because the piano wasn't amplified, and so those horns could very well cover up for me. Once I played at a place called the Day and Night Club, about six miles north of Clarksdale. That was a white joint. And I played there a long time with a guy called Kid Derby. He was a banjo player. He couldn't sing, but he knew a whole lot of popular tunes, and he was very popular.

LB: He was a black banjo player?

EB: Oh, yeah, in those days there wasn't no such thing as no black and white cat working together, if they wanted to. It was just that racist down there. When I was playing with Derby, we played at the Night and Day Club for about seven months. That was a good gig. I made $10 a week there and all my food. And it was a Greek running the place at that time, so he'd give us enough food to take home, to last you till you come back. So I really could say I was getting my board and $10 a week. And that was a fortune, man. I lived like a king then. You could buy a car and anything like that on time if you had a job like that.

Now, I have worked on the same stage that some hillbillies worked on, with that same group. With Derby and his band. At this time it was a white man running that club. I mean, a Greek is white, too, but but down South in those days, man, a Greek was white when he compare me and the Greek. But when he compare a Englishman or Irish or Dutch or something, that Greek was a Greek, you understand. So, they had a little dressing room out back of the club, and this white man, he put a strand of hay-baling wire across there and hung a whole string of potato sacks up there and put on one side "Niggers," and (on the other side) "White Folks" (laughs). Those white boys took a knife and cut that sack down from end to end and piled it up in front of that nightclub and poured kerosene on it and set it afire. That was the hillbilly boys. That's why I have never been able to be no racist, because I learned better than that early. 'Cause there's a lot of people doesn't understand that how good some people is, and how real. 'Cause these cats didn't have to do that, man. They were Mississippians and that was in Mississippi. They really had a funny way of talking, 'cause they were uneducated cats, man, they played those fiddles and banjos. But they could play, man, and sing those hillbilly songs. He said, "What the hell this son of a bitch talkin' about? Putting a damn sheet up here between us and y'all. It ain't hardly steppin' room in here. We play on the same stage. He don't know music is natural international, don't give a damn what color he is." I say, "Hello, brother, welcome to the club."

And I have seen some white men in the South who have admired some black men for having that gift to progress. Sometime I have been chauffeuring for one big rich white man and he'd be talking to another one. He could talk about anything, even about black people, 'cause he didn't recognize me as nothing but a tool, you know. He said, "Yeah, you know, now I could help old so-and-so. If he had about $40,000 and another 10 years, he'd be worth 2,000,000." 'Cause he watched what this cat started off as a sharecropper and how he made them few little pennies multiply, and now he own a little farm of his own. But he said, "But damn, if that nigger got that much money, shit, he would be able to socialize with us. I can't let him do that." But he would help him to a certain extent. But that was better than one who said, "I want to kill him if I see him progressing."

You know, it's a lot of white people here, man, who hate black people and have never really, *really*, said hello to one, you know. He just look at you and listening to the propaganda and look at all of what happened to the black slaves. I wouldn't say that those people all were dumb. They had their sense about things and their culture, but they were kidnaped and brought over here and *destroyed*, you know. They didn't even let families stay together, man.

LB: Did your older relatives ever talk about slavery?

EB: My father's father used to tell me a lot about that. That's why this Boyd, that's just an identification for me like my social security number. I don't respect that as nothing. 'Cause I'm no Boyd, man. Because my grandfather once was named Calloway all his life till he were 18 years old. Then he was named Boyd 'cause another man bought him and that was his name. So those Boyds and Smiths and all that, man, it's nothing but bull to me. I mean, you have to use it to be identified. You have to wear that brand but you don't have to brag about it. It's nothing for you to be proud about. And so a lot of these people here today have followed that old slaveryism about black people, and they just create some image about you and doesn't know anything about you for real.

From *The Poetry of the Blues*

Samuel Charters

THERE is little social protest in the blues. There is often a note of anger and frustration; sometimes the poverty and the rootlessness in which the singer has lived his life is evident in a word or a phrase, but there is little open protest at the social conditions under which a Negro in the United States is forced to live. There is complaint, but protest has been stifled. Slavery, and the period of semislavery that followed the Civil War, was a period of helpless bewilderment for the Negroes who found themselves swept into it. Their tribal beliefs were useless, and they were deprived of the education that might have given them some understanding of the social situation around them. When education finally did come they found that there was still almost no encouragement for them to enter fully into American life. The young Negro, whatever his ambitions or social attitudes, is driven into an unwilling acceptance of what is little more than a semicitizenship. If he is unable to accept it he has little choice except to either leave the country or to become a social rebel and express his frustrations in a brief burst of violence. Much of the fear that the southerner has for the Negro is his awareness of the brutality of his treatment of the Negro and the realization that in a moment the smoldering animosities could flare up into an open rage.

It is almost impossible for the white American to realize how tightly he has united against his black fellow citizens. The oppressive weight of prejudice is so constricting that it is not surprising to find little protest in the blues. It is surprising to find even an indirect protest. The white Americans who think of themselves as liberals are often impatient with what they feel to be the failure of the black men and women that they meet to either be more militant in their demands for equality or to respond to a lessening of the pressure. They have, to some extent, overcome much of their own prejudice, but they forget that the Negro still faces a hostile wall of hate and distrust. If a black man or woman is able to get an adequate education there is still little chance that there will be any kind of employment opportunity. If there is a job that pays well there is still the difficulty of finding a home. Even if a Negro has achieved some measure of success he is still restricted in his choice of hotels, restau-

---

Reprinted from *The Poetry of the Blues*, by Samuel Charters (New York: Avon, 1963), 152–73.

rants, neighborhoods, friends, and, in many areas, in his right to vote and his legal rights as a citizen. For the blues singer, at the lowest level of society, the situation is so intolerable that if he even thought about it for a period of time he would be destroyed as an individual. In the rural South, where most of the singers still live, every Negro is a marked man. If he protests, his job, his home, his family, and even his life, are at the mercy of his white neighbors, whose attempts to blind themselves to the situation with a meaningless paternal charity have only taken them closer and closer to the violence they have feared for so many years.

Even singers who have had considerable success have found it difficult to develop a social attitude in their blues. Big Bill [Broonzy] and Josh White both sang several blues which expressed their anger at the situation, but these came in their later years, when they were appearing before sympathetic audiences, often in Europe. Sometimes at a party a southern singer will begin drinking and his voice will take on an edge of anger, but his blues are still the personal expression of his loves and travels and disappointments. If he does become more general he will probably sing one of the two or three verses that are so widely known in the South that there will be no trouble.

> The nigger and the white man
> Playing Seven up,
> The nigger win the pot,
> But he's afraid to pick it up.

An old folk song is also well known, the references changed to suit the singer's own social background.

> The white man he rides in a great big car,
> The brownskin man does the same,
> The black man he rides around in a T-Model Ford,
> But he gets there just the same.

As Son House sang, at the persistent request of a field collector for the folk song archives of the Library of Congress,

> Down South when you do anything that's wrong,
> Down South when you do anything that's wrong,
> Down South when you do anything that's wrong,
> They'll sure put you down on the country farm.
>
> Put you down under a man called Captain Jack.
> Put you under a man called Captain Jack.
> Put you under a man they call Captain Jack.
> He'll sure write his name up and down your back.
>
> Put you down in a ditch with a great big spade.
> Put you down in a ditch with a great big spade.
> Put you down in a ditch with a great big spade.
> Wish to God you hadn't ever been made.

In the blues, however, can be seen some of the attitudes which the social pressure has built up in the Negro. It is not social protest, or even complaint, but in its implications there is reflected some of the difficulty of the continual adjustment to the insult and the injustice of the color line. There is a continual concern in some blues with the varying shades of skin color. Since it was the blackness of the skin that marked the Negro it became associated with evil. One-String sang,

Well, that jet black woman like to scare my mule to death.
That jet black woman like to scare my mule to death.
If I had not had that special, man, I would have run myself.

"Special" is a term for revolver. Cat-Iron repeated a commonly held notion that the black woman is a sorceress.

I don't want no black woman, fryin' no meat for me.
I don't want no black woman, fryin' no meat for me.

For she studies evil, she's liable to poison me.

Among the woman singers there was often a concern with the relationship between the color of their man's skin and his ideas of fidelity. Since a man with light skin was closer to social acceptance they often felt that he would be difficult to keep.

I don't want no brownskin, he won't do me no good.
I don't want no brownskin, he won't do me no good.
He'll fool 'round with other women, won't come home when he should.

They felt that a man with darker skin would be more grateful for their attention.

Going to find me a black man somewhere in this town.
Going to find me a black man somewhere in this town.
Black man will stay by you when your brownskin throws you down.

But the concern with skin color is a minor strain in the blues. Related to it is the difficulty which Negroes from rural areas had adjusting to the life of the cities both in the North and South. Sophistication, like a light skin color, represents a step away from the lowest level of society. Rabbit Brown, a street entertainer in New Orleans, sang,

'Cause I was born in the country she thinks I'm easy to rule.
'Cause I was born in the country she thinks I'm easy to rule.
She tried to hitch me to a wagon she tried to drive me like a mule.

Furry Lewis had the same comment.

When I had my money it was hello sugar pie.
When I had my money it was hello sugar pie.
Now I done got broke it's so long country guy.

The most complete break that someone could make with the life in the South was to move to a northern city, but it was a frightening trip for a man or a woman who had little social experience and knew little about life outside the county where they had been born and raised. They found themselves without jobs, sometimes without even anyone to help them, usually living in a crowded tenement in a crumbling slum area. It was difficult to stick it out during the first months. During the depression years thousands were driven back to the South. Often in the North they found themselves ridiculed by people who had arrived a year or so earlier, and had already acquired some knowledge of the city life. In a reference to the yearly payments which a sharecropper was used to receiving, Jazz Gillum sang,

> You want a whole lot of credit
> To pay off once a year,
> But you owe the salary you make
> For just liquor and beer.
> You better go back to the country,
> 'Way back out in the woods.
> I'm tired of hearin' you hollerin' City Lights ain't no good . . .

They found, too, that the life was still difficult.

> I would stay up North, but nothing here that I can do,
> I would stay up North, but nothing here that I can do.
> Just stand around the corner and sing my lonesome blues.

The women found that they couldn't handle the city men. Ida Cox complained,

> When I was down South I wouldn't take no one's advice.
> When I was down South I wouldn't take no one's advice.
> But I won't let that same bee sting me twice.
>
> I don't want no northern yellow, no northern black or brown.
> I don't want no northern yellow, no northern black or brown.
> Southern men will stick by you when the northern men can't be found.

Sometimes alcohol was used as an escape from the situation. Furry Lewis tried to reason with his woman.

> Now you know you didn't want me when you laid down across my bed,
> Drinking your white lightning and talking all out of your head.
> You know you didn't want me when you laid down across my bed.
> Drinking your white lightning and talking all out of your head.

J. D. Short referred to wine, the common drink with impoverished alcoholics, white and black.

> Knees got the rickets, head got to rolling.
> Keep on drinking, sweet Lucy, life won't last me long.
> I drink so much wine,
> Yes, so much wine.

Black Ace warned his woman that if she didn't stop drinking she'd find "the deal gone down," meaning that their relationship would be over.

> You know you spent all your money for Seagram "Seven Crown."
> You know you spent all your money for Seagram "Seven Crown."
> Now if you ever gets sober, mama, you will find that the deal's gone down.

For many of the singers, footloose wanderers at the edges of society, prison is a harsh reality. In the smaller towns of the South any unfamiliar Negro could be picked up for vagrancy. There was a continual need for labor on the roads and for city maintenance; so local sheriffs had no hesitation in making arrests. Behind the police brutality and intimidation there was also the fear of the Negro, and the helplessness of the lone black man as he tried to stand up against the corruption and the dishonesty of southern "law enforcement" was one of the most demoralizing aspects of his situation. It was an unwritten law in many areas that a Negro who had a white man behind him could commit almost any crime against another Negro without fear of the law. The most serious crime was to be without a white man willing to talk to the sheriff and the judge. Sleepy John Estes referred to this in his "Jailhouse Blues."

> Now, I was sitting in jail with my eyes all full of tears.
> Now, I was sitting in jail with my eyes all full of tears.
> You know I'm glad I didn't get lifetime, boys, that I 'scaped the 'lectric chair.
>
> Now, I consulted lawyers, and I know darn well I was wrong.
> Now, I consulted lawyers, and I know darn well I was wrong.
> You know I could not get a white man in Brownsville, yes, to even go my bond.

In 1959 Dr. Harry Oster of Louisiana State University recorded prisoners in the penitentiary at Angola, Louisiana, and in their blues was a desolate cry of defeat, of anger, and of despair. They were men for whom time had become only a monotonous succession of days without meaning or hope. Guitar Welch sang,

> I'm gonna shake hands with my partner, I'm gonna ask him how come he here,
> I'm gonna shake hands with my partner, I'm gonna ask him how come he here.
> You know I had a wreck in my family, they're gonna send me to the old electric chair.
>
> Wonder why they electrocute a man at the one o'clock hour at night?
> Wonder why they electrocute a man, baby, Lord, at the one o'clock hour at night?
> The current much stronger, people turn out all the light . . .

Hogman Maxey felt his weariness and pain at the end of the long prison day.

> Oh, black night fallin', my pains comin' down again.
> Oh, black night fallin', my pains comin' down again.
> Oh, I feel so lonesome, oh I ain't got no friend.
>
> Oh, oh, just another pain, oh Lord, it hurts so bad.
> Man, just another pain, oh Lord, oh it hurts so bad.
> Lord, I feel so lonesome, baby, lost the best friend I ever had.
>
> Oh, sheets and pillow cases torn all to pieces, baby, bloodstain all over the wall.
> Mm, sheets and pillows torn all to pieces, baby, and bloodstain all on the wall.
> Oh, Lord, I wasn't aiming when I left, baby, and the telephone wasn't in the hall . . .

For Robert Pete Williams, the blues were an expression of his feeling at the injustice that had been done to him.

Some got six months, some got a solid year,
But me and my buddy, we got life time here.
Some got six months, some got a solid year,
But me and my buddy, we got life time here.

Six months, oh baby, let me go to bed.
I've drunk white lightning, gone to my head.
It gone to my head.

I've got so much of time, darling,
It worryin' me, oh babe.
You know this time killin' me,
But I just can't help it, darling, I just got to roll.

You know that old judge must been mad.
Yeh, that old judge must been mad, darling.
When he gave me my sentence he throwed the book at me.

First time in trouble I done get no fair trial at all, oh Lord.
Seem like to me, baby, they locked the poor boy in jail.

When there is complaint in the blues it usually is personal, even if it concerns the drudgery of the laboring jobs that are often the best a Negro can hope to get.

I do more work, Lord, than a pair of twins.
I do more work, Lord, than a pair of twins.
My body's aching from my head down to my shins.

Bessie Smith complained of the washwoman's life.

Sorry I do washing just to make my livelihood.
Sorry I do washing just to make my livelihood.
Oh the washwoman's life it ain't a bit of good.

Rather be a scullion, cooking in some white folks' yard.
Rather be a scullion, cooking in some white folks' yard.
I could eat up plenty, wouldn't have to work so hard.

But even the life of a cook was difficult. For Clara Smith it meant the scorn of other women.

Women talk about me, they lies on me, call me out of my name.
They talk about me, lies on me, call me out of my name.
All their men come to see me just the same.

I'm just a workin' gal, oh workin' gal, kitchen mechanic is what they say,
I'm just a workin' gal, oh workin' gal, kitchen mechanic is what they say,
But I'll have an honest dollar on that rainy day . . .

Sometimes the complaint was more general, at the W. P. A., or at unemployment. In nearly all of these blues, however, the complaint is still personal, or the larger social theme is only used to introduce one of the common blues attitudes. A W. P. A. blues will often have as little real social consciousness as a blues of infidelity. The first verse may mention the subject,

W. P. A. done tore my baby's playhouse down.
W. P. A. done tore my baby's playhouse down.
Done took my baby, she's nowhere around,

but the verses that follow usually return to a standard blues pattern.

I wonder where's my baby, I wonder where could she be,
I wonder where's my baby, I wonder where could she be,
She's gone somewheres, she's gone and left poor me.

In 1930 Bo Carter sang of the first months of the depression, but three of the six verses are concerned with problems that this has raised between men and women, and one concerns his own sexual relationships. The other two directly mention the difficulties of the period, but each verse ends with a refrain insisting that Carter isn't going to worry about it.

These times and days, I can't understand.
Just 'cause times is hard the women want to change men.
'Cause times is hard, but I don't worry.
I got the whole world in my hand.

These times and days worried everybody's mind.
You often find men who haven't got a dime.
'Cause times is hard, but I don't worry.
I got the whole world in my hand.

I'm tellin' you the truth, as the good Lord who's above,
The women all 'stand, can't live off of love.
'Cause times is hard, but I don't worry.
I got the whole world in my hand.

Let me tell you one thing, woman, surely true,
That as you change men you won't have no more.
'Cause times is hard, but I don't worry.
I got the whole world in my hand.

The clothes in rags, no shoes on my feet,
But that ain't the main question, they want something to eat.
'Cause times is hard, but I don't worry.
I got the whole world in my hand.

It was late last night, hear my baby cry,
You know it's all night long, daddy, please take your time.
'Cause times is hard, but I don't worry.
You got the whole world in your hand.

The momentary reference to the social conditions is immediately vivid, but it is almost lost in the emotional emphasis of the blues. There are a few singers who try to deal with social problems, but even in their own compositions it is still love, and its pain and disappointment, that dominate the blues. One of the few songs which makes a fundamental attack on the American system is, ironically, an attack on the economic system rather than on the social justice. Bessie Smith would have found it difficult to record a song that dealt with racial intolerance, but she was able to sing a blues that is openly socialistic.

> Mr. Rich Man, Mr. Rich Man, open up your heart and mind.
> Mr. Rich Man, Mr. Rich Man, open up your heart and mind.
> Give the poor man a chance, help stop these hard, hard times.
>
> While you living in your mansion you don't know what hard times means.
> While you living in your mansion you don't know what hard times means.
> Poor working man's wife is starving while your wife is living like a queen.
>
> Please listen to my pleading, 'cause I can't stand these hard times long.
> Oh, listen to my pleading, can't stand these hard times long.
> They'll make an honest man to think that you know is wrong.
>
> If all men thought the better a man would start again today.
> If all men thought the better a man would start again today.
> He would do anything you ask him in the name of the U.S.A.
>
> When the war is over all men must live the same as you.
> And the war is over all men must live the same as you.
> If it wasn't for the poor man, Mr. Rich Man, what would you do?

The blues, however, has lost little by its lack of concern with social protest and comment. The greatness of poetry is its power to express the individual emotion, the personal response to the reality of experience. It is the cry of pain, the shout of joy, the whisper of love, and the murmur of despair at separation and death. Even in the poorest poetry it is the momentary emotion which is usually the poet's concern, rather than the opinions and details of social commentary. As Archibald MacLeish expressed it,

> "The things of the poet are done to a man alone . . ."

In the greatest blues there is often a reflection of the social restrictions which encircle the singer, but in the situation he is able to find the things ". . . done to a man alone . . ." In his "Crossroads Blues" Robert Johnson cries out to someone to save him as he stands at a crossroad trying to get a ride. There is nowhere for him to go. He doesn't know of any women living nearby. In desperation he calls to someone passing to tell his friend Willie Brown, another singer from Clarksdale, that he is ". . . sinking down." The reason for his desperation is that he is in a Mississippi county that jails any Negro found on the roads after dark. But instead of an explanation he only cries out in his fear, and it is the intensity of his cry that gives his blues its poetic strength.

> I went to the crossroads, fell down on my knees.
> I went to the crossroads, fell down on my knees.
> I asked the Lord above, have mercy, save poor Bob if you please.
>
> Uumh, standing at the crossroads I tried to flag a ride.
> Standing at the crossroads I tried to flag a ride.
> Ain't nobody seem to know me, everybody pass me by.

And the sun going down, boys, dark gone catch me here.
Uumh, oh dark gone catch me here.
I haven't got no loving sweet woman, that love will be near.

You can run, you can run, tell my friend poor Willie Brown,
You can run, tell my friend poor Willie Brown,
Lord, that I'm standing at the crossroads, babe, I believe I'm sinking down.

There will be social change, too, in the United States, and if the blues simply mirrored the protest of the moment they would finally have little more than an historical interest, like the songs of the suffragettes or the Grange movement. Instead, as the Negro in America has struggled to find a life on the other side of the racial line he has turned to the blues as the expression of his personal and immediate experience, and in their directness and in their concern with what the singers call the ". . . true feeling" the blues express a larger human reality. In the honesty of their emotion is an insistent reminder that on either side of the racial line live only other men and women, who find the same moments of pain and joy in the experience of life.

From "The Songs
Formulaic Structure and Meaning in Early Downhome Blues"

Jeff Todd Titon

FANTASY in blues lyrics may be linked to racial protest. Listeners have been perplexed because they cannot find much overt racial or social protest in blues lyrics. A number of explanations are possible. It has been argued that blues singers were not angry, since they were well treated, entertaining whites as well as blacks. But the assumption that the singers did not feel white hostility and the constraints of the plantations system, or that they were not aware of the anger of their fellows, goes against so much else in oral black culture that it is most unlikely. Rather, this is the wishful thinking of those who would turn downhome life into plantation pastoral.

If the blues singer did feel anger, why did he not express this overtly in his lyrics? I suggested earlier that as long as there were other outlets for protest, the relatively newer blues songs may simply not have been thought of as a proper protest vehicle. Because blues, at an early stage in its development, was made available by vaudeville singers and then through W. C. Handy's popular songs, their themes as well as their forms were fixed in the minds of others who took blues up. Singers learned that the proper subject of a blues song was the pain and joy of love, not racial protest. One possible explanation for the paucity of protest themes in *recorded* blues is that since the singer, whose name was on the record, could be traced, caught, and punished, he would have exercised self-censorship. While this is a reasonable argument, singers probably did not censor their lyrics in the recording studio. For one thing, the formulaic process of blues composition makes it difficult to ascribe to the singer the ability to censor lyrics at will. Undoubtedly, some protest phrases would have crept in despite the singers' best efforts. Furthermore, where we know that lyrics were substituted, anti-black phrases were, as Tony Russell has pointed out, "usually directed against sections of the black public."[1] Here, for instance, is a common-stock American folksong couplet at least as old as its appearance in the 1867 collection *Slave Songs of the United States:*

> Some folks say a Nigger won't steal
> I caught one in my cornfield.[2]

Reprinted from Jeff Todd Titon, *Early Downhome Blues: A Musical and Cultural Analysis* (Urbana: University of Illinois Press, 1977), 186–89. Used by permission of the author.

In his 1931 recording of "Preachers Blues" (Vocalion 1643), Kansas Joe McCoy used the line

> Some folks say a preacher won't steal

which fits the folk stereotype (one that crosses racial boundaries) of the preacher. This does not rule out the possibility that the line was on occasion sung

> Some folks say Mister Charlie won't steal

in live performance to black audiences, confirming their suspicion that the white boss was not to be trusted.

In a recent essay, William Ferris, Jr., attempts to show that blues singers' repertoires for black audiences contain obscene lyrics and racial protest not sung in front of white audiences.[3] But his case is clouded by the history of black singers like Leadbelly and Big Bill Broonzy, who composed blues songs on protest subjects after they were discovered by white folklorists and promoted for northern, white audiences sympathetic to the Civil Rights movement and other liberal causes. Even so, their repertoires did not contain very much overt protest. And who can imagine that Leadbelly did not have some help composing "Bourgeois Blues"?[4] That is not to deny that he was angry about housing discrimination in Washington, D.C., but it is to suggest that his expressing that anger in a blues song may have issued from his desire to please his new audience.

If blues lyrics contain little overt protest, could they contain coded messages, covert protest? If so, the messages are so well hidden that one doubts the code's existence. Blues songs carry sexual messages, often obscene by contemporary standards, in a series of quite obvious and frequently hilarious metaphors for the sex act (e.g., Memphis Minnie's "Sting me bumble bee until I get enough"). But part of a code's effectiveness in songs, or in any form of entertainment designed to please a large audience, depends upon most of the audience deciphering it. Besides occasional reference to "Mr. Charlie," I can find little evidence of a protest code in the vast majority of blues lyrics.

Covert protest need not be presented in code; its expression may be unconscious. It might be argued, for example, that the songs offer an unwitting allegory in which deception in love signifies treachery in race relations. Perhaps the boasts and bluffs of the singer are sublimations of racial hostility. Richard Wright observed that "a submerged theme of guilt, psychological in nature, seems to run through [blues songs]. Could this guilt have stemmed from the burden of renounced rebellious impulses?"[5] Paul Oliver goes a step further, claiming that in the blues of lost love the "singer has found, consciously or subconsciously, a vehicle for protest. . . . Neither the blues singer or his listener is likely to be aware of the function of the songs as a sublimation of frustrated desires. . . . But . . . they sublimate hostility and canalize aggressive instincts against a mythical common enemy, the 'cheater.' "[6]

This is an appealing theory. The mistreating lover is transformed into the mistreating white plantation owner, the sheriff, and other authority figures, while the drama of the song revolves around the victim's response to mistreatment. Experiments have shown that people who are nonaggressive tend to exhibit more aggression in Thematic Apperception Tests than do people who are aggressive.[7] But plantation-system blacks had outlets among themselves for aggression even if they had to show deference among whites. There is hostility expressed between lovers in blues songs; but it may simply be a reflection, not a sublimation, since, after all, lovers did mistreat one another, argue, and fight. Nor is aggression a dominant theme in early downhome blues lyrics. (It becomes much more important in blues songs of the Depression and the post–World War II era.) Finally, it is one thing to say that aggression is a sublimation of racial hostility, and quite another to speculate that it must therefore be an expression of racial *protest*.

Viewed as a sublimator of racial hostility, the blues singer performs a negative role in the black community, feeding fantasies and diverting energy into forms (including art) which allow racial injustice to continue. The character Clay in LeRoi Jones's play *Dutchman* observes, for example, that if Charlie Parker had not blown his violence into his horn, he would have murdered whites on the street. But viewed as an artist, the blues singer plays a positive role. He offers his listeners an imitation of life, an imitation so real that the traditional wisdom of blues lyrics becomes proverbial expression and offers explanations as well as directives. Linear, temporal logic is replaced by an endless circular structure, the parts of which may be interchanged to provide different perspectives each time they are sung, each time they are lived. James Baldwin's account of the novelist as artist serves also to indicate the positive function of the blues singer (or the preacher, for that matter) in the black community:

> You [the artist] are compelled . . . into dealing with whatever it is that hurts you. . . . You must find some way of using this to connect you with everyone else alive. . . . You must understand that your pain is trivial except insofar as you can use it to connect with other people's pain; and insofar as you can do that with your pain, you can be released from it. And then hopefully it works the other way around, too; insofar as I can tell you what it is like to suffer, perhaps I can help you to suffer less.[8]

Art gives us order. But it also gives us disorder—a great deal more than life does, for we put life's perceptions into preconceived constructions of reality. The disorder of painful experience, the gap between what we hope for and what happens, can be prolonged and experienced at will only through art. The more we experience it—connect our pain with other people's pain—the more we can adjust and adapt, learn and grow.

Notes

1. Tony Russell, *Blacks, Whites, and Blues* (London: Studio Vista, 1970), p. 18.
2. William F. Allen, Charles P. Ware, and Lucy M. Garrison, *Slave Songs of the United States* (1867; reprint, Freeport, N.Y.: Books for Libraries, 1971), p. 89.
3. William Ferris, Jr., "Racial Repertoires among Blues Performers," *Ethnomusicology* 14 (September 1970): 439–49. A balanced discussion of protest themes in blues lyrics can be found in Samuel Charters, *The Poetry of the Blues* (New York: Oak, 1963), pp. 98–110.
4. The text is given by Moses Asch and Alan Lomax in *The Leadbelly Songbook* (New York: Oak, 1962), p. 24.
5. Richard Wright, foreword to *Blues Fell This Morning* (New York: Collier, 1963), by Paul Oliver, p. 9.
6. Paul Oliver, *Screening the Blues: Aspects of the Blues Tradition* (London: Cassell, 1968), p. 258.
7. Eric Klinger, *Structure and Functions of Fantasy* (New York: Wiley, 1971), pp. 326ff.
8. James Baldwin, Buddah 2004, *The Struggle*.

8 On the Record

JOHNNY Parth's Document reissue program has pushed back to 1890 the date that African American music made its audio recorded debut. However, it was not until 1920 that African American recordings of the blues finally emerged on phonograph records. In "The Social Context of Black Swan Records," Ted Vincent offers a fascinating portrait of the variety of conflicting economic and sociopolitical pressures—particularly class pressures and prejudices—that shaped the policies and output of Harry Pace's Black Swan Records, self-described as "The Only Phonograph Company Owned and Operated by Colored People" in its time, and a significant forerunner to the operations of such African American recording industry entrepreneurs as Berry Gordy of Motown Records. By examining the backgrounds and aesthetics of Black Swan's board of directors, as well as their social agenda for African Americans, Vincent demonstrates the additional pressures, sometimes self-imposed, under which the company operated as it attempted to market its favored classical music in the face of undeniable evidence that its jazz and blues would be much more profitable. It is a compelling and instructive glimpse into the operations of a groundbreaking organization that unfortunately found its business at odds with its aesthetic and social values and vision and, combined with the unfair advantages that larger companies enjoyed in the market, found itself unable to compete and survive, though not before making some valuable contributions to American music.

Of course, the emergence and success of blues on record is of great significance since, in a market-driven economy, that which does not sell is quickly eliminated, so that early success, which produced recordings that have significance in and of themselves, also helped make possible subsequent recordings by blues artists who might never have been recorded at all.

Naturally, not everybody has responded gratefully to the recording industry's economically motivated efforts, not only on account of its frequent exploitation of African American performers (as explored in Barry Lee Pearson's excerpt about the perception of rampant rip-offs in the recording industry with regard to recordings) and dissemination of racist stereotypes in race record advertisements (see Jeff Titon's *Early Downhome Blues*, pp. 218–60 for an in-depth discussion), but also because of the influence that the industry had on the nature of the forms and subject matter of the blues. Some critics have suggested, for example, that the 12-bar AAB form became entrenched at the expense of other patterns—by the frequent recording of that form, which was then in turn imitated by other performers who heard it and were asked to perform it live. Additionally, the length restrictions of the 78 rpm record—2 ½ to 3 minutes or so—might also have influenced composers and performers to develop songs of such a brief length, as might have a desire on the part of record company executives for the blues song to develop a story thematically rather than proceed associationally in the lyrics. As we have already said in the introduction to the folklore section, some early folklorists and scholars lamented what they saw as the overemphasis on prurient subjects or sophomoric metaphors when dealing with sexuality, while others sorrowed at the replacement of the performance in its original social context with a flat, brittle, dizzyingly spinning platter with a hole bored in its center. Ultimately, however, it seems that the widespread dissemination of the blues and the convenience offered by the recorded artifact to those who might not otherwise have the opportunity or wherewithal to encounter live all of the various blues performers they wished to hear offset, or at least soften overall, the negatives that may have been brought to the tradition by the industry, though of course the extensive distribution of some element that is false or embarrassingly racist cannot be perceived as a positive.

Recommended Further Reading

Jeff Todd Titon. *Early Downhome Blues.* Urbana: University of Illinois Press, 1977. 218–60.

The Social Context of Black Swan Records

Ted Vincent

HARLEM-BASED Black Swan Records of Harry H. Pace, proudly owned and managed by "members of the race," pioneered in getting black artists in jazz and blues recorded during the initial years of the Jazz Age. Between its founding early in 1921 and its demise late in 1923, Black Swan produced over 180 records. The only other black-run record companies of the time produced 12 and three records respectively. And while Black Swan produced enough of the revolutionary jazz sounds to have a major impact upon jazz and blues, the company also inaugurated the recording of black performers in classical music.

Music historians, however, dutifully mention Black Swan's role while failing to give details. One likely cause of the omission is a hesitance to elaborate on the almost embarrassing social environment around the Black Swan offices. It was a company led by—for lack of a better term—"Wannabees." With filmmaker Spike Lee and others now focusing attention on this group, the full Black Swan story seems about due.

The first months of Black Swan in 1921 were followed with eager anticipation in the black press of the day. One report quoted founder Harry Pace declaring: "There are 12 million colored people in the U.S. and in that number there is hid a wonderful amount of musical ability. We propose to spare no expense in the search for and developing of the best singers and musicians among the 12 million."

The first recordings were cut in late February and early March of 1921 and released in May. Pace had started in a one-room basement office, and by the end of the company's first year he had developed a thriving business with a three-story office in Harlem. A problem of inadequate record pressing facilities was solved in mid-1922 after Black Swan moved into a partnership with Olympic Records.

A large majority of the first "jazz records" was in the form of blues. In the summer of 1920 Mamie Smith broke through on the OKeh label to become the first black singer to release a blues record. The next two years would be a critically formative period in a decade-long musical bonanza in blues records. At the end of 1922 Black Swan had played

---

Reprinted from *Living Blues* 86 (May–June 1989): 34–40. Used by permission of the author.

a major part in the new phenomenon. The discographies show the company put on record 91 blues or blues-related songs, a total for Black Swan that put it in second place behind the 105 of OKeh Records, the much larger company that was a division of the German-financed General Phonograph Corporation. Black Swan blues production was well ahead of its nearest challengers—Columbia with 43, Arto with 33, Paramount with 18, and the French-financed Pathé with 14.

Competition was fierce. Between July 1920 and December 1922 at least 13 record companies recorded black blues singers; and by 1924, eight of the 13 were either out of business or had failed and been reorganized. A number of additional failures comprised many of the small companies that had leased blues record masters from the 13 that did the actual recording sessions.

The black vocalists recording blues and jazz in this period were almost always female—in part out of racist fears of a black male crooner being listened to by a white woman. Black Swan helped to break this taboo, recording two male singers in its blues record series.

In 1921 the record market was being flooded with hundreds of dance band records. All but a small fraction of the dance records were from white groups, and most of the output was quite forgettable musically. Black Swan began business with poor facilities for recording more than one or two musicians at a time, but Pace nonetheless managed to record 23 sides of instrumental blues and jazz by black performers—in the process showing white companies that there was a commercial market to be tapped. By the end of 1922, Black Swan's 23 instrumentals by black performers were barely behind the industry leader Emerson, and well ahead of third place OKeh, which had 14.

Black Swan's instrumentals included the first recorded piano solo by "the father of stride piano," James P. Johnson, and a Black Swan piano solo by Fletcher Henderson may have been the first piano recording with a boogie woogie walking bass. The impact of Pace's records on the dance mania of the period was suggested in a *Billboard* magazine gossip column item that told of a Hollywood movie industry matron bragging that her parties were more fun because she had a collection of Black Swan records.

The musical impact of Black Swan was, however, relegated to an early experimental period of the Jazz Age. The best music was very definitely to come later, on the records of other companies. Then, too, the quality of Black Swan music is hard to gauge because the recording facilities were not the best—although one historian who commented on the studio problems did note that the records were nonetheless "well produced." Perhaps the most relevant data is in the tabulations of numbers of records produced, which shows impressive numerical strength for the one major black-owned record company as of the end of 1922. The following year would see jazz and blues recording explode—both numerically and in quality.

The year 1923 ushered many a future star into the recording end of the business, including the two best-remembered blues singers of the era, Bessie Smith and Ma Rainey. The year also marked the first recordings of such historic jazz groups as King Oliver (with Louis Armstrong) and the first Jelly Roll Morton bands.

The number of black women blues singers recorded went from 19 in the last six months of 1922 to 38 in the first six months of 1923, and 42 in the last half of the year, these being the figures from the standard discographies of Brian Rust, Tom Lord, Robert Dixon, and other sources.

Harry Pace's Black Swan company helped prepare the way for the breakthroughs of 1923, but it would share little in the great boom year. The company made its last records in August 1923 and officially sold out to Paramount in March 1924.

For a brief time the Black Swan Record Company had exemplified the best of black effort to market black culture, the best of what "black capitalism" could offer in the United States. Harry Pace became a popular "inspirational" speaker, as in the *Chicago Defender* report of Pace giving a lecture on "self-reliance" to a group of black business people in Brooklyn.

The company's floundering, just when the big stars and big money were starting to flow through the business, was in part related to serious problems in the social setting of Black Swan. But before elaborating on those aspects of the story the economic setting needs further details.

The bottom line for Black Swan was that it was a small company in a new industry (its monthly production was about a tenth or less of the giant Victor). As in so many other new industries, when the giants get interested in a product line, the essentially unfair nature of capitalism comes to the surface—insofar as the smaller companies are concerned.

For instance, publicity on the initial financial success of Black Swan, including accounts in the *Chicago Defender* and the national show business weekly *Billboard*, on how Pace was paying top salary to his lead blues singer Ethel Waters appears to have been noticed by the big companies. As the major companies with their superior banking connections became interested in black music, the pressures mounted on Black Swan.

By mid-1923 the input from the big companies was clearly evident in advertising in the leading black weeklies, such as the *Chicago Defender*, where Victor, Paramount, OKeh, Emerson, and other majors regularly ran ads two to three times the size of the ads for Black Swan. A year earlier Black Swan's ads had been quite comparable in size.

But beyond the economic hurdles, the story of Black Swan reflects the sharp and debilitating class and cultural division within black America of the 1920s, a schism expressed in the music world as a conflict between those who felt the future of black American music lay in jazz and blues, and those who wanted the emphasis on classical and other forms of "cultural" rather than "popular" music.

In 1921 the various degrees of "hot" to "cool" black music had yet to be defined. There were style differences between the generally younger musicians who liked jazz and the older musicians in the New York area who played in a ragtime style. One segment of the younger crowd tended to hang out with or work in the offices of Clarence Williams. In August 1922, Williams founded his "Home of the Blues" the Clarence Williams Music Company, a sheet music and music copyrighting concern. Clarence Williams' songwriting associates included Spencer Williams, Fats Waller, and Porter Grainger—the author of *T' Ain't Nobody's Business If I Do* and other classics. Williams marketed the blues successfully enough so that when his health began to fail in 1943 he was able to sell two-thirds control of his company to Decca Records for a reported $50,000—comparable to almost a quarter million in today's dollars.

Clarence Williams' blues taste stemmed from his background in Louisiana, where his father played blues guitar, and the young Clarence tap-danced for dimes on corners, when he wasn't working at sweeping floors at the local dance hall and brothel.

One of the problems for Black Swan was that the company's interest in jazz and the blues was compromised by the friendships and business connections the company had with people associated with that sizable segment in black society that was hostile to just about all the popular black musical forms, be they jazz, ragtime, or blues. Loosely representing this group was the two-year-old National Association of Negro Musicians (NANM), which included musicians of all fields but was dominated by college and school music teachers who were determined to push classical music. The classical music produced by Black Swan Records included performances by two performer/music teacher officers of the NANM, Florence Cole Talbert and Kemper Harreld. Typically, the black music teachers, like their white counterparts in this era, felt that "serious" training was essential. And while there were many sophisticated and jazz-oriented black music teachers, there were also those who seemed to share the notions of the majority of white music teachers that blues artists, who had yet to learn to read a symphony score, were not "real musicians."

It is in this context that one has to understand Black Swan Records, a company presided over by Harry Pace—a former college professor in Greek and Latin. The question around Pace's studio at Black Swan wasn't so much what kind of pop music would be recorded, but how far the company could profitably go with pushing classical music and avoiding pop.

Black Swan's difficulties were compounded by the company board of directors. Harry Pace appears to have been the only board member with any experience in the area of popular music. Pace had worked for almost a decade in partnership with the "father of the blues," W. C. Handy, in the Pace & Handy Music Company, the first sizable black sheet music concern. But for fellow Black Swan board members, Pace was surrounded by individuals with quite high-class musical tastes. The directors' list published in the February 24, 1923, issue of *Billboard* included: Dr. W.E.B. Du Bois, editor of the NAACP monthly, *The Crisis*; Dr. M. V. Boutte of Meharry Medical School; Dr. Godfrey Nurse, prominent physician and realtor; Dr. W. H. Willis, head of the Washington, D.C. medical association; Truman K. Gibson, insurance and banking executive; and among others, John E. Nail, reputedly the nation's wealthiest black realtor, with massive holdings in Harlem. Nail was brother-in-law of NAACP National Secretary James Weldon Johnson.

The input of the board is suggested in Black Swan advertising in the NAACP monthly, *The Crisis*. *The Crisis* was then a general interest monthly with much of its readership in the black colleges, the market of the young well-to-do in black America. For *The Crisis*, the ads of Black Swan had special emphasis on the company's "serious" and "classical" production (quite the opposite of the advertising in the mass circulation *Chicago Defender* and *Pittsburgh Courier*, where Black Swan featured the company's blues singers and rarely even mentioned that there were classical numbers). On the other hand, a full-page November 1921 spread in *The Crisis* divided the listings into four categories. At the top was "High Class"—classical records. Below the classical records was "Dance Numbers." Below them "Male Quartette," and at the bottom, "Blues."

The ad bias toward the classics was most strongly displayed in the January 1923 *Crisis*, and in the January through June 1923 issues of the black monthly of the cultural/left, *The Messenger*, where the following appeared:

> "Colored People don't Want Classic Music!"
> So Our Dealers write us. "Give Em Blues and Jazz. That's all we can sell."

> We Believe the Dealer is Wrong. But unless we furnish him with
> What he has Demand for, he will not handle our Goods.
>
> If you—the person reading this advertisement—earnestly want to Do Something for Negro Music, Go to your Record Dealer and ask for the Better Class of Records by Colored Artists. If there is a Demand he will keep Them. Try this list of the Better Class. . . .

The list included classical numbers and, among others, Stephen Foster's *Swanee River* in the form of a violin solo by Kemper Harreld.

It was quite clear within the first few months of Black Swan's record production that recordings of blues and jazz sold, while the attempts to market black recordings of serious music, including opera, failed. Nonetheless, much of the company's advertising continued to focus upon its classical singers.

Ironically, Black Swan wasn't able to sign the very top black concert stars of the time, such as tenor Roland Hayes, who began recording early in 1923 with a company in England.

The uneconomical advertising policy of pushing classics should be seen in light of the deep frustration among black lovers of the classics, music lovers who resented the reluctance of white record companies to record black performers of serious music. There were certainly good serious performers to be recorded. By the 1940s, according to historian Eileen Southern, four of the seven highest paid concert performers in the U.S. were black Americans. Until Black Swan, these performers had not been able to perform serious music on records. Then in May 1921 Black Swan's first two releases were classical numbers by Revella Hughes and C. Carrol Clark.

With the financially costly but explainable push for the classics in mind, many other decisions at Black Swan have a certain logic. For instance, when it came to choosing personnel at Black Swan, President Pace was less interested in jazz experience than in collecting musical talent that fit the definitions of talent handed down by the music teachers. So, to serve as Black Swan musical director Pace selected Fletcher Henderson, classically trained at Atlanta University. Henderson would go on to become a prominent jazz band leader and the nearest thing there was to an official father of swing music. It may be noted that swing leaned heavily toward the easy listening end of the spectrum, as opposed to hot jazz.

For the arranging of the music Pace selected William Grant Still, a not-very-jazzy individual, but certainly a well-qualified choice, considering Still's immense musical future as arranger for and writer of symphonies, scores for Hollywood movies, and the music for television shows, including the original "Perry Mason" and "Gunsmoke." Other officers of the company came out of backgrounds in music teaching, vaudeville, or musical show business.

Probably the strongest jazz influence was among the horn players and other sidemen hired to back up blues singers on Black Swan. The sidemen included a great many individuals who went on to long and illustrious careers in jazz and blues—including Don Redman, Joe Smith, Gus and Bud Aikens, Garvin Bushell, and Ralph Escudero.

The jazz histories include scenes of debate at Black Swan over just how much jazz and blues the company should produce. Ethel Waters, the best known of Black Swan's blues singers, recalled in her autobiography her first visit to the studios. "I found Fletcher Henderson sitting behind a desk and looking very prissy and important. . . There was much discussion of whether I should sing popular or 'cultural' numbers. They finally decided on popular . . . That first Black Swan record I made had *Down Home Blues* on side one, *Oh Daddy* on the other. It proved a great success . . . got Black Swan out of the red." Waters went on to become Black Swan's most-recorded blues singer. The company could have used more like her, for historians Charters and Kunstadt note that Waters was one of the very few Black Swan blues singers with "the rough, earthy touch that the audience was looking for." Charters and Kunstadt explain that Harry Pace "was in an awkward position. The Negro business community felt that the role of Black Swan Records should be to show the Negro at his best, and the music that was selling records, jazz music, and the blues, was considered degrading by many of Pace's friends. He tried recording novelties, but these were more in the style of the old minstrel show walk-around than anything else." Pace also tried classical music and Broadway show tunes, even West Indian calypso and march music.

Charters and Kunstadt are but two among many jazz historians who have commented on Black Swan's role in a light and breezy manner, taking literary advantage of the foibles of youth committed by the young staff, and getting the most out of anecdotes, such as the one on how Harry Pace lost the chance to be the first one to get Bessie Smith on record. Allegedly, the fastidious Pace threw Smith out of the Black Swan studio in the middle of her first cut, after he walked by and overheard the gruff Bessie say, "Hold it a minute, boys, while I spit." Historian George Hoefer adds, sarcastically, "Bessie went on, six months later, to pull Columbia out of receivership while Black Swan went bankrupt."

One has to keep in mind that collecting star performers was only part of what was needed for success.

There were distribution problems, there were problems of not making the right secret agreements with competitors to divide up parts of the market, and there were problems of having too many or too few records of the fast-changing dance crazes. It should be kept in mind that giant Columbia Records went broke even before little Black Swan's goof with Bessie Smith gave Columbia the chance for resurrection. That is, to understand the recording industry is to understand its basic instability.

Take the marketing problem, for example. For Black Swan to have produced records continuously from February 1921 through August 1923 has to be considered an achievement when one takes into account that Black Swan was marketing to a very economically disadvantaged population. And the distribution problems were compounded by the lack of either black-owned retail outlets, or a sufficient number of white-owned "ghetto" shops that would deal with a black company. The big white companies sold records at neighborhood "5 & Dime" stores, as seen in the Paramount ad saying its records were available at Kress Stores. Black Swan distributor lists did not show dime store ties.

Black Swan felt it had a special burden of showing "good taste" in order to fight the moral majority–type crusaders who were claiming that the "jungle rhythms" of jazz and "Negro music" in general, were turning America to a life of debauchery. "Did Jazz Put the Sin in Syncopation?" asked *Ladies Home Journal* in one of its many journalistic tirades against the new music. And it wasn't only whites who were critical. Most black ministers of that time seemed to think of jazz and blues as "that devil music."

Related to wild charges that jazz music was creating "a holocaust" of illegitimate births and other improprieties, there was the stereotype of black music as "shouts" and "stomps." Black Swan musical director Fletcher Henderson's reputation for over-orchestrated jazz and blues has to be seen in light of the understandable attempt to display complex structure. In the process, musicians like Henderson helped break new ground in melding European and African musical forms—as can be seen in the complex introductions and breaks in the classic blues that was the product of Bessie Smith, Ethel Waters, Rosa Henderson, Ida Cox, Ma Rainey, and the other recorded singers of the '20s.

In the case of Black Swan, the added frills on its jazz and blues numbers tended to kill some of the intensity. The result was generally too mellow to be memorable, and consequently Black Swan's recordings fall into forgettable "easy listening" modes and few have been reissued. Ironically, there were a sizable number of graduates from Black Swan's restrictive musical environment who went on with other companies to make a great flood of hot recordings that have been widely reissued and are available today in libraries and record stores. These performers include blues singers Alberta Hunter, Ethel Waters and Eva Taylor; pianist James P. Johnson; bandleader Henderson; cornetist Joe Smith and the other aforementioned sidemen.

Had Black Swan been launched a bit later in the decade, when a semblance of order came over the record industry, there might have been room for the two goals of pushing classical music (to a black public that didn't generally attend symphonies or the opera), and trying to turn a profit by producing enough of the music that the black public was buying.

But Black Swan came on the scene at a time of cutthroat desperate competition among companies. It was necessary for survival to make deals, Machiavellian alliances of sorts. It is in this context that we can try to understand the economic arrangement in April 1922 that put Harry Pace's Black Swan in partnership with the bankrupt white-owned Olympic Record Company. This peculiar deal opened Black Swan to the superior record-pressing facilities of defunct Olympic, in return for which Black Swan reissued old failed dance band records from the Olympic label. But the rereleased white bands now appeared on a black label, with fictitious band names, including the names of well-known black band leaders, as in "James P. Johnson's All-Stars" (without James P. Johnson or his friends) and "Henderson's Dance Players" (without Fletcher Henderson).

From the very beginning of the company Pace had advertised, as he did in the July 1921 *Crisis* monthly of the NAACP, that "Black Swan Records Are Made By The Only Phonograph Company in the World Owned and Operated by Colored People . . . The Only records made using exclusively Colored Singers and Musicians." By July 1922 Pace was no longer advertising exclusive black ownership and management, but the Black Swan advertisement in *The Crisis* that month still claimed, "The Only Records Using Colored Singers and Musicians Exclusively." And yet, under the heading "July Releases" were three dance band reissues of white bands.

Record companies of 1922 quite commonly switched labels on dance bands, in order to appear to be presenting a broader range, or to appear to have some "hot" group that had sold well for some other company. Since the bands themselves frequently used assumed names in order to get out from under an exclusive contract there were plenty of names of "alleged" top bands to go around.

However, Pace's blatantly fraudulent racial line had to hurt public confidence in his product, in the long run. The false labeling finally extended to having Fletcher Henderson record a dance record under a white name for a new Olympic Records series. And then, on the very last Black Swan record issued, "Pace really outsmarted himself," notes Fletcher Henderson's biographer Walter Allen. Pace released a Henderson dance record on Black Swan under one of the fictitious names he had been using as cover for the old Olympic white bands.

One of the achievements of Black Swan was to show the record industry that there was a sizable black market to be tapped, to prove that the popularity of blues singer Mamie Smith on OKeh in 1920 was no fluke.

Ironically, the Black Swan example helped get work for blues experts from the black community at the white companies, experts who made it possible for those companies to find and record the blues stars who were swamping the market, so far as Black Swan was concerned in 1923. Generally, these black employees for the big companies came from funkier social roots than did the crowd around the Black Swan studios. There was Clarence Williams up from the New Orleans street scene. Another talent scout for the big companies was Mamie Smith's songwriter Perry Bradford, who began his music career in the tough one-night-stand touring circuit around the turn of the century.

Some comparisons of musical emphasis can be made between Black Swan and the sheet music companies of Williams, Bradford, and Pace's old partner W. C. Handy. Black Swan had about one-third of its record production in blues, or blues-related items. Clarence Williams' large sheet music company appears to have had in this period a good three-fourths of his company's output in blues numbers. Blues appears to have comprised about two-thirds of W. C. Handy's sheet music offerings in these years. And Bradford appears to have had about 90 percent of his output in blues songs.

If Clarence Williams, W. C. Handy, and Perry Bradford could see that "the classic blues" was superior music deserving of emphasis, then why couldn't Harry Pace and company see it? Pace had worked with Handy in 1919 when Handy was telling the press that he "intends . . . to show that these blues can be woven into beautiful symphonies and a truly higher art." Blues and jazz musicians of the '20s seemed ever ready to state flatly that their music was qualitatively the equal of anybody's, as in the October 18, 1924, issue of Marcus Garvey's *Negro World*, where pianist-composer Eubie Blake declared that "we are giving the world real American folk songs and dances that will go down with the years as distinctive as the Russian or any other pronounced type of art."

Black Swan could point to its goal of elevating all forms of black music, but the argument was shallow. Pace and company had to know the "hot" new music was special. Their problem was that the most earthy and rough blues and jazz didn't fit their class prejudices. Pace and the others around the Black Swan studios were not really poor judges of talent, so much as they were too proper, too fearful of being too different from the norm. All record companies struggled with questions of taste. From 1920 through 1922 Victor brought many a blues singer into the studio for a trial, and rejected every one of them. It may be noted that Bessie Smith had been considered a bit too different or raw for some *proper* folks at OKeh, and allegedly at Emerson, before getting rejected at Black Swan. And there were others from among the more "funky" blues singers that had to wait until late in the game to get recorded—Ma Rainey, for instance, didn't make it until December 1923.

If Harry Pace was a lesser talent scout than some others, he still should get some credit for being much more generous than the other record company executives of 1921 and 1922 in putting out a record or two for most of the singers who came into the studio for a trial. The largesse in this area is evident in the following chart:

	Jan.–June 1921	July–Dec. 1921	Jan.–June 1922	July–Dec. 1922	Jan.–June 1923	July–Dec. 1923
Artists recorded on Black Swan	5	5	4	10	8	1
Artists recorded on all other companies	8	13	8	10	31	42

(the bottom number includes some singers also with Black Swan at the same time)

Harry Pace had much less success in keeping top talent at Black Swan than he did in giving the talent a start. Of the blues singers who started their recording between 1920 and 1922 there were 17 singers with 10 or more songs cut during their career. Of the 17, eight had recorded at the start or early in their career for Black Swan. But by the end of 1923, as Black Swan was about to go under, only two of the eight were still with the company.

Of the musicians who left Black Swan, some jumped quickly to another company, while others appear to have gone searching only after having waited and waited for Black Swan to take them back into the studio. Jazz and blues pianist James P. Johnson may have left Black Swan because of the choice of material he had been given to record. After getting to do one piano solo, Pace had him backing show tunes and comedy.

To be fair to Black Swan it is important to add to the history the social context in which Pace and company operated. With that context explained, the resulting picture is one of a group of music promoters who may have had misguided priorities (classical instead of jazz), but they were not stupid. They were members of a distinct social class and reflected its priorities—as in the *Billboard* gossip column mention that Black Swan's singer of the classics, Florence Cole Talbert, was to give a private recital for the prominent black banker in Chicago, Jesse Binga.

An understanding of Black Swan is also helped by placing its personnel in the political setting of the day.

The decline of Black Swan in 1923, for example, was no doubt influenced to some degree by the highly public conflict between the largely working class black movement of Marcus Garvey—the Universal Negro Improvement Association—and the NAACP and Urban League officials around Black Swan.

The bitter antagonism between Black Swan board member Du Bois and Marcus Garvey was a major topic of the black press of that time and the subject of large articles and whole chapters in black history texts.

In January 1923 Black Swan president Harry Pace and board member John E. Nail also became outspoken enemies of the militant black nationalist from Jamaica. Pace and Nail were two of eight signers of a letter to U.S. Attorney General Daugherty demanding the deportation of Marcus Garvey. The widely republished letter angrily derided Garvey and insulted his followers. In one section of the letter, the membership of Garvey's million-strong organization was compared with the Ku Klux Klan and with the conclusion that the Garveyites group "is just as objectionable and even more dangerous, inasmuch as it naturally attracts an even lower type of cranks, crooks and racial bigots among whom suggestibility to violent crime is much greater."

Garvey retorted to this letter by noting that the tone was that of people who seemed to hate their own race. Speaking of Harry Pace, specifically, Garvey called him "a business exploiter who endeavors to appeal to the patriotism of the race by selling us commodities at a higher rate than are charged in the ordinary . . . markets." And Garvey labeled Black Swan board member and Harlem realtor John Nail "a real estate shark who delights, under the guise of race patriotism, to raise the rent of poor colored people even beyond that of white landlords. . . ."

In musical taste, Marcus Garvey was known to share with Harry Pace, John E. Nail, and Dr. Du Bois a preference for classical and other serious composition. Early in 1922, in fact, Pace had given a lecture on music at Garvey's New York Liberty Hall.

But the very bitter social division between upper class and working class black America of the '20s led to intense conflict between, on the one hand, the college-trained NAACP types who read *The Crisis* with its Black Swan ads for "the Better Class" of black music, and, on the other hand, the tenement-dwelling blues-record-buying alleged "dupes" of the "demagogue" Marcus Garvey.

While Pace and company fraternized at the annual NAACP ball, where the music was from the likes of Smith's Society Orchestra, Garveyites frequented their Liberty Hall, which featured functions like the Ethiopian Barndance, at which the music was advertised to be "American and West Indian Blues."

From "Wasn't only my songs, they got my music too"

Barry Lee Pearson

THE musician copes with a world eager to cheat him. Stories of rip-offs, though slightly less dramatic than tales of violence, are all too common. Working two jobs, musicians have relied on others—usually fellow musicians—to find them work. But they have also placed themselves in the hands of agents, managers, producers, and club owners, generally to the musician's disadvantage. Cast as villains, management figures are portrayed as lining their pockets at the musician's expense. But musicians continue to need help to get beyond the small tavern circuit. Having been burned so often, however, they develop a healthy suspicion. Wild Child Butler spoke of his caution:

"You run up on all kind of people in this business. That's why I'm really funny about who I talk to, you know, or fool with, cause there really some bad peoples out here in this business. I been got and I have paid so many dues. I really did that. I don't know when they'll stop. I'm still paying them. I don't know what's going to come out of it."[1]

Ripped off across the board—personally, collectively, culturally—the complaint "I never saw a penny" describes the history of the blues. Rip-offs occur at all levels of the bluesman's work: writing, recording, and performing. Once again the stereotype of the down-and-out artist, his work, stolen, paid off with a bottle of booze, corresponds to real corruption. Sunnyland Slim expressed the cynical realism of the blues artist who has learned his lesson the hard way:

"You can't write—you can't, man, can't write, can't claim nothin and don't get no paper for it, you know what I mean. It's not yours, no matter what anybody do—You can't claim nothin if you ain't got the papers on it. You can't. That ain't your coat there if you ain't got nothing to show for it."[2]

Sunnyland is still angry. It's hard to be ripped off, whether it's having been beaten out of some money or having your life's work stolen. While most artists complain about being

---

Reprinted from "*Sounds So Good to Me*": *The Bluesman's Story*, by Barry Lee Pearson (Philadelphia: University of Pennsylvania Press, 1984), 104–8.

cheated financially, others, like Sunnyland, are angry about being denied their place in history. When someone has a song stolen, the bitterness is twofold: it hurts the businessman financially, but it hurts the artist by cheating him out of his due credit. Harmonica Frank Floyd also complained of being cheated:

"I try to be honest, fair and square, with everybody. That's my motto. And can't none of them say I've crooked anyone and can't stand people that crook me. However, these people have done it and —— of Nashville Tennessee is another hasn't paid off for the record that he's got out. He said he'd pay for it later, but he didn't pay a god derned penny—and I didn't give no permission for none of them guys to record my records. So I should have a little say over what belongs to me, it looks to me like. Wasn't only my songs—they got my music too. See what I mean."[3]

His indictment of the music business sounds discouragingly familiar. Yet I took the option of deleting—or as the bluesman says—"not calling no names." Generally careful about mentioning names in interviews, people get angry when they talk of being ripped off. But careless comments can wind up costing the musician in the future. Wild Child Butler was still so angry he wanted me to talk about his nemesis:

"Well, all my songs now, I never got a dime for no writing and they copyright it, —— Enterprises. Mercury sent me some things that said they gave me a piece of money, but they said they're lying, that Mercury never gave them no money, but I never even got nothin for a line I wrote. Yeah, it really is. I never got nothin for nothin I wrote. On the L.P. I ain't never got a dime out of nothing I wrote. I ain't never got nothing.

"And by the way, I didn't have no special pay. I had my file lying there in the cabinet. They wouldn't even give me my copyrights when I got my release from them. The guy tell me, 'I'm gonna send them, I'll mail them.' Every time I call them they lie to me. The great ——, I hope you talk about him—He's a big—I didn't think he would lie to me like that. They tell me, 'All right, we gonna send em, we gonna send em,' and I know she had them down at the office, but they don't even send me the copyrights."[4]

Even in this case, however, Eddie Taylor's admonition—"Don't talk too much yap, yap, yap. You know, say the wrong thing at the wrong time at the wrong place. You know, that can ruin you."[5]—may be applicable.

Although blues artists talk about their records with pride in their story, they complain that the record industry rips them off as well. Generally treated like a replaceable part in a badly run machine, the blues artist sees his sessions as poorly planned, cheap, slipshod affairs. But to be honest, blues records get little distribution and almost no air play. So while thousands of records are produced, few people actually get rich, least of all the artist.[6]

Artists know that their records, "Money Taking Woman" or "Build Myself a Cave," provide a frame of reference for their fans, and so they can supply names, dates, and labels. Speaking of records is akin to listing publications, and even if the artist "never saw a penny," if the record was released it would show up in the hands of a collector and the artist would be asked about it. So he keeps his recording history in order as with Wild Child Butler ("My first record was 'Aching All Over,' and the flip 'Dying Chill' on a small label, Sharpshot"[7]) or Byther Smith ("My first recording was 'Thank You, Mr. Kennedy' and 'Champion Girl'"[8]).

First recordings, like first guitars, first paychecks, or even first interviews, tend to stand out in memory at least as a convenient beginning. Recordings that do not sell present different problems. Painfully aware that record sales determine fame and fortune and are an artistic judgment as well, musicians rationalize a record's failure or even cite conspiracy—the figures were juggled or it was held back in favor of another artist's lesser record.

They reasonably believe that if they make a good record the public should want it, and they tell unusual tales about how their record hit the top ten in Puerto Rico or Canada. They know this because they heard it from a friend who heard it on the radio.

Paranoia—"My record would have been a hit if not for so and so" or "I could have had a big break if not for so and so"—has been justified in the blues business. This was especially true in the early 1960s, where a combination of recording monopolies and a diminishing market placed the artist's future in the hands of a few powerful people. Eddie Taylor claimed:

"Course I could call names of important people. Before —— died, he had ABC, and Columbia were asking for me and [he] told them they couldn't get me cause I was his man, I had a contract with him. And I never had a contract with him, you know."[9]

Traditionally in a weak bargaining position, the bluesman copes with the situation as best he can and stoically takes work where he can find it. This often means giving up artistic control, but as Eddie Taylor rationalizes, it's up to the man with the money:

"If I'm recording for you, you paying for the studio, you paying the fellows, you paying me. I can't get in the studio and quit just because I feel bad about that. I just go ahead and do the best I can."[10]

But the inequities of the system drive some artists out of the business. Fed up with the hassles of being cheated and tired of being angry, Big Chief Ellis quit:

"The reason I had to give it up cause I was getting ripped off. Practically every record company I recorded for owes me money right now. In fact, I had to threaten a couple of them to even get money from them. I went down to wreck this company. He knew I meant business. He made me out a check right then. He knew I was out to wreck this company. I had got tired of getting ripped off, and that's the reason I had to give it up, cause they'll record you, pay you for the recording, then you don't hear no more. This mostly happens to blues and religious."[11]

He returned to music later on but retained his suspicious nature.

Even in day-to-day performance the bluesman gets ripped off. On one end of the spectrum James Thomas spoke of working small rural cafes:

"Oh, they tough and you can charge fifty cents at the door. Well, cause who you have at the door, they gonna cheat you out of some of that. So it's tough everywhere you go. Somebody gonna slip in, some stay until they get tired, go out, and give the ticket to some of his friends. They there till they get ready to go. It's always ways to slip in."[12]

On the other end of the spectrum, Wild Child Butler spoke of a blues superstar being taken by his own manager who booked him in a major Chicago club:

"She books him, she gonna get him thirty-five hundred dollars a week and he gets—his manager—they say he went down there and booked him for twenty-six hundred dollars and took the whole gig over. She booked him for thirty-five hundred dollars, and his own man went down and booked him for twenty-six hundred dollars and took the whole gig over."[13]

Byther Smith passes on another lesson:

"Don't have em charge anything, because there are so many peoples behind that counter at different clubs and different places I've known. People do it—they get the band fellows to drinking and they gonna charge. You come in here, you buy one drink, and they buy, say, 'This is on me, here.' But they gonna put it on the band's tab. That's in order—Because you're a customer, that's gonna make you come back, say, 'Gee, I went to the club over at such and such a place and I bought one drink and then they give me a set, see."[14]

But losing can also make a good story if a clever con is involved and the difficulties are now settled. Blues musicians appreciate the ability to be able to "take it" and may even con each other. And as Byther Smith points out, even the victim should appreciate a truly bold or clever move:

"So I get dressed and go on out there. I get there about five minutes before work time. Sammy Lawhorn was sitting up there. When I walked in, Sammy says, 'Hot dog. Here comes my baby. Everybody gotta bring it in for my baby.' I was bringing my guitar and amplifier in. Sammy says, 'Queen Bee, gives me Smitty's money now. I'm gonna drink it up.' And that woman paid Sammy. See, he's sitting at the bar, he's not working, he's just sitting at the bar. So she goes and pays him. [Laughter.]"[15]

Notes

1. Wild Child Butler, in my car, Chicago, Illinois, July 1974.
2. Sunnyland Slim, Childe Harold, Washington, D.C., February 1978.
3. Harmonica Frank Floyd, Smithsonian Folklife Festival, The Mall, Washington, D.C., August 1976.
4. Wild Child Butler, 1974.
5. Eddie Taylor, Northeastern Illinois University, Chicago, Illinois, December 1974.
6. There are exceptions: high-quality records, bad records redeemed by great performances, and even successful recording stars. Yet it is interesting to note that the artists who bragged most about their records generally referred to past successes or to a record yet to come out. For example, Roosevelt Sykes bragged: "The first records I put out was in '36, and I got royalty on them. Five cents on the dollar I reckon. Do you know I was drawing seventy or eighty dollars a month? Well, you know they were sellin some of those records?" (Ann Arbor Blues Festival, Ann Arbor, Michigan, August 1969). And Sam Chatmon stated: "Well, I started making records in 1929, fourteenth of June, 1929. So I was playing four, five, eight years or so before I started recording. After I made the record, the first number I made was a hit, 'Forty-Four Blues,' and every record I made was a star ever since" (Smithsonian Folklife Festival, The Mall, Washington, D.C., September 1976).
7. Wild Child Butler, 1974.
8. Byther Smith, at his home, Chicago, Illinois, December 1974.
9. Eddie Taylor, 1974.

10. Ibid.
11. Big Chief Ellis to Susan Day, at his home, Washington, D.C., April 1977.
12. James Thomas, at my home, Bloomington, Indiana, March 1973.
13. Wild Child Butler, 1974.
14. Byther Smith, 1974.
15. Ibid.

9 Literature, Criticism, and the Blues

WHEN late eighteenth- and nineteenth-century Romantic artists began defining their work less in terms of formal elements and more by the spiritual and passionate energy generated out of the process of imagining and creating in the liminal gulf between the ideal and the real, implicitly they affirmed the feeling that the poetic sentiment was expressed not just in words and sounds but in sights and motions and textures as well. In this, they began blurring the boundaries between genres and endorsing transgenre pollination to produce art that was conceptually related but not slavishly imitative. The resources of the blues performer have inspired artists in a myriad of genres in numerous ways who have blended ideas and emotions learned from the blues with their own visions and sensibilities to generate their own distinctive works.

The most obvious influence has been on creative writing, especially poetry, since the blues is a form of poetry, but also on fiction, drama, and nonfiction, as well as in the area of literary criticism, where critics have attempted to gauge the importance of the vernacular tradition to the literature of African Americans. However, the same ways in which literary artists employ the blues may be translatable to sculptors, painters, quilters, and others, so any discussion of poetry specifically can be pertinent to other musical and nonmusical genres as well. It can be difficult to nail down just where and how much the blues has had an influence on another work. The judgment is, after all, very subjective. If we wish to characterize a poem as a "blues poem" or blues-influenced poem, we must first acknowledge that the blues have so many different characteristics from which to draw—one or more of which may be present in the poem—that the determination of the nature and extent of influence can be very complicated. The poem may draw upon or adhere to the blues tradition in one sense, and depart from or expand it in another. It may draw upon the southeastern prewar blues tradition, or that of postwar Chicago, or rhythm and blues, or it may be "filtered" through another related form of music such as some style of jazz or gospel. And because the poem will, out of convenience, primarily be part of the written rather than the oral tradition—or perhaps more accurately an alliance of the two—we must consider the effect of that transference on the performance experience, energy, inflections, persona, and audience response.

The blues tend to be manifested in poetry in the following ways: there are poems that

1. seek to define the blues and its philosophy;
2. celebrate the blues as a source of inspiration and transcendence;
3. employ blues as an emotional, psychic, spiritual, community, political resource;
4. use the traditional forms of the blues;
5. experiment with the forms of the blues;
6. use the traditional subject matter of the blues;
7. use nontraditional subject matter in combination with other identifiable blues elements;
8. pay tribute to a particular blues performer;
9. depict the exploitation and suffering of a performer or an archetypal blues figure;
10. depict the exploitation and suffering of a person or group of people;
11. challenge the currently prevailing notion of order, propriety, and morality.

There are, of course, poems that employ more than one of these strategies at a time, and the strategies may be employed either literally or figuratively. For example, the antiphonal nature of the blues stanza may be literally reproduced, or it may be produced less formally by the echo of a sentiment followed by a response or resolution to it. The literary critic, then, must attempt to identify the nature of the oral blues tradition, and then open up to the multiplicitous ways that those characteristics may be engaged, re-envisioned, and utilized by a writer. Distinguished creative writers such as Langston Hughes, Zora Neale Hurston, Sterling Brown, William Carlos Williams, Robert Lowell, James Baldwin, Allen Ginsberg, Jack Kerouac, Amiri Baraka, Bob Kaufman, Ralph Ellison, Alice Walker, Toni Morrison, Sherley Anne Williams, Jayne Cortez, Michael Harper, and August Wilson have gone to the well repeatedly and employed the blues variously in their work. It is, in fact, a tribute to the breadth and resilience of the blues that what has been characterized by some as a limited form and tradition has neither died out nor dried up as a source of inspiration throughout the world.

"Songs Called the Blues" is Langston Hughes's quick take on the state of the blues, 1941. The essay reflects his own preference for urban blues of a somewhat more sophisticated variety as reflected in the performers he names as among the best active, and yet also acknowledges the thorough grounding of the blues in the lives of those Hughes called the "low-down folks," whose lives and art were an inspiration to Hughes in his own life and art as he outlined in his manifesto "The Negro Artist and the Racial Mountain." Setting the blues side by side with the Spirituals, whose contributions had for decades been recognized and championed by a number of commentators, James Weldon Johnson and Alain Locke among them, Hughes seeks to emphasize the variety and function of the blues, their international contributions to American culture, and the potential they demonstrate for providing the creative artist with valuable material to employ, without losing sight of their origin in the despair and hope, the mundane experiences, of the African American.

James Baldwin's short story masterpiece "Sonny's Blues" portrays the deleterious effects of a ghetto environment on two very different brothers, the older a middle-class African American high school math teacher struggling with his exacting sense of propriety and responsibility and the death of his daughter, the other a junkie ex-con jazz musician searching for his voice and identity on his own terms. Through a series of Manichaean dichotomies—light and darkness, order and chaos, formal and informal education, sacred and secular music, sin and redemption—Baldwin explores the relationship of the brothers to each other, to the community, and to their vocations. As he does so, he challenges facile observations and conclusions concerning their lives, but ultimately finds for them a shared field of energy and communion in a ritualistic baptismal and communal ceremony acted out in a darkened neighborhood bar. There Sonny, in his circle of light in the darkness he finds surrounding him, unites himself with his brother and his community by transmuting their shared suffering into new and transcendent art, guided by the bassist Creole, polestar of the rhythm, who acts as the supportive father/big brother figure he has lost/lacked in his family life. Baldwin's story places the blues beautifully in psychological, sociological, communal, and artistic contexts to provide one of the most trenchant portrayals of the value and function of the blues.

In his influential book *The Poetry of the Blues*, Samuel Charters seeks to understand the artistry of the blues performer in relation to devices employed in the English poetic tradition, though of course not all of the devices that Charters describes are exclusive to that tradition, nor was it likely that the performers about whom Charters wrote picked up those devices from that tradition (and of course Charters does not make that claim). His brief but specific discussions outline how such elements as simile, metaphor, personification, apostrophe, metonymy, and patterns of imagery and symbolism are utilized skillfully and meaningfully by blues singers to create poetry of surpassing depth and beauty. While some critics such as Paul Garon have seen Charters's discussions to be "a mere catalog of poetic devices" (*Blues and the Poetic Spirit,* 30) that misses the essence of what is important about poetry and art, Charters's book was an early attempt to treat with seriousness the poetic skill of the blues performer and helped usher blues lyrics, for good or ill—and there have been many a serious argument about this—into the arena of academic consideration.

By way of contrast, Black Aesthetic theoretician, cultural critic, and artist Larry Neal attempts to associate the blues not with the traditions of Western poetry but with black liberation through self-definition and self-determination. For Neal, "Black Music, in all its forms, represents the highest artistic achievement of the race." Therefore committed black artists must draw on this "Soul Force" of the race in order to speak from and to black people and establish a black identity and deliver a black message as an antidote to the identity and message imposed by a morally and artistically exhausted Western viewpoint. Thus, Neal views the blues as crucially connected to the message and mission of the black church—"Keeper of the Memory" of the Homeland—only "thrust into the eyes of life's raw realities." The Black Aesthetic, then, is a spiritual movement that is both constructive in its championing resistance and rebellion, and destructive in its aim to destroy "white ways of looking at the world." The black artist can accomplish both goals by writing "a blues that takes us to a more meaningful level of consciousness and aspiration." A passionate and articulate spokesman for African American art, Neal's was a challenging, assertive, and celebratory voice, tragically silenced in his mid-forties by a heart attack in 1981, but not before leaving behind some thought-provoking messages about African American culture.

The manner in which blues song lyrics express reality and socialize listeners into characteristic ways of dealing with the world is the focus of S. I. Hayakawa's "Popular Songs vs. The Facts of Life." Taking as his thesis that pop songs tend to be sentimental, full of fanciful and unrealistic notions about love that fail to prepare listeners to deal with adult relationships, Hayakawa counters that blues lyrics, because they portray love realistically and unsentimentally, are healthier brokers of intimate social intercourse. The problem with Hayakawa's thesis is that, while there are many blues songs that are realistic, even to the point of cynicism, in their lyrics, there are also numerous songs that are exaggerated, fantastic, even delusional in their dealings with love. Stanley Edgar Hyman, for example, in his article "The Folk Tradition," lists "compensatory grandiose fantasy" among his five major pervasive themes in blues music, and though Hyman's categories can be a bit abstract and vague, this one does point importantly to the element of fantasy and its place in the blues tradition. Still, the seriousness with which Hayakawa treats the effects of the lyrics of pop and blues songs, culminating in his description of the "IFD disease," illuminates the function and effect of the blues lyric as it is disseminated to a listening audience absorbing the attitudes of the performer toward life.

In "The Blues Roots of Contemporary Afro-American Poetry," Sherley A. Williams examines the blues and the ways in which the blues have been employed by Afro-American poets from Langston Hughes to Lucille Clifton. Drawing on Stephen Henderson's discussion of the employment of the African American vernacular tradition in African American poetry, including the "interior dynamism" lent to the written word by folk art, Williams relates the function and structure of the blues to effects rendered in print by African American poets. In the "Transformation" section of her article, Williams asserts that the blues are "seldom metaphoric or symbolic except in sexual and physical terms," a notion with which critics who see the lyrics of the blues as containing a strong sociopolitical message beneath the literal surface would vehemently disagree; however, her discussion of Henderson's "mascon" or "massive concentration of black experiential energy" as it is employed from the blues tradition in African American poetry makes some specific and pertinent points regarding both the literal and the metaphoric uses to which poets might put the blues.

Houston Baker's *Blues, Ideology, and Afro-American Literature* is a heroic attempt to wed the vernacular blues tradition with contemporary literary theory in the examination of the African American literary tradition. In this work Baker switches from his strategy in *The Journey Back* of focusing on a "speaking subject" who creates a language (code) to be deciphered to focusing on the language (code) which itself speaks the subject. For Baker, the subject is what he terms "the economics of slavery," a system that exploited and dehumanized African labor while it created and sustained a mythology of a patriarchal, racial, and cultural superiority, and the language is the vernacular as expressed in the blues matrix, a "point of ceaseless input and output" on which literary artists draw for inspiration. Though it sometimes seems that Baker treats the blues as too much of a trope or abstract source rather than an art form significant in and of itself, and that his definition of the blues and his characterization of the blues performer's "signatory coda" as being "atopic" are somewhat incomplete—constructed for his argument—Baker's vigorous, stimulating discussions of music, criticism, and literature force the reader into considering the blues in a different, and fascinating, intellectual light, employing deconstruction, semiotics, and Marxist criticism in his examination of literary artists connected crucially to the blues.

In "It Jus Be's Dat Way Sometime," an article unfortunately not available for inclusion in this volume, Hazel Carby seeks to identify the function and importance of the female blues singer both in her own time and in the subsequent literary tradition through the study of the singers' treatment of sexuality in their material. Seeing the singers' lyric discourses as meditations on "conventional and unconventional sexuality," Carby identifies a sexual autonomy and independence in their lyrics, a space cleared out where women were free to explore and express their sexuality unfettered. Critics would argue that while this is undoubtedly true of some female blues singers and their songs, others do not sing with a consistently "assertive and demanding" voice, nor do they revel in gender- or boundary-breaking roles in their performances. Ultimately, it is undoubtedly true that blues singers had the freedom and opportunity to express a broader range of attitudes toward sexuality—and other subjects such as violence as well—in their songs, and as such provided women with the occasion to raise issues and arguments that might otherwise be suppressed or ignored. A comprehensive transcription and examination of the lyrics of female blues singers as they have been made available in Johnny Parth's Document reissue series should yield some valuable information on the percentage of lyrics that model assertive roles as opposed to submissive ones (understood in relation to the gender of the composer, of course). Unfortunately, such a specific project has not yet been undertaken, though R. R. MacLeod's series of lyric transcriptions for the Yazoo and Document series will eventually include all of the female blues material from the prewar era.

In the recent *Blues Legacies and Black Feminism*, Angela Y. Davis examines the women's blues tradition as reflected in the work of Ma Rainey, Bessie Smith, and Billie Holiday. Through specific discussions of the lyrics sung by Rainey and Smith (all of which are transcribed in full in the text) and selected material by Holiday, Davis argues that female blues singers like the three under discussion helped shape and articulate a convention-challenging, liberating African American working-class ethos that was in conflict with the emerging, social-uplift bourgeois consciousness of the "club" women of the African American middle class. Agreeing with Carby, Davis believes these singers helped create a cultural space for expression of issues otherwise marginalized in everyday discourse, and as such demonstrate the very prominent and important role that protest has in the female blues tradition. Some critics have argued that Davis's work does not pay sufficient attention to the role of male tunesmiths who wrote some of the songs sung by these performers and thus are responsible for some of the sentiments; that these women were performers and not political agents; that Davis ignores the biographies of her subjects because of some inconvenient details; and that her thesis sometimes causes her to force lyrics into strange interpretations for support (Francis Davis in the *New York Times Book Review* 147 [March 8, 1998]: 16, and Lance A. Williams in *Blues Revue* 41 [October 1998]: 78). However, Davis provides careful transcriptions, well-researched scholarship, and a feminist revisioning of the roles of female blues singers that is provocative and valuable for a reexamination of the blues in its sociopolitical and artistic settings.

Recommended Further Readings

Kimberly Benston. "Tragic Aspects of the Blues." *Phylon* 36:2 (June 1975: 164–76.

Sterling Brown. "The Blues as Folk Poetry." In *Folk-Say I*, ed. B. A. Botkin. Norman: University of Oklahoma Press, 1930.

Hazel Carby. "It Jus Be's Dat Way Sometime: The Sexual Politics of Women's Blues." In *Feminisms: An Anthology of Literary Theory and Criticism*, ed. Robyn R. Warhol and Diane Prince Herndl. New Brunswick, N.J.: Rutgers University Press, 1991.

Ralph Ellison. *The Collected Essays of Ralph Ellison*. New York: Modern Library, 1995.

Paul Garon. *Blues and the Poetic Spirit*. London: Eddison Press Ltd., 1975.

Henry Louis Gates, Jr. *The Signifying Monkey*. New York: Oxford University Press, 1988.

Stephen Henderson. *Understanding the New Black Poetry*. New York: William Morrow, 1973.

Langston Hughes. "The Negro Artist and the Racial Mountain." *Nation* 122 (1926): 692–94.

Stanley Edgar Hyman. "The Folk Tradition." In *Mother Wit from the Laughing Barrel*, ed. Alan Dundes. Englewood Cliffs, N.J.: Prentice Hall, 1973.

Franklin Rosemont et al. "Surrealism and Blues: Special Supplement." *Living Blues* 25 (Jan.–Feb. 1976): 19–34.

Steven C. Tracy. *Langston Hughes and the Blues*. Urbana: University of Illinois Press, 1988.

——. "William Carlos Williams and *Blues: A Magazine of New Rhythms*." *William Carlos Williams Review* 15:2 (Fall 1989): 17–29.

Richard Wright. "Foreword." In Paul Oliver, *Blues Fell This Morning*. 1960. Rpt. Cambridge: Cambridge University Press, 1994.

Songs Called the Blues

Langston Hughes

THE BLUES are folk-songs born out of heartache. They are songs of the black South, particularly the city South. Songs of the poor streets and back alleys of Memphis and Birmingham, Atlanta and Galveston, out of black, beaten, but unbeatable throats, from the strings of pawn-shop guitars, and the chords of pianos with no ivory on the keys.

The Blues and the Spirituals are two great Negro gifts to American music. The Spirituals are group songs, but the Blues are songs you sing alone. The Spirituals are religious songs, born in camp meetings and remote plantation districts. But the Blues are *city* songs rising from the crowded streets of big towns, or beating against the lonely walls of hall bed-rooms where you can't sleep at night. The Spirituals are escape songs, looking toward heaven, tomorrow, and God. But the Blues are today songs, here and now, broke and broken-hearted, when you're troubled in mind and don't know what to do, and nobody cares.

There are many kinds of Blues. There are the family Blues, when a man and woman have quarreled, and the quarrel can't be patched up. There's the loveless Blues, when you haven't even got anybody to quarrel with. And there's the left-lonesome Blues, when the one you care for's gone away. Then there's also the broke-and-hungry Blues, a stranger in a strange town. And the desperate going-to-the-river Blues that say:

> I'm goin' down to de river
> And take ma rockin' chair—
> If the Blues overcome me,
> I'm gonna rock on away from here!

But it's not always as bad as that, because there's another verse that declares:

> Goin' down to de railroad,
> Lay ma head on de track.

Reprinted from *Phylon* 2, no. 2 (Summer 1941): 143–45. Reprinted by permission of Harold Ober Associates.

> I'm goin' to de railroad,
> Lay ma head on de track—
> But if I see de train a-comin'
> I'm gonna jerk it back!

For sad as Blues may be, there's almost always something humorous about them—even if it's the kind of humor that laughs to keep from crying. You know,

> I went to de gypsy's
> To get ma fortune told.
> Went to de gypsy's
> To get ma fortune told,
> But the gypsy said, dog-gone
> Your un-hard-lucky soul!

In America, during the last quarter of a century, there have been many great singers of the Blues, but the finest of all were the three famous Smiths—no relation, one to another—Mamie Smith, Clara Smith, and the astonishing Bessie Smith. Clara and Bessie are both dead now, and Mamie no longer sings, but thousands of Blues collectors in the United States and abroad prize their records. Today a girl named Georgia White carries on the old tradition of the Blues in the folk manner. And Midge Williams, of the Louis Armstrong band, sings them in a more polished, but effective way. Of the men, Lonnie Johnson is perhaps the finest living male singer of the Blues, although that portly fellow Jimmy Rushing in Count Basie's orchestra is a runner-up. And Lead Belly, of course, is in a class by himself.

The most famous Blues, as everybody knows, is the *St. Louis Blues*, that Mr. W. C. Handy wrote down one night in the corner of a bar on a levee street in St. Louis thirty years ago, and which has since gone all over the world. The *St. Louis Blues* is sung more than any other song on the air waves, is known in Shanghai and Buenos Aires, Paris and Berlin—in fact, is heard so often in Europe that a great many Europeans think it must be the American National Anthem.

Less popular, but equally beautiful are the Blues, *Troubled In Mind, Memphis Blues, Yellow Dog Blues*, and the never to be surpassed *Gulf Coast Blues*, which begins with one of the loneliest lines in all the realm of song:

> The mail man passed but
> He didn't leave no news . . .

Blues are still being made. One of the newest authentic Blues to come up out of the South, by way of the colored boys in the government work camps, is the *DuPree Blues*, that sad story of a man who wanted to give his girl a diamond ring, but had none to give her, so he took his gun and went to the jewelry store where, instead of getting the diamond ring, he got the jewelry man, jail, and the noose.

The real Negro Blues are as fine as any folk music we have, and I'm hoping that the day will come when famous concert singers like Marian Anderson and Paul Robeson will include a group of Blues on their programs as well as the Spirituals which they now sing so effectively.

A young dancer in New York, Felicia Sorel, is already using the Blues as a background for the creation of new dance forms. I see no reason why great dances could not be born of the Blues. Great American dances containing all the laughter and pain, hunger and heartaches, search and reality of the contemporary scenes—for the Blues have something that goes beyond race or sectional limits, that appeals to the ear and heart of people everywhere—otherwise, how could it be that in a Tokio restaurant one night I heard a Louis Armstrong record of the *St. Louis Blues* played over and over for a crowd of Japanese diners there? You don't have to understand the words to know the meaning of the Blues, or to feel their sadness, or to hope their hopes:

Troubled in mind, I'm blue!
But I won't be blue always:
De sun's gonna shine
In my back door someday!

Sonny's Blues

James Baldwin

I READ about it in the paper, in the subway, on my way to work. I read it, and I couldn't believe it, and I read it again. Then perhaps I just stared at it, at the newsprint spelling out his name, spelling out the story. I stared at it in the swinging lights of the subway car, and in the faces and bodies of the people, and in my own face, trapped in the darkness which roared outside.

It was not to be believed and I kept telling myself that, as I walked from the subway station to the high school. And at the same time I couldn't doubt it. I was scared, scared for Sonny. He became real to me again. A great block of ice got settled in my belly and kept melting there slowly all day long, while I taught my classes algebra. It was a special kind of ice. It kept melting, sending trickles of ice water all up and down my veins, but it never got less. Sometimes it hardened and seemed to expand until I felt my guts were going to come spilling out or that I was going to choke or scream. This would always be at a moment when I was remembering some specific thing Sonny had once said or done.

When he was about as old as the boys in my classes his face had been bright and open, there was a lot of copper in it; and he'd had wonderfully direct brown eyes, and great gentleness and privacy. I wondered what he looked like now. He had been picked up, the evening before, in a raid on an apartment downtown, for peddling and using heroin.

I couldn't believe it: but what I mean by that is that I couldn't find any room for it anywhere inside me. I had kept it outside me for a long time. I hadn't wanted to know. I had had suspicions, but I didn't name them, I kept putting them away. I told myself that Sonny was wild, but he wasn't crazy. And he'd always been a good boy, he hadn't ever turned hard or evil or disrespectful, the way kids can, so quick, so quick, especially in Harlem. I didn't want to believe that I'd ever see my brother going down, coming to nothing, all that light in his face gone out, in the condition I'd already seen so many others. Yet it had happened and here I was, talking about algebra to a lot of boys who might, every one of them for all I knew, be popping off needles every time they went to the head. Maybe it did more for them than algebra could.

I was sure that the first time Sonny had ever had horse, he couldn't have been much older than these boys were now. These boys, now, were living as we'd been living then, they were growing up with a rush and their heads bumped abruptly against the low ceiling of their actual possibilities. They were filled with rage. All they really knew were two darknesses, the darkness of their lives, which was now closing in on them, and the darkness of the movies, which had blinded them to that other darkness, and in which they now, vindictively, dreamed, at once more together than they were at any other time, and more alone.

When the last bell rang, the last class ended, I let out my breath. It seemed I'd been holding it for all that time. My clothes were wet—I may have looked as though I'd been sitting in a steam bath, all dressed up, all afternoon. I sat alone in the classroom a long time. I listened to the boys outside, downstairs, shouting and cursing and laughing. Their laughter struck me for perhaps the first time. It was not the joyous laughter which—God knows why—one associates with children. It was mocking and insular, its intent to denigrate. It was disenchanted, and in this, also, lay the authority of their curses. Perhaps I was listening to them because I was thinking about my brother and in them I heard my brother. And myself.

One boy was whistling a tune, at once very complicated and very simple, it seemed to be pouring out of him as though he were a bird, and it sounded very cool and moving through all that harsh, bright air, only just holding its own through all those other sounds.

I stood up and walked over to the window and looked down into the courtyard. It was the beginning of the spring and the sap was rising in the boys. A teacher passed through them every now and again, quickly, as though he or she couldn't wait to get out of that courtyard, to get those boys out of their sight and off their minds. I started collecting my stuff. I thought I'd better get home and talk to Isabel.

The courtyard was almost deserted by the time I got downstairs. I saw this boy standing in the shadow of a doorway, looking just like Sonny. I almost called his name. Then I saw that it wasn't Sonny, but somebody we used to know, a boy from around our block. He'd been Sonny's friend. He'd never been mine, having been too young for me, and, anyway, I'd never liked him. And now, even though he was a grown-up man, he still hung around that block, still spent hours on the street corners, was always high and raggy. I used to run into him from time to time and he'd often work around to asking me for a quarter or fifty cents. He always had some real good excuse, too, and I always gave it to him, I don't know why.

But now, abruptly, I hated him. I couldn't stand the way he looked at me, partly like a dog, partly like a cunning child. I wanted to ask him what the hell he was doing in the school courtyard.

He sort of shuffled over to me, and he said, "I see you got the papers. So you already know about it."

"You mean about Sonny? Yes, I already know about it. How come they didn't get you?"

He grinned. It made him repulsive and it also brought to mind what he'd looked like as a kid. "I wasn't there. I stay away from them people."

"Good for you." I offered him a cigarette and I watched him through the smoke. "You come all the way down here just to tell me about Sonny?"

"That's right." He was short of shaking his head and his eyes looked strange, as though they were about to cross. The bright sun deadened his damp dark brown skin and it made his eyes look yellow and showed up the dirt in his kinked hair. He smelled funky. I moved a little away from him and I said, "Well, thanks. But I already know about it and I got to get home."

"I'll walk you a little ways," he said. We started walking. There were a couple of kids still loitering in the courtyard and one of them said goodnight to me and looked strangely at the boy beside me.

"What're you going to do?" he asked me. "I mean, about Sonny?"

"Look. I haven't seen Sonny for over a year, I'm not sure I'm going to do anything. Anyway, what the hell *can* I do?"

"That's right," he said quickly, "ain't nothing you can do. Can't much help old Sonny no more, I guess."

It was what I was thinking and so it seemed to me he had no right to say it.

"I'm surprised at Sonny, though," he went on—he had a funny way of talking, he looked straight ahead as though he were talking to himself—"I thought Sonny was a smart boy, I thought he was too smart to get hung."

"I guess he thought so too," I said sharply, "and that's how he got hung. And now about you? You're pretty goddamn smart, I bet."

Then he looked directly at me, just for a minute. "I ain't smart," he said. "If I was smart, I'd have reached for a pistol a long time ago."

"Look. Don't tell *me* your sad story, if it was up to me, I'd give you one." Then I felt guilty—guilty, probably, for never having supposed that the poor bastard *had* a story of his own, much less a sad one, and I asked, quickly, "What's going to happen to him now?"

He didn't answer this. He was off by himself some place. "Funny thing," he said, and from his tone we might have been discussing the quickest way to get to Brooklyn, "when I saw the papers this morning, the first thing I asked myself was if I had anything to do with it. I felt sort of responsible."

I began to listen more carefully. The subway station was on the corner, just before us, and I stopped. He stopped, too. We were in front of a bar and he ducked slightly, peering in, but whoever he was looking for didn't seem to be there. The juke box was blasting away with something black and bouncy and I half watched the barmaid as she danced her way from the juke box to her place behind the bar. And I watched her face as she laughingly responded to something someone said to her, still keeping time to the music. When she smiled one saw the little girl, one sensed the doomed, still-struggling woman beneath the battered face of the semi-whore.

"I never *give* Sonny nothing," the boy said finally, "but a long time ago I come to school high and Sonny asked me how it felt." He paused, I couldn't bear to watch him, I watched the barmaid, and I listened to the music which seemed to be causing the pavement to shake. "I told him it felt great." The music stopped, the barmaid paused and watched the juke box until the music began again. "It did."

All this was carrying me some place I didn't want to go. I certainly didn't want to know how it felt. It filled everything, the people, the houses, the music, the dark, quicksilver barmaid, with menace; and this menace was their reality.

"What's going to happen to him now?" I asked again.

"They'll send him away some place and they'll try to cure him." He shook his head. "Maybe he'll even think he's kicked the habit. Then they'll let him loose"—he gestured throwing his cigarette into the gutter. "That's all."

"What do you mean, that's *all?*"

But I knew what he meant.

"I *mean*, that's *all*." He turned his head and looked at me, pulling down the corners of his mouth. "Don't you know what I mean?" he asked, softly.

"How the hell *would* I know what you mean?" I almost whispered it, I don't know why.

"That's right," he said to the air, "how would *he* know what I mean?" He turned toward me again, patient and calm, and yet I somehow felt him shaking, shaking as though he were going to fall apart. I felt that ice in my guts again, the dread I'd felt all afternoon; and again I watched the barmaid, moving about the bar, washing glasses, and singing. "Listen. They'll let him out and then it'll just start all over again. That's what I mean."

"You mean—they'll let him out. And then he'll just start working his way back in again. You mean he'll never kick the habit. Is that what you mean?"

"That's right," he said, cheerfully. "*You* see what I mean."

"Tell me," I said at last, "why does he want to die? He must want to die, he's killing himself, why does he want to die?"

He looked at me in surprise. He licked his lips. "He don't want to die. He wants to live. Don't nobody want to die, ever."

Then I wanted to ask him—too many things. He could not have answered, or if he had, I could not have borne the answers. I started walking. "Well, I guess it's none of my business."

"It's going to be rough on old Sonny," he said. We reached the subway station. "This is your station?" he asked. I nodded. I took one step down. "Damn!" he said, suddenly. I looked up at him. He grinned again. "Damn it if I didn't leave all my money home. You ain't got a dollar on you, have you? Just for a couple of days, is all."

All at once something inside gave and threatened to come pouring out of me. I didn't hate him any more. I felt that in another moment I'd start crying like a child.

"Sure," I said. "Don't sweat." I looked in my wallet and didn't have a dollar, I only had a five. "Here," I said. "That hold you?"

He didn't look at it—he didn't want to look at it. A terrible closed look came over his face, as though he were keeping the number on the bill a secret from him and me. "Thanks," he said, and now he was dying to see me go. "Don't worry about Sonny. Maybe I'll write him or something."

"Sure," I said. "You do that. So long."

"Be seeing you," he said. I went on down the steps.

And I didn't write Sonny or send him anything for a long time. When I finally did, it was just after my little girl died, he wrote me back a letter which made me feel like a bastard.

Here's what he said:

Dear brother,

You don't know how much I needed to hear from you. I wanted to write you many a time but I dug how much I must have hurt you and so I didn't write. But now I feel like a man who's been trying to climb up out of some deep, real deep and funky hole and just saw the sun up there, outside. I got to get outside.

I can't tell you much about how I got here. I mean I don't know how to tell you. I guess I was afraid of something or I was trying to escape from something and you know I have never been very strong in the head (smile). I'm glad Mama and Daddy are dead and can't see what's happened to their son and I swear if I'd known what I was doing I would never have hurt you so, you and a lot of other fine people who were nice to me and who believed in me.

I don't want you to think it had anything to do with me being a musician. It's more than that. Or maybe less than that. I can't get anything straight in my head down here and I try not to think about what's going to happen to me when I get outside again. Sometime I think I'm going to flip and *never* get outside and sometime I think I'll come straight back. I tell you one thing, though, I'd rather blow my brains out than go through this again. But that's what they all say, so they tell me. If I tell you when I'm coming to New York and if you could meet me, I sure would appreciate it. Give my love to Isabel and the kids and I was sure sorry to hear about little Gracie. I wish I could be like Mama and say the Lord's will be done, but I don't know it seems to me that trouble is the one thing that never does get stopped and I don't know what good it does to blame it on the Lord. But maybe it does some good if you believe it.

Your brother,
Sonny

Then I kept in constant touch with him and I sent him whatever I could and I went to meet him when he came back to New York. When I saw him many things I thought I had forgotten came flooding back to me. This was because I had begun, finally, to wonder about Sonny, about the life that Sonny lived inside. This life, whatever it was, had made him older and thinner and it had deepened the distant stillness in which he had always moved. He looked very unlike my baby brother. Yet, when he smiled, when we shook hands, the baby brother I'd never known looked out from the depths of his private life, like an animal waiting to be coaxed into the light.

"How you been keeping?" he asked me.

"All right. And you?"

"Just fine." He was smiling all over his face. "It's good to see you again."

"It's good to see you."

The seven years' difference in our ages lay between us like a chasm: I wondered if these years would ever operate between us as a bridge. I was remembering, and it made it hard to catch my breath, that I had been there when he was born; and I had heard the first words he had ever spoken. When he started to walk, he walked from our mother straight to me. I caught him just before he fell when he took the first steps he ever took in this world.

"How's Isabel?"

"Just fine. She's dying to see you."

"And the boys?"

"They're fine, too. They're anxious to see their uncle."

"Oh, come on. You know they don't remember me."

"Are you kidding? Of course they remember you."

He grinned again. We got into a taxi. We had a lot to say to each other, far too much to know how to begin.

As the taxi began to move, I asked, "You still want to go to India?"

He laughed. "You still remember that. Hell, no. This place is Indian enough for me."

"It used to belong to them," I said.

And he laughed again. "They damn sure knew what they were doing when they got rid of it."

Years ago, when he was around fourteen, he'd been all hipped on the idea of going to India. He read books about people sitting on rocks, naked, in all kinds of weather, but mostly bad, naturally, and walking barefoot through hot coals and arriving at wisdom. I used to say that it sounded to me as though they were getting away from wisdom as fast as they could. I think he sort of looked down on me for that.

"Do you mind," he asked, "if we have the driver drive alongside the park? On the west side—I haven't seen the city in so long."

"Of course not," I said. I was afraid that I might sound as though I were humoring him, but I hoped he wouldn't take it that way.

So we drove along, between the green of the park and the stony, lifeless elegance of hotels and apartment buildings, toward the vivid, killing streets of our childhood. These streets hadn't changed, though housing projects jutted up out of them now like rocks in the middle of a boiling sea. Most of the houses in which we had grown up had vanished, as had the stores from which we had stolen, the basements in which we had first tried sex, the rooftops from which we had hurled tin cans and bricks. But houses exactly like the houses of our past yet dominated the landscape, boys exactly like the boys we once had been found themselves smothering in these houses, came down into the streets for light and air and found themselves encircled by disaster. Some escaped the trap, most didn't. Those who got out always left something of themselves behind, as some animals amputate a leg and leave it in the trap. It might be said, perhaps, that I had escaped, after all, I was a school teacher; or that Sonny had, he hadn't lived in Harlem for years. Yet, as the cab moved uptown through streets which seemed, with a rush, to darken with dark people, and as I covertly studied Sonny's face, it came to me that what we both were seeking through our separate cab windows was that part of ourselves which had been left behind. It's always at the hour of trouble and confrontation that the missing member aches.

We hit 110th Street and started rolling up Lenox Avenue. And I'd known this avenue all my life, but it seemed to me again, as it had seemed on the day I'd first heard about Sonny's trouble, filled with a hidden menace which was its very breath of life.

"We almost there," said Sonny.

"Almost." We were both too nervous to say anything more.

We live in a housing project. It hasn't been up long. A few days after it was up it seemed uninhabitably new, now, of course, it's already rundown. It looks like a parody of the good, clean, faceless life—God knows the people who live in it do their best to make it a parody. The beat-looking grass lying around isn't enough to make their lives green, the hedges will never hold out the streets, and they know it. The big windows fool no one, they aren't big enough to make space out of no space. They don't bother with the windows, they watch the TV screen instead. The playground is most popular with the children who don't play at jacks, or skip rope, or roller skate, or swing, and they can be found in it after dark. We moved in partly because it's not too far from where I teach, and partly for the kids; but it's really just like the houses in which Sonny and I grew up. The same things happen, they'll have the same things to remember. The moment Sonny and I started into the house I had the feeling that I was simply bringing him back into the danger he had almost died trying to escape.

Sonny had never been talkative. So I don't know why I was sure he'd be dying to talk to me when supper was over the first night. Everything went fine, the oldest boy remembered him, and the youngest boy liked him, and Sonny had remembered to bring something for each of them; and Isabel, who is really much nicer than I am, more open and giving, had gone to a lot of trouble about dinner and was genuinely glad to see him. And she's always been able to tease Sonny in a way that I haven't. It was nice to see her face so vivid again and to hear her laugh and watch her make Sonny laugh. She wasn't, or, anyway, she didn't seem to be, at all uneasy or embarrassed. She chatted as though there were no subject which had to be avoided and she got Sonny past his first, faint stiffness. And thank God she was there, for I was filled with that icy dread again. Everything I did seemed awkward to me, and everything I said sounded freighted with hidden meaning. I was trying to remember everything I'd heard about dope addiction and I couldn't help watching Sonny for signs. I wasn't doing it out of malice. I was trying to find out something about my brother. I was dying to hear him tell me he was safe.

"Safe!" my father grunted, whenever Mama suggested trying to move to a neighborhood which might be safer for children. "Safe, hell! Ain't no place safe for kids, nor nobody."

He always went on like this, but he wasn't, ever, really as bad as he sounded, not even on weekends, when he got drunk. As a matter of fact, he was always on the lookout for "something a little better," but he died before he found it. He died suddenly, during a drunken weekend in the middle of the war, when Sonny was fifteen. He and Sonny hadn't ever got on too well. And this was partly because Sonny was the apple of his father's eye. It was because he loved Sonny so much and was frightened for him, that he was always fighting with him. It doesn't do any good to fight with Sonny. Sonny just moves back, inside himself, where he can't be reached. But the principal reason that they never hit it off is that they were so much alike. Daddy was big and rough and loud-talking, just the opposite of Sonny, but they both had—that same privacy.

Mama tried to tell me something about this, just after Daddy died. I was home on leave from the army.

This was the last time I ever saw my mother alive. Just the same, this picture gets all mixed up in my mind with pictures I had of her when she was younger. The way I always see her is the way she used to be on a Sunday afternoon, say, when the old folks were talking after the big Sunday dinner. I always see her wearing pale blue. She'd be sitting on the sofa. And my father would be sitting in the easy chair, not far from her. And the living room would be full of church folks and relatives. There they sit, in chairs all around the living room, and the night is creeping up outside, but nobody knows it yet. You can see the darkness growing against the windowpanes and you hear the street noises every now and again, or maybe the jangling beat of a tambourine from one of the churches close by, but it's real quiet in the room. For a moment nobody's talking, but every face looks darkening, like the sky outside. And my mother rocks a little from the waist, and my father's eyes are closed. Everyone is looking at something a child can't see. For a minute they've forgotten the children. Maybe a kid is lying on the rug, half asleep. Maybe somebody's got a kid in his lap and is absent-mindedly stroking the kid's head. Maybe there's a kid, quiet and big-eyed, curled up in a big chair in the corner. The silence, the darkness coming, and the darkness in the faces frightens the child obscurely. He hopes that the hand which strokes his forehead will never stop—will never die. He hopes that there will never come a time when the old folks won't be sitting around the living room, talking about where they've come from, and what they've seen, and what's happening to them and their kinfolk.

But something deep and watchful in the child knows that this is bound to end, is already ending. In a moment someone will get up and turn on the light. Then the old folks will remember the children and they won't talk any more that day. And when light fills the room, the child is filled with darkness. He knows that everytime this happens he's moved just a little closer to that darkness outside. The darkness outside is what the old folks have been talking about. It's what they've come from. It's what they endure. The child knows that they won't talk any more because if he knows too much about what's happened to *them*, he'll know too much too soon, about what's going to happen to *him*.

The last time I talked to my mother, I remember I was restless. I wanted to get out and see Isabel. We weren't married then and we had a lot to straighten out between us.

There Mama sat, in black, by the window. She was humming an old church song, *Lord, you brought me from a long ways off.* Sonny was out somewhere. Mama kept watching the streets.

"I don't know," she said, "if I'll ever see you again, after you go off from here. But I hope you'll remember the things I tried to teach you."

"Don't talk like that," I said, and smiled. "You'll be here a long time yet."

She smiled, too, but she said nothing. She was quiet for a long time. And I said, "Mama, don't you worry about nothing. I'll be writing all the time, and you be getting the checks. . . ."

"I want to talk to you about your brother," she said, suddenly. "If anything happens to me he ain't going to have nobody to look out for him."

"Mama," I said, "ain't nothing going to happen to you *or* Sonny. Sonny's all right. He's a good boy and he's got good sense."

"It ain't a question of his being a good boy," Mama said, "nor of his having good sense. It ain't only the bad ones, nor yet the dumb ones that gets sucked under." She stopped, looking at me. "Your Daddy once had a brother," she said, and she smiled in a way that made me feel she was in pain. "You didn't never know that, did you?"

"No," I said, "I never knew that," and I watched her face.

"Oh, yes," she said, "your Daddy had a brother." She looked out of the window again. "I know you never saw your Daddy cry. But *I* did—many a time, through all these years."

I asked her, "What happened to his brother? How come nobody's ever talked about him?"

This was the first time I ever saw my mother look old.

"His brother got killed," she said, "when he was just a little younger than you are now. I knew him. He was a fine boy. He was maybe a little full of the devil, but he didn't mean nobody no harm."

Then she stopped and the room was silent, exactly as it had sometimes been on those Sunday afternoons. Mama kept looking out into the streets.

"He used to have a job in the mill," she said, "and, like all young folks, he just liked to perform on Saturday nights. Saturday nights, him and your father would drift around to different places, go to dances and things like that, or just sit around with people they knew, and your father's brother would sing, he had a fine voice, and play along with himself on his guitar. Well, this particular Saturday night, him and your father was coming home from some place, and they were both a little drunk and there was a moon that night, it was bright like day. Your father's brother was feeling kind of good, and he was whistling to himself, and he had his guitar slung over his shoulder. They was coming down a hill and beneath them was a road that turned off from the highway. Well, your father's brother, being always kind of frisky, decided to run down this hill, and he did, with that guitar banging and clanging behind him, and he ran across the road, and he was making water behind a tree. And your father was sort of amused at him and he was still coming down the hill, kind of slow. Then he heard a car motor and that same minute his brother stepped from behind the tree, into the road, in the moonlight. And he started to cross the road. And your father started to run down the hill, he says he don't know why. This car was full of white men. They was all drunk, and when they seen your father's brother they let out a great whoop and holler and they aimed the car straight at him. They was having fun, they just wanted to scare him, the way they do sometimes, you know. But they was drunk. And I guess the boy, being drunk, too, and scared, kind of lost his head. By the time he jumped it was too late. Your father says he heard his brother scream when the car rolled over him, and he heard the wood of that guitar when it give, and he heard them strings go flying, and he heard them white men shouting, and the car kept on a-going and it ain't stopped till this day. And, time your father got down the hill, his brother weren't nothing but blood and pulp."

Tears were gleaming on my mother's face. There wasn't anything I could say.

"He never mentioned it," she said, "because I never let him mention it before you children. Your Daddy was like a crazy man that night and for many a night thereafter. He says he never in his life seen anything as dark as that road after the lights of that car had gone away. Weren't nothing, weren't nobody on that road, just your Daddy and his brother and that busted guitar. Oh, yes. Your Daddy never did really get right again. Till the day he died he weren't sure but that every white man he saw was the man that killed his brother."

She stopped and took out her handkerchief and dried her eyes and looked at me.

"I ain't telling you all this," she said, "to make you scared or bitter or to make you hate nobody. I'm telling you this because you got a brother. And the world ain't changed."

I guess I didn't want to believe this. I guess she saw this in my face. She turned away from me, toward the window again, searching those streets.

"But I praise my Redeemer," she said at last, "that He called your Daddy home before me. I ain't saying it to throw no flowers at myself, but, I declare, it keeps me from feeling too cast down to know I helped your father get safely through this world. You father always acted like he was the roughest, strongest man on earth. And everybody took him to be like that. But if he hadn't had *me* there—to see his tears!"

She was crying again. Still, I couldn't move. I said, "Lord, Lord, Mama, I didn't know it was like that."

"Oh, honey," she said, "there's a lot that you don't know. But you are going to find it out." She stood up from the window and came over to me. "You got to hold on to your brother," she said, "and don't let him fall, no matter what it looks like is happening to him and no matter how evil you gets with him. You going to be evil with him many a time. But don't you forget what I told you, you hear?"

"I won't forget," I said. "Don't you worry, I won't forget. I won't let nothing happen to Sonny."

My mother smiled as though she were amused at something she saw in my face. Then, "You may not be able to stop nothing from happening. But you got to let him know you's *there.*"

Two days later I was married, and then I was gone. And I had a lot of things on my mind and I pretty well forgot my promise to Mama until I got shipped home on a special furlough for her funeral.

And, after the funeral, with just Sonny and me alone in the empty kitchen, I tried to find out something about him.

"What do you want to do?" I asked him.

"I'm going to be a musician," he said.

For he had graduated, in the time I had been away, from dancing to the juke box to finding out who was playing what, and what they were doing with it, and he had bought himself a set of drums.

"You mean, you want to be a drummer?" I somehow had the feeling that being a drummer might be all right for other people but not for my brother Sonny.

"I don't think," he said, looking at me very gravely, "that I'll ever be a good drummer. But I think I can play a piano."

I frowned. I'd never played the role of the older brother quite so seriously before, had scarcely ever, in fact, *asked* Sonny a damn thing. I sensed myself in the presence of something I didn't really know how to handle, didn't understand. So I made my frown a little deeper as I asked: "What kind of musician do you want to be?"

He grinned. "How many kinds do you think there are?"

"Be *serious,*" I said.

He laughed, throwing his head back, and then looked at me. "I *am* serious."

"Well, then, for Christ's sake, stop kidding around and answer a serious question. I mean, do you want to be a concert pianist, you want to play classical music and all that, or—or what?" Long before I finished he was laughing again. "For Christ's *sake,* Sonny!"

He sobered, but with difficulty. "I'm sorry. But you sound so—*scared!*" and he was off again.

"Well, you may think it's funny now, baby, but it's not going to be so funny when you have to make your living at it, let me tell you *that.*" I was furious because I knew he was laughing at me and I didn't know why.

"No," he said, very sober now, and afraid, perhaps, that he'd hurt me, "I don't want to be a classical pianist. That isn't what interests me. I mean"—he paused, looking hard at me, as though his eyes would help me to understand, and then gestured helplessly, as though perhaps his hand would help—"I mean, I'll have a lot of studying to do, and I'll have to study *everything,* but, I mean, I want to play *with*—jazz musicians." He stopped. "I want to play jazz," he said.

Well, the word had never before sounded as heavy, as real, as it sounded that afternoon in Sonny's mouth. I just looked at him and I was probably frowning a real frown by this time. I simply couldn't see why on earth he'd want to spend his time hanging around nightclubs, clowning around on bandstands, while people pushed each other around a dance floor. It seemed—beneath him, somehow. I had never thought about it before, had never been forced to, but I suppose I had always put jazz musicians in a class with what Daddy called "good-time people."

"Are you *serious?*"

"Hell, *yes*, I'm serious."

He looked more helpless than ever, and annoyed, and deeply hurt.

I suggested, helpfully: "You mean—like Louis Armstrong?"

His face closed as though I'd struck him. "No. I'm not talking about none of that old-time, down home crap."

"Well, look, Sonny, I'm sorry, don't get mad. I just don't altogether get it, that's all. Name somebody—you know, a jazz musician you admire."

"Bird."

"Who?"

"Bird! Charlie Parker! Don't they teach you nothing in the goddamn army?"

I lit a cigarette. I was surprised and then a little amused to discover that I was trembling. "I've been out of touch," I said. "You'll have to be patient with me. Now. Who's this Parker character?"

"He's just one of the greatest jazz musicians alive," said Sonny, sullenly, his hands in his pockets, his back to me. "Maybe *the* greatest," he added, bitterly, "that's probably why *you* never heard of him."

"All right," I said, "I'm ignorant. I'm sorry. I'll go out and buy all the cat's records right away, all right?"

"It don't," said Sonny, with dignity, "make any difference to me. I don't care what you listen to. Don't do me no favors."

I was beginning to realize that I'd never seen him so upset before. With another part of my mind I was thinking that this would probably turn out to be one of those things kids go through and that I shouldn't make it seem important by pushing it too hard. Still, I didn't think it would do any harm to ask: "Doesn't all this take a lot of time? Can you make a living at it?"

He turned back to me and half leaned, half sat, on the kitchen table. "Everything takes time," he said, "and—well, yes, sure, I can make a living at it. But what I don't seem to be able to make you understand is that it's the only thing I want to do."

"Well, Sonny," I said, gently, "you know people can't always do exactly what they *want* to do—"

"No, I don't know that," said Sonny, surprising me. "I think people *ought* to do what they want to do, what else are they alive for?"

"You getting to be a big boy," I said desperately, "it's time you started thinking about your future."

"I'm thinking about my future," said Sonny, grimly. "I think about it all the time."

I gave up. I decided, if he didn't change his mind, that we could always talk about it later. "In the meantime," I said, "you got to finish school." We had already decided that he'd have to move in with Isabel and her folks. I knew this wasn't the ideal arrangement because Isabel's folks are inclined to be dicty and they hadn't especially wanted Isabel to marry me. But I didn't know what else to do. "And we have to get you fixed up at Isabel's."

There was a long silence. He moved from the kitchen table to the window. "That's a terrible idea. You know it yourself."

"Do you have a *better* idea?"

He just walked up and down the kitchen for a minute. He was as tall as I was. He had started to shave. I suddenly had the feeling that I didn't know him at all.

He stopped at the kitchen table and picked up my cigarettes. Looking at me with a kind of mocking, amused defiance, he put one between his lips. "You mind?"

"You smoking already?"

He lit the cigarette and nodded, watching me through the smoke. "I just wanted to see if I'd have the courage to smoke in front of you." He grinned and blew a great cloud of smoke to the ceiling. "It was easy." He looked at my face. "Come on, now. I bet you was smoking at my age, tell the truth."

I didn't say anything but the truth was on my face, and he laughed. But now there was something very strained in his laugh. "Sure. And I bet that ain't all you was doing."

He was frightening me a little. "Cut the crap," I said. "We already decided that you was going to go and live at Isabel's. Now what's got into you all of a sudden?"

"*You* decided it," he pointed out. "*I* didn't decide nothing." He stopped in front of me, leaning against the stove, arms loosely folded. "Look, brother. I don't want to stay in Harlem no more, I really don't." He was very earnest. He looked at me, then over toward the kitchen window. There was something in his eyes I'd never seen before, some thoughtfulness, some worry all his own. He rubbed the muscle of one arm. "It's time I was getting out of here."

"Where do you want to *go*, Sonny?"

"I want to join the army. Or the navy, I don't care. If I say I'm old enough, they'll believe me."

Then I got mad. It was because I was so scared. "You must be crazy. You goddamn fool, what the hell do you want to go and join the *army* for?"

"I just told you. To get out of Harlem."

"Sonny, you haven't even finished *school*. And if you really want to be a musician, how do you expect to study if you're in the *army*?"

He looked at me, trapped, and in anguish. "There's ways. I might be able to work out some kind of deal. Anyway, I'll have the G.I. Bill when I come out."

"*If* you come out." We stared at each other. "Sonny, please. Be reasonable. I know the setup is far from perfect. But we got to do the best we can."

"I ain't learning nothing in school," he said. "Even when I go." He turned away from me and opened the window and threw his cigarette out into the narrow alley. I watched his back. "At least, I ain't learning nothing you'd want me to learn." He slammed the window so hard I thought the glass would fly out, and turned back to me. "And I'm sick of the stink of these garbage cans!"

"Sonny," I said, "I know how you feel. But if you don't finish school now, you're going to be sorry later that you didn't." I grabbed him by the shoulders. "And you only got another year. It ain't so bad. And I'll come back and I swear I'll help you do *whatever* you want to do. Just try to put up with it till I come back. Will you please do that? For me?"

He didn't answer and he wouldn't look at me.

"Sonny. You hear me?"

He pulled away. "I hear you. But you never hear anything *I* say."

I didn't know what to say to that. He looked out of the window and then back at me. "OK," he said, and sighed. "I'll try."

Then I said, trying to cheer him up a little, "They got a piano at Isabel's. You can practice on it."

And as a matter of fact, it did cheer him up for a minute. "That's right," he said to himself. "I forgot that." His face relaxed a little. But the worry, the thoughtfulness, played on it still, the way shadows play on a face which is staring into the fire.

But I thought I'd never hear the end of that piano. At first, Isabel would write me, saying how nice it was that Sonny was so serious about his music and how, as soon as he came in from school, or wherever he had been when he was supposed to be at school, he went straight to that piano and stayed there until suppertime. And, after supper, he went back to that piano and stayed there until everybody went to bed. He was at the piano all day Saturday and all day Sunday. Then he bought a record player and started playing records. He'd play one record over and over again, all day long sometimes, and he'd improvise along with it on the piano. Or he'd play one section of the record, one chord, one change, one progression, then he'd do it on the piano. Then back to the record. Then back to the piano.

Well, I really don't know how they stood it. Isabel finally confessed that it wasn't like living with a person at all, it was like living with sound. And the sound didn't make any sense to her, didn't make any sense to any of them—naturally. They began, in a way, to be afflicted by this presence that was living in their home. It was as though Sonny were some sort of god, or monster. He moved in an atmosphere which wasn't like theirs at all. They fed him and he ate, he washed himself, he walked in and out of their door; he certainly wasn't nasty or unpleasant or rude, Sonny isn't any of those things; but it was as though he were all wrapped up in some cloud, some fire, some vision all his own; and there wasn't any way to reach him.

At the same time, he wasn't really a man yet, he was still a child, and they had to watch out for him in all kinds of ways. They certainly couldn't throw him out. Neither did they dare to make a great scene about that piano because even they dimly sensed, as I sensed, from so many thousands of miles away, that Sonny was at that piano playing for his life.

But he hadn't been going to school. One day a letter came from the school board and Isabel's mother got it—there had, apparently, been other letters but Sonny had torn them up. This day, when Sonny came in, Isabel's mother showed him the letter and asked where he'd been spending his time. And she finally got it out of him that he'd been down in Greenwich Village, with musicians and other characters, in a white girl's apartment. And this scared her and she started to scream at him and what came up, once she began—though she denies it to this day—was what sacrifices they were making to give Sonny a decent home and how little he appreciated it.

Sonny didn't play the piano that day. By evening, Isabel's mother had calmed down but then there was the old man to deal with, and Isabel herself. Isabel says she did her best to be calm but she broke down and started crying. She says she just watched Sonny's face. She could tell, by watching him, what was happening with him. And what was happening was that they penetrated his cloud, they had reached him. Even if their fingers had been a thousand times more gentle than human fingers ever are, he could hardly help feeling that they had stripped him naked and were spitting on that nakedness. For he also had to see that his presence, that music, which was life or death to him, had been torture for them and that they had endured it, not at all for his sake, but only for mine. And Sonny couldn't take that. He can take it a little better today than he could then but he's still not very good at it and, frankly, I don't know anybody who is.

The silence of the next few days must have been louder than the sound of all the music ever played since time began. One morning, before she went to work, Isabel was in his room for something and she suddenly realized that all of his records were gone. And she knew for certain that he was gone. And he was. He went as far as the navy would carry him. He finally sent me a postcard from some place in Greece and that was the first I knew that Sonny was still alive. I didn't see him any more until we were both back in New York and the war had long been over.

He was a man by then, of course, but I wasn't willing to see it. He came by the house from time to time, but we fought almost every time we met. I didn't like the way he carried himself, loose and dreamlike all the time, and I didn't like his friends, and his music seemed to be merely an excuse for the life he led. It sounded just that weird and disordered.

Then we had a fight, a pretty awful fight, and I didn't see him for months. By and by I looked him up, where he was living, in a furnished room in the Village, and I tried to make it up. But there were lots of people in the room and Sonny just lay on his bed, and he wouldn't come downstairs with me, and he treated these other people as though they were his family and I weren't. So I got mad and then he got mad, and then I told him that he might just as well be dead as live the way he was living. Then he stood up and he told me not to worry about him any more in life, that he *was* dead as far as I was concerned. Then he pushed me to the door and the other people looked on as though nothing were happening, and he slammed the door behind me. I stood in the hallway, staring at the door. I heard somebody laugh in the room and then the tears came to my eyes. I started down the steps, whistling to keep from crying, I kept whistling to myself, *You going to need me, baby, one of these cold, rainy days.*

I read about Sonny's trouble in the spring. Little Grace died in the fall. She was a beautiful little girl. But she only lived a little over two years. She died of polio and she suffered. She had a slight fever for a couple of days, but it didn't seem like anything and we just kept her in bed. And we would certainly have called the doctor, but the fever dropped, she seemed to be all right. So we thought it had just been a cold. Then, one day, she was up, playing, Isabel was in the kitchen fixing lunch for the two boys when they'd come in from school, and she heard Grace fall down in the living room. When you have a lot of children you don't always start running when one of them falls, unless they start screaming or something. And, this time, Grace was quiet. Yet, Isabel says that when she heard that *thump* and then that silence, something happened in her to make her afraid. And she ran to the living room and there was little Grace on the floor, all twisted up, and the reason she hadn't screamed was that she couldn't get her breath. And when she did scream, it was the worst sound, Isabel says, that she'd ever heard in all her life, and she still hears it sometimes in her dreams. Isabel will sometimes wake me up with a low, moaning, strangled sound and I have to be quick to awaken her and hold her to me and where Isabel is weeping against me seems a mortal wound.

I think I may have written Sonny the very day that little Grace was buried. I was sitting in the living room in the dark, by myself, and I suddenly thought of Sonny. My trouble made his real.

One Saturday afternoon, when Sonny had been living with us, or, anyway, been in our house, for nearly two weeks, I found myself wandering aimlessly about the living room, drinking from a can of beer, and trying to work up the courage to search Sonny's room. He was out, he was usually out whenever I was home, and Isabel had taken the children to see their grandparents. Suddenly I was standing still in front of the living room window, watching Seventh Avenue. The idea of searching Sonny's room made me still. I scarcely dared to admit to myself what I'd be searching for. I didn't know what I'd do if I found it. Or if I didn't.

On the sidewalk across from me, near the entrance to a barbecue joint, some people were holding an old-fashioned revival meeting. The barbecue cook, wearing a dirty white apron, his conked hair reddish and metallic in the pale sun, and a cigarette between his lips, stood in the doorway, watching them. Kids and older people paused in their errands and stood there, along with some older men and a couple of very tough-looking women who watched everything that happened on the avenue, as though they owned it, or were maybe owned by it. Well, they were watching this, too. The revival was being carried on by three sisters in black, and a brother. All they had were their voices and their Bibles and a tambourine. The brother was testifying and while he testified two of the sisters stood together, seeming to say, amen, and the third sister walked around with the tambourine outstretched and a couple of people dropped coins into it. Then the brother's testimony ended and the sister who had been taking up the collection dumped the coins into her palm and transferred them to the pocket of her long black robe. Then she raised both hands, striking the tambourine against the air, and then against one hand, and she started to sing. And the two other sisters and the brother joined in.

It was strange, suddenly, to watch, though I had been seeing these street meetings all my life. So, of course, had everybody else down there. Yet, they paused and watched and listened and I stood still at the window. "*Tis the old ship of Zion,*" they sang, and the sister with the tambourine kept a steady, jangling beat, "*it has rescued many a thousand!*" Not a soul under the sound of their voices was hearing this song for the first time, not one of them had been rescued. Nor had they seen much in the way of rescue work being done around them. Neither did they especially believe in the holiness of the three sisters and the brother, they knew too much about them, knew where they lived, and how. The woman with the tambourine, whose voice dominated the air, whose face was bright with joy, was divided by very little from the woman who stood watching her, a cigarette between her heavy, chapped lips, her hair a cuckoo's nest, her face scarred and swollen from many beatings, and her black eyes glittering like coal. Perhaps they both knew this, which was why, when, as rarely, they addressed each other, they addressed each other as Sister. As the singing filled the air the watching, listening faces underwent a change, the eyes focusing on something within; the music seemed to soothe a poison out of them; and time seemed, nearly, to fall away from the sullen, belligerent, battered faces, as though they were fleeing back to their first condition, while dreaming of their last. The barbecue cook half shook his head and smiled, and dropped his cigarette and disappeared into his joint. A man fumbled in his pockets for change and stood holding it in his hand impatiently, as though he had just remembered a pressing appointment further up the avenue. He looked furious. Then I saw Sonny, standing on the edge of the crowd. He was carrying a wide, flat notebook with a green cover, and it made him look, from where I was standing, almost like a schoolboy. The coppery sun brought out the copper in his skin, he was very faintly smiling, standing very still. Then the singing stopped, the tambourine turned into a collection plate again. The furious man dropped in his coins and vanished, so did a couple of the women, and Sonny dropped some change in the plate, looking directly at the woman with a little smile. He started across the avenue, toward the house. He has a slow, loping walk, something like the way Harlem hipsters walk, only he's imposed on this his own half-beat. I had never really noticed it before.

I stayed at the window, both relieved and apprehensive. As Sonny disappeared from my sight, they began singing again. And they were still singing when his key turned in the lock.

"Hey," he said.

"Hey, yourself. You want some beer?"

"No. Well, maybe." But he came up to the window and stood beside me, looking out. "What a warm voice," he said.

They were singing *If I could only hear my mother pray again!*

"Yes," I said, "and she can sure beat that tambourine."

"But what a terrible song," he said, and laughed. He dropped his notebook on the sofa and disappeared into the kitchen. "Where's Isabel and the kids?"

"I think they went to see their grandparents. You hungry?"

"No." He came back into the living room with his can of beer. "You want to come some place with me tonight?"

I sensed, I don't know how, that I couldn't possibly say no. "Sure. Where?"

He sat down on the sofa and picked up his notebook and started leafing through it. "I'm going to sit in with some fellows in a joint in the Village."

"You mean, you're going to play, tonight?"

"That's right." He took a swallow of his beer and moved back to the window. He gave me a sidelong look. "If you can stand it."

"I'll try," I said.

He smiled to himself and we both watched as the meeting across the way broke up. The three sisters and the brother, heads bowed, were singing *God be with you till we meet again.* The faces around them were very quiet. Then the song ended. The small crowd dispersed. We watched the three women and the lone man walk slowly up the avenue.

"When she was singing before," said Sonny, abruptly, "her voice reminded me for a minute of what heroin feels like sometimes—when it's in your veins. It makes you feel sort of warm and cool at the same time. And distant. And—and sure." He sipped his beer, very deliberately not looking at me. I watched his face. "It makes you feel—in control. Sometimes you've got to have that feeling."

"Do you?" I sat down slowly in the easy chair.

"Sometimes." He went to the sofa and picked up his notebook again. "Some people do."

"In order," I asked, "to play?" And my voice was very ugly, full of contempt and anger.

"Well"—he looked at me with great, troubled eyes, as though, in fact, he hoped his eyes would tell me things he could never otherwise say—"they *think* so. And *if* they think so—!"

"And what do *you* think?" I asked.

He sat on the sofa and put his can of beer on the floor. "I don't know," he said, and I couldn't be sure if he were answering my question or pursuing his thoughts. His face didn't tell me. "It's not so much to *play*. It's to *stand* it, to be able to make it at all. On any level." He frowned and smiled: "In order to keep from shaking to pieces."

"But these friends of yours," I said, "they seem to shake themselves to pieces pretty goddamn fast."

"Maybe." He played with the notebook. And something told me that I should curb my tongue, that Sonny was doing his best to talk, that I should listen. "But of course you only know the ones that've gone to pieces. Some don't—or at least they haven't *yet* and that's just about all *any* of us can say." He paused. "And then there are some who just live, really, in hell, and they know it and they see what's happening and they go right on. I don't know." He sighed, dropped the notebook, folded his arms. "Some guys, you can tell from the way they play, they on something *all* the time. And you can see that, well, it makes something real for them. But of course," he picked up his beer from the floor and sipped it and put the can down again, "they *want* to, too, you've got to see that. Even some of them that say they don't—*some*, not all."

"And what about you?" I asked—I couldn't help it. "What about you? Do *you* want to?"

He stood up and walked to the window and remained silent for a long time. Then he sighed. "Me," he said. Then: "While I was downstairs before, on my way here, listening to that woman sing, it struck me all of a sudden how much suffering she must have had to go through—to sing like that. It's *repulsive* to think you have to suffer that much."

I said: "But there's no way not to suffer—is there, Sonny?"

"I believe not," he said and smiled, "but that's never stopped anyone from trying." He looked at me. "Has it?" I realized, with this mocking look, that there stood between us, forever, beyond the power of time or forgiveness, the fact that I had held silence—so long!—when he had needed human speech to help him. He turned back to the window. "No, there's no way not to suffer. But you try all kinds of ways to keep from drowning in it, to keep on top of it, and to make it seem—well, like *you*. Like you did something, all right, and now you're suffering for it. You know?" I said nothing. "Well you know," he said, impatiently, "why *do* people suffer? Maybe it's better to do something to give it a reason, *any* reason."

"But we just agreed," I said, "that there's no way not to suffer. Isn't it better, then, just to—take it?"

"But nobody just takes it," Sonny cried, "that's what I'm telling you! *Everybody* tries not to. You're just hung up on the *way* some people try—it's not *your* way!"

The hair on my face began to itch, my face felt wet. "That's not true," I said, "that's not true. I don't give a damn what other people do, I don't even care how they suffer. I just care how *you* suffer." And he looked at me. "Please believe me," I said, "I don't want to see you—die—trying not to suffer."

"I won't," he said, flatly, "die trying not to suffer. At least, not any faster than anybody else."

"But there's no need," I said, trying to laugh, "is there? in killing yourself."

I wanted to say more, but I couldn't. I wanted to talk about will power and how life could be—well, beautiful. I wanted to say that it was all within; but was it? or, rather, wasn't that exactly the trouble? And I wanted to promise that I would never fail him again. But it would all have sounded—empty words and lies.

So I made the promise to myself and prayed that I would keep it.

"It's terrible sometimes, inside," he said, "that's what's the trouble. You walk these streets, black and funky and cold, and there's not really a living ass to talk to, and there's nothing shaking, and there's no way of getting it out—that storm inside. You can't talk it and you can't make love with it, and when you finally try to get with it and play it, you realize *nobody's* listening. So *you've* got to listen. You got to find a way to listen."

And then he walked away from the window and sat on the sofa again, as though all the wind had suddenly been knocked out of him. "Sometimes you'll do *anything* to play, even cut your mother's throat." He laughed and looked at me. "Or your brother's." Then he sobered. "Or your own." Then: "Don't worry. I'm all right now and I think I'll *be* all right. But I can't forget—where I've been. I don't mean just the physical place I've been, I mean where I've *been*. And *what* I've been."

"What have you been, Sonny?" I asked.

He smiled—but sat sideways on the sofa, his elbow resting on the back, his fingers playing with his mouth and chin, not looking at me. "I've been something I didn't recognize, didn't know I could be. Didn't know anybody could be." He stopped, looking inward, looking helplessly young, looking old. "I'm not talking about it now because I feel *guilty* or anything like that—maybe it would be better if I did, I don't know. Anyway, I can't really talk about it. Not to you, not to anybody," and now he turned and faced me. "Sometimes, you know, and it was actually when I was most *out* of the world, I felt that I was in it, that I was *with* it, really, and I could play or I didn't really have to *play*, it just came out of me, it was there. And I don't know how I played, thinking about it now, but I know I did awful things, those times, sometimes, to people. Or it wasn't that I *did* anything to them—it was that they weren't real." He picked up the beer can; it was empty; he rolled it between his palms: "And other times—well, I needed a fix, I needed to find a place to lean, I needed to clear a space to *listen*—and I couldn't find it, and I—went crazy, I did terrible things to *me*, I was terrible *for* me." He began pressing the beer can between his hands, I watched the metal begin to give. It glittered, as he played with it, like a knife, and I was afraid he would cut himself, but I said nothing. "Oh well. I can never tell you. I was all by myself at the bottom of something, stinking and sweating and crying and shaking, and I smelled it, you know? *my* stink, and I thought I'd die if I couldn't get away from it and yet, all the same, I knew that everything I was doing was just locking me in with it. And I didn't know," he paused, still flattening the beer can, "I didn't know, I still *don't* know, something kept telling me that maybe it was good to smell your own stink, but I didn't think that *that* was what I'd been trying to do—and—who can stand it?" and he abruptly dropped the ruined beer can, looking at me with a small, still smile, and then rose, walking to the window as though it were the lodestone rock. I watched his face, he watched the avenue. "I couldn't tell you when Mama died—but the reason I wanted to leave Harlem so bad was to get away from drugs. And then, when I ran away, that's what I was running from—really. When I came back, nothing had changed, *I* hadn't changed, I was just—older." And he stopped, drumming with his fingers on the windowpane. The sun had vanished, soon darkness would fall. I watched his face. "It can come again," he said, almost as though speaking to himself. Then he turned to me. "It can come again," he repeated. "I just want you to know that."

"All right," I said, at last. "So it can come again, All right."

He smiled, but the smile was sorrowful. "I had to try to tell you," he said.

"Yes," I said. "I understand that."

"You're my brother," he said, looking straight at me, and not smiling at all.

"Yes," I repeated, "yes. I understand that."

He turned back to the window, looking out. "All that hatred down there," he said, "all that hatred and misery and love. It's a wonder it doesn't blow the avenue apart."

We went to the only nightclub on a short, dark street, downtown. We squeezed through the narrow, chattering, jam-packed bar to the entrance of the big room, where the bandstand was. And we stood there for a moment, for the lights were very dim in this room and we couldn't see. Then, "Hello, boy," said a voice and an enormous black man, much older than Sonny or myself, erupted out of all that atmospheric lighting and put an arm around Sonny's shoulder. "I been sitting right here," he said, "waiting for you."

He had a big voice, too, and heads in the darkness turned toward us.

Sonny grinned and pulled a little away, and said, "Creole, this is my brother. I told you about him."

Creole shook my hand. "I'm glad to meet you, son," he said, and it was clear that he was glad to meet me *there*, for Sonny's sake. And he smiled, "You got a real musician in *your* family," and he took his arm from Sonny's shoulder and slapped him, lightly, affectionately, with the back of his hand.

"Well. Now I've heard it all," said a voice behind us. This was another musician, and a friend of Sonny's, a coal-black, cheerful-looking man, built close to the ground. He immediately began confiding to me, at the top of his lungs, the most terrible things about Sonny, his teeth gleaming like a lighthouse and his laugh coming up out of him like the beginning of an earthquake. And it turned out that everyone at the bar knew Sonny, or almost everyone; some were musicians, working there, or nearby, or not working, some were simply hangers-on, and some were there to hear Sonny play. I was introduced to all of them and they were all very polite to me. Yet, it was clear that, for them, I was only Sonny's brother. Here, I was in Sonny's world. Or, rather: his kingdom. Here, it was not even a question that his veins bore royal blood.

They were going to play soon and Creole installed me, by myself, at a table in a dark corner. Then I watched them, Creole, and the little black man, and Sonny, and the others, while they horsed around, standing just below the bandstand. The light from the bandstand spilled just a little short of them and, watching them laughing and gesturing and moving about, I had the feeling that they, nevertheless, were being most careful not to step into that circle of light too suddenly: that if they moved into the light too suddenly, without thinking, they would perish in flame. Then, while I watched, one of them, the small, black man, moved into the light and crossed the bandstand and started fooling around with his drums. Then—being funny and being, also, extremely ceremonious—Creole took Sonny by the arm and led him to the piano. A woman's voice called Sonny's name and a few hands started clapping. And Sonny, also being funny and being ceremonious, and so touched, I think, that he could have cried, but neither hiding it nor showing it, riding it like a man, grinned, and put both hands to his heart and bowed from the waist.

Creole then went to the bass fiddle and a lean, very bright-skinned brown man jumped up on the bandstand and picked up his horn. So there they were, and the atmosphere on the bandstand and in the room began to change and tighten. Someone stepped up to the microphone and announced them. Then there were all kinds of murmurs. Some people at the bar shushed others. The waitress ran around, frantically getting in the last orders, guys and chicks got closer to each other, and the lights on the bandstand, on the quartet, turned to a kind of indigo. Then they all looked different there. Creole looked about him for the last time, as though he were making certain that all his chickens were in the coop, and then he—jumped and stuck the fiddle. And there they were.

All I know about music is that not many people ever really hear it. And even then, on the rare occasions when something opens within, and the music enters, what we mainly hear, or hear corroborated, are personal, private, vanishing evocations. But the man who creates the music is hearing something else, is dealing with the roar rising from the void and imposing order on it as it hits the air. What is evoked in him, then, is of another order, more terrible because it has no words, and triumphant, too, for that same reason. And his triumph, when he triumphs, is ours. I just watched Sonny's face. His face was troubled, he was working hard, but he wasn't with it. And I had the feeling that, in a way, everyone on the bandstand was waiting for him, both waiting for him and pushing him along. But as I began to watch Creole, I realized that it was Creole who held them all back. He had them on a short rein. Up there, keeping the beat with his whole body, wailing on the fiddle, with his eyes half closed, he was listening to everything, but he was listening to Sonny. He was having a dialogue with Sonny. He wanted Sonny to leave the shoreline and strike out for the deep water. He was Sonny's witness that deep water and drowning were not the same thing—he had been there, and he knew. And he wanted Sonny to know. He was waiting for Sonny to do the things on the keys which would let Creole know that Sonny was in the water.

And, while Creole listened, Sonny moved, deep within, exactly like someone in torment. I had never before thought of how awful the relationship must be between the musician and his instrument. He has to fill it, this instrument, with the breath of life, his own. He has to make it do what he wants it to do. And a piano is just a piano. It's made out of so much wood and wires and little hammers and big ones, and ivory. While there's only so much you can do with it, the only way to find this out is to try; to try and make it do everything.

And Sonny hadn't been near a piano for over a year. And he wasn't on much better terms with his life, not the life that stretched before him now. He and the piano stammered, started one way, got scared, stopped; started another way, panicked, marked time, started again; then seemed to have found a direction, panicked again, got stuck. And the face I saw on Sonny I'd never seen before. Everything had been burned out of it, and, at the same time, things usually hidden were being burned in, by the fire and fury of the battle which was occurring in him up there.

Yet, watching Creole's face as they neared the end of the first set, I had the feeling that something had happened, something I hadn't heard. Then they finished, there was scattered applause, and then, without an instant's warning, Creole started into something else, it was almost sardonic, it was *Am I Blue*. And, as though he commanded, Sonny began to play. Something began to happen. And Creole let out the reins. The dry, low, black man said something awful on the drums, Creole answered, and the drums talked back. Then the horn insisted, sweet and high, slightly detached perhaps, and Creole listened, commenting now and then, dry, and driving, beautiful and calm and old. Then they all came together again, and Sonny was part of the family again. I could tell this from his face. He seemed to have found, right there beneath his fingers, a damn brand-new piano. It seemed that he couldn't get over it. Then, for awhile, just being happy with Sonny, they seemed to be agreeing with him that brand-new pianos certainly were a gas.

Then Creole stepped forward to remind them that what they were playing was the blues. He hit something in all of them, he hit something in me, myself, and the music tightened and deepened, apprehension began to beat the air. Creole began to tell us what the blues were all about. They were not about anything very new. He and his boys up there were keeping it new, at the risk of ruin, destruction, madness, and death, in order to find new ways to make us listen. For, while the tale of how we suffer, and how we are delighted, and how we may triumph is never new, it always must be heard. There isn't any other tale to tell, it's the only light we've got in all this darkness.

And this tale, according to that face, that body, those strong hands on those strings, has another aspect in every country, and a new depth in every generation. Listen, Creole seemed to be saying, listen. Now these are Sonny's blues. He made the little black man on the drums know it, and the bright, brown man on the horn. Creole wasn't trying any longer to get Sonny in the water. He was wishing him Godspeed. Then he stepped back, very slowly, filling the air with the immense suggestion that Sonny speak for himself.

Then they all gathered around Sonny and Sonny played. Every now and again one of them seemed to say, amen. Sonny's fingers filled the air with life, his life. But that life contained so many others. And Sonny went all the way back, he really began with the spare, flat statement of the opening phrase of the song. Then he began to make it his. It was very beautiful because it wasn't hurried and it was no longer a lament. I seemed to hear with what burning he had made it his, with what burning we had yet to make it ours, how we could cease lamenting. Freedom lurked around us and I understood, at last, that he could help us to be free if we would listen, that he would never be free until we did. Yet, there was no battle in his face now. I heard what he had gone through, and would continue to go through until he came to rest in earth. He had made it his: that long line, of which we knew only Mama and Daddy. And he was giving it back, as everything must be given back, so that, passing through death, it can live forever. I saw my mother's face again, and felt, for the first time, how the stones of the road she had walked on must have bruised her feet. I saw the moonlit road where my father's brother died. And it brought something else back to me, and carried me past it. I saw my little girl again and felt Isabel's tears again, and I felt my own tears begin to rise. And I was yet aware that this was only a moment, that the world waited outside, as hungry as a tiger, and that trouble stretched above us, longer than the sky.

Then it was over. Creole and Sonny let out their breath, both soaking wet, and grinning. There was a lot of applause and some of it was real. In the dark, the girl came by and I asked her to take drinks to the bandstand. There was a long pause, while they talked up there in the indigo light and after awhile I saw the girl put a Scotch and milk on top of the piano for Sonny. He didn't seem to notice it, but just before they started playing again, he sipped from it and looked toward me, and nodded. Then he put it back on top of the piano. For me, then, as they began to play again, it glowed and shook above my brother's head like the very cup of trembling.

From *Poetry of the Blues*

Samuel Charters

WITHIN the blues there is a conscious use of the poetic devices that have been for centuries part of the English poetic tradition. Although the idea of a blues verse may be relatively simple the language which expresses it has often a marked sophistication. The directness and immediacy of the experience is heightened with an imagery and a symbolism that is itself drawn from the reality of the life. It is a poetic idiom that finds its images in the cabins and the tenements, in the fields, the empty roads, and the crowded streets of American Negro life.

The simile, the direct comparison, is used often in blues verses. One of the earliest lines, used in blues in every part of the South, was the well-known,

> My woman has a heart like a stone cast in the sea . . .

A line still used in Mississippi and Tennessee is the vivid,

> Put your arms around me like the circle 'round the sun . . .

The singer who first compared the "circle 'round the sun" with the warmth and the intensity of an embrace found his comparison in the sun over his head as he stood in the summer fields, just as Blind Lemon Jefferson, in describing a woman, found his comparison in the movements of the squirrels in the brush along the stream beds in Texas where he had been raised.

> She's a fair made woman, cunning as a squirrel . . .

The metaphor, the indirect comparison, is less often used, but it still is found in many blues. Big Joe Williams sings,

---

Reprinted from *The Poetry of the Blues*, by Samuel Charters (New York: Avon, 1963), 43–56.

Before I be your dog, before I be your dog,
'Fore I be your dog, if I had my way,
Make you walk the log . . .

Like much of blues metaphor this could be read as an image, rather than an indirect comparison, but the distinction between the two is often slight and depends on the singer's interpretation. If Big Joe meant "Before I be (like) your dog," then the phrase is a metaphor, but if he meant, "Before I (let you treat me the way you treat) your dog," then he intended it as an image. There is such an extended use of imagery in the blues that it has taken the place of metaphor as a dominant poetic device.

Personification, giving to an object or an idea the characteristics of a human being, has always been important in the blues, and even in some early work song verses the "blues" itself has already become almost human. By the late 1920's Lonnie Johnson could sing,

People, I've stood these blues 'bout as long as I can.
I walked all night with these blues, we both joined hand in hand.
And they travelled my heart through, just like a natural man.

referring to the blues as someone he could walk all night with ". . . joined hand in hand." In other verses, however, the word is still used in the Elizabethan sense of "blue devils." It is this meaning that is intended in the widely known verse,

Woke up this morning, blues all 'round my bed,
Woke up this morning, blues all 'round my bed,
Picked up my pillow, blues all under my head.

In Blind Willie McTell's verse,

Blues grabbed me at midnight, didn't turn me loose 'til day,
Blues grabbed me at midnight, didn't turn me loose 'til day,
I didn't have no mama to drive these blues away,

it could be the blues personified as a human figure that seized him, or the "blue devils," or simply the mood of the blues. One of the most vivid of the personifications of the blues is Ma Rainey's "Yonder Comes The Blues," in which she seems to suggest that the blues is a loiterer, lounging after her when she tries to ignore his presence.

I worry all day, I worry all night,
Everytime my man comes home he wants to fuss and fight,
When I pick up the paper to try to read the news,
Just when I'm satisfied, yonder comes the blues.

I went down to the river each and every day,
Trying to keep from throwing myself away.
I walked and I walked 'til I wore out my shoes,
I can't walk no further, yonder comes the blues . . .

People have the different blues and think they're mighty sad,
But blues about a man the worst I ever had.

I been disgusted and all confused,
Every time I look around, yonder comes the blues.

There is as much use made of the closely related technique of apostrophe, in which something inanimate is addressed as human. A prison gang, working in a ragged line in the afternoon heat, sings to "Old Hannah," the sun.

Oh, go down, old Hannah,
   Well, well, well
Don't you rise no more.
   Don't you rise no more.
Why don't you go down, old Hannah,
   Old Hannah,
Don't you rise,
   No more.

Hociel Thomas, accompanying herself on the piano, sings,

Go down, sunshine, and see what tomorrow brings.
Go down, sunshine, and see what tomorrow brings.
Lord, he might bring sunshine, then again he might bring rain.

With the extended train imagery of many blues there is often a verse in which the singer addresses the train, trying to make it listen to him as it pulls away from the station with his woman.

I'm crying, "Train, train, bring my baby back to me."
Hear me crying, "Train, train, bring my baby back to me.
Can't bring back my baby just bring me my used-to-be."

Even the less-well-known technique of metonymy, the use of a related idea for the idea itself, is often found in the blues. The expression "I'm going to put on my traveling shoes," has become almost a cliché, but the use of the word "traveling" to imply that the singer is thinking of leaving is an obvious use of metonymy. The phrase has been used so often that "traveling" has little more effect than an adjective, but a similar phrase in a less familiar blues still has the vividness of the stronger figure of speech. As Sleepy John Estes sings,

I'm going upstairs and pack my leaving trunk . . .

The imagery of the blues has a rich variety of expression, and in it is the directness of an immediately imagined poetic idea. Cat-Iron, an intense Mississippi singer recorded by Frederic Ramsey Jr. in Natchez, knew what it meant to be left by someone, and he knew the sound of muffled crying in the night. Instead of singing,

I got something to tell you going to make you cry . . .

he sang,

I got something to tell you, woman, make the hair rise on your head.

I got something to tell you, woman, make the hair rise on your head.
I got something to tell you, woman, make the spring cry on your bed . . .

Furry Lewis, instead of promising his woman that he would make her rich, promises her that he will make her money grow like the grass on a spring field.

> If you'll be my woman I will turn your money green.
> If you'll be my woman I will turn your money green.
> Show you more money, baby, than Rockefeller ever seen.

Tommy McClennan, standing beside a road in the Mississippi delta, waiting for a bus, sees it coming toward him and for a moment the swaying Greyhound becomes, in his imagination, a dog running along the road in the hot sun.

> Here comes that Greyhound with his tongue hanging out on the side.
> Here comes that Greyhound with his tongue hanging out on the side.
> You have to buy a ticket if you want to ride.

In the pain of separation Gertrude Perkins feels the desolation of a winter wind.

> The cold wind howling, howling in my heart.
> The wind howling, howling in my heart.
> For the best of friends, Lord, they have got to part.

Will Shade, sitting in his shabby room behind Beale Street in Memphis, tries to show the pain that his woman has caused him.

> If I could just take
> My heart in my hand,
> I could show you, woman,
> How you treat a man . . .

The Black Ace, recording for Chris Strachwitz with his old-fashioned steel guitar in his home in Fort Worth, uses the language of the card game to tell his woman that she won't find a better man.

> I'm the Black Ace, I'm the boss card in your hand.
> I'm the Black Ace, I'm the boss card in your hand.
> But I'll play for you, mama, if you please let me be your man.

The imagery of the blues still has a vitality and strength of expression.

In some of the greatest blues the imagery has been extended into a symbolism in which the image becomes something beyond itself, in which it has a meaning beyond the immediate reality. Much of the sexual poetry of the blues uses a colorful imagery and an irrepressible symbolism, and it is such a rich area of the blues that it will need a fuller discussion to do it justice. In many well-known blues, however, there is an intense symbolism. In a folk culture, where little is written and there isn't a concern with precise meanings, the symbolism often becomes confused, but it continues to have some meaning for the singer who uses it, even though he would have a difficult time explaining it. Sometimes the symbol becomes so loose in its interpretation that the meaning changes within a few verses. The ballad song, "Careless Love," is sung by many blues performers, and as they alter it to the blues idiom there is considerable confusion about the term "careless love" itself. Although it seems to be a synonym for a heedless infatuation and has become

"Kelly's love" in some versions, in others it seems to mean the sexual embrace, and in an imaginative version by Lonnie Johnson it becomes the symbol of everything that has menaced his life. Careless love has "robbed me out of my silver and gold," "caused my father to lose his mind," "drove me out in the ice and snow," and in the final verse Lonnie finally turns on this personification of his misfortunes with the words,

> . . . Damn you, I'm going to shoot you.
> Shoot you four or five times.
> Then stand over you until you finish dying.

Even in the blues which have a consistent symbolism there is often an elaboration of the original idea which confuses the meaning, but in a language which is still developing there is often more variety than consistency. In one of her finest blues Bessie Smith uses the "long old road" as a symbol for the passing years, and in her first verse seems to have almost a religious intent as she sings of meeting a friend. It is similar to many spiritual verses.

> It's a long old road, but I'm gonna find the end.
> It's a long old road, but I'm gonna find the end.
> And when I get there I'm gonna shake hands with a friend.

She continues to develop the symbol of the road in a blues of great clarity and power.

> On the side of the road I sat underneath the tree.
> On the side of the road I sat underneath the tree.
> Nobody knows the thoughts that come over me.
>
> Weepin' and cryin', tears falling on the ground.
> Weepin' and cryin', tears falling on the ground.
> When I got to the end I was so worried down.
>
> Picked up my bag, baby, and I tried it again.
> Picked up my bag, baby, and I tried it again.
> I got to make it, I've got to find the end.

In the third verse there is a momentary confusion. She sings, "When I got to the end I was so worried down." She seems to imply that she's reached the end of the road, but in the fourth verse she ". . . tried it again . . . I've got to find the end," so the line seems to mean that she reached the end of her momentary depression, that she has cried away her despair and is ready to begin walking again. It is a moving use of a symbol to express an involved idea of the passage of life and the difficulty of going on with it, and the thought is complete within its handful of lines. It is often sung with this meaning, and with this symbolism implied in the performance. Bessie, however, sings one more verse, and almost succeeds in stripping it of any poetic intent. Her last verse finishes,

> You can't trust nobody, you might as well be alone.
> You can't trust nobody, you might as well be alone.
> Found my lost friend, and I might as well stayed at home.

The literalness of the last verse implies that she never intended to describe anything more than walking along a road with a suitcase to see a friend, and that there is no symbolic meaning to the difficult journey she has started. The blues, however, still has the strength of inconsistency, and other singers have used her symbol of the "long old road" for their own lives, overlooking the intent of her last verse. The most imaginative of the singers have a technical control of their idiom which enables them to use not only the words and phrases of simile and metaphor, of personification, apostrophe and metonymy, but also the longer forms of the image and the symbol. For Robert Johnson the road, in his phrase the "passway," became an intense and moving symbolic expression of the struggles that haunted his short life:

> I got stones in my passway, and my road seems dark as night.
> I got stones in my passway, and my road seems dark as night.
> I have pains in my heart, they have taken my appetite.
>
> I have a bird to whistle, and I have a bird to sing.
> Have a bird to whistle, and I have a bird to sing.
> I got a woman that I'm loving, boy, but she don't mean a thing.
>
> My enemies have betrayed me, have overtaken poor Bob at last.
> My enemies have betrayed me, have overtaken poor Bob at last.
> And there's one thing certain, they have stones all in my path.
>
> Now you are trying to take my life
> And all my loving too.
> You laid the passway for me,
> Now what are you trying to do?
> I'm crying, "Please, please, let us be friends,
> And when you hear the howling in my passway, honey, please don't let me in."

Any Day Now

Black Art and Black Liberation

Larry Neal

"I was born by the river in a little old tent,
and just like the river, I've been running ever since.
It's been a long time, but I know change is gonna come. . . ."

—Sam Cooke

WE BEAR witness to a profound change in the way we now see ourselves and the world. And this has been an ongoing change. A steady, certain march toward a collective sense of who we are, and what we must now be about to liberate ourselves. Liberation is impossible if we fail to see ourselves in more positive terms. For without a change of vision, we are slaves to the oppressor's ideas and values—ideas and values that finally attack the very core of our existence. Therefore, we must see the world in terms of our own realities.

Black Plower, in its most fundamental sense, stands for the principle of Self-Definition and Self-Determination. Black Power teaches us that we must have ultimate control over our own lives. It teaches us that we must make a place on this Earth for ourselves, and that we must construct, through struggle, a world that is compatible with our highest visions.

This was the gut essence of the Black Power philosophy before the political butchers and the civil rights hustlers got into the game, confusing everybody and the issues. Black Power is essentially a nationalistic concept; it speaks to the suppressed need of Afro-Americans for true liberation, for Nationhood. The forerunners of the current movement were such nineteenth-century thinkers as David Walker, Edward Blyden, and Martin Delaney. The movement takes its revolutionary zeal from Gabriel Prosser and Nat Turner. It takes its Third World outlook from W.E.B. Du Bois, Marcus Garvey, Malcolm X, and Frantz Fanon. And on its weaker side, it takes its economic and institutional philosophy from Booker T. Washington. Therefore, when Brother Stokely Carmichael invoked the slogan "Black Power" on the Meredith March, it was these voices speaking through him.

Reprinted from Woodie King and Earl Anthony, eds., *Black Poets and Prophets: The Theory, Practice, and Esthetics of the Pan-Africanist Revolution* (New York: Mentor, 1972), 148–65. Reprinted by permission of Evelyn Neal.

Now along with the Black Power movement, there has been developing a movement among Black artists. This movement we call the Black Arts. This movement, in many ways, is older than the current Black Power movement. It is primarily concerned with the cultural and spiritual liberation of Black America. It takes upon itself the task of expressing, through various art forms, the Soul of the Black Nation. And like the Black Power Movement, it seeks to define the world of art and culture in its own terms. The Black Arts movement seeks to link, in a highly conscious manner, art and politics in order to assist in the liberation of Black people. The Black Arts movement, therefore, reasons that this linking must take place along lines that are rooted in an Afro-American and Third World historical and cultural sensibility. By "Third World," we mean that we see our struggle in the context of the global confrontations occurring in Africa, Asia, and Latin America. We identify with all of the righteous forces in those places which are struggling for human dignity.

Lately, Black artists have been concerned with the development, for lack of a better term, of a "Black Esthetic." Esthetic sounds like some kind of medical term. It might just as well be for all that its dictionary definition tells us: "Esthetic: 1) A branch of philosophy relating to the nature of forms of beauty, especially found in the fine arts. 2) Study of the mental and emotional responses to the beauty in art, nature, etc."—*Standard College Dictionary.*

For the most part, this definition is worthless. What the Western white man calls an "esthetic" is fundamentally a dry assembly of dead ideas based on a dead people; a people whose ideas have been found meaningless in light of contemporary history. We need new values, new ways of living. We need a new system of moral and philosophical thought. Dig: There is nothing in the above quoted definition about *people.* It is a cold, lifeless corpse they speak of; the emanations of a dead world trying to define and justify itself.

Therefore, today we bear witness to the moral and philosophical decay of a corrupt civilization. Europe and America are the new Babylons. Today, we see white artists wallowing in the sudden discovery of the body, of sex. These hypocritical puritans now play with themselves like new-born babies. They have suddenly discovered the body, which, for centuries, they denied existed. Art and the body. Sexploitation. Andy Warhol madness. America has become one great big dirty movie. Like suddenly sex, one of man's most natural urges, has become controversial; or at least, they would have us believe so. What's so controversial about sex? Nothing, we know.

I raise these questions to illustrate the impasse that Western art has reached. They fall back on the sex thing because they are unable to deal with the political, spiritual, and cultural liberation of Man. They are unable within the confines of even their ideas of art to deal with the real issues confronting Man today. And the most important of which is the liberation of the majority of Mankind. So they steal and suck Black energy, an energy which in the slop jars of their minds they distort and corrupt in their own sick images.

And backed up by a powerful and oppressive political system, he tries to force Black people to measure up to his standards. Thus, we are constantly forced to see ourselves through white eyes. We are made to evaluate our innermost impulses against his. And in the process, we do ourselves great spiritual and psychological harm. The Black Arts movement seeks to give a total vision of ourselves. Not the split vision that Du Bois called the "Double Consciousness": ". . . this sense of always looking at one's self through the eyes of others, of measuring one's soul by the tape of a world that looks on in amused contempt and pity. One ever feels his two-ness—an American, a Negro—two souls, two thoughts, two unreconciled strivings; two warring ideals in one dark body, whose dogged strength alone keeps it from being torn asunder. . . ."

These words are from *The Souls of Black Folk,* which was published in 1903. Now, in 1969, Du Bois' sons and daughters in the Black Arts movement go forth to destroy the Double Consciousness, go forth to merge these "warring ideals" into One Committed Soul integrated with itself and taking its own place in the world. Can you dig it?

But this is no new thing. It is the road that all oppressed peoples take en route to total liberation. In the history of Black America, the current ideas of the Black Arts movement can be said to have their roots in the so-called Negro Renaissance of the nineteen-twenties. The twenties was a key period in the rising historical and cultural consciousness of Black people. This period grooved with the rise of Garvey's Black Nationalism, danced and made love to the music of Louis Armstrong, Bessie Smith, Jelly Roll Morton, King Oliver, Perry Bradford, Fats Waller, and the Holy Father, Duke Ellington. There was a flowering of black poets, writers and artists. And there was the ascendancy of hip, blues-talking, Langston Hughes, who came on singing songs about Africa, Haiti, and Harlem:

"Droning a drowsy syncopated tune,
Rocking back and forth to a mellow croon,
   I heard a Negro play.
Down on Lenox Avenue the other night
By the pale dull pallor of an old gas light
   He did a lazy sway. . . .
   He did a lazy sway. . . .
To the tune o' those weary Blues . . ."

There were other writers of that period: Claude McKay, Jean Toomer, James Weldon Johnson, Countee Cullen. . . . But Langston best personifies the Black artist who is clearly intent upon developing a style of poetry which springs forcefully and recognizably from a Black life style; a poetry whose very tone and concrete points of reference is informed by the feelings of the people as expressed in the gospel and blues songs.

It is here that any discussion of a Black esthetic must begin. Because Black music, in all of its forms, represents the highest artistic achievement of the race. It is the memory of Africa that we hear in the churning energy of the gospels. The memory of the Motherland that lingers behind the Christian references to Moses, Jesus, and Daniel. The Black Holy Ghost roaring into some shack of a church in the South, seizing the congregation with an ancient energy and power. The Black Church, therefore, represents and embodies the transplanted African memory. The Black Church is the Keeper of that Memory, the spiritual bank of our almost forgotten visions of the Homeland. The Black Church was the institutionalized form that Black people used to protect themselves from the spiritual and psychological brutality of the slavemasters. She gave us a music, a literature and a very valid and essential poetry. And when she ceased to be relevant, for some of us, we sang the blues: *"They call it stormy Monday, but Tuesday's just as bad; call it stormy Monday, but Tuesday's just as bad. Wednesday's worse, but Thursday's also sad. . . ."*

At the pulsating core of their emotional center, the blues are the spiritual and ritual energy of the church thrust into the eyes of life's raw realities. Even though they appear primarily to concern themselves with the secular experience, the relationships between males and females, between boss and worker, between nature and Man, they are, in fact, extensions of the deepest, most pragmatic spiritual and moral realities. Even though they primarily deal with the world as flesh, they are essentially religious. Because they finally celebrate life and the ability of man to control and shape his destiny. The blues don't jive. They reach way down into the maw of the individual and collective experience. Sonny Terry and Brownie McGhee sing: *"If you lose your money, please don't lose your mind; If you lose your woman, please don't mess with mine."*

Taken together, the blues represent an epic cycle of awesome propositions—one song (poem) after the other expressing the daily confrontations of Black people with themselves and the world. They are not merely entertainment. They act to clarify and make more bearable the human experience, especially when the context of that experience is oppressive. A man that doesn't watch his "happy home" is in a whole world of trouble. Therefore, the blues singer is teaching an ethical standard in much the same way as the poet. Only the psychic strength of most of the blues singers is often times more intensely focused than that of the poet's. We must often strain for images like: *"I walked out in the Milky Way and I reached for a star. I looked across the cosmic way and my lover, she wasn't very far. . . ."*

That's Jimmy Reed. As poetry, the blues act to link Man to a past informed by the Spirit. A past in which art served as a means of connecting our ancestors with the Unknown psychic forces which they knew to exist in the Universe. Yeah. Forces which they somehow felt were related to the natural operation of the Universe. (*He's a Deep Sea Diver with a stroke that can't go wrong.*) The blues are a deep-down thing, always trying to get to the nitty-gritty of human experience.

Therefore, no matter how you cut it, the blues and the people who create them are the Soul Force of the race, the emotional current of the Nation. And that is why Langston Hughes and Ralph Ellison based their esthetic on them. The Black Arts movement strives for the same kind of intimacy with the people. It strives to be a movement that is rooted in the fundamental experiences of the Nation.

The blues singer is not an alienated artist moaning songs of self-pity and defeat to an infidel mob. He is the voice of the community, its historian, and one of the shapers of its morality. He may claim to speak for himself only, but his ideas and values are, in fact, merely expressions of the general psychology of his people. He is the bearer of the group's working myths, aspirations, and values. And like the preacher, he has been called on by the Spirit to rap about life in the sharpest, the harshest terms possible. Also like the preacher, he may have gotten the calling early in life. He may have even sung in the church like Ray Charles and James Brown.

It is the ultimate urge to communicate the private pain to the collective that drives and pushes the blues singer from place to place, from job to job, from one fast-moving freight train to the other. All kinds of cities and people moving through the blues experience. All kinds of human tragedies and circumstances find their way into the blues singer's repertoire. It is all about feeling. All about people. All about Truth.

Contemporary Black music and the living folklore of the people are, therefore, the most obvious examples of the Black esthetic. Because these forms are the truest expressions of our pain, aspirations, and group wisdom. These elements decidedly constitute a culture. And a culture expresses a definite feeling about the world. Otis Redding, Sam Cooke,

Little Willie John, Blind Lemon, Bessie Smith, Billie Holiday, Charlie Parker, Coleman Hawkins, Eric Dolphy, and John Coltrane are, in the minds of Black people, more than entertainers. They are the poets and philosophers of Black America. Each of these artists devoted his life to expressing what Du Bois referred to as the "Souls of Black Folk." They along with the Black church are the keepers of our memory, the tribal historians, soothsayers, and poets. In them, more so than in literature, we find the purest and most powerful expression of the Black experience in America. These artists have set the standards, and the current movement attempts to meet them and, where possible, to create new and more demanding ones.

So when *we* speak of an esthetic, we mean *more* than the process of making art, of telling stories, of writing poems, of performing plays. We also mean the destruction of the white thing. We mean the destruction of white ways of looking at the world. For surely, if we assert that Black people are fighting for liberation, then everything that we are about, as people, somehow relates to it.

Let me be more precise: When artists like LeRoi Jones, Quincy Troupe, Stanley Crouch, Joe Goncalves, Etheridge Knight, Sonia Sanchez, Ed Spriggs, Carolyn Rodgers, Don L. Lee, Sun Ra, Max Roach, Abbey Lincoln, Willie Kgositsile, Arthur Pfister . . . assert that Black Art must speak to the lives and the psychic survival of Black People, they are not speaking of "protest" art. They are not speaking of an art that screams and masturbates before white audiences. That is the path of Negro literature and civil rights literature. No, they are not speaking about that kind of thing, even though that is what some Negro writers of the past have done. Instead, they are speaking of an art that addresses itself directly to Black people; an art that speaks to us in terms of our feelings and ideas about the world; an art that validates the positive aspects of our life style. Dig: An art that opens us up to the beauty and ugliness within us; that makes us understand our condition and each other in a more profound manner; that unites us, exposing us to our painful weaknesses and strengths; and finally, an art that posits for us the Vision of a Liberated Future.

So the function of artistic technique and a Black esthetic is to make the goal of communication and liberation more possible. Therefore, Black poets dig the blues and Black music in order to find in them the means of making their address to Black America more understandable. The Black artist studies Afro-American culture, history, and politics and uses their secrets to open the way for the brothers with the heavy and necessary political rap. We know that art alone will not liberate us. We know that culture as an abstract thing within itself will not give us Self-Determination and Nationhood. And that is really what we all want, even though we fail often to admit it openly. We want to rule ourselves. Can you dig it? I know you can.

But a cultureless revolution is a bullcrap tip. It means that in the process of making the revolution, we lose our vision. We lose the soft, undulating side of ourselves—those unknown beauties lurking rhythmically below the level of material needs. In short, a revolution without a culture would destroy the very thing that now unites us; the very thing we are trying to save along with our lives. That is, the *feeling* and *love-sense* of the blues and other forms of Black music. The *feeling* of a James Brown or an Aretha Franklin. That is the *feeling* that unites us and makes it more possible for us to move and groove together, to do whatever is necessary to liberate ourselves. John Coltrane's music must unquestionably be a part of any future revolutionary society, or something is diabolically wrong with the fools who make the revolution. A revolution that would have Leonard Bernstein, Bobby Dylan, or the Beatles at the top of its cultural hierarchy would mean that in the process of making the revolution, the so-called revolutionaries had spiritually murdered Black people. (Bobby Seale, are you listening?) A future society without the implied force and memory of Bessie Smith, Charlie Parker, Sun Ra, Cecil Taylor, Pharoah Sanders, and Charlie Mingus is almost inconceivable.

The artists carry the past and the future memory of the race, of the Nation. They represent our various identities. They link us to the deepest, most profound aspects of our ancestry. Charlie Parker was a genius and an oppressed Black man. His is certainly a memory worth fighting for, as is the memory of Malcolm X, King, Du Bois, Garvey, Fanon, Richard Wright, Jean Toomer, Claude McKay, Conrad Kent Rivers, Henry Dumas (killed by a pig in a New York subway), Booker T. Washington (him too), Cinque, Nat Turner, Denmark Vesey, Leadbelly, Stagalee, Shine, The Signifying Monkey, Sojourner Truth, Frederick Douglass, Harriet Tubman . . . and all of our Mothers and Fathers.

The Black Arts movement is rooted in a spiritual ethic. In saying that the function of art is to liberate Man, we propose a function for art which is now dead in the West and which is in keeping with our most ancient traditions and with our needs. Because, at base, art is religious and ritualistic; and ritual moves to liberate Man and to connect him to the Greater Forces. Thus Man becomes stronger psychically, and is thus more able to create a world that is an extension of his spirituality—his positive humanity. We say that the function of art is to liberate Man. And we only have to look out of the window to see that we need liberation. Right on, Brothers. And God Shango, help us!

This is what's on Amiri Baraka's (LeRoi Jones) mind. He could have been the pawed-over genius of the white literary establishment. But he peeped that they were dead, and that they finally had nothing to give—the future ultimately did not include them. It was LeRoi who first used the term "Black Art" in a positive sense. In the Western world view, it is connected with the "evil," "dark" forces of witchcraft and demonology. It was LeRoi who first shifted and elevated its meaning, giving it new significance in the context of a Black esthetic.

In a poem entitled "Black Art" he sings that Poem is the Black nation:

> ". . . . We want a black poem. And a Black world. Let the world be a Black
> Poem . . ."

Therefore, the poem comes to stand for the collective consciousness of Black America—the will toward Nationhood which is the unconscious motivation in back of the Black Power movement. It comes to stand for a radical reordering of the nature and function of both art and the artist.

But LeRoi is only one part of the developing consciousness. Let's check out some other Brothers and Sisters. Here is James Brown reminding us of our past. The hit song, "There Was A Time," traces the history of a people through their dances, and achieves in the process something of a rhythm-and-blues epic poem:

> ". . . There was a dance—
> Dig this:
> There was a dance

I used to do
They call the Mash Patater.

There was a day.
Now dig this:
There was a dance.
Now dig this:
They call the jerk,
Everybody relax and watch me work. . . ."

The esthetic is both the activity and the memory of the activity. The movement, the energy that is actual and real. Not merely what happens on the page. Quoting these lyrics hardly does justice to Brown's genius. He invokes dances like the Camelwalk and the Boogaloo. Each dance conjuring up a definite feeling and memory. Black poetry is best understood, as the powerful force that it is, when it is recited and danced.

And in a bar called The Shalimar in Harlem, on Seventh Avenue, Gylan Kain understands that there is:

"a sense of coolness
at midday
as passerby
        pass in
        an' out
a bar they call
The Shalimar
day blackens into night
and night blackens in day
and soul
        blazes into flames/of

PINKS and GREENS and YELLOWS and REDS and BLUES—and
BROWN and OPALS and SOUNDS and SHADOWS—

protrude outward
into alligator shoes/lepard skins
funny kind of hats that slant
downward and sideward
that in some funny kind of way
become ultra hip
the voodoo, who do
what you don't dare do people . . ."

Dig on Carolyn Rodgers singing about the kind of poem she wants:

". . . I want a poem for the eternal Red, Big Red, dead
Red, a-live Red in our hearts, his ending,
our beginning, yeah

I want a poem that don't be cryin
or scream/preachin/rappin
for the end of scream/preachin/rappin

or protestin for the cause of protestin
or lyin for the white pigs,
  I want a mean poem."

Ed Spriggs wants magic to happen:

"witch doctor
come uptown
come tennis-shoed
come sucking on a short neck
come holding onto a tit in mt morris pk
come lick sweet on some caldonia's ears
(where ever you find them)
come hear what black rose hymns
into the altar of our afro'd ears . . .
do sukey jumps or the boogaloo but come on
turkey us cats in hero bones
shoot your shit from starless roof
spread magic substances
pour it on our hymnals
on our tenement radiator pulse
candle the interior our mammy's womb
fatten it with roots of sassafras
witch doctor come up here . . ."

Arthur Pfister uses street rhythms to get this:

"Mouths ain't guns
& tongues ain't missiles.
Eyes ain't suns
& hairs ain't thistles.
Poems ain't knives, or grenades to sling,
but dig me brother,
  we gon'
    do our thing . . ."

Singer Chuck Jackson sees "blue shadows" falling all over town; and Smokey Robinson, with pain in his voice, tells his baby about tracks of his tears and the smile that is not really there. Marvin Gaye and Tammi Terrell affirm the love that we have for each other, singing, "You're all I need to get by." Jerry Butler teaches us that Only the Strong Survive. The Last Poets sing and dance power poems about Black love, the Third World, and Black Liberation. Willie Kgositsile reminds us:

". . . What does my hunger
have to do with a gawdamn poem?
THIS WIND YOU HEAR IS THE BIRTH OF MEMORY. WHEN THE MOMENT HATCHES IN TIME'S WOMB THERE WILL BE NO ART TALK. THE ONLY POEM YOU WILL HEAR WILL BE THE SPEARPOINT PIVOTED IN THE PUNCTURED MARROW OF THE VILLAIN; THE TIMELESS NATIVE SON DANCING LIKE CRAZY TO THE RETRIEVED RHYTHMS OF DESIRE FADING INTO MEMORY."

The Black Arts movement preaches that liberation is inextricably bound up with politics and culture. The culture gives us a revolutionary moral vision and a system of values and a methodology around which to shape the political movement. When we say "culture," we do not merely mean artistic forms. We mean, instead, the values, the life styles, and the feelings of the people as expressed in everyday life. The total liberation of Blues People cannot be affected if we do not have a value system, a point of reference, a way of understanding what we see and hear every day around us. If we do not have a value system that is, in reality, more moral than the oppressor's, then we cannot hope to change society. We will end up taking each other off, and in our confusion and ignorance, calling the murders of each other revolutionary. A value system helps us to establish models for Black people to emulate; makes it more possible for us to deeply understand our people, and to be understood by them.

Further, the Black Arts movement proposes a new "mythology." What musician-poet Jimmy Stewart calls a "Black Cosmology," a Black World-View that is informed by the living Spirit. According to Stewart, such a world view would make easier and more natural the shaping of the Black artistic, cultural, and political forms. This idea has fantastic implications for religion, as the Hon. Elijah Muhammad and Detroit's Rev. Albert Cleage have demonstrated.

Like can you dig it: We have been praying to the wrong God. And who is God, anyway, but the awesomely beautiful forces of the Universe? The Black Sun exploding semen into Her dark body. Your ancestors are the Gods who have actually walked this planet. Those who have tried to liberate us. Nat Turner, Harriet Tubman, Malcolm X, they are surely Gods. They preached Black Liberation. And Black Liberation is far more important than some Alice-in-Wonderland Heaven.

Black Art must sing the praises of the true gods of the planet. We don't need any soulless Hebrew God. We need to see ourselves reflected in our religions. For prayer is poetry; and like poetry it acts to reinforce the group's vision of itself. If that vision is rooted in a hypocritical alien force, we do ourselves great psychic and psychological harm by adhering to it. For example, one of the first things the Algerians did when they began to fight the French was to cease allowing the colonial authorities to conduct their marriage ceremonies.

Like Black Art, Black religion should be about strengthening group unity and making radical change. If your minister is not, in some way, engaged in the job of achieving Black freedom, he is a con man. Cut him loose quick.

The text of my sermon is the Life and Death of Charlie Parker. People loved him and called him Bird. His life was confusion in the midst of artistic creation. In some ways, you could say he was a sinner. But like us he lived and did the best that he could do under the circumstances. And after my sermon, Brother Sun Ra will perform some songs about the nature of the universe; and after that we will have some words from the Self-Defense Committee.

Religion, therefore, like politics, can embrace all of the ideological features of the liberation struggle. What is needed, however, is a change of references. A hippy Jesus won't do. A change of references is needed in black popular music also. Like: We can't go into the future singing: "Who's Making Love to Your Old Lady" or "It's Your Thang, Do With It What You Wanna Do."

It is the task of the Black artist to place before his people images and references that go beyond merely reflecting the oppression and the conditions engendered by the oppression. Don't condemn the people for singing the blues. Write a blues that takes us to a more meaningful level of consciousness and aspiration. But also understand the realities of the human condition that are posed by the blues. Take the energy and the feeling of the blues, the mangled bodies, the broken marriages, the moaning nights, the shouting, the violence, the love cheating, the lonely sounding train whistles, and shape these into an art that stands for the spiritual helpmate of the Black Nation. Make a form that uses the Soul Force of Black culture, its life styles, its rhythms, its energy, and direct that form toward the liberation of Black people. Don't go off playing Jimi Hendrix or something like that. Respect and understand the culture. Don't exploit it.

Put it into meaningful institutions that are run and controlled by Black People with a vision. What Amiri is trying to do in Newark. What Clarence Reed and the beautiful young Brothers of the Harlem Youth Federation are trying to do at the Black Mind in Harlem. What Jacques and Cecilia and the other Liberators of the National Black Theatre work hard at daily. Give to the culture temples like the East Wind where you can see the Last Poets. Build something like Gaston Neal's school in Washington, D.C. Let us see theaters like the new Lafayette springing up wherever Black people live and work. Construct Black Universities like Abdul, A. B. Spellman, and Vincent Harding are tying to do. Because these attempts at building Black Institutions are not merely *cultural* in the narrow sense of that word. They are finally about the physical and spiritual survival of Black America. In the context of our struggle *here*, they are as important as the gun.

Yeah. While on the subject of the gun. If de war comes, and, dis being America, it probably will—whose images and songs will flicker on the film of your brain: Billie Holiday's or Janis Joplin's? Whose pain and suffering whistles past your ears in the gas-filled night, Malcolm X's or Josef Stalin's? Check it out. . . . (This is mean, ain't it?)

The Black Arts movement supplies the political brothers with an arsenal of feelings, images, and myths.

Brother Rap: *This is the role of culture. Don't let the political brothers in the naturals and blue dashikis hang you up. Everybody who is aware knows that this thing goes beyond hair styles and African clothing. The most brainwashed brother on the street is hip to that. That's why some of the meanest, most potentially revolutionary niggers still wear processes.*

The new references of clothing and hair are essentially visions of ourselves perfected; they are sign posts on the road to eventual Self-Determination. For a Sister to wear her hair natural asserts the sacred and essentially holy nature of her body. The natural, in its most positive sense, symbolizes the Sister's willingness to determine her own destiny. It is an act of love for herself and her people. The natural helps psychologically to liberate the Sister. It prepares her for the message of a Rap Brown, a Robert Williams, a Huey Newton, a Maulana Karenga. The Sister's natural helps to destroy the "Double Consciousness" Du Bois spoke of. It gives her what Eldridge Cleaver calls a "Unitary Image" of herself. That is, she comes to see herself as a more spiritually total person.

If Black Revolutionary Cultural Consciousness is perverted by jive Negro hustlers and Madison Avenue freaks, it is our job to illustrate how that very perversion is consistent with the nature of the capitalistic, colonialistic, and imperialistic monsters that now rule the planet. To merely point out to Black people the economic and political nature of our oppression is not enough. Why is it not enough? It is so because people are *more* than just the sum total of economic and political factors. Man must exist on a more cosmic plane than that. This is what Cecil Taylor, Phil Cochran, Aretha Franklin, Milford Graves, Abdul Rahman, James Snead, Loften Mitchell, Evan Walker, Ed Bullins, Ron Milner, Maya Angelou, Jacob Lawrence, Tony Northern, Charlie Fuller, Romare Bearden, Eleo Pomare, Judi Dearing, John Parks, and all of the names I have forgotten teach us. Yeah.

The Blues God knows that he will cease to exist if his people cease to exist. He knows that being Black and Beautiful is not enough. He knows that the oppressor cares nothing about our beauty. And I'm certain that He will back me up in this. Right, Stanley and Black Arthur?

This is what the Black Arts movement is all about. What I believe to be its most vital core. However, there *are* people out there bullcrapping, but that don't matter—the Black Boogaloo will blow them away. What we got to do is to dig into this thing that tugs at our souls—this blue yearning to make a way of our own.

Black people you are Black Art. You are the poem, as Amiri Baraka teaches us. You are Dahomey smile. You are slave ship and field holler. You are Blues and Gospel and Be-Bop and New Music. You are Carolyn's poem, and Eleo Pomare's dance. You are Buddy Bolden's memory; you heard him play in Funky Butt Hall and Preservation Hall and in Congo Square. You are both memory and flesh. Black Liberation to you Baby. Hey Now!

Black Liberation for the ditty-bopping hip ones; for all of the righteous sinners and hustlers; for Chaka Zulu and Honky Tonk Bud, the hip cat's stud. Black Liberation for Cinque, for Bo Diddley, for Bobby Hutton and James Powell. Black Liberation for William T. Dawson, Albert Murray, Ralph Ellison, Margaret Walker, Rosa Guy, John Clarke, John Killens, James Brown, James Baldwin; for Barbecue Bob and Big Fat Fannie; for Shine and Sugar Ray Robinson; for the Signifying Monkey and Kid Gavilan and Kid Chocolate; for Jack Johnson and High John The Conqueror. Black Liberation for Otis Redding and Wilson Pickett, for Jerry Butler, for Joe Louis, for Roy Campanella, for Helen and Malik, for Marybelle and Jeanette. Black Liberation for our unknown Fathers and your Mammy's Mammy; for ashy legs and early trim, for hopping freight trains, for the Hannibals and the Adefumis and the Ahmeds and the Paul Robesons and the Ben Davises and the Max Stanfords and the Huey Newtons. Black Liberation for all political prisoners everywhere.

Right on. Black Liberation for the sea deaths and the chains, for long stretches of desert and pyramids, for drums, for folk tales, and the hot breathing earth, and the spiraling Father Snake and the Primeval Sperm. Black Liberation to you Baby—Check out everybody's political program carefully. Black Liberation for cotton death, for Emmett Till death, for Mack Parker death, for Leonard Deadwyler death, Medgar Evers death, for Malcom death; Black Liberation for Mamma and Evelyn and Charles and Melvin and Robbie and Joe and Howard and Charlie and Marybelle and Rose and Stanley and Ace and Martha and Sam and Carol and Frostie and Gerrie, and for all of my various families.

So the Blues God spoke to me, told me to hip you to what you have always secretly known. Listen carefully to the following: This is the death of the white lie that our ancestors prophesied. This is the death of the double-consciousness. Listen: under the songs and the moaning night, they plotted their deaths and worked ju-ju on the Beasts; they spoke to us and fortified us against their insane machinations; they plotted his death under the spirituals and the blues; they invoked the Future Memory which is us, and it is to that Memory that we dance and fight and sing.

They invoked the Future Memory while baring their behinds to cracker whips and jack boots. They were visionaries and warriors; they were Niggers and Toms. They were mean Poppa Stoppas. They were pimps and prostitutes. They were railroad men and mackdaddys. They were college presidents and porters. They were mucked-up intellectuals and exploited workers, gun-toting ministers, and lolligagging mommas and numbers runners, and shuffling waiters, and drifters.

They were loud and raunchy, macking in dark corners. They were invisible men, sliding into putrid sewers of the mind. They were doctors and con-men, running the murphy on lonely old ladies in mourning shawls. Were high yellow debutantes and mulatto clarinet players. They were Sunday tea and the Rinky Dinks and the Jack and Jills and the Elks and the Masons and jack-leg preachers and Seventh-Day Adventists and Baptists and Methodists and Holy Roller and Sanctified. They wore wigs and day glow drawers. Moved to Lincoln Drive and to Mobile and to Chicago and to Harlem and to Paris. They were an oppressed Nation in the Neon Diaspora (thank you, David). They worked in the Post Offices and sent their daughters and sons to Negro colleges. And we love them. And we love them. And we will struggle and dedicate our lives to them (thank you, Marvin Gaye and Tammi). And we love them, even though sometimes we stabbed and shot each other for flimsy dimes, falling on the wine-stained pavements; even though we shot shit into our Black arms, dying our sag deaths in funky hallways, in penthouses, in the Rivieras of aristocratic old faggots and bitches. They were Big Daddy and Big Momma. And we love them, even though sometimes we did not know it.

ALL PRAISES DUE TO THE BLACK MAN.
SHO' NUFF, CHILD. . . .

Popular Songs vs. The Facts of Life

S. I. Hayakawa

BECAUSE I have long been interested in jazz—its history, its implications, its present developments—I also listen to some extent to popular songs, which are, of course, far from being the same thing.[1] My present subject is an attempt to examine, from a semantic point of view, the words of popular songs and jazz songs in order to discover their underlying assumptions, orientations, and implied attitudes.

First, let me clarify the distinction between popular songs and jazz. In "true" jazz, as the jazz connoisseur understands the term, the basic interest on the part of both musician and listener is in the music as music. Originality and inventiveness in improvisation are highly prized, as are the qualities of instrumentation and of rhythm. Popular music, on the other hand, stands in about the same relationship to jazz as the so-called "semi-classics" stand in relation to Bach, Beethoven, and Brahms. Just as the musical ideas of the classics are diluted, often to a point of insanity, in the "semi-classics," so are the ideas of jazz (and of semi-classics) diluted in popular music—diluted, sweetened, sentimentalized, and trivialized.

Now the contrast between the musical sincerity of jazz and the musical slop of much of popular music is interestingly paralleled in the contrast between the literary sincerity of the words of blues songs (and the blues are the basic source of jazz inspiration) and the literary slop in the majority of popular songs. The words of true jazz songs, especially the Negro blues, tend to be unsentimental and realistic in their statements about life. (In saying "Negro blues," I should add that most of these are written by Negroes, but some have been written by whites under Negro inspiration.) The words of popular songs, on the other hand, largely (but not altogether) the product of white song-writers for predominantly white audiences, tend towards wishful thinking, dreamy and ineffectual nostalgia, unrealistic fantasy, self-pity, and sentimental clichés masquerading as emotion.

We have been taught—and rightly—to be more than cautious about making racial distinctions. Hence let me hasten to explain that the differences between (predominantly Negro) blues and (predominantly white) popular songs can, in my opinion, be satisfac-

Reprinted from *Etc: A Review of General Semantics* 12, no. 2 (Winter 1955): 83–95. Used with permission of the International Society for General Semantics, Concord, California.

torily accounted for without "racial" explanations. The blues arise from the experiences of a largely agricultural and working-class Negro minority with a social and cultural history different from that of the white majority. Furthermore, the blues—a folk music which underwent urbanization (in New Orleans, Chicago, New York, Memphis, Kansas City, and elsewhere)—developed in an economic or market situation different from that in which popular songs, aimed at mass markets through mass entertainment media, developed.[2] With these cultural and economic conditions in mind, let me restate the thesis of this paper, using this time the terminology of general semantics: The blues tend to be *extensionally* oriented, while popular songs tend to exhibit grave, even pathological, *intensional* orientations.

Perhaps I can make my thesis come to life by discussing a specific area of emotion about which songs are written, namely, love in the light of what Wendell Johnson calls the IFD disease—the triple-threat semantic disorder of Idealization (the making of impossible and ideal demands upon life), which leads to Frustration (as the result of the demands not being met), which in turn leads to Demoralization (or Disorganization, or Despair).[3] What Johnson says in *People in Quandaries* is repeatedly illustrated in the attitudes toward love expressed in popular songs.

First, in looking forward to love, there is an enormous amount of unrealistic idealization—the creation in one's mind, as the object of love's search, a dream girl (or dream boy) the fleshly counterpart of which never existed on earth:

> Will I ever find the girl in my mind,
> The girl who is my ideal?[4]
>
> Every night I dream a little dream,
> And of course Prince Charming is the theme,
> The he for me . . .[5]

Next, of course, one meets a not-altogether-unattractive person of the other sex, and the psychological process called *projection* begins, in which one attributes to a real individual the sum-total of the imaginary perfections one has dreamed about:

> I look one look at you,
> That's all I meant to do,
> And then my heart stood still . . .[6]
>
> You were meant for me, and I was meant for you.
> Nature fashioned you and when she was done,
> You were all the sweet things rolled up in one . . .
> I confess, the angels must have sent you,
> And they meant you just for me.[7]

Wendell Johnson has commented frequently on what he calls a prevalent belief in magic.[8] Some of his clients in his speech clinic at the University of Iowa, he says, will do no drills, perform no exercises, read no books, carry out no recommendations; they simply seem to expect that now that they have come to *the* right speech clinic their stuttering will somehow magically go away. The essence of magic is the belief that you don't have to do anything—the right magic makes all effort unnecessary.

Love is depicted in most popular songs as just this kind of magic. There is rarely an indication in the accounts of love-euphoria commonly to be found in these songs that, having found the dream-girl or dream-man, one's problems are just beginning. Rather it is explicitly stated that, having found one's ideal, all problems are solved:

> We'll have a blue room, a new room, for two room,
> Where every day's a holiday, because you're married to me . . .[9]

The "Blue Room" song hints at what other songs often state, namely, that not only are emotional problems (and apparently economic problems) automatically solved by finding "the sweetheart of all my dreams"; the housing problem is also solved:

> You'll find a smiling face, a fireplace, a cozy room,
> A little nest that's nestled where the roses bloom . . .[10]

> In a bungalow all covered with roses,
> I will settle down I vow,
> I'm looking at the world thru rose-colored glasses,
> And everything is rosy now.[11]

That, then, is the idealization. And students of general semantics know from reading Wendell Johnson what that leads to. The unrealistic expectations—for love is never expected to last for any shorter a period than "forever"—result inevitably in disappointment, disenchantment, frustration, and, most importantly, self-pity. Hence:

> I'm all alone every evening,
> All alone, feeling blue,
> Wondering where you are, and how you are,
> And if you are all alone too.[12]

What if it turns out that he wasn't all alone at all, but two-timing her? She complains bitterly:

> You were only fooling,
> While I was falling in love.[13]

> Little you care for the vows that you made,
> Little you care how much I have paid . . .[14]

But in spite of the disappointments he has caused, she still loves him:

> Yesterday's kisses are bringing me pain,
> Yesterday's sunshine has turned into rain,
> I'm alone because I love you,
> Love you with all my heart.[15]

> Am I blue, am I blue,
> Ain't these tears in these eyes telling you?[16]

> How can I go on living, now that we're apart?[17]

She admits vociferously, "I'm a fool to care," but she wallows nevertheless in self-commiseration:

> No day or night goes by,
> That I don't have my cry . . .[18]

The next stage in the progress from disenchantment to demoralization and despair is, of course, another popular song theme, "I'm through with love, I'll never love again"—a theme which has such variants as these:

> I'll never love again,
> I'm so in love with you.
> I'll never thrill again
> To somebody new . . .[19]

> And if I never fall in love again,
> That's soon enough for me,
> I'm gonna lock my heart and throw away the key.[20]

And what is the final stage? Students of general semantics are familiar enough with psychiatric concepts to know that when the world of reality proves unmanageable, a common practice is to retreat into a symbolic world, since symbols are more manageable and predictable than the extensional realities for which they stand. The psychiatric profession classifies this retreat as schizophrenia, but that does not prevent it from being the theme of a popular song:

> I'm going to buy myself a paper doll to call my own,
> A doll that other fellows cannot steal. . . .
> When I come home at night she will be waiting,
> She'll be the truest doll in all the world.
> I'd rather have a paper doll to call my own
> Than a fickle-minded real live girl.[21]

This, then, is the picture of love's unhappy progress, as presented by the song writers of the commercial song-publishing world. The unrealistic emotions and the bathos of popular songs have, of course, long been notorious. It may well be asked if songs can be otherwise and yet be popular.

In answer to this question, let me next present the problems of love as seen by the writers of blues songs, such as are the basis of jazz. The first thing to be noticed is that the object of love is not idealized, but is looked at fairly realistically. It is one thing to call a pretty girl an angel, but quite another to look at angels as they are seen in "Harlem Blues":

> Now you can have your Broadway, give me Lenox Avenue,
> Angels from the skies stroll Seventh, and for that thanks are due
> To Madam Walker's Beauty Shops and the Poro System too,
> That made them angels without any doubt.[22]

Shortcomings of character or appearance in the object of one's love are candidly acknowledged:

The man I love's got lowdown ways for true,
Well, I am hinkty and I'm lowdown too.[23]

You're so mean and evil, you do things you ought not to do,
But you've got my brand of honey, so I guess I'll have to put up with you.[24]

In other words, there is no to-do made about looking and looking for an ideal girl or man—one adjusts oneself to the kind of women and men that actually exist. Refraining from "always chasing rainbows," the people depicted in the blues appear to save themselves a vast amount of emotional energy.

The loved one's imperfections, however, do not appear to stand in the way either of the intensity or durability of one's affections, as is indicated in this lament over a woman's death:

I went down to St. James Infirmary,
Heard my baby groan,
I felt so broken-hearted,
She used to be my own.

I tried to keep from cryin'
My heart felt just like lead,
She was all I had to live for,
I wish that it was me instead . . .

Though she treated me mean and lowdown,
Somehow I didn't care.
My soul is sick and weary,
I hope we'll meet again up there.[25]

Furthermore, there is no magical attitude toward love indicated in the blues. Love means a mutual human relationship, and therefore there are duties and responsibilities, no less than there are rewards. In its crudest and most elementary statement, the duty is financial:

You want to be my man you got to give me $40 down,
If you don't be my man, your baby's gonna shake this town.[26]

You sittin' down wonderin' what it's all about,
If you ain't got no money, they will put you out,
Why don't you do right, like other men do?
Get out of here, and get me some money too.[27]

In general the duties described are those of living up to one's obligations as a mate, of providing that minimum of dependability that makes, as they say, a house a home:

Kind treatment make me love you, be mean and you'll drive me away,
You're gonna long for me baby, one of these old rainy days.
Yes, I love you, baby, but you don't treat me right,
Walk the streets all day, baby, and never come home at night.[28]

And the famous blues singer, Bessie Smith, gives the following advice to girls—advice which is full of the sense of one's own responsibility in a love situation:

So if your man is nice, take my advice,
Hug him in the morning, kiss him every night,
Give him plenty loving, treat him right,
For a good man nowadays is hard to find.[29]

The physical basis of love is more candidly acknowledged in the blues than in most popular songs. I am indebted to Dr. Russell Meyers of the University of Iowa Hospitals for the following observation about Jelly Roll Morton's "Winin' Boy Blues," in which there occurs the line, "Pick it up and shake it, life's sweet stavin' chain."[30] Dr. Meyers equates this line to Herrick's "Gather ye rosebuds while ye may," translating thus: "A stavin' chain is the heavy chain used by loggers to bind together logs to be floated down river, so that it is metaphorically that which binds together, i.e., sexuality; the idea is, as in Herrick, that you shake it now, while you are still able."

Popular songs, to be sure, also refer to the physical basis of love, but usually in extremely abstract periphrasis, as in "All of me, why not take all of me?" In the blues, however, as in the Elizabethan lyric, the subject is treated metaphorically. The following is from a song made famous by Bessie Smith:

You better get yourself to a blacksmith shop to get yourself overhauled,
There ain't nothing about you to make a good woman bawl.
Nobody wants a baby when a real man can be found,
You been a good ol' wagon, but you done broke down.[31]

So there are disappointments in love in the blues, no less than in popular songs. But the quality of disappointment is different. The inevitability of change in a changing world appears to be accepted. Conditions change, people change, and in spite of all one can do to preserve a valued relationship, failure may result:

Folks I love my man, I kiss him morning, noon and night,
I wash his clothes and keep him dry and try to treat him right.
Now he's gone and left me, after all I've tried to do,
The way he treat me, girls, he'll do the same thing to you.
That's the reason I got those weeping willow blues.[32]

I've got a hard-working man,
The way he treats me I can't understand,
He works hard every day,
And on Sat'day he throws away his pay.
Now I don't want that man,
Because he's done gone cold in hand.

Now I've tried hard to treat him kind,
But it seems to me his love has gone blind,
The man I've got must have lost his mind,
The way he treats me I can't understand.
I'm gonna get myself another man,
Because the one I've got done gone cold in hand.[33]

The most vivid statement of a sudden change of situation, involving desertion and heartbreak, is made in "Young Woman's Blues," by Bessie Smith:

Woke up this morning when the chickens were crowin' for day,
Looked on the right side of my pillow, my man had gone away.
By the pillow he left a note,
Reading, "I'm sorry, Jane, you got my goat" . . .

Her reaction to this blow, however, is not, as in popular songs, any giving away to self-pity. The song continues:

I'm a young woman, and I ain't done running round.[34]

In other words, she may be hurt, but she is far from demoralized. This refusal to be demoralized under conditions which in popular songs call for the utmost in wailing and self-commiseration is repeatedly to be found in the blues. Instead of the self-abasement that we find in the "kick-me-in-the-face-again-because-I-love-you" school of thought, the heartbroken men and women of the blues songs regroup their emotional forces and carry on without breakdown of morale. The end of a love relationship is by no means the end of life. As Pearl Bailey has sung:

Gonna truck downtown and spend my moo,
Get some short-vamp shoes and a new guy too . . .
Cause I'm tired, mighty tired, of you.[35]

There is then, considerable tough-mindedness in the blues—a willingness, often absent in popular songs, to acknowledge the facts of life. Consequently, one finds in the blues comments on many problems other than those of love, for example, the problem of urban congestion, as in "I'm going to move to the outskirts of town," or of alcoholism, as in the song, "Ignorant Oil." There is also much folk wisdom in the blues, as in "Nobody knows you when you're down and out," or in such observations as:

Now if a woman gets the blues, Lawd, she hangs her head and cries,
But if a man gets the blues, Lawd, he grabs a train and rides.[36]

I am often reminded by the words of blues songs of Kenneth Burke's famous description of poetry as "equipment for living." In the form in which they developed in Negro communities, the blues are equipment for living humble, laborious, and precarious lives of low social status or no status at all—nevertheless, they are valid equipment, in the sense that they are the opposite of escape literature. "Rock Pile Blues" states explicitly what the blues are for:

My hammer's heavy, feels just like a ton of lead,
If they keeps me slaving someone's gonna find me dead.
Don't mind the rock pile, but the days are oh so long,
Ain't no end of misery, that is why I sing this song.[37]

As a student of general semantics, I am concerned here with two functions which literary and poetic symbols perform with respect to our emotional life. First, by means of literary symbols we may be introduced vicariously to the emotions and situations which we have not yet had occasion to experience; in this sense, literature is preparation. Secondly, symbols enable us to organize the experiences we have had, make us aware of them, and therefore help us to come to terms with them; in this sense, literature is learning.

If our symbolic representations give a false or misleading impression of what life is likely to be, we are worse prepared for life than we would have been had we not been exposed to them at all. The frustration and demoralization of which Wendell Johnson writes are of necessity preceded by the expectations created by unrealistic idealizations. This is not to say, of course, that idealizations are in themselves unhealthy; they are a necessary and inescapable product of the human processes of abstraction and symbolization, and without idealizations we should be swine indeed. But there is a world of difference in the semantogenic effects of possible and impossible ideals. The ideals of love, as depicted in popular songs, are usually impossible ideals.

Hence the question arises: do popular songs, listened to, often memorized and sung in the course of adolescent and youthful courtship, make the attainment of emotional maturity more difficult than it need be? It is almost impossible to resist having an opinion on this question, although it would be hard to substantiate one's opinion except on the basis of considerable experience in contact with the emotional problems of young people. Mr. Roy E. Dickerson, executive secretary of the Cincinnati Social Hygiene Society, who has had this experience, has offered the following comment on the thesis of this paper:

> In my judgment there is no doubt about the unfortunate influence of IFD upon the younger generation today. I detected it, I think, in even such a highly selected group as the delegates to the Seventh National Hi-Y-Tri-Hi-Y Congress held under the auspices of the National Council of YMCA's at Miami University recently. I had the pleasure of handling the group of the section of the Congress which gave attention to courtship and marriage. It was still necessary to debunk some super-romantic concepts.
>
> I am up to my eyes in marriage counseling. I feel that I am consulted again and again about ill-considered marriages based upon very superficial and inadequate ideas regarding the nature of love and how it is recognized.[38]

The existence of the blues, like the existence of occasional popular songs with love themes which do not exhibit the IFD pattern, demonstrates that it is at least possible for songs to be both reasonably healthy in psychological content and widely sung and enjoyed. But the blues cannot, of course, take over the entire domain of popular song because, as widely known as some of them have been, their chief appeal, for cultural reasons has been to Negro audiences—and even these audiences have been diminishing with the progressive advancement of Negroes and their assimilation of values and tastes in common with the white, middle-class majority. Furthermore, while there is lyricism to be found in blues tunes and their musical treatment, the words of blues songs are notoriously lacking in either lyricism or delicacy of sentiment—and it would seem that popular songs must, to some degree, supply the need for lyrical expression, especially about matters of love.

With all their limitations, however, the blues demonstrate that a popular art can function as "equipment for living." Cannot our poets and our songwriters try to do at least as much for our young people as Bessie Smith did for her audiences, namely, provide them with symbolic experiences which will help them understand, organize, and better cope with their problems? Or, if that is too much to ask (and perhaps it is, since Bessie Smith was, in her own way, an authentic genius), can they not at least cease and desist from further spreading the all-too-prevalent IFD disease?

Notes

1. Originally presented at the Second Conference on General Semantics, held under the auspices of Washington University and the St. Louis Chapter of the International Society for General Semantics, at St. Louis, Missouri, June 12, 1954.

This paper was also presented before the Associated Students of San Francisco State College at Nourse Auditorium, San Francisco, July 8, 1954. On this occasion the lecture was illustrated by music performed by the Bob Scobey Frisco Jazz Band and Claire Austin. I wish to thank again, for their excellent and spirited contribution to the program, the performers of that evening: Bob Scobey (trumpet), Fred Higuera (drums), Dick Lammi (bass), Bill Napier (clarinet), Wally Rose (piano), Jack Buck (trombone), and Clancey Hayes (banjo and voice). Whatever was left unclear in the speech was made more than clear by the skilful interpretive singing of Mr. Hayes and the deeply felt blues-singing of Mrs. Austin.

The materials of this paper were again presented at the Folk and Jazz Festival at Music Inn, Lenox, Massachusetts, September 5, 1954. Music on this occasion was supplied by the Sammy Price Trio, with blues-singing by Jimmy Rushing and Myra Johnson. I am deeply indebted to these gifted performers for their help, and for their sympathetic understanding of the argument of this paper.

2. I might add that I do not know enough about folk music among the whites (hillbilly music, cowboy songs, etc.) to be able to include these in my discussion. Hence in comparing folk blues with commercial popular songs, I am comparing two genres which are not strictly comparable.

3. Wendell Johnson, *People in Quandaries:* (New York: Harper, 1946), pp. 14–20.

4. "My Ideal," by Leo Robin, Richard Whiting, and Newell Chase. Copyright, 1930, by Famous Music Co.

5. "The Man I Love," by George and Ira Gershwin. Copyright, 1924, by Harms, Inc.

6. "My Heart Stood Still," by Lorenz Hart and Richard Rodgers. Copyright, 1927, by Harms, Inc.

7. "You Were Meant for Me," with lyrics by Arthur Freed, melody by Nacio Herb Brown. Copyright, 1929, by Robbins Music Corp.

8. For example, at a lecture at University College, University of Chicago, May 14, 1954, under the auspices of the Chicago Chapter of the International Society for General Semantics.

9. "Blue Room," by Lorenz Hart and Richard Rodgers. Copyright, 1926, by Harms, Inc.

10. "My Blue Heaven," by George Whiting and Walter Donaldson. Copyright, 1927, by Leo Feist, Inc.

11. "Looking at the World Thru Rose Colored Glasses," by Tommy Malie and Jimmy Steiger. Copyright, 1926, by Pickwick Music Corp.

12. "All Alone," by Irving Berlin. Copyright, 1924, by Irving Berlin.

13. "You Were Only Fooling," with words by Billy Faber and Fred Meadows, music by Larry Fotine. Copyright, 1948, by Shapiro, Bernstein & Co.

14. "Somebody Else Is Taking My Place," by Dick Howard, Bob Ellsworth, and Russ Morgan. Copyright, 1937, by the Back Bay Music Co.—assigned to Shapiro, Bernstein & Co. Copyright, 1941, by Shapiro, Bernstein & Co.

15. "I'm Alone Because I Love You," words and music by Joe Young. Copyright, 1930, by M. Witmark & Sons.

16. "Am I Blue," by Grant Clarke and Harry Akst. Copyright, 1929, by M. Witmark & Sons.

17. "Have You Ever Been Lonely?" with words by George Brown (Billy Hill) and music by Peter de Rose. Copyright, 1933, by Shapiro, Bernstein & Co., Inc.

18. "I Need You Now," by Jimmy Crane and Al Jacobs. Copyright, 1953, by Miller Music Corp.

19. "I'll Never Smile Again," with words and music by Ruth Lowe. Copyright, 1939, by Pickwick Music Corp.

20. "I'm Gonna Lock My Heart," by Jimmy Eaton and Terry Shand. Copyright, 1938, by Shapiro, Bernstein & Co., Inc.

21. "Paper Doll," by Johnny Black. Copyright, 1915, by E. B. Marks.

22. "Harlem Blues," by W. C. Handy. Copyright, 1922, by W. C. Handy; copyright renewed. Included in *A Treasury of the Blues*, ed. W. C. Handy (New York: Simon and Schuster, 1949).

23. "The Basement Blues," by W. C. Handy. Copyright, 1924, by Handy Bros. Music Co., Inc.

24. "Goin' to Chicago Blues," by Jimmy Rushing and Count Basie. Copyright, 1941, by Bregman, Vocco and Conn, Inc.

25. "St. James Infirmary," by Joe Primrose. Copyright, 1930, by Gotham Music Co.

26. "The Memphis Blues," by W. C. Handy. Copyright, 1912, by W. C. Handy. (Included in *A Treasury of the Blues.*) When the lecture on which this paper was based was delivered in San Francisco, it was extensively reported in the San Francisco *News*. In the correspondence columns of the *News* a few days later, there appeared a protest from a reader who remarked regarding my quotation of these lines, "It is good to know that our future teachers (at San Francisco State College) are acquiring moral and spiritual values by getting the good honest feel of the brothel." Mr. Ralph Gleason, writing in the musicians' magazine, *Downbeat*, and taking his interpretation of my lecture from the letter-writer in the *News*, worked himself up into quite a moralistic lather against what he imagined to be my recommendation of love on a cash-down basis over white middle-class morality. I trust it is not necessary to explain to readers of *Etc.* that what I am doing here is attempting to draw a humorous contrast between love regarded as magic and love (including facsimiles thereof) regarded as involving mutual obligations. The statement that love involves obligations is not entirely absent, of course, from popular songs. A recent example is "Little Things Mean a Lot," by Edith Lindeman and Carl Stutz (New York: Leo Feist, 1954), which, as sung by Kitty Kallen, has recently enjoyed vast popularity.

27. "Why Don't You Do Right?" by Joe McCoy. Copyright, 1942, by Mayfair Music Corp.

28. "Blues in the Dark," by Jimmy Rushing and Count Basie. Copyright, 1943, by Bregman, Vocco and Conn, Inc.

29. "A Good Man Is Hard to Find," by Eddie Green. Copyright, 1917, by Mayfair Music Corp. This song is not of Negro composition and is not, strictly speaking, a blues. However, ever since its famous rendition by Bessie Smith (Columbia 14250-D), it has been part of the blues repertory.

30. See General 4004-A, in the album *New Orleans Memories*, by Jelly Roll Morton.

31. "You've Been a Good Ole Wagon" (Smith-Balcom), sung by Bessie Smith (Columbia 14079-D; re-issue, Columbia 35672).

32. For this and several other quotations from blues songs in this paper, I am indebted to Professor John Ball of the Department of English, Miami University, Oxford, Ohio, who, as a student of jazz, has transcribed from his record collection the words of many blues songs, including many which have never appeared in print.

33. "Cold in Hand Blues" (Gee-Longshaw), sung by Bessie Smith (Columbia 14064-D; re-issue, Columbia 35672).

34. "Young Woman's Blues" (Bessie Smith), sung by Bessie Smith (Columbia 14179-D; re-issue, Columbia 35673).

35. "Tired" (Roberts and Fisher), sung by Pearl Bailey (Columbia 36837).

36. See note 32. Memo to Professor Ball: Where on earth did you find this, John?

37. "Rock Pile Blues," by Spencer Williams. Copyright, 1925, by Lincoln Music Co. (Included in *A Treasury of the Blues.*)

38. From a personal letter dated July 13, 1954.

The Blues Roots of Contemporary Afro-American Poetry

Sherley A. Williams

ETHNOPOETICS is for me the study of the new forms of poetry which develop as a result of the interfaces or confrontations between different cultures. The spirituals, play and work songs, cakewalks and hoe-downs, and the blues are the first recorded artifacts to grow out of the complex relationship between Africans and Europeans on the North American continent. Afro-American oral tradition, of which these lyric forms are a part, combines with white American literature whose traditions are rooted more in the literate cultures of the West than in the oral traditions, either indigenous or transplanted, of the New World. Afro-American literature is thus created within the framework of multiple relationships, and the tension between the white literary and the black oral traditions informs and influences the best contemporary Afro-American poetry at the level of structure as well as theme. The themes of the poetry are usually accessible to non-black audiences, but the poets' attempts to own the traditions to which they are heir create technical transformations which cannot be analyzed, much less evaluated, solely within the context of their European roots. Most critics pay lip service to the idea that Afro-American music, speech and life-styles influence the form and structure of Afro-American writing. Thus Stephen Henderson's discussion, in *Understanding the New Black Poetry* (1973), of some of the techniques of Afro-American speech and singing which have been carried over virtually unchanged into Afro-American poetry is rare in its concrete descriptions of these devices. This paper builds on his work, concentrating on the transformations which result when the blues of Afro-American oral tradition interfaces with the "poetry" of European literary tradition.

Blues is essentially an oral form meant to be heard rather than read; and the techniques and structures used to such powerful purpose in the songs cannot always be transferred directly to the literary traditions within which, by definition, Afro-American poets write. Blues is viewed here as a verbal—as distinct from musical—genre which developed out of the statement (or call) and response patterns of collective work groups. Blues culminated in a "classic" form (heard most consistently in the early blues recordings of Bessie Smith,

---

Reprinted from Michael Harper and Robert B. Stepto, eds., *Chant of Saints: A Gathering of Afro-American Literature, Art, and Scholarship* (Urbana: University of Illinois Press, 1979), 123–35.

Ma Rainey and the other "classic blues" singers) which embodies the distinctive features of Afro-American song forms in a standardized structure. In some contemporary Afro-American poetry, the devices and structures of the classic blues form are transformed, thus allowing the poetry to function in much the same way as blues forms once functioned within the black communities across the country.

I. Function

Afro-American music still functions to some extent as a reflector of a wide range of values in the national black community and often serves as a catalyst for discussions, reviews and revisions of these values. The immediacy of this process has been diminished by the advent of huge impersonal concerts, but records and local "soul" stations keep alive this supra-entertainment function of the music. The professional songwriter had modified what used to be a very close and personal relationship among singer, song, and the group tradition on which all depended for the act of creation and which the act of creation affirms and extends. In an age where almost everyone is singing someone else's song, performance has to some extent taken the place of authorship. Thus Otis Redding's version of "Respect," while very popular, was never made into the metaphor of Black Man/Black Woman or, just as importantly, Black/White relationships that Aretha Franklin's version became. Of course, Aretha was right on time, but there was also something about the way Aretha characterized respect as something given with force and great effort and cost. And when she even went so far as to spell the word "respect," we just knew that this sister wasn't playing around about getting Respect and keeping it. Early blues singers and their growing repertoire of songs probably helped to solidify community values and heighten community morale in the late nineteenth and early twentieth centuries. The singers provided welcome entertainment and a necessary reminder that there had to be more to the lives of the audience than the struggle for material subsistence—if they were ever to achieve and enjoy the day the sun would shine in their back door. Michael S. Harper, in his liner notes to the album *John Coltrane*, alludes to the communal nature of the relationship between blues singer and blues audience when he speaks of the audience which assumes "we" even though the blues singer sings "I." Blues singers have also been aware of this function of their art, for as Henry Townsend said in an interview with Samuel B. Charters (*The Poetry of the Blues*, 1963):

> You know I'm going to put this a little blunt. I don't know if I should say it or not, because it might hurt the religious type of people, but when I sing the blues, I sing the truth. The religious type of people may not believe that it's good, because they think the blues is not the truth; but the blues, from a point of explaining yourself as facts, is the truth and I don't feel that the truth should be condemned. . . .

Unlike sacred music, the blues deals with a world where the inability to solve a problem does not necessarily mean that one can, or ought to, transcend it. The internal strategy of the blues is action, rather than contemplation, for the song itself is the creation of reflection. And while not all blues actions achieve the desired result, the impulse to action is inherent in any blues which functions out of a collective purpose. But while the gospels, for example, are created for the purpose of preparing the congregation to receive the Holy Spirit and become possessed by it, the blues singer strives to create an atmosphere in which analysis can take place. This necessary analytic distance is achieved through the use of verbal and musical irony seldom found in the singing of the spirituals or the gospels. Thus Billie Holiday, in "Fine and Mellow," concludes the recital of the wrongs her man has done her with the mocking observation that

> Love is like a faucet
> it turns off and on
> Sometimes when you think it's on, baby
> it have turned off and gone.

The persona pointedly reminds her man that her patience with his trifling ways has its limits at the same time that she suggests that she might be in her present difficulties because she wasn't alert to the signs that her well was going dry. The self-mockery and irony of the blues pull one away from a total surrender to the emotions generated by the concreteness of the experiences and situations described in the song. Even where the verbal content of the song is straightforward and taken at face value, the singer has musical techniques which create ironic effects.

The vocal techniques of Afro-American music—melisma, intentional stutters and hesitations, repetitions of words and phrases, and the interjection of exclamatory phrases and sounds—are used in the spirituals and gospels to facilitate emotional involvement. In blues singing, however, these same devices are often used in a deliberately random manner which emphasizes unimportant phrases or words as often as it does key ones. The devices themselves, especially melisma and changes in stress, have become standardized enough to have formed a substantial part of the artistry of Billie Holiday. At their worst, the devices become no more than meaningless vocal calisthenics, but at their best they disengage meaning from feeling. Put another way, the singer objectifies, almost symbolizes, the emotional content of the song through the use of melisma, stuttering and variations in stress, and, in so doing, places the situation in stark relief as an object for discussion. Thus, a member of the blues audience shouts "Tell it like it is" rather than "Amen" or "Yes, Jesus" as a response to a particularly pungent or witty truth, for the emphasis is on thinking, not tripping.

Charles Keil's analysis (*The Urban Blues*, 1966) of a Bobby Blue Bland performance illustrates how even the selection of songs in a blues performance underscores the relationship of singer and audience and the manner in which communal values are incorporated into the presentation of the blues performer's act. Many contemporary Afro-American poets consciously assume the role of people's voices—see, for example, Marvin X's second volume of poetry *The Son of Man*—and ask black people (rather than whites) to affirm their stance. That initial gesture may have grown out of the learned intellectual model provided by Marx and Herskovits; once having made it, however, it became real for many poets, at more than just the level of rhetoric and "kill the honkey" poems. We witness this realness in the increasing sureness with which Afro-American poets challenge the primacy of European forms.

II. Structure

A number of Afro-American poets have written poems based on the less structured blues forms; few, however, have attempted to utilize the deceptively simple classic blues structure. Langston Hughes is an exception. The sophistication of meaning and form which characterizes Hughes's poem "Young Gal's Blues" is, of course, characteristic of classic blues at its best and the literary sophistication is in fact made possible by the existence of such songs as "Backwater Blues" or the more contemporary variation on the classic form "Your Friends." "Young Gal's Blues," in which a young woman tries to fortify herself against the prospect of death (which can come at any time) and the loneliness of old age (which will certainly catch her if death don't do it first), is an example of an oral form moving unchanged into literary tradition:

I'm gonna walk to the graveyard
'Hind ma friend, Miss Cora Lee
Gonna walk to de graveyard
'Hind ma dear friend Cora Lee

Cause when I'm dead some
Body'll have to walk behind me.

Hughes worries the first line by dropping "I'm" in the repetition of the first half line and adding "dear" when he repeats the second half-line. Repetition in blues is seldom word for word and the definition of worrying the line includes changes in stress and pitch, the addition of exclamatory phrases, changes in word order, repetitions of phrases within the line itself, and the wordless blues cries which often punctuate the performance of the songs. The response to this opening statement repeats and broadens the idea of death even as it justifies and explains the blues persona's action. Ideally, each half line is a complete phrase or clause; but Hughes, even in breaking the line between "some" and "body" rather than after "dead," keeps within the convention of half lines on which the classic structure is based. The stanza is a closed unit without run-over lines or run-over thoughts; and the same pattern, response justifying the statement, is followed in the second stanza in which the persona tells of her determination to visit old Aunt Clew in "de po' house" because "When I'm old an' ugly / I'll want to see somebody, too." The "po' house" evokes the known social and political conditions rather than stating them directly.

In evoking rather than stating these conditions, Hughes makes the same assumption about his audience that a blues singer makes: both poet (singer) and audience share the same reality. The lives of the audience are bound by the same grim social reality in which one faces an old age characterized by the same grinding poverty which destroys youth before it can flower and makes the fact that while working is still necessary, one is no longer capable of doing it—this being the only distinction between middle and old age. The particularized, individual experience rooted in a common reality is the primary thematic characteristic of all blues songs no matter what their structure. The classic song form itself internalizes and echoes, through the statement/response pattern, the thematic relationship between individual and group experience which is implied in these evocations of social and political reality.

De po' house is lonely
an' de grave is cold.
O, de po' house is lonely
De grave is cold.
But I'd rather be dead than to
be ugly and old

The statement in this stanza is more general than the statement in either of the first two stanzas and while the stanza is self-contained, it places the personal reflection of the preceding stanza within a larger context. The response returns to the first person, the subjective testimony, as the persona says quite frankly that she would rather die than be ugly. It is also Hughes's definition of what it is to be young; to care more for the quality of one's life than the fact of life itself. Thus the response in this stanza makes explicit the persona's choices in life. But neither choice, death at an early age or an old age endured in poverty and loneliness, is particularly happy and the persona, recognizing that love is one of the few things which make any life bearable, concludes the fourth stanza and the poem with the plea "Keep on a-lovin me, daddy / Cause I don't want to be blue."

The response can also be the antithesis of the statement as in the opening stanza of "Billie's Blues,"

> I love my man
>   I'm a lie if I say I don't
> But I'll quit my man
>   I'm a lie if I say I won't,

where the paradox also provides the frame for the distinctions which the persona later makes between being a slave, which she is quite prepared to be for her man, and a "dog" which she refuses to become, between mere good looks typified by white features ("I ain't good looking and my hair ain't curled") and the confidence, the affirmation of self necessary to get one through the world.

The change in focus from individual to communal reality may be done as in the Hughes poem or through simply worrying the line as in the blues standard "The Things I Used to Do": "The things I used to do / I won't do no more. / Lawd the things I used to *I'm tryna tell yo' all* / I won't do no more," where the singer appeals directly to the audience to witness his situation and, in effect, to affirm his solution to his problem. The abrupt change of subject or theme as in "Sweet Sixteen" serves the same purpose. The persona describes his love for a flighty, headstrong young girl who has run away from her home and now wants to "run away from old me, too." The persona is now desperate and the song is really a plea to the woman to do right, love him as he loves her. The third stanza ends with the line, "Seems like everything I do [to try and keep you with me] is in vain."

Then, in a dramatic shift in subject and perspective:

> My brother's in Korea
>   My sister's down in New Orleans
> You know I'm having so much trouble, people
>   I wonder what in the world's gonna happen to me.

At the level of the love theme, the absence of family ties underscores the persona's loneliness; hence his dependence on this relationship. His scattered family exists within the framework of the ruptured family relationships, caused by the oppressive and repressive system of the country, which characterizes too much of the Afro-American experience. The response to this statement of loneliness is one of complete despair, addressed to "people," the audience whose private pains are set within the same kind of collective experience. The next stanza is again addressed to the woman and reiterates, at the level of their personal relationship, the persona's realization that he has lost pride, dignity, and a necessary sense of himself as a result of this relationship:

> Treat me mean, baby,
>   but I'll keep on loving you anyway
> But one of these old days, baby,
>   you're gonna give a lot of money to hear someone call my name.

Billie Pierce's version of "Married Man Blues," recorded by Samuel B. Charters in New Orleans in 1954, uses what had become a traditional statement/response description of the problems of loving a married man to place the song within a more universal context. The persona has loved only one man, a married man, in her life. And despite the fact that she "stole him from his wife" she is still in trouble because she has stolen only his affection, not his continued presence. The traditional verse is used to summarize her situation:

> Girls it's awful hard
>   to love another woman's man
> Cause you can't get him when you wanna
>   have to catch catch as catch's can.

The last half-line in the response is Billie's personal variation on the standardized wording, "got to catch him when you can," and the rhythmical variation plays nicely against the established rhythm of the statement. The stanza, in addition, serves as a transition, tying together the fictive first person experiences and the more "real" first person admonitions of the last part of the song.

The second portion of the song opens with an assertion of individuality: "My first name is Billie / and my last name is Pierce." The assertion of individuality and the implied assertion—as action, not mere verbal statement—of self is an important dimension of the blues. Janheinz Jahn (*Neo-African Literature*, 1968) is essentially correct when he describes the blues in terms of this assertion of life-force rather than the usual ones of melancholy and pain. The assertion of self usually comes at the end of the blues song after the description/analysis of the situation or problem and is often the only solution to that problem or situation. In "Married Man Blues," Billie's assertive stance is underscored in successive stanzas which imply some of the values inherent in a good love relationship:

> Aw, you want me to do right there, Little Dee Dee
>   And you ain't doing right yourself
> Well you get yourself another woman
>   And I'll get me somebody else.
>
> Well, at my first time leaving you, baby
>   Crying ain't gone make me stay
> Cause the more you cry Dee Dee, baby
>   Well the more you gonna drive little Billie away.

The sting of the stanzas is balanced by the fact that they are part of the anonymous oral tradition, and Billie Pierce was a master at combining such traditional verses with written songs ("Saint Louis Woman," "Careless Love," for example) to create her own personal versions of these songs. Here, she also underscores the closeness of her musical relationship with her husband, Dee Dee Pierce, who accompanies her on trumpet, by the encouragements spoken throughout this portion of the song to, "Play it nice, play it the way I like it Dee Dee, baby."

This complex interweaving of general and specific, individual and group, finds no direct correspondence in Afro-American literature except in the literary blues. But the evocation of certain first person experiences and the extensive use of multiple voices in Afro-American poetry may be, at least in part, an outgrowth from this characteristic of the blues. Nikki Giovanni's "The Great Pax Whitey" which seems a rather pedestrian and undigested patchwork of folk and personal legend and black nationalist philosophy becomes, when viewed (or better yet, read) as a poem in which a congregation of voices speaks, a brilliant literary approximation of the kind of collective dialogue which has been going on underground in the black community at least since the nineteenth century and of which the blues in its various forms was an important part.

III. Transformation

Blues songs are almost always literal, seldom metaphoric or symbolic except in sexual and physical terms. And, while similes are used extensively, much of the verbal strength of the blues resides in the directness with which the songs confront experience and in what Stephen Henderson identifies as "mascon images," Afro-American archetypes which represent "a *mas*sive *con*centration of black experiential energy." Often the mascons are not really images in the literary sense of the word, rather they are verbal expressions which evoke a powerful response in the listener because of their direct relationship to concepts and events in the collective experience. Thus the graveyard and the po'house in "Young Gal's Blues" might be described as universal archetypes or mascons, while the calling of the names in "Sweet Sixteen" is a specifically black one. The latter expression grows directly out of traditional people's belief in the strong relationship between name and personal essence and the corresponding Afro-American preoccupation with titles (Miss, Mr., Mrs. and, with great deliberation and care, Ms.), with the naming of children and the acquisition of nicknames and sobriquets—and who may use them. In such an atmosphere, to call someone out of their names, as the Monkey tells the Lion that the Elephant has done him in the "Signifying Monkey," is punishable, in children, by a beating. And the changing of one's names as most blacks did after emancipation and many more did during the sixties takes on an added significance.

Very often, the meanings of mascons cut across areas of experience usually thought of as separate but which in Afro-American experiences are not mutually exclusive. Thus the term "jelly roll," as Henderson illustrates, moves at a number of different levels, while the expressions centered in the concept of "home" move at both a spiritual and material level, and "The Streets," which has developed into a mascon as a result of the Afro-American urban experience, involves both pleasure and pain. Despite the fact that these expressions are used over and over again by blacks in everyday conversations as well as in more self-conscious verbal events, they escape being clichés because their meanings are deeply rooted in a constantly renewed and thus *living* reality. They are distinguished from the vernacular vocabulary of black speech in that the vernacular rests on the idea that the standard English version of a word, say "bad" or "dig," has one meaning and the standard black version has another, often contradictory, meaning: excellent and understand. Mascons, on the contrary, concentrate their massive force within the frame of the literal meaning of the standard English word. And it is this literal yet figuratively complex relationship which makes the response in the final stanza of "Sweet Sixteen" such a powerful climax to the song. But one of these old days, the persona tells his woman, you would even get up off some money, just to have back the man I was when I met you, the man that loving you destroyed. Thus mascons are a compression, as well as a concentration, whose power is released through the first person experience.

When Harriet Tubman, in Robert Hayden's "Runagate Runagate Runagate" invites us to "ride my train," it is not merely the thought of the Underground Railroad to which blacks respond. But Harriet's "train" is also the train whose tracks throughout the South were laid by black men who also worked on them as cooks, porters, and red caps and which many blacks rode to the promised land of the North. And despite the fact that trains are no longer a significant part of our day to day reality, they live on in the metaphors of the "Gospel Train" which many plan to ride to glory and the "Soul Trains" which proclaim the black musical presence in the world. It is the stored energy of this mascon which enables Afro-American poets to play so lovingly and meaningfully with John Coltrane's name and they capture something of his function as an artist in their use of his nickname, Trane.

Many Afro-American poets have used techniques which approximate or parallel various blues devices and Lucille Clifton, in her first volume of poems, *Good Times,* uses these transformations consistently and successfully. Like the blues, her poems are firmly based in a living black reality which is more concerned with itself than with direct confrontations with white society and its values. There are several poems about whites in the volume, but even here, the impression is of a black person, involved in a conversation with other blacks, who occasionally tosses a comment to the white man she knows is waiting in the wings. His presence does not cause her to bite her tongue, however, and the opening poem "in the inner city," is addressed as much to the white man in the wings as it is to the black audience.

> in the inner city
> or
> like we call it
> home
> we think a lot about uptown
> and the silent nights
> and the houses straight as
> dead men
> and the pastel lights
> and we hang on to our no place
> happy to be alive
> and in the inner city
> or
> like we call it
> home

Clifton's poems are created out of the collective experience which culminates in and is transformed by the inner city. Those experiences in their broader outlines are evoked rather than stated, through vignettes told in the first person; and the individual experience plays against the assumed knowledge of that collective history in much the same way that the communal pattern of statement and response plays against the individual experience expressed in the blues. The inner city of which Clifton speaks is neither that of the "deviants" who inhabit most sociological studies about blacks nor the statistics which politicians manipulate so skillfully for their own gains; it is the community, home. "Inner city" becomes both the literal ghetto and the metaphoric inner landscape of black hearts which has seldom been explored so sensitively and revealingly as in Clifton's *Good Times*.

The spareness of Clifton's poetry depends in part on mascon images. "Pushing," a mascon of enormous contemporary force, is used to climax "For deLawd," Clifton's tribute to the long "line / of black and going on women" from which she comes. Grief for murdered brothers, murdered husbands, murdered sons has kept on pushing them, kept them "for their still alive sons / for their sons coming / for their sons gone / just pushing." And pushing is both the will to struggle on toward a long sought goal, even in the face of enormous odds (as Curtis Mayfield and The Impressions exhort us to do in "Keep on Pushing") and the double consciousness which blacks have of this country and its institutions—a consciousness which many would rather not have for it often highlights the futility of trying to "make it" in America (the expression, "I'm so pushed" is used interchangeably with "I'm hipped"). And this reading of "pushing" complements the ironic use of "making it." For it is against the background of the collective experience of "making it through . . . sons" murdered literally and figuratively by the society and the individual prospect of what can happen to her sons that the persona knowingly goes on about her business. The ability to keep on pushing, to keep on keeping on, to go on about one's business is the life-force, the assertion of self amidst collective and individual destruction which comes directly out of the blues tradition. This is what the persona's mother in "Billie's Blues" passes on to her daughter and what makes the closing of that song so delightful:

Some men call me honey
Some think that I've got money
Some men like me cause I'm snappy
Some because I'm happy
Some men tell me, Billie
Baby, you're built for speed
Now when you put that all together
It makes me everything a good man need.

The loss of that sense of vitality makes the persona in "Sweet Sixteen" a tragic figure. Clifton expresses this life force again and again, and it provides a continuing frame for and necessary counterpoint to the often fatal despair which also stalks the inner city.

The power of first person experiences is balanced by distancing techniques—shifts in diction, voice, and focus which parallel the ways in which distance is achieved in the blues. After a series of first person poems whose diction hovers marvelously between the standard and the black dialects (and thus embodies both), Clifton will place a poem written from a third person perspective in precise standard diction. The shift in viewpoint immediately makes the subject of the poem its subject.

Robert

was born obedient
without questions

did a dance called
picking grapes
sticking his butt out
for pennies

married a master
who whipped his mind
until he died

until he died
the color of his life
was nigger

"Robert" as both poem and person is such an object and comes after a series of poems in which a female persona talks about members of her immediate and extended family who have lost the battle for psychic survival in the society. The focus within this series of four poems (which begins with "My mamma moved among the days") shifts from the destruction of these others to the survival of the persona, and the series ends with the lines, "I stand up / through your destruction / I stand up." The reference is not only to the destruction of Miss Rosie, who is the subject of this poem, but to the persona's mother, father, and sister who have each appeared in previous poems. Clifton implies that the only thing which makes the destruction of these others somewhat bearable is the persona's ability to stand up, to affirm herself because these others have died that she might live. Robert is an immediate contrast to the lives sketched in these mini-portraits for he begins his existence in defeat and "until he died / the color of his life / was nigger." This poem further enlarges the context in which each poem in the series exists and its impersonal, objective stance returns, at a more abstract level, to the general/collective tone of "in the inner city," the poem which serves as introduction to this sequence and to the volume as a whole. The shift from first to third person perspective provides both an inner and outer view of the inner city and creates an atmosphere which encourages one to enter into and understand the experiences presented in the poems at both an emotional and analytic level. Sequences of poems are used to develop themes beyond the limits of a single poem; and individual poems come, in fact, to function in much the same way that individual classic blues stanzas function within the classic song. The individual expression is always seen within the context of the collective experience.

Lucille Clifton and other poets who work or even attempt to work in a similar mode extend the verbal traditions of the blues in the same way that the Swing of Count Basie and the bebop of Charlie Parker extend the instrumental traditions of the blues, making those traditions "classic" in a recognizably Western sense while remaining true to the black experiences and black perceptions which are their most important sources. But unlike the oral lyrics which, of necessity, preserve their group traditions only in their forms or structures and need a separate history to preserve a concrete sense of the collective life styles, values, and experiences which they represent, poetry, as a written form, carries with it the possibility of functioning simultaneously on both levels. Thus while B. B. King in "Sweet Sixteen" can allude to, even symbolize, collective experiences or internalize the necessary and sustaining relationship between group and individual in the statement/response pattern and structures, Clifton, in her poetry incorporates elements of the older oral traditions, re-asserts the collective at concrete levels even as she deals, through subjective testimony, with individual experiences. And this is the beginning of a new tradition built on a synthesis of black oral traditions and Western literate forms.

Introduction to *Blues, Ideology, and Afro-American Literature*

Houston Baker

Standing at the crossroads, tried to flag a ride,
Standing at the crossroads, tried to flag a ride,
Ain't nobody seem to know me, everybody passed me by.

—Crossroad Blues

In every case the result of an untrue mode of knowledge must not be allowed to run away into an empty nothing, but must necessarily be grasped as the nothing *of that from which it results*—a result which contains what was true in the preceding knowledge.

—Hegel, *Phenomenology of Spirit*

So perhaps we shy from confronting our cultural wholeness because it offers no easily recognizable points of rest, no facile certainties as to who, what, or where (culturally or historically) we are. Instead, the whole is always in cacophonic motion.

—Ralph Ellison, "The Little Man at the Chehaw Station"

. . . maybe one day, you'll find they actually do understand exactly what you are talking about, all these fantasy people. All these blues people.

—Amiri Baraka, *Dutchman*

From Symbol to Ideology

IN MY book *The Journey Back: Issues in Black Literature and Criticism* (1980),[1] I envisioned the "speaking subject" creating language (a code) to be deciphered by the present-day commentator. In my current study, I envision language (the code) "speaking" the subject. The subject is "decentered." My quest during the past decade has been for the distinctive, the culturally specific aspects of Afro-American literature and culture. I

Reprinted from Houston Baker, *Blues, Ideology, and Afro-American Literature: A Vernacular Theory* (Chicago: University of Chicago Press, 1984), 1–14.

was convinced that I had found such specificity in a peculiar subjectivity, but the objectivity of economics and the sound lessons of poststructuralism arose to reorient my thinking. I was also convinced that the symbolic, and quite specifically the symbolically anthropological, offered avenues to the comprehension of Afro-American expressive culture in its plenitude.[2] I discovered that the symbolic's antithesis—practical reason, or the material—is as necessary for understanding Afro-American discourse as the cultural-in-itself.

My shift from a centered to a decentered subject, from an exclusively symbolic to a more inclusively expressive perspective, was prompted by the curious force of dialectical thought. My access to the study of such thought came from attentive readings of Fredric Jameson, Hayden White, Marshall Sahlins, and others. While profiting from observations by these scholars, I also began to attend meetings of a study group devoted to Hegel's *Phenomenology of Spirit.*

Having journeyed with the aid of symbolic anthropology to what appeared to be the soundest possible observations on Afro-American art, I found myself confronted suddenly by a figure-to-ground reversal. A fitting image for the effect of my reorientation is the gestalt illustration of the Greek hydria (a water vase with curved handles) that transforms itself into two faces in profile. John Keats's "Ode on a Grecian Urn," with its familiar detailing of the economies of "art" and human emotion, can be considered one moment in the shift. Contrasting with Keats's romantic figurations are the emergent faces of a venerable ancestry. The shift from Greek hydrias to ancestral faces is a shift from high art to vernacular expression.

The "vernacular" in relation to human beings signals "a slave born on his master's estate." In expressive terms, vernacular indicates "arts native or peculiar to a particular country or locale." The material conditions of slavery in the United States and the rhythms of Afro-American blues combined and emerged from my revised materialistic perspective as an ancestral matrix that has produced a forceful and indigenous American creativity. The moment of emergence of economic and vernacular concerns left me, as the French say, *entre les deux:* suspended somewhere between symbolic anthropology and analytical strategies that Fredric Jameson calls the "ideology of form."[3]

Ideology, Semiotics, and the Material

In acknowledging a concern for the ideology of form, however, I do not want to imply that my symbolic-anthropological orientation was untrue, in the sense of deluded or deceived.[4] This symbolic orientation was simply one moment in my experiencing of Afro-American culture—a moment superseded now by a prospect that constitutes its determinate negation.[5] What was true in my prior framework remains so in my current concern for the ideology of form. Certainly the mode of ideological investigation proposed by Jameson is an analysis that escapes all hints of "vulgar Marxism" through its studious attention to modern critiques of political economy, and also through its shrewd incorporation of poststructuralist thought.[6]

In chapters that follow, I too attempt to avoid a native Marxism. I do not believe, for example, that a fruitful correlation exists when one merely claims that certain black folk seculars are determinate results of agricultural gang labor. Such attributions simply privilege the material as a substrate while failing to provide detailed accounts of processes leading from an apparent substrate to a peculiar expressive form. A faith of enormous magnitude is required to accept such crude formulations as adequate explanations. The "material" is shifty ground, and current critiques of political economy suggest that postulates based on this ground can be understood only in "semiotic" terms. Hence, the employment of ideology as an analytical category begins with the awareness that "production" as well as "modes of production" must be grasped in terms of the sign. An example of a persuasive case for "political economy" as a code existing in a relationship of identity with language can be found in Jean Baudrillard's *For a Critique of the Political Economy of the Sign.*[7] To read economics as a semiotic process leads to the realization that ideological analyses may be as decidedly intertextual as, say, analyses of the relationship between Afro-American vernacular expression and more sophisticated forms of verbal art. If what is normally categorized as *material* (e.g., "raw material," "consumer goods") can be interpreted semiotically, then any collection of such entities and their defining interrelationships may be defines as a *text.*[8]

In the chapters in this book, however, I do not write about or interpret the *material* in exclusively semiotic terms. Although I am fully aware of insights to be gained from semiotics, my analyses focus directly on the living and laboring conditions of people designated as "the desperate class" by James Weldon Johnson's narrator in *The Autobiography of an Ex-Colored Man.* Such people constitute the vernacular in the United States. Their lives have always been sharply conditioned by an "economics of slavery" as they worked the agricultural rows, searing furnaces, rolling levees, bustling roundhouses, and piney-woods logging camps of America. A sense of "production" and "modes of production" that foregrounds such Afro-American labor seems an appropriate inscription of the material.

The Matrix as Blues

The guiding presupposition of the chapters that follow is that Afro-American culture is a complex, reflexive enterprise which finds its proper figuration in blues conceived as a matrix. A matrix is a womb, a network, a fossil-bearing rock, a rocky trace of a gemstone's removal, a principal metal in an alloy, a mat or plate for reproducing print or phonograph records. The matrix is a point of ceaseless input and output, a web of intersecting, crisscrossing impulses always in productive transit. Afro-American blues constitute such a vibrant network. They are what Jacques Derrida might describe as the "always already" of Afro-American culture.[9] They are the multiplex, enabling *script* in which Afro-American cultural discourse is inscribed.

First arranged, scored, and published for commercial distribution early in the twentieth century when Hart Wand, Arthur "Baby" Seals, and W. C. Handy released their first compositions, the blues defy narrow definition. For they exist, not as a function of formal inscription, but as a forceful condition of Afro-American inscription itself. They were for Handy a "found" folk signifier, awakening him from (perhaps) a dream of American form in Tutwiler, Mississippi, in 1903.[10] At a railroad juncture deep in the southern night, Handy dozed restlessly as he awaited the arrival of a much-delayed train. A guitar's bottleneck resonance suddenly jolted him to consciousness, as a lean, loose-jointed, shabbily clad black man sang:

Goin' where the Southern cross the Dog.
Goin' where the Southern cross the Dog.
Goin' where the Southern cross the Dog.

This haunting invocation of railroad crossings in bottleneck tones left Handy stupified and inspired. In 1914, he published his own Yellow Dog Blues.

But the autobiographical account of the man who has been called the "Father of the Blues" offers only a simplistic detailing of *a progress*, describing, as it were, the elevation of a "primitive" folk ditty to the status of "art" in America. Handy's rendering leaves unexamined, therefore, myriad corridors, mainroads, and way-stations of an extraordinary and elusive Afro-American cultural phenomenon.

Defining Blues

The task of adequately describing the blues is equivalent to the labor of describing a world class athlete's awesome gymnastics. Adequate appreciation demands comprehensive attention. An investigator had to *be* there, to follow a course recommended by one of the African writer Wole Soyinka's ironic narrators to a London landlord: "See for yourself."

The elaborations of the blues may begin in an austere self-accusation: "Now this trouble I'm having, I brought it all on myself." But the accusation seamlessly fades into humorous acknowledgment of duplicity's always duplicitous triumph: "You know the woman that I love, I stoled her from my best friend, / But you know that fool done got lucky and stole her back again." Simple provisos for the troubled mind are commonplace, and drear exactions of crushing manual labor are objects of wry, *in situ* commentary. Numinous invocation punctuates a guitar's resonant back beat with: "Lawd, Lawd, Lawd . . . have mercy on me / Please send me someone, to end this misery." Existential declarations of lack combine with lustily macabre prophecies of the subject's demise. If a "matchbox" will hold his clothes, surely the roadside of much-traveled highways will be his memorial plot: "You can bury my body down by the highway side / So my old devil spirit can catch a Greyhound bus and ride." Conative formulations of a brighter future (sun shining in the back door some day, wind rising to blow the blues away) join with a slow-moving *askesis* of present, amorous imprisonment: "You leavin' now, baby, but you hangin' crepe on my door," or "She got a mortgage on my body, and a lien on my soul." Self-deprecating confession and slack-strumming growls of violent solutions combine: "My lead mule's cripple, you know my off mule's blind / You know I can't drive nobody / Bring me a loaded .39 (I'm go'n pop him, pop that mule!)." The wish for a river of whiskey where if a man were a "divin' duck" he would submerge himself and never "come up" is a function of a world in which "when you lose yo' eyesight, yo' best friend's gone / Sometimes yo' own dear people don't want to fool with you long."

Like a streamlined athlete's awesomely dazzling explosions of prowess, the blues song erupts, creating a veritable playful festival of meaning. Rather than a rigidly personalized form, the blues offer a phylogenetic recapitulation—a nonlinear, freely associative, nonsequential meditation—of species experience. What emerges is not a filled subject, but an anonymous (nameless) voice issuing from the black (w)hole.[11] The blues singer's signatory coda is always *atopic*, placeless: "If anybody ask you who sang this song / Tell 'em X done been here and gone." The "signature" is a space already "X"(ed), a trace of the already "gone"—a fissure rejoined. Nevertheless, the "you" (audience) addressed is always free to invoke the X(ed) spot in the body's absence.[12] For the signature comprises a scripted authentication of "your" feelings. Its mark is an invitation to energizing intersubjectivity. Its implied (in)junction reads: Here is my body meant for (a phylogenetically conceived) you.

The blues are a synthesis (albeit one always synthesizing rather than one already hypostatized). Combining work songs, group seculars, field hollers, sacred harmonies, proverbial wisdom, folk philosophy, political commentary, ribald humor, elegiac lament, and much more, they constitute an amalgam that seems always to have been in motion in America—always becoming, shaping, transforming, displacing the peculiar experiences of Africans in the New World.

Blues as Code and Force

One way of describing the blues is to claim their amalgam as a code radically conditioning Afro-America's cultural signifying. Such a description implies a prospect in which any aspect of the blues—a guitar's growling vamp or a stanza's sardonic boast of heroically backbreaking labor—"stands," in Umberto Eco's words, "for something else" in virtue of a systematic set of conventional procedures.[13] The materiality of any blues manifestation, such as a guitar's walking bass or a French harp's "whoop" of motion seen, is, one might say, enciphered in ways that enable the material to escape into a named or coded, blues signification. The material, thus, slips into irreversible difference. And as phenomena named and set in a meaningful relation by a blues code, both the harmonica's whoop and the guitar's bass can recapitulate vast dimensions of experience. For such discrete blues instances are always intertextually related by the blues code as a whole. Moreover, they are involved in the code's manifold interconnections with other codes of Afro-American culture.

A further characterization of blues suggests that they are equivalent to Hegelian "force."[14] In the *Phenomenology*, Hegel speaks of a flux in which there is "only *difference* as a *universal* difference, or as a difference into which the many antitheses have been resolved. This difference, as a *universal* difference, is consequently the *simple element in the play of Force itself* and what is true in it. It is the *law of Force*" (p. 90). Force is thus defined as a relational matrix where *difference* is the law. Finally the blues, employed as an image for the investigation of culture, represents a *force* not unlike electricity. Hegel writes:

> Of course, given *positive* electricity, negative too is given *in principle;* for the positive *is*, only as related to a negative, or, the positive is *in its own self* the difference from itself; and similarly with the negative. But that electricity as such should divide itself in this way is not in itself a necessity. Electricity, as *simple Force*, is indifferent to its law—*to be* positive and negative; and if we call the former its *Notion* but the latter its being, then its Notion is indifferent to its being. It merely *has* this property, which just means that this property is not *in itself* necessary to it. . . . It is only with law as a law that we are to compare its *Notion* as Notion, or its necessity. But in all these forms, necessity has shown itself to be only an empty word. [P. 93]

Metaphorically extending Hegel's formulation vis-à-vis electricity, one might say that a traditional property of cultural study may well be the kind of dichotomy inscribed in terms like "culture" and "practical reason." But even if such dichotomies are raised to the status of law, they never constitute the necessity or "determinant instances" of cultural study and explanation conceived in terms of *force*—envisioned, that is, in the analytic notion of a blues matrix as force. The blues, therefore, comprise a mediational site where familiar antinomies are resolved (or dissolved) in the office of adequate cultural understanding.

Blues Translation at the Junction

To suggest a trope for the blues as a forceful matrix in cultural understanding is to summon an image of the black blues singer at the railway junction lustily transforming experiences of a durative (unceasingly oppressive) landscape into the energies of rhythmic song. The railway juncture is marked by transience. Its inhabitants are always travelers—a multifarious assembly in transit. The "X" of crossing roadbeds signals the multi-directionality of the juncture and is simply a single instance in a boundless network that redoubles and circles, makes sidings and ladders, forms Y's and branches over the vastness of hundreds of thousands of American miles. Polymorphous and multidirectional, scene of arrivals and departures, place betwixt and between (ever *entre les deux*), the juncture is the way-station of the blues.

The singer and his production are always at this intersection, this crossing, codifying force, providing resonance for experience's multiplicities. Singer and song never arrest transience—fix it in "transcendent form." Instead they provide expressive equivalence for the juncture's ceaseless flux. Hence, they may be conceived as translators.[15]

Like translators of written texts, blues and its sundry performers offer interpretations of the experiencing of experience. To experience the juncture's ever-changing scenes, like successive readings of ever-varying texts by conventional translators, is to produce vibrantly polyvalent interpretations encoded as blues. The singer's product, like the railway juncture itself (or a successful translator's original), constitutes a lively scene, a robust matrix, where endless antinomies are mediated and understanding and explanation find conditions of possibility.

The durative—transliterated as lyrical statements of injustice, despair, loss, absence, denial, and so forth—is complemented in blues performance by an instrumental energy (guitar, harmonica, fiddle, gut-bucket bass, molasses jug, washboard) that employs locomotive rhythms, train bells, and whistles as onomatopoeic references. In *A Theory of Semiotics*, Eco writes:

> Music presents, on the one hand, the problem of a semiotic system without a semantic level (or a content plane): on the other hand, however, there are musical "signs" (or syntagms) with an explicit denotative value (trumpet signals in the army) and there are syntagms or entire "texts" possessing pre-culturalized connotative value ("pastoral" or "thrilling" music, etc.). [P. 111]

The absence of a content plane noted by Eco implies what is commonly referred to as the "abstractness" of instrumental music. The "musical sign," on the other hand, suggests cultural signals that function onomatopoeically by calling to mind "natural" sounds or sounds "naturally" associated with common human situations. Surely, though, it would be a mistake to claim that onomatopoeia is in any sense "natural," for different cultures encode even the "same" natural sounds in varying ways. (A rooster onomatopoeically sounded in Puerto Rican Spanish is phonically unrecognizable in United States English, as a classic Puerto Rican short story makes hilariously clear.)

If onomatopoeia is taken as cultural mimesis, however, it is possible to apply the semiotician's observations to blues by pointing out that the dominant blues syntagm in America is an instrumental imitation of *train-wheels-over-track-junctures*. This sound is the "sign," as it were, of the blues, and it combines an intriguing melange of phonics: rattling gondolas, clattering flatbeds, quilling whistles, clanging bells, rumbling boxcars, and other railroad sounds. A blues text may thus announce itself by the onomatopoeia of the train's whistle sounded on the indrawn breath of a harmonica or a train's bell tinkled on the high keys of an upright piano. The blues stanzas may then roll through an extended meditative repertoire with a steady train-wheels-over-track-junctures guitar back beat as a traditional, syntagmatic complement. If desire and absence are driving conditions of blues performance, the amelioration of such conditions is implied by the onomatopoeic *training* of blues voice and instrument. Only a *trained* voice can sing the blues.[16]

At the junctures, the intersections of experience where roads cross and diverge, the blues singer and his performance serve as codifiers, absorbing and transforming discontinuous experience into formal expressive instances that bear only the trace of origins, refusing to be pinned down to any final, dualistic significance. Even as they speak of paralyzing absence and ineradicable desire, their instrumental rhythms suggest change, movement, action, continuance, unlimited and unending possibility. Like signification itself, blues are always nomadically wandering. Like the freight-hopping hobo, they are ever on the move, ceaselessly summing novel experience.

Antinomies and Blues Mediation

The blues performance is further suggestive if economic conditions of Afro-American existence are brought to mind. Standing at the juncture, or railhead, the singer draws into his repertoire hollers, cries, whoops, and moans of black men and women working in fields without recompense. The performance can be cryptically conceived, therefore, in terms suggested by the bluesman Booker White, who said, "The foundation of the blues is working behind a mule way back in slavery time."[17] As a force, the blues matrix defines itself as a network mediating poverty and abundance in much the same manner that it reconciles durative and kinetic. Many instances of the blues performance contain lyrical inscriptions of both lack and commercial possibility. The performance that sings of abysmal poverty and deprivation may be recompensed by sumptuous food and stimulating beverage at a country picnic, amorous favors from an attentive listener, enhanced Afro-American communality, or Yankee dollars from representatives of record companies traveling the South in search of blues as commodifiable entertainment. The performance, therefore, mediates one of the most prevalent of all antinomies in cultural investigation—creativity and commerce.

As driving force, the blues matrix thus avoids simple dualities. It perpetually achieves its effects as a fluid and multivalent network. It is only when "understanding"—the analytical work of a translator who translates the infinite changes of the blues—converges with such blues "force," however, that adequate explanatory perception (and half-creation) occurs. The matrix effectively functions toward cultural understanding, that is, only when an investigator brings an inventive attention to bear.

The Investigator, Relativity, and Blues Effect

The blues matrix is a "cultural invention": a "negative symbol" that generates (or obliges one to invent) its own referents.[18] As an inventive trope, this matrix provides for my following chapters the type of image or model that is always present in accounts of culture and cultural products. If the analyses that I provide are successful, the blues matrix will have *taken effect* (and *affect*) through me.

To "take effect," of course, is not identical with to "come into existence" or to "demonstrate serviceability for the first time." Because what I have defined as a blues matrix is so demonstrably anterior to any single instance of its cultural-explanatory employment, my predecessors as effectors are obviously legion. "Take effect," therefore, does not signify discovery in the traditional sense of that word. Rather, it signals the tropological nature of my uses of an already extant matrix.

Ordinarily, accounts of art, literature, and culture fail to acknowledge their governing theories; further, they invariably conceal the *inventive* character of such theories. Nevertheless, all accounts of art, expressive culture, or culture in general are indisputably functions of their creators' tropological energies. When such creators talk of "art," for example, they are never dealing with existential givens. Rather, they are summoning objects, processes, or events defined by a model that they have created (by and for themselves) as a picture of art. Such models, or tropes, are continually invoked to constitute and explain phenomena inaccessible to the senses. Any single model, or any complementary set of inventive tropes, therefore, will offer only a selective account of experience—a partial reading, as it were, of the world. While the single account temporarily reduces chaos to ordered plan, all such accounts are eternally troubled by "remainders."

Where literary art is concerned, for example, a single, ordering, investigative model or trope will necessarily exclude phenomena that an alternative model or trope privileges as a definitive artistic instance. Recognizing the determinacy of "invention" in cultural explanation entails the acknowledgment of what might be called a *normative relativity.* To acknowledge relativity in our post-Heisenbergian universe is, of course, far from original. Neither, however, is it an occasion for the skeptics or the conservatives to heroically assume the critical stage.

The assumption of normative relativity, far from being a call to abandonment or retrenchment in the critical arena, constitutes an invitation to speculative explorations that are aware both of their own partiality and their heuristic transitions from suggestive (sometimes dramatic) images to inscribed concepts. The openness implied by relativity enables, say, the literary critic to *re-cognize* his endeavors, presupposing from the outset that such labors are not directed toward independent, observable, empirical phenomena but rather toward processes, objects, and events that he or she half-creates (and privileges as "art") through his or her own speculative, inventive energies and interests.

One axiological extrapolation from these observations on invention and relativity is that no object, process, or single element possesses *intrinsic aesthetic value*. The "art object" as well as its value are selective *constructions* of the critic's tropes and models. A radicalizing uncertainty may thus be said to mark cultural explanation. This uncertainty is similar in kind to the always selective endeavors of, say, the particle physicist.[19]

The physicist is always compelled to choose between velocity and position.[20] Similarly, an investigator of Afro-American expressive culture is ceaselessly compelled to forgo manifold variables in order to apply intensive energy to a selected array.

Continuing the metaphor, one might say that if the investigator's efforts are sufficiently charged with blues energy,[21] he is almost certain to remodel elements and events appearing in traditional, Anglo-American space-time in ways that make them "jump" several rings toward blackness and the vernacular. The blues-oriented observer (the *trained* critic) necessarily "heats up" the observational space by his or her very presence.[22]

An inventive, tropological, investigative model such as that proposed by *Blues, Ideology, and Afro-American Literature* entails not only awareness of the metaphorical nature of the blues matrix, but also a willingness on my own part to do more than merely hear, read, or see the blues. I must also play (with and on) them. Since the explanatory possibilities of a blues matrix—like analytical possibilities of a delimited set of forces in unified field theory—are hypothetically unbounded, the blues challenge investigative *understanding* to an unlimited play.

Blues and Vernacular Expression in America

The blues should be privileged in the study of American culture to precisely the extent that inventive understanding successfully converges with blues force to yield accounts that persuasively and playfully refigure expressive geographies in the United States. My own ludic uses of the blues are various, and each figuration implies the valorization of vernacular facets of American culture. The Afro-American writer James Alan McPherson is, I think, the commentator who most brilliantly and encouragingly coalesces blues, vernacular, and cultural geographies of the United States in his introduction to *Railroad: Trains and Train People in American Culture*.[23]

Having described a fiduciary reaction to the steam locomotive by nineteenth-century financiers and an adverse artistic response by such traditional American writers as Melville, Hawthorne, and Thoreau, McPherson details the reaction of another sector of the United States population to the railroad:

> To a third group of people, those not bound by the assumptions of either business or classical traditions in art, the shrill whistle might have spoken of new possibilities. These were the backwoodsmen and Africans and recent immigrants—the people who comprised the vernacular level of American society. To them the machine might have been loud and frightening, but its whistle and its wheels promised movement. And since a commitment to both freedom and movement was the basic promise of democracy, it was probable that such people would view the locomotive as a challenge to the integrative powers of their imaginations. [P. 6]

Afro-Americans—at the bottom even of the vernacular ladder in America—responded to the railroad as a "meaningful symbol offering both economic progress and the possibility of aesthetic expression" (p. 9). This possibility came from the locomotive's drive and thrust, its promise of unrestrained mobility and unlimited freedom. The blues musician at the crossing, as I have already suggested, became an expert at reproducing or translating these locomotive energies. With the birth of the blues, the vernacular realm of American culture acquired a music that had "wide appeal because it expressed a toughness of spirit and resilience, a willingness to transcend difficulties which was strikingly familiar to those whites who remembered their own history" (p. 16). The signal expressive achievement of blues, then, lay in their translation of technological innovativeness, unsettling demographic fluidity, and boundless frontier energy into expression which attracted avid interest from the American masses. By the 1920s, American financiers had become aware of commercial possibilities not only of railroads but also of black music deriving from them.

A "race record" market flourished during the twenties. Major companies issued blues releases under labels such as Columbia, Vocalion, OKeh, Gennett, and Victor. Sometimes as many as ten blues releases appeared in a single week; their sales (aided by radio's dissemination of the music) climbed to hundreds of thousands. The onset of the Great Depression ended this phenomenal boom. During their heyday, however, the blues unequivocally signified a ludic predominance of the vernacular with that sassy, growling, moaning, whooping confidence that marks their finest performances.

McPherson's assessment seems fully justified. It serves, in fact, as a suggestive play in the overall project of refiguring American expressive geographies. Resonantly complementing the insights of such astute commentators as Albert Murray, Paul Oliver, Samuel Charters, Amiri Baraka, and others,[24] McPherson's judgments highlight the value of a blues matrix for cultural analysis in the United States.

In harmony with other brilliant commentators on the blues already noted, Ralph Ellison selects the railroad way-station (the "Chehaw Station") as his topos for the American "little man."[25] In "The Little Man at the Chehaw Station,"[26] he autobiographically details his own confirmation of his Tuskegee music teacher's observation that in the United States

> You must *always* play your best, even if it's only in the waiting room at Chehaw Station, because in this country there'll always be a little man hidden behind the stove . . . and he'll know the *music*, and the *tradition*, and the standards of *musicianship* required for whatever you set out to perform. [P. 25]

When Hazel Harrison made this statement to the young Ellison, he felt that she was joking. But as he matured and moved through a diversity of American scenes, Ellison realized that the inhabitants of the "drab, utilitarian structure" of the American vernacular do far more than respond in expressive ways to "blues-echoing, train-whistle rhapsodies blared by fast express trains as they thundered past" the junction. At the vernacular level, according to Ellison, people possess a "cultivated taste" that asserts its "authority out of obscurity" (p. 26). The "little man" finally comes to represent, therefore, "that unknown quality which renders the American audience far more than a receptive instrument that may be dominated through a skillful exercise of the sheerly 'rhetorical' elements—the flash and filigree—of the artist's craft" (p. 26).

From Ellison's opening gambit and wonderfully illustrative succeeding examples, I infer that the vernacular (in its expressive adequacy and adept critical facility) always *absorbs* "classical" elements of American life and art. Indeed, Ellison seems to imply that expressive performers in America who ignore the judgments of the vernacular are destined to failure.

Although his injunctions are intended principally to advocate a traditional "melting pot" ideal in American "high art," Ellison's observations ultimately valorize a comprehensive, vernacular expressiveness in America. Though he seldom loses sight of the possibilities of a classically "transcendent" American high art, he derives his most forceful examples from the vernacular: Blues seem implicitly to comprise the *All* of American culture.

Blues Moments in Afro-American Expression

In the chapters that follow, I attempt to provide suggestive accounts of moments in Afro-American discourse when personae, protagonists, autobiographical narrators, or literary critics successfully negotiate an obdurate "economics of slavery" and achieve a resonant, improvisational, expressive dignity. Such moments and successful analyses of them provide cogent examples of the blues matrix at work.

The expressive instances that I have in mind occur in passages such as the conclusion of the *Narrative of the Life of Frederick Douglass.* Standing at a Nantucket convention, riffing (in the "break" suddenly confronting him) on the *personal* troubles he has seen and successfully negotiated in a "prisonhouse of American bondage," Douglass achieves a profoundly dignified blues voice. Zora Neale Hurston's protagonist Janie in the novel *Their Eyes Were Watching God*—as she lyrically and idiomatically relates a tale of personal suffering and triumph that begins in the sexual exploitations of slavery—is a blues artist par excellence. Her wisdom might well be joined to that of Amiri Baraka's Walker Vessels (a "locomotive container" of blues?), whose chameleon code-switching from academic philosophy to blues insight makes him a veritable incarnation of the absorptively vernacular. The narrator of Richard Wright's *Black Boy* inscribes a black blues life's lean desire (as I shall demonstrate in chapter 3) and suggests yet a further instance of the blues matrix's expressive energies. Ellison's invisible man and Baraka's narrator in *The System of Dante's Hell* (whose blues book produces dance) provide additional examples. Finally, Toni Morrison's Milkman Deal in *Song of Solomon* discovers through "Sugarman's" song that an awesomely expressive blues response may well consist of improvisational and serendipitous surrender to the air: "As fleet and bright as a lodestar he wheeled toward Guitar and it did not matter which one of them would give up his ghost in the killing arms of his brother. For now he knew what Shalimar knew: If you surrendered to the air, you could *ride* it."[27]

Such blues moments are but random instances of the blues matrix at work in Afro-American cultural expression. In my study as a whole, I attempt persuasively to demonstrate that a blues matrix (as a vernacular trope for American cultural explanation in general) possesses enormous force for the study of literature, criticism, and culture. I know that I have appropriated the vastness of the vernacular in the United States to a single matrix. But I trust that my necessary selectivity will be interpreted, not as a sign of myopic exclusiveness, but as an invitation to inventive play. The success of my efforts would be effectively signaled in the following chapters, I think, by the transformation of my "I" into a juncture where readers could freely improvise their own distinctive tropes for cultural explanation. A closing that in fact opened on such inventive possibilities (like the close of these introductory remarks) would be appropriately marked by the crossing sign's inviting "X."

Notes

1. Chicago: University of Chicago Press, 1980.

2. Though a great many sources were involved in my reoriented cultural thinking, certainly the terminology employed in my discussion at this point derives from Marshall Sahlins's wonderfully lucid *Culture and Practical Reason* (Chicago: University of Chicago Press, 1976). Sahlins delineates two modes of thinking that have characterized anthropology from its inception. These two poles are "symbolic" and "functionalist." He resolves the dichotomy suggested by these terms through the middle term "cultural proposition," a phrase that he defines as a cultural mediating ground where the material and symbolic, the useful and the ineffable, ceaselessly converge and depart.

3. The "ideology of form" as a description of Jameson's project derives from the essay "The Symbolic Inference; or, Kenneth Burke and Ideological Analysis," *Critical Inquiry* 4 (1978): 507–23. Surely, though, Jameson's most recent study, *The Political Unconscious: Narrative as a Socially Symbolic Act* (Ithaca, N.Y.: Cornell University Press, 1981), offers the fullest description of his views on ways in which cultural texts formally inscribe material/historical conditions of their production, distribution, and consumption.

4. In *The Journey Back*, I define my project as follows: "The phrase ['the anthropology of art'] expresses for me the notion that art must be studied with an attention to the methods and findings of disciplines which enable one to address such concerns as the status of the artistic object, the relationship of art to other cultural systems, and the nature and function of artistic creation and perception in a given society" (p. xvi). The project's privileging of "symbolic anthropology" and "art" under the sign *interdisciplinary* involved exclusions that were ironical and (I now realize) somewhat disabling where a full description of expressive culture is sought.

5. The Hegelian epigraph that marks the beginning of these introductory remarks offers the best definition I know of "determinate negation." The epigraph is taken from the *Phenomenology of Spirit*.

6. I have in mind Louis Althusser and Étienne Balibar, *Reading Capital* (London: New Left Books, 1977), and Jean Baudrillard's *For a Critique of the Political Economy of the Sign* (1972; St. Louis: Telos Press, 1981) and *The Mirror of Production* (1973; St. Louis: Telos Press, 1975). By "poststructuralist" thought, I have in mind the universe of discourse constituted by *deconstruction*. Jacques Derrida's *Of Grammatology* (1967; Baltimore: Johns Hopkins University Press, 1976) is perhaps the locus classicus of the deconstructionist project. One of the more helpful accounts of deconstruction is Christopher Norris's *Deconstruction: Theory and Practice* (London: Methuen, 1982). Of course, there is a certain collapsing of poststructuralism and political economy in the sources cited previously.

7. For a full citation of Baudrillard, see note 6.

8. Ibid.

9. In *Of Grammatology*, Derrida defines a problematic in which *writing*, conceived as an iterable *differe(a)nce*, is held to be *always already* instituted (or, in motion) when a traditionally designated *Man* begins to speak. Hence, *script* is anterior to speech, and absence and *differe(a)nce* displace presence and identity (conceived as "Intention") in philosophical discourse.

10. The story appears in W. C. Handy, *Father of the Blues*, ed. Arna Bontemps (New York: Macmillan Co., 1941), p. 78. Other defining sources of blues include: Paul Oliver, *The Story of*

the Blues (London: Chilton, 1969); Samuel B. Charters, *The Country Blues* (New York: Rinehart, 1959); Giles Oakley, *The Devil's Music: A History of the Country Blues* (New York: Harcourt Brace Jovanovich, 1976); Amiri Baraka, *Blues People: Negro Music in White America* (New York: William E. Morrow, 1963) [excerpts reprinted herein]; Albert Murray, *Stomping the Blues* (New York: McGraw-Hill Book Co., 1976); and William Ferris, *Blues from the Delta* (New York: Anchor Books, 1979).

11. The description at this point is coextensive with the "decentering" of the subject mentioned at the outset of my introduction. What I wish to effect by noting a "subject" who is not *filled* is a displacement of the notion that knowledge, or "art," or "song," are manifestations of an ever more clearly defined individual consciousness of *Man.* In accord with Michel Foucault's explorations in his *Archaeology of Knowledge* (1969; New York: Harper & Row, 1972), I want to claim that blues is like a discourse that comprises the "already said" of Afro-America. Blues' governing statements and sites are thus vastly more interesting in the process of cultural investigation than either a history of ideas or a history of individual, subjective consciousness vis-à-vis blues. When I move to the "X" of the trace and the body as host, I am invoking Mark Taylor's formulations in a suggestive deconstructive essay toward radical christology called "The Text as Victim," in *Deconstruction and Theology* (New York: Crossroad, 1982), pp. 58–78.

12. The terms used in "The Text as Victim," ibid., are "host" and "parasite." The words of the blues are hostlike in the sense of a christological Logos-as-Host. But without the dialogical action of the parasite, of course, there could be no Host. Host is, thus, parasitic on a parasite's citation. Both, in Taylor's statement of the matter, are *para-sites.*

13. The definition of "code" is drawn from A *Theory of Semiotics* (Bloomington: Indiana University Press, 1976). All references to Eco refer to this work and are hereafter marked by page numbers in parentheses.

14. *The Phenomenology of Spirit,* trans. A. V. Miller (New York: Oxford University Press, 1977). While it is true that the material dimensions of the dialectic are of primary importance to my current study, it is also true that the locus classicus of the dialectic, in and for itself, is the *Phenomenology.* Marx may well have stood Hegel on his feet through a materialist inversion of the *Phenomenology,* but subsequent generations have always looked at that uprighted figure—Hegel himself—as an authentic host.

15. Having heard John Felstiner in a session at the 1982 Modern Language Association Convention present a masterful paper defining "translation" as a process of preserving "something of value" by keeping it in motion, I decided that the blues were apt translators of experience. Felstiner, it seemed to me, sought to demonstrate that *translation* was a process equivalent to gift-giving in Mauss's classic definition of that activity. The value of the gift of translation is never fixed because, say, the poem, is always in a transliterational motion, moving from one alphabet to another, always renewing and being *re-newed* in the process. Translation forestalls fixity. It calls attention always to the *translated's* excess—to its complex multivalence.

16. One of the most inspiring and intriguing descriptions of the relationship between blues voice and sounds of the railroad is Albert Murray's lyrical exposition in *Stomping the Blues.*

17. Quoted in Oakley, *The Devil's Music,* p. 7.

18. I have appropriated the term "negative symbol" from Roy Wagner's *The Invention of Culture* (Chicago: University of Chicago Press, 1975), p. xvi.

19. My references to a "post-Heisenbergian universe" and to the "particle physicist" were made possible by a joyful reading of Gary Zukav's *The Dancing Wu Li Masters: An Overview of the New Physics* (New York: William E. Morrow, 1979).

20. Zukav, ibid., writes: "According to the uncertainty principle, we cannot measure accu-

rately, at the same time, both the position *and* the momentum of a moving particle. The more precisely we determine one of these properties, the less we know about the other. If we precisely determine the position of the particle, then, strange as it sounds, there is *nothing* that we can know about its momentum. If we precisely determine the momentum of the particle, there is no way to determine its position" (p. 111). Briefly, if we bring to bear enough energy actually to "see" the imagined "particle," that energy has always already *moved* the particle from its *position* (which is one of the aspects of its existence that one attempts to *determine*) when we take our measurement. Indeterminacy thus becomes normative.

21. The "blues force" is my translational equivalent in investigative "energy" for the investigative energy delineated by Heisenberg's formulations. See note 20.

22. Eco (*A Theory of Semiotics*, p. 29) employs the metaphor of "ecological variation" in his discussions of the semiotic investigation of culture to describe observer effect in the mapping of experience.

23. New York: Random House, 1976. All citations refer to this edition and are hereafter marked by page numbers in parentheses.

24. See note 9.

25. The Chehaw Station is a whistle-stop near Tuskegee, Alabama. It was a feature of the landscape of Tuskegee Institute, where Ellison studied music (and much else).

26. *American Scholar* 47 (1978): 24–48. All citations refer to this version and are hereafter marked by page numbers in parentheses.

27. *Song of Solomon* (New York: Alfred A. Knopf, 1977), p. 337.

I Used To Be Your Sweet Mama

Ideology, Sexuality, and Domesticity

Angela Y. Davis

You've had your chance and proved unfaithful
So now I'm gonna be real mean and hateful
I used to be your sweet mama, sweet papa
But now I'm just as sour as can be.

—"I Used to Be Your Sweet Mama"[1]

LIKE most forms of popular music, African-American blues lyrics talk about love. What is distinctive about the blues, however, particularly in relation to other American popular musical forms of the 1920s and 1930s, is their intellectual independence and representational freedom. One of the most obvious ways in which blues lyrics deviated from that era's established popular musical culture was their provocative and pervasive sexual—including homosexual—imagery.[2]

By contrast, the popular song formulas of the period demanded saccharine and idealized nonsexual depictions of heterosexual love relationships.[3] Those aspects of lived love relationships that were not compatible with the dominant, etherealized ideology of love—such as extramarital relationships, domestic violence, and the ephemerality of many sexual partnerships—were largely banished from the established popular musical culture. Yet these very themes pervade the blues. What is even more striking is the fact that initially the professional performers of this music—the most widely heard individual purveyors of the blues—were women. Bessie Smith earned the title "Empress of the Blues" not least through the sale of three-quarters of a million copies of her first record.[4]

The historical context within which the blues developed a tradition of openly addressing both female and male sexuality reveals an ideological framework that was specifically African-American.[5] Emerging during the decades following the abolition of slavery, the

---

blues gave musical expression to the new social and sexual realities encountered by African Americans as free women and men. The former slaves' economic status had not undergone a radical transformation—they were no less impoverished than they had been during slavery.[6] It was the status of their personal relationships that was revolutionized. For the first time in the history of the African presence in North America, masses of black women and men were in a position to make autonomous decisions regarding the sexual partnerships into which they entered.[7] Sexuality thus was one of the most tangible domains in which emancipation was acted upon and through which its meanings were expressed. Sovereignty in sexual matters marked an important divide between life during slavery and life after emancipation.

Themes of individual sexual love rarely appear in the musical forms produced during slavery. Whatever the reasons for this—and it may have been due to the slave system's economic management of procreation, which did not tolerate and often severely punished the public exhibition of self-initiated sexual relationships—I am interested here in the disparity between the individualistic, "private" nature of sexuality and the collective forms and nature of the music that was produced and performed during slavery. Sexuality after emancipation could not be adequately expressed or addressed through the musical forms existing under slavery. The spirituals and the work songs confirm that the individual concerns of black people expressed through music during slavery centered on a collective desire for an end to the system that enslaved them. This does not mean there was an absence of sexual meanings in the music produced by African-American slaves.[8] It means that slave music—both religious and secular—was quintessentially collective music. It was collectively performed and it gave expression to the community's yearning for freedom.[9]

The blues, on the other hand, the predominant postslavery African-American musical form, articulated a new valuation of individual emotional needs and desires. The birth of the blues was aesthetic evidence of new psychosocial realities within the black population. This music was presented by individuals singing alone, accompanying themselves on such instruments as the banjo or guitar. The blues therefore marked the advent of a popular culture of performance, with the borders of performer and audience becoming increasingly differentiated.[10] Through the emergence of the professional blues singer—a predominantly female figure accompanied by small and large instrumental ensembles—as part of the rise of the black entertainment industry, this individualized mode of presenting popular music crystallized into a performance culture that has had an enduring influence on African-American music.

The spirituals, as they survived and were transformed during the post-slavery era, were both intensely religious and the aesthetic bearers of the slaves' collective aspirations for worldly freedom.[11] Under changed historical circumstances in which former slaves had closer contact with the religious practices and ideologies of the dominant culture, sacred music began to be increasingly enclosed within institutionalized religious spaces. Slave religious practices were inseparable from other aspects of everyday life—work, family, sabotage, escape. Postslavery religion gradually lost some of this fluidity and came to be dependent on the church. As sacred music evolved from spirituals to gospel, it increasingly concentrated on the hereafter. Historian Lawrence Levine characterizes the nature of this development succinctly. "The overriding thrust of the gospel songs," he writes,

> was otherworldly. Emphasis was almost wholly upon God with whom Man's relationship was one of total dependence. . . . Jesus rather than the Hebrew children dominated the gospel songs. And it was not the warrior Jesus of the spirituals but a benevolent spirit who promised His children rest and peace and justice in the hereafter.[12]

The blues rose to become the most prominent secular genre in early twentieth-century black American music. As it came to displace sacred music in the everyday lives of black people, it both reflected and helped to construct a new black consciousness. This consciousness interpreted God as the opposite of the Devil, religion as the not-secular, and the secular as largely sexual. With the blues came the designations "God's music" and "the Devil's music." The former was performed in church—although it could also accompany work[13]—while the latter was performed in jook joints, circuses, and traveling shows.[14] Despite the new salience of this binary opposition in the everyday lives of black people, it is important to underscore the close relationship between the old music and the new. The new music had old roots, and the old music reflected a new ideological grounding of black religion. Both were deeply rooted in a shared history and culture.

God and the Devil had cohabited the same universe during slavery, not as polar opposites but rather as complex characters who had different powers and who both entered into relationships with human beings. They also sometimes engaged with each other on fairly equal terms. As Henry Louis Gates, Jr., and others have argued, the Devil was often associated with the trickster orisha Legba, or Elegua, in Yoruba religions.[15] Some of the folk-tales Zora Neale Hurston presents in *Mules and Men* portray the Devil not as evil incarnate but as a character with whom it was possible to identify in humorous situations.[16]

In describing the religious household in which she was reared, veteran blues woman Ida Goodson emphasizes that the blues were banned from her childhood home. Nevertheless, she and her playmates often played and sang the blues when her parents were away. On those occasions when her parents showed up unexpectedly, they easily made the transition to gospel music without missing a beat:

> My mother and father were religious persons. And they liked music, but they liked church music. They didn't like jazz like we do. And of course we could not even play jazz in our home while they were there. But just the moment they would turn their back, go to their society or church somewhere or another, we'd get our neighborhood children to come in there and we'd get to playing the blues and having a good time. But still we'd have one girl on the door watching to see when Mr. Goodson's coming back home or Mrs. Goodson. Because I knew if they came and caught us what we would get. . . . Whenever we'd see my father or my mother coming back home, the girl be saying, "There come Mr. Goodson 'nem." And they'd be so close up on us, we'd change the blues, singing "Jesus keep me near the cross." After that my mother and father would join us and we'd all get to singing church songs.[17]

As if reconciling the two positions—that of herself as a young musician and that of her religious parents—Goodson later explains that "the Devil got his work and God got his work."

During slavery, the sacred universe was virtually all-embracing. Spirituals helped to construct community among the slaves and infused this imagined community with hope for a better life. They retold Old Testament narratives about the Hebrew people's struggle against Pharaoh's oppression, and thereby established a community narrative of African people enslaved in North America that simultaneously transcended the slave system and encouraged its abolition. Under the conditions of U.S. slavery, the sacred—and especially sacred music—was an important means of preserving African cultural memory. Karl Marx's comments on religion as the "opium of the people"[18] notwithstanding, the spirituals attest to the fact that religious consciousness can itself play a transformative role. As Sojourner Truth and other abolitionists demonstrated—as well as insurrectionary leaders Nat Turner, Denmark Vesey, and the Underground Railroad conductor Harriet Tubman—religion was far more than Marx's "illusory sun." Spirituals were embedded in and gave expression to a powerful yearning for freedom.[19] Religion was indeed, in Marx's words, the "soul" of "soulless conditions."[20]

The spirituals articulated the hopes of black slaves in religious terms. In the vast disappointment that followed emancipation—when economic and political liberation must have seemed more unattainable than ever—blues created a discourse[21] that represented freedom in more immediate and accessible terms. While the material conditions for the freedom about which the slaves had sung in their spirituals seemed no closer after slavery than they had seemed before, there were nevertheless distinct differences between the slaves' personal status under slavery and during the post–Civil War period. In three major respects, emancipation radically transformed their personal lives: (1) there was no longer a proscription on free individual travel; (2) education was now a realizable goal for individual men and women; (3) sexuality could be explored freely by individuals who now could enter into autonomously chosen personal relationships. The new blues consciousness was shaped by and gave expression to at least two of these three transformations: travel and sexuality. In both male and female blues, travel and sexuality are ubiquitous themes, handled both separately and together. But what finally is most striking is the way the blues registered sexuality as a tangible expression of freedom; it was this dimension that most profoundly marked and defined the secularity of the blues.

Theologian James Cone offers the following definition of the blues, agreeing with C. Eric Lincoln's succinct characterization of them as "secular spirituals." Cone writes:

> They are secular in the same sense that they confine their attention solely to the immediate and affirm the bodily expression of black soul, including its sexual manifestations. They are spirituals because they are impelled by the same search for the truth of black experience.[22]

It is not necessary to accede to Cone's essentialist invocation of a single metaphysical "truth" of black experience to gain from his description a key insight into why the blues were condemned as the Devil's music: it was because they drew upon and incorporated sacred consciousness and thereby posed a serious threat to religious attitudes.

Levine emphasizes the blurring of the sacred and the secular in both gospel music and the blues. It may not have been the secularity of the blues that produced such castigation by the church, he argues, but rather precisely their sacred nature. He writes:

> The blues was threatening not primarily because it was secular; other forms of secular music were objected to less strenuously and often not at all. Blues was threatening because its spokesmen and its ritual too frequently provided the expressive communal channels of relief that had been largely the province of religion in the past.[23]

Although both Cone and Levine make references to Mamie Smith, Ma Rainey, Bessie Smith, and other women who composed and performed blues songs, they, like most scholars, tend to view women as marginal to the production of the blues. Note that in the passage quoted above, Levine refers quite explicitly to the "spokesmen" of the blues. With the simple substitution of "spokeswomen," his argument would become more compelling and more revealing of the new religious consciousness about which he writes.

Blues practices, as Levine asserts, did tend to appropriate previously religious channels of expression, and this appropriation was associated with women's voices. Women summoned sacred responses to their messages about sexuality.[24] During this period, religious consciousness came increasingly under the control of institutionalized churches, and male dominance over the religious process came to be taken for granted. At the same time that male ministers were becoming a professional caste, women blues singers were performing as professional artists and attracting large audiences at revival-like gatherings. Gertrude "Ma" Rainey and Bessie Smith were the most widely known of these women. They preached about sexual love, and in so doing they articulated a collective experience of freedom, giving voice to the most powerful evidence there was for many black people that slavery no longer existed.

The expression of socially unfulfilled dreams in the language and imagery of individual sexual love is, of course, not peculiar to the African-American experience. As part of the capitalist schism between the public and private realms within European-derived American popular culture, however, themes of romantic love had quite different ideological implications from themes of sexuality within postslavery African-American cultural expression. In the context of the consolidation of industrial capitalism, the sphere of personal love and domestic life in mainstream American culture came to be increasingly idealized as the arena in which happiness was to be sought.[25] This held a special significance for women, since love and domesticity were supposed to constitute the outermost limits of their lives. Full membership in the public community was the exclusive domain of men. Therefore, European-American popular songs have to be interpreted within this context and as contributing to patriarchal hegemony.

The blues did not entirely escape the influences that shaped the role of romantic love in the popular songs of the dominant culture. Nevertheless, the incorporation of personal relationships into the blues has its own historical meanings and social and political resonances. Love was not represented as an idealized realm to which unfulfilled dreams of happiness were relegated. The historical African-American vision of individual sexual love linked it inextricably with possibilities of social freedom in the economic and political realms. Unfreedom during slavery involved, among other things, a prohibition of freely chosen, enduring family relationships. Because slaves were legally defined as commodities, women of childbearing age were valued in accordance with their breeding potential and were often forced to copulate with men—viewed as "bucks"—chosen by their owners for the sole purpose of producing valuable progeny.[26] Moreover, direct sexual exploitation of African women by their white masters was a constant feature of slavery.[27] What tenuous permanence in familial relationships the slaves did manage to construct was always subject to the whim of their masters and the potential profits to be reaped from sale. The suffering caused by forced ruptures of slave families has been abundantly documented.[28]

Given this context, it is understandable that the personal and sexual dimensions of freedom acquired an expansive importance, especially since the economic and political components of freedom were largely denied to black people in the aftermath of slavery. The focus on sexual love in blues music was thus quite different in meaning from the prevailing idealization of romantic love in mainstream popular music. For recently emancipated slaves, freely chosen sexual love became a mediator between historical disappointment and the new social realities of an evolving African-American community. Ralph Ellison alludes to this dimension of the blues, I think, when he notes "their mysteriousness . . . their ability to imply far more than they state outright and their capacity to make the details of sex convey meanings which touch on the metaphysical."[29]

Sexuality was central in both men's and women's blues. During the earliest phases of their history, blues were essentially a male phenomenon. The archetypal blues singer was a solitary wandering man accompanied by his banjo or guitar, and, in the words of blues scholar Giles Oakley, his principal theme "is the sexual relationship. Almost all other themes, leaving town, train rides, work trouble, general dissatisfaction, sooner or later revert to the central concern."[30] In women's blues, which became a crucial element of the rising black entertainment industry, there was an even more pronounced emphasis on love and sexuality.

The representations of love and sexuality in women's blues often blatantly contradicted mainstream ideological assumptions regarding women and being in love. They also challenged the notion that women's "place" was in the domestic sphere. Such notions were based on the social realities of middle-class white women's lives, but were incongruously applied to all women, regardless of race or class.[31] This led to inevitable contradictions between prevailing social expectations and black women's social realities. Women of that era were expected to seek fulfillment within the confines of marriage, with their husbands functioning as providers and their children as evidence of their worth as human beings. The sparsity of allusions to marriage and domesticity in women's blues therefore becomes highly significant.

In Bessie Smith's rendition of "Sam Jones Blues," which contains one of the few commentaries on marriage to be found in her body of work, the subject is acknowledged only in relation to its dissolution. Her performance of this song satirically accentuates the contrast between the dominant cultural construction of marriage and the stance of economic independence black women were compelled to assume for their sheer survival:

> Sam Jones left his lovely wife just to step around
> Came back home 'bout a year, lookin' for his high brown
>
> Went to his accustomed door and he knocked his knuckles sore
> His wife she came, but to his shame, she knew his face no more
>
> Sam said, "I'm your husband, dear."
> But she said, "Dear, that's strange to hear
> You ain't talking to Mrs. Jones, you speakin' to Miss Wilson now
>
> "I used to be your lofty mate
> But the judge done changed my fate

"Was a time you could have walked right in and called this place your home
sweet home
But now it's all mine for all time, I'm free and livin' all alone

. . . .

"Say, hand me the key that unlocks my front door
Because that bell don't read 'Sam Jones' no more, no
You ain't talkin' to Mrs. Jones, you speakin' to Miss Wilson now."[32]

Although the written lyrics reveal a conversation between "proper" English and black working-class English, only by listening to the song do we experience the full impact of Smith's manipulation of language in her recording. References to marriage as perceived by the dominant white culture are couched in irony. She mocks the notion of eternal matrimony—"I used to be your lofty mate"—singing genteel words with a teasing intonation to evoke white cultural conceptions. On the other hand, when she indicates the perspective of the black women, Miss Wilson—who "used to be Mrs. Jones"—she sings in a comfortable, bluesy black English. This song is remarkable for the way Smith translates into musical contrast and contention the clash between two cultures' perceptions of marriage, and particularly women's place within the institution. It is easy to imagine the testifying responses Smith no doubt evoked in her female audiences, responses that affirmed working-class black women's sense of themselves as relatively emancipated, if not from marriage itself, then at least from some of its most confining ideological constraints.

The protagonists in women's blues are seldom wives and almost never mothers. One explanation for the absence of direct allusions to marriage may be the different words mainstream and African-American cultures use to signify "male spouse." African-American working-class argot refers to both husbands and male lovers—and even in some cases female lovers—as "my man" or "my daddy." But these different linguistic practices cannot be considered in isolation from the social realities they represent, for they point to divergent perspectives regarding the institution of marriage.

During Bessie Smith's era, most black heterosexual couples—married or not—had children. However, blues women rarely sang about mothers, fathers, and children. In the subject index to her book *Black Pearls*, black studies scholar Daphne Duval Harrison lists the following themes: advice to other women; alcohol; betrayal or abandonment; broken or failed love affairs; death; departure; dilemma of staying with man or returning to family; disease and afflictions; erotica; hell; homosexuality; infidelity; injustice; jail and serving time; loss of lover; love; men; mistreatment; murder; other woman; poverty; promiscuity; sadness; sex; suicide; supernatural; trains; traveling; unfaithfulness; vengeance; weariness, depression, and disillusionment; weight loss.[33] It is revealing that she does not include children, domestic life, husband, and marriage.

The absence of the mother figure in the blues does not imply a rejection of motherhood as such, but rather suggests that blues women found the mainstream cult of motherhood irrelevant to the realities of their lives.[34] The female figures evoked in women's blues are independent women free of the domestic orthodoxy of the prevailing representations of womanhood through which female subjects of the era were constructed.

In 252 songs recorded by Bessie Smith and Ma Rainey, there are only four—all by

Bessie Smith—that refer to marriage within a relatively neutral context or in a way that takes the marital relationship for granted. In "Poor Man's Blues," mention is made of the gross disparities between the economic conditions of the working man's wife and the rich man's wife: "Poor working man's wife is starvin', your wife's livin' like a queen."[35] In "Pinchback Blues," advice is offered to women with respect to the foremost quality they should seek in a husband—namely, that he be a working man. Bessie Smith sings the following phrases in a way that demands she be taken seriously:

> . . . girls, take this tip from me
> Get a workin' man when you marry, and let all these sweet men be
> . . . .
> There's one thing about this married life that these young girls have got to know
> If a sweet man enter your front gate, turn out your lights and lock your door.[36]

Even though this song assumes that most women listeners will get married, it does not evoke the romantic expectations usually associated with marriage. Instead, it warns women not to enter into marriages in which they will end up supporting an exploitative man—a "sweet man" or a "pinchback."

"Take Me for a Buggy Ride," a popular song filled with sexual innuendo and recorded in 1933 during the very last session of Bessie Smith's career, contain a passing uncritical reference to marriage:

> Daddy, you as sweet as you can be when you take me for a buggy ride
> When you set me down upon your knee and ask me to be your bride.[37]

Even these explicit references to marriage may be attributed to the fact that Smith was seeking ways to cross over into mainstream musical culture. She herself decided to record no blues during what would be her final recording session. She wanted to sing only popular songs, all of which were composed by the husband-and-wife team of Leola B. Wilson and Wesley "Socks" Wilson.[38] Her producer, John Hammond, may also have had something to do with this decision to exclude blues songs. After a hiatus in her recording career—occasioned both by the anticipated obsolescence of the blues and the 1929 stock market crash that left the recording industry in shambles—there were obvious economic reasons for wanting to appeal to as broad an audience as possible.

The sexual allusions in these songs, along with songs recorded earlier in the thirties, have caused them to be labeled quasi-pornographic. While sexual metaphors abound in these songs, the female characters are clearly in control of their sexuality in ways that exploit neither their partners nor themselves. It is misleading, I think, to refer to songs such as "Need a Little Sugar in My Bowl" as pornographic. Nevertheless, Hammond is probably correct in his contention that, given their superficial approach to sexuality, "they do not compare with Bessie's own material of the twenties."[39] The reference to marriage in "Take Me for a Buggy Ride" may very well be a result of Bessie Smith's attempt to cross over into a cultural space that required her to position herself in greater ideological proximity to white audiences, while maintaining her connection with black fans. Having put together a swing accompaniment for this last session consisting of black and white musicians—Buck Washington, Jack Teagarden, Chu Berry, Frankie Newton, Billy Taylor, and Bobby Johnson, with Benny Goodman playing on one number—John Hammond certainly was expecting to see these records distributed outside the "race records" market.

Gertrude "Ma" Rainey, a pioneer on the black entertainment circuit and the person responsible for shaping women's blues for many generations of blues women, received her title "Mother of the Blues" before she made her first recording. In the songs she recorded, the institution of monogamous marriage often was cavalierly repudiated with the kind of attitude that is usually gendered as male. "Blame It on the Blues," for example, implicitly rejects the sexual exclusivity of marriage. Reflecting on the source of her distress, the protagonist finds that she can blame it neither on her "husband," her "man," nor her "lover." The lyrics of this song—and the tragicomic way Rainey sings them—refuse to privilege marriage over non- or extramarital sexual partnerships:

> Can't blame my mother, can't blame my dad
> Can't blame my brother for the trouble I've had
> Can't blame my lover that held my hand
> Can't blame my husband, can't blame my man.[40]

In "Shave 'Em Dry," a song rich in provocative sexual metaphors, Rainey sings about a woman involved with a married man.[41] "When your wife comes," she sings with unflappable seriousness, "tell her I don't mean no harm." And in the spoken introduction to "Gone Daddy Blues," the woman who has left her husband for another man seems to play with the notion of convincing him to take her back:

> Unknown man: Who's that knocking on that door?
> Rainey: It's me, baby.
> Man: Me who?
> Rainey: Don't you know I'm your wife?
> Man: What?! Wife?!
> Rainey: Yeah!
> Man: Ain't that awful? I don't let no woman quit me but one time.
> Rainey: But I just quit one li'l old time, just one time!
> Man: You left here with that other man, why didn't you stay?[42]

"Misery Blues" is the only one of Rainey's songs in which the woman appears truly oppressed by the expectations associated with the institution of marriage. She is singing the "misery blues" because she has allowed herself to be deceived by a man who promised to marry her, that is, to support her in the traditional patriarchal way. She expected marriage to free her from her daily toil. The husband-to-be in this song not only reneges on his promise of marriage, but absconds with all her money:

> I love my brownskin, indeed I do
> Folks I know used to me being a fool
> I'm going to tell you what I went and done
> I give him all my money just to have some fun
>
> He told me that he loved me, loved me so
> If I would marry him, I needn't to work no mo'

Now I'm grievin', almost dyin'
Just because I didn't know that he was lyin'.[43]

While Rainey's performance mournfully emphasizes the woman's grief, "Misery Blues" can be construed as an "advice" song that cautions women who might similarly be deceived by the romantic expectations associated with the bourgeois, patriarchal institution of marriage.

Bessie Smith's work poses more explicit challenges to the male dominance that ideologically inheres in this institution. In "Money Blues," for example, the wife makes life unbearable for her husband with her incessant demands for money and high living.[44] The husband, Samuel Brown, has "beer money," but his wife demands champagne. (As is often the case, the "blues" in the title notwithstanding, this is a popular song, not a twelve-bar blues.) In "Young Woman's Blues," one of Smith's own compositions, the protagonist is simply not interested in marriage. Smith's performance of the following verse exudes a self-confident sense of female independence and unabashed embrace of sexual pleasure:

No time to marry, no time to settle down
I'm a young woman and ain't done runnin' 'round.

The same sentiment is definitively restated in the closing lines of the song:

I ain't no high yella, I'm a deep killer brown
I ain't gonna marry, ain't gon' settle down
I'm gon' drink good moonshine and run these browns down
See that long lonesome road, Lord, you know it's gotta end
And I'm a good woman and I can get plenty men.[45]

In what is undoubtedly the most disturbing reference to marriage in Bessie Smith's work, the narrator of "Hateful Blues" threatens to use the butcher knife she received as a wedding present to carve up her fickle husband.[46]

Early women's blues contain few uninflected references to marriage. Evocations of traditional female domesticity, whether associated with marriage or not, are equally rare. When women are portrayed as having fulfilled the domestic requirements socially expected of women in relationships with men, it is often to make the point that the women have been abused or abandoned. In Bessie Smith's "Weeping Willow Blues," the narrator proclaims:

Folks, I love my man, I kiss him mornin', noon, and night
I wash his clothes and keep him clean and try to treat him right
Now he's gone and left me after all I've tried to do.[47]

Smith sings these lines with convincing sincerity, thus debunking the notion that the fulfillment of conventional female domestic responsibilities is the basis for happiness in marriage. On the other hand, "Yes, Indeed He Do" is full of irony in its references to domesticity, implicitly criticizing the stultifying household work women are compelled to do for their men:

I don't have to do no work except to wash his clothes
And darn his socks and press his pants and scrub the kitchen floor.[48]

The sardonic "Safety Mama," another Smith composition, humorously critiques the sexual division of labor that confines women to the household. The song contains an inverted image of domesticity, in which the man is compelled by the woman to take on what are assumed to be female household chores as punishment for his sexist behavior in the relationship:

> So wait awhile, I'll show you, child, just how to treat a no-good man
> Make him stay at home, wash and iron
> Tell all the neighbors he done lost his mind.[49]

The manner in which Bessie Smith creates this musical caricature of domesticity reveals the beginnings of an oppositional attitude toward patriarchal ideology.

There are important historical reasons that romanticized images of marriage—and the permanency in personal relationships implied by this social institution—are absent from women's blues. Normative representations of marriage as the defining goal of women's lives blatantly contradicted black social realities during the half-century following emancipation. A poor black woman of the era who found herself deserted or rejected by a male lover was not merely experiencing private troubles; she also was caught in a complex web of historical circumstances. However smoothly a personal relationship may have been progressing, a recently emancipated black man was compelled to find work, and even if he found a job near the neighborhood where he and his partner had settled, he nevertheless might be seduced by new possibilities of travel. In search of work—and also in search of the perpetually elusive guarantees of security and happiness—men jumped freight trains and wandered from town to town, from state to state, from region to region. There were imperative economic reasons for undertaking journeys away from home, yet even when jobs were not to be found and available employment was backbreaking and poorly compensated, the very process of traveling must have generated a feeling of exhilaration and freedom in individuals whose ancestors had been chained for centuries to geographical sites dictated by slave masters.[50] This impulse to travel would infect great numbers of black men as a socio-historically initiated compulsion, and would later be rendered in song in Robert Johnson's "Hellhound on My Trail":

> I got to keep moving, I got to keep moving
> Blues falling down like hail, blues falling down like hail
> I can't keep no money, hellhound on my trail
> Hellhound on my trail, hellhound on my trail.[51]

Many of the absconding and unfaithful lovers memorialized by blues women were in pursuit of that fleeting glimpse of freedom offered by the new historical possibility of self-initiated travel. Most women, on the other hand, were denied the option of taking to the road. In his "C. & A. Blues," Peetie Wheatstraw offered one of the many blues versions of this disparity between the male and female conditions. He portrayed the man assuaging his pain through travel and the woman assuaging hers with tears:

> When a woman gets the blues, she hangs her head and cries
> When a man gets the blues, he flags a freight train and rides.[52]

A few songs recorded by Bessie Smith—"Chicago Bound Blues" is one[53]—support the masculinist view of men's and women's divergent responses to new forms of emotional pain in the postslavery era. In general, however, blues women did not acquiesce to the idea—which appears in various forms in male country blues—that men take to the road and women resort to tears. The women who sang the blues did not typically affirm female resignation and powerlessness, nor did they accept the relegation of women to private and interior spaces.

Although women generally were not socially entitled to travel on as wide a scale as men, significantly, blues women overcame this restriction.[54] Likewise, in their music, they found ways to express themselves that were at variance with the prevailing standards of femininity. Even as they may have shed tears, they found the courage to lift their heads and fight back, asserting their right to be respected not as appendages or victims of men but as truly independent human beings with vividly articulated sexual desires. Blues women provided emphatic examples of black female independence.

A significant number of songs in Gertrude "Ma" Rainey's recorded legacy suggest ways in which the structures of gender politics in black communities deviated from those of the dominant culture. In the call-and-response tradition, many of her love- and sex-oriented songs mirror or furnish responses to songs associated with the male country blues tradition. Male blues deal with a wider range of experiences, many accumulated on the job or on the road. But those that revolve around sexuality or include observations on love relationships are not radically different from their female counterparts in the behavior they describe and the images they evoke. Contrary to prevailing assumptions, as Sandra Lieb, author of *Mother of the Blues: A Study of Ma Rainey*, has observed, relatively few of Rainey's songs evoke women so incapacitated by their lover's infidelity, desertion, or mistreatment that they are bereft of agency or driven to the brink of self-destruction. "Only thirteen of her [ninety-two recorded] songs describe a women in abject sorrow, lying in bed and weeping for her absent man."[55] Far more typical are songs in which women explicitly celebrate their right to conduct themselves as expansively and even as undesirably as men. The protagonists in Ma Rainey's blues often abandon their men and routinely and cavalierly threaten them, even to the point of violence.

While the overwhelming majority of Bessie Smith's 160[56] available recorded songs allude to rejection, abuse, desertion, and unfaithful lovers, the preponderant emotional stance of the singer-protagonist—also true of Ma Rainey—is far from resignation and despair. On the contrary, the most frequent stance assumed by the women in these songs is independence and assertiveness—indeed defiance—bordering on and sometimes erupting into violence. The first song Bessie Smith recorded, a cover of Alberta Hunter's popular "Down Hearted Blues," portrays a heartbroken woman whose love for a man was answered with mistreatment and rejection. But her bout with the blues does not result in her dejectedly "hanging her head and crying." Smith represents this woman as proud and even contemptuous of the man who has mistreated her, accentuating, in the following lines, the woman's self-respect:

> It may be a week, it may be a month or two
> It may be a week, it may be a month or two
> But the day you quit me, honey, it's comin' home to you.[57]

It may be true, as Paul Garon has observed, that "[t]he blues is . . . a self-centered music, highly personalized, wherein the effects of everyday life are recounted in terms of the singers' reactions."[58] At the same time, however, the blues give expression to larger considerations reflecting worldviews specific to black working-class communities. Thus, "Down Hearted Blues" does not conclude with the implicit threat made against the man who has mistreated and deserted the female protagonist. Instead, it ends with an address to men in general—a bold, perhaps implicitly feminist contestation of patriarchal rule:

I got the world in a jug, the stopper's in my hand
I got the world in a jug, the stopper's in my hand
I'm gonna hold it until you men come under my command.[59]

An equally bold challenge can be found in Ma Rainey's wonderfully humorous "Barrel House Blues," which celebrates women's desires for alcohol and good times and their prerogative as the equals of men to engage in acts of infidelity:

Papa likes his sherry, mama likes her port
Papa likes to shimmy, mama likes to sport
Papa likes his bourbon, mama likes her gin
Papa likes his outside women, mama like her outside men.[60]

This signifying blues, in drawing parallels between male and female desire, between their similar inclinations toward intoxication, dance, and sex, launches a brazen challenge to dominant notions of women's subordination. "Barrel House Blues" sketches a portrait of a good-time "mama" no less at ease with her body and her sexuality than her "papa." Such glimpses of women who assert their sexual equality with men recur again and again in the work of the classic blues singers.[61] Indeed, some of these fictional portraits probably reflect actual experiences of black women who traveled the professional entertainment circuits. Ma Rainey was notorious for being able to outshine any man with her amazing sexual voracity—and Bessie Smith was known for being able to trounce any man who challenged her to a drinking duel.

In Gertrude "Ma" Rainey's and Bessie Smith's times, women's blues bore witness to the contradictory historical demands made of black American women. On the one hand, by virtue of their femaleness, they faced ideological expectations of domesticity and subordination emanating from the dominant culture. On the other hand, given the political, economic, and emotional transformations occasioned by the disestablishment of slavery, their lived experiences rendered such ideological assumptions flagrantly incongruous. In the blues, therefore, gender relationships are stretched to their limits and beyond. A typical example is one of Bessie Smith's early songs, "Mistreatin' Daddy," which opens with an address to an abusive and insensitive lover:

Daddy, mama's got the blues, the kind of blues that's hard to lose.
'Cause you mistreated me and drove me from your door.

Smith sings these lines as if to convince us that this woman has attempted to make the relationship work, and is utterly despondent about having been abused by a man she may have loved. Before long, however, she menacingly informs him,

If you see me setting on another daddy's knee
Don't bother me, I'm as mean as can be

> I'm like the butcher right down the street
> I can cut you all to pieces like I would a piece of meat.[62]

Fearless, unadorned realism is a distinctive feature of the blues. Their representations of sexual relationships are not constructed in accordance with the sentimentality of the American popular song tradition. Romantic love is seldom romanticized in the blues. No authentic blues woman could, in good faith, sing with conviction about a dashing prince whisking her into the "happily-ever-after." Only a few songs among Bessie Smith's recorded performances—and none in Rainey's—situate love relationships and sexual desire within a strictly masculinist discursive framework. The classic blues women sang of female aspirations for happiness and frequently associated these aspirations with sexual desire, but they rarely ignored the attendant ambiguities and contradictions. In "Honey, Where You Been So Long?" for example, Ma Rainey evokes a woman who is overjoyed that her man is returning:

> He'll soon be returning and glad tidings he will bring
> Then I'll throw my arms around him, then begin to sing.

But she does not attempt to pretend that this man is a paragon of perfection:

> Honey, where you been so long?
> Never thought you would treat me wrong
> Look how you have dragged me down.[63]

Note a language that mocks the dominant white culture with down-home black English. Bessie Smith's "Sam Jones Blues" uses the same technique to highlight cultural contradictions black women experienced when comparing their own attitudes toward love and sex with the idealizations of the dominant culture.

The woman in Ma Rainey's "Lawd, Send Me a Man Blues" harbors no illusions about the relationship she desires with a man. She is lonely and wonders "who gonna pay my board bill now." Appealing for any man she can get, she pleads with a bluesy zeal:

> Send me a Zulu, a voodoo, any old man
> I'm not particular, boys, I'll take what I can.[64]

Bessie Smith's "Baby Doll" conveys a similar message:

> I wanna be somebody's baby doll so I can get my lovin' all the time
> I wanna be somebody's baby doll to ease my mind
> He can be ugly, he can be black, so long as he can eagle rock and ball the jack.[65]

These blues women had no qualms about announcing female desire. Their songs express women's intention to "get their loving." Such affirmations of sexual autonomy and open expressions of female sexual desire give historical voice to possibilities of equality not articulated elsewhere. Women's blues and the cultural politics lived out in the careers of the blues queens put these new possibilities on the historical agenda.

The realism of the blues does not confine us to literal interpretations. On the contrary, blues contain many layers of meanings and are often astounding in their complexity and profundity. Precisely because the blues confront raw emotional and sexual matters associated with a very specific historical reality, they make complex statements that transcend the particularities of their origins. There is a core of meaning in the texts of the classic blues women that, although prefeminist in a historical sense, reveals that black women of that era were acknowledging and addressing issues central to contemporary feminist discourse.

By focusing on the issue of misogynist violence, the first activist moments of the second-wave twentieth-century women's movement exposed the centrality of the ideological separation of the public and private spheres to the structure of male domination. In the early 1970s, women began to speak publicly about their experiences of rape, battery, and the violation of their reproductive rights. Obscured by a shroud of silence, these assaults against women traditionally had been regarded as a fact of private life to be shielded at all costs from scrutiny in the public sphere. That this cover-up would no longer be tolerated was the explosive meaning behind feminists' defiant notion that "the personal is political."[66]

The performances of the classic blues women—especially Bessie Smith—were one of the few cultural spaces in which a tradition of public discourse on male violence had been previously established. One explanation for the fact that the blues women of the 1920s—and the texts they present—fail to respect the taboo on speaking publicly about domestic violence is that the blues as a genre never acknowledges the discursive and ideological boundaries separating the private sphere from the public. Historically, there has been no great body of literature on battering because well-to-do white women who were in a position to write about their experiences in abusive relationships only recently have been convinced that such privately executed violence is a suitable subject of public discourse.

There is, however, a body of preserved oral culture—or "orature," to use a term employed by some scholars[67]—about domestic abuse in the songs of blues women like Gertrude Rainey and Bessie Smith. Violence against women was always an appropriate topic of women's blues. The contemporary urge to break the silence surrounding misogynist violence and the organized political movement challenging violence against women has an aesthetic precursor in the work of the classic blues singers.

Women's blues have been accused of promoting acquiescent and therefore antifeminist responses to misogynist abuse. It is true that some of the songs recorded by Rainey and Smith seem to exemplify acceptance of male violence—and sometimes even masochistic delight in being the target of lovers' beatings. Such claims do not take into account the extent to which blues meaning is manipulated and transformed—sometimes even into its opposite—in blues performance. Blues make abundant use of humor, satire, and irony, revealing their historic roots in slave music, wherein indirect methods of expression were the only means by which the oppression of slavery could be denounced. In this sense, the blues genre is a direct descendant of work songs, which often relied on indirection and irony to highlight the inhumanity of slave owners so that their targets were sure to misunderstand the intended meaning.[68]

Bessie Smith sings a number of songs whose lyrics may be interpreted as accepting emotional and physical abuse as attendant hazards for women involved in sexual partnerships. But close attention to her musical presentation of these songs persuades the listener that they contain implicit critiques of male abuse. In "Yes, Indeed He Do," Smith's sarcastic presentation of the lyrics transforms observations on an unfaithful, abusive, and exploitative lover into a scathing critique of male violence:

Is he true as stars above me? What kind of fool is you?
He don't stay from home all night more than six times a week
No, I know that I'm his Sheba, and I know that he's my sheik
And when I ask him where he's been, he grabs a rocking chair
Then he knocks me down and says, "It's just a little love lick, dear."

. . . .

If he beats me or mistreats me, what is that to you?
I don't have to do no work except to wash his clothes
And darn his socks and press his pants and scrub the kitchen floor
I wouldn't take a million for my sweet, sweet daddy Jim
And I wouldn't give a quarter for another man like him

Gee, ain't it great to have a man that's crazy over you?
Oh, do my sweet, sweet daddy love me? Yes, indeed he do.[69]

Edward Brooks, in *The Bessie Smith Companion*, makes the following comment about this song:

> Bessie delivers the song with growling gusto, as if it were really a panegyric to an exemplary lover; she relates his wrongs with the approval of virtues and it comes as a jolt when the exultation in her voice is compared with her actual words.[70]

Brooks's analysis assumes that Smith was unselfconscious in her performance of this song. He therefore misses its intentional ambiguity and complexity. Smith was an accomplished performer, actor, and comedian and was therefore well acquainted with the uses of humor and irony. It is much more plausible to characterize her decision to sing "Yes, Indeed He Do" with mock praise and elation as a conscious effort to highlight, in the most effective way possible, the inhumanity and misogyny of male batterers.

"Yes, Indeed He Do" was recorded in 1928, five years after Smith began her career as a recording artist. In 1923, she recorded "Outside of That," a song about a man who was regularly abusive, but also a superb lover. The sarcasm in "Yes, Indeed He Do" is far more conspicuous than in the earlier song, but "Outside of That" also deserves a close examination. The protagonist enthusiastically proclaims her love for a man who batters her, and who becomes especially violent in response to her announcement—in jest, claims the narrator—that she no longer loves him:

I love him as true as stars above
He beats me up but how he can love
I never loved like that since the day I was born.

I said for fun I don't want you no more
And when I said that I made sweet papa sore
He blacked my eye, I couldn't see
Then he pawned the things he gave to me
But outside of that, he's all right with me.

I said for fun I don't want you no more
And when I said that I made sweet papa sore
When he pawned my things, I said you dirty old thief

> Child, then he turned around and knocked out both of my teeth
> Outside of that, he's all right with me.[71]

At first glance, this song appears to embrace—and even glorify—male violence. It is often interpreted as overtly condoning sadomasochistic relationships. But when one considers the lyrics carefully—even apart from Smith's interpretation—there is no convincing evidence that the woman derives pleasure from the beatings she receives. On the contrary, she lauds her lover for his sexual expertise and proclaims that she loves him despite the brutality he inflicts upon her. Smith's presentation of "Outside of That" is somewhat more subtle than in "Yes, Indeed He Do," but a close listening does confirm that she uses her voice to ironize and criticize the woman—even if she herself happens to be that woman—who would embrace with such enthusiasm a partnership so injurious to her physical and emotional well-being.

The historically omnipresent secrecy and silence regarding male violence is linked to its social construction as a private problem sequestered behind impermeable domestic walls, rather than a social problem deserving political attention. Until very recently, it was so effectively confined to the private sphere that habitually police officers would intervene in "domestic disputes" only in "life and death" situations. Even in the 1990s, police intervention, when it does occur, is still accompanied by a serious reluctance to insert the public force of the state into the private affairs of individuals.[72] "Outside of That" effectively presents violence against women as a problem to be reckoned with publicly. The song names the problem in the voice of the woman who is the target of the battering: "He beats me up . . . He blacked my eye, I couldn't see . . . he turned around and knocked out both of my teeth." It names domestic violence in the collective context of blues performance and therefore defines it as a problem worthy of public discourse. Hearing this song, women who were victims of such abuse consequently could perceive it as a shared and thus social condition.

Whether individual women in Bessie Smith's audience were able to use her performance as a basis for developing more critical attitudes toward the violence they suffered is a matter for speculation. Certainly, the organized campaign to eradicate domestic violence did not emerge in the United States until the 1970s. Women involved in these early efforts borrowed a "consciousness-raising" strategy from the Chinese women's movement referred to as "speak bitterness," or "speak pains to recall pains."[73] This strategy resonates strikingly with blues practices. Among black working-class women, the blues made oppositional stances to male violence culturally possible, at least at the level of individual experience. The lyrics indicate resistance by the victim: "I said for fun I don't want you no more . . . When he pawned my things, I said you dirty old thief." Though these comments are offered in a humorous vein, they nevertheless imply that the victim does not cower before the batterer but rather challenges his right to assault her with impunity. In Bessie Smith's rendering of this song, the recurring phrase "outside of that, he's all right with me" is sung with a satirical edge, implying that its significance may be precisely the opposite of its literal meaning.

Ma Rainey's "Black Eye Blues," a comic presentation of the issue of domestic violence, describes a woman named Miss Nancy who assumes a posture of defiance toward her abusive partner:

I went down the alley, other night
Nancy and her man had just had a fight
He beat Miss Nancy 'cross the head
When she rose to her feet, she said

"You low down alligator, just watch me
Sooner or later gonna catch you with your britches down
You 'buse me and you cheat me, you dog around and beat me
Still I'm gonna hang around

"Take all my money, blacken both of my eyes
Give it to another woman, come home and tell me lies
You low down alligator, just watch me
Sooner or later gonna catch you with your britches down
I mean, gonna catch you with your britches down."[74]

Women's blues suggest emergent feminist insurgency in that they unabashedly name the problem of male violence and so usher it out of the shadows of domestic life where society had kept it hidden and beyond public or political scrutiny. Even when she does not offer a critical perspective, Bessie Smith names the problem and the ambivalence it occasions. In "Please Help Me Get Him off My Mind," for example, the protagonist consults a Gypsy about her emotional entanglement with a violent man, whose influence she wishes to exorcise.[75]

Other explicit references to physical abuse in Smith's work can be found in "It Won't Be You,"[76] "Slow and Easy Man,"[77] "Eavesdropper's Blues,"[78] "Love Me Daddy Blues,"[79] "Hard Driving Papa,"[80] and " 'Tain't Nobody's Bizness If I Do."[81] In the first song, the protagonist sardonically celebrates her decision to leave her man by informing him that if in fact her next partner "beats me and breaks my heart," at least "it won't be you." "Slow and Easy Man" presents a woman who presumably delights in the sexual pleasures offered her by a partner, but there is a casual reference to the fact that this man "curses and fights."

We can assume that the woman in "Eavesdropper's Blues" is the target of verbal and physical abuse since the man turns her "eyes all blue" if she has no money to offer him. In "Love Me Daddy Blues," as in "Please Help Me Get Him off My Mind," the woman experiences the dilemma typical of battered wives who continue to love their abusers.

Edward Brooks describes the last lines of "Hard Driving Papa" as "a celebration of masochism."[82] But when Bessie Smith sings "Because I love him, 'cause there's no one can beat me like he do," it is clear from her performance that far from relishing the beatings she has received, she is expressing utter desperation about her predicament. The penultimate line, "I'm going to the river feelin' so sad and blue" is delivered with such melancholy that we are all but certain the protagonist is intent upon suicide. This is a rare moment of unmitigated despair in Smith's work. To interpret the reference to battering as a celebration of masochism ignores the larger truth-telling and complexity in the song.

Bessie Smith's recorded performance of Porter Grainger's " 'Tain't Nobody's Bizness If I Do"—a song also associated with Billie Holiday—is one of Smith's most widely known recordings. Like "Outside of That," it has been interpreted as sanctioning female masochism. It is indeed extremely painful to hear Smith and Holiday sing the following verse so convincingly:

Well, I'd rather my man would hit me than to jump right up and quit me
'Taint nobody's bizness if I do, do, do, do
I swear I won't call no copper if I'm beat up by my papa
'Tain't nobody's bizness if I do, if I do.[83]

The lyrics of this song touched a chord in black women's lives that cannot be ignored. While it contradicts the prevailing stance in most of Bessie Smith's work, which emphasizes women's strength and equality, it certainly does not annul the latter's sincerity and authenticity. Moreover, the song's seeming acquiescence to battering occurs within a larger affirmation of women's right as individuals to conduct themselves however they wish—however idiosyncratic their behavior might seem and regardless of the possible consequences. The song begins:

There ain't nothin' I can do or nothin' I can say
That folks don't criticize me
But I'm going to do just as I want to anyway
And don't care if they all despise me.[84]

Violence against women remains pandemic. Almost equally pandemic—although fortunately less so today than during previous eras—is women's inability to extricate themselves from this web of violence. The conduct defended by the woman in this male-authored song is not so unconventional after all. " 'Tain't Nobody's Bizness If I Do" may well have been a catalyst for introspective criticism on the part of many women in Bessie Smith's listening audience who found themselves entrapped in similar situations. To name that situation so directly and openly may itself have made misogynist violence available for criticism.

Gertrude Rainey's "Sweet Rough Man"[85] has been described as a "classic expression of the 'hit me, I love you' tradition of masochistic women's songs." In her analysis, Sandra Lieb argues that this song is an exception within the body of Rainey's work for its presentation of "a cruel, virile man abusing a helpless, passive woman."[86] Feminist literary critic Hazel Carby calls it "the most explicit description of sexual brutality in [Rainey's] repertoire," emphasizing that it was composed by a man and reiterating Lieb's argument that there are differing responses to male violence in female- and male-authored blues.[87] The lyrics to "Sweet Rough Man" include the following lines:

I woke up this mornin', my head was sore as a boil
I woke up this mornin', my head was sore as a boil
My man beat me last night with five feet of copper coil

He keeps my lips split, my eyes as black as jet
He keeps my lips split, my eyes as black as jet
But the way he love me makes me soon forget

Every night for five years, I've got a beatin' from my man
Every night for five years, I've got a beatin' from my man
People says I'm crazy, I'll explain and you'll understand

. . . .

Lord, it ain't no maybe 'bout my man bein' rough

> Lord, it ain't no maybe 'bout my man bein' rough
> But when it comes to lovin', he sure can strut his stuff.[88]

Of all the songs recorded by Bessie Smith and Gertrude Rainey, this one is the most graphic in its evocation of domestic violence and goes farthest in revealing women's contradictory attitudes toward violent relationships. Though it was composed by a man, Rainey chose to sing it enthusiastically. We should recognize that to sing the song at all was to rescue the issue of men's violence toward woman from the silent realm of the private sphere and reconstruct it as a public problem. The woman in the song assumes a stance which is at once "normal" and pathological. It is pathological to desire to continue a relationship in which one is being systematically abused, but given the prevailing presumptions of female acquiescence to male superiority, it is "normal" for women to harbor self-deprecatory ideas. Rainey's rendering of "Sweet Rough Man" does not challenge sexist conduct in any obvious way, but it does present the issue as a problem women confront. The female character acknowledges that "people says I'm crazy" for loving such a brutal man, and the song very clearly states the dilemma facing women who tolerate violence for the sake of feeling loved.

Naming issues that pose a threat to the physical or psychological well-being of the individual is a central function of the blues. Indeed, the musical genre is called the "blues" not only because it employs a musical scale containing "blue notes" but also because it names, in myriad ways, the social and psychic afflictions and aspirations of African Americans. The blues preserve and transform the West African philosophical centrality of the naming process. In the Dogon, Yoruba, and other West African cultural traditions, the process of nommo—naming things, forces, and modes—is a means of establishing magical (or, in the case of the blues, aesthetic) control over the object of the naming process.[89] Through the blues, menacing problems are ferreted out from the isolated individual experience and restructured as problems shared by the community. As shared problems, threats can be met and addressed within a public and collective context.

In Ma Rainey's and especially in Bessie Smith's blues, the problem of male violence is named, and varied patterns of implied or explicit criticism and resistance are woven into the artists' performance of them. Lacking, however, is a naming or analysis of the social forces responsible for black men's propensity (and indeed the male propensity in general) to inflict violence on their female partners. The blues accomplish what they can within the confines of their form. The political analysis must be developed elsewhere.

There are no references to sexual assault in either Rainey's or Smith's music. Certainly, black women of that era suffered sexual abuse—both by strangers and acquaintances. It is tempting to speculate why the blues do not name this particular problem. One possibility, of course, is that "rape" was still an unacknowledged and unarticulated dimension of domestic violence, and that black public discourse on rape was firmly linked to the campaign against racist violence. The birth of the blues coincided with a period of militant activism by middle-class black women directed at white racists for whom rape was a weapon of terror, and at white employers who routinely used sexual violence as a racialized means of asserting power over their female domestic help. Leaders like Mary Church Terrell and Ida B. Wells, who were instrumental in the creation of the black women's club movement,[90] linked the rape of black women by white men to the manipulative use of false rape charges against black men as a justification for the widespread lynchings of the period.[91] Black men were habitually represented as savage, sex-crazed rapists, bent on violating the physical and spiritual purity of white womanhood.[92] It may well be that the discourse on rape was so thoroughly influenced by the prevailing racism that intraracial rape could not be named. The difficult and delayed emergence of the beginnings of a collective consciousness around sexual harassment, rape, and incest within the black community is indicative of how hard it has been to acknowledge abuse perpetrated by the abused.[93]

Another explanation for the absence of allusions to rape within women's blues may be the very nature of female blues discourse. Even in their most despairing moods, the female characters memorialized in women's blues songs do not fit the mold of the typical victim of abuse. The independent women of blues lore do not think twice about wielding weapons against men who they feel have mistreated them. They frequently brandish their razors and guns, and dare men to cross the lines they draw. While acknowledging the physical mistreatment they have received at the hands of their male lovers, they do not perceive or define themselves as powerless in face of such violence. Indeed, they fight back passionately. In many songs Ma Rainey and Bessie Smith pay tribute to fearless women who attempt to avenge themselves when their lovers have been unfaithful. In "Black Mountain Blues," Bessie Smith sings:

> Had a man in Black Mountain, sweetest man in town
> Had a man in Black Mountain, the sweetest man in town
> He met a city gal, and he throwed me down
>
> I'm bound for Black Mountain, me and my razor and my gun
> Lord, I'm bound for Black Mountain, me and my razor and my gun
> I'm gonna shoot him if he stands still, and cut him if he run.[94]

In Smith's "Sinful Blues," a woman's rage also turns into violence:

> I got my opinion and my man won't act right
> So I'm gonna get hard on him right from this very night
> Gonna get me a gun long as my right arm
> Shoot that man because he done me wrong.
> Lord, now I've got them sinful blues.[95]

In Ma Rainey's "See See Rider Blues," the protagonist who has discovered that her man has another woman friend announces her intention to buy herself a pistol and to "kill my man and catch the Cannonball."[96] Her concluding resolution is: "If he don't have me, he won't have no gal at all." In Rainey's "Rough and Tumble Blues," the woman attacks not the man, but the women who have attempted to seduce him:

> I got rough and killed three women 'fore the police got the news
> 'Cause mama's on the warpath with those rough and tumble blues.[97]

In Rainey's "Sleep Talking Blues," the woman threatens to kill her man if he mentions another woman's name in his sleep. The woman in Smith's "Them's Graveyard Words" responds to her lover's confession that he has acquired a new woman friend with the murderous threat "them's graveyard words":

> I done polished up my pistol, my razor's sharpened too
> He'll think the world done fell on him when my dirty work is through.[98]

In some songs, the woman actually does kill her partner and is condemned to prison—or to death. Frequently, she kills out of jealousy, but sometimes, as in Rainey's "Cell Bound Blues," she kills in self-defense, protecting herself from her man's violent blows.[99] In two of Bessie Smith's songs—"Sing Sing Prison Blues" and "Send Me to the 'Lectric Chair"—when she comes before the criminal justice system, the woman is ready and willing to pay the consequences for having killed her man. In the former, directing her words to the judge, the woman says:

> You can send me up the river or send me to that mean old jail
> You can send me up the river or send me to that mean old jail
> I killed my man and I don't need no bail.[100]

In "Send Me to the 'Lectric Chair," the woman pleads with the judge to give her the death penalty. She is not prepared to spend the rest of her life in prison and she is willing to accept the punishment she deserves for having "cut her good man's throat." The striking postures assumed by these women offer not even a hint of repentance for having taken their lovers' lives. In "Send Me to the 'Lectric Chair," the woman sardonically describes the details of her crime:

> I cut him with my barlow, I kicked him in the side
> I stood there laughing over him while he wallowed 'round and died.[101]

These rowdy and hardened women are not simply female incarnations of stereotypical male aggressiveness. Women's blues cannot be understood apart from their role in the molding of an emotional community based on the affirmation of black people's—and in particular black women's—absolute and irreducible humanity. The blues woman challenges in her own way the imposition of gender-based inferiority. When she paints blues portraits of tough women, she offers psychic defenses and interrupts and discredits the routine internalization of male dominance. In Bessie Smith's "Hateful Blues" the woman is responding to a male partner who has skipped out on her. She is feeling "low down," but she does not hesitate to inform us that "nothin' ever worries me long." Although she has cried and cried, she persuades herself to stop: "I ain't gonna cry no more." And, with increased determination, she announces that "if he can stand to leave me, I can stand to see him go." Finally, she entertains thoughts of violent revenge:

> If I see him I'm gon' beat him, gon' kick and bite him, too
> Gonna take my weddin' butcher, gonna cut him two in two.[102]

This rough-and-tumble, sexually aware woman is capable of issuing intimidating threats to men who have mistreated her, and she is more than willing to follow through on them; she is a spiritual descendant of Harriet Tubman, who, it is said, always warned her passengers on the Underground Railroad that no one would be permitted to turn back, that they would all forge onward or die at her hands. This was the only way to guarantee confidentiality regarding their route of escape. The female portraits created by the early blues women served as reminders of African-American women's tradition of womanhood, a tradition that directly challenged prevailing notions of femininity.

The lives of many of the blues women of the twenties resembled those of the fearless women memorialized in their songs. We know that at times Bessie Smith was a victim of male violence and also that she would not hesitate to hurl violent threats—which she sometimes carried out—at the men who betrayed her. Nor was she afraid to confront the most feared embodiments of white racist terror. One evening in July of 1927, robed and hooded Ku Klux Klansmen attempted to disrupt her tent performance by pulling up the tent stakes and collapsing the entire structure. When Smith was informed of the trouble, she immediately left the tent and, according to her biographer,

> ran toward the intruders, stopped within ten feet of them, placed one hand on her hip, and shook a clenched fist at the Klansmen. "What the fuck you think you're doin'," she shouted above the sound of the band. "I'll get the whole damn tent out here if I have to. You just pick up them sheets and run!"
>
> The Klansmen, apparently too surprised to move, just stood there and gawked. Bessie hurled obscenities at them until they finally turned and disappeared quietly into the darkness. . . .
>
> Then she went back into the tent as if she had just settled a routine matter.[103]

Daphne Duval Harrison has noted that women's blues in the 1920s "introduced a new, different model of black women—more assertive, sexy, sexually aware, independent, realistic, complex, alive." Her explication of the blues' importance for redefining black women's self-understanding deserves extensive quotation:

> The blues women of Ida Cox's era brought to their lyrics and performances new meaning as they interpreted and reformulated the black experience from their unique perspective in American society as black females. They saw a world that did not protect the sanctity of black womanhood, as espoused in the bourgeois ideology; only white middle- or upper-class women were protected by it. They saw and experienced injustice as jobs they held were snatched away when white women refused to work with them or white men returned from war to reclaim them. They pointed out the pain of sexual and physical abuse and abandonment.[104]

Blues women were expected to deviate from the norms defining orthodox female behavior, which is why they were revered by both men and women in black working-class communities. Ida Cox's "Wild Women Don't Have the Blues" became the most famous portrait of the nonconforming, independent woman, and her "wild woman" has become virtually synonymous with the blues queen herself:

> I've got a disposition and a way of my own
> When my man starts kicking, I let him find another home
> I get full of good liquor and walk the street all night
> Go home and put my man out if he don't treat me right
> Wild women don't worry, wild women don't have the blues

You never get nothing by being an angel child
You'd better change your ways and get real wild
I want to tell you something, I wouldn't tell you no lie
Wild women are the only kind that really get by
'Cause wild women don't worry, wild women don't have the blues.[105]

In "Easy Come, Easy Go Blues," Bessie Smith also explored the theme of the "wild woman"—the woman who consciously rejects mainstream values, especially those prescribing passivity in relations with men. This song is about a woman who refuses to allow the mistreatment she has suffered at the hands of a man to plunge her into depression. She refuses to take love so seriously that its loss threatens her very essence:

If my sweet man trifles, or if he don't
I'll get someone to love me anytime he won't.

She concludes with a summary statement of her bold position:

This world owe me a plenty lovin', hear what I say
Believe me, I go out collectin' 'most every day
I'm overflowing with those easy come, easy go blues.[106]

"Prove It on Me Blues," composed by Gertrude Rainey, portrays just such a "wild woman," who affirms her independence from the orthodox norms of womanhood by boldly flaunting her lesbianism. Rainey's sexual involvement with women was no secret among her colleagues and her audiences. The advertisement for the release of "Prove It on Me Blues" showed the blues woman sporting a man's hat, jacket, and tie and, while a policeman looked on, obviously attempting to seduce two women on a street corner. The song's lyrics include the following:

They said I do it, ain't nobody caught me
Sure got to prove it on me
Went out last night with a crowd of my friends
They must've been women, 'cause I don't like no men

It's true I wear a collar and a tie
Make the wind blow all the while
'Cause they say I do it, ain't nobody caught me
They sure got to prove it on me

. . . .
Wear my clothes just like a fan
Talk to the gals just like any old man
'Cause they say I do it, ain't nobody caught me
Sure got to prove it on me.[107]

Sandra Lieb has described this song as a "powerful statement of lesbian defiance and self-worth."[108] "Prove It on Me Blues" is a cultural precursor to the lesbian cultural movement of the 1970s, which began to crystallize around the performance and recording of lesbian-affirming songs. In fact, in 1977 Teresa Trull recorded a cover of Ma Rainey's song for an album entitled *Lesbian Concentrate*.[109]

Hazel Carby has insightfully observed that "Prove It on Me Blues"

> vacillates between the subversive hidden activity of women loving women [and] a public declaration of lesbianism. The words express a contempt for a society that rejected lesbians. . . . But at the same time the song is a reclamation of lesbianism as long as the woman publicly names her sexual preference for herself. . . .

Carby argues that this song "engag[es] directly in defining issues of sexual preference as a contradictory struggle of social relations."[110]

"Prove It on Me Blues" suggests how the iconoclastic blues women of the twenties were pioneers for later historical developments. The response to this song also suggests that homophobia within the black community did not prevent blues women from challenging stereotypical conceptions of women's lives. They did not allow themselves to be enshrined by the silence imposed by mainstream society.

Memphis Willie B. (Borum)'s song "Bad Girl Blues" is one example of how lesbianism was addressed by blues men. The lyrics lack any hint of moral condemnation:

> Women loving each other, man, they don't think about no man
> Women loving each other and they don't think about no man
> They ain't playing no secret no more, these women playing it a wide open hand.[111]

Ma Rainey's "Sissy Blues" similarly recognizes the existence of male homosexuality in the black community without betraying any moral disapprobation. As is generally the case with the blues, the issue is simply named:

> I dreamed last night I was far from harm
> Woke up and found my man in a sissy's arms
>
> . . . .
>
> My man's got a sissy, his name is Miss Kate
> He shook that thing like jelly on a plate
>
> . . . .
>
> Now all the people ask me why I'm all alone
> A sissy shook that thing and took my man from home.[112]

The blues songs recorded by Gertrude Rainey and Bessie Smith offer us a privileged glimpse of the prevailing perceptions of love and sexuality in postslavery black communities in the United States. Both women were role models for untold thousands of their sisters to whom they delivered messages that defied the male dominance encouraged by mainstream culture. The blues women openly challenged the gender politics implicit in traditional cultural representations of marriage and heterosexual love relationships. Refusing, in the blues tradition of raw realism, to romanticize romantic relationships, they instead exposed the stereotypes and explored the contradictions of those relationships. By so doing, they redefined women's "place." They forged and memorialized images of tough, resilient, and independent women who were afraid neither of their own vulnerability nor of defending their right to be respected as autonomous human beings.

Notes

1. Bessie Smith, "I Used to Be Your Sweet Mama," Columbia 14292-D, Feb. 9, 1928. Reissued on *Empty Bed Blues*, Columbia CG 30450, 1972.

2. According to Hazel Carby, "[w]hat has been called the 'Classic Blues,' the women's blues of the twenties and early thirties, is a discourse that articulates a cultural and political struggle over sexual relations: a struggle that is directed against the objectification of female sexuality within a patriarchal order but which also tries to reclaim women's bodies as the sexual and sensuous objects of song." "It Jus Be's Day Way Sometime: The Sexual Politics of Women's Blues," *Radical America* 20, no. 4 (June–July 1986), p. 12.

3. See Henry Pleasants, *The Great American Popular Singers* (New York: Simon & Schuster, 1974). According to Lawrence Levine, "the physical side of love which, aside from some tepid hand holding and lip pecking, was largely missing from popular music, was strongly felt in the blues." *Black Culture and Black Consciousness: Afro-American Thought from Slavery to Freedom* (New York: Oxford University Press, 1975), p. 279.

4. Bessie Smith's first recording, a cover of Alberta Hunter's "Down Hearted Blues," sold 780,000 copies in less than six months. Chris Albertson, *Bessie* (New York: Stein & Day, 1972), p. 46.

5. The central place of the blues in the elaboration of a postslavery black cultural consciousness has been examined widely in works like LeRoi Jones's pioneering *Blues People* and Lawrence Levine's engaging study *Black Culture and Black Consciousness.* While both suggest important approaches to the understanding of racial dimensions of African-American culture, scant attention is accorded gender consciousness. Daphne Duval Harrison's trailblazing study *Black Pearls* reveals, in fact, how rich women's blues can be as a terrain for explorations of the place gender occupies in black cultural consciousness.

6. See W. E. B. Du Bois, *Black Reconstruction in America* (New York: Harcourt, Brace, 1935).

7. See Herbert Gutman, *The Black Family in Slavery and Freedom, 1750–1925* (New York: Pantheon, 1976), chap. 9.

8. Lawrence Levine cites a rowing song heard by Frances Kemble in the late 1830s and characterized by her as nonsensical, but interpreted by Chadwick Hansen as containing hidden sexual meanings.

> Jenny shake her toe at me,
>   Jenny gone away;
> Jenny shake her toe at me,
>   Jenny gone away.
> Hurrah! Miss Susy, oh!
>   Jenny gone away;
> Hurrah! Miss Susy, oh!
>   Jenny gone away.

Black Culture and Black Consciousness, p. 11. (Frances Anne Kemble, *Journal of a Residence on a Georgian Plantation in 1838–1839* [1863; reprint, New York: Knopf, 1961], pp. 163–164.) "Chadwick Hansen [in "Jenny's Tow: Negro Shaking Dances in America," *American Quarterly* 19 (1967), pp. 554–63] has shown that in all probability what Miss Kemble heard was not the English word 'toe' but an African-derived word referring to the buttocks." The Jenny of whom the slaves were singing with such obvious pleasure was shaking something more interesting and provocative than her foot.

9. According to James Cone, "The spiritual . . . is the spirit of the people struggling to be free . . . [it] is the people's response to the societal contradictions. It is the people facing trouble and affirming, 'I ain't tired yet.' But the spiritual is more than dealing with trouble. It is a joyful experience, a vibrant affirmation of life and its possibilities in an appropriate esthetic form. The

spiritual is the community in rhythm, swinging to the movement of life." *The Spirituals and the Blues: An Interpretation* (New York: Seabury, 1972), pp. 32–33. [Excerpt reprinted herein.]

10. Popular musical culture in the African-American tradition continues to actively involve the audience in the performance of the music. The distinction, therefore, is not between the relatively active and relatively passive stances of the audience. Rather it is between a mode of musical presentation in which everyone involved is considered a "performer"—or perhaps in which no one, the song leader included, is considered a "performer"—and one in which the producer of the music plays a privileged role in calling forth the responses of the audience.

11. See James Cone's discussion of the liberation content of the spirituals. John Lovell, Jr. (*Black Song: The Forge and the Flame* [New York: Macmillan, 1972]) also emphasizes the relationship between the slave community's yearning for liberation and the music it produced in the religious tradition of Christianity.

12. Levine, p. 175.

13. Religious themes are to be found in some of the prison work songs recorded by folklorists such as Alan Lomax during the thirties, forties, and fifties.

14. See Giles Oakley, *The Devil's Music: A History of the Blues* (New York and London: Harcourt Brace Jovanovich, 1976), pp. 97–99.

15. See Henry Louis Gates, Jr., *The Signifying Monkey: A Theory of African-American Literary Criticism* (New York: Oxford University Press, 1988), chap. 1.

16. See Zora Neale Hurston, *Mules and Men* (Bloomington: Indiana University Press, 1978), stories on Jack and the Devil, p. 164, and about "unh hunh" as a word the Devil made up, p. 169.

17. *Wild Women Don't Have the Blues*, dir. Christine Dall, Calliope Film Resources, 1989, videocassette.

18. When applied to the religious contours and content of slave-initiated cultural community, the infamous observation by the young Karl Marx that religion is the "opium of the people" elucidates the utopian potential of slave religion; but, in this context, Marx's observation simultaneously goes too far and not far enough.

> Religious *suffering is at the same time an* expression *of real suffering and a protest against real suffering. Religion is the sigh of the oppressed creature, the sentiment of a heartless world, and the soul of soulless conditions. It is the* opium *of the people. . . . Religion is only the illusory sun around which man revolves so long as he does not revolve around himself.*

Karl Marx, "The Critique of Hegel's Philosophy of Right" in Karl Marx, *Early Writings*, ed. T. B. Bottomore (New York: McGraw-Hill, 1963), pp. 43–44.

Marx goes too far in the sense that he assumes a necessarily and exclusively ideological relationship between religious consciousness and material conditions, i.e., that religion is fundamentally false consciousness and that the "self" or community it articulates is necessarily an illusion. Such an all-embracing conception of religion cannot account for its extrareligious dimensions. On the other hand, he does not go far enough when he dismisses the revolutionary potential of religious consciousness.

19. See Lovell, chaps. 17 and 18.

20. Marx, p. 44.

21. See Houston A. Baker, Jr., *Blues, Ideology, and Afro-American Literature* (Chicago: University of Chicago Press, 1984). [Excerpt reprinted herein.]

22. Cone, p. 112. C. Eric Lincoln originated the term "secular spirituals."

23. Levine, p. 237.

24. Julio Finn argues that "the jook joint is to the blues what the church is to the spiritual,

and the bluesman on stage is in his pulpit. Contrary to the 'holy' atmosphere which reigns in the church, the jook joint is characterized by its rowdiness—the noise and smoke and drinking are necessities without which its character would be fatally altered, for that would alter the music, which is in no small way shaped by it." Julio Finn, *The Bluesman* (London: Quartet, 1986), p. 202. Unfortunately, Finn confines his discussion to blues men and does not consider the role of women.

25. See Joan Landes, "The Public and the Private Sphere: A Feminist Reconsideration," in Johanna Meehan, ed., *Feminists Read Habermas* (London: Routledge, 1995). According to Aida Hurtado in "Relating to Privilege: Seduction and Rejection in the Subordination of White Women and Women of Color" (*Signs: A Journal of Women and Culture in Society*, 14, no. 4 [Summer 1989]), "the public/private distinction is relevant only for the white middle and upper classes since historically the American state has intervened constantly in the private lives and domestic arrangements of the working class. Women of Color have not had the benefit of the economic conditions that underlie the public/private distinction. Instead the political consciousness of women of Color stems from an awareness that the public is *personally* political."

26. Du Bois points out that in many border states, slave-breeding became a main industry: "The deliberate breeding of a strong, big field-hand stock could be carried out by selecting proper males, and giving them the run of the likeliest females. This in many Border States became a regular policy and fed the slave trade." *Black Reconstruction in America*, p. 44.

27. Gutman, pp. 80 and 388.

28. Slave narratives by Frederick Douglass, Solomon Northrup, and Harriet Jacobs contain poignant descriptions of family separations. See also Gutman, chap. 8.

29. Ralph Ellison, *Shadow and Act* (New York: Vintage, 1972), p. 245.

30. Oakley, p. 59.

31. Angela Y. Davis, *Women, Race, and Class* (New York: Random House, 1981).

32. Bessie Smith, "Sam Jones Blues," Columbia 13005-D, Sept. 24, 1923. Reissued on *Any Woman's Blues*, Columbia G 30126, 1972.

33. Harrison, *Black Pearls*, p. 287.

34. See Mary P. Ryan's discussion of the cult of motherhood in *Womanhood in America: From Colonial Times to the Present* (New York: Franklin Watts, 1975).

35. Bessie Smith, "Poor Man's Blues," Columbia 14399-D, Aug. 24, 1928. Reissued on *Empty Bed Blues*, Columbia CG 30450, 1972.

36. Bessie Smith, "Pinchback Blues," Columbia 14025-D, Apr. 4, 1924. Reissued on *Empty Bed Blues*, Columbia CG 30450, 1972.

37. Bessie Smith, "Take Me for a Buggy Ride," Okeh 8945, Nov. 24, 1933. Reissued on *The World's Greatest Blues Singer*, Columbia CG 33, 1972.

38. Albertson, p. 188. The four songs she recorded on November 24, 1933, were "Do Your Duty," "Gimme a Pigfoot," "Take Me for a Buggy Ride," and "I'm Down in the Dumps."

39. See Edward Brooks, *The Bessie Smith Companion* (New York: Da Capo, 1982), pp. 224–25. [Excerpt reprinted herein.]

40. Gertrude "Ma" Rainey, "Blame It on the Blues," Paramount 12760, Sept. 1928. Reissued on *Ma Rainey*, Milestone M-47021, 1974.

41. Gertrude "Ma" Rainey, "Shave 'Em Dry," Paramount 12222, 1924. Reissued on *Ma Rainey's Black Bottom*, Yazoo 1071, n.d.

42. Gertrude "Ma" Rainey, "Gone Daddy Blues," Paramount 12526, Aug. 1927. Reissued on *Ma Rainey*, Milestone M-47021, 1974.

43. Gertrude "Ma" Rainey, "Misery Blues," Paramount 12508, Aug. 1927. Reissued on *Blues the World Forgot*, Biograph BLP-12001, n.d.

44. Bessie Smith, "Money Blues," Columbia 14137-D, May 4, 1926. Reissued on *Nobody's Blues but Mine*, Columbia CG 31093, 1972.

45. Bessie Smith, "Young Woman's Blues," Columbia 14179-D, Oct. 1926. Reissued on *Nobody's Blues but Mine*, Columbia CG 31093, 1972.

46. Bessie Smith, "Hateful Blues," Columbia 14023-D, Apr. 9, 1924. Reissued on *Empty Bed Blues*, Columbia CG 30450, 1972.

47. Bessie Smith, "Weeping Willow Blues," Columbia 14042-D, Sept. 26, 1924. Reissued on *Empty Bed Blues*, Columbia CG 30450, 1972.

48. Bessie Smith, "Yes, Indeed He Do," Columbia 14354-D, Aug. 24, 1928. Reissued on *Empty Bed Blues*, Columbia CG 30450, 1972.

49. Bessie Smith, "Safety Mama," Columbia 14634-D, Nov. 20, 1931. Reissued on *The World's Greatest Blues Singer*, Columbia CG 33, 1972.

50. See chap. 3 herein for a more comprehensive discussion of the role of travel in the postslavery male experience and, consequently, in the shaping of the blues. According to Houston Baker, "Afro-Americans—at the bottom even of the vernacular ladder in America—responded to the railroad as a 'meaningful symbol offering both economic progress and the possibility of aesthetic expression.' [James Alan McPherson, *Railroad: Trains and Train People in American Culture* (New York: Random House, 1976), p. 9.] This possibility came from the locomotive's drive and thrust, its promise of unrestrained mobility and unlimited freedom. The blues musician at the crossing . . . became an expert at reproducing or translating these locomotive energies." Baker, *Blues, Ideology, and Afro-American Literature*, p. 11. [Excerpt reprinted herein.]

51. Robert Johnson, "Hellhound on My Trail." Reissued on Robert Johnson, *The Complete Recordings*, Columbia compact discs C2K 46222, CK 46234, 1990.

52. See Paul Oliver, *The Meaning of the Blues* (New York: Collier, 1960), p. 85.

53. Bessie Smith, "Chicago Bound Blues," Columbia 14000-D, Dec. 4, 1923. Reissued on *Any Woman's Blues*, Columbia G 30126, 1972.

54. Chap. 3 herein examines themes of travel in Gertrude Rainey's blues.

55. Sandra Lieb, *Mother of the Blues: A Study of Ma Rainey* (Amherst: University of Massachusetts Press, 1983), p. 83.

56. A total of 160 Bessie Smith recordings are available today. However, if parts I and II of "Empty Bed Blues" are counted as one song—which they are in some instances (Brooks, for example)—then the total may be given as 159.

57. Alberta Hunter, "Down Hearted Blues"; Bessie Smith, "Down Hearted Blues," Columbia A3844, Feb. 16, 1923. Reissued on *The World's Greatest Blues Singer*, Columbia CG 33, 1972.

58. Paul Garon, *Blues and the Poetic Spirit* (New York: Da Capo, 1978), p. 33. [Excerpts reprinted herein.]

59. Bessie Smith, "Down Hearted Blues."

60. Gertrude "Ma" Rainey, "Barrel House Blues," Paramount 12082, Dec. 1923. Reissued on *Queen of the Blues*, Biograph BLP-12032, n.d.

61. Daphne Duval Harrison points out that women "employed the bragging, signifying language of males to boast of fine physical attributes and high-powered sexual ability. . . . The prurient nature of many of these blues led to a spate of community activism seeking to ban them. Black newspapers waged the battle against performers who included them in their repertoire and accused them of using lewd lyrics as a substitute for talent. This was clearly not the case because the best of the blues women sang sexual blues sometimes. Admittedly, some were openly lascivious and left little to the imagination." *Black Pearls*, p. 106.

62. Bessie Smith, "Mistreatin' Daddy." Columbia 14000-D, Dec. 4, 1923. Reissued on *Any Woman's Blues*, Columbia G 30126, 1972.

63. Gertrude "Ma" Rainey, "Honey, Where You Been So Long?" Paramount 12200, Mar. 1924. Reissued on *Queen of the Blues*, Biograph BLP-12032, n.d.

64. Gertrude "Ma" Rainey, "Lawd, Send Me a Man Blues," Paramount 12227, May 1924. Reissued on *Queen of the Blues*, Biograph BLP-12032, n.d.

65. Bessie Smith, "Baby Doll," Columbia 14147-D, May 4, 1926. Reissued on *Nobody's Blues but Mine*, Columbia CG 31093, 1972.

66. See Sara Evans's study, *Personal Politics: The Roots of Women's Liberation in the Civil Rights Movement and the New Left* (New York: Knopf, 1979).

67. See Michere Githae Mugo, *Orature and Human Rights* (Rome: Institute of South African Development Studies, NUL, Lesotho, 1991).

68. See Oakley's discussion of work and song, pp. 36–46.

69. Bessie Smith, "Yes, Indeed He Do."

70. Brooks, p. 143. [Excerpt reprinted herein.]

71. Bessie Smith, "Outside of That," Columbia A 3900, Apr. 30, 1923. Reissued on *The World's Greatest Blues Singer*, Columbia CG 33, 1972.

72. See Susan Schechter, *Women and Male Violence: The Visions and Struggles of the Battered Women's Movement* (Boston: South End, 1982), for an examination of the early anti-violence movement. An excellent recent study, specifically focusing on black women and domestic violence, is Beth Richie's *Compelled to Crime: The Gender Entrapment of Battered Women* (New York: Routledge, 1996).

73. References to the Chinese women's revolutionary tactic "speak bitterness" or "speak pains to recall pains" can be found in many of the second-wave feminist writings on consciousness-raising. See, for example, Robin Morgan's *Sisterhood Is Powerful: An Anthology of Writings from the Women's Liberation Movement* (New York: Vintage, 1970), p. xxv. See also Irene Pesliki's widely circulated document, "Resistances to Consciousness." It can be found in Morgan's *Sisterhood Is Powerful* and Leslie B. Tanner's edited volume *Voices from Women's Liberation* (New York: Signet, 1971).

74. Gertrude "Ma" Rainey, "Black Eye Blues," Paramount, 12963, Sept. 1928. Reissued on *Ma Rainey*, Milestone M-47021, 1974.

75. Bessie Smith. "Please Help Me Get Him off My Mind," Columbia 14375, Aug. 24, 1928. Reissued on *Empty Bed Blues*, Columbia CG 30450, 1972.

76. Bessie Smith, "It Won't Be You," Columbia 14338-D, Feb. 21, 1928. Reissued on *Empty Bed Blues*, Columbia CG 30450, 1972.

77. Bessie Smith, "Slow and Easy Man," Columbia 14384-D, Aug. 24, 1928. Reissued on *Empty Bed Blues*, Columbia CG 30450, 1972.

78. Bessie Smith, "Eavesdropper's Blues," Columbia 14010-D, Jan. 9, 1924. Reissued on *Any Women's Blues*, Columbia C 30126, 1972.

79. Bessie Smith, "Love Me Daddy Blues," Columbia 14060-D, Dec. 12, 1924. Reissued on *The Empress*, Columbia CG 30818, 1972.

80. Bessie Smith, "Hard Driving Papa," Columbia 14137-D, May 4, 1926. Reissued on *Nobody's Blues but Mine*, Columbia CG 31093, 1972.

81. Bessie Smith, "'Tain't Nobody's Bizness If I Do," Columbia A3898, Apr. 26, 1923. Reissued on *The World's Greatest Blues Singer*, Columbia CG 33, 1972.

82. Brooks, p. 109. [Excerpt reprinted herein.]

83. Bessie Smith, "'Tain't Nobody's Bizness If I Do."

84. Ibid.

85. Gertrude "Ma" Rainey, "Sweet Rough Man," Paramount 12926, Sept. 1928. Reissued on *Ma Rainey*, Milestone M-47021, 1974.

86. Lieb, p. 120.

87. Carby, p. 18.

88. Rainey, "Sweet Rough Man."

89. "All magic is word magic, incantation and exorcism, blessing and curse. Through Nommo, the word, man establishes his mastery over things. 'In the beginning was the Word, and the Word was with God, and the Word was God,' so begins the gospel according to St. John, and it looks as if Nommo and the *logos* of St. John agreed. Yet the apostle continues: 'The same (i.e. the word) was in the beginning with God. All things were made by it and without it was not anything made that was made.' In the gospels the word remains with God, and man has to testify to it and proclaim it. Nommo, on the other hand, was also, admittedly, with Amma, or God, in the beginning, but beyond that everything comes into being only through the word, and as there is Muntu [human being], the word is with the muntu. Nommo does not stand above and beyond the earthly world. *Logos* becomes flesh only in Christ, but Nommo becomes 'flesh' everywhere. According to the apostle, *Logos* has made all things, once for all, to become as they are, and since then all generated things remain as they are, and undergo no further transformation. Nommo, on the other hand, goes on unceasingly creating and procreating, creating even gods." Janheinz Jahn, *Muntu: The New African Culture* (New York: Grove, 1961), p. 132. [Excerpt reprinted herein.]

90. Paula Giddings, *When and Where I Enter: The Impact of Black Women on Race and Sex in America* (New York: Morrow, 1984). See chaps. 5 and 6.

91. See Ida B. Wells, *Crusade for Justice: The Autobiography of Ida B. Wells*, ed. Alfreda M. Duster (Chicago and London: University of Chicago Press, 1970).

92. See Paula Giddings for a historical account of the origins of the myth of the black rapist as a political weapon (p. 27).

93. See Alice Walker's discussion of the attack on *The Color Purple* by prominent black men in *The Same River Twice: Honoring the Difficult: A Meditation on Life, Spirit, Art, and the Making of the Film "The Color Purple," Ten Years Later* (New York: Simon & Schuster, 1996).

94. Bessie Smith, "Black Mountain Blues," Columbia 14554-D, June 22, 1930. Reissued on *The World's Greatest Blues Singer*, Columbia CG 33, 1972.

95. Bessie Smith, "Sinful Blues," Columbia 114052-D, Dec. 11, 1924. Reissued on *The Empress*, Columbia CG 30818, 1972.

96. Gertrude "Ma" Rainey, "See See Rider Blues," Paramount 12252, Dec. 1925. Reissued on *Ma Rainey*, Milestone M-47021, 1974.

97. Gertrude "Ma" Rainey, "Rough and Tumble Blues," Paramount 12303, 1926. Reissued on *The Immortal Ma Rainey*, Milestone MLP-2001, 1966.

98. Bessie Smith, "Them's Graveyard Words," Columbia 14209-D, Mar. 3, 1927. Reissued on *The Empress*, Columbia CG 30818, 1972.

99. Gertrude "Ma" Rainey, "Cell Bound Blues," Paramount 12257, 1925. Reissued on *The Immortal Ma Rainey*, Milestone MLP-2001, 1966.

100. Bessie Smith, "Sing Sing Prison Blues," Columbia 14051-D, Dec. 6, 1924. Reissued on *The Empress*, Columbia CG 30818, 1972.

101. Bessie Smith, "Send Me to the 'Lectric Chair," Columbia 14209-D, Mar. 3, 1927. Reissued on *The Empress*, Columbia, CG 30818, 1972. A barlow is a large pocketknife with one blade.

102. Bessie Smith, "Hateful Blues."

103. Albertson, pp. 132–33.

104. Harrison, pp. 111, 64.

105. Ida Cox, "Wild Women Don't Have the Blues," Paramount 12228, 1924. Reissued on *Wild Women Don't Have the Blues*, Riverside RLP 9374, n.d.

106. Bessie Smith, "Easy Come, Easy Go Blues," Columbia 14005-D, Jan. 10, 1924. Reissued on *Any Woman's Blues*, Columbia G 30126, 1972.

107. Gertrude "Ma" Rainey, "Prove It on Me Blues," Paramount 12668, June 1928. Reissued on *Ma Rainey*, Milestone M-47021, 1974.

108. Lieb, p. 125.

109. *Lesbian Concentrate: A Lesbianthology of Songs and Poems*, Olivia Records MU 29729, 1977.

110. Carby, p. 18.

111. See text of Memphis Willie B. Borum's "Bad Girl Blues" in Eric Sackheim, ed., *The Blues Line* (New York: Schirmer, 1968), p. 288.

112. Gertrude "Ma" Rainey, "Sissy Blues," Paramount 12384, 1928. Reissued on *Oh My Babe Blues*, Biograph BLP-12011, n.d.

10 The Blues as Influence

IN addition to infusing energy into literature, the blues have invigorated the work of artists in other fields such as painting, sculpture, and other types of music. Jazz commentators have long recognized that our greatest jazz musicians have almost to a person been expert blues players, mining in this bedrock form for ideas they could mold and develop into an emotionally satisfying style, as Martin Williams elucidates beautifully in his exposition of the blues core of Charlie Parker's work (and Edward Brooks in his discussion of Louis Armstrong's work in the section on style). The father of gospel music, the venerable Thomas A. Dorsey, himself spent his early recording days in the bands of Ma Rainey and Tampa Red, and his gospel music is infused with a blues feel (though, it should be pointed out, the blues has drawn some of its stylistic inspiration from the church as well—see the introduction to "The Blues and Religion"). Mahalia Jackson, too, was enthralled by the blues tradition, haunted by the singing of Bessie Smith, and the "Queen of Gospel" applied some of Smith's techniques in her own performances. Rhythm and blues, country, rock and roll, rock, folk, heavy metal, rap—none would be what they are today without the blues. A short list of those in other genres heavily influenced by the blues would include the following important figures:

Country and Bluegrass	*Western Swing*	*Pop*
Jimmy Rodgers	Bob Wills	Peggy Lee
Merle Travis	Milton Brown	The Boswell Sisters
Hank Williams	Smokey Wood	Louis Prima

Bill Monroe	Cliff Bruner	Frank Sinatra
Earl Scruggs	Bob Dunn	Billy Eckstine

Many in rock and roll, from Chuck Berry, Little Richard, Fats Domino, Elvis Presley, and Jerry Lee Lewis on down would be included as well. Charles Wolfe's survey of white country singers in the blues idiom brings to the fore a number of talented musicians who, rather than being merely imitative, personalized the blues so that it reflected their own artistic aesthetic, most prominent among them the "Father of Country Music," Jimmie Rodgers. Rodgers in turn inspired many imitators of his trademark blue yodels, including material such as Walter Vincson's 1930 recording of "Mississippi Yodelin' Blues" on down to John Jackson's various recordings of Rodgers's songs, completing the cycle of coming from the African American musical tradition through Rodgers and back into the tradition.

As Eric von Schmidt and Jim Rooney describe, those in the folk constellation who drew upon the blues for inspiration celebrated it wholeheartedly. However, some could be well-meaning starry-eyed romantics, occasionally misguided, insensitive, and even selfish even as they helped usher in an era of unprecedented white appreciation of the blues. Still, such giants of the folk music scene as Woody Guthrie, Pete Seeger, Dave van Ronk, John Fahey, Bob Dylan, Doc Watson, Richie Havens, Davy Graham, JoAnn Kelly, and Rory Block have succeeded in translating the blues into their own idioms.

European and American composers in the classical tradition have also been attracted by the blues allure. We think of the ballet *La Creation Du Monde* (1923) by Darius Milhaud, by turns exotic and swirling, heavy and dejected, and longingly nostalgic—and contrastingly cacophonous and euphonious—in its positioning of a blues tonality as part of the process and product of creation. George Gershwin produced an explosive mix of Liszt, jazz, and blues in his triumphant *Rhapsody in Blue* (1924)—commissioned by the so-called King of Jazz, Paul Whiteman and premiered at jazz's society coming out party "An Experiment in Modern Music" at Aeolian Hall—and his sonorous "Andante con moto e poco rubato" from *Preludes for Piano* (1926) is a marvel of understatement and control. William Grant Still's *Lenox Avenue* (1937), a ballet set in Harlem sporting a blues sequence at a house rent party, is only one of more than 150 works by the composer, many of which drew on his African American heritage, though he saw himself not as a black composer but "an American composer who happens to be a Negro." Igor Stravinsky's *Ebony Concerto* (1945), commissioned by Woody Herman and recorded under Stravinsky's direction by the Columbia Jazz Combo with

Benny Goodman as featured soloist; Leonard Bernstein's *Prelude, Fugue, and Riffs* (1949), also commissioned by Herman and recorded by Goodman; the William Russo composition recorded featuring the Siegel-Schwall Band, *Three Pieces for Blues Band and Symphony Orchestra* (1968)—and, conversely, blues pianist–harp-player Corky Siegel's fascinating *Chamber Blues* (Alligator CD 4824); and the Pulitzer Prize-winning *Blood on the Fields* (1994) and "In This House, On This Morning" (1992) of Wynton Marsalis: these people have also followed their composers' fascination with the blues tradition as an antidote to the stale, the stodgy, the sluggish, the shrinking musical culture with which they struggled as they followed their muses unabashedly into vernacular territory. Indeed, we have not explored here theatrical works, such as Kurt Weill's opera *Street Scene* (1947), with its first act "Blues: I Got a Marble and a Star," libretto by Langston Hughes, or the work of distinguished jazz composers and arrangers in the great Fletcher Henderson–Duke Ellington tradition such as John Carisi ("Israel"), George Russell ("Jack's Blues"), Gil Evans ("Blues For Pablo"), Oliver Nelson ("Blues and the Abstract Truth"), and Quincy Jones, some of whom also worked on pop sessions and in TV and film, all of which serves to indicate the inroads blues was making on a comprehensive cross-section of American culture. While some critics have lamented the forays of classical music into blues territory as producing uneasy grafts at best and a culturally traitorous pandering to the condescending haughtiness of the guardians of taste and culture at worst, others see the entree of the blues into the upper echelons of high society and culture as evidence of their communicative power and a vindication of the claim to legitimacy as a serious art form.

Visual artists have also made the pilgrimage to the blues; Winold Reiss, Aaron Douglas, Archibald Motley, Jr., Romare Bearden, Jackson Pollock, and James Thomas, to name a few. Art historian and curator Richard J. Powell has discussed the ways in which a blues aesthetic—which he characterizes as relating to twentieth-century art associated with African American "issues and ideals," grass-roots values, rhythms, and humanism—informs and invigorates various visual artists. For Powell, the descriptive term "blues" encompasses the breadth of Afro-American musical forms such as ragtime, be-bop, doo-wop, and hip-hop, being an "affecting, evocative presence" in them all and thus standing out as an enduring presence in its own right and a fertile, prolific taproot in the clearing. It is, in fact, a tribute to the breadth and resilience of the blues that what has been characterized by some as a limited form and tradition has neither died out or dried out or dried up as a source of inspiration throughout the world.

One of the most controversial issues regarding influence in the blues world is that of the legitimacy and value of blues by white artists. There have been versions/imitations/rip-offs (write your own caption) of blues by white artists since very early in the history of recorded blues, inevitable given the nature of the milieu in which old-time singers traded "common stock" tunes (such as "John Henry," "Bully of the Town," "Careless Love," and many fiddle and banjo songs) that were widely performed in a variety of settings, especially the minstrel, medicine, and road shows, but also just informal street-corner and country dance settings. White performers, attracted by the hypnotic lure of such an expressive, fixed but flexible form, began adding blues to their repertoires, some in imitation of African American performers, others with an original take of their own on the genre, but most clearly distinguishable from African American performers. Over the years, common strategies have been to imitate a performance or recording (as in Eric Clapton's *From the Cradle*), imitate the style of an artist or "school" of blues performers (Jeremy Spencer's Elmore James, Stevie Ray Vaughan's Albert King), combine the blues with country (Jimmie Rodgers and Tommy Duncan) or jazz (George Barnes and Mose Allison) influences, or employ the trappings and techniques of rock and heavy metal, themselves gleaned from blues innovations (Roy Buchanan and Stevie Ray Vaughan). In fact, there have been African American artists who have approached the blues in this fashion as well.

Those who question the authenticity of white blues artists (represented here by Paul Garon's sharply worded section from *Blues and the Poetic Spirit*) point out the sociopolitical and aesthetic origins of the blues in African American experience that renders the soul of the music unattainable to any but those who have actually lived as African Americans. For them, white blues performances are a continuation of the tradition of commercial rip-offs that is represented by the often racist minstrel tradition. In this instance, imitation is the sincerest form of battery, committing artistic and economic violence on the creators and longtime sustainers of the music, since the unfair advantage of greater access to a variety of commercial venues makes success more accessible to white performers than African American ones, extending a long tradition of whites reaping what African Americans have sown. Not only that, but the appropriation of the blues by whites can also be seen as changing the original meaning and purpose of the blues tradition, since its role as an expressive art frequently served in the African American community as a (sometimes covert, sometimes overt) vehicle for protest, an expression of solidarity, and an expression of pride in the beauty of African American art and the indomitable will to survive. This appropriation creates the ironic situation of the "oppressor" employing the sociopolitical and aesthetic vehicle that the oppressed uses to object to the oppressor and affirm themselves—and reaps the benefits from the exploitation once again. These opponents argue that most white performers implicitly acknowledge their illegitimacy by straining after their idea of an African American singing style or stage manner, reinforcing the notion that they cannot sound like themselves and still be blues artists. Ironically, since one of the major aims of the blues is to sound like oneself, to generate one's own distinctive voice and sound, the strategy is an egregious violation of the aesthetic of the tradition itself. As Amiri Baraka summed up succinctly in *The Music: Reflections on Jazz and Blues,* "Blues is African-American" (262).

On the other hand, defenders of white blues point out that art is art, that it does not construct restrictive boundaries to render itself unavailable to anyone, and that such dismissive notions actually violate the spirit of artistic creation. If we can enjoy the performance as performance, blindfolded to "extraneous" issues such as ethnicity and time period (some see the performance rendered in a style created in/associated with an earlier era as, additionally, anachronistic and objectionable), then we should not concern ourselves with issues irrelevant to the performed art itself. Furthermore, the notion of "soul" as a defining mark of the blues is esoteric and ambiguous, definable in a variety of subjective ways, but always in the "ear of the behearer." And one must not downplay the role of technique in the production of blues either formally or "soulfully," and technique is something that can be learned and passed on cross-culturally and cross-generationally. They point out that a number of African Americans have appreciated, even been "fooled by," the work of white performers (such as John Jackson thinking that Uncle Dave Macon was black), and since the 1960s a number of well-known blues artists, Muddy Waters, B. B. King, and John Lee Hooker among them, have employed, accepted, and/or praised white blues performers, instrumentalists in particular (but sometimes stopping short of lauding their vocal abilities—one recalls Zora Neale Hurston's disdain for "the white damsels who try to sing the blues" in "Characteristics of Negro Expression"). For them, music is music, and the notion that whites are unable to sing the blues is racist and exclusionary, counterproductive to unifying blacks and whites. It is likewise counter to the tradition that blues and rhythm and blues have had of breaking down the racial barriers symbolized concretely by the ropes and barriers that separated whites from blacks at southern dances, which a number of artists report sometimes gave way to the joyous abandon produced by the blues performers on stage. Such irreconcilable differences will likely forever divorce the "purists" from the "progressives," bifurcating an audience that, each side, takes its arguments, and its music, as seriously as the other.

The logical extension of this question as it has been debated over and over by scholars was raised by Alan Dundes in *Mother Wit from the Laughing Barrel,* and it is worth dropping the bomb here, in the midst of a volume where a good portion of the material would be rendered weak and/or useless if we respond to Dundes' musing in the affirmative: "If being a Negro is a prerequisite to playing the blues, it may also be one for understanding all the nuances of the blues" (470).

Recommended Further Readings

Amiri Baraka. *The Music: Reflections on Jazz and Blues.* New York: William Morrow, 1987.
William Ferris. "Vision in Afro-American Folk Art: The Sculpture of James Thomas." *Journal of American Folklore* 88 (1975).
Paul Garon. "White Blues." Joel Slotnikoff's Blues World, www.bluesworld.com.
Lawrence Hoffman. "Guest Editorial." *Guitar Player* (August 1990): 18.
Bob Margolin. "Blues and Race." *Blues Revue Quarterly* 13 (Summer 1994): 9–10.
Peter van der Merwe. *Origins of the Popular Style.* Oxford: Clarendon, 1989.
Richard J. Powell, ed. *The Blues Aesthetic: Black Culture and Modernism.* Washington, D.C.: Washington Project for the Arts, 1989.
Tony Russell. *Blacks, Whites, and Blues.* London: Studio Vista, 1970.

From "Charlie Parker
The Burden of Innovation"

Martin Williams

A GREAT deal of misinformation has been put into print about music in which Parker was a major figure. It was at first called, onomatopoetically, bebop, then modern jazz. It has been said that the boppers often made their compositions by adopting the chord sequences of standard popular songs and writing new melody lines to them. So they did, and so had at least two generations of jazzmen before them. It has been said that they undertook the similar practice of improvising with only a chord sequence as their guide, with no reference to a theme melody itself—in classicist terms "harmonic variations," in the terms of jazz critic André Hodeir "chorus phrase." But the practice had become a norm and commonplace by the late 'thirties to men like Teddy Wilson, Henry "Red" Allen, Roy Eldridge, Johnny Hodges, Ben Webster, Lester Young, Coleman Hawkins, Charlie Christian, and hundreds of others; indeed one might say that in their work it had reached a kind of deadlock of perfection. For that matter, one can find choruses of nonthematic improvising in the recordings of players who were leaders in the 'twenties and earlier—Louis Armstrong, Earl Hines, Bix Beiderbecke, Jack Teagarden, Sidney Bechet, even Bunk Johnson.

The practices are, basically, as old as the blues. Certainly King Oliver's three classic 1923 choruses on *Dippermouth Blues* have no thematic reference to the melody of that piece. One might say that jazz musicians spent the late 'twenties and the 'thirties discovering that they could "play the blues" on chords of *Sweet Sue, I Ain't Got Nobody, Sweet Georgia Brown, You're Driving Me Crazy, I Got Rhythm, Tea for Two,* and the rest.

What Parker and bebop provided was a renewed musical language (or at least a renewed dialect) with which the old practices could be replenished and continued. The renewed language came, in part, as have all innovations in jazz, from an assimilation of devices from European music. But a deliberate effort to import "classical" harmony or melodic devices might have led jazzmen to all sorts of affectation and spuriousness.

Like Louis Armstrong before him, Charlie Parker was called on to change the language of jazz, to reinterpret its fundamentals and give it a way to continue. He did that with

---

a musical brilliance that was irrevocable. But he did it simply by following his own artistic impulses, and Parker's innovations represent a truly organic growth for jazz and have little to do with the spurious impositions of a self-consciously "progressive" jazzman.

The music of Charlie Parker and Dizzy Gillespie represented a way for jazz to continue, but that way was not just a matter of new devices; it also had to do with a change in even the function of the music. Parker's work implied that jazz could no longer be thought of only as an energetic background for the barroom, as a kind of vaudeville, as a vehicle for dancers. From now on it was somehow a music to be listened to, as many of its partisans had said it should have been all along. We will make it that, Parker seemed to say, or it will perish. The knowledge that he was sending it along the road must have been at times a difficult burden to carry.

Today we are apt to see Parker as the most important of the pioneer modernists, chiefly because his influence has proved more general, widespread, and lasting; and because, for most of his brief and falling-star career, his talent grew and his invention seemed constant. Rightly or wrongly, we are apt to think of Dizzy Gillespie's influence as chiefly on brassmen, Parker's on everyone. And we know that Thelonious Monk's ideas were rather different from either Parker's or Gillespie's, and that their real importance would emerge only later.

It is perhaps hard for some of us to realize now, so long after the fact, what a bitter controversy modern jazz brought about, but it is instructive to look briefly at that controversy. Among other things, its opponents declared that the modernists had introduced harmonic values that were alien to jazz. Well, once jazz has embraced European harmony in any aspect, as it did far longer ago than 1900, it has by implication embraced it all, as long as the right players came along to show just how it could be unpretentiously included and assimilated into the jazz idiom. But the curiousness of this argument is clearly dramatized in the fact that bop's opponents are apt to approve of pianist Art Tatum and tenor saxophonist Don Byas, both of whom were harmonically as sophisticated and knowledgeable as Parker and Gillespie. But Byas does not really *sound* like a modernist, because rhythmically he is not a modernist. And rhythm is the crux of the matter.

The crucial thing about the bebop style is that its basis came from the resources of jazz itself, and it came about in much the same way that innovation had come about in the past. That basis is rhythmic, and it involves rhythmic subdivision. Any other way would surely have been disastrous. We should not talk about harmonic exactness or substitute chords and the rest before we have talked about rhythm.

Like Louis Armstrong, Charlie Parker expanded jazz rhythmically and, although his rhythmic changes are intricately and subtly bound up with his ideas of harmony and melody, the rhythmic change is fundamental. "Bebop," however unfortunate a name for the music, does represent it rhythmically and hence rather accurately, much as "swing" accurately represents the rhythmic momentum that Armstrong introduced.

We may say that Armstrong's rhythms are based on a quarter-note. Parker's idea of rhythm is based on an eighth-note. Of course I am speaking of melodic rhythm, the rhythm that the players' accents make as they offer their melodies, not of the basic time or the basic percussion.

For that matter, to speak of rhythm, melodic line, and harmony as if they were entities is a critic's necessary delusion. But such separations can clarify much. To many ears attuned to the music of Coleman Hawkins or Roy Eldridge and the rhythmic conceptions they use, Parker's music seemed at first pointlessly fussy and decorative—a flurry of technique. Players at first found Parker's sophisticated blues lines like *Relaxin' at Camarillo* and *Billie's Bounce* almost impossible to play, not because of their notes but because their strong melodic lines demanded such a fresh way of accenting and phrasing. But once one is in touch with Parker rhythmically, every note, every phrase, becomes direct, functional musical expression. And of course I am giving only a rough rule of thumb; each style is more complex than such a description makes it seem. Parker, who showed that his notes and accents might land on heavy beats, weak beats, and the various places in between beats, was the most imaginative player rhythmically in jazz history, as his one dazzlingly intricate chorus on *Ornithology* might easily attest.

I do not think that one can hear the impeccable swing of a player like Lionel Hampton without sensing that some sort of future crisis was at hand in the music, that—to exaggerate only slightly—a kind of jazz as melodically dull as a set of tone drums might well be in the offing. In guitarist Charlie Christian, it seems to me, one hears both the problem and the basis for its solution, a basis which Lester Young had helped provide him with. Christian's swing was perfect. He was an outstanding melodist. And at times his rhythmic imagination carried him to the verge of some new discoveries.

To say that fresh rhythmic invention is basic to Parker's music is not to ignore the fact that he also possessed one of the most fertile harmonic imaginations that jazz has ever known. In this respect one can mention only Art Tatum in the same paragraph with him. Tatum must have been an enormous influence, one feels sure, harmonically and even in note values. But Tatum's imagination was harmonic and ornamental, and Parker—although he had a melodic vocabulary in which (as with most musicians) certain phrases recur—was perhaps the greatest *inventor* of melodies jazz has seen.

Still, one is brought up short by the realization that a "typical" Parker phrase turns out to be much the same phrase one had heard years before from, say, Ben Webster. The secret is of course that Parker inflects, accents, and pronounces that phrase so differently that one simply may not recognize it.

What was Parker's heritage? Such questions are always vexing for so original a talent. Someone has suggested that he combined on alto the two tenor saxophone traditions: the sophisticated and precise harmonic sense of Coleman Hawkins and his follower, Don Byas; and the rhythmic originality, variety, and looseness of phrase and penchant for horizontal, linear melody of Lester Young and his follower, guitarist Charlie Christian. But the closest thing on previous jazz records to Parker's mature phrasing that I know of are a handful of Louis Armstrong's most brilliant trumpet solos—*West End Blues* from 1928, *Sweethearts On Parade* from 1930, *Between the Devil and the Deep Blue Sea* from 1931, *Basin Street Blues* from 1933. In them we clearly hear Parker's melodic rhythm in embryo. No one jazzman, not even Roy Eldridge, undertook to develop that aspect of Armstrong until Charlie Parker.

However, it is fitting that Parker's first recorded solo, on *Swingmatism* with Jay McShann, does owe so much to Lester Young. Whatever his debt to others (and to himself) for the genius of his style, Parker had obviously absorbed Young's language soundly and thoroughly. Charlie Parker's second recorded solo is also indicative—brilliant but perhaps exasperating. On McShann's *Hootie Blues* he played what might have been a beautifully developed and rhythmically striking chorus, one which introduces almost everything Parker was to spend the rest of his life refining. But the solo is not finally satisfactory; he interrupts it in the seventh bar to interpolate a trite riff figure. Granted that he showed the sound intuition of knowing that a contrastingly simple idea was precisely right at that moment in his melody, a simply commonplace one was not.

The best introduction to Parker's music is probably his remarkable pair of choruses on *Lady Be Good.* Stylistically he begins rather conservatively, in a late swing period manner rather like Lester Young's, and he gradually transforms this into the style that Parker himself offered jazz.

These choruses are melodically fascinating in another aspect. Just as *Embraceable You* is organized around the interweaving and permutation of one melodic fragment, *Lady Be Good* uses several which emerge as the choruses unfold. Parker's first few notes are Gershwin's, but he uses these notes as the opening to quite a different melodic phrase. His second phrase is a simple riff. His third phrase echoes his opening Gershwin-esque line, but in a kind of reverse-echo reassortment of its notes, and it also has something of the character of his second riff phrase—in a sense it combines and continues both. And so on.

At the same time this brilliance was delivered in the most adverse circumstances, at a "Jazz at the Philharmonic" concert in the spring of 1946 in Los Angeles. The solo thereby refutes what is patently true, that Parker's playing really belonged only in the small improvising quintets he established as the norm. The circumstances were made even more trying by the fact that, as Parker begins to move further away from the conventions of an earlier style, moving in his own direction, he is rewarded with a wholly unnecessary background riff from the other musicians on the stage at the time. It is apt to distract a listener, but it apparently did not distract Parker. Still, the solo is delivered with a kind of personal and technical strain and pressure in his alto sound that was foreign to Parker at his best.

Almost opposite to the "classic" development of a *Lady Be Good* is another public recording made with a far more appropriate group, the Carnegie Hall concert of 1947 with Dizzy Gillespie. Here is Parker the daring romantic, using passing and altered harmonies, complex movements and countermovements of rhythm, unexpected turns of melody. Much of it is delivered with an emotional directness that makes the complexity functional and necessary. The celebrated stop-time break on *A Night in Tunisia* played on the same occasion shows Parker's intuitive sense of balance at its best: an alternation of tensions and releases so rapid, terse, and complete that it may seem to condense all of his best work into one melodic leap of four bars. One knows that on this occasion Parker was out to "get" his friend and rival Gillespie, and Gillespie was playing as if he were not to be gotten. This personal element influences the aesthetics of the music, sometimes for the worse. There was at times a sharper than usual edge, an apparent strain, to Parker's sound.

No one who has listened with receptive ears to Charlie Parker play the blues could doubt that aspect of his authenticity as a jazzman. Nor should one fail to understand after hearing his music that the emotional basis of his work is the urban, Southwestern blues idiom that we also hear running through every performance by the Basie orchestra of the late 'thirties. *Parker's Mood* (especially take 1) is as indigenously the blues as a Bessie Smith record, more so than several James P. Johnson records. But one also senses immediately the increase in the emotional range of the idiom that Parker's technical innovations make possible.

Charlie Parker was a bluesman, a great *natural* bluesman without calculated funkiness or rustic posturing. It has been said that all the great jazzmen can play the blues, but that is obviously not so. Earl Hines has played wonderful solos in the blues form, but with little blues feeling. Neither did James P. Johnson, Fats Waller, nor any of the classic "stride" men. Johnny Hodges can play the blues; Benny Carter not. But without counting, one would guess that perhaps 40 per cent of Parker's recordings were blues. The best of them are reassessments and lyric expansions of traditional blues phrases and ideas, ideas reevaluated by Parker's particular sensibility. The classic example is probably *Parker's Mood,* but there are dozens of others. And his "written" (more properly, memorized) blues melodies are also a valid introduction to his work. On the first record date under his own name he produced two blues. *Now's the Time* is an obviously traditional piece (so traditional that its riff became a rhythm-and-blues hit as *The Hucklebuck*) which is given an original twist or two by Parker, particularly in its last couple of bars. But *Billie's Bounce* is a strikingly original, continuous twelve-bar melody, in which phrases and fragments of phrases repeat and echo and organize the line, and in which traditional riffs and ideas leap in and out rephrased, reaccented, and formed into something striking, fresh, and unequalled.

A Lighter Shade of Blue
White Country Blues

Charles Wolfe

IT WAS a rainy Friday morning in early November, and at the temporary recording studio on Peachtree Street in downtown Atlanta, engineers were busy checking their equipment for another day's work. Frank Walker, who was in charge of Columbia's field recording unit, and his assistant Bill Brown, a small, sharp-tongued man who was Walker's liaison with the local talent, were looking over the list of performers scheduled for the 4th. The team had been in town for a week, and they had already recorded some fifty-five masters; today they hoped to get at least twenty more. Though the idea of taking a portable unit into various southern cities to get more authentic examples of blues, gospel, and hillbilly music was still new, it was already proving its worth. A couple of years before, Columbia, like most other major labels, had created a separate series of "race" recordings and another of "hillbilly" music. Columbia referred to the former as its 14000 series, and the latter as the 15000 series ("Old Familiar Tunes"). A couple of hundred records had been issued in each series, many of them selling surprisingly well. But, though the music was segregated when it came out on disk, in the field it was a different story. As Walker later recalled, "If you were recording in Texas, well, you might have a week in which you recorded your country music; cowboy music thrown in and a little Spanish music from across the border. . . . And the next week might be devoted to so-called 'race music,' because they both came from the same area, and with the same general ideas."

Today's schedule in Atlanta was even more varied. First up was a set of sweet string-band sides by McMichen's Melody Man; next came a set of blues by Charlie Lincoln (Laughing Charlie Hicks), the brother of "Barbecue Bob" Hicks, one of Columbia's more successful blues singers. Brown had approved six songs for Lincoln, including "Hard Luck Blues" and "Chain Gang Blues." After lunch came Riley Puckett, the blind yodeler and singer who had become the best-known country artist in the 15000 series. Finally, there were the Allen Brothers, Lee and Austin. They were something quite different.

Walker had recorded them the previous spring, and their release of "Salty Dog Blues," issued a couple of months earlier, was selling very well. (It would eventually sell around

---

Reprinted from Lawrence Cohn, ed., *Nothing but the Blues: The Music and the Musicians* (New York: Abbeville Press, 1993), 233–63. Used by permission of the author.

18,000 copies, making it a modest hit by 1920s standards.) Although it was called a blues, and although it bore some relation to the version of "Salty Dog" recorded by the venerable bluesman Papa Charlie Jackson, it didn't sound much like the classic country blues Walker was familiar with. Buoyed by Austin's vocal solo, propelled by a tenor banjo, kazoo, and guitar, it bounced along at a brisk tempo, full of jivey patter, asides, and hey hey heys. Nonetheless, it was selling, and the Allens seemed to have a lot of other pieces like it. Today they were scheduled for four songs, three of which were called blues: "Chattanooga Blues," "Coal Mine Blues," and "Laughin' and Cryin' Blues."

After lunch, the two young Allens appeared in the studio. They didn't fit the stereotype of blues singers. They looked like a couple of well-mannered college students, dressed in double-breasted suits, Austin's cowlick drooping over his left eye, instruments carefully tuned. And they were young. Lee was only twenty-one, Austin (who did most of the singing) twenty-six. They had been born on Monteagle Mountain, about fifty miles north of Chattanooga. Lee had even attended the prestigious St. Andrews prep school there, at about the same time as James Agee did—the famed writer who would produce the classic work on Depression America, *Let Us Now Praise Famous Men.* The Allens had grown up listening to the old ballads and sentimental songs their mother sang, but they heard little of the blues until they had grown up and moved on down to Chattanooga. That town was hardly a blues center—though it had produced Bessie Smith—but the Allens did get a chance to hear guitarist May Bell, who performed on riverboats in the area, and the busking team of Evans and McClain, who were later to record as the Two Poor Boys. They were fascinated and soon created their own particular style of the blues. Now, on November 4, 1927, they were ready for the next chapter of their recording career.

They waited for the engineer to turn on the little green light, and the Allens launched into take one of what they thought was their best new song, "Chattanooga Blues":

> Oh I thought I heard my baby cry,
> Wow wow wow-wow, wow wow wow-wow,
> Thought I heard my baby cry,
> Oh she cried like she never cried before.

The lyrics were hardly original or even evocative, but Austin's strong, heavily accented voice carried them through. Lee took a break, forging a raggy, infectious kazoo solo. "Percolate, mama, percolate," urged Austin. There were a few more topical references to give the commonplace stanzas some sense of identity: references to Chattanooga's hospitality, and to the "lock and dam" of the Tennessee River. Then the yellow light went on in the studio, and the brothers wound down. That take was history.

After a couple of hours, the Allens finished their four recordings, and left the studio. On their way out, Walker gave them the monthly catalog supplement to the new Columbia releases, showing them that Columbia 15175, their "Salty Dog Blues," was featured on the new list. The Allens left pleased, their dreams of a record career a good deal stronger. They returned to their circuit of radio broadcasts and theater dates around Chattanooga, and to their work with rural medicine shows. Walker, for his part, didn't think much of two of the songs cut that day, but he judged that "Chattanooga Blues" had as much of a chance of hitting well as "Salty Dog." He packed the wax masters for shipment to New York and went on with his session.

Then something odd happened. Columbia's New York office, overwhelmed by the dozens of masters Walker was shipping up, familiar with neither southern accents nor music, listened to the Allens' sides and decided the pair was black. Accordingly, their next coupling, "Chattanooga Blues" and "Laughin' and Cryin' Blues," was issued on the 14000 Race series (14266). It was rushed out on December 20, 1927, just six weeks after the session. Back in Chattanooga, the Allens were overjoyed at how soon their new record was out—until they noticed it was in what the local record dealer called the Race Series. They frantically wired Walker to ask him to correct the mistake before it went any further, but over six thousand records had already been pressed, and there was not much he could do. The brothers then contacted a local attorney, who initiated on their behalf a $250,000 lawsuit against Columbia for damaging their reputations.

The suit got Walker to thinking that he might be able to issue the record in the 15000 series as well as the 14000 series. The Allens decided to go to the spring sessions in Atlanta, which went off well enough, but, after a final talk with Walker, the brothers decided to sever their ties with Columbia. A few weeks later, they dropped the lawsuit and signed with Victor.

The Allens recorded a total of thirty-six releases (seventy-two songs) on Columbia, Victor, and Vocalion. They became known for their topical blues, such as "Chain Store Blues" (a diatribe against early supermarket chains), "Tipple Blues" (about a coal-mining camp in Lynch, Kentucky), "Roll Down the Line" (derived from the convict-lease system of the 1890s), "Price of Cotton Blues," and (for Victor in 1930) "Jake Walk Blues"—about an epidemic of palsy caused by drinking Jamaica Ginger during the height of Prohibition. The record sold over twenty thousand copies, making it one of Victor's best sellers for the year. Their version of "A New Salty Dog" also sold well, staying in print on Bluebird and Montgomery Ward reissues well into the 1930s. In the latter half of their career, which ended in 1934, the Allens also developed a taste for the rowdy, double-entendre blues similar to the kind of stuff turned out by groups like the Hokum Boys. These included "Slide, Daddy, Slide," "Pile-Drivin' Papa," "Shake It, Ida, Shake It," "Warm Knees Blues," and "Misbehavin' Mama." Their version of "(Mama Don't Allow) No Low Down Hanging Around" (1930), with its well-known line, "Come here mama, just look at Kate, / She's doing her loving in a Cadillac Eight," sold well and was copied by other singers. But the peak of the Allens' creativity, 1930–32, happened to coincide with the worst years of the Depression, and their later records simply had no chance. "Shanghai Rooster Blues" sold only 3,500 copies in 1930, and "Price of Cotton Blues" sold a meager 2,700. Many of the later Victors sold fewer than 2,000 copies—no worse than other releases in the series, but not enough to support a career. After a stint in the theater, the brothers broke up, Austin staying in New York, Lee returning to Tennessee to work as an electrical contractor. After a final "reunion" session in 1934 for Vocalion-ARC in New York, in which they rerecorded some of their biggest hits, the brothers retired, never to perform together again.

The case of the Allen Brothers, while dramatic, was not all that unusual in the history of early country music. Just as white jazz bands eagerly tacked the label "blues" on almost any dance tune, early country artists were quick to add the "blues" suffix to a variety of songs of all types. Yet, although the major record companies maintained segregated series for blues and country recordings in the 1920s, and although racial dividing lines were generally well maintained, the field sessions that recorded the music were themselves quite integrated. Black songsters sat waiting next to white gospel quartets; black blues singers took their turns with white fiddle bands. The give and take between white and black music "in the field" was always greater than the segregated record series implied; what had upset the Allen brothers in their lawsuit was not so much that their music had been mistaken for the work of African-Americans, but that they themselves had been mistaken for blacks. "We were trying to get into vaudeville back then," recalled Lee Allen. "It would have hurt us in getting dates if people who didn't know us thought we were black." But the Allens were only one out of many hillbilly performers in the 1920s who knew what real blues was, who did not tack the label on to any song or tune, and though few of these performers tried to emulate authentic blues singers exactly (in the way, for instance, that white urban folksingers in the 1960s did), they found in the blues rich inspiration. As they adapted and reworked both material from the city blues and the more indigenous country blues, they soon forged their own version of the music: a genre called white blues. From 1925 to 1940, this genre defined itself as one of the most interesting—and most commercial—subtypes of early country music.

There were forms of blues in country music from its earliest days. Most historians agree that the first country instrumental was fiddler Eck Robertson's 1922 Victor cut of "Arkansas Traveler," and that the first real country vocal was Fiddlin' John Carson's "Little Old Log Cabin in the Lane" for Okeh in 1923. We now know, however, that Virginia millhand Henry Whitter had recorded several sides for Okeh as early as March 1923, before Carson, and that one of these was "Lonesome Road Blues." The sides were issued only after Carson's sales had shown there was a market for such music, and "Lonesome Road Blues," coupled with "The Wreck on the Southern Old 97," was issued in March 1924, becoming one of the year's best-sellers. No one knows where Whitter learned "Lonesome Road Blues," with its famous opening line, "Going down the road feeling bad," or if, in fact, he had composed it himself. With its incessant guitar and high, nasal voice, Whitter's record sounded little like any black blues, but the song was in the standard blues form, and stanzas of it had apparently been circulating in black and white folk traditions. It became very popular, due in part to the success of "Old 97" on its flip side, and soon other singers like George Reneau were starting to cover it. (It remains a bluegrass standard even today.)

During the next couple of years, as record companies tried to get a handle on just what their new working-class southern audience wanted—and how the companies could find it—other pioneers of Whitter's generation included an occasional blues in their recorded repertoire. A few months after Whitter's first record was released, banjoist and singer Uncle Dave Macon traveled to New York to make his first sides for Vocalion. Macon was from rural middle Tennessee and had a huge repertoire that included a very large number of songs he had learned from black singers; in the middle of some of his later records (which were often designed as medleys in the vaudeville manner) he does passable imitations of a country blues singer, a black preacher, and a gospel singer. But one of his earliest sides was "Hill Billie Blues," a reworking of W. C. Handy's popular "Hesitation Blues." It was the first song actually to use the word hillbilly in its title and was probably drawn from the touring vaudeville act Macon had at the time, "Uncle Dave Macon and his Hillbillies." Though he was to keep "Hesitation Blues" in his repertoire through his later career and through his long stint as a star of the Grand Ole Opry, Macon later dropped the references to "hillbilly" in the piece.

There were other isolated early blues hits by artists who never really tried to specialize in the genre. One such was "Blue Ridge Mountain Blues," first recorded by Riley Puckett, the Georgia singer, late in 1924; within a few months, all the major companies rushed out cover versions by singers like Ernest Stoneman (Okeh), Vernon Dalhart (Victor), and Uncle Dave Macon's back-up man, Sid Harkreader (Vocalion). It, too, has survived into the modern era, a staple with bluegrass and honky-tonk bands. There was Roba Stanley, a very young woman from north Georgia who became the first woman soloist to sing on country records; in 1924 she had done a surprisingly strong version of "All Night Long" for Okeh. Two members of the popular radio string band the Hill Billies recorded an influential and moving instrumental called "Bristol Tennessee Blues" for Vocalion in 1926. Though issued under the name the Hill Billies, the disk featured the fiddling of Fred Roe, a native of upper east Tennessee. It resembles a country blues more than anything else recorded during this era, with its sharp, acerbic tone and brother Henry Roe's finger-picked guitar accompaniment. Unfortunately, Roe never followed up on this style of playing, and most of his later records were conventional, if well played, hoedowns and songs.

None of these early performers from the 1922–27 period specialized in blues, and few of them really sounded like blues singers. Most were using the term blues cavalierly, tacking it on to any jazzy song, or any song that had the suggestion of a lament or of double entendre. This all changed in the watershed year of 1927, a year that saw the apogee of old-time recorded music. By 1927, the major record companies were releasing dozens of new hillbilly records every week and sending their field-recording units into southern cities on a regular basis. The result was a series of dramatic recordings that celebrated everything from Cajun to gospel music, and that also celebrated white blues. In fact, the year saw the emergence of a number of singers who specialized, one way or another, in the blues, and whose intense popularity did much to define the genre we now call "white blues." In addition to the Allen Brothers, these included banjoist-singer Dock Boggs, slide guitarist and singer Frank Hutchison, Georgians Tom Darby and Jimmie Tarlton, and famed "blue yodeler" Jimmie Rodgers.

The first of these to record was a sometime West Virginia miner named Frank Hutchison. He was reared in Logan County, a rugged and isolated region near the border of West Virginia and eastern Kentucky. This Appalachian area was to become a fertile pocket for the developing genre of white blues, producing singers like Dock Boggs and Dick Justice, as well as Roy Harvey, the Shepherd Brothers, and, somewhat later, Roscoe Holcomb. Logan County itself, surrounded by mountains and dense hardwood forests, had become a center for coal mining by the turn of the century. When Hutchison was a teenager, several local residents were killed in what was called the Battle of Blair Mountain, a fight between federal troops and miners trying to unionize. It was a place where many of the miners, both black and white, living in company towns and doing some of the most dangerous work in the country, felt a sense of desperation and frustration akin to what black sharecroppers in the Mississippi Delta felt. It was a place that nurtured the blues.

Hutchison was born in 1897, and almost at once he was attracted to the black music in the area. When he was seven or eight he met one of the black railroad workers who were coming into the county to lay tracks for the mines. The man's name—as preserved by family folklore—was Henry Vaughn, and he could play the blues on the guitar. Frank soon picked some of this up, and soon was playing his guitar with a knife, sliding the strings the way he had seen Vaughn do. A little later he met a "crippled Negro living back in the hills" named Bill Hunt; Hunt was about fifty at the time and was apparently a songster as well as a bluesman. He taught young Frank dozens of songs from his repertoire of nineteenth-century traditional tunes that blacks and whites had shared before the blues became fashionable. By 1920, Hutchison's repertoire contained a bagful of rare old songs: rags, blues, traditional ballads, and novelties like "Coney Isle," about a giant amusement park, not in Brooklyn, New York, but near Cincinnati, Ohio.

By the early 1920s, Hutchison was good enough to eke out a living with his music, playing small stage shows he set up in mining camps, at political rallies, at private parties, and at movie theaters to introduce and even accompany silent films. Though his few surviving publicity pictures show him as an intense, brooding young man, he was apparently pretty lively. Pioneer recording star Pop Stoneman remembered him as "a big red-headed Irishman," and one of his sidemen remembered mainly the kinds of jokes he would tell on his shows. (Much of the rural vaudeville aspect comes out in his records, which are full of asides and quips.) But all agreed with one of his banjo players that Frank "always specialized in the blues. Just blues of all kinds." He traveled often, but seldom left the West Virginia–Kentucky area, sensing that his blues style would be best received there.

Somehow, late in 1926, Hutchison got hold of Okeh Records and traveled to New York to record his first two sides, "Worried Blues" and "The Train That Carried My Girl from Town." Both featured Hutchison using his pocket knife as a guitar slide, the instrument tuned to D, which so impressed later mountain musicians. "Worried Blues" is a classic blues in its lyric form, with a number of stanzas that Hutchison could have borrowed from a variety of sources. Some stanzas, such as "When you got the blues you can't eat nor sleep / You'll walk around like a police on his beat," and one that mentions him left "to sing my ragtime song," have a decidedly urban feel to them, a reference to a world far away from Logan County. Later songs, though, were more topical. As Okeh continued to call him back again and again for sessions that would eventually account for some thirty-two sides, he did songs like "Miner's Blues." Here Hutchison sings "Ain't gonna work on no tipple," and backs it with a series of distinctive runs in an E-natural tuning. His "Cannon Ball Blues" (1929) was probably based on Furry Lewis's Victor recording, and his odd narrative about the Titanic ("The Last Scene of the Titanic," 1927) might have been adapted from a black "toast" (an oral narrative poem) on the subject. (Miners both black and white knew and enjoyed these long, often bawdy, toasts.) Hutchison's records continued to sell well through the late 1920s (though almost half of them date from 1927), and most of them were blues of some sort, either vocals or guitar instrumentals. There was "Stackalee," "All Night Long," "The Deal" ("Don't Let Your Deal Go Down"), "Old Rachel," and a version of "John Henry" he called "K. C. Blues." He was popular enough that when Okeh decided to put together an all-star skit called "The Okeh Medicine Show" for a six-part record series, Hutchison was chosen to join the label's biggest stars: Fiddlin' John Carson, Narmour and Smith, Emmett Miller, and others. He told friends that he would have recorded more blues if the label had let him, but the A & R men at Okeh seemed to want him to diversify, and on one of his last sessions they insisted he join a fiddler for a series of breakdowns. Possibly for this reason, but more likely because of the Depression, Hutchison stopped recording after the "Medicine Show" skits, and stopped making music altogether.

He spent his later life as a storekeeper, and eventually moved to Columbus, Ohio, where he died in 1945.

Some eighty miles southeast of Logan, at Norton, Virginia, was the home of the second major white blues figure to emerge in 1927, Dock Boggs. He did his first sides for Brunswick in March, and though there were only a handful of them, they proved about as influential as Hutchison's. In some ways, Boggs's background was typical of that of many mountain musicians: he first learned to play the old clawhammer banjo-style, to sing traditional ballads like "Poor Ellen Smith," and to sight-read old gospel songs. Yet the area where he was born (in 1898) was already a grimy coal mining and railroad center. Immigrants and blacks were moving into the area to work alongside white mountaineers, who were seeing their old ways of farming and logging give way to the newer world of unions, mining bosses, and company stores. There was more give and take between blacks and whites in this region than might be expected; both shared work in the mines, and both were exploited by mining companies. They shared music in a number of ways; ledgers that have survived from storekeepers who sold records in places like War and Richland show that country blues records, especially the Paramount label featuring singers like Blind Lemon Jefferson, sold as well as fiddle records and hillbilly songs.

Unlike Hutchison, who only occasionally worked in the mines, Boggs was working in the mines full-time by 1910. He was also trying to balance his love of music (which he considered a hobby) with his need to make a living. As a boy, he would occasionally escape from the mines and go to nearby black communities, such as Dorchester, to listen to the kind of string-band music that was played there. Shyly standing on the edge of a crowd of dancers, he listened intently to the things the banjo player did. Years later, he recalled, "I heard this fellow play the banjo. . . . And I said to myself—I didn't tell anybody else—if I ever, I want to learn how to play the banjo kinda like that fellow does. I don't want to play like my sister and brother. I am going to learn how to pick with my fingers." Later he followed and learned from other black musicians in the area, one called Go Lightning, another named Jim White, and pillaged the large record collection of his brother-in-law. Soon he was creating a new style of banjo finger picking and an intense, moaning method of singing. He had a powerful voice and a keen sense for the kind of vocal embellishments he heard on the blues records.

In 1926, Boggs went to a Brunswick "talent audition" in Norton, Virginia, and was surprised to find that he was one of three acts chosen to record—out of a field of seventy-five that even included A. P. Carter. One of Boggs's first releases was "Down South Blues," which he had adapted from a 1923 Vocalion disk by city blues singer Rosa Henderson. Boggs turned the regular, rather predictable rhythm of a mediocre city blues singer into a complex redaction of raw, urgent force—mountain blues at its best. Later in the same session he did "Sugar Baby," "Country Blues" (an old traditional song called "Hustling Gamblers"), "New Prisoner's Song," and "Sammie, Where Have You Been So Long." He cut eight sides in all. The Brunswick people, astounded by their luck in finding a white coal miner who could sing with such power, begged him to record more, but Boggs was afraid of being cheated by the company, and demurred. The songs he did do were not all blues, but most of them were at least stylistically close. "Country Blues" and "Down South Blues" were especially potent, and two generations of banjoists copied them as models of the "high, lonesome sound" that soon came to characterize mountain blues. Boggs knew exactly what he was doing with his music; he once commented that he wished he had been given the gift to play the guitar instead of the banjo, so he could copy the music of his favorite, Mississippi John Hurt. Another time he said, "I put so much of myself into some pieces that I very nearly broke down emotionally."

The Brunswick records were successful in every way, but for a variety of reasons Boggs was unable to capitalize on his success. Shortly after he returned from New York, he returned to his job in the mines. It was a hard life and, in the wake of the miners' struggles to unionize, a dangerous one. Dock saw many of his friends killed in the mines or shot to death in mining camps and on mountain trails. Yet he seemed unable to venture out on his own, to try to make it as a professional musician.

When he finally did try, it was too late. The Depression hit, devastating not only the mining economy but the record and entertainment industry. On one occasion, Boggs had lined up a new recording session for Victor in June 1931, but couldn't scrape up the money to get there. Another time he went to Atlanta to record for Okeh, but froze in front of the mike on a radio-show audition and lost out there as well. He signed to record for an independent West Virginia label called Lonesome Ace, but was forced to record compositions by the label's owner, a local lawyer named W. E. Myers; it made little difference, since the records, produced in 1929, didn't get out until after the stock market crashed. By the time Roosevelt was in the White House, Boggs had given up and was back at work in the mines. In the 1960s he was rediscovered by folklorists, did a series of albums for Folkways, and performed at festivals. He still played very well and still had a remarkable feel for the blues, but his shot at real fame was little more than a memory.

The mountain blues of Hutchison and Boggs was matched in the Deep South by a team who actually sold more records than both of them combined: Tom Darby and Jimmie Tarlton. They recorded over sixty sides for three major labels in the period from 1927 to 1933, making them among the most prolific of the early country artists who took their blues seriously. To casual fans, Darby and Tarlton were best known for their two-sided Columbia hit record of "Birmingham Jail" and "Columbus Stockade Blues," one of the biggest selling old-time records of the decade. Their style was built on Darby's soulful singing and Tarlton's superb slide guitar work, and it was one of the loosest, least formulaic sounds in classic country music. Their repertoire was equally quirky, eclectic, and vast, and in some ways summed up the best aspects of white blues.

Jimmie Tarlton, who seems to have been the dominant member of the duo, was born in Chesterfield County, South Carolina, in 1892. The son of sharecropper parents, he learned to play the fretless banjo from his father, and to sing old ballads from his mother. By the time he was twelve, he was playing the guitar in both the open tuning and in the slide style he had learned from black musicians in North and South Carolina, and in Georgia, where his family had traveled in search of work. When he was seventeen, he left home, determined to try to make a living as a musician. For a time he worked in the textile mills in the Piedmont, North Carolina, then took off "busking"—going around the country, playing on street corners, at fairs, in bars, wherever he could find an audience. He got a lot farther than many of his contemporaries who went this route, getting to Oklahoma, to California, and back to New York. As he went, he picked up new songs and other musical styles. During World War I, in fact, he played his guitar in bars in New York and Hoboken. About 1922, on the West Coast, he met the famed Hawaiian guitarist Frank Ferera; this was during the height of Hawaiian music's popularity, and Ferera taught Jimmie how to use a better slide, a piece of highly polished steel that allowed him to note with more dexterity. He also taught him a lot about adapting old pop songs to the steel guitar's sound. By the mid 1920s, when Jimmie had returned to the South to settle near Columbus, Georgia, he had been exposed to a wider range of musical styles than most of his fellow old-time musicians. He quickly set about synthesizing what he had heard into his own unique style.

In 1927 he teamed up with another guitarist from Columbus, Tom Darby. Though Darby was the same age as Tarlton, he had traveled very little—stints to Georgia and Florida—and performed in public even less; his guitar playing and singing style were adopted almost completely from musicians he had heard in and around Columbus. Darby's singing featured a very strong blues component, replete with a harrowing falsetto, tendency to improvise around the melody, and a complex sense of rhythm. Darby's parents had come from the mountains in north Georgia, and he was second cousin to Skillet Lickers star Riley Puckett. His grandfather and some of his uncles were apparently full-blooded Cherokees, and he recalled hearing his uncles play fiddle music at family gatherings. A local talent scout persuaded Darby to team up with Tarlton and got them an audition for Columbia records. Their first Columbia release, a send-up of Florida land speculators called "Down on Florida on a Hog," coupled with "Birmingham Town," was cut on April 5, 1927 and sold well enough that Columbia's A & R man, Frank Walker, invited them back to the Atlanta sessions that fall.

Thus it was that on November 10, 1927, the pair once again recorded, this time doing "Birmingham Jail" and "Columbus Stockade Blues." Both had traditional roots, but both had been substantially reworked by the singers to the point where even today it is not clear how much they had created and how much they had borrowed. In later years, Tarlton liked to say that he wrote "Birmingham Jail" in 1925 when he had been given an eighty-five-day sentence in the Birmingham jail for moonshining. He was allowed to keep his guitar, he said, and as he sat in his cell thinking of his girlfriend Bessie, he created the song. The guards and warden were so impressed that they got a pardon for Jimmie, and in 1937, when the city dedicated a new jail, Tarlton was asked to return for the ceremonies. All of which showed, if nothing else, just how popular this first record had become. It sold almost two hundred thousand copies for Columbia, making it one of the best-selling entries in their Old Familiar Tunes catalog. Both singers would have been rich had they taken royalties on the song, but Darby talked Tarlton into accepting a flat fee for their work—a lump sum of $75 each.

Though "Columbus" became a country standard and was repopularized by Jimmie Davis (in the 1940s) and by Willie Nelson and Danny Davis (in the 1960s), in the 1920s Columbia thought "Birmingham Jail" was the bigger hit. They encouraged Tarlton to come up with two sequels, "Birmingham Jail No. 2" (in 1928) and "New Birmingham Jail" (in 1930). The former, backed by "Lonesome Railroad," became the team's second-best-selling record. Their other Columbia hits included two down-and-dirty country blues pieces, "Traveling Yodel Blues" and "Heavy Hearted Blues"; a bizarre, uptempo version of the Victorian chestnut "After the Ball"; a Civil War song, "Rainbow Division"; an uptempo guitar instrumental called "Birmingham Rag"; and an intense, almost rhythm and blues "Sweet Sarah." These lesser hits sold between fifteen and forty thousand each. Other records, which did not sell as well but became favorites with later fans, included "My Little

Blue Heaven" (derived from the Gene Austin hit), "Captain Won't Let Me Go Home," "Lowe Bonnie," "Ft. Benning Blues," and "The Weaver's Blues." By late 1929, the team was having contract disagreements with Columbia, and in April 1930 they did their last session for the firm. In the next few years, each man did separate sessions (Tarlton for Columbia, Darby for Victor), and got back together for two unsuccessful sessions in 1932 and 1933. But the magic was gone and the glory days were over.

The team had traveled with some of the best-known figures in the music—from the Skillet Lickers to the Delmore Brothers to the Dixon Brothers—but the new slick harmony sounds of the mid-1930s made the free-wheeling sound of Darby and Tarlton obsolete. By 1935 both men were retired. Then, in the 1960s, they were rediscovered by young enthusiasts of the folk revival movement. Tarlton was found in Phenix City, Alabama, and made a brief comeback that included stints at folk clubs around the country and a new solo LP on the Testament label. (It remains an astounding album even today, showing that Tarlton had lost little of his skill and creativity.) Soon after, Tom Darby was also "discovered," but only a few concerts were scheduled featuring the reunited team. It was learned that Tarlton had tried various comebacks before, even appearing for a time in a medicine show with Hank and Audrey Williams. The 1960s appeared to presage better things, and soon he was appearing at the Newport Folk Festival, and seeing a reissue of the original Darby and Tarlton sides on the Old Timey label. But it was, after all, late. Jimmie died in 1973, Darby in 1971, having barely tasted the fruits of their new careers.

On November 30, 1927, twenty days after Darby and Tarlton recorded "Columbus Stockade Blues" in Atlanta, the next chapter in white blues unfolded in the old Trinity Baptist Church in Camden, New Jersey. The old church, with its remarkable acoustics, had been converted into Studio #1 by the Victor Talking Machine Company, and on that afternoon it was hosting a session by a brash, hawk-faced young man named Jimmie Rodgers. He had been born in 1897 in southern Mississippi, had started working on the Mobile and Ohio Railroad when he was fourteen, contracted what was later diagnosed as tuberculosis a year later, and started out in music by doing black-face comedy in a tent show in 1923. During the next few years, he worked with a number of vaudeville and string-band groups, eventually winding up in Asheville, North Carolina, in the spring of 1927. That summer he auditioned for Victor's talent scout, Ralph Peer, who set up a field studio in the mountain town of Bristol, Tennessee. At this time Peer had just joined Victor, moving there from Okeh, where he had helped pioneer blues recording by releasing Mamie Smith's "Crazy Blues" in 1920. Blues had proved to be a bonanza for Peer, and now he was hoping to repeat his success by developing another genre of southern music, "hillbilly," or what the Victor publicists liked to call "Native American Melodies." He still recorded blues—usually going to Memphis for that—but he wasn't sure where to go for hillbilly material. He chose Bristol because, he told a newspaper writer at the time, "in no section of the South have the prewar melodies and old mountaineer songs been better preserved than in the mountains of east Tennessee and Southwest Virginia."

At first, it seemed, Rodgers was hardly doing that. Peer later recalled that "in order to earn a living in Asheville, he was singing mostly songs originated by New York publishers—the current hits." This Peer didn't want, in part because it was not "old-time" enough for his series, in part because he wanted original or public domain songs to which he could get publishing rights. Rodgers eventually came up with two sentimental songs that were passable; Peer paid him a hundred dollars on account and went on with the session. The record was issued in October and sold fairly well for a new artist, yet Peer did not call Rodgers back for more. So the singer took it upon himself to go to New York, check into a hotel (billing the room to Victor), and telephone Peer. Looking over the sales figures for the first disk, Peer shrugged and agreed to schedule a session at Camden. He soon found that Rodgers didn't really have much material ready to record; he chose three songs that seemed old-time enough, but for the fourth he reluctantly agreed to try something else. Peer recalled years later, "We did not have enough material and I decided to use [one] of his blues songs to 'fill in.'" Rodgers called this song "T for Texas," but it was eventually released by Victor as "Blue Yodel."

No one knows exactly where Rodgers got the set of blues stanzas he used for "T for Texas." Growing up in an area with a large black population, meeting numerous black musicians in his travels as a brakeman, he was certainly exposed to a wider range of black music than were people like Boggs and Hutchison. Some evidence suggests that he knew singers Ishman Bracey and Tommy Johnson, and stanzas that he used for this and his later "blue yodels" also show up in records by Peetie Wheatstraw, "Ma" Rainey, Bo Carter, Sadie McKinney, and other black singers. But the full extent of specific interaction between Rodgers and other bluesmen of the 1920s and 1930s will probably never be known. Rodgers quickly mastered the rhetoric of the country blues—catchphrases like "good gal," "sweet loving daddy," "whole wide world"—and used it to patch together lyrics that had the effect, if not the intensity, of blues. When "T for Texas" ("Blue Yodel") was issued, on February 3, 1928, publicity agents and reviewers were not sure what to call the new music. Victor ads described the release as "Popular Song for Comedian with Guitar" and praised Rodgers for his "grotesque style." Edward Abbe Niles, a Wall Street lawyer who wrote surprisingly hep reviews for *The Bookman*, called the song "engaging, melodious, and bloodthirsty"; a few months later he was describing Rodgers as "White man gone black"—an epithet that would be used three decades later to describe Elvis Presley.

"Blue Yodel" (Victor 21142) became in many respects the seminal record for white blues. It almost certainly actually sold over a million copies—one of the very few early country discs to do so—and established Rodgers as the premier singer of early country music. The balance of 1928 saw Victor issue no fewer than seven more Rodgers records, though only six of the fourteen songs were actually in the vein of "Blue Yodel." (Rodgers's blues songs have fascinated modern historians and folklorists, but his sentimental songs and railroad ballads were about as popular in his own day.) He recorded until just a few days before he died in 1933, having laid down some 110 songs, of which 13 were in the "Blue Yodel" series, and 25 others were related blues pieces—about a third of this recorded repertoire. Peer himself was convinced, though, that the blues was the key to Rodgers' sales and insisted he record more and more blues. The most popular included "In the Jailhouse Now" (1928, similar to earlier songs by Blind Blake and radio singer Ernest Rogers); "Blue Yodel No. 4 (California Blues)" (released in early 1929 and selling 365,000 copies); "Brakeman's Blues" (1928, subtitled "Portland, Maine Is Just the Same as Sunny Tennessee"); "Desert Blues" (1929, with sales of 200,000); and "Blue Yodel No. 8" ("Mule Skinner's Blues," 1931). As Peer realized that the Rodgers records were "crossing over"—appealing to a pop audience in addition to hillbilly and blues audiences—he began experimenting with a variety of studio back-up bands. While many of the biggest hits featured Rodgers alone with his guitar or with a small string band, starting in October 1928, Peer set him up with a small jazz band and by early 1929 was backing him with Victor studio orchestras. Genuine jazz and blues figures soon followed. Louis Armstrong and Lil Hardin Armstrong backed him on "Blue Yodel No. 9" (1930), though the newspaper ads failed to mention them, in spite of the fact that Armstrong was one of the biggest jazz names in the country. Clifford Hayes's Louisville Jug Band served as his band for "My Good Gal's Gone Blues" (1931), and the fine St. Louis guitarist Clifford Gibson backed him on "Let Me Be Your Side Track" (1931); the issued take of this number only featured Rodgers's own guitar, and for years it had been assumed that the Gibson takes were lost. Recently, however, they have been discovered and have been issued on the Rounder/Bear Family set of Rodgers's complete works. Sadly, some of Rodgers's best blues, in the most challenging settings, were done in the depths of the Depression and were hardly heard by anyone. "Let Me Be Your Side Track," for instance, sold only about thirteen thousand copies in its original edition.

Rodgers's biographer Nolan Porterfield has written, "While no one could seriously suggest that Jimmie Rodgers was another Blind Lemon Jefferson or Robert Johnson or even Furry Lewis, his performance of 'Blue Yodel,' insofar as it is a direct, serious, and authentic rendering of the material, is scarcely distinguishable from that heard on dozens of black blues recordings of the time." The most important thing Rodgers added to the blues conventions was his yodel; this is what held together most of his blues stanzas, and this was the thing that his imitators tried to emulate. No one really knows how Rodgers came up with it, but it was distinctly different from the pseudo-Alpine yodel that earlier singers like Riley Puckett adopted, and different, too, from the cowboy yodels. It might have borrowed something from the falsetto singing of certain Delta blues singers, or even from black field hollers and work songs. One source that might have been closer to Rodgers than any of these, however, was a well-defined tradition of black-face singing that had emerged on the vaudeville and medicine show circuits shortly before World War I. Such singing was part black-face parody, part exaggeration, part vocal contortion, and part sincere imitation. One of its first stars was Lasses White, who recorded and featured a song called "Nigger Blues" about 1916, and who later starred on the Grand Ole Opry in the 1930s. But the singer who really developed the style on records and who influenced two generations of country singers was a man named Emmett Miller.

Though Miller seldom appeared on radio and confined much of his activity to the live vaudeville circuit, he left behind an impressive series of recordings, done between 1924 and 1936, which reveal him to be adept at the kind of falsetto singing and "blue yodeling" that Rodgers later did. Miller was born in Macon, Georgia, in 1903 and grew up mimicking the black dialects he heard there and in other southern towns. By 1919, when he was sixteen, he began doing black-face shows with Dan Fitch and within a few years was starring in the show at New York's Hippodrome along with Cliff Edwards and the team of Smith and Dale. By 1924, Billboard was referring to Miller's "trick singing stunt" that almost stopped the show and won him "encore after encore." The "trick singing" was in part Miller's ability to break into a falsetto in the middle of a word, and in 1924 he committed this technique to wax for the first time when he recorded "Anytime" for Okeh.

By 1925, Miller had relocated to Asheville, North Carolina, where he worked in clubs, and where he impressed local singers. A young duo named the Callahan Brothers heard him there and adopted his version of "St. Louis Blues," with an eerie falsetto chorus, to their duet style. In 1934 they recorded their version for ARC, giving that label its biggest hit of the decade and challenging all later harmony duet singers. Miller might also have met Rodgers in Asheville—his singing partner Turk McBee said he did—and there taught Rodgers some of the "trick singing." Miller also recorded again in Asheville, doing a version of a song that would become his trademark and a country standard, "Lovesick Blues." Soon he was touring again, with the Al G. Field show, the newspapers describing him as a "comedian unexcelled in the impersonation of the southern Negro."

During 1928, in a flurry of activity, Miller began recording in earnest for Okeh. Often backed by a studio band he called the Georgia Crackers and that sometimes included jazzmen Tommy Dorsey, Eddie Lang, and Gene Krupa, he rerecorded his two big hits, "Anytime" and "Lovesick Blues," in the new electrical process. He also did his version of "St. Louis Blues" and "I Ain't Got Nobody," with his famous descending yodel built on the syllable "I." The next year, 1929, he did three others that became standards, "Right or Wrong" (which western swing singers took over), "Big Bad Bill Is Sweet William Now," and "The Blues Singer from Alabam." Occasionally the Okeh producers tried to force him to record a ballad like "She's Funny That Way," but he resisted, complaining to his friends that the company was "trying to make another damned Gene Austin out of me." All told, Miller cut some twenty-eight sides featuring music (plus others done as skits and a set in "The Okeh Medicine Show").

It was a small body of work, but surprisingly powerful. Down in Fort Worth, young fiddler Bob Wills painstakingly copied into his notebook the words to many of Miller's records and added them to his repertoire. When he hired his famous singer Tommy Duncan a couple of years later, Wills tested him by asking him to do Miller's version of "I Ain't Got Nobody." Duncan passed with flying colors and shortly after recorded the piece with Wills. In Alabama, singer Rex Griffin watched Miller do a live show in a club, and then adapted "Lovesick Blues" to his own country style. He had a major hit with it on his own for Decca in 1935, which inspired Hank Williams to do his version in 1949. By the 1950s (when Miller, ironically, was doing his last attempt at vaudeville in a touring show called "Dixiana"), "Lovesick Blues," an old Tin Pan Alley song, had become the most famous white blues in modern country music. Later singers like Merle Haggard and Leon Redbone dedicated entire LPs to Miller and his work; and though none of his records were really designed either for the specific blues or old-time market, Miller's many fans found him, and appropriated his loose, sinuous, double-jointed vocal style for their own. Unfortunately, Miller saw little of this recognition, and until recently has been an enigma to both country and blues fans.

With the spectacular success of Rodgers's "Blue Yodel" and the surprising sales of Darby and Tarlton's "Columbus Stockade Blues," the major companies began a feeding frenzy to find and record more white blues. Ralph Peer, seeing his own royalties from Rodgers's publishing roll in so fast he had to set up a dummy corporation to manage the profits, was especially eager. Some of his artists, such as the Allen Brothers, got upset with him because he began insisting they do blues to the exclusion of almost everything else. Other companies rushed to find Rodgers clones, and for the next ten years yodeling became almost synonymous with country music. Young Gene Autry, fresh from Oklahoma, started off doing superb Rodgers covers and pastiches for Gennett and Victor before he found his cowboy image. Howard Keesee (Gennett) and Bill Bruner (Okeh) came so close to Rodgers's style that their own careers lacked any real sense of identity. Dwight Butcher (Victor), Daddy John Love (Bluebird), Jerry Behrens (Okeh), and Jimmie's own cousin Jesse Rogers (Bluebird) all began their careers as serious Rodgers devotees. Ramblin' Red Lowery (ARC), a native of west Tennessee who worked over Memphis radio, moved further away from the Rodgers style than did many, yet the handful of records he did in the mid-1930s, such as "Ramblin' Red's Memphis Yodel—No. 1" (Vocalion, 1934), showed how a singer could still merge some of Rodgers's mannerisms with a more authentic blues sensibility. Young Jimmie Davis, five years before he won national fame (and eventually a governorship) with the sentimental "Nobody's Darlin' But Mine," did a series of Rodgers sound-alikes for Victor. But he also did a set of racier titles, such as "Sewing Machine Blues" (1932), "Red Nightgown Blues" (1932), "Yo Yo Mama" (1932), and "She's a Hum Dum Dinger from Dingersville" (1930). On many of these he was accompanied by two well-known black musicians from Shreveport, Buddy Woods and Ed Schaffer, as well as Buddy Jones—all of whom had recorded on their own.

Another who built a career on the Rodgers style, but who successfully parlayed it into an extensive series of recordings, was West Virginia radio singer Bill Cox (1897–1968). Known as the Dixie Songbird, Cox started off as a worker in an axe factory in Charleston (West Virginia); he began singing over station WOBU in 1927 and soon had a local reputation as a good guitarist, harmonica player, and singer of rowdy songs. He began recording for Gennett in 1929, first doing many Rodgers covers and then recording some of his own pieces in the Rodgers style. At first, these included comedy songs like "Rollin' Pin Woman" and "Alimony Woman," but later he began to do more serious pieces like "East Cairo Street Blues." By 1933 he was recording for the American Record Company, becoming one of the first to do "Midnight Special" (1933) and having a real hit with "NRA Blues" (1933), a protest song from the early New Deal days. In 1934 he injured his hand, and Cox hired as a temporary sideman a teenager named Cliff Hobbs to help out. At the suggestion of A & R man Art Satherly, Cox taught Hobbs how to sing tenor, and the two started recording as a duet. From 1933 to 1941, Cox recorded over sixty solo sides for ARC, and seventy duets with Hobbs. These included such topical songs as "Franklin D. Roosevelt's Back Again" (1936), off-color pieces like "Sally, Let Your Bands Hang Down" (1936), later country standards like "Filipino Baby," and covers of "Didi Wa Didi" (1939). The only major hit from all these was a piece called "Sparkling Brown Eyes" (1937), and Cox, unable or unwilling to work the kind of live tours that would have made him a decent living, slowly faded into obscurity. In 1965 he was discovered living in a tiny converted chickenhouse in the slums of Charleston, scarcely aware of the effect his old records had had on listeners, fans, and other singers.

As prolific a record maker as Cox was the Kentucky singer Cliff Carlisle (1904–83), who was not only a remarkable singer and composer but one of the first old-time artists to understand and feature the Hawaiian steel guitar. "My music," he once said, "is a cross between hillbilly and blues—even Hawaiian music has sort of blues to it." Unlike many early hillbilly guitarists, Carlisle started playing the steel from the very beginning, patterning his work on the records of Sol Hoopii and Frank Ferera, Hawaiian guitarists whose popularity was especially strong in the South. He won his first record contract (for Gennett) by doing Rodgers covers, but soon was producing his own Rodgers-like songs and billing himself as "The Yodeling Hobo." Like Cox, he moved over to the American Record Company in the early 1930s and began recording everything from murder ballads to a series of zany songs about domestic violence, such as "Pay Day Fight" (1937) and "Wildcat Woman and a Tomcat Man" (1936). Among his most popular, though, was a series of double-entendre pieces like "Shanghai Rooster Yodel" (1931) and "Tom Cat Blues" (1932). The latter featured the well-known lines:

> Here comes a ring-tail tom,
> He's boss around the town,
> And if you got your heat turned up,
> You better turn your damper down.

Chickens were favorite images, showing up in "Chicken Roost Blues" (1934) and "It Takes a Old Hen to Deliver the Goods" (1937); frogs were eulogized with "When I Feel Froggie, I'm Gonna Hop." Two 1933 songs, "Mouse's Ear Blues" and "Sal's Got a Meatskin," were about deflowering virgins. And pieces like "Copper Head Mama" and "Onion Eating Mama" (both 1934) went far to dispel the delicate, sentimental country lass described in earlier country songs. Many of the gamier songs were released under a pseudonym ("Bob Clifford"), a practice that didn't seem to affect sales but allowed Carlisle also to release items like "Valley of Peace" and "Jesus My All."

Other varieties of white blues, though, took forms quite different from the Rodgers model. One that became ubiquitous among radio singers in the 1930s was the so-called talking blues. Though casual fans often associate it with folksinger Woody Guthrie, its roots were a generation deeper than that. In April 1926 a young mandolin player named Chris Bouchillon appeared with his brothers for a try-out at a Columbia field session; they were from Greenville, South Carolina, and all worked at a foundry there. Frank Walker was not overly impressed with them, and when Chris tried to sing what he called his "blues thing," Walker stopped him. "I thought his singing was the worst thing I had heard, but I liked his voice. I liked the way he talked to me. I said, 'Don't sing it. Just talk it. Tell them about the blues but don't sing it." Backed by his brother, guitarist Uris, Bouchillon did as he was told and created "Talking Blues," with its famous opening line, "If you want to get to Heaven, let me tell you how to do it." The record was issued in early 1927, and soon became one of the year's biggest hits. It would eventually sell over ninety thousand copies, and soon Chris was back in the studios doing a series of follow-ups: "Born in Hard Luck," "New Taking Blues," and "My Fat Girl." Several stanzas of Bouchillon's original "Talking Blues" had been collected previously by folklorists from black informants, and early recordings by Talking Billy Anderson and by Coley Jones suggest the genre may have been known in black tradition.

During the next decade, old-time performers added to their repertoires a wide variety of talking blues. Lonnie Glosson, Curly Fox, Buddy Jones, the Prairie Ramblers, and others all recorded forms of talking blues, but the performer who became best known for it was Robert Lunn, a fixture on Nashville's "Grand Ole Opry" through the 1930s and 1940s. Born in Franklin, Tennessee, in 1912, Lunn spent his youth in vaudeville, where he somehow picked up Bouchillon's "song." By 1935 he was on the Opry, performing his "Talking Blues" every Saturday night before a nationwide audience; he used Bouchillon's verses at first, then began adding new ones, including topical material, until he had over a hundred verses in his repertoire. Fans loved it, and in 1936 they voted Lunn the show's most popular performer. Seven extra clerks were hired just to take care of the mail he was receiving. Though he never got around to recording the piece until the 1950s, Lunn did publish in various songbooks and helped spread the talking blues across the country to other entertainers like young Woody Guthrie.

Another variety of white blues was centered on the fiddle. Though the fiddle was the primary instrument of nineteenth-century folk culture, both with whites and blacks, not all that many of the early country fiddlers from the late 1920s and 1930s specialized in blues. The one exception would probably be the distinctive Mississippi fiddler Willie T. Narmour (1889–1961). A native of rural Carroll County in north-central Mississippi (the same area John Hurt came from), Narmour and his guitarist Shellie Smith grew up learning a rich collection of unusual, bluesy fiddle tunes. Like many Mississippi fiddlers, Narmour preferred the more deliberate "long bow" technique to the "jiggy bow" (fast, choppy strokes) of mountain fiddlers. This gave his playing an unusual tone and allowed him to experiment with nuances of expression and rhythm that gave his music such a distinctive sound. He and Smith did thirty-one tunes for Okeh in 1928–30 (recording many of them for Bluebird in 1934), but the most famous were "Carroll County Blues" (1929) and "Charleston No. 1" (1929). The former was Narmour's adaptation of a tune he heard a black fieldhand humming; the latter was not a version of the dance step, but a local piece named after Charleston, Mississippi, a county seat to the north of Carroll County. Both became standards with southern fiddlers and bluegrass bands, and both are still heard in fiddle contests today.

There were other blues fiddle tunes that won fame in the 1930s, though many of them were from fiddlers not necessarily known for the blues. The "train piece" format, in which a song built slowly through a series of alternating drone and breakdown passages, came from two records by east Tennessee mountain fiddler G. B. Grayson. These were "Train 45" (Victor and Gennett, 1927) and "Going Down the Lee Highway" (Victor, 1929). Tommy Magness, a veteran north Georgia fiddler who later played with both Bill Monroe and Roy Acuff, popularized "Natural Bridge Blues" and "Polecat Blues" (both Victor, 1940) in records he made with Roy Hall and his Blue Ridge Entertainers. Arthur Smith, probably the most famous fiddler in the 1930s through his work on the Opry and records for Bluebird, had a number of jazzy tunes (like "House of David Blues") that he called blues. He also made some more serious efforts, replete with his sliding notes and patented E-string double stops, including "Chittlin's Bookin' Time in Cheatham County" (Bluebird, 1936), his version of "St. James Infirmary," and "Florida Blues" (Bluebird, 1937), a driving, swinging workout that impressed two generations of fiddlers. Fellow Opry star Kirk McGee, who played all manner of music on guitar and banjo, reserved his fiddle work for blues and was judged by many critics to be the very finest of old-time blues fiddlers. His "Salt Lake City Blues" and "Salty Dog Blues" (both Vocalion, 1927) were both adapted directly from a Papa Charlie Jackson record, and "Milkcow Blues" he learned from Kokomo Arnold.

Early country music also produced a number of individual guitarists who, among their other accomplishments, recorded examples of country blues that were far more faithful to the original than anything Rodgers produced. Dick Justice (ca. 1900–ca. 1955), a friend of

Frank Hutchison's from Logan County, West Virginia, recorded a version of "Cocaine" and a pastiche he called "Brown Skin Blues" (both Brunswick, 1929). The former was a redoing of Luke Jordan's 1927 record, while the latter seems to have been drawn from a Lemon Jefferson side. Unfortunately, Justice recorded only one session before dropping into obscurity. Larry Hensley (1912–73), the guitarist and mandolin player for the well-known southern Kentucky band Walker's Corbin Ramblers, recorded a version of "Match Box Blues" (ARC, 1934). It was derived from Lemon Jefferson's recording and elaborates not only on Jefferson's vocal, but also on his guitar style. Sam McGee (1894–1975), another early Opry star and long-time companion of Uncle Dave Macon, contributed his masterpiece with "Railroad Blues" (Gennett, 1934). Here, too, the guitar work overshadows the singing. The guitar choruses are full of pulls, bent notes, choked chords, and even a high falsetto vocal done in unison with the guitar, in the manner of Delta bluesmen. McGee continued to play this and similar numbers well into the 1960s and 1970s, as he was discovered by the folk revival movement. By the mid-1930s some guitarists had gotten their hands on the dobro, and pioneers like Clell Summey were exploring its possibilities. Summey, from Knoxville, was a member of Roy Acuff's first band and was featured on some of Acuff's first releases, such as "Steel Guitar Chimes" and "Steel Guitar Blues" (both ARC, 1937).

As the 1930s drew to a close, the blues was assimilated into more and more forms of commercial country music. The "blue yodel" was gone, a victim of overexposure, and there were no longer many country artists who thought of themselves as blues specialists. Yet as the records and radio shows proliferated, taking country music far from the mountain mining camps or country vaudeville shows, the newer groups routinely added blues songs and styles to their repertoire. Milton Brown and then Bob Wills defined western swing in part through reworkings of "Sitting on Top of the World," "Joe Turner Blues," "Brain Cloudy Blues," and "Steel Guitar Rag" (the latter derived from Sylvester Weaver's 1923 "Guitar Rag"). Duet singing and blues were first merged by the Memphis team of Reece Fleming and Respers Townsend, and then by the more technically adept Delmore Brothers; their "Brown's Ferry Blues" (Bluebird 1933) had become one of Bluebird's best-selling records by 1935, and it anticipated the Delmores' even heavier involvement with blues after the war. October 1940 brought another taste of things to come, when Kentucky mandolin player Bill Monroe made his first recordings with a band he called the Blue Grass Boys. At the Kimball Hotel in Atlanta, under the direction of veteran Frank Walker, Monroe did "Mule Skinner Blues," "Dog House Blues," and "Tennessee Blues," giving notice that "the taste of the blues," as he put it, would be a major part of the new music he was inventing. The notion of white blues was no longer novel, and producers no longer thought of it as an automatic ticket to big sales, but it was on its way to becoming a part of the deep fabric of country music. The universal appeal of the blues was merely being validated once again.

Fixin' to Die

Eric von Schmidt and Jim Rooney

EVERYONE was going to Newport. After a two-year hiatus, the Newport Folk Festival had been revived through the combined efforts of George Wein, Pete Seeger, Manny Greenhill, and many of the members of the New York folk community. The idea was to make the Festival as representative as possible of the many levels of the growing folk music world. It would have been the best of the commercial folk groups like Peter, Paul, and Mary and the Tarriers; the best young artists like Joan Baez and Bob Dylan; the best of the traditional artists like Bill Monroe and Jean Ritchie; and, of course, those who considered themselves the "parents" of this whole revival—Pete Seeger, Oscar Brand, and Theo Bikel. Hovering over the Festival was the spirit of Woody Guthrie. It was going to be a celebration of the culmination of the long struggle to bring the people's music back to the people. The songs of the time were "Blowin' in the Wind" and "We Shall Overcome." The song for all time was "This Land Is Your Land."

A lot had happened since the last festival in 1960, and the Cambridge folks were ready to join in the celebration. Betsy Siggins was hanging out with Joan Baez and got to meet Bob Dylan and Jack Elliott's mother and father. Bob Siggins and Jim Rooney were at a bluegrass workshop taking pictures of Bill Keith playing with Bill Monroe. Fritz and Mitch Greenhill backed Jackie Washington on the "New Folks" concert. Robert L. Jones had a friend in Newport who was restoring an old mansion built by some industrialist in the middle of Jamestown Bay on a big rock; the house became party headquarters. The nighttime concerts were held in Freebody Park in town, and in the daytime there were music workshops there and next door on the grounds of the Newport Casino, one of the grand old tennis clubs of the world. If he could have been there, Woody Guthrie would have loved it—all these guitar pickers sitting around where the Vanderbilts used to play.

Eric von Schmidt was at the Casino on Saturday afternoon at a workshop on blues. He was listening to Mississippi John Hurt sing "Spike Driver Blues." It was unreal. John Hurt was dead. *Had* to be. All those guys on that Harry Smith Anthology were dead. They'd all recorded back in the twenties and thirties. They'd never been seen or heard from since.

Reprinted from Eric von Schmidt and Jim Rooney, *Baby, Let Me Follow You Down: The Illustrated Story of the Cambridge Folk Years* (Amherst: University of Massachusetts Press, 1993), 189–99.

But there was no denying that the man singing so sweet and playing so beautifully was *the* John Hurt. He had a face—and what a face. He had a hat that he wore like a halo. In another place, in another time, Eric might well have got on his knees, but he didn't. After the workshop was over, he went up to Mississippi John Hurt, shook his hand, and said, "Mister Hurt, I just want to tell you how much I enjoy your music. You know, one time I built a boat, and I named it after you." John Hurt smiled, looked at Eric with his Jiminy Cricket eyes, and said, "Oooh? Thass NICE!"

There was nothing quite like Newport at night. It was cool and sometimes the wind blew the fog in off the water. The combination of the fog and the colored stage lights would make the artists look like they were almost illusions. Ralph Rinzler brought Clarence Ashley and Mike Seeger brought Dock Boggs. A blues collector named Tom Hoskins brought John Hurt. They were not ghosts up there. They were absolutely real. Seeing them all on the stage like that was as if someone had suddenly turned the lights on in a room that had been dark for years. There they all were, still singing and playing just as they had over thirty years earlier. It was a minor miracle.

How did it happen? That was the question that intrigued Phil Spiro as he sat listening to John Hurt. Phil had gradually involved himself in the folk world for the last three years and had a radio show that he shared with Dave Wilson on the M.I.T. radio station WTBS.

> Geoff Muldaur is the one who really turned me on to country blues. I heard him play one night at the Turk's Head on Charles Street. He was still at B.U., and afterwards we went back to his dorm. He played some records, including some Blind Willie Johnson—stuff that really turned on something in my head. I guess it had something to do with the simplicity of the music. From that point on, I really got into country blues.
>
> I listened to a lot of records, and I also went to hear some of the young, white blues singers who were around. There were lots of guys who played blues who left me totally cold, and there were some who I thought were fantastic. Geoff was a beautiful singer. Eric von Schmidt is one of the finest blues musicians I've ever heard. To do what he did with "Galveston Flood," "Grizzly Bear," and "He Was a Friend of Mine" showed a mastery of the idiom. He took something from within the idiom and transformed it in such a way that nobody could tell that it wasn't always that way. Eric set a standard for me by which I judged many others.
>
> Before 1963, the idea that the bluesmen we listened to on old records might still be alive somewhere hadn't really occurred to us. That all changed when Tom Hoskins rediscovered Mississippi John Hurt. The first contact I had with anybody who was involved in looking for these old guys was when I met Hoskins at Newport. I asked him how it had happened, and it turned out that he had just acted on a hunch. One of John's songs was "Avalon Blues" and it had the line, "Avalon's my hometown, always on my mind." So Hoskins went to Avalon, Mississippi, on the off chance that he would still be living there, and he was! It was that simple.
>
> At about the same time I had met Hobart Smith at the Club 47. He did a radio show, and we became good friends, so I visited him in Saltville a couple of times when I was on my way to Florida to see my parents. Hobart had a friend named John Gallaher who played "St. Louis Tickle" which he had learned from Blind Lemon Jefferson when he was through there one time. They didn't draw a hell of a lot of distinction between black

music and white music in their minds. Hobart also played some beautiful stuff on the piano at home. You haven't lived if you haven't heard him play "Pretty Polly" on the piano. The thing about all of this was that I didn't have a tape recorder with me, and there was all this great music happening. It certainly made me think about going out in the field to collect and record the music out there. I remember Hobart saying that Alan Lomax, who had recorded him, was a good man, and that he'd come into your house, and you'd feel right at home with him, and he'd put his feet up and be one of the family—but watch him.

The whole story of the rediscovery of all these bluesmen after so long is pretty weird. I remember Geoff Muldaur telling me that they had found Booker White and how. John Fahey and Ed Denson, who were blues fanatics from California, addressed a card to: "Bukka White—Old Blues Singer, Aberdeen, Mississippi." They were hoping to pull off another John Hurt, because Booker (Bukka was a typo mistake on the old record label) had recorded a song about *his* hometown called "Aberdeen Blues". Booker wasn't living there any more, but somebody carried the card to him up in Memphis. It said: "Hi. If you're alive and well, call us collect. We want you to come out here and make a record." He called; they sent money for him to go to California, and that's how that happened. Geoff couldn't believe it and neither could I. It just electrified me.

When Booker came to Boston to play at the "Y" I saw to it that he stayed with me, pushy kid that I was. I was sharing an apartment on Roberts Road with Al Wilson who later went on to be called "Blind Owl" in Canned Heat. I met Al through Laurie Forti, who had a very good blues collection. At the time I met him, Al was an accomplished guitarist. He had already gone through Muddy Waters' records and John Lee Hooker's records. He was very melodically oriented. He was already open for country blues. It was a time when everybody was just digging in. The Origins of Jazz Library records were coming out. We'd sit around and listen to those and could hardly wait until the next one came out. Neither of us were collectors though; we were really interested in the music.

Al occasionally worked for his father's construction firm as a bricklayer. The crew thought he was a hippie because he wore glasses! He was very happy to get out of there and somehow make another kind of living. He made a little money teaching, collected some unemployment, and every so often he'd grit his teeth and go back and lay bricks. He had the blues. He had good reason. If you're looking for a persecuted minority, try the minority of one sometime.

When I moved in with Al, I didn't quite know what I was getting into. I'm not the world's neatest person, but he was something else. Al cleaned house twice. Once when Booker came to stay with us; once when Son House came. His method of cleaning was quite simple. He would bring in the three trashcans from outside and start filling them up. He would then take the cans back outside, and the room would be clean. We didn't have a phone. We didn't have any plates. We had a fork. When we decided to eat in, we'd put a hot dog on a fork and cook it over the burner.

While Booker was staying with us, Al talked to him a lot about his music. Al was exceptional in his ability to relate and empathize with older musicians. He was so in tune with whatever spirit there was in blues that they would play with him and talk to him as a fellow musician. He had no ego. He was into music for its own sake, and that's how he was able to communicate so well. He wasn't interested in finding out what someone had for lunch thirty years ago when he recorded such and such; he was more interested in how he felt about his music. They discussed how Booker approached the problem of writing a song; why he preferred certain techniques to others on the guitar;

what qualities he admired in other bluesmen; and so on. Naturally, the conversation would get around to musicians that Booker knew and had known in the old days.

Booker didn't care too much for Robert Johnson or anyone with a high voice, as I recall, but he enjoyed listening to the records of one of his boyhood idols, Charlie Patton. Eventually, Al played some of Son House's old records. Booker really took an interest. He didn't recognize Son's music at first, but when Al identified it as Son House, Booker went into deep thought. After a while, he recalled that a friend of his in Memphis had casually mentioned seeing Son House last year.

Both Al and I were astonished to hear this, for blues collectors had been looking for Son House for over ten years. The only information known about him was that his first name was Eugene, he had lived in Robinsonville, Mississippi, was a part-time preacher, and sometimes wore a white cowboy hat. He had recorded commercially for Paramount in 1930 and again for the Library of Congress in the early forties. No one had seen him since.

Through Booker, we got in touch with the woman who had seen Son in Memphis—Ma Rainey. Not *the* Ma Rainey, but a woman who is such a fine blues singer that her friends call her "Ma Rainey" out of respect for her abilities. I called Ma (her real name is Lillian Glover) and she said, yes, she had seen Son House last year. No, she didn't find out where he was living, but she would be glad to help look for him. Off to Memphis! I had two weeks vacation beginning the second week of June, so I was ready. Al was playing at the Club 47 during that period and couldn't go. I contacted Nick Perls who was a blues record collector from New York. He was into old records and tapes more than living bluesmen who have problems like food and board, but he had a car and wanted to look for old '78's. He also had a gigantic tape recorder. It came in sections, both of which weighed about eighty pounds. I also talked to Dick Waterman about going. He was a good photographer and journalist, and he, too, had been fascinated by the "rediscovery" phenomenon which started with John Hurt.

Like so many others who eventually got drawn into the folk world, Dick Waterman had started out to do something else.

I went to Boston University's School of Public Relations and Communications to study journalism. Out the back door of the SPRC was the "Golden Vanity." This was in 1959–60. So I naturally drifted over there and got acquainted with people like Robert L. Jones and got some exposure to folk music.

I worked for newspapers in Bridgeport, Connecticut, and Miami. I was basically a sportswriter and sports photographer. In 1963, I came back from Miami. I was doing some freelance writing for the *National Observer.* By this time, the folk revival was in full swing, and I convinced the *Observer* that this was going to be a major story. So I went to Newport and covered the festival for them. From then on, I started hanging out at the Club 47, all the time.

In February of '64, Mississippi John Hurt needed a place to play in Boston. Dave Wilson and I became partners and rented the Cafe Yana for a week. I had met John briefly at Newport, and he had immediately captivated me. He was a charming, wonderful man, and that's why I wanted to help put him on. So he came in and sold out every night for six nights. We were blessed with good weather; immediately after we closed, there was a blizzard.

A couple of months later Phil Spiro told me that he thought there was a good chance that another of the old bluesmen who everybody thought was dead was somewhere down in Memphis. It was Son House. He wanted to know if I'd be interested in coming along on the trip. I couldn't pass up a story like that, and the next thing we knew we were down in Memphis!

Rev. Robert Wilkins, another rediscovered bluesman, was an old friend of Son's, and he offered to help us look for him down around Lake Cormorant, Mississippi, where we heard he had once lived. Without his help we would never have gotten anywhere. We were going around from house to house and farm to farm. We were down in the delta between Highway 61 and the river. We were in there for days, looking for Son and people who knew him. We were four in a Volkswagen with a New York license plate. It was insufferably hot. Spiro and me with our Boston accents, Perls with his New York accent, travelling with a black minister. Wallace was running for President, and the white people in Mississippi were with him all the way. The daily newspapers were full of reports of people being trained to come in to help with voter registration. So people in Mississippi knew who we were and why we were there. We were just not welcome there because of the way we looked and sounded, and when we said what we wanted, they didn't like that either. "What do you want that nigger music for? You come down here with a machine to record . . ." And we're talking about the Library of Congress and about this music being an art form. They didn't want to hear about it.

One day we were riding along. Perls was driving. Reverend Wilkins was in the front seat. Spiro and I were crushed up in the back seat. We're going down this country dirt road. We needed directions. We pulled up in front of a barn with a fence running alongside of it. There were two young guys—big, heavy, beefy, red-faced guys with their hair cut short, almost to the skull, with big, beefy arms—just standing there.

We stopped the car. They were on the driver's side. Reverend Wilkins opened the door and said over the top of the Volkswagen, "Can you tell us how to get to so and so's house?"

They just looked at him for the longest time and then spat straight down in contempt. Spiro and I looked at each other. We were totally helpless in the back seat. The guys walked over and stood and looked right across the roof of the car at Reverend Wilkins. He had his coat off, was wearing a white shirt, a tie, and steel-rimmed spectacles. If there ever was calm, this man had it. He was so in possession and control of himself. He looked across and said very deliberately, "We're looking for so and so. He's around here somewhere."

They just looked at him, full of loathing and hatred. The air just crackled. They finally said, "Third farm down," and they turned and walked away. As they walked away, Reverend Wilkins said, "Thank you," and got back into the car.

June of '64 in the delta was a serious time. The day we finally talked to Son on the phone from Mississippi to Rochester, New York—June 21, 1964—was the day that Goodman, Schwerner, and Chaney were killed.

We spoke to people in Indianapolis who put us on to people in Detroit, who put us on to people in Rochester. We called him and asked, "Are you the Son House who recorded for Paramount Records and the Library of Congress?"

He said, "Yeah, that's me."

We said, "Don't go anywhere, we're coming."

We left Memphis the following day and drove straight to Rochester. When we got there we drove up to a four-story apartment building at 61 Grieg Street. We had sent a telegram so we knew he would be expecting us. He was supposed to be a short, fat man.

There was a thin man sitting on the stoop with a woman. Spiro asked him if he knew which apartment Son House lived in.

"This is him," said Son House.

Interestingly enough, on that same day, Tuesday, the 23rd, Bill Barth, Henry Vestine, and John Fahey found Skip James in Tunica, Mississippi, about five miles from where we had been looking for Son. We had been looking for Skip, too, but when you played a record of Skip James for somebody, they'd look at you and say, "Nobody sounds like that." Skip had that high falsetto and those strange tunings, and he didn't really play into the guitar. He sort of brushed the strings and would play things like "I'm So Glad" incredibly fast. There was simply nobody who played like Skip.

As soon as we found Son, we called Ralph Rinzler at Newport. We made a tape of two or three songs in Rochester and rushed it down to him. Son went to Newport, but he got sick and did not perform that year. The Newport Folk Festival of '64 was the greatest collection of country blues singers except for the '69 Ann Arbor Blues Festival. There was Robert Pete Williams, Sleepy John Estes with Hammy Nixon and Yank Rachel, Mississippi John Hurt, Skip James, Libba Cotten, Reverend Robert Wilkins, Fred McDowell. It was just incredible. Sam Charters and Dr. Willis James hosted the workshops.

One of the great recollections I have of those workshops is when Skip James came in. He was wearing a hat and a heavy jacket. He had on a badge that said "Kin" (you were either "Performer," "Staff," or "Kin"). No one had heard him play except for the people who had discovered him. They brought him in, and he was sort of a presence on the grounds for the first day or so. People would say, "That's Skip James." He was very quiet, almost mysterious. Finally it came his time on this workshop. There was a little wooden pallet on the grass, and there was a chair on the pallet. Everyone was sitting around on the grass. There were maybe a couple of thousand people gathered around—all very attentive. These were the real folkies—the people who hung out at the 47 in Cambridge, the "Gaslight" in New York, and the "2nd Fret" in Philadelphia.

Skip sat down, and put his guitar on his leg. He set himself, doing a little finger manipulation with his left hand, then he set his fingers by the sound hole, sighed, and hit the first note of "I'd Rather Be The Devil Than Be That Woman's Man." He took that first note up in falsetto all the way, and the hairs on the back of my neck went up, and all up and down my arms, the hairs just went right up. Even now I get a reaction to that note when I listen to the recording of it on "Blues at Newport." It's such an eerie note. It's almost a wail. It's a cry.

There was an audible gasp from the audience. That to me is what it's all about. It was the same with Son when I first brought him to the Club 47 on the way to Newport. I sat him down in a chair on the stage, and handed him the guitar, which he held with the neck down lower than the body. He got himself set, and he lay the slide way down and then just ripped that slide up the neck and quivered it up near the body. Everybody went "AHH!" I looked around, and I could see that he had an ability to communicate powerfully. He could absolutely transfix people. And I said to myself, "What the hell did I get myself into?" I was in it then. I had turned a corner in my life, and there was no looking back from that point.

If Waterman was in it, at least it was as the result of his own choice. Imagine what the phenomenon of rediscovery meant to the rediscovered. That was the other side of the dream—and what a strange dream it was. Imagine what it must have felt like to be confronted with these young, white, college-educated kids who materialized out of the blue to tell you that something you did thirty years ago on an afternoon had changed their lives, and then to be taken to a place far away where hundreds or even thousands more awaited you and expected you to change their lives, too. On one level it was sheer magic between an artist and those who deeply loved his art. That communication knows no boundaries be they geographical, social, racial—whatever. But what happened the rest of the time? What happened with the rest of the audience to whom you are some kind of curiosity? Peter Guralnick had grown up in the Cambridge area and had gradually become a blues fan. At one point Joe Boyd put together a concert at Eliot House at Harvard with the recently rediscovered bluesman Sleepy John Estes and his partner Hammy Nixon. Peter was in New York when he found out about it.

> I had a friend at Harvard, and he called me one day to tell me that Sleepy John Estes was going to play at Eliot House. I said, "That's impossible! He must be one hundred and three years old!" We hadn't heard of anyone being rediscovered at this point. I was in New York going to Columbia, and I came back on the bus just to go to this concert.
>
> Seeing Sleepy John and Hammy Nixon was a thrill for me, but it was very bizarre being in the audience at Eliot House. Estes never said a word. Hammy Nixon hammed it up. Some people in the audience were yelling, "Put it in the alley!" "Let's hear those blues, baby!" Other people were saying, "Shh. Shh." I felt between the two. I'd never had exposure to this kind of thing. I found out later that the best way to hear the music was where it occurred naturally when I went down south or to Chicago. Of course, there I'm an outsider, too. But at least the performer is comfortable, which is probably the better thing.

After that concert Joe Boyd, Geoff Muldaur, Eric von Schmidt, and a bunch of people took Sleepy John and Hammy to a party at Fritz's parents house in Newton. For Geoff it was a thrill just to be with them. For them it was probably strange. Newton is a long way from Brownsville, Tennessee, but everyone managed to have a pretty good time—especially Geoff.

> It was a great party. They went to bed late at night with a bottle of Jack Daniels. When they woke up it was gone. They drank it in their sleep! They showed Fritz how to paint his jug. You had to put paint on the jug or it wouldn't have the right tune. At about two in the morning John went into his spiritual trip and started healing everybody. Nancy Wardwell was there and he got hold of her and sang blues to her. His thing was making up blues right on the spot. I went to shake his hand and say goodbye, and he sang:
>
> "Ohhhh Geoff . . . I won't ever see you no more . . ." I just couldn't stand it.

In the course of the next few years it became clear to Phil Spiro that rediscovering someone was very much of a mixed blessing, and he had some second thoughts about it.

> I'm half inclined today to say that if I had to do it all over again, I wouldn't do it. For someone like a Bill Monroe, who is primarily a performer, to drop into obscurity and then be rediscovered—that's life again. But for somebody who maybe recorded four or five records and who sat around with his buddies on the back porch and maybe played once in a while at a local joint, it's a whole other world which has a whole other set of values. To be sure, many of the ones who were found got their rocks off in their old age,

> at a time when they had no reasonable expectation of anything more exciting than a Social Security check. But what was the price we asked of them? And what did we give them? For the ones who had recorded before, like Son and Skip and Booker, we kept comparing them to their younger selves, and they knew it. How could they help knowing, when perhaps three-quarters of the people that they met were asking them questions about what color shirt they wore on that muggy delta day in 1931 when . . . Nobody seemed to give a flying fuck that they were *still* living on the wrong side of this poverty line, and that the income from their music was not enough to significantly improve their lot over welfare in most cases.
>
> We also consciously or unconsciously tried to shape the music that they played on stage. The same statement could be made for the guys running Paramount during the thirties, but at least their motive was simple profit, which motive the artist shared. Our motivation was a strange combination of ego, scholasticism, and power. I wonder now what would have happened if we had just left them alone instead of telling them what songs to sing and what instrument to play them on.
>
> The rediscoverers fought over the artists. Spotswood and Hoskins fought Denson and Fahey over Skip James. Hoskins and Waterman were at odds over John Hurt. We ended up embroiling these old guys in a lot of problems. Money problems, mainly. Most of them wound up feeling they had been cheated. They had no way of assessing what their true worth was. It was something they weren't prepared to deal with, didn't know how to deal with, and, for the most part, didn't deal with well.
>
> Worst of all, aside from a couple of people like Chris Strachwitz and Dick Waterman, the rediscoverers all too often didn't see the old guys as real, breathing, feeling, intelligent people. In general, we were collectors of people, who we tended to treat as if they were the very rarest of records—only one copy known to exist.

Within a year after discovering Son House, Dick Waterman was well aware that he was up to his ears in the story he had set out to cover. If it was too late to put the genie back in the bottle, he could at least try to give it some shape and direction which would benefit the various bluesmen who suddenly found themselves in some form of show business, and at the mercy of some pretty dishonest, coldhearted types.

> Nearly a year after the Newport Festival I was at the one and only New York Folk Festival. We were staying at the Henry Hudson Hotel, and I formed Avalon Productions in the bar of the hotel. Until that time, bluesmen were being managed and booked by people who had little record companies. People from Music Research had John Hurt, people from Takoma had Bukka White, people from Delmark had Sleepy John Estes. So I got everyone together and offered to book everyone and to make managerial and booking decisions. I said I would not get into the record business at all; I would route everyone. They would play more dates in more cities. The record people would know where they were playing and would be better able to promote and advertise their records. I was to represent Son, Skip, Bukka, Libba Cotten, Sleepy John, and Babe Stovall.
>
> I said that I would set a minimum price. Then I went to the bluesmen and said that they would have to see to it that no one circumvented me. I knew that people would be calling them at home, telling them that I was asking too much and trying to sweet-talk them into working cheap. Some folkie from Cambridge could work for $50.00/day and come out ahead, but these men were a long way from home—always on the ground, never in planes. They'd spend fifteen hours on a bus, play somewhere for fifty or one hundred dollars, get a place to stay, breakfast, and then they'd be right back on the bus.

So I set up Avalon Productions and started booking. The people that stood by our agreement did well, and I continued to work with them. Those who repeatedly went around me, I let go. Years later, John Hurt confided in me. He had spoken to Son House and Skip James and the others, and they had said, "Dick is fair. We go in and we get paid. Dick makes sure the money is good, and Dick gives us the money. We always know what we're going to get paid." Then John came to me, and we were moving towards a legal action when John died. Later, Tom Hoskins got a $280,000.00 settlement from Vanguard. He got money, back masters, copyrights, the works. For some people the rediscovery business turned out to be very profitable.

My attitude is that I toil hard for living people. I do the very best that I can for widows and children. However, once the bluesman is gone, I'm depressed by the almost ghoulish grave-robber aspect of it: ne'er-do-well children of former wives—people who never did anything for him in his lifetime—come in after the royalties or the copyrights.

For most of the bluesmen this experience was like the flare of a candle just before it goes out. For those of us who were lucky enough to be there, the light was a blessing and perhaps was enough to enable our own candles to burn a little bit brighter, a little bit longer. For some, like Al Wilson, the experience was what he needed to become himself.

If you talk in a certain way—in my case, like a person who spent the first twenty-two years of his life in a suburb of Boston—you talk in a whole different way—and, if only subconsciously, you attempt to sing the lyrics of a song with an inflection or any other simulation of any dialect you've heard, it creates a situation in which the very sentence, as divorced from music, cannot proceed in a natural, loose, and relaxed way. This is why I think there's an advantage in getting away from the traditional words and using the way you talk yourself—though I definitely would have to agree that the way they talk in Arlington, Mass., is lacking in the poetic quality I hear in the way they talk in Mississippi. Nonetheless, there's nothing gained in attempting to simulate that. You just have to use your own way.

From "Whites Versus Blacks"

Paul Garon

WE HAVE now to consider the psychological relevance of the black man to the white man and what effect this has on the evolution of the blues. As a starting point, I would like to quote the psychoanalyst Richard Sterba (1947): 'The male Negro as he appeared in dreams of white people . . . often had to be recognised as representative of the dreamer's father, particularly the father at night or in his nocturnal activities' (416). Sterba also pointed out how blacks come to unconsciously represent siblings to the whites.

Dream symbols, of course, do not refer only to dream life, but are in fact one of the few indications we have of the nature of the unconscious activity that exists in us night *and* day. The dream is not the unconscious, but it gives us occasional glimpses of how our unconscious operates when we are awake as well as when we sleep. Later we shall discuss symbolism at length, but at this juncture it is worthwhile to establish a few basic points. Individuals do not choose what a symbol represents to their unconscious, although they can in a sense choose (again not consciously) which symbol they may use. In spite of the multiplicity of symbols, those ideas which are symbolised are very few indeed: birth, death, the self, members of one's family, parts of the body, etc. Additionally, symbols have a universal meaning, not through 'archetypal inheritance' as Jung would have it, but through individuals who create symbols for themselves out of their common experience. Thus, it is the common ontogenetic development of mankind (and not *necessarily* the phylogenetic development) that gives symbols their universal meaning.

Symbol interpretation, in spite of its being one of the few areas in which psychoanalysis can look to other fields (folklore, mythology, art, etc.) for confirmation, is considered by many to be the most far-fetched aspect of psychoanalysis. In analytic patients, symbol interpretation is usually met with total disbelief or disgust. Some critics feel that to interpret symbols is to rob life of its more varied meanings, for indeed what have we left if everything we relate to is only our fathers, mothers, sisters, brothers, birth or death? Perhaps no one has answered this objection better than Roheim (1950): 'I never think it necessary to emphasize the obvious. It is fairly obvious that a grown man is not quite the

---

Reprinted from Paul Garon, *Blues and the Poetic Spirit* (London: Eddison Press Ltd., 1975), 54–61. Used by permission of the author.

same as a five year old child, and that the President of the United States is not really the father of all the patients in whose dreams he might occur in that role. After Freud managed to dive to the bottom of the ocean, people now tell us that the ocean has a surface' (450). And thus, simply, I am not suggesting that the black man is *only* father, or brother, to the white. Rather, it is an additional unconscious dimension of black/white relations, a dimension the analysis of which will, I hope, illuminate several trends that run through the 'white blues' world.[1]

If it is true that the black man is unconsciously identified with the father by whites, we can expect the whites' attitudes towards the blacks to reflect this identification. It is my feeling that this unconscious identification contributes to certain tendencies in the 'white blues' world, tendencies which place the highest premium on those aspects of the blues most divorced from creativity. I feel, also, that this unconscious identification with the father (or brother) manifests itself in relation to the ideas of success, competition, and fear of success, all of which may operate unconsciously, but which nevertheless contribute in large measure to the peculiar position of the 'white blues' performer.

To be more explicit, numerous whites who are devoted to playing country blues guitar consider it the highest mark of their achievement to be able to play a tune, note-for-note, exactly as it was played by the original recording artist. I would say that in America, this sort of performer completely dominates the higher echelons of the 'white country blues' milieu. Creativity, imagination, improvisation, all are ignored and demeaned in pursuit of faultless imitation. In contrast, those 'white blues' instrumentalists who are drawn to the more urban (electric) blues, almost invariably do something to identify themselves to the listener as white. The most favoured mechanisms are having the entire band perform lead solos at the same time; playing much louder than any black blues band;[2] trying to jam many more notes into every bar of every solo; or providing a harmonic background or melodic lead that is of such a nature as to label the performance distinctively as rock rather than blues.

When it is recalled that nearly all those *country* blues guitarists who are imitated so ardently are dead, and when it is realised that the majority of the great *urban* blues guitar stylists are still alive, it becomes less hazardous to suggest that, indeed, unconscious identifications play a large part in the life of the 'white blues' musician, and that these identifications make themselves known by determining certain patterns relating to competition, success, and fear of competition and success.[3]

The purpose of these observations is not so much to expose certain tendencies that may operate in the unconscious of more than one 'white blues' performer; rather, it is my intention to try to clarify exactly why it is that 'white blues' finds it so difficult to exceed the bounds of stupefying mediocrity. Indeed, it's either because the performer finds himself bound (unconsciously) to not create, to not imagine, but to only imitate, or because imitation itself become slightly hazardous, and originality therefore invariably carries the performer outside the framework which can easily be recognised as *blues*, i.e. outside the framework of competitive success. In exceedingly few cases do we find fresh, inventive, creative, poetic, original work which could, without the most irresponsible generalisations, be still considered blues.

In short, then, unconscious determinants, whereby the black blues man comes to represent the father or brother of the white, contribute in a significant way to the wholesale inadequacy of 'white blues'. Other factors contribute to this, to be sure: there is no doubt, for example, that through the same process of identification (with the black man as father=superior strength), the 'white bluesman' gains enormously in self-esteem, thus reaffirming his masculinity, etc. Also, it would be only slightly unfair to leave out the more conscious, superficial determinants, all of which have their own unconscious connections. For example, whether the young white enthusiast will be attracted more to urban blues than to country blues depends partly on whether or not the music that provided the most pleasure before exposure to blues was jazz, rock and roll, rhythm and blues, or acoustic guitar music like hillbilly or folk music, from the Carter Family to Pete Seeger to the Kingston Trio. Again, of course, one would like to know how these earlier tastes came into being. Financial considerations also prevail since it's far less expensive to buy an acoustic guitar than an electric guitar and amplifier.

Yet we are studying blues as a mental activity, and a few words must be said, again, regarding the various levels of mental functioning, our analysis of such levels, and the reactions that such an analysis is bound to engender.

While we have suggested that a multiplicity of factors is responsible for the appeal of blues to young whites, it can be predicted that the revelation of those factors which relate to unconscious determinants and which have been revealed by psychoanalysis will call forth the most ardent disbelief, revulsion, and rejection. Similarly, revealing those factors which seem more 'sociological' will produce no emotional response whatsoever, but rather a smattering of quasi-academic approval, for such is the nature of the resistances to psychoanalysis and the current academic fondness for 'observables'. Regarding the popular tendency to reject certain findings of psychoanalysis while willingly confirming others, Freud (1918) said:

> If we look a little closer, to see which group of factors it is that has been given preference, we shall find that it is the one that contains material already known from other sources or what can be most easily related to that material . . . What is left over, however, and rejected as false, is precisely what is new in psychoanalysis and peculiar to it. This is the easiest method of repelling the revolutionary and inconvenient advances of psychoanalysis (53).

Psychoanalysts have rarely investigated black music, but there have been several articles by analysts on jazz. In one of these articles Dr. A. Esman (1951) suggests that the anxiety created in the bourgeoisie by the very existence of jazz (and, of course, blues) is due to 'a return of the repressed—a universal source of anxiety' (222). He goes on to suggest how the bourgeoisie defends itself against jazz in much the same manner as the individual defends himself against anxiety; by 'reinforced repressions and denial. Many intellectuals rationalized their defenses by regarding jazz as an "inferior" form of music, a "popular diversion", unworthy of consideration by those whose interest lay in the realm of the fine arts'. To Esman, jazz represents 'the id drives that the super-ego of the bourgeois culture sought to repress', a formulation with which I am in complete agreement.[4]

It should surprise no one, then, to find that young whites, infuriated not only by their parents' alienation and bourgeois mentality but also by their attempts to inflict this predominant mode of mental servility on their children as well, would be attracted by jazz and blues. To the ideas proposed by Esman, Margolis (1954) has added that adolescents are attracted to jazz partly because it functions as a protest group and it provides group solidarity; its improvisational nature, moreover, is attractive as a means of free expression.

To the above roster of charms we must add a dimension which is often considered characteristic of the blues: its open treatment of sexuality. There is no doubt that sexuality operates as an attractive force in the blues, and while we will return to this subject many times, it is here that one must give in to the temptation to describe one of the more comic aspects of 'white bluesdom'.

The male chauvinism that is so manifest in the blues in not without an historical base which makes it more easily understandable. Yet the 'white blues' world, while sharing this historical base to a certain extent, could, with its connections with the 'counter-culture', be expected to be in touch with other currents as well, not the least of which would be the women's liberation movement. Still, this has not prevented the 'white bluesmen' and rock singers, in a pathetic attempt to reinforce their own self-esteem and masculinity, from borrowing from their black 'fathers' precisely those lyrics and songs containing the most derogatory estimations of women's potential. Removed from their historical base and their socio-economic setting, these songs as purveyed by white adolescents are sickly, pale and offensive.

Without attempting a thorough discussion of interracial sexual dynamics, it should still be clear that it is exactly those mechanisms which we have discussed (from the aesthetic disguise to the father identifications to the return of the repressed), and which make the blues so appealing to whites, that also operate to make 'white blues', even at its worst, more appealing to some whites than black blues. And just as some whites have always been attracted to jazz primarily because it is a music of black men, so there are whites whose personal requirements for pleasure, in terms of the aesthetic illusion and alienation, prohibit their enjoyment of black music. For many, any sort of association with black people becomes associated with 'the repressed' and thereby prevents their pleasure, and for these people black music must be served up by whites. These people also supply 'white blues' with its *raison d'etre*.

It is tempting to explain the relationship between the 'white blues' musicians and their audience with the phrase 'Let the dead bury their dead', but in view of the fact that 'white blues' has a rather large following, and in defence of those black musicians who play and sing the blues, as well as those who understand that the blues realises its essence only through its fullest participation in the milieu from which it came, it would be more pertinent to develop more fully our discussion of the 'white blues' world.

The most baffling aspect of the entire phenomenon of 'white blues' is the legitimacy and relevance with which its perpetuators would like to see it endowed. This single fact is evidence of the cretinously low level of mental activity which is forced upon us under the guise of the creative process in so-called youth culture today (perhaps it should be recalled here that the very concept 'youth culture' is a protofascist mystification devised in pre-Hitlerian Germany), for in 'white blues' creativity rarely makes an appearance. But can anyone pretend that 'white blues' are any more creative and any less imitative than, say, reproductions of Eskimo sculptures turned out by white suburbanites? And what of these reproductions? Are they not death? Is it not clear that they are totally devoid of imagination and creativity? The same must be said for 'white blues'. Removed from the unique historical configurations that produced the blues, that is, the socio-economic and cultural conditions through which blues came into being, the melodic similarities produced by the white imitators appear weak, trivial, spineless and without substance. Their audience is won through the interplay of several factors, most of which I have alluded to above, but all of which are supported by a monumental dysfunction of the critical faculties. Thus, 'art for art's sake' becomes 'do your own thing' while both adages remain no more than the flimsiest excuses for the perpetuation of mediocrity and dullness. As Charles Radcliffe (1965) wrote in an early critique of the 'white blues' phenomenon: 'The British singers argue . . . that no music is sacrosanct, that if they wish to play what they like and publicly champion, that is their affair. So it is. It is also the critic's right to assess their music . . . in terms of the Negro tradition and find it wanting ' (133).

The question, then, is not 'Can whites play (or sing) the blues?' but simply, 'Why do they bother, and who cares?' Since the subject of this book is the blues, and not its peripheral pathology, and since we have only begun to explore what the blues is, it would be senseless to devote any more space to what is, after all, only a symptom or a side-effect.

Notes

1. A dream reported to me by a young white blues fan produced much embarrassment in the dreamer. While he was sleeping, someone put on a record by Howling Wolf. He immediately began to dream of a jungle with large apes swinging noisily through the trees. His embarrassment stemmed from his feeling that the dream revealed hidden prejudice, but it also seemed likely that the dream-work had made use of this tendency to allow one symbol for the father (Howling Wolf) to be replaced by another (the apes).

2. I once attended a Howling Wolf club date with the members of an extremely popular 'white blues' band. When we left, one of the band members approached me and said rather boastingly, pointing back at Wolf, 'Shit, man, we play twice as loud as that!'

3. It should not be thought that I am suggesting that all musicians of one sort are victims of a particular oedipal resolution while other sorts of musicians are victims of another—this might be true, but the evidence is lacking. Rather, it should be remembered that patterns of competition are established through the resolution of the oedipus complex as well as through one's early relations with one's siblings. Thus the ideas being dealt with here are present in all of us, and it is the specific way of dealing with these ideas, defence mechanisms as well as character structure, that attracts our interest. Once again, no attempt is being made to assert that in certain styles of musicianship certain defence styles predominate, although this may be the case.

4. It's interesting to ask why psychoanalysts have almost totally ignored jazz and blues; as we noticed earlier, Kohut took note of jazz only to disparage it. The analyses of Esman and Margolis, however, clearly establish the basis for this phenomenon of evasion by pointing to the irreducibly anti-bourgeois content of jazz and blues.

Works Cited

Esman, A. H. 1951. 'Jazz: a Study in Cultural Conflict.' *American Imago* VIII , 219–26.

Freud, Sigmund. 1918. 'From the History of an Infantile Neurosis.' *Standard Edition* XVII (Hogarth Press, London, 1955), 7–122.

Margolis, N. 1954. 'A Theory on the Psychology of Jazz.' *American Imago* XI, 263–91.

Radcliffe, Charles. 1965. 'The Blues in Archway Road.' *Anarchy* 5 (Freedom Press, London, 1965), 129–33. [Published under the pseudonym Ben Covington.]

Roheim, Geza. 1950. *Psychoanalysis and Anthropology.* International Universities Press, New York, 1950.

Sterba, Richard. 1947. 'Some Psychological Factors in Negro Race Hatred and in Anti-Negro Riots.' *Psychoanalysis and the Social Sciences* I, ed. Geza Roheim (International Universities Press, New York, 1947), 411–27.

A Blues Discography

THE following is an extensive discography of blues and blues-related recordings issued and reissued during the century. Some might argue that a shorter, more selective list would be more valuable. But there are a number of reasons why the lists are so long. Most important, there have been a great many excellent blues recordings produced since 1920, in a variety of styles; to cover as many important elements and developments as possible, the list must be both broad and deep. Since these recordings have been released over the years on a variety of labels, both domestic and imported, large label and small, the recordings have not always remained in print, or will not remain in print for long in the future. Thus I include some duplicate listings of important artists and recordings so the reader might pursue alternatives. Also domestic and foreign listings will give readers from a variety of countries a chance to locate recordings manufactured closer to home. Another advantage to inclusiveness is that since some larger libraries are beginning to increase their blues record holdings, the likelihood of finding out-of-print releases may be greater. Finally, there is the relevant issue of bootleg releases, dealt with below.

Compiling a selected discography is also a difficult task in the sense that it is such a subjective process: all listeners have their favorite recordings. Although I do not shy away from stating my own preferences, I still feel it necessary to acknowledge recordings that have garnered critical or popular acclaim as well. Despite the fact that this list is so long, I can still say confidently that it is only a starting place, that the blues tradition is so stunning and vibrant that many other worthy recordings not on this list await the audiences of the present and future.

Additionally, there are problems inherent in the categorizations of blues styles that I have offered in my list. There are artists, for example, who began recording in the prewar era, continued recording in the postwar, and even on into the 1990s. As a result, we find Son House, Sonny Terry and Brownie McGhee, Lonnie Johnson, and others listed in more than one section. Then there are the artists such as Big Joe Turner, Bobby Bland, and Earl Hooker who changed their region or style. Furthermore, it is awfully difficult sometimes to separate Texas and West Coast blues from rhythm and blues (those categories should be read and consulted together precisely for that reason, and I have a sense that the categories could be in many cases interchangeable). Still, the list seems a bit more manageable for people wishing to explore different types of blues, and as long as the categories are not approached as absolutes, the benefits seem to outweigh the drawbacks. In fact, by drawing attention to the difficulties of categorization, the categories may very well serve an extremely useful corrective function. Ultimately, the list is intended to help celebrate both the unity and diversity of the blues tradition.

Finally, "inclusive" does not mean "all-inclusive." Readers will no doubt recommend additions.

Bootleg Recordings

Anyone professing to care about the blues and its practitioners will be concerned in some way about the issue of "bootleg" reissues. Wherever one comes down, the problems are varied and complex. Since a number of bootleg recordings are contained in this discography, a brief discussion of those issues is warranted. Defenders of blues bootleg reissues argue that their releases have often made material available that would not have been reissued legally. As a result, those releases would not be competing with legal products. Beyond that, they argue that record companies' reluctance to reissue blues recordings actually highlights the great service that bootlegs have done for the blues commercially. That is, bootlegs, particularly those released in the 1950s and 1960s, helped create a market among whites by making them aware of the wealth of great blues recordings. This helped bring about a "blues revival" that increased revenue for blues artists in a variety of ways: (1) awakening major labels to the viability of blues on the reissue market, and thus increasing major label reissues; (2) bringing about a renewed interest that generated new recordings; (3) increasing bookings at clubs, coffeehouses, and festivals in this country and abroad; (4) increasing radio, television, and advertising exposure; (5) increasing awareness of African American cultural contributions in a variety of areas; (6) initiating or resuscitating musicians' careers. Furthermore, defenders argue that bootleg reissues rarely made money for the reissuers (in fact, the recordings may not have made any money for the original companies, an argument used to defend the original companies against charges of rampant dishonesty). They were, rather, "labors of love" by collector/aficionados paying tribute to their musical heroes, so to brand producers of bootleg blues reissues as exploiters ignores the purpose and intent of their ventures.

Critics of bootleg reissues have countered that frequently, though not always, the original recordings were produced under exploitative conditions, including low pay for sides recorded and issued, stolen author credits or false co-credits, and pirated copyrights. Therefore even legal reissues can rest very uneasily on the sometimes questionable ethics of the original arrangement between company and artist. Bootleg reissues continue this racist and exploitative practice. Re-release without permission, payment, or royalties not only extends the exploitation but also removes control over the release from both artist and record company, so that neither can determine what should be released, the quality of the sound, and the nature of the packaging, collection, and description of the music in the liner notes. Certainly, opponents argue, if exploitative conditions have left the artist without a legal right to royalties, the reissuers who profess to love the blues should feel some moral or ethical responsibility, and the removal of control over the elements listed above from the artist's hands is a paternalistic and demeaning practice. Since reissue companies have often been white-owned or white-run, there may be some white arrogance involved. The artist, as creator and performer of the material, deserves control over it.

There are, of course, reissue companies who have paid royalties to the artists, as well as some who have refused to reissue without the artist's consent, so it would be unfair to paint all companies with the same broad brush of insensitivity, if not arrogance and exploitation. One must not assume, either, that all blues recording artists wholly oppose all bootleg reissues, though it is likely that many, if not most, do. Additionally, reissuing older recordings by legally licensing them from the original companies would in some cases not have brought the artist any new revenues (and we are often less worried about cheating big companies than we are about ripping off individuals). Still others would argue that more money, new and increased venues, and mainstream commercialization have not been aesthetically positive for the blues tradition. The social, political, psychological, and aesthetic issues abound, rebound, and resound. Ultimately one must practice as one's own conscience dictates, buying that which conforms to one's own philosophical response to the issues.

Select Discography: Pre–World War II Blues

African Backgrounds

African Journey: A Search for the Roots of the Blues. Vanguard LP SRV73014/5.
African Music: Rhythm in the Jungle. Victor 78 rpm P 10 84-89.
Savannah Syncopators: African Retentions in the Blues. CBS (UK) LP 52799.

Before and Alongside the Blues

American Primitive Vol. 1: Raw Pre-War Gospel (1926–1936). Revenant 206.
Before the Blues Vols. 1–3. Yazoo 2015-2017.
Blacks, Whites, and Blues. CBS (UK) LP 52796.
Blues in the Mississippi Night. Rykodisc 90155.
Cap'n, You're So Mean. Rounder LP 4013.
The Earliest Negro Vocal Quartets/Groups Vols. 1–4. Document 5061/5288/5355/5531.
Field Recordings Vols. 10–11. Document 5600 (features some interviews with ex-slaves).
Forty Years of Women in Jazz. Jass CD 9-10.
Get Your Ass in the Water and Swim Like Me. Rounder 2014.
The Gospel Sound. Columbia C2K 57160 (2 CDs).
The Greatest Songsters (1927–1929). Document 5003.
How Can I Keep From Singing Vols. 1–2. Yazoo 2020-2021.
John and Old Marster: Negro Folk Tales. Flyright (UK) EP 01.
The Last Medicine Show. Flyright (UK) LP 507/508.
Murderous Home. Rounder 1714.
Negro Songs of Protest. Rounder LP 4004.
Preachin' the Gospel: Holy Blues. Columbia CK 46779.
The Smithsonian Collection of Classic Jazz. Smithsonian 033 (5CDs).
The Songster Tradition (1927–1935). Document 5045.
String Bands (1926–1929). Document 5167.
Wake up Dead Man: Black Convict Work Songs from Texas Prisons. Rounder LP 2013.

Louis Armstrong: Portrait of the Artist As a Young Man. Columbia 57176 (4 CDs).
The Complete Blue Note Recordings of Sidney Bechet. Mosaic MD4-110 (4 CDs).

Arizona Dranes (1926–1929). Document 5186.
Duke Ellington. *Playing the Blues.* Black and Blue LP.
Reverend J. M. Gates Vol. 1 (1926). Document 5114.
Golden Gate Jubilee Quartet Vols. 1–4 (1937–1943). Document 5472-5475.
W. C. Handy Narrates and Sings His Immortal Songs. Mark 56 LP 684.
The Complete Blind Willie Johnson. Columbia C2K 52835.
The Complete Recorded Works of Washington Phillips. Yazoo 2003.
William Grant Still Conducts William Grant Still. Glendale LP 8011.
Sister Rosetta Tharpe Vols. 1–2 (1938–1944). Document 5334/5335.

General Anthologies

The Blues: The Smithsonian Collection of Classic Blues Singers. Smithsonian RD101 (4CDs).
Blues Classics. MCA MCAD 3 (3CDs).
The Copulatin' Blues Compact Disc. Jass CD-1.
Country Blues Bottleneck Guitar Classics. Yazoo 1026.
Essential Blues Piano. House of Blues 51416 1313 2 (2 CDs).
Fattenin' Frogs for Snakes: The Essential Recordings of the Blues Ladies. Indigo 2042.
I Can't Be Satisfied: Early American Women Blues Singers Vols. 1–2. Yazoo 2026/2027.
News and the Blues. Columbia CK 46217.
Roosevelt's Blues: African-American Blues and Gospel Songs on FDR. Agram 2017.
Roots and the Blues: The Retrospective. Columbia 47911 (4 CDs).
Roots of Rap. Yazoo 2018.
Roots of Rock. Yazoo 1063.
Ruckus Juice and Chitlins: The Great Jug Bands Vols. 1–2. Yazoo 2032/2033.
Sissy Man Blues. Jass CD-13.
Slide Guitar Blues. Indigo 2030.
Southern Country Blues. Starsounds 3712-2 (3 CDs).
Street Walkin' Blues. Jass CD-626.
36 Masterpieces of Blues 1927–1942. Fremeaux and Associates 033 (2 CDs).
Urban Blues. Indigo 2040.

Regional Recordings/Instrumental Practitioners

See "Acoustic Blues" in the postwar discography for more recordings by some of these artists and their disciples.

Alabama

Alabama: Black Country Dance Bands (1924–1949). Document 5166.
Alabama: Black Secular and Religious Music (1927–1934). Document 5165.
Alabama Blues. Yazoo 1006.

Ed Bell (1927–1930). Document 5090.
Lucille Bogan Vols. 1–3 (1923–1935). Document 6036-6038.
Jaybird Coleman and the Birmingham Jug Band (1927–1930). Document 5140.
Clifford Gibson (1929–1931). Document 6015.
Walter Roland Vols. 1–2 (1933–1935). Document 5144/5145.

Chicago

Chicago Blues Vol. 1 (1939–1951). Document 5270.
Chicago Blues Vol. 2 (1941–1944). Document 5444.
Chicago Piano (1929–1936). Document 5191.

Big Bill Broonzy Vols. 1–12 (1927–1947). Document 5050-5052, 5126-5133, 6047.
The Young Big Bill Broonzy. Yazoo 1011.
Doctor (Peter) Clayton (1935–1942). Document 5179.
Doctor Clayton and His Buddies (1946/1947). Old Tramp 05.
Arthur "Big Boy" Crudup Vols. 1–4 (1941–1954). Document 5201-5204.
——. *That's All Right Mama*. BMG Bluebird 61043-2.
Georgia Tom Dorsey Vols. 1–2 (1928–1934). Document 6021-6022.
Bill "Jazz" Gillum. *The Bluebird Recordings 1934–1938*. RCA 07863 66717-2.
——. *Jazz Gillum Vols. 1–4 (1936–1949)*. Document 5197-5200.
Lil Green. *Why Don't You Do Right? (1940–1942)*. EPM 158212.
——. *Lil Green (1946–1951)*. JPCD 1527-2.
Lil Johnson Vols. 1–3 (1929–1937). Document 5307-5309.
Merline Johnson Vols. 1–3 (1937–1940). Document 5292-5294.
Memphis Slim: The Bluebird Recordings 1940–1941. RCA 07863 66720-2.
Tampa Red Vols. 1–15 (1928–1953). Document 5073-5077, 5206-5215.
——. *The Bluebird Recordings Vols. 1–2 (1934–1938)*. RCA 07863 66721-2/66722-2.
——. *Bottleneck Guitar 1928–1937*. Yazoo 1029.
——. *The Guitar Wizard 1932–1934*. Sony 53235.
Washboard Sam Vols. 1–7 (1935–1949). Document 5171-5177.
——. *Rockin' My Blues Away*. BMG Bluebird 61042-2.
Casey Bill Weldon Vols. 1–3 (1935–1938). Document 5217-5219.
Georgia White Vols. 1–4 (1930–1941). Document 5301-5304.
Sonny Boy Williamson Vols. 1–5 (1937–1947). Document 5055-5059.
——. *The Bluebird Recordings 1937–1938*. RCA 07863 66723-2.
——. *The Bluebird Recordings 1938*. RCA 07863 66796-2.

Harmonica

See also recordings by Sonny Boy Williamson and Jazz Gillum in the Chicago section, Sonny Terry in the Southeast section, and the Memphis Jug Band and Gus Cannon in the Tennessee section.

Blues Harmonica. Indigo 2032.
The Great Harp Players (1927–1936). Document 5100.
Harmonica Blues. Yazoo 1053.
Harmonica Masters. Yazoo 2019.
Harp Blowers (1925–1936). Document 5164.

Indianapolis

Scrapper Blackwell Vols. 1–2 (1928–1958). Document 6029-6030.
Leroy Carr Vols. 1–6 (1928–1935). Document 5134-5139.
——. *Blues Before Sunrise*. Sony 44122.

Kansas City

Kansas City Blues. Capitol 52047 (3 CDs).
Kansas City Blues (1924–1929). Document 5152.

Kansas City Piano. Decca LP 79226.
The Real Kansas City. Columbia CK 64859.

Count Basie: The Complete Decca Recordings. GRD 611.
Bennie Moten's Kansas City Orchestra (1929–1932). RCA 9768-2-RB.
The Chronological Joe Turner (1941–1946). Classics 940.
——. *Every Day in the Week*. Decca GRD 621.
——. *I've Been to Kansas City*. MCAD 42351.

Kentucky and Ohio

Cincinnati Blues (1928–1936). Story of Blues 3519-2.

John Byrd and Walter Taylor. Story of Blues 3517-2.
Clifford Hayes and the Louisville Jug Band Vols. 1–4 (1924–1931). JPCD 1501-1504.
Stovepipe No. 1 and David Crockett (1924–1930). Document 5269.

Mississippi

Canned Heat Blues. BMG Bluebird 61047-2.
Down the Dirt Road: The Essential Recordings of Mississippi Blues. Indigo 2039.
Son House and the Great Delta Blues Singers (1928–1930). Document 5002.
Mississippi Blues (1935–1951). Wolf 005.
Mississippi Blues Vol. 1 (1928–1937). Document 5157.
Mississippi Blues Vol. 2 (1928–1930). Document 5158.
Mississippi Masters. Yazoo 2007.

Ishman Bracey and Charley Taylor (1928–1929). Document 5049.
Bo Carter Vols. 1–5 (1928–1940). Document 5078-5082.
——. *Twist It Babe*. Yazoo 1034.
Mississippi John Hurt: 1928 Sessions. Yazoo 1065.
Skip James (1931). Document 5005.
Robert Johnson: The Complete Recordings. Columbia C2K 64916 (2 CDs).
Tommy Johnson (1928–1929). Document 5001.
Tommy McClennan: The Bluebird Recordings 1939–1942. RCA 07863 67430-2 (2 CDs).
Robert Lee McCoy: The Bluebird Recordings. RCA 07863 67416-2.
Mississippi Sheiks Vols. 1–4 (1930–1936). Document 5083–5086.
Charlie Patton Vols. 1–3 (1929–1934). Document 5009–5011.
——. *Founder of the Delta Blues*. Yazoo 1020.
——. *King of the Delta Blues*. Yazoo 2001.
Bukka White (1930–1940). Travelin' Man 03.
——. *The Complete Bukka White (1937–1940)*. Columbia CK 52782.
Big Joe Williams Vols. 1–2 (1935–1949). Document 6003-6004.

Piano

See also Texas, St. Louis, Chicago, and Kansas City for regional piano anthologies.

Barrelhouse Boogie. RCA 8334-2-RB.
Barrelhouse Piano 1927–1936. Yazoo 1028.
Barrelhouse Piano Blues and Stomps (1929–1933). Document 5193.
Boogie Woogie Vol. 1 Piano Soloists. Jasmine 2538.

Boogie Woogie Vol. 2 The Small Groups. Jasmine 2539.
Boogie Woogie Vol. 3—The Big Bands. Jasmine 2540.
Boogie Woogie and Barrelhouse Piano Vols. 1–2 (1928–1932). Document 5102-5103.
Deep South Blues Piano (1935–1937). Document 5233.
Mama Don't Allow No Easy Riders Here. Yazoo 2034.
Piano Blues Vol. 1 (1927–1936). Document 5192.
Piano Blues Vol. 2 (1927–1940). Document 5220.
Piano Blues Vol. 3 (1924–1940s). Document 5314.
Piano Blues Vol. 4 (1923–1928). Document 5336.
Piano Blues Vol. 5 (1929–1936). Document 5337.
Piano Blues and Boogie. Indigo 2031.
Shake Your Wicked Knees. Yazoo 2035.

The Chronological Albert Ammons (1936–1939). Classics 715.
The Chronological Albert Ammons (1939–1946). Classics 927.
Cow Cow Davenport Vols. 1–2 (1925–1945). Document 5141-5142.
Will Ezell (1927–1931). Document 6033.
The Chronological Pete Johnson (1938–1939). Classics 656.
The Chronological Pete Johnson (1939–1941). Classics 665.
The Chronological Pete Johnson (1944–1946). Classics 933.
The Chronological Meade Lux Lewis (1927–1939). Classics 722.
The Chronological Meade Lux Lewis (1939–1941). Classics 743.
The Chronological Meade Lux Lewis (1941–1944). Classics 841.
Cripple Clarence Lofton Vols. 1–2 (1935–1943). Document 6006-6007.
Big Maceo: The Bluebird Recordings 1941–1942. RCA 07863 66715-2.
Big Maceo: The Bluebird Recordings 1945–1947. RCA 07863 66716-2.
Red Nelson (1935–1947). Old Tramp 06.
Sammy Price and the Blues Singers (1929–1950). Wolf WBJ 007 (4 CDs).
Roosevelt Sykes Vols. 1–10 (1929–1957). Document 5116-5122, 6048-6050.
Jimmy Yancey Vols. 1–3 (1939–1950). Document 5041-5043.

The Southeast

Carolina Blues (1937–1947). Document 5168.
Carolina Blues Guitars (1936–1939). Old Tramp 03.
Georgia Blues (1928–1933). Document 5110.
Georgia Blues and Gospel (1927–1931). Document 5160.
Mama Let Me Lay It on You. Yazoo 1040.
Raggin' the Blues: The Essential Recordings of East Coast Blues. Indigo 2044.
Ragtime Blues Guitar (1927–1930). Document 5062.
Virginia Traditions: Western Piedmont Blues. Global Village 1003.

Barbecue Bob Vols. 1–3 (1927–1930). Document 5046-5048.
——. *Chocolate to the Bone*. Yazoo 2005.
Blind Blake Vols. 1–4 (1926–1932). Document 5024-5027.
——. *Ragtime Guitar's Foremost Fingerpicker*. Yazoo 1068.
Gary Davis: The Complete Early Recordings. Yazoo 2011.
Blind Boy Fuller Vols. 1–6 (1935–1940). Document 5091-5096.
——. *East Coast Piedmont Style*. Sony 46777.
Charlie Lincoln and Willie Baker (1927–1930). Document 6027.

Carl Martin and Willie "61" Blackwell (1930–1941). Document 5229.
The Complete Brownie McGhee. Columbia C2K 52933 (2 CDs).
Blind Willie McTell Vols. 1–3 (1927–1935). Document 5006-5008.
Blind Willie McTell (1940). Document 6001.
——. *Atlanta Twelve String*. Atlantic 7 82366-2.
——. *The Definitive Blind Willie McTell*. Columbia C2K 53234 (2 CDs).
——. *The Early Years*. Yazoo 1005.
——. *The Victor Recordings 1927–1934*. RCA 66718.
Buddy Moss Vols. 1–3 (1933–1941). Document 5123–5125.
Sonny Terry (1938–1945). Document 5230.
——. *Whoopin' the Blues*. Capitol D 108936.
Josh White Vols. 1–6 (1929–1944). Document 5194-5196, 5405, 5571-5572.
Josh White: Blues Singer, 1932–1936. Columbia CK 67001.
——. *Free and Equal Blues*. Smithsonian Folkways 40081.

St. Louis

St. Louis (1927–1933). Document 5181.
St. Louis Barrelhouse Piano (1929–1934). Document 5104.
St. Louis Country Blues (1929–1937). Document 5147.
St. Louis Girls (1927–1934). Document 5182.

Walter Davis Vols. 1–7 (1933–1952). Document 5281-5287.
——. *First Recordings (1930–1932)*. JSP 605.
Lonnie Johnson Vols. 1–7 (1925–1932). Document 5063-5069.
Lonnie Johnson Vols. 1–3 (1937–1947). Document 6024-6026.
——. *He's a Jelly Roll Baker*. BMG Bluebird 66064-2.
——. *Steppin' on the Blues*. Sony 46221.
Mary Johnson (1929–1936). Document 5305.
Charley Jordan Vols. 1–3 (1930–1937). Document 5097-5099.
St. Louis Bessie and Alice Moore Vols. 1–2 (1927–1941). Document 5290/5291.
Peetie Wheatstraw Vols. 1–7 (1930–1941). Document 5241-5247.

Tennessee

Frank Stokes' Dream: The Memphis Blues. Yazoo 1008.
Memphis Blues (1927–1938). Document 5159.
Memphis Blues (1928–1935). Document 5014.
Memphis Masters. Yazoo 2008.

The Beale Street Sheiks (1927–1929). Document 5012.
Gus Cannon Vols. 1–2 (1927–1930). Document 5032/5033.
Sleepy John Estes. *I Ain't Gonna Be Worried No More*. Yazoo 2004.
Jim Jackson Vols. 1–2 (1927–1930). Document 5114/5115.
Jack Kelly and the South Memphis Jug Band (1933–1939). Document 6005.
Furry Lewis (1927–1929). Document 5004.
Memphis Jug Band. Yazoo 1067.
Memphis Jug Band (1932–1934). Document 6002.
Memphis Jug Band Vols. 1–3 (1927–1930). Document 5021-5023.
Memphis Jug Band and Associates (1927–1930). Wolf 004.
Memphis Minnie Vols. 1–5 (1935–1941). Document 6008-6012.
Memphis Minnie Vols. 1–3 (1944–1953). Wolf 008-010.

——. *Hoodoo Lady 1933–1937*. Columbia CK 46775.
——. *I Ain't No Bad Gal*. Sony 44072.
Memphis Minnie and Kansas Joe Vols. 1–4 (1929–1934). Document 5028-5031.
Frank Stokes (1928–1929). Document 5013. (See also the Beale Street Sheiks.)

Texas

Easin' In: The Essential Recordings of Texas Blues. Indigo 2043.
San Antonio Blues (1937). Document 5232.
Texas: Black Country Dance Music (1927–1935). Document 5162.
Texas Blues (1927–1937). Document 5161.
Texas Blues: Blues Masters Vol. 3. Rhino 71123.
Texas Girls (1926–1929). Document 5163.
Texas Piano Vols. 1–2 (1923–1938). Document 5224/5225.

Texas Alexander Vols. 1–3 (1927–1950). Matchbox 2001-2003.
Blind Lemon Jefferson Vols. 1–4 (1925–1929). Document 5017-5020.
——. *King of the Country Blues*. Yazoo 1069.
Leadbelly. Columbia CK 30035.
Leadbelly: King of the 12-String Guitar. Columbia CK 46776.
Joe Pullum Vols. 1–2 (1934–1941). Document 5393-5394.
J. T. "Funny Paper" Smith (1930–1931). Document 6016.
Henry Thomas: Texas Worried Blues. Yazoo 1080/1.
Ramblin' Thomas and the Dallas Blues Singers (1928–1932). Document 5107.
Oscar Woods and Black Ace (1929–1938). Document 5143.

Noncommercial Field Recordings/Library of Congress

Black String Band Music "Altamont." Rounder 0238.
Field Recordings Vol. 1: Virginia (1936–1941). Document 5575.
Field Recordings Vol. 2: North and South Carolina, Georgia, Tennessee, Arkansas (1926–1943). Document 5576.
Field Recordings Vol. 3: Mississippi (1936–1942). Document 5577.
Field Recordings Vol. 4: Mississippi and Alabama (1934–1942). Document 5578.
Field Recordings Vol. 5: Louisiana, Texas, Bahamas (1933–1940). Document 5579.
Field Recordings Vol. 6: Texas (1933–1958). Document 5580.
Field Recordings Vol. 7: Florida (1935–1936). Document 5587.
Field Recordings Vol. 8: Louisiana, Alabama, Mississippi (1934–1947). Document 5598.
Field Recordings Vol. 9: Georgia, South and North Carolina, Virginia, Kentucky (1924–1939). Document 5599.
Field Recordings Vols. 10/11 (1933–1941). Document 5600-1/2.
I Can Eagle Rock (1940–1941). Travelin' Man 09.
Mississippi Blues (1940–1942). Travelin' Man 07.
Mississippi Blues and Gospel (1934–1942 Field Recordings). Document 5320.
Red River Blues (1934–1943). Travelin' Man 08.
Southern Journey Vol. 3—61 Highway Mississippi. Rounder 1703.
Texas Field Recordings (1934/1939). Document 5231.

Albert Ammons, Pete Johnson, and Meade Lux Lewis. *The Boogie Woogie Boys (1938)*. Document 6046.
David "Honeyboy" Edwards (1942–1991). Indigo 2003.

Calvin Frazier: Library of Congress Recordings (1938). Laurie 7001.
Son House: The Complete Library of Congress Sessions (1941–1942). Travelin' Man 02.
Sampson Pittman: Library of Congress Recordings (1938). Laurie 7002.
Muddy Waters: The Library of Congress Field Recordings (1941–1942). MCA Chess 9344.

Vaudeville Blues/Women Blues Performers

See also St. Louis and Texas sections for regional women's blues anthologies, and all categories for regional women blues performers.

Barrel House Women Vols. 1–2 (1924–1930). Document 5378/5497.
Better Boot That Thing. RCA 66065-2.
Blue Ladies: Classic Blues Performances 1922–1925. Memphis Archives 7017.
The Blues Ladies. Indigo 2042.
Classic Blues Women: Blues Masters Vol. 11. Rhino 71134.
Empty Bed Blues. Pulse 115.
Female Blues Singers Vols. 1–14 (1920–1935). Document 5505-5518.
Four Women Blues. RCA 66719.
Mean Mothers: Independent Women's Blues Vol. 1. Rosetta 1300.

Ida Cox Vols. 1–4 (1923–1938). Document 5322-5325.
Ida Cox (1939–1940). Affinity 1015.
Lucille Hegamin Vols. 1–3 (1920–1932). Document 5419-5421.
Rosa Henderson Vols. 1–4 (1923–1931). Document 5401-5404.
Bertha "Chippie" Hill (1925–1929). Document 5330.
Alberta Hunter Vols. 1–4 (1921–1946). Document 5422-5425.
Sara Martin Vols. 1–4 (1922–1928). Document 5395-5398.
Ma Rainey Vols. 1–5 (1923–1928). Document 5156, 5581-5584.
Bessie Smith: The Complete Recordings Vols. 1–5. Columbia C2K47091/47471/47474/52838/57546 (10CDs).
Clara Smith Vols. 1–6 (1923–1932). Document 5364-5369.
Mamie Smith Vols. 1–4 (1920–1942). Document 5357-5360.
Trixie Smith Vols. 1–2 (1922–1939). Document 5332-5333.
Victoria Spivey Vols. 1–4 (1926–1937). Document 5316-5319.
Sippie Wallace Vols. 1–2 (1923–1945). Document 5399-5400.

White Blues

White Country Blues 1926–1938. Columbia C2K 47466 (2 CDs).
Hillbilly Blues 1928–1946. Fremeaux and Associates 065.

Cliff Carlisle. *Blues Yodeler and Steel Guitar Wizard.* Arhoolie-Folklyric 7039.
Darby and Tarleton: Complete Recordings. Bear Family BCD 15764 (3 CDs).
Jimmie Davis. *Nobody's Darlin' but Mine.* Bear Family BCD 15943 (5 CDs).
Frank Hutchinson Vols. 1–2 (1926–1929). Document 8003/8004.
Jimmie Rodgers. *The Singing Brakeman.* Bear Family BCD 15540 (6 CDs).
Bob Wills and His Texas Playboys. *Anthology.* Rhino 70744.
——. *The Tiffany Transcriptions Vol. 3.* Rhino R2 71471.

Select Discography: Post–World War II Blues, Rhythm and Blues, and Jazz

General Anthologies

The Aladdin Records Story. EMI E2 30882 (2CDs).
American Folk Blues Festival '63. LR CD-2023.
Atlantic Blues: Guitar. Atlantic 81695-2.
Atlantic Blues: Vocalists. Atlantic 81696-2.
Blues, Boogie, and Bop: The 1940s Mercury Sessions. Polygram 314 525 609-2 (7 CDs).
Blues Guitar Blasters. Ace CDCH 232.
Blues Piano Orgy. Delmark 626.
Defiance Blues. House of Blues 51416-13402-4.
Essential Blues Piano. House of Blues 51416-1313-2 (2 CDs).
Guitar Player Presents Legends of Guitar: Electric Blues. Rhino 70716.
Harmonica Classics: Blues Masters Vol. 4. Rhino 71124.
Harp Blues. Ace CDCH 710.
If It Ain't a Hit, I'll Eat My . . . Baby. ZuZazz 2009.
Kings of the Blues. Ace CDCH 276.
Mean Old World. Smithsonian RD 110 MSD4-35974 (4 CDs).
The Mercury Blues 'n' Rhythm Story 1945–1955. Mercury 314 528 292-2 (8 CDs).
Motown's Blue Evolution. Motown 31453-0613-2.
The R&B Hits 1942–1945. Indigo 100.
The R&B Hits 1946. Indigo 2060.
The Real Blues Brothers. Dunhill Compact Classics DZS-026.
The Real Blues Brothers Vol. 2. Dunhill Compact Classics DZS-159.
The Roots of Rock: 1945–1956. Time-Life 302.
The Roots of Rock II. Time-Life 432.
The Roots of Rock 'n Roll. Savoy LP 2221 (2 LPs).
Rural Blues Vols. 1 & 2. BGO 384 (single CD release of two Imperial LPs).
Rural Blues Vol. 3—Down Home Stomp. Imperial LP 94006.
Superblues—All-Time Classic Blues Hits Vol. 3. Stax SCD 8595-2.

(Since a number of the artists listed in the following regional/stylistic sections continued to record in the 1970s–1990s, please consult that section for further recordings by those listed here.)

Regional Recordings

Chicago

Blues Is Killin' Me. Paula PCD 19.
The Blues World of Little Walter. Delmark 648.
Chess Blues. MCA Chess 9340 (4 CDs).
Chess Blues Classics 1947–1956. MCA Chess 9369.
Chess Blues Classics 1957–1967. MCA Chess 9368.
Chess Blues Piano Greats. MCA Chess CHD2-4385 (2 CDs).
Chicago Blues Masters Vol. 3. Capitol CDP7243 8 36288 2 (2 CDs).
Chicago Blues of the 1950s. Paula PCD 22.
Chicago Blues of the 1960s. Paula PCD 23.
Chicago Blues—The Chance Era. Charly 146 (2 CDs).
Chicago Blues—The Vee-Jay Era. Charly 145 (2 CDs).
Chicago/The Blues/Today Vols. 1–3. Vanguard 79216-79218 (3 CDs).
Chicago Boogie. P-Vine PCD 1888.
The Cobra Records Story. Capricorn 42012 (2 CDs).
Drop Down Mama. MCA Chess 93002.

James Cotton. *The Best of the Verve Years.* Verve 314 527 371-2.
Buddy Guy. *Buddy's Blues.* Chess CHD 9374.
Earl Hooker. *Blue Guitar.* Paula 18.
——. *Two Bugs and a Roach.* Arhoolie 324.
Howlin' Wolf: The Complete Recordings 1951–1969. Charly CD RED BOX 7 (7 CDs).
——. *His Best.* Chess CHD 9375.
——. *Howling Wolf Rides Again.* Flair V2-86295.
Elmore James. *The Classic Early Recordings 1951–1956.* Ace ABOXCD 4 (3 CDs).
——. *Complete Chess, Chief, Fire Sessions.* Chess Box 4 (4 CDs).
——. *The Complete Fire and Enjoy Recordings.* Collectables 8829 (3 CDs).
J. B. Lenoir. *His JOB Recordings.* Flyright CD 04.
——. *Vietnam Blues.* Evidence 26068.
Little Walter. *Blues With a Feeling.* MCA Chess CHD2-9357.
——. *The Chess Years 1952–1963.* Charly CD RED BOX 5 (4 CDs).
Magic Sam. *West Side Guitar Vol. 1.* Paula 02.
——. *West Side Guitar Vol. 2.* Paula 341.
The Complete Muddy Waters 1947–1967. Charly CD RED BOX 3 (9 CDs).
——. *His Best 1947–1956.* Chess CHD 9370.
——. *His Best 1956–1964.* Chess CHD 9380.
Robert Nighthawk. *Bricks in My Pillow.* Delmark 711.
Jimmy Reed. *The Classic Recordings.* Rhino 71660 (4 CDs).
Jimmy Reed/Eddie Taylor. *Ride 'Em on Down.* Charly 171.
Jimmy Rogers. *The Complete Chess Recordings.* MCA Chess CHD2-9372.
Otis Rush. *His Cobra Recordings Vol. 1.* Paula 01.
——. *His Cobra Recordings Vol. 2.* Paula 343.
Johnny Shines and Robert Lockwood. Flyright CD 10.
Otis Spann. *The Complete Candid Otis Spann/Lightnin' Hopkins Sessions.* Mosaic MD3-139 (3 CDs).
——. *Good Morning Mr. Blues.* Analog 3016.
Koko Taylor. *The Chess Years.* Chess 9328.

Junior Wells. *Blues Hit Big Town.* Delmark 640.
——. *It's My Life Baby.* Vanguard 73120.
Sonny Boy Williamson: The Chess Years. Charly CD RED BOX 1 (4 CDs).
——. *His Best.* Chess CHD 9377.

Deep South

Arkansas Blues. P-Vine PCD 3040.
Blues from the Deep South. P-Vine PCD 3038.
Delta Blues—1951. Acoustic Archives Trumpet AA 702.
Goin' in Your Direction. Acoustic Archives Trumpet 801.
Mississippi Blues. P-Vine PCD 3041.

Papa Lightfoot and Sammy Myers. *Blues Harmonica Wizards.* Official 5254.

Detroit

Danceland Years. Pointblank 40116.
Detroit after Hours. Trix 3311.
A *Fortune of Blues Vol. 1.* Regency 119.
A *Fortune of Blues Vol.* 2 Regency 120.

John Lee Hooker. *Graveyard Blues.* Specialty 7018.
——. *His Best Sides.* Chess CHD 9383.
——. *The Vee Jay Years.* Charly Box 6.
Little Sonny. *New King of the Blues Harmonica/Hard Goin' Up.* Stax CDSXD 968.
Baby Boy Warren. *Detroit Blues.* Kingfish LP 1001.

East Coast

Blues Masters Vol. 13: New York City Blues. Rhino 71131.
East Coast Blues. Collectables 5324.
The Fire and Fury Story. Capricorn CDLAB 102 (2 CDs).
Jubilee Jezebels. Sequel NEM CD 750.
Jubilee Jezebels Vol. 2. Sequel NEM CD 916.
Jumpin' at Jubilee. Sequel NEM CD 749.
Old Town Blues Vol. 1. Ace (UK) 469.
Saxophony! Jubilee Honkers and Shouters. Sequel NEM CD 748.

Buster Brown. *New King of the Blues.* Collectables 5110.
Dan Burley. *South Side Shake.* Wolf 008.
Carolina Slim (1950–1952). Document 6043.
Bob Gaddy. *Harlem Blues Operator.* Ace (UK) 407.
Stick McGhee and His Spo-Dee-O-Dee Buddies. *New York Blues.* Ace 502.
Sammy Price. *Rib Joint.* Savoy 4417 (with King Curtis and Mickey Baker).
Wild Jimmy Spruill. *The Hard Grind Bluesman.* Krazy Kat 7429.
Sonny Terry and Brownie McGhee. *Whoopin' the Blues.* Capitol D 108936.
Ralph Willis Vols. 1–2 (1944–1953). Document 5256/5257.

Louisiana

The Best of Excello Records. Excello 4203.
Louisiana Swamp Blues. Capitol 7243 8 52046 2.

Louisiana Swamp Blues. Flyright CD 09.
Troubles Troubles: New Orleans Blues from Ric and Ron. Rhino 7113.
Urban Blues Vol. 2: New Orleans Bounce. Imperial LP 94004.

Clifton Chenier. *Bon Ton Roulet*. Arhoolie 345.
——. *Zodico, Blues, and Boogie*. Specialty 7039.
Fats Domino. *"They Call Me the Fat Man. . . ."* EMI E2-7-96784-2 (4 CDs).
Champion Jack Dupree. *Blues for Everybody*. Gusto LP GD 5037 (2 LPs).
——. *Blues from the Gutter*. WEA 82434.
Snooks Eaglin. *Complete Imperial Recordings*. Capitol 33918.
Slim Harpo. *Hip Shakin'*. Excello 2001 (2 CDs).
Silas Hogan. *Trouble*. Excello 3005.
Earl King. *Earl's Pearls*. Westside 520.
Smiley Lewis Vols. 1–2. KC CD 01-02.
Lightnin' Slim. *I'm Evil*. Excello 3002.
Lonesome Sundown. *I'm a Mojo Man*. Excello 3004.
Professor Longhair. *New Orleans Piano*. Atlantic 7225-2.
——. *Rock and Roll Gumbo*. Dancing Cat 3006.
Katie Webster. Paula 13.

Missouri

East St. Louis Blues—The Stevens Sessions. Sequel NEM CD 940.
Kansas City Blues. Capitol 52047.
St. Louis Blues Review—The Bobbin Sessions. Ace 633.

Julia Lee. *Gotta Gimme What'cha Got*. President 560.
——. *Kansas City Star*. Bear Family 15770 (5 CDs).
Big Joe Turner. *The Complete Aladdin and Imperial Recordings*. EMI E2 99293.
——. *Have No Fear, Big Joe Turner Is Here*. Savoy Jazz SV 0265.
——. *The R&B Years*. Atlantic 781663.

Tennessee

Big Bad Blues—25 Sun Blues Classics. Charly 8272.
Blue Guitar. Charly CD SUN 29.
No Jive: Authentic Southern Country Blues. Ace (UK) 652.
Sun Records The Blues Years 1950–1958. Charly CDSUNBOX 7 (8 CDs).
Wail Daddy! Nashville Jump Blues. Ace (UK) 653.

Bobby Bland. *I Pity the Fool: The Duke Recordings Vol. 1* MCA 10665 (2 CDs).
——. *The Duke Recordings Vol. 2*. MCA 10957 (2 CDs).
——. *The Duke Recordings Vol. 3*. MCA 11444 (2 CDs).
Walter Horton. *Mouth Harp Maestro*. Flair V2-86297.
B. B. King. *The Best of B. B. King Vol. 1*. Ace 908.
——. *The Best of B. B. King Vol. 2*. Ace 199.
——. *King of the Blues*. MCAD4-10677 (4 CDs).
——. *Live at the Regal*. Mobile Fidelity UDCD 548.
Little Milton. *Greatest Hits*. Chess CHD 9386.
——. *The Sun Masters*. Rounder CD SS 35.
Junior Parker. *Junior's Blues*. MCAD 10669.

Texas/West Coast

All Night Long They Played the Blues. Specialty 7029-2.
Atlantic Honkers. Atlantic LP 81666-1 (2 LPs).
The Best of Duke-Peacock Blues. MCAD 10667.
Honkers and Screamers. Savoy LP 2234 (2 LPs).
Shouting the Blues. Specialty 7028-2.
Super Black Blues. Bluestime LP 9003. (Big Joe Turner, T-Bone Walker, Otis Spann et al.)
The Swing Time Records Story. Capricorn 9 42024-2 (2 CDs).
Swing Time Sisters. Night Train 7012.
Texas Blues Vols. 1–2. P-Vine PCD 2519.
Texas Blueswoman: Specialty Legends of Boogie Woogie. Specialty 7019.

Big Maybelle. *Candy*. Savoy Jazz SV-0262.
——. *The Complete Okeh Sessions*. Legacy 53417.
The Complete Aladdin Recordings of Charles Brown. Mosaic MD5-153 (5 CDs).
——. *Best of Driftin' Blues*. Collectables 5631.
Clarence "Gatemouth" Brown. *The Original Peacock Recordings*. Rounder 2039.
Cleo Brown. *Bless You*. President 548.
Pee Wee Crayton: The Complete Aladdin and Imperial Recordings. Capitol 7243 8 36292 2D (2 CDs).
Lowell Fulson: The Complete Chess Masters. Chess CHD 9394.
——. *My First Recordings*. Arhoolie 443.
Lightnin' Hopkins. *The Complete Aladdin Recordings*. EMI CDP-7-96843-2 (2 CDs).
——. *The Gold Star Sessions Vols. 1–2*. Arhoolie 330/337.
Camille Howard. *Rock Me Daddy*. Specialty 7046-2.
Lil Son Jackson. *Complete Imperial Recordings*. Capitol 31744 (2 CDs).
Albert King. *King of the Blues Guitar*. Atlantic 8213-2.
——. *Let's Have a Natural Ball*. Modern Blues Recordings 723.
Freddy King Sings. Modern Blues Recordings 722.
——. *Hideaway: The Best of Freddy King*. Rhino R2 71510.
——. *Just Pickin'*. Modern Blues Recordings 721.
Percy Mayfield. *Memory Pain*. Specialty 7027.
——. *Poet of the Blues*. Specialty 7001.
Jimmy McCracklin. *The Walk: Jimmy McCracklin at his Best*. Razor and Tie 2124-2.
Amos Milburn. *Blues, Barrelhouse, and Boogie Woogie*. Capitol 8 36879-2.
——. *The Complete Aladdin Recordings of Amos Milburn*. Mosaic MD7-155 (7 CDS).
Roy Milton and His Solid Senders. Specialty 7004.
The Original Johnny Otis Show. Savoy Jazz SV 0266.
The Original Johnny Otis Show Vol. 2. Savoy SJL 2252.
Esther Phillips. *Bad Baad Girl*. Charly CD 47.
——. *Better Beware*. Charly CD 248.
——. *The Complete Savoy Recordings*. Savoy 4403.
Big Mama Thornton: The Peacock Recordings. MCA Peacock 10668.
T-Bone Walker: The Complete Capitol/Black and White Recordings. Capitol 7243 8 29379 2.
——. *The Complete Recordings of T-Bone Walker 1940–1954*. Mosaic MD6-130 (6 CDs).
Mercy Dee Walton. *One Room Country Shack*. Specialty 7036-2.
Johnny Watson. *I Heard That!* Charly CD 48.
——. *Three Hours Past Midnight*. Ace CDCH 909.

Hop Wilson. *Houston Ghetto Blues.* P-Vine PCD 1607.
Jimmy Witherspoon. *Blowin' in From Kansas City.* Flair V2-86299.

Rhythm and Blues/Jump Blues

Don't You Feel My Leg. Delmark 683.
Honkers and Screamers. Savoy 2234.
Jumpin' and Jivin'. Specialty 7065.
Jumpin' Like Mad. Capitol 7243 8 52051-2.
The King R&B Box Set. King KBSCD 7002 (4 CDs).
Ladies Sing the Blues. Savoy 2223.
Let's Have a Ball Tonight!: The Pioneers of Rhythm and Blues. Natasha Imports 4025.
Okeh Rhythm and Blues Box. Sony 48912 (3 CDs).
RCA Victor Rhythm and Blues Review. RCD 86279.
The Shouters. Savoy 2244.
Specialty Legends of Jump Blues. Specialty 7058-2.
The Specialty Story. Specialty 5SPCD 4412-2 (5 CDs).
1942–1945 The R&B Hits. Indigo 100 (2 CDs).
1946 The R&B Hits. Indigo 2060.
1947 The R&B Hits. Indigo 2081.

Chuck Berry in London. Chess LP 1495.
The Best of Earl Bostic. King 500.
Earl Bostic Blows a Fuse. Charly CD 241.
Tiny Bradshaw. *Breaking Up the House.* Charly 1092.
James Brown. *Messing with the Blues.* Polydor 847 258-2 (2 CDs).
Roy Brown. *Blues DeLuxe.* Charly 289.
——. *Laughing but Crying.* Route 66 RBD 2.
——. *Mighty Mighty Man.* Ace 459.
Ruth Brown. *Miss Rhythm: Greatest Hits and More.* Atlantic 7 82061-2.
Ray Charles. *The Best of Ray Charles: The Atlantic Years.* Rhino R2 71722.
——. *The Birth of a Legend 1949–1952.* Ebony 8001-8002 (2 CDs).
Sam Cooke. *The Rhythm and the Blues.* RCA 07863 66760-2.
Willie Dixon and the Big Three Trio. Sony 46216.
Wynonie Harris. *Everybody Boogie.* Delmark 683.
——. *Good Rockin' Blues.* Charly 244.
——. *Mr. Blues Is Coming to Town.* Route 66 CD 3.
——. *Women, Whiskey, and Fishtails.* Ace 437.
Ivory Joe Hunter Sings Sixteen of His Greatest Hits. King 605.
Etta James: Her Best. Chess CHD 9367.
Lonnie Johnson. *Me and My Crazy Self.* Charly 266. (See also St. Louis section of pre-war discography.)
——. *Originator of the Modern Blues Guitar.* Blues Boy 300.
Louis Jordan. *The Best of Louis Jordan.* MCA 4079.
——. *Let the Good Times Roll.* Bear Family 15557 (9 CDs).
Little Richard. *The Formative Years 1951–1953.* Bear Family 15448.
Big Jay McNeely. *Big Jay in 3-D.* King 650.
Memphis Slim. *Messin' Around with the Blues.* Gusto LP 5038X (2 CDs). (See also Piano section of prewar discography and Acoustic artists section.)

Sonny Thompson. *Jam Sonny Jam*. Sequel 900.
The Best of Ike Turner. Rhino R2 71819.
Dinah Washington. *The Complete Mercury Recordings Vol. 1*. Polygram 832444 (2 CDs).
——. *The Complete Mercury Recordings Vol. 2*. Polygram 832448 (2 CDs).
——. *Mellow Mama*. Delmark 451.

The 1970s–1990s: A Sampling

The Best of Ecko Records Vol. 1. Ecko 1010.
Blues Fest: Modern Blues of the 70s. Rhino R2 72191.
Blues Fest: Modern Blues of the 80s. Rhino R2 72192.
Blues Fest: Modern Blues of the 90s. Rhino R2 72193.
Deep Blue: The Rounder 25th Anniversary Blues Anthology. Rounder AN20.
Not the Same Old Blues Crap. Fat Possum 80312-2.
One Nation under the Blues. Hip-O 40125.
Southern Shades of Blue Vol. 2. Waldoxy WCD 1901.
Swamp Blues. Excello LP 8015/8016.

Luther Allison. *Reckless*. Alligator 4849.
Carey Bell. *Good Luck Man*. Alligator 4854.
Lurrie Bell. *Mercurial Son*. Delmark 679.
Big Bad Smitty. *Mean Disposition*. Genes 4128.
Bobby Blue Bland. *"Live" On Beale Street*. Malaco 7489.
Clarence "Gatemouth" Brown. *Texas Swing*. Rounder 11527.
Ruth Brown. *R+B=Ruth Brown*. Bullseye Blues 9583.
Eddie C. Campbell. *King of the Jungle*. Rooster Blues 2602.
Albert Collins. *Deluxe Edition*. Alligator 5601.
Albert Collins, Robert Cray, and Johnny Copeland. *Showdown*. Alligator/Mobile Fidelity 620.
Johnny Copeland. *Copeland Special*. Rounder LP 2025.
Shemekia Copeland. *Turn the Heat Up*. Alligator 4857.
Robert Cray. *Strong Persuader*. Mobile Fidelity 564.
Buddy Guy. *Damn Right I've Got the Blues*. RCA 1462.
Jessie Mae Hemphill. *Feelin' Good*. High Water/HMG 6502.
Jimi Hendrix. *Blues*. UNI/MCA 11060.
Michael Hill's Blues Mob. *Have Mercy*. Alligator 4845.
Howlin' Wolf. *The Back Door Wolf*. MCA Chess 9358.
Long John Hunter. *Swinging from the Rafters*. Alligator 4853.
Johnny "Yard Dog" Jones. *Ain't Gonna Worry*. Earwig 4937.
Junior Kimbrough. *All Night Long*. Fat Possum/Capricorn 942 085.
Eddie King. *Another Cow's Dead*. Roesch RR-0035.
Denise LaSalle. *Still Bad*. Malaco 7475.
Magic Slim and the Teardrops. *Raw Magic*. Alligator LP 4728.
Johnny Mars. *Mighty Mars*. JSP LP1023.
Muddy Waters. *Can't Get No Grindin'*. Chess 9319.
——. *Fathers and Sons*. Vogue VG 651 600134.
Jay McShann. *Hootie's Jumpin' Blues*. Stony Plain 1237.
The Johnny Otis Show. *Live at Monterey*. Edsel ED 266.
John Primer. *The Real Deal*. Atlantic/Code Blue 82863-2.

Fenton Robinson. *I Hear Some Blues Downstairs.* Alligator 4710.
Jimmy Rogers. *Blue Bird.* Analogue Productions Originals 2001.
Roomful of Blues with Joe Turner/Eddie "Cleanhead" Vinson. 32 Blues 32015.
Freddie Roulette. *Back in Chicago.* Hi Horse 4044.
Otis Rush. *Right Place Wrong Time.* Hightone 8007.
The Raw Harmonica Blues of Charlie Sayles. Dusty Road LP 701.
Son Seals. *Midnight Son.* Alligator 4708.
Byther Smith. *Housefire.* Bullseye Blues 9503.
Super Chikan. *Blues Come Home to Roost.* Rooster Blues 2634.
Hound Dog Taylor and the House Rockers. Alligator 4701.
Koko Taylor. *I Got What It Takes.* Alligator 4701.
Chris Thomas. *21st Century Blues—From Da 'Hood.* Private 0100 582123-2.
Rufus Thomas. *Blues Thang.* Sequel 1054-2.
Joe Louis Walker. *Cold Is the Night.* Hightone LP 8006.
——. *Great Guitars.* Verve 314 537 141-2.
Johnny "Big Moose" Walker. *Ramblin' Woman.* Bluesway LP6036.
Junior Wells. *Southside Blues Jam.* Delmark 628.

Acoustic Blues

Artists listed here with an asterisk also recorded in the prewar era. Consult the prewar section of this discography for more recordings by these artists.

Bluesville Volume 1: Folk Blues. Ace CDCH 247.
The Bluesville Years Vol. 4: In the Key of Blues. Prestige 9908 (Memphis).
The Bluesville Years Vol. 6: Blues Sweet Carolina Blues. Prestige 9914.
The Bluesville Years Vol. 8: Roll Over Ms. Beethoven. Prestige 9916 (Vaudeville blues).
I Have to Paint My Face. Arhoolie 432.
Play My Juke Box. Flyright 45 (Southeast).
Southern Highway Vol. 3–61 Highway Mississippi. Rounder 1603.

DeFord Bailey. *Country Music's First Black Star.* Tennessee Folklore Society 122.*
Boogie Woogie Red. *Red Hot.* Blind Pig BP 003-77.
Big Bill Broonzy. *Big Bill Blues.* Vogue VG 651 600041.*
Big Chief Ellis. Trix 3316.
Corey Harris. *Fish Ain't Bitin.* Alligator 4850.
Alvin Youngblood Hart. *Big Mama's Door.* Okeh 67593.
The Hopkins Brothers: Lightning, Joel, and John Henry. Arhoolie 340.
Son House. *Father of the Delta Blues: The Complete 1965 Sessions.* Columbia C2K 48867 (2 CDs).*
The Best of Mississippi John Hurt. Vanguard VCD-19/20.*
Henry Johnson. *The Union County Flash.* Trix LP 3304.
Larry Johnson. *Fast and Funky.* Baltimore Blues Society no. #.
John Lee. *Down at the Depot.* Rounder LP 2010.
Fred McDowell. *Mississippi Delta Blues.* Arhoolie 304.
Memphis Slim. *The Real Boogie Woogie.* Folkways LP 3524.*
Keb Mo. Sony 57863.
Peg Leg Sam. *Medicine Show Man.* Trix LP3302.

"Philadelphia" Jerry Ricks. *Deep in the Well.* Rooster Blues R2636.
Sonny Terry and Brownie McGhee. *Back to New Orleans.* Fantasy 24708.*
Taj Mahal. *Recycling the Blues and Other Related Stuff.* Mobile Fidelity Sound Lab 764.
Henry Townsend. *Mule.* Nighthawk 201.*
Reverend Robert Wilkins. *Memphis Gospel Singer.* Piedmont LP 13162.*
Robert Pete Williams. *Free Again.* Original Blues Classics 553.

White Blues

There are some whites who play on some of the recordings listed above, and some African Americans who play on some of the recordings listed below. See the introduction to "Blues as Influence" for some comments on this issue.

Country Blues Guitar. Kicking Mule LP 145.

Allman Brothers Band. *The Fillmore Concerts.* Polydor 314 517 294-2 (2 CDs).
Rory Block. *Gone Woman Blues.* Rounder 11575.
Roy Bookbinder. *Travelin' Man.* Adelphi/Genes 1017.
Paul Butterfield. *Best of the Elektra Years.* WEA 62124 (2 CDs).
Canned Heat. *Boogie with Canned Heat.* See for Miles CD 62.
——. *Livin' the Blues.* See for Miles CD 97.
Eric Clapton. *Crossroads.* Polygram 835261 (4 CDs).
The Paul de Lay Band. *Take It from the Turnaround.* Evidence 26076-2.
The Delmore Brothers. *Freight Train Boogie.* Ace 435.
Dr. John. *Gumbo.* Rhino 7006.
Ronnie Earl. *Plays Big Blues.* Black Top BTEL 7002.
Otis Grand. *The Blues Sessions 1990–1994.* JSPCD294.
Stefan Grossman. *Shake That Thing.* Shanachie 97027.
King Biscuit Boy with Crowbar. *Official Music.* Stony Plain 1220.
Little Charlie and the Night Cats. *Deluxe Edition.* Alligator 5603.
David Maxwell. *Maximum Blues Piano.* ToneCool 1160.
Ella Mae Morse. *Barrelhouse, Boogie and Blues.* Bear Family 16117.
Charlie Musselwhite. *Memphis Charlie.* Arhoolie CD 303.
Rod Piazza and the Mighty Flyers. *Live at B. B. King's Blues Club.* Big Mo 10262.
Elvis Presley. *Reconsider Baby.* RCA 5418.
Charlie Rich. *Feel Like Going Home.* Epic E2K 64762 (2 CDs).
The Siegel-Schwall Band. . . . *Where We Walked (1966–1970).* Vanguard VCD 135-36.
Inside Dave Van Ronk. Fantasy 24710.
Stevie Ray Vaughan. *Live at Carnegie Hall.* CBS 68163.
Hank Williams. *Low Down Blues.* Polydor 532737.
Johnny Winter. Columbia CK 9826.

Jazz and the Blues—a Sampling

John Coltrane. *Blue Train: John Coltrane Plays the Blues.* Fantasy 11005.
Miles Davis. *Bluing: Miles Davis Plays the Blues.* Fantasy 11004.
Duke Ellington. *At Newport.* Columbia CK 40587.
Ella Fitzgerald. *Bluella—Ella Sings the Blues.* Fantasy 2310960.

Lionel Hampton. *Hamp: The Legendary Decca Recordings.* Decca GRD-2-652 (2 CDs).
Coleman Hawkins. *Blues Wail: Coleman Hawkins Plays the Blues.* Fantasy 11006.
Billie Holiday. *Billie's Blues.* Blue Note CDP 7 48786 2.
Wynton Marsalis. *Levee Low Moan.* Columbia 47975.
Charles Mingus. *Blues and Roots.* Atlantic 1305-2.
——. *Oh Yeah.* WEA 90667.
Oliver Nelson. *Blues and the Abstract Truth.* Impulse 154.
Charlie Parker. *Plays the Blues.* Polydor 511391.
Jimmy Smith. *The Complete February 1957 Jimmy Smith Blue Note Sessions.* Mosaic MD3-154 (3CDs).
Sonny Stitt. *Only the Blues.* Verve Elite Edition.
The Complete Ben Webster on EmArcy. EmArcy 824 836-2 (2 CDs).

Blues, Jazz, and Classical Music

Goodman, Benny. *Compositions and Collaborations.* CBS Masterworks MK 42227 (Bernstein, Copland, Stravinsky, Gould, Bartok).
Johnson, James P. *Victory Stride: The Symphonic Music of James P. Johnson.* Musicmaster 67140.
Kronos Quartet. *The Complete Landmark Sessions.* 32 Jazz 32011 (Thelonious Monk, Bill Evans).
Lateef, Yusef, and Adam Rudolph. *The World at Peace.* YAL/Meta 753.
Marsalis, Wynton. *Blood on the Fields.* Columbia 57694.
New World Symphony. *New World Jazz.* BMG BG2 68798 (Adams, Gershwin, Bernstein, Milhaud, Stravinsky, Hindemith, Antheil, Raksin).
Oldham, Denver. *Africa: Piano Music of William Grant Still.* Kock International Classics 3-7084-2 H1.
Ozawa, Seiji. *Bernstein/Russo.* Deutsche Grammophon LP 2530 309 (with the Siegel-Schwall Band on the Russo composition).
——. *Gershwin/Bernstein/Russo.* Deutsche Grammophon 419 625-2 (with Corky Siegel, harmonica on the Russo composition).
Rattle, Simon. *The Jazz Album.* EMI D 172226 (Milhaud, Gershwin, Stravinsky, Bernstein).
Roberts, Marcus. *Portraits in Blue.* Sony Classical 7862493 (Gershwin, J. P. Johnson).
Siegel, Corky. *Corky Siegel's Chamber Blues.* Alligator ALCD 4824.
Still, William Grant. *William Grant Still Conducts William Grant Still.* Glendale LP 8011.
Thomas, Michael Tilson. *Gershwin: Rhapsodies, Preludes, Unpublished Piano Works.* CBS Masterworks MK 34699.
Various Artists. *The Birth of the Third Stream.* Columbia CK 64929 (Schuller, Mingus, Russell, Lewis, Johnson, Giuffre).

Literature and Blues Recordings

Sterling Brown. *The Poetry of Sterling A. Brown.* Smithsonian 47002.
Jayne Cortez. *Taking the Blues Back Home.* PGD Verve 31918.
Allen Ginsberg. *Holy Soul Jelly Roll.* Rhino Word Beat R2 71693 (4 CDs).
Langston Hughes. *The Voice of Langston Hughes.* Smithsonian 47001.
——. *Weary Blues with Langston Hughes.* Verve 841 660-2.
The Jack Kerouac Collection. Rhino Word Beat R 70939 (3 CDs).

Ishmael Reed. *Conjure: Cab Calloway Stands in for the Moon.* American Clave 1015.
——. *Conjure: Music for the Texts of Ishmael Reed.* American Clave AMCL 1006.

The Blues Foundation of Memphis, Tennessee, has a yearly W. C. Handy Awards ceremony at which time they announce awards for blues performers, recordings, and media. *Living Blues Magazine,* Center for the Study of Southern Culture, University of Mississippi, University, Mississippi 38677-9836, has also initiated annual readers' and critics' awards, reported yearly in the magazine.

For educational activities, contact the Blues Educational Center, the education arm of the Blues Heaven Foundation established by Willie Dixon and housed in the old Chess studio building, 2120 S. Michigan Ave., Chicago, Illinois 60616.

Blues: A Selected Bibliography of Primary and Secondary Materials

This bibliography has been divided into the following sections:

Bibliography or Index
General Histories/Commentary
African Roots
Before and Alongside the Blues
Studies/Collections by Early Folklorists
Important Later Articles on Folklore
The Blues and Religion
Regional/Stylistic/Genre Studies
Discussions of Blues Lyrics
Interaction between the Blues and Other Musics
Interviews
Biographies/Autobiographies
Discographies
Collections of Blues Lyrics
Dictionaries and Concordances
The Blues and Literature
The Blues as Influence
Guides to Recorded Blues
Journals

Bibliography or Index

Aldin, Mary Katherine, comp. *Blues Magazine Selective Index*. Hollywood: privately published, 1998. (Includes 78 *Quarterly, Blues Access, Blues and Rhythm, Juke Blues, Living Blues.*)

Ford, Robert, comp. *A Blues Bibliography: The Literature of the Afro-American Musical Heritage*. London: RIS, 1999.

Hart, Mary L. *The Blues: A Bibliographical Guide*. New York: Garland. 1989.

General Histories/Commentary

Barlow, William. *Looking Up at Down: The Emergence of Blues Culture*. Philadelphia: Temple University Press, 1989.

Cohn, Lawrence. *Nothing But the Blues.* New York: Abbeville, 1993.

Davis, Francis. *The History of the Blues: The Roots, the Music, the People.* New York: Hyperion, 1995.

Dixon, R. M. W., and John Godrich. *Recording the Blues.* London: StudioVista, 1970.

Finn, Julio. *The Bluesman.* New York: Interlink, 1992.

Jones, Leroi. *Blues People.* New York: William Morrow, 1963.

Lomax, Alan. *The Land Where the Blues Began.* New York: Pantheon, 1993.

Murray. Albert. *The Hero and the Blues.* Columbia: University of Missouri Press, 1973.

——. *Stomping the Blues.* New York: Vintage, 1976.

Oakley, Giles. *The Devil's Music: A History of the Blues.* New York: Taplinger, 1970.

Oliver, Paul. *The Story of the Blues.* Philadelphia: Chilton, 1973.

Spencer, Jon Michael. *Blues and Evil.* Knoxville: University of Tennessee Press, 1993.

Wardlow, Gayle Dean. *Chasin' the Devil's Music.* San Francisco: Miller Freeman, 1998.

African Roots

Charters, Samuel. *The Roots of the Blues: An African Search.* New York: Perigee, 1981.

Evans, David. "Africa and the Blues." *Living Blues* 10 (1972): 27–29.

——. "African Elements in Twentieth-Century United States Black Folk Music." *Jazzforschung* 10 (1978): 85–110.

Jahn, Janheinz. *A History of Neo-African Literature.* New York: Grove, 1968.

——. *Muntu.* London: Faber and Faber, 1961.

Lomax, Alan. "The Homogeneity of African-American Musical Style." In *Afro-American Anthropology,* ed. Norman E. Whitten, Jr., and John F. Szwed. New York: Free Press, 1970: 181–201.

Oliver, Paul. "African Influence on the Blues." *Living Blues* 8 (Spring 1972): 13–17.

——. "Echoes of the Jungle?" *Living Blues* 13 (Summer 1973): 29–32.

——. *Savannah Syncopators: African Retentions in the Blues.* New York: Stein and Day, 1970.

Waterman, Richard Alan. "Comments On Paul Oliver's *Savannah Syncopators.*" *Living Blues* 6 (1971): 30–36.

Before and Alongside the Blues—Other African American Sources

Berlin, Edward A. *Ragtime. A Musical and Cultural History.* Berkeley: University of California Press, 1980.

Cone, James H. *The Spirituals and the Blues.* New York: Seabury, 1972.

Dundes, Alan, ed. *Mother Wit from the Laughing Barrel.* Englewood Cliffs, N.J.: Prentice-Hall, 1973.

Epstein, Dena J. *Sinful Tunes and Spirituals.* Urbana: University of Illinois Press, 1977.

Fletcher, Tom. *100 Years of the Negro in Show Business.* 1954. Rpt. New York: Da Capo, 1984.

Gioia, Ted. *The History of Jazz.* New York: Oxford University Press, 1997.

Hasse, John Edward, ed. *Ragtime: Its History, Composers, and Music.* New York: Schirmer, 1985.

Levine, Lawrence. *Black Culture and Black Consciousness.* New York: Oxford University Press, 1977.

Lovell, John, Jr. *Black Song: The Forge and the Flame.* New York: Macmillan, 1972.

Morgan, Thomas, and William Barlow. *From Cakewalks to Concert Halls: An Illustrated History of African-American Music from 1895 to 1930.* Washington, D.C.: Elliott and Clark, 1992.

Oliver, Paul. *Songsters and Saints: Vocal Traditions on Race Records.* Cambridge: Cambridge University Press, 1984.

Rosenberg, Bruce A. *The Art of the American Folk Preacher*. New York: Oxford University Press, 1970.
Simond, Ike. *Old Slack's Reminiscence*. Chicago, 1892. Rpt. Bowling Green, Ohio: Bowling Green University Press, 1974.
Tirro, Frank. *Jazz: A History*. New York: W. W. Norton, 1977.
Toll, Robert. *Blacking Up: The Minstrel Show in Nineteenth-Century America*. New York: Oxford University Press, 1974.

Studies/Collections by Early Folklorists

Davis, Henry C. "Negro Folk-Lore in South Carolina." *Journal of American Folklore* 27 (1914): 241–54 (hereafter *JAF*).
Johnson, Guy B. "Double Meaning in the Popular Negro Blues." *Journal of Abnormal and Social Psychology* 22 (1) (1927): 12–20.
Krehbiel, H. E. *Afro-American Folksongs*. New York: Schirmer, 1914.
Lomax, Alan. "I Got the Blues." *Common Ground* 8 (Summer 1948): 38–52.
Lomax, John A. "Self-Pity in Negro Folk-Songs." *The Nation* 105 (July–Dec. 1917): 141–45.
Lomax, John A., and Alan Lomax. *American Ballads and Folk Songs*. New York: Macmillan, 1934.
Odum, Howard W. "Folk-Song and Folk-Poetry as Found in the Secular Songs of the Southern Negroes." *JAF* 24 (1911): 255–94.
——. *Negro Workaday Songs*. Chapel Hill: University of North Carolina Press, 1925.
Odum, Howard W., and Guy B. Johnson. *The Negro and His Songs*. Chapel Hill: University of North Carolina Press, 1925.
Perrow, E. C. "Songs and Rhymes from the South." *JAF* 25 (1912): 137–55; 26 (1913): 123–73; 28 (1915): 129–90.
Scarborough, Dorothy. *On the Trail of Negro Folk-Songs*. Cambridge, Mass.: Harvard University Press, 1923.
Thomas, Gates. "South Texas Negro Work Songs." In *Rainbow in the Morning*, ed. J. F. Dobie. Rpt. Hatboro, Pa.: Folklore Associates, 1965.
Thomas, Will. *Some Current Folk-Songs of the Negro*. Austin: Folklore Society of Texas, 1912.
Webb, W. Prescott. "Notes on Folk-Lore of Texas." *JAF* 28 (1915): 291–96.
White, Newman I. *American Negro Folk-Songs*. Cambridge: Harvard University Press, 1928.
Work, John. *American Negro Songs and Spirituals*. New York: Crown, 1940.

Important Later Articles on Folklore

Barnie, John. "Oral Formulas in the Country Blues." *Southern Folklore Quarterly* 42 (1) (1978): 39–52.
Evans, David. "Fieldwork with Blues Singers: The Unintentionally Induced Natural Context." *Southern Folklore Quarterly* 42 (1) (1978): 9–16.
Jarrett, Dennis. "The Singer and the Bluesman: Formulations of Personality in the Lyrics of the Blues." *Southern Folklore Quarterly* 42 (1) (1978): 31–37.

The Blues and Religion

Cone, James H. *The Spirituals and the Blues*. New York: Seabury Press, 1972.
Gruver, Rod. "The Blues as a Secular Religion." *Blues World* 29 (April 1970): 3–6; 30 (May 1970): 4–7; 31 (June 1970); 5–7; 32 (July 1970): 7–9.

Hughes, Langston. "My Adventures as a Social Poet." *Phylon* 8 (3) (1947): 206.
Spencer, Jon Michael. *Blues and Evil.* Knoxville: University of Tennessee Press, 1993.

Regional/Stylistic/Genre Studies

Bastin, Bruce. *Red River Blues: The Blues Tradition in the Southeast.* Urbana: University of Illinois Press, 1986.
Broven, John. *Rhythm and Blues in New Orleans.* Gretna, La.: Pelican, 1978.
Cantor, Louis. *Wheelin' on Beale.* New York: Pharos Books, 1992.
Evans, David. *Big Road Blues: Tradition and Creativity in the Folk Blues.* Berkeley: University of California Press, 1982.
Ferris, William. *Blues from the Delta.* Garden City, N.Y.: Doubleday, 1978.
Field, Kim. *Harmonicas, Harps, and Heavy Breathers.* New York: Fireside, 1993.
Harrison, Daphne Duval. *Black Pearls.* New Brunswick, N.J.: Rutgers University Press, 1988.
Hoffman, Lawrence. "The Blues Harp Pt. 1." *Living Blues* (Sept.–Oct. 1991): 24–31.
——. "The Blues Harp Pt. 2." *Living Blues* (Nov.–Dec. 1991): 43–48.
——. "The Blues Slide Guitar Pt. 1." *Living Blues* (July–Aug. 1992): 24–34.
——. "The Blues Slide Guitar Pt. 2." *Living Blues* (Sept.–Oct. 1992): 28–33.
Keil, Charles. *Urban Blues.* Chicago: University of Chicago Press, 1966.
Lomax, Alan. *The Land Where the Blues Began.* New York: Pantheon, 1993.
McKee, Margaret, and Fred Chisenhall. *Beale Black and Blue.* Baton Rouge: Louisiana State University Press, 1981.
Mitchell, George. *Blow My Blues Away.* Baton Rouge: Louisiana State University Press, 1971.
Olsson, Bengt. *Memphis Blues.* London: Studio Vista, 1970.
Oster, Harry. *Living Country Blues.* Detroit: Folklore Associates, 1969.
Palmer, Robert. *Deep Blues.* New York: Viking, 1981.
Richards, Tim. *Improvising Blues Piano.* London: Scott Educational Publications, 1998.
Rowe, Mike. *Chicago Breakdown.* London: Eddison, 1973.
Ryan, Marc. *Trumpet Records: An Illustrated History with Discography.* Milford, N.H.: Big Nickel, 1992.
Shaw, Arnold. *Honkers and Shouters.* New York: Macmillan, 1978.
Silvester, Peter. *A Left Hand Like God: A Study of Boogie Woogie.* New York: DaCapo, 1989.
Stewart-Baxter, Derrick. *Ma Rainey and the Classic Blues Singers.* New York: Stein and Day, 1970.
Titon, Jeff. *Early Downhome Blues: A Musical and Cultural Analysis.* Urbana: University of Illinois Press, 1978.
Tracy, Steven C. *Going To Cincinnati.* Urbana: University of Illinois Press, 1993.
Vincent, Ted. "The Social Context of Black Swan Records." *Living Blues* 86 (May/June 1989): 36–40.
Zur Heide, Karl Gert. Deep South Piano. London: Studio Vista, 1970.

Discussions of Blues Lyrics

Charters, Samuel. *The Poetry of the Blues.* New York: Avon, 1970.
Oliver, Paul. *The Meaning of the Blues.* 1960. Rpt. New York: Collier, 1963.
——. *Screening the Blues.* London: Cassell, 1968.
van Rijn, Guido. *Roosevelt's Blues.* Oxford: University of Mississippi Press, 1996.

Interaction between the Blues and Other Musics

Evans, David. "Black Musicians Remember Jimmie Rodgers." *Old Time Music* 7 (Winter 1972–1973): 12–14.

Porterfield, Nolan. *Jimmie Rodgers: The Life and Times of America's Blue Yodeler.* Urbana: University of Illinois Press, 1979.

Russell, Tony. *Blacks, Whites, and Blues.* London: Studio Vista, 1970.

Interviews

Alyn, Glen, with Mance Lipscomb. *I Say Me for a Parable.* New York: Da Capo, 1994.

Oliver, Paul. *Conversation with the Blues.* 1965. Rpt. Cambridge: Cambridge University Press, 1997.

Pearson, Barry Lee. *Sounds So Good to Me: The Bluesman's Story.* Philadelphia: University of Pennsylvania Press, 1984.

——. *Virginia Piedmont Blues.* Philadelphia: University of Pennsylvania Press, 1990.

Biographies/Autobiographies

Albertson, Chris. *Bessie.* New York: Scarborough, 1982.

Bradford, Perry. *Born With the Blues.* New York: Oak, 1965.

Brooks, Edward. *The Bessie Smith Companion.* New York: Da Capo, 1982.

Broonzy, Big Bill, and Yannick Bruynoghe. *Big Bill Blues.* New York: Oak, 1964.

Brown, Ruth, and Andrew Yule. *Miss Rhythm: The Autobiography of Ruth Brown, Rhythm and Blues Legend.* New York: Donald I. Fine, 1997.

Calt, Stephen. *I'd Rather Be the Devil: Skip James and the Blues.* New York: Da Capo, 1994.

Calt, Stephen, and Gayle Dean Wardlow. *King of the Delta Blues: The Life and Music of Charlie Patton.* Newton, N.J.: Rock Chapel Press, 1988.

Charters, Samuel. *The Bluesmen.* New York: Oak, 1967.

Collins, Tony. *Rock Mr. Blues.* Milford, N.H.: Big Nickel, 1994. (Wynonie Harris)

Dance, Helen. *Stormy Monday: The T-Bone Walker Story.* Baton Rouge: Louisiana State University Press, 1987.

Dixon, Willie. *I Am the Blues.* New York: Da Capo, 1989.

Edwards, David. *The World Don't Owe Me Nothing: The Life and Times of Delta Bluesman Honeyboy Edwards.* Chicago: Chicago Review Press, 1997.

Fahey, John. *Charley Patton.* London: Studio Vista, 1970.

Garon, Paul. *The Devil's Son-in-Law: The Story of Peetie Wheatstraw and His Songs.* London: Studio Vista, 1978.

Garon, Paul, and Beth Garon. *Woman with Guitar.* New York: Da Capo, 1992. (Memphis Minnie)

Handy, W. C. *Father of the Blues.* New York: Collier, 1941.

Harris, Michael W. *The Rise of the Gospel Blues: The Music of Thomas Andrew Dorsey in the Urban Church.* Oxford: Oxford University Press, 1992.

Harris, Sheldon. *Blues Who's Who.* New Rochelle, N.Y.: Arlington House, 1979.

King, B. B., and David Ritz. *Blues All around Me: The Autobiography of B. B. King.* New York: Avon, 1997.

Kostelanetz, Richard, ed. *The B. B. King Companion.* New York: Schirmer, 1997.

Lance, Cousin Herb. "Notes to *black is brown and brown is beautiful.*" Skye LP SK-13.

Leadbitter, Mike. "Juke Boy's Blues." *Blues Unlimited* 111 (December–January 1974–75): 6.
Lieb, Sandra. *Mother of the Blues: A Study of Ma Rainey*. Amherst: University of Massachusetts Press, 1981.
Lord, Tom. *Clarence Williams*. Chigwell, Essex: Storyville Publications, 1976.
Porterfield, Nolan. *Jimmie Rodgers: The Life and Times of America's Blue Yodeler*. Urbana: University of Illinois Press, 1979.
Sacre, Robert, ed. *The Voice of the Delta: Charley Patton*. Liege, Belgium: University Press of Liege, 1987.
Santelli, Robert. *The Big Book of Blues*. New York: Penguin, 1993.
Sawyer, Charles. *The Arrival of B. B. King*. New York: Da Capo, 1980.
Tooze, Sandra B. *Muddy Waters: The Mojo Man*. Toronto: ECW Press, 1997.
Wilcock, Donald, with Buddy Guy. *Damn Right I've Got the Blues*. New York: Woodford, 1993.
Wolfe, Charles, and Kip Lornell. *The Life and Legend of Leadbelly*. New York: HarperCollins, 1992.

Discographies

Dixon, R. M. W., John Godrich, and Howard Rye. *Blues and Gospel Records, 1895–1942*. 2d ed. New York: Oxford University Press, 1997.
Fancourt, Les. *B. B. King, Albert & Freddy: A Discography*. London: Retrack Books, 1993.
Leadbitter, Mike, Leslie Fancourt, and Paul Pelletier. *Blues Records 1943–1970*. Vol. 2. London: RIS, 1994.
Leadbitter, Mike, and Neil Slaven. *Blues Records 1943–1970*. Vol. 1. London: RIS, 1987.
Lornell, Kip. *Virginia's Blues, Country, and Gospel Records 1902–1943*. Lexington: University of Kentucky Press, 1989.
Mahony, Dan. *The Columbia 13/14000D Series*. Stanhope, N.J.: Walter Allen, 1966.
Ruppli, Michel. *The King Labels: A Discography*. Westport, Conn.: Greenwood, 1985.
Vreede, Max E. *Paramount 12000/13000 Series*. London: Storyville, 1971.

Collections of Blues Lyrics

Bourgeois, Anna Strong. *Blueswomen: Profiles and Lyrics, 1920–1945*. Jefferson, N.C.: McFarland, 1996.
Handy, W. C. *Blues: An Anthology*. New York: Boni, 1926.
Macleod, R. R., transcriber. *Blues Document*. Edinburgh: Pat Publications, 1997.
——. *Document Blues 1*. Edinburgh: Pat Publications, 1994.
——. *Document Blues 2*. Edinburgh: Pat Publications, 1995.
——. *Document-Blues 3*. Edinburgh: Pat Publications, 1995.
——. *Document Blues 4*. Edinburgh: Pat Publications, 1996.
——. *Document Blues 5*. Edinburgh: Pat Publications, 1998.
——. *Yazoo 1–20*. Edinburgh: Pat Publications, 1988.
——. *Yazoo 21–83*. Edinburgh: Pat Publications, 1988.
Oliver, Paul. *Early Blues Songbook*. New York: Music Sales Co., 1992.
Sackheim, Eric, ed. *The Blues Line*. New York: Schirmer, 1975.
Taft, Michael. *Blues Lyric Poetry: An Anthology*. New York: Garland, 1983.
Titon, Jeff. *Downhome Blues Lyrics*. Boston: Twayne, 1981.

Dictionaries and Concordances

Gold, Robert. *Jazz Talk.* New York: Da Capo, 1982.

Major, Clarence. *Juba to Jive.* New York: Viking, 1994.

Taft, Michael. *Blues Lyric Poetry.* New York: Garland, 1984.

Townley, Eric. *Tell Your Story.* Chigwell, Essex: Storyville, 1976.

The Blues and Literature

Baker, Houston. *Blues, Ideology, and Afro-American Literature.* Chicago: University of Chicago Press, 1984.

Baldwin, James. "Sonny's Blues." In *Going to Meet the Man.* New York: Dial, 1965.

Brown, Sterling. "The Blues as Folk Poetry." In *Folk-Say,* ed. B. A. Botkin. Norman: University of Oklahoma Press, 1930.

——. *The Collected Poems of Sterling Brown.* New York: HarperCollins, 1980.

Carby, Hazel. "It Just Be's Dat Way Sometime: The Sexual Politics of Women's Blues." In *Feminisms: An Anthology of Literary Theory and Criticism,* ed. Robyn R. Warhol and Diane Prince Herndl. New Brunswick, N.J.: Rutgers University Press, 1991.

Davis, Angela Y. *Blues Legacies and Black Feminism.* New York: Pantheon, 1998.

Ellison, Ralph. *Shadow and Act.* New York: Random House, 1964.

Garon, Paul. *Blues and the Poetic Spirit.* London: Eddison, 1975.

Gates, Henry Louis. *The Signifying Monkey.* New York: Oxford University Press, 1988.

Henderson, Stephen. *Understanding the New Black Poetry.* New York: William Morrow, 1973.

Hughes, Langston. "Happy New Year! with Memphis Minnie." *Chicago Defender,* January 9, 1943.

——. "Songs Called the Blues." *Phylon* 2 (2) (Summer 1941): 143–45.

Neal, Larry. "Any Day Now: Black Art and Black Liberation." In *Black Poets and Prophets,* ed. Woodie King and Earl Anthony. New York: Mentor, 1972.

Rosemont, Franklin, et al. *Surrealism and Blues: Special Supplement. Living Blues* 25 (Jan.–Feb. 1976): 19–34.

Tracy, Steven C. *Langston Hughes and the Blues.* Urbana: University of Illinois Press, 1988.

Williams, Sherley A. "The Blues Roots of Contemporary Afro-American Poetry." In *Chant of Saints,* ed. Michael Harper and Robert Stepto. Chicago: University of Chicago Press, 1979.

The Blues as Influence

Hoffman, Lawrence. "Guest Editorial." *Guitar Player* (August 1990): 18.

Margolin, Bob. "Blues and Race." *Blues Revue Quarterly* 13 (Summer 1994): 9–10.

Powell, Richard J., ed. *The Blues Aesthetic.* Washington, D.C.: Washington Project for the Arts, 1989.

Von Schmidt, Eric, and Jim Rooney. *Baby Let Me Follow You Down.* Amherst: University of Massachusetts Press, 1993.

Williams, Martin. *The Jazz Tradition.* Oxford: Oxford University Press, 1983.

Wolfe, Charles. "A Lighter Shade of Blue." In *Nothing But the Blues,* ed. Lawrence Cohn. New York: Abbeville Press, 1993.

Guides to Recorded Blues

Oliver, Paul, ed. *The Blackwell Guide to Recorded Blues,* rev. ed. Cambridge: Cambridge University Press, 1991.

Scott, Frank, ed. *The Down Home Guide to the Blues.* Pennington, N.J.: A Capella Books, 1991.

Journals (still in publication and out of print)

Block (Netherlands)
Blues Access (US)
Blues and Rhythm (UK)
Blues Life (Austria)
Blues Revue (US)
Blues Unlimited (UK)
Blues World (UK)
Il Blues (Italy)
Jefferson (Sweden)
Juke Blues (UK)
Living Blues (US)
78 Quarterly (US)

Videography

The following is a list of selected video releases featuring blues performers in formal and informal performances, being interviewed, and being discussed as documentary subjects. A broad overview of African Americans in the movies and in music is available in the two-video set *That's Black Entertainment.* Readers may also be interested in full-length feature films such as King Vidor's *Hallelujah* (including Jim Jackson, Gus Cannon, and Victoria Spivey) and *Reet, Petite, and Gone* (including Louis Jordan). See the film index in Sheldon Harris's *Blues Who's Who* for more listings of films and TV performances, many of which are not currently available on videotape.

Performances and Documentaries

African Guitar. Vestapol 13017.
An American Songster: John Jackson. Rhapsody 8013.
And This Is Free. Shanachie 1403.
The!!!!Beat. Vestapol 13014. (Freddy King)
Bessie Smith and Friends. MUL 055109.
Big City Blues. Rhapsody 8020.
The Blues. VIDJAZZ 13. (Bessie Smith, Big Bill Broonzy, Sonny Boy Williamson II, T-Bone Walker, et al.)
The Blues Accordin' to Lightnin' Hopkins. Flower Films.
The Blues as Social History. A Singh Production.
Blues Houseparty. Houseparty Productions.
Blues Masters Vol. 1. Rhino 2101. (Leadbelly, Bessie Smith, Mamie Smith, Roy Milton, et al.)
The Blues Summit Concert. MCAV-10847 (B. B. King, Ruth Brown, Albert Collins, et al.)
Blues Up the Country. Vestapol 13037. (Gary Davis, Pink Anderson, John Jackson, et al.)
Born with the Blues. Vestapol 13060. (Brownie McGhee)
Chicago Blues. Rhapsody 9012. (Muddy Waters, Buddy Guy, Junior Wells, J. B. Hutto, et al.)
Classic Jazz. VIDJAZZ 20. (Meade Lux Lewis, Louis Armstrong, Red Allen, et al.)
Delta Blues, Cajun Two-Step. Vestapol 13050. (Skip James, Son House, Bukka White)
Devil Got My Woman. Vestapol 13049. (Howlin' Wolf, Skip James, Son House, et al.)
Elizabeth Cotten. Vestapol 13019.
Good Mornin' Blues. Yazoo 505. (B. B. King, Big Joe Williams, Gus Cannon, et al.)

Hubert Sumlin: Living the Blues. Juke Joint Films.
It's a Mean Old World to Live In/Born in the Blues. Shanachie 1401. (Pearly Brown, Big Boy Crudup)
Jazz on a Summer's Day. New Yorker Video 16590. (Big Maybelle, Dinah Washington, et al.)
John Lee Hooker and Friends 1984–1992. Vestapol 13054.
John Lee Hooker: Rare Performances 1960–1984. Vestapol 13035.
The Land Where the Blues Began. Vestapol 13078 (R. L. Burnside, Sam Chatmon, et al.)
The Last of the Blue Devils. Rhapsody 8039. (Count Basie, Big Joe Turner, Jay McShann)
Legends of Bottleneck Blues Guitar. Vestapol 13002. (Son House, Furry Lewis, et al.)
Legends of Country Blues Guitar. Vestapol 13003. (Bill Broonzy, John Hurt, et al.)
Legends of Country Blues Guitar Vol. 2. Vestapol 13016. (Leadbelly, Bukka White, et al.)
Legends of the Delta Blues. Vestapol 13038. (Son House, John Lee Hooker, et al.)
Lightnin' Hopkins 1960–1979: Rare Performances. Vestapol 13022.
Louis Jordan and The Tympani Five. MUL 027572.
Mance Lipscomb In Concert. Vestapol 13022.
Mance Lipscomb/Lightnin' Hopkins. Yazoo 502.
The Many Faces of Billie Holiday. MVD J467.
Masters of the Country Blues: Big Bill Broonzy/Roosevelt Sykes. Yazoo 518.
Masters of the Country Blues: John Lee Hooker/Furry Lewis. Yazoo 519.
My Castle's Rockin'. ARK 1331. (Alberta Hunter)
Out of the Blacks, Into the Blues Pt. 1. Yazoo 506. (Roosevelt Sykes, Brownie McGhee, et al.)
Out of the Blacks, Into the Blues Pt. 2. Yazoo 507. (B. B. King, Willie Dixon, et al.)
Percy Mayfield: The Poet Laureate of the Blues. Winner 113.
Piano Players Rarely Ever Play Together. Stevenson Productions Inc. (Professor Longhair, Tuts Washington, Allen Toussaint)
Red River Blues. Vestapol 13056. (Brownie McGhee and Sonny Terry)
Sippie. Rhapsody 8054. (Sippie Wallace)
Times Ain't Like They Used to Be. Yazoo 512. (Whistler's Jug Band, Jimmie Rodgers, et al.)
Whoopin' the Blues. Vestapol 13057. (Sonny Terry)
Zydeco Gumbo. Rhapsody 8062. (Clifton Chenier, Boozoo Chavis, et al.)

Blues Instructional Videos

Gaye Adegbalola. *Learn to Sing the Blues.* Homespun Video.
Rory Block. *The Power of Delta Blues Guitar.* Homespun Video (2 videotapes).
Billy Branch. *Beginning Blues Harp.* Mountain Top.
Bob Brozman. *Learn to Play Bottleneck Blues Guitar.* Homespun Video (3 videotapes).
Paul Butterfield Teaches Blues Harmonica Master Class. Homespun Video.
Stefan Grossman. *Bottleneck Blues Guitar.* Guitar Workshop Video 902.
——. *Country Blues Guitar Parts 1–3.* Guitar Workshop Video 904-906.
——. *Fingerpicking Country Blues Guitar.* Guitar Workshop Video 931.
——. *How to Play Blues Guitar.* Guitar Workshop Video 903.
John Jackson. *The Fingerpicking Blues of John Jackson.* Homespun Video.
Woody Mann. *Fingerstyle Blues Guitar.* Guitar Workshop Video 914.
Jerry Portnoy's Blues Harmonica Masterclass. International Blues Management.
Kenny Ray. *Blues Guitar Videos Parts 1–6.* PO Box 844, Menlo Park, CA 94026.
Gary Smith *Amplified Blues Harp De-mystified.* Mountain Top.
Keith Wyatt. *Introducing Acoustic Blues Guitar.* Warner Brothers Publications.

The Blues Internet Connection

The Alabama Blues Project site: http://www.dbtech.net/ventblues
Blue Highway: www.thebluehighway.com
Blues Access Magazine: www.bluesaccess.com/ba-home.html
Blues Chat Room: www.BluesChat.com
Blues Link: www.blues-link.com
Blues-L List (free discussion group): listservAbrownvm.brown.edu
In the message space type: subscribe blues-L (your name).
Detroit Blues: www.detroitblues.com
The House of Blues: www.hob.com
Legends Blues Wear: Legendsonline.com
Library of Congress American Folklore Center: Icweb.loc.gov/folklife/afc.html
Living Blues: imp.cssc.olemiss.edu/blues.html
Joel Slotnikoff's *Blues World* e-mag: www.bluesworld.com
Washington, D.C., Blues Society: intelus.com.80/DCblues/
www.fred.net/turtle/blues.html
www.island.net/~blues
www.memphismojo.com
www.tristateblues.com

R. R. MacLeod has also established an Internet site for the purpose of including composer credits for his series of books transcribing the lyrics of recordings released on the Yazoo and Documents labels. See http://www.bluesworld.com/RRMcleod.html

CD-Rom/Enhanced CD

Blues MusicRom Perspectives. Selectware.
The Downhome Blues and the Uptown Blues. Philips Media Cd-i.
On the Road with B. B. King. MCA CD-Rom.
Pinetop Perkins. *Born in the Delta.* Telarc 83418.

Index

General Index

Musical Composition and Recording Index